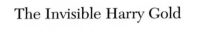

The Invisible Harry Gold

THE INVISIBLE HARRY GOLD

The Man
Who Gave the
Soviets the
Atom Bomb

Allen M. Hornblum

Yale UNIVERSITY PRESS
NEW HAVEN AND LONDON

Published with assistance from the foundation established in memory of Henry Weldon Barnes of the Class of 1882, Yale College.

Yale University Press books may be purchased in quantity for educational, business, or promotional use. For information, please e-mail sales.press@yale.edu (U.S. office) or sales@yaleup.co.uk (U.K. office).

Designed by James J. Johnson and set in New Caledonia type by The Composing Room of Michigan, Inc., Grand Rapids, Michigan.
Printed in the United States of America by Sheridan Books, Ann Arbor, Michigan.

Library of Congress Cataloging-in-Publication Data

Hornblum, Allen M.
　The invisible Harry Gold : the man who gave the Soviets the atom bomb / Allen M. Hornblum.
　　p. cm.
　Includes bibliographical references and index.
　ISBN 978-0-300-15676-8 (cloth : alk. paper)

　1. Gold, Harry.　2. Spies—United States—Biography.　3. Chemists—Pennsylvania—Philadelphia—Biography.　4. Prisoners—Pennsylvania—Biography.　5. Espionage, Soviet—United States—History.　6. Atomic bomb—United States—History.　7. Manhattan Project (U.S.)—History.　8. Soviet Union—Relations—United States.　9. United States—Relations—Soviet Union.　I. Title.
　E748.G63H67 2010
　327.1′2092—dc22
　[B]

2010017515

A catalogue record for this book is available from the British Library.

This paper meets the requirements of ANSI/NISO Z39.48-1992 (Permanence of Paper).

10　9　8　7　6　5　4　3　2　1

To Gregory M. Harvey

Who follows John D. M. Hamilton and Augustus S. Ballard in maintaining the
highest standards of the Philadelphia Bar

'Tis education forms the common mind,
Just as the twig is bent, the tree's inclined.

—ALEXANDER POPE, *Epistle to Cobham* (1734)

Contents

photo gallery follows page 162

Preface

Everyone was there that warm August day in 1972: doctors and nurses, medical technicians from the pathology lab, blood bank workers, and others, from administration to housekeeping, who staffed John F. Kennedy Hospital in Northeast Philadelphia. They had come to pay their last respects to a unique and cherished colleague. The hospital's chief chemist, well known for his generosity and patience, was about to be lowered into his final resting place, a few yards from his beloved mother at Har Nebo Cemetery.

Some mourners had no idea that the dead man was anything other than an endearing, if slightly eccentric, member of the hospital's medical team. But most of the people now shedding tears and holding each other's hands were aware that their friend, mentor, and colleague had an infamous past. Despite his singularly unimpressive exterior, Harry Gold had been a gifted and devoted secret agent who spent years providing the Soviet Union with industrial and military secrets, including the greatest prize of all: the secrets to the atomic bomb.

Gold's dutiful and substantive work won him the Order of the Red Star, one of the Soviet Union's highest honors. The FBI's director J. Edgar Hoover had called him a "master Soviet spy" and described the nation-wide manhunt that preceded his arrest as "the toughest case the FBI ever faced."[1] The portly, amiable, occasionally absent-minded chemist was the antithesis of the suave, physically imposing James Bond, but whereas Bond was fiction, Gold was the real deal. It was not a fact that was easily assimilated. Dumbfounded by the realization that his innocuous-looking neighbor was a former secret agent—one who was said to have significantly jeopardized his countrymen—Northeast Philadelphia resident Milton Bolno exclaimed, "You'd never in a million years believe this guy was a spy."[2] But Gold was not only an accomplished agent and Soviet courier. He was the centerpiece of what Hoover would call "the crime of the century."[3]

That he was an enigma is beyond question, but the mystery of Harry Gold is deeper than the obvious paradox of a kind, apolitical sugar refinery worker rising to the high ranks of a foreign power's clandestine operations. Granted, the thought of a shy nebbish pulling off cloak-and-dagger capers is intriguing, and his ability to carry them off so expertly for so long is a story in itself, but Gold was also one of the most denounced, slandered, and demonized figures in twentieth-century America. Labeled a "pathological liar," a "forlorn creature," a "weakling," an "inveterate liar," a "twisted and degenerate mind," and a "fantasist" by political opponents posing as investigative journalists, he was subjected to long-distance amateur diagnoses of "pseudologia fantastica" and labeled a "pathologic imposter whose only means of gratifying a lifetime of starved emotional needs was in the acting out of a spy career based on nothing more than his fantasy wish-fulfillments."[4] It is safe to say that no one at Har Nebo Cemetery on the day of his burial would have recognized their friend in this bizarre and cruel description.

How had the person one co-worker called "an adorable little pet we all wanted to take care of" become the object of such scorn and outrage?[5] The calumny heaped upon Gold during his life and long after his death was only partially due to his disloyalty and criminal acts. It had far more to do with his confession to those acts and his naming of others who had similarly served the Soviet Union. Harry Gold was the human tripwire that brought down a host of Americans who had spied for the Soviet Union during the 1930s and 1940s. The most famous of these were Julius and Ethel Rosenberg, executed in June 1953. Upon being put to death at Sing Sing Prison, they immediately became martyrs to millions of Americans who desperately wanted to imagine the young couple as innocent victims of a hysteria that was destroying the nation's liberal and democratic principles. Anti-Communist paranoia had polluted the land, these people argued, and right-wing lawmakers and a reactionary fanaticism personified by Hoover's FBI were working to root out not only New Deal liberalism but every form of progressive thought in America.

Within a few years, a vibrant cottage industry of authors and researchers, magazine and newspaper columnists, pamphleteers, and eventually documentary filmmakers emerged to exonerate the Rosenbergs and vilify their accusers. A key witness against the Rosenbergs, and the man whose credibility it was most necessary to destroy, was Harry Gold. As one of the former associates he sent to prison said, "This little man set off an explosion that is still reverberating around the world."[6]

Like his fellow spy Elizabeth Bentley five years earlier, Gold had told all. But whereas Bentley's confession resulted in relatively few criminal prosecutions, Gold's was a windfall. According to one high-ranking FBI agent, Gold's knowledge of Soviet operations led to cases "breaking everywhere—dozens of them every day." In quantity and quality, the information "devolving from the confession of Harry Gold was enormous."[7] As spectacular arrests, trials, and convictions accumulated during 1950 and 1951, more and more observers grew curious about the timid, sad-eyed Philadelphia bachelor who had inspired the investigations and would prove equally effective as a prosecution witness.

Regrettably for Gold, the Rosenbergs' defenders did a far more effective job of defining him than did the government or the news media. Motivated by a religious fervor to discredit the ones who had destroyed the Rosenbergs, they targeted the informers for abuse. Like Whittaker Chambers and Elizabeth Bentley before him, Gold would be mauled by partisan wordsmiths until lifelong friends and co-workers had difficulty recognizing him. In addition to naming names, he had conceded his guilt without even putting up a fight. Extraordinary detective work nailed Gold, not hard evidence. Without his cooperation and confession, it is very unlikely he would have been convicted. Even if Klaus Fuchs had been willing to testify against him—which is doubtful—the British government would never have let Fuchs appear in an American courtroom. Gold could have walked, and without him many others would not have been indicted, imprisoned, or executed. His actions destroyed the lives of many clandestine Communist activists in America.

Once he started to talk, Gold could be seen in two ways: either he was a traitor who had sold his country down the river or he was a delusional psychotic whose "pathological needs" propelled him to become "a pseudologist of the first rank."[8] In the eyes of the public, he would become both. The criminal justice system confirmed the former identity, and defenders of the Rosenbergs worked diligently to brand him as the latter. Their campaign was facilitated by Gold's shy manner and short stature. He seemed made to order for bullies, whether they were neighborhood ruffians who beat him up with their fists or polysyllabic political activists who used a pen and typewriter.

The short, overweight Gold, with his odd gait and obsessive personality, offered a striking contrast with the dashing, handsome, distinguished-looking Alger Hiss and William Remington—two contemporaries who also led double lives and eventually became tenants of Lewisburg Penitentiary, though for much shorter terms than Gold. Gold did not graduate from an elite prep school and prestigious Ivy League university or have a distinguished family lineage. Introverted and isolated, he was relatively easy to stigmatize.

Yet it was Gold who told the truth about his career as a spy, and Julius Rosenberg who lied about his commitment and actions on behalf of Communism and the Soviet Union. Interestingly, both men devoted years of their lives to the Soviet cause—Harry even longer than Julius—but whereas Gold grew weary of his covert activities and dubious about Russia's "grand experiment," Rosenberg remained firm in his commitment and willing to give his life for the cause. When both were caught in 1950, Gold divulged everything; Rosenberg denied everything.

For the rest of the century, dueling authors and scholars would remain intransigent on the guilt or innocence of the Rosenbergs. Harry Gold remained central to the story but was increasingly viewed as a mystifying oddball. Where others—such as Chambers, Bentley, Hiss, Harry Dexter White, Judith Coplon, Remington, and Joel Barr—had their lives and motivations fully fleshed out in biographies, Gold remained a scholarly orphan, an intriguing Zelig who seemed to be everywhere, and the lone figure from that era still denied an accurate historical account rather than a politically motivated caricature. It is gratifying to rectify this half-century-long sin of omission by helping throw "a shaft of light . . . upon the life of Harry Gold."[9]

Since the fall of the Soviet Union in the early 1990s, a steady stream of once-secret Soviet and American documents, KGB memoirs, and independent scholarship has added fresh evidence to what we knew about Soviet espionage in America. The revelations in 1992 by Vasili Mitrokhin, a former KGB agent; the National Security Agency's 1995 release of the Venona decrypts (World War II KGB and GRU cables); Alexander Feklisov's account of his KGB career in 2001; and most recently the notebooks of Alexander Vassiliev, a former KGB agent, which opened an extensive portion of KGB archives to public scrutiny—all these have not only contributed a better understanding of Soviet spy missions in America but have also confirmed the hundreds of U.S. citizens who chose to work secretly for Soviet intelligence organizations. Such documentation should make the scholarly study of Communism and the Cold War less of a brutal ideological battlefield.

Harry Gold's significant role in KGB operations in America and his subsequent role in their destruction are delineated in these newly released documents. My own research and interviews with Gold-era associates might also contribute to a better understanding of this period. Some will continue to reject these sources and cling to comfortable decades-old canards. During my research, I came into contact with a number of people whose minds seemed shackled by 1950s and 60s notions of Gold as a "fantasist" and "FBI dupe," as propounded by John Wexley and Walter and Miriam Schneir.

This mindset seems immune to new scholarship and recent archival discoveries. In my university office between classes a few years ago, for instance, I received a telephone call from a woman who wanted to know if I was "the Allen Hornblum who is writing a biography of Harry Gold." I was surprised, since there had been no publicity about my intention, and I had told only a few friends and colleagues about my research. I asked her how she had learned I was involved in such a book project, but she declined to answer. She also refused to tell me her name. But she did ask whether I intended the Gold book as follow-up to an earlier book of mine entitled *Acres of Skin.* Now I was really mystified; I had no idea what the caller was talking about. *Acres of Skin* is an exposé and history concerning the use of prison inmates as test subjects for medical experiments. I could not see its relationship to World War II spying and Harry Gold. When I told her I didn't understand her question, she proceeded to inform me that Gold had been used as a human guinea pig by the FBI while incarcerated in Philadelphia's Holmesburg Prison. He had been programmed to recite a narrative of his involvement in Soviet spy missions according to a script he had been given. When I told her that in all my years of research on both the Holmesburg medical experiments and Harry Gold I had seen no evidence to support her story, she became quite upset. I had either not researched the subject thoroughly enough, she suggested, or I was hiding evidence. She was certain Gold had been subjected to government experiments in mind control. That is the only reason he would have admitted to things he didn't do and testified against an innocent couple, Ethel and Julius Rosenberg.

Other comments were a little more grounded in reality. A friend, a retired public school principal, expressed dismay that I was writing a book about Harry Gold. His concern had to do with revisiting a dark chapter in the lives of many American Jews, who found it embarrassing that so many Jewish Americans had gravitated to the Communist banner in the 1930s and 40s and were even willing to spy for the Soviet Union. Why, my friend asked, did I have to write about that subject. It was only going to reopen old wounds and get people thinking about Jews and Communism again.

With all due deference to those who share my friend's concern, I do not subscribe to the notion that history should be written to fit one's ideological needs or that truth should be suppressed, twisted, or slanted to foster one's political agenda. Why American Jews and others were drawn to Communism in the face of the Great Depression and the rise of Fascism in Europe is a legitimate issue for exploration and debate. The life of Harry Gold is a good vehicle for examining that issue.

Like many other first-generation Americans early in the last century, Harry Gold led a life fraught with difficulty and hardship. He was an intelligent, highly motivated youth from a good family who approached the world with the best of intentions, but his life took a bizarre and ultimately heartbreaking turn from which he would never recover. The enigma of Harry Gold, the world's most unlikely secret agent, is long overdue for serious examination. Samson Golodnitsky envisioned great things for his son in America, but a couple of missteps led his bright, inquisitive, and hardworking golden boy on a singularly tragic journey.

Part 1
The Spy

. . . .

CHAPTER 1

South Philadelphia

S amson Golodnitsky grew up accustomed to slightly more comfortable circumstances than most of his hard-pressed Jewish neighbors in Smila, on the Tyasmyn River in central Ukraine. His father was a relatively prosperous businessman. Even the wealthiest and most accomplished Jewish families were saddled with governmental restrictions and social constraints, but Samson went to good schools and showed promise, particularly in mathematics.

While at school, Samson became greatly influenced—"infected" was the term used by one subsequent observer—by the life, works, and philosophy of the Russian novelist Leo Tolstoy. During the late nineteenth century, Tolstoy "preached the idea of the nobility of labor." "Any man could look God or himself in the eye . . . who worked with his hands toward the welfare of the community," Samson's son would later recall.[1] By the 1890s, with most of his greatest literary works behind him, Tolstoy was involved in a spiritual quest that caused him to "identify with the poor and the oppressed, to abandon his wealth, to live in peace and forgiveness with all men."[2]

The Russian literary giant's search for truth and meaning not only influenced many of his countrymen but also drew adherents around the world. Samson Golodnitsky was one of his converts, so taken with Tol-

stoy's pronouncements that he renounced his family's wealth, resisted his
father's plans for him, and set about to make his way using his own hands.
Sent to Switzerland for more schooling, he rarely attended classes and
began to earn his own living as a woodworker, believing, as Tolstoy
preached, that "the only men of stature in the community were those
who worked with their hands."[3] Though he would never renounce that
viewpoint, Samson would soon fall in love with a young woman in
Switzerland who would replace Tolstoy as the dominant force in his life.

Celia Ominsky was born into a large Jewish family in a small town in
central Ukraine in 1881. Her father, a carpenter, was "an extremely pious
man." He often found it difficult to provide for his family, but he was devoted to the faith of his fathers and in times of need was heard to say "*Got
veln tsushteln*" ("God will provide"). The oldest female of seventeen siblings, Celia was "quite precocious" as a child and had not only "learned
to read and write Hebrew, Yiddish and Russian" but by fourteen was giving Hebrew lessons to children in her village. She was sent to Kiev to further her education, but lack of funds and the societal constraints on Jews
in tsarist Russia greatly restricted her educational possibilities.[4]

According to her son's recollection a half-century later, Celia worked
part time in a bakery and dutifully completed her gymnasium assignments but was gradually radicalized by Russia's harsh political and economic conditions. In the 1890s she became a supporter of the rapidly
growing Zionist movement. But she quickly grew disillusioned and joined
the Socialist Workers before switching to a "revolutionary" group. According to family legend, her participation involved some dangerous political intrigue—as when an attractive young revolutionary officer persuaded her to transport bombs in a market basket.[5]

Frustrated by the lack of opportunity in her native country, Celia
Ominsky left Russia for Paris while still a teenager and enrolled herself
in a "mechanical dentistry" program. Bright, energetic, and possessed
with a desire to improve her lot in life, Celia did well in her coursework,
but after two years her funds were nearly depleted. For the time being
her formal education came to an end.[6] Focusing now on economic survival, Celia left Paris for Switzerland and what she hoped would be a temporary job rolling cigars and cigarettes. With luck she might save enough
money to return to Paris and complete her dental studies.

It was in Bern that the two young Ukrainian Jews met and fell in love.
Samson was immediately smitten with Celia's comely features, her spirit,
her desire for knowledge, and her self-assurance. Celia was equally taken
with Samson's quiet, unassuming manner, the handsome figure he cut

with his stylish Kaiser Wilhelm mustache, and his regal bearing on the rare occasions when he was attired in the fashionable clothes of the day.[7] Samson and Celia were married in 1907 or 1908 and set about making a home for themselves. Life was not easy, and soon they had an extra mouth to feed. On December 12, 1910, Heinrich Golodnitsky was born in Bumplitz, a suburb of Bern.[8] With his "long and very blond curls," penchant for chocolate, and doting parents, little Heinrich should have been a happy child, but his subsequent recollections show that he was aware of his parents' daily struggles and "dismal" prospects. His father had promised to "go to night school in nearby Zurich" where a "famous Polytechnic Institute" was located, but he never did. His mother was still working for a modest wage in the cigarette factory.

By early 1914 the Golodnitskys had "come to the conclusion that the future in Switzerland was extremely limited." They decided, like millions of others across the continent, to start over in the New World.[9]

Golodnitskys Become Golds

With hopes for a better life and a good bit of trepidation, Samson Golodnitsky, aged thirty-three, Celia, thirty-two, and three-year old Heinrich boarded the S.S. *Lapland* in Antwerp, Belgium, and sailed for America.[10] The *Lapland,* along with its cargo of mostly Russian and central European immigrants, arrived in New York Harbor on July 13, 1914.[11] It was at Ellis Island, according to Gold, that the family's awkward last name was anglicized. When a U.S. immigration official suggested to Samson— who barely spoke English—"Why don't you change your name to something simple, so you won't always be plagued with this spelling difficulty —something, say, like 'Gold'"? Samson, "ever willing to oblige," agreed, and little Heinrich Golodnitsky became Harry Gold.[12]

The Golds traveled to Chicago, where they stayed for just under a year in "pretty miserable" circumstances. Gold recalls his family sharing "a ramshackle hovel" with another family while his mother went to work in a tobacco factory. His father did heavy manual labor in a Chicago coal yard for "pitifully low wages" because his "non-existent English kept him from explaining to the people at the employment agency that he had skills as a woodworker, and at mathematics and bookkeeping."[13] The brutally cold winters and scorching summers did little to endear the area to the Golds.

In 1915, the family decided to move again. Samson heard that there was work available in the shipyards of Norfolk, Virginia, where he had some wealthy relatives who were long established in the retail business.

But Celia decided on a more cautious approach and took her son to Philadelphia, where her brother Shama had settled. If the Norfolk venture did not pan out, some members of the family would already be situated in their next likely destination.[14]

That's exactly how things turned out. Work in the shipyards was sporadic, living conditions in Norfolk "were horrible," and the well-off relatives took no interest in the latest Golodnitsky to arrive. The Golds reunited in Philadelphia, one of the oldest and largest industrial towns in America.

Philadelphia in the early years of the twentieth century was a noisy, hazy brew of bustling factories, smoke-belching chimneys, horse-drawn delivery wagons, crowded streetcars, and ethnically diverse neighborhoods. European immigration was placing its stamp on the city's residential landscape, and like the vast majority of their *landsmanshaft*, the Golds gravitated to South Philadelphia. Bounded by the Delaware and Schuylkill rivers to its east, west, and south, and with Center City Philadelphia to its north, South Philadelphia was home to a rich mixture of Italian, Irish, Polish, and Jewish immigrants. From the nearby docks where the big European ships dropped their wretched but hopeful human cargo, many Jews fanned out through the neighborhood's Jewish quarter looking for friends and relatives who could help with shelter and employment.

Eastern European Jews had been coming to America in significant numbers since the 1880s, and the section of South Philly between Third and Tenth streets, and between Snyder and Oregon avenues, may have been—with the exception of New York's Lower East Side—the heart of Jewish religious, commercial, and residential life in America. By 1920, nearly a hundred thousand Jews lived in South Philadelphia, and though the numbers would gradually decline as Jews looked to newer, less congested neighborhoods like Strawberry Mansion, Mt. Airy, or Overbrook Park, a portion of South Philly would retain a distinctive Jewish ambience well past mid-century.[15]

The Jewish quarter was flanked by Italians to the west and Irish to the east. To its south was "the Neck," home to a rough collection of hog tenders and subsistence farmers. South Philly real estate was staked out along ethnic and religious lines, and woe to those who forgot it.[16] Interethnic relations were "far from peaceful, and territory was often defended" to the point of bloodshed. Most American-born Jewish residents had vivid memories of anti-Semitic insults and of being frequently attacked on the way to school.[17]

Sam and Celia Gold, however, were not expecting rose petals to be tossed at their feet. They were familiar with the harsh realities of life and only asked for a roof over their heads and the opportunity to earn a living. The Golds lived for a few months with Celia's brother, who presided over his own brood of eight adults and children in a six-room row house on the 2500 block of South Sixth Street. Sam Gold found work at a succession of firms, including the Lester Piano Company, the Pooley cabinet-making firm, and the Belber Trunk and Bag Company. Celia found a job outside the neighborhood in an Arch Street sweatshop. The income allowed the Golds to move from their single room to three rooms in another South Sixth Street residence, and in 1916, to one of the newly built homes on the 2600 block of South Second Street. Though they were still renting and had to share the house with another family, each move represented a step up. From 1917 until well into the 1930s, the Gold family resided in a series of rented homes on the 2500 and 2600 blocks of South Philip Street, in the extreme southeast corner of the city. A local historian describes the streetscape: "50 twelve-foot-wide rowhouses, 25 to a side, . . . lined every street. Like sardines there were one hundred and fifty neatly stacked two and three story dwellings with cellars in each block."[18] The street's inhabitants were largely Russian and Jewish, bordered by the Irish to the east and the "Neckers" below Oregon Avenue.

Hazardous Business

The 2500 and 2600 blocks of Philip Street would be the geographical hub of young Harry's world. When the Golds moved onto the block, the street was unleveled and unpaved, with irregular mounds of clay making it all but impassable for horse-drawn wagons and the few hand-cranked automobiles in the area.

Oregon Avenue was for all practical purposes the end of the city and a major thoroughfare for freight trains traveling to and from piers along the Delaware River. A latticework of steel track gave a final warning to all who stepped across it that they were leaving the civilized part of the city. Philip Street residents became used to the rattle of dishes in kitchen cupboards when a train passed by, and it was "customary for boys (and men) to hitch rides on the freight cars" and "pry open the box car doors and steal" whatever of value could be carried off. Pilfering coal during the winter was thought by most area residents to be "one of the rights of man."

The train hopping and thievery were hazardous business, thanks to the unexpected jolting stops and "toughness of the railroad detectives." Lacking the physical coordination and nerve to hop the moving box cars, young Harry would stare enviously at the other boys' feats of bravery but admitted, "I could never quite bring myself to jump for a handrail." The challenge became all the more daunting when a neighborhood youth would lose his grip and be carried off missing an appendage or two. The sight of Charlie Bilker being brought home while an older boy carried "Charlie's hand with its bleeding stumps of fingers" and "Louie Horn's scream as the wheel of a freight passed over his leg" did much to reinforce his mother's prohibition against playing around with trains.[19]

Sometime before 1920, Sam was hired as a cabinetmaker by the Victor Talking Machine Company. Based just across the Delaware River in Camden, New Jersey, the growing company was thought to be a good place to work. Some described it as run in a "benevolently paternalistic fashion"—decent wages, periodic bonuses, free turkeys at Thanksgiving, and other gifts at Christmas.

On February 10, 1917, Celia Gold gave birth to a second son—a "bitter disappointment" for Sam, who very much wanted a girl and was "resentful" for "a very long time."[20] This may be why Harry, then six years old, considered himself his father's favorite son, even though he saw such favoritism as "unfortunate." His mother, however, was "rigidly impartial."

Yussel (Yiddish for Joseph) Gold was named after a grandfather who ordered his children, "When I die and you name a child after me, do not dare to use a Gentile version of my name—it must be *Yussel.*"[21] Though his friends, teachers, and neighbors all knew him as Joe, his brother and parents never called him anything but Yus or Yussel.

"They were a very strange family"

Although they had much in common with the other residents of Philip Street, the Golds stood out. As a number of former neighbors recalled, "They were just different." It wasn't that they exhibited bizarre behavior or a flashy lifestyle, or were threatening in any way; they were just different. Dr. Arthur Coltman, a longtime resident of the neighborhood whose family owned a popular kosher butcher shop, recalls the Golds as "very quiet people. . . . The Gold family didn't socialize very much. They kept to themselves."[22]

"They were a very strange family," adds Yetta Silverstein, who grew up on Philip Street and was in the Gold home often. "It was a very somber household. They were sort of stand-offish, certainly not typical of the other Jewish families on the street." Philip Street in the 1920s, she recalls, was like any other street in the Jewish quarter of South Philadelphia.[23] People gossiped and shared birthdays and other special events;

the streets were narrow asphalt playgrounds. "It was a small street and there were no cars. The kids played ball in the street all day and the mothers were always in each other's houses cooking, baking, sewing, and talking about the latest developments in their lives. Everybody seemed to know everybody's business on the street, but not the Golds."

According to Mrs. Silverstein, "they weren't involved with other people, not even their next door neighbors. Mr. Gold rarely talked and Mrs. Gold was not very friendly with the other women on the street. They spoke English in the house, but they'd also speak a lot of Russian to each other. I didn't always understand what they were saying. They never talked about their lives, didn't socialize, and never seemed to have arguments amongst themselves like other families. They were just very quiet, very strange people. Not your typical Jewish family. They were very poor and lacked a lot. They would talk very secretly and didn't really bother with anybody. They pretty much just kept to themselves."[24]

"No point in protesting"

Sam Gold taught his older son to work hard without complaining and to persevere despite obstacles. A short, handsome man who continued to sport a stylish mustache, with a stoical demeanor and modest ambitions, he enjoyed working with his hands, appreciated good tools, and appeared most content when turning a block of wood into something attractive and useful. He was said to be a master craftsman and was no doubt quite content sculpting finely detailed wooden cabinets for an array of RCA products (Victor Talking Machines became Radio Corporation of America in the mid-1920s). Yet his employment at the Camden-based company also exposed him to unrelenting anti-Semitism.

Sam's early years at the company were rewarding: if not financially, at least socially. Things took a dramatic turn for the worse after the First World War. After 1920 a "mass influx of Italian workers . . . needed in the changeover from the old craftsman technique to large scale production" resulted in considerably more workplace prejudice.[25] The newcomers, Sam's son recalled, "were crudely anti-Semitic," and Gold, "one of the few Jewish workers," became a target. They complained that he worked too fast and made them look bad. They would "badger him," steal his tools, put glue on his planes, chisels, and clothes, and in general made his life miserable. The shop foreman was "fully as intolerant" as his workmen, so there was "no point in protesting." Harry watched his father "suffer uncomplainingly over many years."

For much of his childhood, Harry said, he was unaware of his father's difficulties at work, but over the years he overheard enough conversations between his parents "to construct a dishearteningly accurate picture" of the problem. In the mid-1920s an Irish foreman at RCA, "a man who was more bitterly intolerant than anyone he had yet encountered," told Sam: "You son-of-a-bitch, I'm going to make you quit." He proceeded to assign him to a "specially speeded-up production line" where he was "the only one sanding cabinets" by hand.[26]

The result was hard to conceal. Each night Sam Gold would return from work "with his fingertips raw and bleeding and with the skin partially rubbed off." Harry and his younger brother would then watch the evening ritual of his mother bathing "the wounded members and then putting ointment on them." Though shaken by his father's daily travail—Harry considered his father's life at RCA a "veritable hell"—he was proud that his father "never quit. . . . Nor did he ever utter one word of complaint." The old man's stoicism was a lesson for his son.[27]

Despite his skills as a craftsman, impressive work ethic, and general meticulousness, Sam proved a modest wage earner at best. Reluctant to "take advantage of his skills in mathematics and in bookkeeping," he had a history of rejecting well-paid positions and "stubbornly resisted any attempt to get him to improve his spoken English." His "passion for tools" and working with his hands dominated his life. On the rare occasions when there was any extra money in his paycheck, he would make "extravagant purchases of diverse shiny wood-planes, chisels and miter-saws." Celia "would be sorely disappointed" with such expenditures and voice her displeasure, but her husband would reply that the tools would pay for themselves with the extra jobs he could now procure as a handyman. But as Harry admitted, his father "was the world's poorest businessman" and "customarily lost money" doing odd jobs for neighbors.[28] Trying to earn extra money by building screened porches for his neighbors, Sam offered cut-rate prices to attract business. According to Harry, his "father lost money on every one of these jobs" yet had to listen to neighbors' "complaints that the cost was exorbitant."

Harry grew up with a similar disregard for business and "lack of veneration for money"—but he had a deep respect for his father's work ethic. Harry admired Sam's commitment to providing for his family despite abuse from co-workers and bosses at RCA and assignments designed to drive him out of the plant. Even when he was laid off, Sam would leave the house "dragging one of his enormously heavy tool chests" at "the fantastic hour of five A.M. so as to be the first in line" for a job seen in a want

ad. Moreover, he would "invariably walk both back and forth from whatever temporary work he happened to have, this sometimes a total distance of seven or eight miles, merely to save fifteen cents carfare." That
extra measure of self-sacrifice would also be passed from father to son.

"Die Rebbetzin"

As anyone who grew up on Philip Street between World War I and World
War II could tell you (and as John D.M. Hamilton, Harry Gold's attorney,
informed the court many years later): "The dominating influence of the
[Gold] home was the mother."[29] Sam Gold may have been the breadwinner, but Celia was the moral, intellectual, and spiritual force within
the family. Proud, educated, and opinionated, she was a stern, imposing
woman who impressed everyone who entered her orbit. Known by many
by the descriptive, if inaccurate, title of *"die Rebbetzin"* (the rabbi's wife),
Mrs. Gold supplemented the family income by giving Hebrew and Yiddish lessons to neighborhood children. Numerous Hebrew schools in the
Jewish quarter offered language lessons and bar mitzvah training according to the traditional rote method. Celia charged twenty-five or fifty
cents a week to teach children at her kitchen table, where she treated
them as individuals and augmented the lessons with Hebrew literature
and Jewish folklore, offering sweet baked goods as a reward.[30] The result
was rapid student progress, a growing clientele, and seven or eight extra
dollars a week. Mrs. Gold's reputation as a Hebrew teacher was "known
throughout the entire vicinity."[31]

She left a deep impression on many of her students; Yetta Silverstein,
who spent many afternoons in the Gold kitchen learning to read and
speak Hebrew and Yiddish in the mid-1920s, was one of them. "I loved
Mrs. Gold," she says. "I began to feel like a daughter to her. She was an
attractive, good-looking woman, with nice skin and pretty curly hair. She
was not a housewife like the other mothers on the street and wasn't baking and cooking all the time. She wasn't very friendly with the other
women. Mr. Gold never talked. He was very quiet and not sociable at all,
but I still looked forward to going there after school. Mrs. Gold was a
very bright woman, very educated. I loved her.

"Girls weren't *Bat Mitzvah* in those days so getting such training was
something special. Mrs. Gold could be very stern, but she was always very
nice to me. She never had a daughter and I think that had something to
do with it. She baked cookies for me and was very pleasant. She was a very
smart woman; I admired her."[32]

Harry was less enthusiastic about living in a de facto Talmud Torah school. He was proud that his mother, a "natural teacher," was respected and paid for her intellectual talents, but he "bitterly hated" seeing his home invaded by strangers—children and occasionally adults—every day from four to eight in the evening. He didn't like eating dinner in the living room while students learned Yiddish and Hebrew in the kitchen. He resented being "deprived" of his mother's "fascinating and amusing company," so he turned to "books and sports" for other "sources of entertainment."[33]

Curiously, while Celia Gold earned money fostering the Hebrew language and Jewish tradition, and was constantly reading Bible stories to her children, she herself wasn't altogether sold on the business of faith. Though Harry would describe his mother as a "deeply religious person," he recognized she had evolved into a "Social Democrat" and "practicing agnostic"; she "despised hypocrisy" and the "putting on of airs." It's fairly clear that Mrs. Gold grew increasingly suspicious of organized religion.[34] This was especially the case at the "tiny house of worship at the corner of Philip and Porter Streets," dominated by "arbitrary administration," "wealthy bootleggers," and "businessmen" who "cheated their neighbors."

Reared in a devout family, appreciative of the "pure beauty of Biblical tales" and well versed in their historical origin, Celia Gold was also aware of the "absurd extremes of the strictly orthodox Hebrew faith" and didn't bother concealing her doubts from her children.[35] Her agnosticism and distaste for established authority may not have interfered with her sons being bar mitzvah, but that ceremonial passage to manhood also concluded their formal participation in the Jewish religion. Never again would they be part of any synagogue activity.

Any resulting spiritual void was filled by Celia's sobering lectures on the family's Old World history, aphorisms regarding the human condition, and lessons on the importance of discerning right from wrong. God, she reminded them, looked more favorably upon "worthwhile work that contributed to the welfare of society," no matter how menial the task, than upon the empty declarations of pompous, self-important, "psalm-singing, breast-beating hypocrites." Some of the "world's greatest men," she told her sons, may have "labored in comparative obscurity," but by contributing "original thinking and achievement, these toilers had gained . . . a sort of intimacy and awareness of God."[36]

Celia stressed to Harry and Yus the "fundamental rights of men" and the constant struggle of the "great masses of people" around the world. "He who does not help his fellow men may not look to God," she told them. Harry developed a "sympathy for the underdog."[37] As he admitted years later, "Mom instilled in me the thought that whenever anyone was hurt, anguished, or in trouble, and cried out, I should be there to answer and to extend aid."[38] By all accounts he learned that lesson well.

Another lesson Celia Gold taught her children was self-reliance. Anything that smacked of charity or public handout was to be avoided. Her opposition to charity was so "violent" that she refused the "free baskets of food" and turkeys that were given out at "neighborhood centers at Thanksgiving and Christmas." More extreme yet was her opposition to Harry attending the University of Pennsylvania's summer camp at Green Lane during his last two years of grammar school. He was "pretty sickly a good deal of the time as a child," and his frail constitution was his ticket to the Green Lane summer camp, but his mother needed a good bit of convincing.[39] As her son recalled, "it took an awful lot of persuading" and a few "white lies" by Harry and a public school teacher to persuade her that the program "was in no sense a charity affair, before he was permitted to go."[40] Gold greatly enjoyed his two summers at the camp in 1923 and 1924. He added seven or eight pounds to his "very puny" frame each summer, developed a "tremendous appetite" for the first time in his life, and met and became inspired by the Penn athletes who were camp counselors.

"Harry would never look you in the eye"

By his own account, Harry's early years were happy and secure. He was oblivious to the family's economic struggles and had few cares or wants. Celia regularly told him Bible stories as a toddler, and as he got older she began reading Yiddish folk stories and humorous pieces from the *Jewish Daily Forward*. Harry loved the tales of Sholem Alechim as well as those of B. Kovner in the *Forward*. Taken by the "earthy and wholesome quality of Jewish literature," he came to see the stories as an accurate depiction of the "people themselves," not a "strained" or "artificial" presentation of Jewish life. That some of the stories contained an "undertone of derisiveness" only made them more appealing.[41]

Outside his parents' protective cocoon, the world was a threatening place. Apprehension intruded on the most innocent and mundane events. Once, walking with his mother past the schoolyard of Sharswood Elementary School at Second and Wolf streets during recess, six-year-old Harry was unnerved by the hordes of "screaming, yelling, pushing, and boisterous children." He "shrank against" his mother's side and asked, "Momma, will I have to go there?"

Gold never understood the origin of this "shyness" that had to be "consciously fought." He developed an aversion to "exuberant noise" and rowdy crowds. "Meeting people for the first time" was particularly taxing. He attributed this embarrassing trait to "a fear of being exposed to ridicule"; he could never quite figure out what had precipitated it,[42] but it was all too apparent to others. Yetta Silverstein, who was often in the Gold home for her Hebrew and Yiddish lessons, said, "Harry would never look you in the eye. He was very shy. He would never come close to you and made you feel like you were intruding." About to graduate from high school, in his own home, and eight years older than his mother's young student, Harry was the one who would turn away whenever he and the young girl made eye contact.[43] "Everyone in the neighborhood," said Yetta, "knew that he was smart." Though she "didn't remember him having any friends" or "ever going out with a girl," she does recall that "he had a lot of books. You could tell he was very bright."

Sylvia Weiss and Ted Krakow, both former residents of the neighborhood, have similar memories of the small, shy Gold boy. "He was one of the kids who came in my parents' corner grocery store," recalls Mrs. Weiss. "He was a bit smaller than the other boys his age and was very quiet. He stayed to himself most of the time."[44] Ted Krakow, who lived one street east of Philip, knew Harry as the *Rebbetzin's* son. "He was little and heavy, but everyone knew he was very smart," recalls Krakow.[45]

"He was a real loner," says Mary Frank, another former neighbor. While other kids were out playing in the street, "Harry always seemed to be involved in some intellectual activity."[46]

Considering Harry's obvious discomfort in the company of others, it is not surprising to learn that "he withdrew more and more to himself . . . became a prodigious reader" and evolved into one of those semi-reclusive kids who was more attached to books than to friends.[47] Devouring his first book at an early age, he admitted to an "ineffable feeling of sadness" when he had completed it—"there was no more to read."[48] But there were "other books, many, many others": *The Adventures of Tom Swift, The Rover Boys*, the Frank Merriwell baseball stories, Alexandre Dumas and *The Man in the Iron Mask*, and Ralph Henry Barbour's tales of schoolboy heroics on the athletic field. His joy as a child, he would recount years later, was to sit in his family's "capacious, leather-covered, upholstered chair with a number of hard crusts of pumpernickel bread, on which I had rubbed garlic and sprinkled salt, and to munch aromatically away as I read."[49]

Later, Gold tackled Dickens, Milton, Browning, and Shakespeare.

His intellectual appetite was wide and insatiable: O. Henry's short stories one day, Albert Payson Terhune's "dog stories" of Lassie and Laddie the next, and a Zane Grey western, Jack London adventure, or Conan Doyle mystery the day after. Little Harry's intellectual pursuits may have resonated positively among the intelligentsia of his working-class neighborhood, but they drew sneers and heckling from most children his age. His interest in poetry inspired abuse. "On one occasion," he recalled, "I recited poetry before the assembly in Grammar School and I took a merciless riding from the boys afterwards, got into a couple fights; so, I refused to listen to any of the teachers' entreaties to recite any more poetry. The boys regarded it as very sissyish business."[50]

Gold also developed a passion for movies and theater. He became "enthralled by a drama of any kind"; "the more credible the character portrayal and the more absorbing the story, the better." Though the early film serials of the late 1910s and early 1920s whetted his appetite for the screen adventures of *The Sheik* and *The Sea Hawk*, live theater was where his "real romance" with drama took flight. The rare but exhilarating occasions when his mother would take him to the Arch Street Theatre to see the Yiddish actress Molly Picon, and his seeing *Peter Pan* at the old Broad Street Theatre a few years later, ignited a "passion" for anything dramatic on a stage.[51] Often, Harry admitted, he would exit the theater in a "beatific daze."

He would soon develop a similar interest in music and opera, especially after his father took advantage of his employee discount and "purchased a Victor Talking Machine." Immediately, the Gold family became devoted listeners to everything from "plaintive Yiddish lullabies" to classic Italian operas sung by "Tetrazzini, Caruso, and the famed cantor, Yussell Rosenblatt." Harry wanted to take his growing interest in music to the next level—to learn a musical instrument—but "such was not possible under our [family's] meager circumstances in the early twenties."[52]

"Fear of disgrace or ridicule"

Young Harry wasn't consumed just by the arts and matters of the mind. He also had an "all-absorbing ardor for sports." This infatuation was clearly hampered by his "small and slight" stature, "sickly" constitution, and timidity. Even in high school, Gold still stood just five feet, three inches tall and weighed between ninety and 110 pounds—not the physical hallmarks of athletic achievement. "I would try to be a participant," he would say years later, "but I was much too slight. They just laughed at me. They wouldn't even let me put on a uniform."[53]

Despite these handicaps, Gold loved to "play football on the hard asphalt and pavement of Philip Street and the dump lots" nearby; he relished the "hard, smashing thrill of an open-field tackle." These moments of athletic triumph, however, were few. Gold was considered the "worst player" in the neighborhood, causing teammates "to shudder when they drew [him] as a partner" or team member. Sometimes he was not chosen at all and stood alone on the sidelines. Still, he was a "fanatical" supporter of his high school basketball and football teams, and avidly followed his favorite college and professional players and teams throughout his life—but always as a fan.[54]

If his slight frame and unimpressive athletic ability left him feeling ostracized, his inability to protect himself made him decidedly vulnerable. Gold described his South Philly neighborhood as "a rough one" that endorsed only one method of "proving a boy's superiority"—"a fight." He "avoided fights whenever it could be managed," at other times he took a "shellacking." Small, timorous, and Jewish, Gold became a target for bullies. Sometimes his family's naiveté contributed to the mayhem, as when his mother sent him out to play with other children "dressed . . . in a white sailor suit." Within minutes, not surprisingly, another kid on the block "smeared it with mud and [Harry] ran home in tears."

Gold avoided physical combat except when the alternative was worse —"to admit cowardice." He would later wonder if his "reluctance to fight" was due to his long-standing "fear of disgrace or ridicule in front of a crowd."[55]

The geographic and ethnic landscape only compounded the problem. Though Philip Street was technically in the Jewish quarter, other sizable ethnic communities surrounded it. The Irish were only one block away, on Second Street, and the Neckers were just below the Oregon Avenue train tracks and public dump. Both areas were minefields of religious and ethnic conflict. For Gold, a walk down Stonehouse Lane in the Neck was an "expedition" into the preserve of "some indescribably dirty youngsters" who stoned Gold and his friends, and no doubt were the same ones who committed the sudden "lightning raids" and "brick-throwing, window-smashing forays" against Jewish homes above Oregon Avenue. South Philadelphia Jews liked to believe they too "had a rough crowd" and "could hold their own" with their intimidating neighbors, but one thing was clear—you "never walked alone" through the Neck.[56] "You didn't go down there unless you had to," recalls Ted Krakow, who lived on American Street, just north of Oregon Avenue. "They'd beat the hell out of you. Jews were not welcome down there."[57]

Confrontations closer to home could be just as troubling. A snowball fight with the Catholic kids from Mount Carmel Parochial School, at Third and Wolf, left Gold with a ringing head for two days when one of the snowballs held a concealed rock.[58]

The large and growing Italian community to the west presented its own problems. Borrowing books from the public library at Broad and Porter streets, well over a mile from his home, could be risky. At the age of twelve, Gold was "badly beaten by a group of fifteen Gentile boys at 12th and Shunk Streets while returning from the library."

"From that time on," Gold would write later, his father—"with his not too unwilling agreement"—"insisted on convoying Harry to the library regularly" on Saturday nights, patiently waiting outside while his son chose books. Sam Gold's interest in protecting his son's welfare was admirable, but for Harry the paternal escort service was the height of humiliation. He "took pains to conceal it from the rest of the boys" in the neighborhood. Harry faced a real quandary: either accept the stigma of a parent providing protection on his journeys through South Philadelphia or do without a bodyguard and risk a pummeling by "lurking gangs."[59] For two long, humiliating years, Harry accepted his father as a shield.[60]

The minor but almost daily indignities, along with the more serious confrontations such as those at Mount Carmel and the Broad Street library—not to mention his father's very troubling affairs with bigoted co-workers—left Gold with "tremendous resentment" and an "overwhelming desire to do something active" to fight prejudice. He hoped that one day he'd discover some means "on a much wider and [more] effective scale than by smashing an individual anti-Semite in the face."[61]

Though often the target of bullies and anti-Semites, Gold bought into many of his neighborhood's customs and attitudes. One of the more important and universal principles "was the doctrine that a self-respecting man never became a squealer" or "tattler to the police or cops." Law enforcement officers were considered "corrupt hoodlums, takers of bribes, and sadists" who beat up prisoners and anyone else they decided to lean on. "One really had to live where I did," said Gold, "to fully appreciate the bitter venom and hatred with which a stool pigeon was regarded."[62] Upon his arrest many years later, this tenet of noncooperation with authorities proved initially troubling, but eventually—to his surprise—easy to rationalize away.

"Please make me pass, Harry"

His mother's deep convictions and directives still guided Harry in everything from his beneficent outlook toward his fellow man to his extreme chivalry regarding the opposite sex. The tension between maternal guidance and environmental pressures led to some rather interesting predicaments.

One instance was his penchant for tutoring schoolchildren in the neighborhood. Few were turned away, and it was commonplace for Harry to sit in the homes of other children and assist them with their schoolwork. He occasionally did more than just tutor. Early on, Gold realized he "had the happy faculty of being able to write the English compositions and themes" assigned by his various teachers. It wasn't long before other children asked him to write theirs as well. Gold "happily agreed."[63]

Soon, however, he was "expending all of [his] creative reserve and efforts in doing as many as four or five in one night for other students" and then realizing near midnight that he had "run dry" of ideas and had not begun his own composition. All too frequently Gold would fall asleep, then "stealthily awake" before dawn and "patch together" his own assignment. Never was payment offered or requested for his ghostwriting services. Though he claimed that these services "bored and exasperated" him, he, like his mother, did "enjoy helping people."

As an academic soft touch, Gold was susceptible to some brazen requests. Late in his career at Southern High, for example, his English class was "given a written test based on Shakespeare's *Macbeth*." The instructor, Dr. Farbish, "a holy terror," gave them twenty-five questions requiring one- to three-word answers. The test was designed to provide a lifeline for the many students flunking the course. "Pass this and I'll let you get by" was the teacher's challenge. Gold quickly shot through the quiz but was startled by Dr. Farbish's request that he "help him . . . by doing the grading" that very night. Gold dutifully agreed, but another student "witnessed the transfer of exam sheets" and he was soon "besieged by a group of boys all pleading, 'Please make me pass, Harry.'"

Gold went home and "sat up till after 5 AM filling in missing answers, erased the wrong ones and supplied the correct words, and even went so far as to fake the some twenty-five different varieties of handwriting." By the time he "fell wearily into bed, everyone had passed, every last boy." In what he called a "twisted quirk of expiation," Gold "lowered his own mark a trifle."

Dr. Farbish's reaction on seeing the grades would trouble Gold for years. "The class did very well, did they not, Harry?" he said. Then he turned his back without waiting for an answer and walked away. For decades, Gold felt "the gentle sarcasm of his teacher's remark" and believed he owed him an apology for acting so "shamefully." It wasn't often that his mother's firm dictates about honesty and trustworthiness fell victim to the pressures of the street.[64]

A "Frank Merriwell complex"

The Farbish incident presented Gold with what he called a "real stumbling block." "Why," he asked himself many times, "had I done this for a group of stupid, lazy dolts to who I had no responsibility and no allegiance?"[65] The answer was unavoidable: "gullibility and naiveté." Combined with his "very powerful impulse" to trust in the intrinsic goodness of people (gemütlichkeit) and his strong desire to please, they made for a potent brew of emotions that did not always serve Harry well. "I never stopped being astounded," he would one day write, "upon discovering that the very person who smiled and spoke to me kindly, had nasty, hidden ulterior motives." Though he considered such people "twisted," he "could not get angry" with them. He pitied them, for "they were missing so much of the fun of liking others."[66] Even though he was sometimes taken advantage of, the "desire to help others," according to his attorney, would be "the dominant characteristic of Harry Gold's later life."[67]

Some of these impulses contributed to Gold's "extravagantly chivalrous notions regarding girls." His "mom's teaching that women must be respected and . . . reading Zane Grey and Frank Merriwell" led to a highly inflated view of women and a firm belief in "romantic love." At an early age he was "convinced that if a boy waited long enough, the one he loved would come along." For Gold, "all girls were good and gentle creatures, made specifically for men to cherish and protect."

Years later, Gold realized that these notions did not square with reality. "I was much perturbed to discover that many of the feminine gender were full of malice and meanness, and would lie more often than tell the truth." Until he grasped this sobering truth, however, Gold honored the opposite sex and "always" gave up his seat "on a trolley car" to a woman. In fact, he thought himself "probably the last male in Philadelphia to stop doing so."[68]

Women were not the only ones to scuttle Gold's storybook notions. His propensity to believe in the innate goodness of people could also be rudely shaken by his heroes—athletes. Gold admitted to growing up with a "Frank Merriwell complex"—an adoration of accomplished athletes, who in addition to their physical prowess exemplified honesty and fair play. It came as a "crushing shock" to learn that not every athletic hero was a paragon of virtue.[69] On hearing one of his "great baseball heroes, Al Simmons," unload "a selection of curse words" on a lowly shoeshine boy, "the illusion of a Lancelot . . . a man pure in heart and without blemish of any kind," was quickly and painfully "shattered."[70]

Such idealistic notions were repeatedly crushed. Gold's impulse to trust in people seemed boundless. A healthy suspicion regarding motives and a judicious assessment of credibility—especially when someone was asking him to do something—were resources he never seemed to acquire.

A "fixation . . . so overpowering"

Curiously, though he was without caution in his interpersonal dealings, Harry was quite the opposite in his correspondence and academic work. A fervent list maker, he also rewrote letters, messages, and work assignments—not once or twice but many times. The slightest mistake required another draft. Every note, every personal letter, every report had to be pristine. Gold's "ever-present drive for perfection in a task undertaken" was irresistible. "This fetish of discarding a not-quite-up-to-snuff page troubled" him throughout his academic and professional life, and "remnants of this curious twist," as he referred to it, remained with him until his death.[71] Today, of course, we recognize such behavior as a symptom of an obsessive-compulsive disorder. Gold's list making and rewriting are fairly typical of the disorder.[72]

In addition to these compulsions, Gold also experienced "unwelcome distressing thoughts and mental images." The most troubling was an intense and recurring fear of never being gainfully employed: "Starting at the age of about twelve, I began to fret about my future—in what way would I earn a living, to what sort of work would I be adapted?" Over time, the fear increased, "ceaselessly digging away" at him. "Perhaps I would never actually be able to find a job," he wrote, "maybe no one would want to hire me." Gold admitted that "this fixation became so overpowering" that he "would cry," and his father would have to console him.[73]

This fear was aggravated by his very real inability to find and hold employment during his teenage years. His first job as a "candy-butcher" at the old Broad Street Theatre lasted one performance because he "only sold one box" of candy: he was "too frightened to call out his wares between acts."[74] As a fourteen-year-old, Gold tried selling newspapers like most other boys in the neighborhood, but when assigned a "lonely street corner in far Eastwick"—a section of Southwest Philadelphia—he "sold so few papers" that he was "told not to return." Frightened by reports of neighborhood gangs setting upon outsiders, Gold admitted to being relieved he had been fired.

Even before the Depression, Gold was all too familiar with the difficulty of finding a job. During summers when others were being hired as "errand boys," he made the "round of small shops and wholesale houses in the area of Market, Arch, and Vine streets" but "never as much as got a nibble." Exhausted and depressed from these failures, he would go home "to find solace in Ralph Henry Barbour, Dumas or James Oliver Curwood—plus a liberal supply of mom's cookies."[75]

"I lose all tolerance"

In his solitary existence, beset by insecurities, Gold developed a fast attachment to any who offered their friendship. He would later refer to his "almost puppy-like eagerness to please," and others who came to know him would comment on the same quality. Once he became "fond of a particular person," he would "literally, do anything for him."[76]

As he entered his teens, Gold did begin to open up and develop some serious friendships. And he was proud of them—not surprising, considering that most of his youth had been spent at his mother's side with a wide array of books for companions. Finally "I was one of a very closely bound group of boys, the gang."[77]

Abe Sklar "was the leader." "Small and wiry," he was the "best fighter in the group," according to Gold, and someone whose "counsel always seemed so sensible." Danny Gussick "was the black sheep" of the group, whose father, "a professional gambler," spent more time in New York than in Philadelphia. Izzy Lieberman "was the oldest of eleven children" and left school at an early age to help support his family. "His father was tubercular" and often confined to a sanatorium. Frank Kessler was the "steady-going and solid sort, both mentally and physically," the one whom Harry looked upon as a "reassuring" confidant and whose name he would appropriate when working as a secret agent.[78]

Gold relished being part of his own group of boys. "To say we were close is an understatement," he wrote years later, "for we went everywhere together, played together, and were constantly in one another's homes." It was this group of friends in December 1926, when Gold turned sixteen, who unexpectedly came to his home with gifts—a matching tie and handkerchief, his favorite chocolate-covered cherries, and tickets to a show at the Earle Theatre. These were his first birthday presents from anyone other than his parents. Many years later, Gold would fondly declare, "I shall never forget it."[79]

Gold would make other friends during these years, such as Leon Coltman, Arthur's brother and the bright son of the local kosher butcher, "from the only really comfortably-off family in our street," and Sammy Haftel, a stocky youngster "who could fight like a demon" and "taught others to respect him"—despite the abuse he took because his father was a "drunkard" and his mother worked to support the family. Gold treasured these friendships all his life and was saddened "whatever drifting away occurred" as some of the boys married and he himself went to college.[80]

Though these relationships were slow to emerge, Gold cherished them all, extended himself far beyond the norm when his friends were in need, and "never consciously, except for brief outbursts, hated anyone for long." But there was "one burning exception" to his "powerful impulse" to like and respect people: Fascists.

For Gold, Fascism was a "creed synonymous with that ages-old horror, anti-Semitism. Here I lose all tolerance," he would write. From his early experiences fending off bigoted youth, his father's recurring abuse at the Victor Talking Machine plant, and the increasing reports of religious and political repression in Germany, "it was obvious that there could be no quarter in the fight against anti-Semitism, and no true peace until it was vanquished, no, not beaten, but utterly obliterated."[81]

But as he approached his senior year, what preoccupied Gold was getting a job after high school. He longed to contribute to the household—and if the job could have an element of science or chemistry to it, so much the better. By his mid-teens Gold had developed a keen interest in chemistry. He and Sammy Haftel would often walk to the Center City showrooms of various chemical companies to admire the sophisticated equipment, and when savings allowed, head toward the South Street company warehouses to "purchase a variety of elementary laboratory glassware and chemicals." "From his first high school chemistry course," Gold wrote, "the bond had been sealed."[82]

But for a poor Jewish boy with no work history, a college education and a professional career as a chemist were distant dreams. His first goal was daunting enough—landing a job.

CHAPTER 2

. . . .

A Debt Repaid

I n August 1928, Governor Alfred E. Smith became the Democratic
Party's candidate for president of the United States; Walt Disney
introduced his most popular animated character, Mickey Mouse;
and the New York Yankees were on their way to winning another
World Series. In Paris, the Kellogg-Briand Peace Pact was signed by fifteen nations in an effort to outlaw aggressive warfare. In Philadelphia,
Harry Gold was getting ready to graduate from high school.

Though he would not receive his diploma from South Philadelphia
High School until February 1929, Gold completed his required course
work and left school in August.[1] Unable to find a steady summer job, he
had stayed in school for two consecutive summers and graduated a half-
year ahead of schedule, ranked third in a class of 160.[2]

Soon after graduation, an acquaintance of his father came forward
with a job offer. Gold was hired by "Giftcrafters, a woodworking firm in
the Kensington section of the city whose principal product was ship models." He had grown up watching his father repair and refinish furniture
in the basement and build enclosed porches for neighbors on Philip
Street. Woodworking never became a passion for Harry, but it was a job,
and the $10 a week he was paid at the plant was the first steady money
he ever earned. He guided sanding machines, assembled models with

glue and nails, and became proficient with an array of chisels. The grueling ten-hour days and six-day weeks gave him a new skill, toughened hands, and a meager but growing bank account.[3] At least temporarily, Giftcrafters put a stop to Gold's recurring panic that he would never land a job that paid a regular wage.

"Forty cents an hour for seven days a week"

Gold had no intention of following his father into a career in woodworking. His father's low pay and constantly bruised and bloody fingers—and vile treatment at the hands of anti-Semitic co-workers—inspired Harry to aim higher. If he was going to earn money with his hands, he'd prefer to be handling chemicals and test tubes in a laboratory. He kept his eyes open for new opportunities, and in December 1928 applied for a position with the Pennsylvania Sugar Company, a large refinery plant along the banks of the Delaware River in the Fishtown section of the city.

One of the largest sugar refineries in the world, with sales of more than $31 million and employing almost eleven hundred Philadelphians, Pennsylvania Sugar had been overhauled from a "small, wobbly company" in 1912 into a serious and growing concern. Its three subsidiaries, Pennsylvania Alcohol Corporation, Siboney Distilling Corporation, and the Franco-American Chemical Corporation, were each formidable economic operations that produced everything from Quaker brand alcohol and antifreeze to solvents, paints, lacquers, and rum.[4]

Gold was given an entry level job cleaning spittoons, emptying waste receptacles, and washing dirty equipment, but the facility had a chemistry lab where some significant science was undertaken. Moreover, he was in the presence of college-educated men, some with advanced degrees, who, as Gold's lawyers would say many years later, were "putting into daily practice the sciences in which he was so desperately interested . . . and bringing into commercial reality those things which before had been but text book theories . . . carried out in the school room laboratory."[5] Gold believed he was getting closer to his goal of becoming a man of science.

In addition, he was making money, "forty cents an hour for seven days a week, twelve hours a day." That added up to $33.60 per week, occasionally $40 with overtime, princely sums compared with his wages at Giftcrafters. It contributed mightily to the family's modest income.[6] Gold dutifully brought each check home to his mother, who took a portion for the household, gave her son some spending and transportation money, and put the rest into a bank account she had opened for him. His savings grew quickly—with rarely a day off, he had no time to spend it. But even if he had had the time, the savings would have remained untouched; the family agreed that the money was for Harry's college education.

Gold soaked up as much knowledge as he could, spending more time than he was supposed to in the facility's chemistry lab, and carefully observing the scientists practicing their craft. His keen interest was noted by Dr. Gustave T. Reich, the Pennsylvania Sugar Company's lead researcher. After only six months on the job, the precocious teenager was promoted to "laboratory assistant." Although his pay wasn't increased much, that mattered little; he was no longer cleaning out spittoons but assisting real chemists in serious projects.

"An extreme state of exhaustion"

Gold was also enjoying newfound economic security. That his wages seemed to have little impact on his material possessions or social life bothered him not one bit. "I simply had no time whatsoever to go out" and spend it, he would recall years later of his quickly accumulating savings.[7] By working practically every day of the week and spending almost nothing, Gold managed to save approximately $2,400 by September 1930, when he left the Pennsylvania Sugar Company to enter the University of Pennsylvania.[8] He was now realizing another part of his dream: he had become a college man. Though conscientious and hard working, he was not a brilliant student. He embarked on an ambitious schedule of science, math, and literature courses.[9] It was "all I could do to keep up with my college studies," he later admitted, but he still made time to tutor former high school friends and Sugar Company colleagues who needed help with their studies.[10]

In addition to the demanding course work, Gold attempted to realize another of his dreams—to become an athlete on a college team. Though passionate about sports, he had never distinguished himself on any athletic field. Recognizing his limitations, he steered clear of contact sports and went out for Penn's freshman cross-country team.

Inspired by his vivid recollection of Frank Merriwell's and Ralph Henry Barbour's stories and by the more recent success of the Philadelphia Athletics—winners of the 1929 and 1930 World Series—Gold pushed himself through the long mileage required of competitive distance runners.[11] The rigorous training sessions, combined with his heavy academic load, kept him in "an extreme state of exhaustion" for much of his freshman year. Hindered both by his unimpressive physical gifts and by his lack of high school experience, he had an uphill climb to make the team. A serious ankle sprain just before a big meet in New York sidelined him for several weeks.[12] The injury basically ended his aspirations as a college runner, and he would never again attempt to earn a position on a competitive athletic team.[13]

Athletic disappointment and his mediocre classroom record were soon eclipsed by graver concerns. It was the onset of the Great Depression. Like millions of households across America, the Golds were gradually enveloped in an all-consuming financial struggle.

"The day of reckoning had arrived"

The loss of Harry's weekly wage had hurt, and Celia Gold was occasionally forced to dip into his savings to put food on the table and pay creditors. He gave his mother permission to do as she saw fit. The rent often went unpaid. The family's dilemma grew worse when Sam Gold was laid off from RCA in 1931. It was not the first time the head of the Gold household had been thrown out of work, but this time it was different. The nation was in the midst of a devastating and worsening depression, work was hard or impossible to come by, and the unpaid bills were piling up rapidly.

Sam went out each morning, lugging his heavy toolbox, searching for any kind of work, but he returned home at the end of each day exhausted and penniless. One day Celia, a proud woman unalterably opposed to charity, was devastated to discover him selling apples on a city street corner.

Though preoccupied with his coursework, Harry was aware of the economic conditions affecting the country as well as his family. Yet he may not have felt the full impact until he arrived home one afternoon to discover "a stranger, a city constable, about to take the furniture from the home under a writ" for unpaid rent. It was then that he realized they were practically penniless.[14]

"The day of reckoning had arrived," and Harry did not shirk his responsibility.[15] His bank account depleted, "there was but one source from which funds were available. This was the return of the unearned portion of his tuition for the second semester which had been paid in advance."[16] Though it had been his great dream to attain a college degree and proclaim himself a certified chemist, his family came first. Gold "voluntarily withdrew" from the second semester of his second year at Penn on March

12, 1932. His unselfish act would not only provide the immediate funds for his family; he would now replace his father as the family's chief breadwinner. The next morning he went to his former boss at the Pennsylvania Sugar Company and asked to be rehired.

The company was cutting back its workforce, but Gold was lucky enough to regain a position. Because of across-the-board pay cuts, his wages were significantly lower, and he would be working not in the laboratory but in the distillery plant. His new assignments required more muscle than intellect and proved far less satisfying than lab work. Nevertheless, it was a paycheck, and the Gold household desperately needed it.

"Eagerness to please"

Once his ten- or twelve-hour workdays were over, Gold spent much of his free time assisting co-workers and neighbors with their academic pursuits. He never requested compensation, and refused it on the rare occasions when it was offered. Moreover, these tutoring sessions invariably took place at the home of the student, greatly increasing Harry's expenditure of time and his transportation costs. He seemed oblivious to such concerns. Since grade school, he had helped others in their studies. As his lawyer would say many years later, "these were not casual instances of some friend occasionally helping another, but rather a pattern of conduct in a man who wanted to be of assistance to those who needed help."[17]

Harry also lent money to those in need. Though his generosity had manifested itself during his childhood and adolescence, it took flight now that he was earning a salary while surrounded by cash-strapped co-workers. "Gold made loans to these people," his lawyer recalled, "irrespective of any prior acquaintance and despite the fact his own family was probably in need as much as those to whom he advanced money."[18] What's worse, "he did this when the money was not available to him and in order to obtain it he often borrowed money at usurious rates in order that he might make advances to those who were in need." He rarely asked for the money back. He liked and trusted people, but his "gullibility" often led to problems.[19] In short, he was an easy touch with a seemingly unending line of applicants.[20] Gold knew that these loans were "foolish disbursements," but his "eagerness to please" generally overwhelmed his financial prudence.[21]

As the economy worsened, Harry and his co-workers fretted about their job security, discussed what needed to be done to right the nation, and threw out the names of politicians who could do a better job than President Hoover. Gold was overheard one day telling some pipe fitters that Socialist Party leader Norman Thomas was a "great man." A company superintendent "rebuked" him and warned that there was to be "no further talk of socialism in the plant." Gold complied, but the economic crisis, the threat of additional layoffs, and the lecture from a superior only made him more "obdurate."[22]

Though sympathetic to the Socialist Party's standard bearer and principles, Gold was far from an ideologue or political activist. His politics didn't go much beyond an amorphous "theory of social cooperation." He claimed to be "horrified" and "incredulous" on learning that Davey Zion, a neighborhood friend, had proclaimed himself a Communist and was now giving speeches and handing out party literature at Miflin Park. Though others defended his friend's actions, Gold admitted to "feeling . . . revulsion." For Gold, "Bolshevism or communism was just a name for a wild and vaguely defined phenomenon going on in an 18th century land thousands of miles away."[23]

Politics was a luxury Harry had little time for. With Sam still out of work, the national economy in shambles, his younger brother Yus just entering high school, and his mother struggling to keep food on the table, Harry's modest salary was all that separated them from starvation or eviction. He worked six or seven days a week and could only dream of the day when things would get better and he could return to Penn.

Things were to grow much worse.

In December 1932, just ten days before Christmas, Gold and twenty-five other workers received layoff notices and were told that they had little "hope of being reemployed in the reasonably near future." This was a devastating blow to the entire Gold household, especially Celia. Her dutiful son wasted little time in searching for a new job, but Philadelphia was not a cornucopia of economic opportunity.

"No one had money"

The early years of the Depression in Philadelphia witnessed considerable damage. Unemployment was soaring, and the city's economy was on the verge of collapse. More than fifty banking institutions were forced to close because of "overextended resources, granting credit on insufficient security," and a host of other misguided financial practices. Unemployment councils and shantytowns full of newly homeless men were springing up. City police stations, normally the last refuge of the homeless, were now taking in hundreds of men a night who had nowhere else to turn. In 1932 alone, citywide mortgage foreclosures exceeded nineteen thousand. On one residential street, "thirty-six out of sixty houses were repossessed for debt." The prospect of a similar fate befalling his family frightened Gold tremendously. He needed to find employment quickly, but where in Philadelphia in 1933 did someone find work? Almost 12 percent of white Philadelphians and 16 percent of blacks were unemployed. Foreign-born whites like Gold faired worst of all: 20 percent were jobless.[24] In densely populated South Philadelphia the numbers were even gloomier, "almost one in three workers was out of a job."[25] With his family desperately depending on him, twenty-two-year-old Harry Gold faced a daunting challenge.

Celia painfully decided to return the family's "new parlor suite"— their first in sixteen years—to Lit Brothers Department Store. The $50 refund was "vital and loomed so large" to the Gold family's economic survival.[26] The Golds were not alone in their embarrassment; returning merchandise or, worse, having it repossessed had become commonplace.[27] "Playing eviction in the city's streets" became a new game among children.[28]

"No one had money, it was a terrible time," says Ted Krakow, whose older brother Simon was a friend of Joe Gold's. "We had to beat the sheriff and the constable. They'd come to our house and said if we didn't pay the rent they were going to take the furniture and then put us out on the street." Krakow remembers those emotional times when his family "was on the run." "When we didn't have money to pay the rent, my father would get a horse and wagon, and move us during the night to another house. It happened two or three times."[29]

Sam and Harry Gold looked for work each morning, Sam at the "fantastic hour of 5 a.m. so as to be first in line" for a possible job—but both returned to Philip Street in the evening dejected and voicing increasing despair. Businesses were laying off employees or folding, and furniture cluttered many sidewalks as families were evicted from their homes. With nothing to show for his daily tours of riverfront industrial sites, Kensington textile mills, and Center City businesses, Gold found his teenage nightmares coming back with a vengeance.

His anxiety was evident to his friends. Ferdinand Heller, a research chemist at the Pennsylvania Sugar Company with strong left-wing tendencies, suggested that Harry try something dramatic—he encouraged Gold to leave America and "take [his] family to the Birobidzhan area of the Soviet Russia."[30]

Nestled in a sparsely populated stretch of wilderness the size of Texas between the Bira, Bidzhan, and Amur rivers along the Sino-Soviet border some five thousand miles east of Moscow, Birobidzhan was being promoted as a "national homeland of Soviet Jewry." It would be officially proclaimed the Jewish Autonomous Region (J.A.R.) in May 1934.[31] Despite absent infrastructure, a "harsh climate," and a reputation as "an extremely unattractive territory," Birobidzhan had its advocates, and Jews from all over the world—many captivated by the notion of a homeland of their own—relocated there.[32] Life was fraught with difficulties—some considered the wilderness settlement's obstacles nothing short of "catastrophic"—and Jews were a small minority of the region's inhabitants; yet many of the Jewish faith were drawn to the idea, if not the area itself.[33]

Jews from Philadelphia, Baltimore, and New York City heard the call. "My parents were from Russia and seriously considering going back there during the heart of the Depression," recalled Aaron Libson. "Their doors were open after the revolution. There was potential for a model state, a secular Jewish state, a worker's state where capitalism would be harnessed and life's harshness would be ended. Birbidzhan was definitely known and attractive to Jews."[34]

Doris Kaplan was eleven years old in 1931 when her father came home from work one day and told the family, "We're going to Russia." For her parents, says Kaplan, "Birobidzhan promised a better life—each according to his ability, to each according to his needs."[35] The Kaplans made the exhausting eleven-day trip from New York to Bremen, to Helsinki, to Leningrad and Moscow, and then the long overland journey on the Trans-Siberian Railroad to a lush but remote agricultural community in the middle of nowhere. "It was like going to the country," recalls Kaplan, but this was the real country. She remembers "living in tents, no schools, and great deprivation, but everybody was Jewish and believed in a Socialist system of government." She also remembers "meeting people from France, Argentina, England, Canada."[36]

Life in the grand experiment was difficult, and the promise of a better existence was not always realized. Many believe Birobidzhan "was doomed to failure" from the very beginning.[37] "The poor soil, heavy rains during July and August, when the crop was about to ripen, hordes of mosquitoes and flies, and a very cold winter with little snow were hard on settlers." Predictably, many escaped to more civilized realms or made the disappointing trek back home. Kaplan and her mother departed for Moscow after a few months.[38] Her father joined them the following year. Eventually they would return to America.

Gold had heard of the Birobidzhan experiment and knew of its appeal to some Russian Jews, but for him Fred Heller's well-meaning suggestion was "nonsense."[39] He and his father were out of work and times were hard, but Gold was an American. He had no desire to go anywhere else, and certainly not to the wilds of Siberia. It was just a "hair brained idea" by a well-intentioned friend. "I was not even a communist sympathizer," recalled Gold, or an especially observant Jew.[40] "As bad as things were here," he would subsequently write, "I still considered this my home and liked it very much."

But along with his friends, his familiar Jewish neighborhood, and the American culture he so voraciously imbibed came the dreaded prospect of economic ruin and the "disgraceful specter and the deep ignominy of charity." Though charity cases were growing ever more common on Philip Street and throughout the city, Gold knew his mother's antipathy for handouts.

Yet the Golds were squarely facing economic ruin. They were about to become a charity case—something Harry's mother was "violently against." He had "looked for work frantically" since being laid off, but weeks had passed, it was late February 1933, and bills were going unpaid. The prospect of sheriff's deputies appearing at the front door with an eviction notice was becoming a daily threat.

"Gold must arrive tonight"

One day his friend Fred Heller excitedly came over to his house after work. He was "jubilant"—he had found a job for Gold. Heller explained, "Tom Black, a friend and a former classmate of his at Penn State, was leaving his job at the Holbrook Manufacturing Co., a soap firm in Jersey City, and could possibly arrange for [Gold] to take his place."[41] Black, according to Heller, was taking "a better position at the National Oil Products Co. in Harrison, New Jersey," and the Holbrook outfit would need a replacement. If Gold was interested, Black advised him to give the job serious consideration, since such opportunities were in short supply.

Harry had not taken up his friend's previous suggestion regarding a move to Birobidzhan, but Heller's present announcement was considerably more appealing. The Holbrook opportunity, however, would be as life-altering as relocating to Siberia. It would stave off homelessness for his family, but it would also result in a series of decisions that would precipitate the "crime of the century" and make the name of Harry Gold one of the most reviled in postwar America.[42]

At the time, the only drawback to the Holbrook job was its location
—in Jersey City. Besides two summer camp experiences as a child, Gold
had never lived away from home. But he was in his twenties and the family breadwinner. Circumstances demanded he step up to the plate.

About a week later, a knock on the door notified Gold that there was
a phone call for him at Coltman's Kosher Butcher Shop on Philip Street.
It was Heller, informing him that he had just received a telegram from
Black. The message said, "Gold must arrive tonight" if he wanted the job.
Harry and his mother quickly packed the flimsy cardboard suitcase he
had last used for summer camp a decade earlier. He "borrowed $6 from
Frank Kessler as well as a jacket which closely matched [his] pants
. . . and was bundled off on a Greyhound bus" for North Jersey.[43]

"Capitalism was doomed"

Gold arrived in a snowy Jersey City well after midnight and eventually
found his way to Corbin Avenue, where Black shared an apartment with
Ernie Segressemann. "Tom was waiting for me in the hallway down-
stairs," Gold would report years later. Black had a "huge, friendly grin in
that freckled face crowned with those untamed reddish curls and bear
like grip of his hand."[44] The two men stayed up all night discussing soap
chemistry, politics, and some "complicating circumstances" concerning
the job.[45]

The Holbrook operation was "owned by two venerable and gentle-
manly brothers, Franklin and Stanton Smith," but run by a superintendent named MacIntosh who, Black said, was "very anti-Semitic and would
never consent to hiring a Jew." To get around this impediment, Black
"concocted a jumbled story," arguing that although the name Gold
sounded Jewish, Harry was to say that his grandfather had converted
when he married a Gentile girl many years earlier.[46]

Adding to the "confusing mess" was Black's announcement that
Heller had sent Gold to "Jersey City because as a Socialist he was a likely
recruit to the more militant organization," the Communist Party. That
night Gold "was subjected to a steady barrage of facts to prove that capitalism was doomed . . . in the United States and that the only country to
which the working man owed allegiance was the Soviet Union and that
the only reasonable way of life was communism." Both the fictitious family history and the all-night propaganda session seemed a bit ridiculous to
Gold, but good jobs were hard to come by, especially ones where he
would be a company's "chief chemist."[47]

Although "kindly old Franklin Smith" hired Gold the next day, he was pretty sure that "no one was taken in by" his claim that he was not Jewish, especially MacIntosh, who often spoke of Hitler in admiring terms and once remarked, "All the Jews in America should be put on ships and the goddamn boats sunk in the middle of the ocean." Gold swallowed his resentment "because that wonderful $30 every Saturday kept my family off relief." Of that, he spent $3 each week to rent a room, $4 for food, and $4 for the weekend round-trip train fare between Jersey City and Philadelphia. The remaining $19 was for his parents and brother to live on. His family went "further into debt to . . . the butcher . . . the grocer . . . and their landlord," but they were never evicted or forced to accept charity, "and eventually, all of these people were repaid." For all this, Gold felt extremely "grateful to Tom Black."[48]

Black had relocated to another North Jersey town, but "this new acquaintance rapidly ripened into friendship and the two men saw a great deal of each other."[49] Initially, chemistry and related professional interests were their common ground, but before long their conversations turned to broader issues. Gold's new friend was particularly troubled by "the millions of unemployed throughout the world" and the dysfunctional "economic system, that allowed all that to happen. He preached that something new, something radically different was required to correct the economic rut the world was in. That something for Black was communism: the only ideology where the masses could find security and a viable future." Black "openly expressed his sympathy for the Soviet Republic and also his membership in the Communist Party."[50]

Gold wasn't driven by politics and had never had much interest in Communism. But he also didn't want to offend his new friend, who had kept him and his family off the relief rolls. Black soon moved from economic and political analysis to recruitment. Gold began to feel besieged.[51] Now, in addition to hearing Black constantly advocating "the glories of the Soviet system," he was asked to attend Communist Party meetings. Though he respectfully declined and even, according to Ernie Segressemann, "appeared to be anti-Communist," Black was insistent.[52] Between his gratitude and his natural inclination to please people, it was only a matter of time until Gold relented.

He attended at least two Jersey City party meetings and came away unimpressed. He was pretty much "repelled by the people . . . who belonged to the Communist Party,"[53] a collection of "despicable bohemians who prattled of free love . . . lazy bums who would never work under any economic system," and polysyllabic windbags who loved to hear themselves talk.[54] There was a practically toothless old sailor who "used to get into fights with these big policemen in Jersey City and always lose." And there was "an earnest old Pole who was an ex-anarchist; and a volatile Greek barber" who, bored with the debates over "Marxian dialectics," would jump out of his chair and shout, "To heck with this. Give me six good men and I will take Journal Square by storm."[55] "Nothing was ever accomplished at these meetings," Gold recalled. "They were interminable, and never wound up before 4 a.m. and in spite of Tom's unrestrained enthusiasm, the whole dreary crew seemed to be a very futile threat to even the admittedly unsteady economy of the United States in early 1933." "Frankly," he would write years later, he didn't want to be "seen with people like that."[56]

Clearly, it was going to take a good deal more propagandizing to pull Gold into the Communist Party. Even if he had been philosophically inclined to join, the meetings repelled him. His regard for Black was still strong—he was "pathetically grateful" for the Holbrook job—but there was no way he was joining the party.[57] Black, however, was determined to make the good-natured young Philadelphian a party member.

"A matter of duty and honor"

Tasso Lessing Black was born in Bloomsburg, a small town in central Pennsylvania, on July 5, 1907.[58] His father was a teacher, a scholarly man who loved the classics and passed his love of literature on to his son, whom he had named after an Italian Renaissance poet. Young Black developed an interest in economics, sociology, and philosophy and was "familiar with the writings of Marx, Engels, and Lenin by the time he completed high school," but he set aside the liberal arts to study chemistry in college. It was at Penn State that Black and Fred Heller met. Both shared keen interests in chemistry and left-wing politics.

At the onset of the Great Depression, Black was in his early twenties and earning a decent wage as a chemist in plants in Linden and Jersey City. But he could not escape his "awareness of distress and despair" pervading millions of households around the country. He started reading "the Communist press, especially the more theoretical journals" and began joining groups like the Friends of the Soviet Union and "literary outfits like the John Reed Club and Pen and Hammer."[59] By early 1931 he had recruited himself into the party.

Assigned to a group on the Lower East Side of Manhattan, Black was "properly proletarianized." Not long after, he met Gaik Ovakimian, a high-ranking Soviet spy who was intrigued by the new convert's scientific background. Black expressed an interest in going to Russia and contributing his talents to the new nation, but Ovakimian said he would have to prove himself first. He asked Black to "make reports on some aspects of American industrial chemistry," a suggestion Black found "entirely reasonable."

At their next meeting, Black handed the Soviet spy "several reports" consisting of "a lot of published information and additional data" stolen from his employer concerning "tanning procedures which might not be known in Russia." Ovakimian asked for more, and Black willingly complied.

As Black would recall years later, he would periodically bring up his desire to go to Russia, but his Soviet handler finally put an end to such talk. "The real question he convinced [Black] was how and where [he] could be of most value" to Russia. "There was work of the highest importance to be done right here." Black gradually realized that he was involved "in espionage of some sort," but saw it more as "a matter of duty and honor" than a crime or "moral wrong." Flattered to be told he had the "intelligence and personality" for such an important undertaking, Black tackled his assignments enthusiastically. He was ordered to "stop reading Communist publications, stop seeing Communists, and . . . destroy any Red literature" in his possession. He wasn't to draw any attention to himself.

By 1933, Tasso Lessing Black had become a devout and ardent industrial spy for the Soviet Union. The following year he was asked if he "knew any other friend of the Soviet Union who would like to go there."

"Yes," he answered, "another chemist by the name of Harry Gold."[60]

"How superior was the Soviet way"

Throughout the summer of 1933, Black continued his proselytizing campaign, explaining that new converts needed to be "adequately prepared" before joining the party. He gave Gold "various Marxian textbooks" and encouraged him to "enroll in some of the evening classes for workers run by the Communist Party" near Union Square in New York City.[61] Not wanting to disappoint his friend, one summer evening Gold visited the site, purchased a couple of pamphlets, and made some inquiries. The Communist activists seemed as wary of him as he was of them. He was most struck by the room's decor; the walls were "plastered with those drawings of workmen, all brawny and upright and in overalls . . . with upraised arms, with the fists clenched; and capitalists, with fat cigars and bellies, sitting on huge piles of coins."[62]

In September, Gold heard that Pennsylvania Sugar was hiring again. Roosevelt's National Recovery Act had enabled some businesses to increase their operations and rehire former employees. Gold wasted little time in contacting Dr. Reich and was elated to hear that there was a job for him. The salary would be the same as Holbrook was paying him, but he would be spared the expense of living in Jersey City and would be reunited with his family. Another benefit was that he "would be freed of Tom's importunings to join the Communist Party."

The night before his departure for Philadelphia, Fred Heller, Ernie Segressemann, and Tom Black arrived unexpectedly at his apartment in Heller's "rattletrap, but serviceable Chevrolet" and whisked Gold off to a party in Greenwich Village. The hostess was Vera Kane. Gold thought her "a woman of about 30 . . . very graceful, of medium height and build, with straight black hair framing an oval face, and attractive smile."[63] He was told she was separated from her husband, had a young son who lived with his father, and worked for a New York law firm. She "behaved somewhat as a mother hen" around Black and Segressemann.

This, too, turned into an all-night "gabfest . . . where the ills of the world and needed remedies were discussed," but it was a far more pleasant and harmonious evening than the others Gold had been dragged to, though he continued to be "propagandized by Tom Black" as to the triumphs and successes "of the Soviet system."[64] Edible and intellectual fare consisted of "spaghetti and fried eggs and oysters . . . and the cheap wine of the neighborhood" and listening to "Vera read some incredibly funny stories by Thurber from the *New Yorker* and some rather surprisingly good ones from *New Masses.*" From time to time, the discussion would drift from literature to politics and "how superior was the Soviet way . . . as contrasted with that of the decadent United States." At one point in the evening Gold found himself in a "hotly" contested argument concerning child rearing and the importance of family. As he would recall later, "I was particularly vociferous in my argument against the then existent Soviet idea that children should be raised in state operated homes while their mothers worked in factories because the family has always been very sacred thing to me and we have always been very close in our family."[65] Segressemann complimented Gold on his defense of the traditional family and called his argument particularly persuasive, a quality Gold attributed to the "added incentive of, that very day, returning to [his] home in Philadelphia."[66]

And so in September 1933 Gold returned to his hometown, his neighborhood, his family, and his former employer, the Pennsylvania Sugar Company. But he "was not through with Tom by any means." Whenever Black visited his old college friend, Fred Heller, he would go out of his way to stop by the Gold household in South Philadelphia. The "family was naturally happy to meet the man who . . . had been [their] economic savior," and with his cheerful, "hearty ways," he "quickly endeared himself to them."[67] His warm reception encouraged him to "propagandize" Sam and Celia as well, but there too his recruitment campaign proved unsuccessful.

Despite Black's best efforts, Gold "never made any inquiries in Philadelphia . . . about becoming a Communist." To Gold, Communists were "a shabby and shoddy lot, run through with informers and opportunists, and were great characters for putting other people on a spot." Black, however, seemed impervious to his friend's obstinacy and continued "urging" him to "do the right thing." When Gold visited Black in Newark, they'd eventually wind up at Vera Kane's in Greenwich Village, where both Kane and Black would present "a steady tidal wave of facts and pictures and information . . . regarding the splendid future of communism in the glorious Soviet Union." "Tom and Vera," wrote Gold years later, "never let up."

Gold felt guilty about repeatedly rejecting his friend's requests to join the party, attend meetings, and come out for demonstrations. In addition to keeping the Gold family solvent, Black was an accomplished chemist whom he admired for his academic training and laboratory professionalism. He had been "a favorite student of the late, great chemist, Frank Whitmore, at Penn State" and was "one of the more remarkable chemists" Gold had seen. He was "a superb lab man" who had "uncanny dexterity" and was always able "to think a problem through without making any mistakes," while Gold felt his own work displayed "every possible error in the book."[68] Black had become a heroic figure for Gold, who didn't like disappointing him.

In January 1934, Gold reconstructed another part of his disrupted life—he returned to school. Tuition for the University of Pennsylvania was out of the question, but Philadelphia's Drexel Institute of Technology offered night courses in chemistry. Gold enrolled in a two-year non-degree program in chemical engineering.[69] He switched to night work at Pennsylvania Sugar and soldiered through a physically taxing regimen that would be good preparation for his future career as a secret agent.

As he later described his hectic schedule, "I would leave work at 8 or

8:30 in the morning, go home and go to sleep. Get up early in the afternoon and do my studying . . . have supper and leave the house about 5:30 or 6 and go to Drexel for classes at 7. Classes continued until about 10:15 at night. This would give me just enough time to get home to South Philadelphia and get a cup of coffee, and then go back to work from 12 until 8 or 8:30 the following morning."[70]

It was a demanding schedule that had him crisscrossing the city, but Gold was not intimidated by long hours, hard work, or demanding bosses. He was back home, going to school, and earning a living—things could be worse.

"There is something you can do"

By spring, Gold noticed that Tom Black was no longer beseeching him to join the Communist Party. He was both pleased and made curious by his friend's apparent change of heart, but he dared not ask why for fear of reenergizing the recruitment drive. He would discover the reason soon enough. Many years later, Gold would recognize that moment as the one that turned his life around.

One day in April 1934, when Black was visiting Gold in Philadelphia, Black confronted him: "Harry, you've been stalling me. You have been trying to get out of joining the Communist Party." The reprieve was obviously over; Gold prepared himself for another barrage of Communist propaganda. Surprisingly, his friend took an entirely different tack.

Maybe Harry was right, Black said. As "scientific men," maybe they "didn't belong" in politics. "But there is something you can do," said Black. "There is something that would be very helpful to the Soviet Union and something in which you can take pride." Gold listened, intrigued by this new approach.

"The Pennsylvania Sugar Company," said Black, "has processes, processes on industrial solvents. These are materials of the type, which are used in various finishes and lacquers. The people of the Soviet Union need these processes.

"If you will obtain as many of them as you can in complete detail and give them to me," he continued, "I will see to it that those processes are turned over to the Soviet Union and that they will be utilized" by and for the Russian people.[71] Although these products were commonplace in America, they were not available in Russia, where they could "do much to make the harsh life of those who lived in post-revolution Russia a little more bearable." They "would be doing something illegal," Black acknowledged, but "in the long run [they] would be doing good because [they] would be helping a people who desperately needed it."[72]

"Inevitability"

Amazingly, Gold did not flinch at this shocking suggestion. A law-abiding citizen, never politically active, he found himself reacting favorably to the request. When Black finished making his appeal, Gold told him he "would think it over," but he had already made up his mind. In fact, he was eager to participate and was already visualizing how he could slip company documents and blueprints into a briefcase or hide them on his person, walk out of the plant, copy them at home, and return them the next day undetected.

Gold's reaction is most curious. Though he had resisted his friend's recruitment efforts and was clearly unimpressed with "parlor pinks," "intelligentsia leftists," and the "Bohemian atmosphere of Greenwich Village," the earnest plea to pilfer company documents and processes for the downtrodden Russian people struck a chord.[73] He would offer a mix of rational and emotional reasons for complying, yet one cannot discount the altruistic mind-set that pervaded the Gold household. Celia Gold's descriptions of the harsh struggle to survive in tsarist Russia and her oft-repeated admonition, "No man may look to God who has not helped his fellowmen," informed her son's view of the world.[74] So did Sam's belief in Tolstoy's "brotherhood of man" and his stories of his own "discouragements, disillusions, and disappointments" as a poor immigrant youth. Harry's attorney would argue fifteen years later that there was a certain "inevitability" about his fateful decision.[75]

"Impelled" was the term Gold used to describe his reaction to Black's request. Although there were two prime reasons for this uncharacteristic breach of ethics, namely, his debt of "gratitude to Tom Black" and his "genuine desire to help the people of the Soviet Union," additional factors "exerted far more power."[76] Many years later, he would provide a Senate committee with a numbered list of motives.

First, the Soviet Union had become the first nation to make "anti-Semitism a crime against the state." Tom Black and Vera Kane continually argued that Russia was the "one bulwark against the further encroachment of that ever-growing monstrosity, fascism." For Gold this was no small matter; "nazism and fascism and anti-Semitism were identical" and demanded immediate and overwhelming opposition. He would write years later from his prison cell that "this was the age-old enemy, the evil, bloody stench of the Roman arena, of the medieval ghetto, of the Inquisition, of pogroms, and now of the concentration camp."

His parents' stories of life in the Ukraine, his father's callous treatment by co-workers at RCA Victor, and his own bouts with neighborhood bullies fostered admiration and appreciation for the one country that condemned anti-Semitism as a "crime against the state." "Anything that was against anti-Semitism I was for," Gold would write, "and so the chance to help strengthen the Soviet Union appeared as such a wonderful opportunity."[77]

The second factor was internal—"a certain basic lack of discipline." At the oddest times, Gold admitted, this "almost suicidal impulse" could take a "drastic," even "illegal" turn, as it was now doing. His decision in high school to sabotage his professor's trust in him by altering the test scores of his classmates was one "such foolish action." His decision to "work outside of the laws of this country for the benefit of the Soviet Union" was a more dramatic example. Gold did not try to fool himself: he knew he would be "committing a crime—but it seemed that the greater overall good of the objective justified" the act.[78]

Third was a "definite lack of faith in democratic processes." The Depression had taken a severe toll. With the threat of poverty and eviction hanging over his home, Gold had been forced to leave school and do menial work to support his family. "There were many things badly awry in America": savings wiped out, "shenanigans on the stock market," mass unemployment, increasing homelessness, and despair throughout the land. Gold's faith in the nation, its government, and its institutions had been shaken.[79] Maybe the Bolsheviks could create a better system and achieve the "perfectibility of the New Man."[80]

Fourth, Gold's basic "nature" dictated that when he was "confronted with a desperate situation" something drove him "to immediately react by taking a positive action." He was not one to sit by and complain. When he could not find a summer job like the other kids in the neighborhood, he pushed himself through summer school classes. When he couldn't afford college tuition, he worked until he had raised the necessary funds. And when the Depression hit and his father was laid off, he quit school and went back to work. When Black asked him to aid the Soviet Union, he felt compelled to confront this problem and not flee from it.[81]

Finally, supplying technical data to aid the Russians was "an easy way out for putting an end to Tom's ceaseless entreaties." Gold had "no faith" in the party; it "appalled" him, but he still felt an obligation "to pay back [his] debt for what Tom had done for [his] family."[82]

Driven by these "just under-the-surface impulses," he embarked on a course of action that would have personal and national consequences.[83]

"A good deal of mental anguish"

By the spring of 1935, Gold was sneaking company documents out of the Pennsylvania Sugar lab on practically a daily basis. Papers on an array of "industrial solvents used in the manufacture of lacquers and varnishes such as ethyl acetate, butyl alcohol, butyl propionate, amyl acetate, and certain specialized chemicals as ethyl chloride (used as a local anesthetic, and absolute (100%) alcohol (used to blend motor fuels)" were routinely turned over to Black.[84] Gold found the clandestine work surprisingly easy; the real problem was how to copy all the material he was sneaking out of the plant. He'd spend hours, sometimes an entire day or evening, making copies to give Black. It was a difficult chore, and when stressed by the need to get the documents back where they belonged, Gold would visualize how his efforts were "doing much to make the harsh life of those who lived in post revolution Russia a little more bearable."

If Gold had reservations about his conduct, they stemmed from his abuse of the faith Dr. Reich had placed in him. Gold hated to disappoint people, especially a person of standing and accomplishment who had shown him kindness. Gold was less fearful of being discovered than of "the manner in which Dr. Reich would react." Reich, Gold believed, "liked" and "trusted" him, but despite "a good deal of mental anguish" regarding this breach of trust—not to mention the memory of his mother's stern lectures "against deceit and trickery and thieving"—he continued to steal files from his mentor.[85]

Through the summer and into the fall of 1935, Gold and his confederates, Black and Kane, "fumbled about" trying to copy all the data he was bringing out of Dr. Reich's office. The "blueprints of operating equipment and voluminous plant operating records" were more than they could comfortably handle. "Blueprints for a chemical plant can be exceedingly" large and "detailed . . . and the reports . . . were thick, 50 or 60 pages a piece." "None of us had the money," said Gold, to pay "the photocopying costs," which were prohibitive for such large masses of material. Gold "was making a little over $30 a week and Black about $50." "We just didn't have the funds." "Copying by hand was too impractical—it took too long"—and the risk increased the longer they held the material. "We were up against a stumbling block."[86]

The would-be industrial spies "stumbled amateurishly around" month after month, but their efforts, though inefficient, were far from insignificant. The Russians got word to them that they were "very happy" with their yield and some things had already been placed "in operation." Black's contacts were "very pleased with them."[87]

In November, Black "excitedly" announced some good news. Their "random effort was over": Amtorg (Amerikanskaia torgovaia kompaniia), "the Soviet Union's trading company in America," could offer "excellent facilities for getting information copied." All that was required, Black told his young friend, was "to bring the material to New York City and it would be returned . . . in a few hours at the most."[88] Amtorg would copy all the corporate and scientific information Gold could plunder. But there was even better news.

"Best of all," Gold was informed, "the man who was so generously providing all of this service, a Russian engineer from Amtorg, was very anxious indeed to meet Harry Gold having heard so much" about his efforts on behalf of the Russian people.[89]

Gold appreciated the compliment and was delighted at the prospect of meeting a representative of the Soviet government. The young chemist was about to take his next significant step in becoming a secret agent.

· ·

CHAPTER 3

The Novice Spy

With pride and expectation, Harry Gold traveled to New York City one November evening in 1935 to meet the Amtorg official who would now be providing photocopying services. As far as Gold was concerned, the documents and blueprints he was stealing from his employer were a step closer to enhancing the lives of ordinary Russian citizens.

Gold met his friend Tom Black at Pennsylvania Station a little after 7:00 P.M., and the two men began walking south on Seventh Avenue. They had not gone more than a block or two when a third man joined them. No one said a word. The men continued down the west side of Seventh Avenue as if they were three friends out for a bit of fresh air. The stranger was "short and stocky," with blond hair, an oval face, and "a nose that flared somewhat at the bottom."[1] Gold realized this was all quite unusual, but went along unquestioningly. It only confirmed that their collective efforts were of some consequence—and not totally above board.

Suddenly, the unknown man leaned towards Black, whispered something, and "just sort of shoved him off with his hand." Black drifted off in another direction without saying a word. Gold hesitated, but he felt the hand of his unknown contact assertively grasp his arm, and the two men continued walking down Seventh Avenue. Gold wasn't sure if Black's sudden departure was prearranged, but it unnerved him. The stranger introduced himself as "Paul Smith," which was obviously a pseudonym. Though fluent in English, the man had the "appearance of a Dane" but spoke with what sounded like a "Russian accent." He was also, Gold would quickly learn, cultured, educated, and obviously experienced. He proceeded to issue a series of orders. First, Gold was "to never see Black again . . . unless specifically ordered to do so."

The second thing Smith communicated was his need for "information about various processes that the Pennsylvania Sugar Company had" and any plans they might have for new plants or production items. Whatever a document's size or volume, Gold was "to bring it to New York City," and Smith "would arrange to have it copied."[2] Gold nodded and said this could be done.

Smith's third demand was for "a complete account of [Gold's] life and background up to that time, and the life of [his] parents." The Russian told Gold he wanted to know everything about him, especially his education, and expected the document to be delivered in person several weeks hence in New York City.[3] Again Gold agreed.

Smith told him when and where they would next meet, with extremely detailed contingency plans in case one or both of them could not make it. The plan, designed to maintain contact but deflect suspicion and throw off surveillance, further underscored the nature of their business. Gold was told that if "a meeting place was set in a particular city, say Philadelphia or New York . . . and information to be turned over . . . the meeting would be of the briefest duration, and just for that" purpose. Meetings were "set for a definite hour and at a definite place." If one or the other party didn't show up, "there was a second meeting set roughly a week later, but not for the same hour and not in the same place." If necessary, a third contingency meeting was scheduled for "a different hour, again at a different place."

There was even a fourth contingency, an "emergency set-up" meeting. This too would be at "an entirely different place," a "month or two months apart," and always "scheduled well in advance." This appointment was "for one purpose only," to find out if anything untoward had happened to either of them.[4]

As they approached Greenwich Village, Smith concluded the meeting. He thanked Gold again for his efforts in behalf of his countrymen and said that he looked forward to their next meeting and receiving the items he had requested. Alone now, Gold walked back to Penn Station, reflecting on what had just occurred. Though stunned by the order never to see Tom Black again, he was excited at the prospect of doing something important for "the world's first and only worker-peasant state," the last "hope of progressive mankind."[5]

Smith was considerably different from the "very shoddy" bunch of directionless, "bohemian" characters Gold had met through Black over the past two years. This Amtorg official was knowledgeable, assertive, and obviously in possession of a serious game plan. It was intriguing and certainly exciting. More important, Gold could see that his efforts might translate into tangible results, improving actual lives. That the Soviet Union was civilization's main bulwark against Fascism and anti-Semitism —concerns of paramount importance to Gold—underscored the appeal. Until his arrival back in Philadelphia several hours later, he was unable to think of anything else.

"The Great Illegals"

Harry Gold's gradual seduction into industrial espionage and secret work for the Soviet Union was not unique. A host of sympathetic Americans had become philosophically and psychologically unmoored by the disquieting times.[6] Economic collapse at home and the growing threat of Hitler's Third Reich provoked their apprehension, and America's unimpressive response to these challenges only magnified the concern. The Soviet Union's vigorous, decisive leadership attracted many who looked for action rather than empty rhetoric.[7] As the ex-Marxist philosopher Sidney Hook has said, the Socialist and Communist movements were viewed as "a source of hope in a world of deprivation." Those desperate for solutions "lived in its light" and were "buoyed up by its promise."[8]

Many Philadelphians were intrigued by the social and economic experiment taking place on the other side of the world. "The 1930s were a period of constant economic and political pressure," said Aaron Libson, who would go on to join the Communist Party. "People were working 12 to 14 hours a day and earning only $5 or $6 a week. Complainers were fired and union organizers were blacklisted. And then there was the specter of Fascism looming over Europe. Both were very much a factor" for his interest in the Soviet Union.[9]

"You had to know the poverty in the United States," said Frances Gabow, who would also eventually join the party in the 1930s. "There was hunger in the land. When I was a little girl . . . my mother told us to go to the park and pick dandelions. Jews came here for a better life, but it wasn't much better. People were in the gutter and suffering." "You always had your hand out," agrees Ted Krakow. "People were dependent upon the Jewish federation and other charitable organizations."

In addition, Gabow remembers, anti-Semitism was so prevalent in her neighborhood that she was "scared to death to go to school alone." "Jews looked to the Soviet Union" as "a lighthouse or beacon of hope for the downtrodden." The Communists' propaganda campaign generated thousands of sympathizers and a "large Communist Party membership in Philadelphia."[10]

Jewish historian Murray Friedman, a product of this turbulent period, intimately understood why so many politically progressive Jews found the Soviet Union attractive. "It was a traumatic time," he explains. "You couldn't grow up in a city like New York and Philadelphia and be Jewish and not be political. Politics was the meat and drink of Jewish life, and Communism was one end of the political spectrum."[11] The nation's sick economy combined with Hitler's unimpeded rise in Europe produced an "intense fear that Jews would be highlighted. We worried about the implications," recalls Friedman. "Anti-Semitism was a force" of which American Jews were "intensely conscious." Told that the "Soviet constitution attacked anti-Semitism," many came to believe that Communism offered a positive alternative. "Marxism was the vehicle for the good society," says Friedman. "We grew up in an atmosphere that was drenched in left-wing thought."[12]

Sidney Hook, also a product of the time, has written that many people "were identifying with the Soviet Union—the society in which, allegedly, there was no unemployment, no human want in consequence of the production of plenty, and in which, allegedly, the workers of arm and brain controlled their own destinies." For such people, "the future of mankind required the survival of the U.S.S.R."[13]

The allure of Communism "was in the air," said Joel Barr, a City College of New York graduate and engineer who would one day become a significant part of Soviet espionage operations in the United States. As a Jewish American growing up in the 1930s, Barr had an all-too-personal encounter with the economic devastation affecting the nation. Returning home one day to find "his family's belongings on the sidewalk, guarded by his crying mother," left a "tremendous impression" on the promising student and future spy. As his biographer Steven Usdin writes, "it was difficult" for Barr "to believe that capitalism was the path forward to a prosperous future." When they contrasted "harrowing" evictions with "the fantastic Soviet world depicted in the *Daily Worker*"—sold on street corners throughout New York and Philadelphia and "slipped under apartment doors along with other leftist literature"—many Jews began to look at the experiment going on in Russia as viable and attractive.[14] Supporters portrayed it as "a new world to explore" and a collective effort that fostered heroism. As converts loudly proclaimed, it brought hope into the world. "There is something in the air of Soviet Russia," trumpeted a 1926 *New Masses* publication, "that throbbed in the air of Pericles' Athens; the England of Shakespeare; the France of Danton; the America of Walt Whitman. . . .Where else is there hope in the world?"[15]

Jews were not the only ones to find the new Soviet nation intriguingly seductive. According to the author and documentarian Tim Tzouliadis, "American curiosity to learn about the Soviet experiment was all-consuming," regardless of gender, race, religion or nationality.[16] Dry accounts of Russia's Five-Year Plan became an "unlikely publishing phenomenon" in America as laissez-faire capitalism lost its appeal. Growing numbers saw Communism as the way of the future, especially in large cities where European immigrants predominated. As one observer ironically noted, "Politically, New York became the most interesting part of the Soviet Union."[17]

Stalin, now firmly in control of both the party and the government, took advantage of the situation. Lax security in the West, combined with the Communist state's desire for technological and industrial advancement as well as the contributions of some "remarkably talented" agents of the OGPU (one of the forerunners of the KGB), made for a very rewarding period of "recruitment and intelligence collection."[18] Historian Katherine Sibley has called the 1930s "the heyday of Soviet espionage." Even Whittaker Chambers, another product of the time, acknowledged the spies' achievement: "To this period belongs the recruiting of the best Soviet sources. . . . The Secret Service rode along for almost a decade simply exploiting, and seldom seeking to amplify, this corps of sources until death, casualty and incompetence wore them away."[19]

In this "era of the Great Illegals," as Christopher Andrew and Vasili Mitrokhin call it, secret agents laid the groundwork for many of the Soviet Union's greatest industrial and scientific triumphs.[20] They were "illegals" because they were not tied to a *rezidentura* or official Soviet embassy, consulate, or trade agency like Amtorg. These high wire walkers of the espionage game normally entered the country under false pretenses and with false passports, worked clandestinely, and couldn't rely on legal *rezidents* for camaraderie, guidance, or help in an emergency. Generally multilingual, intelligent, solitary, and committed to worldwide revolution, they enjoyed enormous flexibility and creativity in their espionage activities. Though small in number, they helped the Soviet Union develop the best intelligence-gathering network in the world.[21]

America unwittingly collaborated in the Russian game plan. Like many other Western nations between the world wars, the United States relied on "primitive" security systems, thereby enabling well-trained and seasoned Soviet intelligence agents to harvest both sympathetic Americans and the industrial and governmental material to which they had access. "While security in Moscow became obsessional," write Andrew and Mitrokhin, "much Western security remained feeble." Preoccupied with domestic crime and a rash of bank robberies and high-profile stickups, J. Edgar Hoover's FBI devoted the bulk of its manpower and resources tracking down and capturing gangsters like John Dillinger, Bonnie and Clyde, Pretty Boy Floyd, and Baby Face Nelson. Hunting for foreign spies took a back seat. "To the extent that they [the FBI] made even a passing effort at counterintelligence," said Walter Krivitsky, one of the Soviet Union's great illegals, "it was Nazi agents that the FBI was after."[22]

Krivitsky's ideological colleagues were equally aware of—and pleased with—the FBI's incompetence. According to one knowledgeable source, counterespionage under Hoover "was more conspicuous for failure than for success." Kim Philby, one of Great Britain's highest-ranking intelligence officers and a notorious Soviet agent, argued that Hoover's "ruthless authoritarianism" were "the wrong weapons for the subtle world of intelligence."[23] Given "enormous resources," the FBI "squandered" them.[24] Moreover, the FBI's organizational priorities lay elsewhere. In *Red Spies in America*, Katherine Sibley notes that "the agency had investigated only about 35 espionage cases a year between 1933 and 1937." This would change by the end of the decade.[25]

Further enhancing the Russian advantage were "the Communist parties and their fellow travelers in the West," a veritable army of potential converts that "gave Soviet intelligence a major source of ideological recruits."[26] Many of these recruits were embedded in American industrial, scientific, and governmental bureaucracies. Some didn't even have to be recruited; they walked in off the street and volunteered their services. Tom Black was one of them.

"Only those who violate instructions are caught"

A college graduate and chemist when he first approached the Soviets in 1934, Black was a made-to-order foot soldier. Over the next several years he would be put through one of the more unusual Depression-era apprenticeships, a training program he would later call a "fantastic trade school" for spies. Much of the instruction took place on the heavily trafficked streets of America's largest city. "There was one professor, one pupil, with the sidewalks of New York as the classroom and lessons conducted while walking," said Black after his capture. "Pedestrians saw two ordinary men strolling along, engaged in earnest conversation." But the conversation was not about Primo Carnera's unexpected heavyweight championship or Maxwell Anderson's Pulitzer Prize. It was about "microfilming stolen secrets, the science of meeting new contacts," and the rudiments of the deadly serious business of espionage.[27]

If the information he was taught were written down, said Black, it would have filled a "fat textbook." But these lessons were far too sensitive for transcription and certainly were not for public consumption. Serious penalties were in the offing should they be caught—but Black was told not to be concerned. If he followed his mentors' instructions, no one would ever learn the disturbing nature of their business. "Our methods have been tried all over the world," Paul Smith had once told him. "They're foolproof. Only those who violate instructions are caught. Remember that."[28]

Because the transmission of data and material was the raison d'être of their relationship, meetings between the American supplier and his Soviet handler were the first and most important item on a new agent's checklist. "The precise day, time and place [would be] set in advance—but not the week," said Black. "It might be Thursday at 6:47 in front of the public library. This did not mean next Thursday, but the Thursday following a phone call by the superior agent." The call "might not come through for a month or a year, but when it did, the prearranged time and place still held good. The caller, naturally, talked of trivial things like your health. He might even ask you to get together on Saturday—but it still meant next Thursday."

When agents unknown to each other were ordered to get together, said Black, the process was more complicated. The two strangers "must go about their roles like ordinary people doing ordinary things." One might be instructed to wear "a tie of a certain color," and the other might be told to carry "a current magazine under the right arm." Both would signify "initial identification." Simple everyday phrases or common expressions were also incorporated as secondary codes or signals confirming recognition. An innocent question such as "What time is it, please?" and the equally innocent answer "Sorry, I don't have a watch" were designed to "rule out the remotest chance of coincidence." Moreover, according to Black, there was often a "third unknown" agent lurking nearby to ensure the agents weren't under any type of surveillance. "By means of some simple action," said Black, "such as dropping a newspaper into a trash can or honking his horn a certain way if he were in a car, he warned of danger."[29]

The nuances of photography and microfilming were also taught on New York's crowded sidewalks. Black had a "longstanding interest in photography," but advanced topics like "the swift spoiling of films at the first sign of danger" were completely new to him. So also was the practice of duplicating keys. As a chemist with access to material and data his handlers desired, his success depended on breaking into file cabinets, locked drawers, and laboratory stockrooms. Black became so adept at making a perfect impression of purloined keys in soft wax that he could secretly copy one in his "pocket or in the palm of his hand in ten seconds."

Not all of Black's education consisted of recognition signals and break-in techniques; there was also a strong political component. With equal zeal, Paul Smith elaborated on world politics, the economy, and "the party line of the moment." He offered incisive analyses of events in Moscow and other European capitals, the machinations of Russia's enemies, and the efforts of "ruthless Fascists, Nazis and capitalists . . . to destroy the Soviet homeland." The Soviet Union, it was clear, "must be no less ruthless" in ensuring its own survival.

After dozens of such informative constitutionals through New York's neighborhoods, Black came to believe that he "was being prepared for a vital espionage post." Surely Smith, a high-ranking agent who had been trained by some of Russia's top espionage talent, would not have invested so much effort in his education "without a good reason."[30] Black was enthusiastic, committed, and eager for future assignments; he knew he could do more than just funnel company secrets to his Soviet handlers.

"Smith and I became very fast friends"

Gold, though still a novice at industrial espionage, was equally eager to make a contribution and please the shadowy man from Amtorg. As in all of his undertakings, he was prepared to invest his complete devotion. If he had any qualms about the ethics or legality of what he had embarked on, he kept them to himself. He was tempted to puff out his chest and proclaim this bold venture to his family and close friends like Abe Sklar and Sammy Haftel, but he knew such an initiative would not win their acclaim. His activities were not for public dissemination, and he knew how to keep a confidence.

Gold realized he was engaged in criminal behavior in stealing company secrets, but he rationalized that it was in behalf of a struggling people who needed assistance, in a nation with good intentions. It never crossed his mind to consider his actions unpatriotic. America had recently established diplomatic relations with his parents' homeland, and economic ties between the two countries were growing rapidly. His actions weren't at the expense of his own country, Gold told himself, but "more a question of strengthening the Soviet Union."[31] He harbored an abiding loyalty to the underdog.

If he did have "misgivings," they concerned the very serious breach of trust he was committing. Dr. Gustave T. Reich, the research director of the Pennsylvania Sugar Company, said Gold, had "raised me from a pup." Reich had not only fostered Gold's upward mobility at Pennsylvania Sugar and hired him back—not once but twice—during the depths of the Depression; he had also instilled his love of science and appreciation for the nuances of chemistry and the importance of the scientific method. No matter how Gold tried to repress the notion, he knew he was "violating that man's confidence." He was repeatedly "going into his files . . . stealing from a man who trusted" and mentored him. In the end, however, Gold took the position "that the greater overall good of the objective merited or justified the means."[32] He was proud to be making a contribution to "the world's most gigantic social experiment," its best hope for the future.[33] He continued to take documents from his boss and turn them over to the man calling himself Paul Smith.

Several weeks after his first meeting with Smith, Gold traveled back up to New York City. He carried with him his completed assignment—a lengthy handwritten account of his family's history in Europe, their eleven years in America, and his own life and education. As with all such writing endeavors, Gold had devoted considerable time and thought to it. The document he handed over was the last of several careful drafts.

Smith voiced his appreciation and asked Gold how he thought he could be of most help to the Russian people. What did he have access to at his place of employment that would best serve the needs of the young Soviet nation? The meeting was brief. The two men said their good-byes and parted company, and Gold journeyed back to Philadelphia.

On his next trip to New York, Gold presented Smith with a "list of materials" that "could be obtained at the Pennsylvania Sugar Company." The first item concerned "a process . . . Dr. Reich was working on" to "manufacture absolute ethyl alcohol." The resulting product, according to Gold, would be "100% ethyl alcohol, and would be useful for blend ing" with other products, thereby stretching valuable resources for "greater use." Also on the list were a variety of "manufactured solvents used in varnishes and lacquers," such as "ethyl acetate, diethyl oxilate, butyl acetate and butyl alcohol."[34] Another item was "a local anesthetic called ethyl chloride," which could be used for "minor surgery, such as the removal of warts" and other less serious procedures. Smith seemed particularly interested in "a process for the recovery of CO_2, carbon dioxide from flue gas," on which Reich and Gold had spent considerable time.

Gold spoke authoritatively about each item on the list, explaining its attributes and potential uses. The butyl alcohol process, he said, had been purchased from a French firm and "finally put into operation" at Pennsylvania Sugar's Franco-American Chemical Works in Rutherford, New Jersey. But because a different process had recently made butyl alcohol much cheaper, production had been halted. Smith's interest, however, hadn't waned; he said they "were still interested in the process."[35] The Amtorg agent's desire for this outdated manufacturing process only underscored for Gold how desperate the Russian nation was.

In this and other meetings, Gold went to great lengths to explain what he had access to and how those items might be of value to a recently feudal society trying to catch up to its industrialized neighbors. The combination of subject matter—chemistry—and a backward, needy people made for a compelling case in Gold's mind. For savvy agents like Smith and the more illustrious Gaik Ovakimian and Jacob Golos, men well versed in espionage as well as the nuances of human motivation, individuals like Harry Gold were a rare gift. With his good intentions, submissive personality, and progressive political orientation, Gold was made to order for his handler's purposes. Many an American recruit needed time and training to become "a serving person, a subordinate, a dependent individual" firmly in the hands of his Soviet handler. In time he'd learn how to be "humble, obedient and silent."[36] Gold walked in the door that way.

If Smith was impressed with his new recruit, Gold was no less impressed with his Russian contact. Their meetings were brief when documents were being exchanged, but on other occasions on New York sidewalks or in busy restaurants they could hold a more leisurely, less furtive discussion. In 1936, Gold's "meetings with Paul Smith took place during the day" because he was "working night work in order to be able to go to Drexel Institute in the evening." Normally when he had something for Smith, he'd finish work and either go home and "rest for awhile" and travel "up to New York in the early afternoon" or "not go home at all" and "immediately take a train and go to New York." It was not unusual for him to carry a bulky package of documents and blueprints, hand them to Smith, and then kill "a couple of hours" walking the streets and reading local newspapers in nearby coffee shops nervously waiting for the material to be photocopied. He would carry the originals back to Philadelphia, take them with him to his Drexel classes, and return them to Reich's office that night.[37] The entire process was nerve-racking, but Gold soldiered on.

From the beginning, Smith "insisted that he must reimburse" Gold for his train fare, but Gold always "put him off" with some excuse, such as that he had "already purchased a return ticket." These friendly debates over the Russian's offers to pay travel expenses continued until Smith "gave up the idea of trying to force money" on Gold and adopted "another tack." He tried to ply him with presents—items that a man like Gold would be interested in. Learning that the young Philadelphian was "desirous of building up a fine technical library," Smith purchased for him "Lewkowitsch's three volumes" on "the chemistry and technology of soaps and vegetable oils," a set that Gold estimated as costing between "$36 and $40." Though deeply appreciative, Gold said he refused the gift and "simply left it on the restaurant table," forcing Smith "to go back and pick it up himself."[38] Never particularly motivated by money, especially when a good cause was involved, Gold was determined to show that his sincerity and allegiance were not dependent upon monetary rewards.

Once that point was established, Gold believed that the two men— one Gentile and European, the other American and Jewish—developed mutual respect and a good working relationship. "Smith and I became very fast friends," said Gold, who was well known for seeing more in a relationship than his counterpart did. He quickly grew to like and admire his Russian contact. He thought Smith was "extremely clever" and possessed "an agreeable personality." Though he never learned Smith's real name or even whether he was single or married, Gold believed they had become "extremely good friends."[39]

The Amtorg official's "inborn capacity of being a good host" was regularly on display after they had completed "the business part of their meeting." On those occasions "when there was no passage of information," the two men could stroll through Manhattan discussing a variety of topics or share a meal at a nearby restaurant. On such unpressured occasions, Smith would underscore the importance of never attending a Communist rally, never being seen in a left-wing bookstore, and "never reading Communist literature." Repeatedly he advised Gold "to present the appearance of a normal American."

Smith was teaching Gold the nuances of the spy trade, which punished anyone who forgot or gave short shrift to any of its central tenets. When on a mission, no detail was too insignificant to be attended to. Every synapse must be on high alert, and instinctive reactions must be reined in, if not totally suppressed. A secret agent must become "a taut precision instrument that can spring to understand the most devious manipulations at a nudge from the simplest, most trivial-seeming facts."[40]

Over many sidewalk tutorials, Gold learned additional tenets of spycraft: "meetings between two Soviet agents . . . [should] occur in a crowded place such as a museum or a post office"; when meeting on street corners, the more crowded the intersection the better; punctuality was critical; and passwords were mandatory. Photography was superior to invisible ink, secret documents were best "reduced to microfilm," and "messages in code" through cable "were another favorite means of communication." One of the more prophetic lessons drilled into Gold was that "the central figure of a secret liaison is the courier." Considered "better than the mails as a means of communication," couriers understood the political landscape they worked in and were expected to be resistant to police interrogation. In short, "the hands of a Soviet courier [were] the safest way of transporting the most secret messages to and from Moscow."[41]

"One visit by Paul Smith"

Gold traveled to New York to meet Smith every three to six weeks—occasionally more often. He was forced to master transportation routes and travel schedules, not only New York and Philadelphia mass transit but also the Pennsylvania and Reading railroads. From his home in the farther reaches of South Philadelphia, he would take a forty-minute ride on a Route 9 streetcar from Fourth and Oregon avenues to either the Reading Terminal (Reading Railroad) or Broad Street Station (Pennsylvania Railroad). Upon arriving in New York two hours later, either at Penn Station or in Lower Manhattan, he'd take either a subway, elevated train, streetcar, or taxi to rendezvous with his Amtorg intermediary.[42] Once the rendezvous was over, he'd make the long journey back to Philip Street, Drexel, or his place of employment along the Delaware waterfront. Besides the physical toll of these trips and the time expended on them—rarely less than five hours—there were substantial transportation costs. Railroad fares between the two cities at this time were not more than two dollars, and a subway ride was less than a dime, but Gold's Depression-era wages did not easily support such frequent travel, especially since he was his family's main, and occasionally sole, provider.

His Soviet handlers, however, recognized quickly that a few kind words could offset the young man's concerns about appropriating such large chunks of time and money for such a clandestine undertaking. Smith would periodically tell him that his "work had been received in the Soviet Union" and "judged extremely useful" by Russian scientists.[43] Gold was always delighted to hear that his efforts were improving "the personal comforts of people in the Soviet Union."

Though Gold seemed unperturbed by his taxing schedule—even his lawyer initially found it "dubious" that anyone could maintain such a difficult regimen—his "days more often than not were in the 18 to 20 hour" category.[44] Juggling classes at Drexel, working long days at Pennsylvania Sugar, tutoring neighbors and co-workers, and making frequent trips to New York made for an exhausting life. Those closest to him, such as his family, recognized he was busy, but they had no suspicion anything untoward was occurring. They knew Harry could be consumed by his interests and obligations. His vast amounts of overtime at Pennsylvania Sugar were well established; so was his dedication to his classes and schoolwork. He was a *voyl yingl* (good boy) who had never been in trouble with the law or anybody else, and his absence from the household was noticed but never a cause for worry. Harry was the last person anyone would suspect of being involved something as dark and momentous as undercover work for a foreign power.

For Harry himself, however, his absence from home was a matter of concern. When he had to go to New York on a weekend, he told his doting mother and other family members that he was "going out and didn't specifically say whether [he] was going out with a girl . . . or just going out . . . with a particular friend." Whenever he went "directly from work to New York," he'd usually say that he had to "go to the library to do some studying or to obtain some data" for one of his Drexel courses.[45] He hoped these excuses would satisfactorily explain his long hours away from home.

Although Gold almost invariably did the traveling, there was at least "one visit by Paul Smith" to Philadelphia. He came in early 1936 to meet his new American recruit, but was less than enthusiastic about Philadelphia as a meeting place. Smith thought "the downtown area was much too small" to provide sufficient cover; it didn't lend itself to the successful transfer of information and documents. He thought it near impossible, even for someone as nondescript as Harry Gold, to achieve anonymity in such a comparatively small commercial area as Center City Philadelphia.[46]

Whether Smith really believed this or was just averse to traveling outside the New York area, he not surprisingly got little opposition from Gold, who agreed to do the bulk of the traveling. Gold did, however, agree to accept Smith's offer to cover some of his travel expenses. But even the approximately $40 Smith gave him as reimbursement in 1936 covered only "about fifty or sixty percent" of what Gold had actually spent.[47]

The George W. Childs Scholarship

His time-consuming runs to New York and his nascent industrial espionage activity didn't appear to affect Gold's demeanor, lifestyle, or schoolwork. To most observers, Harry was just being Harry: a dedicated employee who put in long hours, a conscientious student who never short-changed his studies, and a son who was dedicated to his family.

His grades actually improved. Before meeting Smith in November 1935, Gold was earning mostly A's and B's, with only two C's, in courses ranging from organic chemistry and physical chemistry to quantitative analysis. Once he became a full-fledged Soviet agent, he never received less than an A in difficult chemical engineering courses.[48] Gold did so well that he was awarded the George W. Childs Scholarship—an academic honor that entitled exceptional students to "broaden their education by taking courses outside the field of chemistry." After receiving his diploma in chemical engineering, Gold took advantage of the award and returned to Drexel in September 1936 to take courses in psychology and economics.[49]

Though many at the time would have considered his graduation a significant achievement, Gold was dissatisfied. What he truly wanted was not a diploma from a two-year evening school but a college degree in chemical engineering from a respected four-year institution like the University of Pennsylvania. That would not only signal unquestioned intellectual mastery of a subject and earn the respect of his peers, it would also propel him to the professional heights he had always dreamed of. For the time being, however, he would have to content himself with his Drexel diploma.

If espionage had no effect on his grades, it made a noticeable difference in his waistline. In one year as a secret agent he ballooned to 185 pounds. At only five feet, five inches in height, he was becoming grossly overweight, and it was affecting his health.

Celia Gold suffered from hypertension and other heart ailments, and while her younger son seems to have avoided these conditions, Harry was not as fortunate. He was refused a $1,000 insurance policy in 1936 because of his high blood pressure. Dr. F. J. Levitt put the twenty-six-year-old Gold on a strict diet, causing him to shed sixty-five pounds, but this did little for his blood pressure. "If anything," said Gold, "it went up." Hypertension would remain a critical health concern, causing the draft board to turn him down and ultimately contributing to his death.[50]

His financial health also wavered. In early 1936, Gold began "borrowing" money "in connection with the work [he] was doing for the Soviets"; his travel expenses were taking a toll, and his reluctance to accept full compensation only aggravated the situation. He took out a "series of loans" from the Corn Exchange Bank of Philadelphia and did his best to conceal this from his family.[51] His parents and brother already knew Harry was a soft touch for friends and co-workers and kept a watchful eye on his finances. Harry and his mother got along "splendidly," as he put it, but one of their few differences concerned his "constant efforts to help people with whom he worked." She knew co-workers were coming to him for loans. Some began to treat Harry as a liberal credit union that neither charged interest nor expected loans to be repaid.[52] Obviously, such practices led to problems. As Gold increased and extended his journeys as a secret agent, he would eventually be forced to borrow not only from friends but also from Dr. Reich and the Pennsylvania Sugar Company.

In the spring of 1936, during his final term at Drexel, Gold uncharacteristically let down his guard. He faced a conundrum that led him to depart from the tenets of the spy trade. The mistake could have had profound consequences.

Initially, Gold had easy access to Dr. Reich's office and freely searched drawers and cabinets for material he thought would interest the new Russian state. But as winter turned to spring, entry to Reich's office and files became "increasingly difficult." Obtaining the key to the office, once a small concern, had become a problematic venture. The only solution he could think of was to make a duplicate.

As Smith had instructed him on their many tutorial walks, Gold made both an "outline" of the key and a "wax imprint." But who in Philadelphia would make the copy without asking troubling questions?[53] It happened that a fellow Drexel student was more than willing to assist him. Though an unimpressive student, Joe Brodsky was an outspoken member of the Communist Party and actively sought opportunities to become more involved in helping the fledgling Soviet state. Brodsky, who also went by the name Jack Bruin, was constantly pushing his classmates to join the Federation of Architects, Engineers, Chemists, and Technicians.[54] He also regularly asked fellow students for "contributions" for "various left-wing causes." Gold often gave.[55]

During one of their conversations, Gold injudiciously asked Brodsky if he knew someone who would make a key from a wax impression. Brodsky said yes—he knew "another member of the Communist Party" with such skills. But the exchange led Gold, in a moment of weakness, "to tell him what it was for."

"From that time on," according to Gold, "Brodsky kept pestering" him for an introduction to his Soviet contacts. He wanted to be doing more than asking people for money and pushing union membership on classmates. He wanted to do important and daring things like Harry.[56] Gold kept putting Brodsky off; he realized he had been foolish to divulge his highly secret activity to a classmate. He not only feared what Brodsky would do with such explosive information but also worried about his Soviet handler's reaction if word of the blunder got back to him.

. . . .

CHAPTER 4

The Evolution of a Secret Agent

Joseph Brodsky, aka Jack Bruin, was a big talker, constantly engaging people in political discussions, asking for donations for a variety of causes, and encouraging people to join unions and come out to demonstrations. Though his commitment to progressive causes was undeniable, covert work seemed a stretch for him. Yet he couldn't wait to meet an actual undercover Soviet agent, and if he didn't get his introduction, there was no telling what he would do. Gold had a problem, and it was one of his own making.

Brodsky was dumbstruck that mild-mannered Harry Gold, who was reticent about raising his hand in class and never talked politics, was associated with representatives of the Soviet Union. For all of Brodsky's cheerleading, fundraising, and union activity on the Soviets' behalf, Harry was the one doing important secret work. Brodsky was intent on doing the same. Hell, if Gold could do it, so could he. He would pressure Gold for a meeting with his Russian contacts and then impress them with his ardor, reliability, and smarts.

Gold turned to a friend and knowledgeable adviser, someone whose counsel was appropriate for such a dilemma—Thomas Black.

"Not suitable as an espionage agent"

When Gold had been instructed in November 1936 to break off contact with Black, he had protested. Paul Smith was adamant: they needed "to break the link in the chain, so that were one apprehended the only thing that could be done would be possibly to apprehend the second and not complete the ring of three."[1] The two men were never to see each other ever again unless ordered to do so. But Gold was not slavishly obedient to Smith's directives.

The two friends curtailed their communications but remained in touch. They met and socialized, though less freely than before. They would talk about chemistry, how they were getting along, and the latest developments in the news, but little else. The topic of political work was off limits. They were constrained by the seriousness—not to mention illegality—of their respective ventures. Black, according to Gold, was "extremely secretive" and "cagey" in their discussions. Gold was equally circumspect. As the neophyte secret agent would later admit, "Smith's admonitions did have a considerable effect; even though we didn't obey them explicitly."[2] Both would ultimately find their decision to continue meeting—a sin of commission, as it were, that usually engendered "guilty feelings"—a cause of regret.[3]

After Gold admitted his error in judgment in the Brodsky matter, Black helped him design a strategy. Gold would arrange a meeting between Brodsky and Black. If his more experienced friend thought Brodsky had potential as an agent, one of them would inform their Soviet handler and see if a second meeting could be arranged. If, however, Black considered Brodsky inappropriate for clandestine work, he would try to steer him in another direction. If their plan proved unsuccessful, Gold would be back at square one, most likely in the unenviable position of having to admit his mistake and ask Smith if he wanted to meet Brodsky.

Once they met, it didn't take Black long to conclude that Brodsky was "not suitable as an espionage agent." He would subsequently send a memo to his own "espionage superior" explaining the situation and counseling "against accepting Brodsky" into any form of Soviet espionage. Brodsky, he wrote, was so drawn to the bombast and excitement of political activism that he probably "could not isolate himself from mass organizations." The convivial and demonstrative Brodsky clearly didn't have the psychological makeup to perform in the lonely, almost asocial manner that the Soviets expected of their operatives. In their meeting, Black was frank with Brodsky; he told him he'd have to adopt an entirely different demeanor and "disassociate himself from the masses" if he wanted to follow in his classmate's footsteps.[4]

Brodsky was taken aback by Black's assessment, but still enthralled with the prospect of meeting a real Russian operative. He continued to "pester" Gold for an introduction. Gold set about introducing his enthusiastic classmate to his handler. Fortunately, he had just been assigned a new operative, someone less businesslike and more forgiving than the straitlaced Paul Smith. The switch had come most unexpectedly and was awkwardly executed—an occurrence that would be repeated many times during Gold's fifteen years as a secret agent.

During one of their regular meetings in New York City, in the "vicinity of Columbia University," Smith told Gold he had something important to say. "He had to leave very shortly and . . . in the future Gold would report to another individual," as an FBI memo later put it.[5] Gold had little time to digest the news; as they walked across the campus, Smith added that they were about to meet his new handler. They hadn't walked more than a block or two when a large man approached them. Smith introduced the man as Steve Schwartz and a moment later departed without even saying goodbye. As Gold would recall later, his "parting handshake" with Smith was "a very hurried affair" leaving him stunned that a relationship built over sensitive and serious business could be terminated so abruptly. Gold, who took friendships seriously, found the farewell cold and disillusioning, far from the behavior of comrades-in-arms that he had seen on stage and screen. He would never see Smith again, nor ever learn his real name.

"A veritable giant"

Schwartz (or Swartz) was different from Smith in both style and appearance. "A veritable giant" who weighed at least "220 pounds and possibly 6 feet 2 or 3" in height, he was "very well built and very handsome" with his "sandy" hair, "high cheek bones, white teeth, and straight nose." Gold thought he looked like a former athlete or prize fighter. He was also quite the "dude" in Gold's mind, and occasionally wore spats. Though Gold thought he looked comical in such a getup, he felt Schwartz was "too big" for anyone "to tell him about it."[6]

Gold would never be quite sure whether Schwartz was employed at Amtorg or the Soviet embassy, but he had the distinct impression that his new handler was a regular at high-level social functions. When they met in Manhattan, Schwartz was often in formal attire and either coming from or headed to some sort of consular or diplomatic function.[7]

Although intimidating physically, Schwartz had a lenient, "easygoing" manner that Gold appreciated. Unlike Smith, Schwartz was willing to travel to Philadelphia to pick up material purloined from Pennsylvania Sugar. Smith had informed Schwartz that Gold worked "very long hours" and encouraged him "to make things as easy as possible" for him. Schwartz took the advice to heart; at least half of the meetings with his American supplier took place in Philadelphia.[8]

His new Soviet contact's more relaxed style and willingness to travel facilitated Gold's surreptitious work and eased the pressure on his budget and his busy routine. In their personal dealings as well, Schwartz was friendlier and more diplomatic. If he wanted something from Gold, he'd request it, unlike Smith, who had demanded or taken what he wanted— including Gold's Drexel grade and graduation record, which he had never returned.[9]

Gold found Schwartz, despite his size, "gentle" and "shy." He was well read and had an appreciation "for flowers and for art." In their walks around Manhattan they would often discuss lighter subjects. Gold would credit Schwartz with introducing him to the "world of Cezanne and Van Gogh and Monet and Degas and Grant Wood and all of the other great masters."[10]

Schwartz's tenure also coincided with Gold's growing concern for the beleaguered Republican cause in Spain. Gold was proud to be "helping the one country that was helping the Spanish Republicans" in their desperate fight for survival.[11] As he followed daily accounts of the struggle and the gradual entry of foreign powers in the Spanish conflict in 1936 and 1937, Gold received regular pep talks—first from Smith, then from Schwartz—reminding him that anything he did to help the Soviet Union would in turn help foster freedom and justice around the world. Nazi involvement in the domestic conflict of an independent nation was repeatedly offered as an example of capitalist treachery and warmongering. Both of his Soviet contacts repeatedly emphasized "that the only way that capitalism would ever be overthrown was by force and violence." No other path would allow freedom and progressive policies to flourish.

Yet the prospect that the conflict between Communism and capitalism would one day cause enmity between Gold's native country and the one he was spying for never seemed to occur to him. He later said he "just blotted it out." Despite Smith's and Schwartz's ideological pitches and philosophical arguments, Gold would never become "a classical Communist." He had "never read *Das Kapital*" and rarely if ever picked up a copy of the *Daily Worker* unless it was forced on him. He had never bought into the Communist propaganda that Tom Black and Vera Kane bombarded him with earlier in the decade. Gold had been a Socialist, and not a particularly strident one; he appreciated the Soviet Union for its efforts to save the Spanish Republic from a Fascist takeover.[12] His paramount fear was the looming specter of Nazi dominance across Europe. A few years later, when he began to recognize the possibility "there would eventually be a clash between the United States and the Soviet Union" he admitted "not know[ing] what to do about it." But even then, the fear that Nazi Germany would be the "victor" continued to haunt him.[13]

Soviet involvement in world affairs helped smooth over Gold's periodic doubts about his industrial thievery. During these early years as a Soviet operative, Gold was unsure that the value of what he was supplying to the Soviet Union was commensurate with the penalty he'd pay if caught. He considered the company lacquers, solvents, and assorted chemicals he was turning over rather mundane and unimportant. Yet he was "always assured" that the material was "well received" and much appreciated.[14] Could the Russians be so backward industrially, he wondered, that the rudimentary documents and blueprints he was stealing really had value for them?[15]

A more important concern during these early years—and throughout the rest of his career as a spy—was Gold's fear that his exposure would lead to his family's being "completely and horribly disgraced." Since they had no notion of his activities, he knew it would come as a tremendous shock and cause enormous embarrassment.[16] His proud mother and hard-working but simple father would be stunned beyond words if they ever found out what he had been doing. Periodic pep talks by his handlers on the Soviet defense of Spanish loyalists and staunch opposition to Hitler helped alleviate Gold's fears.

Gold withstood Brodsky's badgering for as long as he could. When he finally mentioned the matter to Schwartz in early 1937, he felt fortunate it was he and not Smith he had to apologize to. Smith would undoubtedly have given him a stern lecture; Schwartz was considerably more understanding and, surprisingly, willing to meet with Brodsky. According to Gold, they met twice, once in Philadelphia and once in New York, but it was obvious "the two did not hit it off very well." Though Schwartz may have believed that Brodsky could supply "the names of possible recruits" who had technical experience, nothing ever came of the initiative. Brodsky continued to champion progressive causes and union membership.[17]

Gold was relieved his embarrassing error in judgment had ended so un-
eventfully.

Through that spring and summer, Gold continued to funnel documents,
blueprints, and other items to his Russian contact. It was a harmonious
and profitable relationship; Schwartz received industrial formulas and
methods from one of the world's largest sugar refineries, and Gold had
the satisfaction of knowing he was helping a distressed people get their
industrial base up and running.[18] It didn't hurt that the nation he was
helping was the only one actively fighting Fascism and anti-Semitism
around the world.

By the end of summer, however, after nearly two years' continuous
pilfering of their corporate files, Pennsylvania Sugar and its subsidiaries,
Franco-American Chemical Works and Pennsylvania Alcohol Corporation, had little left to swipe. As Gold would matter-of-factly admit, he and
his Russian partners "had looted them pretty completely."[19] There was
still Dr. Reich's ongoing research into CO_2 recovery—carbon dioxide
from flue gas "so as to make dry ice"—in which the Soviets seemed interested, but Gold had been meticulous in stealing just about everything
else of scientific value.

He could see the end coming. Soon he would be of little value to his
Soviet contacts, and their brief but anxiety-provoking relationship would
come to an end. The prospect did not disappoint him. He was pleased to
have given his help to what he felt was a worthy cause, but he had had
enough. The physical demands and psychological stress of covert activity
would not be missed. The lies he had had to tell his parents to explain his
lengthy absences, the financial cost of his many trips to New York, and the
act itself, stealing trade secrets from his employer and giving them to foreign agents, were burdens he could do without. But the Soviets had no
intention of jettisoning him. They had invested time and energy in his
development; the little chemist from Philadelphia still had value. Gold
wasn't about to be abandoned; the Pennsylvania Sugar Company was.

As historians John Earl Haynes and Harvey Klehr have pointed out,
the Soviets saw "capitalist corporations" as cutting-edge models of industrial efficiency, but also as "illegitimate institutions" that deserved to
have their scientific pockets picked.[20] Humanitarian and ideological
sympathizers like Gold were the politically motivated grifters assigned
to the job.

As early as the spring of 1937, Steve Schwartz began to suggest that
Gold find "other work."[21] Gold was taken aback. He had neither plans

nor a great desire to move on; he had worked at the sugar refinery for nearly a decade and felt comfortable there. A hard-working fellow like Gold could work his way up the corporate ladder for many years, and also pick up valuable knowledge working with Dr. Reich, the company's respected research director. If Gold had any thoughts about his future, they revolved around finishing his education and maybe finding a suitable girl to marry.

Fortunately for Gold, Schwartz didn't press the issue of finding a job elsewhere. There were periodic hints and a friendly suggestion or two, but nothing more. He began asking Gold to research some issues in scientific journals at public libraries. This was less time consuming than trips to New York and much less anxiety provoking than stealing documents from Dr. Reich's office. Gold didn't need any more pressure: he was already under significant strain thanks to a union-management meltdown at Pennsylvania Sugar.

Holding the Fort

The worst of the Great Depression was over, but things were far from good. Employees and employers struggled throughout the 1930s over wages, benefits, working conditions, and a host of related concerns. The Pennsylvania Sugar Company, with its workforce of more than a thousand, was no different. On March 4, 1937, fighting broke out between two hundred striking workers and a "marching line of workers" who refused to honor the strike. Newspapers covering the confrontation described "a shower of bricks and stones" falling on the heads and shoulders of men and women standing in line to enter the plant. Bloodied and dazed bodies were scattered across the refinery's grounds. Simultaneously, a free-for-all broke out on Frankford Avenue near the plant entrance. More than fifty policemen intervened "to stop the battle," in which many employees "were cut and bruised."[22]

The next day, employees opposed to the strike decided on a radical strategy: they would hold the fort and not leave their workstations. Rather than run the strikers' gauntlet of insults and brickbats they would, in the words of plant manager W. H. Hoodless, "work and get paid rather than strike" and get nothing.[23]

In succeeding days, intersections around the plant, such as Delaware and Shackamaxon streets, would become battle zones in which "blackjacks" and "knives" were used, bullets fired, and skulls crushed. In a departure from similar union-management turmoil around the country, the opposing camps at Pennsylvania Sugar reversed their roles, with "loyal employees" staging a "stay-in" at the plant and "those unwilling to work remaining outside."[24] The company claimed that the majority of its workers were on site and working; the union countered that only a few hundred remained inside the plant and the bulk of the workforce was refusing to cross the picket line. With bloodshed an almost hourly occurrence, the tension and anger at the plant reached excruciating levels. It was particularly intense for Harry Gold.

Gold had been repeatedly told by his Soviet handlers to stay out of politics, refrain from reading any controversial literature, and never attend any political gatherings. They weren't difficult orders to follow; the controversial political movements of the day had never been a driving force in his life. But he did have convictions about fairness and justice that weren't easily quashed. One of them was that trade unions were central to the workingman's advancement and the attainment of a fair and just society.

Gold could not sit idly by while a critical, violent struggle over these principles was under way. As a "professional man" with a college education and a good position in one of Pennsylvania Sugar's more elite units, its research department, he was expected to support management and oppose all union initiatives. It was an impossible task.

Management insisted that "all employees remain in the plant while a state of siege ensued." But Gold resented the demand that he and other white-collar professionals "were to try and operate the refinery so as to break the strike" and fatally cripple "the newly formed union." He refused, and Dr. Reich threatened him with "permanent blackballing in the chemical industry."[25]

Risking his job as well as the goodwill of his white-collar colleagues, Gold left the plant and, according to fellow employees, "refused to work until the striking members returned to work."[26] When he returned home that first night, though, Gold was "distraught and wavering," unsure that he had done the right thing. He berated himself for being so cavalier with his family's economic survival. His mother was quick to comfort him, saying, "Son, you did what you knew was right." As she had done so many times in the past, Celia Gold reminded her older son "that whenever anyone was hurt, anguished, or in trouble, and cried out, [he] should be there to answer and to extend aid."[27] The union's goal of uplifting the lives of struggling workers was worth a little self-sacrifice.

Gold's show of solidarity with the striking workers angered plant managers, frustrated his mentor, Dr. Reich, and left an indelible impression on many at the refinery. As the weeks went by and he refused to show up for work, many found his stand detrimental to his own interests. Others thought it principled and rather courageous. A number of colleagues were forced to revise their opinions of the little chemist, who until then had been mostly known as a "conscientious, hard worker" who put in a lot of overtime.[28]

A "strict disciplinarian"

Once the strike was resolved and operations at the sugar refinery returned to normal, Gold was still hard pressed to fulfill his many obligations. He had completed his chemical engineering program and the extra courses he sat in on as a Childs Scholarship recipient.[29] But his evening classes at Drexel were now replaced with nightly excursions to public and university libraries in order "to read current publications and to make notes" on articles and topics of scientific interest to Steve Schwartz.[30] Gold couldn't understand why scientific journals already publicly available would interest the Soviets. Why were they appropriating the valuable time of undercover agents to perform a task any graduate student could easily handle? It was a question that harkened back to a similar curiosity and conversation he had had with Paul Smith.

Weighing the effort and risk of stealing rudimentary processes and easily available formulas from the refinery, Harry had gathered the courage to inquire, "Why couldn't they go ahead and buy these processes from various firms? Wouldn't it be a good deal more simple than all this roundabout way of obtaining the information?"[31]

It was far more complicated than that, Paul explained. "When we approach a firm, either they don't like the Soviet Union . . . and won't sell it to us, or . . . they will only sell us the product. They won't sell us the actual process." And "if they will sell us the process," he went on, "they set an exorbitantly high price, so that we feel we are being swindled." There were even occasions when the Soviets had purchased the process only to find it had been "sabotaged again by someone who didn't like us." But "now we have you," Paul said. "You go and get the process as it is worked. You are a chemist and a chemical engineer" and "give us the complete details of the process as it is worked in the United States."

The Soviet Union was "addicted to processes [that] worked and . . . [were] in actual operation." If "a process is good enough to make a profit in competition in the United States," said Paul, "then that is what we want." Though Harry found it quite surprising, the Soviet Union was not interested in cutting-edge theoretical developments. As Paul repeatedly told him, "We want things which work."[32]

Now that he was spending several evenings a week in libraries reading scientific journals and taking notes for Steve Schwartz, Gold wondered if any of this had a purpose or was just a holding action until something of interest developed at the refinery. But he did as he was instructed.

In October 1937, he was once again assigned to a new Soviet handler. "Fred," as he identified himself, was a small, mustachioed man in his early thirties whose brusque, "arbitrary," and "dictatorial" manner was a radical departure from his predecessor's easygoing style. Less conspicuous than the towering Schwartz, his new contact's "dark hair, piercing black eyes, sagging jowls," and "swarthy" complexion underscored his unfriendly nature. The black mustache that "spread over his entire lip" completed the unattractive image.[33] No longer would Gold enjoy the emotionally rewarding and stimulating relationship he had had with Smith and Schwartz. Fred barked orders, ignored pleasantries, and expected the chemist to dutifully follow his every command. Gold didn't take well to this "strict disciplinarian" who "lived by the book" and displayed little warmth or collegial spirit.[34] Fred would be his least favorite of the many Soviet agents he worked under.

It didn't take long for the two men to develop a firm dislike for each other. Almost immediately, Fred voiced his disappointment with Gold's productivity. Fewer items were now being smuggled out of Pennsylvania Sugar, and he considered his new American supplier a slacker. Gold's excuse—that there was simply "nothing more to give him"—was declared unacceptable. If he truly desired to be of service to the Soviet Union, Fred answered, he "ought to get another job" in an "industry in which they were interested." Gold had heard this line before, but this was not the easygoing Steve Schwartz who rarely pressured him and never issued ultimatums. His new handler, who seemed to have "cultivated the Bolshevik virtue of *tverdost'* (hardness)," was deadly serious.[35] Throughout the early months of their association, Fred was unrelenting in pushing his underperforming Philadelphia contact. He cared little that for the past two years the unassuming chemist had stripped his current employer clean of its trade secrets. He "insisted" that Gold "leave the Pennsylvania Sugar Company and get another job" that would benefit the Soviet Union. If Gold couldn't think of a new employer, Fred already had a few destinations in mind. He directed Gold to pursue a job at "the Philadelphia Navy Yard or the Baldwin Locomotive Works or any firm, any organization, which manufactured military material." As Gold would unhappily learn, "these weren't suggestions," they were "very direct orders."[36]

Gold had never been completely at ease with his work for the Soviets, but these extraordinary demands greatly increased the stakes of his original commitment. He wanted to help the Soviet Union's grand social experiment come to fruition, to foster its industrial development and its valiant stand against Fascism, but he never expected spying to dominate his life. Periodically providing information was one thing; now he was being ordered to leave his job and start over at a totally new firm. He was deeply troubled.

Weeks passed with few new documents coming from the refinery, no progress to report on landing a new job, and worsening tension between the two men. Gold had spent his years since high school in Reich's laboratory. He knew no one at the Philadelphia Navy Yard or any of the steel mills in southeastern Pennsylvania who could help him get in the door. Why would either of those institutions want a chemist, especially one without a college degree?

Like Schwartz before him, Fred came up with a stopgap assignment for his increasingly unproductive agent. He ordered him, Gold later said, to start supplying him with names of "people similar to myself who could give information to the Soviet Union." They didn't have to be chemists, but they should be in some technical field or "critical industry." Fred was "particularly interested" in "anyone who might work at the navy yard."[37]

Gold was again being instructed to do something he found distasteful and distressing. He felt uncomfortable naming friends or colleagues to perform an act that they might find objectionable, if not repugnant. The theft of documents was Gold's personal contribution to the cause. He knew it was wrong, but he did it for what he thought were good reasons. Apart from his Russian handlers, no one else would ever know about it. Now he was being asked to increase his involvement and become a recruiter, thereby exposing himself as a Soviet activist. Gold wasn't prepared for this. His small circle of friends were either uninterested in politics or not in occupations that would be useful to the Russians. He knew a few people who might qualify, but they were distant acquaintances, and, as he would admit years later, he "simply could not approach them." He imagined scenarios where he might open a dialogue with a progressive thinker, somebody who looked at the Russian state as he did, but he was never able to follow through. He just "didn't know how to approach them."[38]

This was not a new phenomenon. As a teenager, Gold quickly lost

jobs hawking candy in Center City theaters or selling newspapers on
street corners because he was too timid to call out his wares. He'd always
had difficulty approaching people and engaging them in conversation.
His tentativeness was particularly apparent when requesting a favor. Now
he was being ordered not only to approach people but even to enlist them
in industrial espionage.

In "desperation," Gold began "to invent fictitious names" of people
and provide them with equally fictitious backgrounds. Some came out
of thin air; others were borrowed from friends or were "composite
names . . . pulled from the telephone directory." Gold didn't know how
long the charade would last, but he was under pressure to "satisfy Fred."[39]

When asked many years later about his willingness to comply with
Fred's orders—or pretend to—Gold admitted to an "extremely unfortunate" and "lifelong" character flaw: his "trait of bending over backwards
to please people." He would go to extreme lengths to assist someone who
asked him for help. When a friend or co-worker asked for a loan and appeared "desperately in need of it," Gold not only quickly agreed but extended himself further by taking "long trolley rides out to their house to
give them the money."[40] Gold recognized how "ridiculous" such acts appeared, but he felt compelled to make sure the individuals got the money
"in time to be able to use it." That same desire to please influenced his
reaction to his Soviet handler's order.

When his need to please people clashed with his extreme reticence,
Gold was sometimes immobilized. On other occasions, the more compelling drive would dominate, as in the case of Howard Dalske, one of the
few genuine names he submitted to Fred. Dalske, a fellow student at
Drexel Institute, worked at the Charles Lennit Company, which made
an assortment of specialized chemicals, such as sodium sulfide, which removed hair from animal hide. Fred was interested in meeting Dalske and
gaining access to his heavy chemical portfolio, but even though Gold became "very friendly" with Dalske and practiced how he would try to co-
opt him, he "was never able to approach him" about becoming a spy.[41]

"Undermining the revolution"

While Gold was attempting to extricate himself from his assignment,
Fred created an additional make-work chore. He directed Gold to start
"keeping tabs on certain people who were supposed to be adherents of
Trotsky" in the Philadelphia area. Karl Buchman, a well-respected musi-
cian and music teacher who lived in Center City near Twenty-second and

Walnut streets, was a known "follower of Trotsky" and was said to have "traveled extensively on the continent." Gold was told to keep tabs on him and to "phone Buchman at his home at certain stated intervals and find out whether Buchman was there."[42] Though he found the assignment disagreeable, he complied.

Fred soon assigned him a second Trotsky supporter to keep an eye on. Leo Tin owned a drug store at Sixth and Jefferson streets in North Philadelphia.[43] Gold was instructed to periodically walk into the store, "buy several items," and "look the place over" without attracting suspicion. He was specifically told to "find out when the man closed the store in the evening" and whether its operations followed any set schedule. Again Gold did as he was told, but he was increasingly unhappy. This work had nothing to do with chemistry and hardly seemed to benefit the Russian people.[44]

Alarmed that he was now being assigned to spy on people and specifically "check on . . . followers of Leon Trotsky," Gold contacted his friend Tom Black. He needed advice, and Black was the only one he could turn to.[45]

Contacting Black was "in direct defiance of . . . orders," but the two men still met at "irregular intervals."[46] Rarely in these surreptitious meetings did they make reference to their respective covert activities, but Gold naturally presumed they were both deep into industrial espionage. On this occasion, however, their undercover work was central to their rendezvous. Gold expressed consternation with his new handler and his unforgiving, dictatorial attitude. Orders to change jobs and submit the names of potential recruits were more than he had bargained for. Now he was assigned to keep an eye on Trotsky's supporters in Philadelphia. Increasingly conflicted, Gold admitted he was at a loss what to do.

To his surprise, his friend knew well what he was facing.

Black, a longtime champion of the Soviets' grand experiment, confessed that he had his own misgivings. The purge trials currently going on in the Soviet Union were deeply disturbing to him and beginning to cause serious reservations. How, he wondered, could "so many of [his] Soviet heroes . . . be scoundrels, assassins, agents of Fascist countries?" He found the courage to ask his Soviet handler, Paul Smith, how such "bizarre charges" could be leveled against the nation's "founding fathers." The trials, he argued, were "undermining the revolution."[47]

Smith "blew his top," but Black did not back down as he had in the past. "For the first time, [Black] stood up" to him and demanded answers. "A long and heated session" ensued, and a "lot of shoe-leather" was spent as the two men carried their animated conversation through the streets of Manhattan. Neither man convinced the other, and as they said goodbye, Black warned that "if such things continue, they might make me a Trotskyist."

The Russian was apoplectic; the American chemist had "committed the great sin of invoking the name of the official devil." They parted angrily, and Black thought "this was the end of the line" for his career as a Soviet secret agent. That assessment appeared confirmed when "the familiar call[s] for a rendezvous did not come through for a month, then a second, and a third." Years later Black would claim he "was filled with a glow of joy" and that a "great weight seemed to lift from my spirits," but in fact his enthusiasm for "the world's most gigantic social experiment" had not completely waned.

"Proceed to Coyoacan"

The obituary for Black's career as a Russian operative was premature. Eventually he received a call and responded just as he was trained to do. Once again he was "pounding the pavements at Paul's side" and, despite his supposed reservations, following his superior's orders. Black thought Paul "strangely friendly," but the only reference to their argument was Paul's unexpected comment that maybe he was right "about becoming a Trotskyist."[48] In fact, that is what the Soviets wanted him to do: "join the Trotskyist movement."

At first Black thought this was an awkward attempt at humor. When Paul insisted he was not joking, Black asked what was so important about the activities of a few insignificant "American Trotskyists." Paul reacted indignantly: "Don't ask questions, you'll get instructions when you're ready. Meanwhile your job is to ingratiate yourself with the Trotskyist leaders here, so that they value and trust you."

The Soviet agent's tone "left no room" for debate. Black, as was customary, did as he was told and soon "enrolled in the Trotskyist wing of the Socialist party." When the Trotskyites subsequently "seceded to form the Socialist Workers Party headed by James Cannon," Black went with them. Although he claimed "not the slightest inkling" of why he had been "ordered to infiltrate the Trotskyist movement," he was no longer in the business of stealing industrial secrets. Now he was working full time on proving himself a loyal disciple of Leon Trotsky.

Months would go by with only infrequent meetings with his Soviet superior. Evidently Smith just wanted to make sure his "sleeper" was still firmly tethered to Moscow. It was appropriate that he should, for Black's political tastes were evolving. According to an account he gave two decades later, he was in fact coming closer to the "Trotsky viewpoint" on a range of issues. As he mixed with Trotsky's disciples and American supporters, he found it increasingly easy to identify with their movement. "When it came to lambasting Stalin and his crimes, in true Trotskyist style, I could put my whole heart into it," he would recount. "The continuing blood-bath of the big purges, turning the Soviet dream into an obscene nightmare, made that easy and heart-warming."[49]

Despite his qualms, Black continued to do as he was told. He made "friends with the anti-Stalin party," participated in group efforts, and donated "generously to Trotskyist [news]papers and causes." He was struck by the irony of using the "Soviet gold" his superiors gave him to "finance Trotskism" in America.

Whatever plans the Russians had for Black were put on hold in early 1938, when he suffered a serious accident at work that nearly killed him. He required hospital care for almost five months. About ten weeks into his lengthy hospital stay, he had a visitor. Black would dramatically refer to the incident as the dark hand of "Red espionage reach[ing] out" for him. The man who entered his room in a businesslike fashion identified himself as "Dr. Schwartz"; he perfunctorily checked Black's medical chart and then examined his burns. Neither man spoke much. Schwartz's authoritative manner left no doubt that he was a physician, but his accent and mannerisms also convinced Black that he was "a Soviet agent come to look me over."[50]

Black's suspicions were proven correct weeks later, after he left the hospital and returned to work. He received a call one day that triggered a "prearranged rendezvous." Surprisingly, it was not his regular Soviet superior who showed up but the mysterious Dr. Schwartz. This time he called himself Robert and asked Black how he was feeling. He then quickly brought up the reason for the meeting and the real purpose of his "long cultivation of friendships in the Trotskyist movement."

"Tom," said the grim Russian, "the time has come for action. You're to quit your job immediately and proceed to Coyoacan near Mexico City. Your Trotskyist friends should be able to help you enter Trotsky's household. We have people there already who will help if necessary."[51]

"A chill went down my spine," Black would recall. He realized that he had been groomed to be part of the crew of "Communist vultures hovering around the exiled leader in Coyoacan" with one thing in mind. Fearing the worst, he argued, "Why must I go there? It's not easy on such short notice."[52] He said he just couldn't quit work after being absent for so long, and he had serious health and financial issues to consider.

He was told to stop making excuses. The decision had already been made. He'd be "contacted and told what [he] needed to know when the time comes." Until then, he was to use his new connections to gain admittance to the Trotsky compound. His superiors would do the rest.

Black continued to protest. He said he needed time; such an abrupt change had to be thought through. "I'll do the thinking," replied Robert, angrily. He told Black this was an order, not a request, and further informed him that "the penalty for disobedience would be drastic."

The two men agreed to meet a week later after Black had "completed preparations" for the trip. During that time Black "racked my brains for a plausible alibi for not going." He feared that the journey to Mexico would end in bloodshed. Well aware that Stalin's agents were hunting the world for Trotsky, his family members, and his closest advisers, Black wanted no part of what many would come to call "the Soviets' boldest clandestine operation yet."[53]

When they next met, Black tried one more time to extract himself from what he perceived as the Trotsky death squad. He vigorously argued that he was about to be "called before the Workman's Compensation Board in connection with substantial claims" resulting from his injury. A considerable amount of money was involved, and there were many outstanding bills to be paid. In addition, his "sudden resignation from a good job, coupled with failure to show up before the board," would spark suspicion. Fellow workers already wary of Black's politics would begin to wonder; an investigation might be launched.

The Russian was angry. Black's resistance was a severe blow to his plans, but he couldn't avoid the logic in the argument. They could not afford to draw suspicion and set off an investigation of Black's activities. Desperate and shaken, Black had managed to win himself a last-minute reprieve.

"Various gentile girls"

When he and Gold met, Black withheld a good bit of what had happened during the past few years of his career as a Soviet operative. He also downplayed his growing disillusionment with such activities, but Gold had garnered enough to be rattled. That "they were going to kill Trotsky" at his Mexican retreat and were angling to involve his friend was particularly frightening. Gold had never imagined that his desire to repay Black for his assistance during the Depression would come to this.

It had all started so innocently. How had the transfer of simple chemical solvents to a progressive nation hoping to achieve industrial parity led to the recruitment of Americans for Trotsky death squads? Gold still supported Russia's grand social experiment, its opposition to Fascism and anti-Semitism, its aid to Spanish freedom fighters, and its desire to lift up workers around the world. But the purge trials were mystifying, as were the whispered allegations of increasing oppression under Stalin's rule. More troubling yet were the new demands being placed on him. Gold hadn't bargained on being told where he could and could not work, or on being pressured to put friends and co-workers forward as potential Soviet agents, or wasting time spying on fellow Philadelphians.

All this came at a time when Gold wanted to move on to the next phase in his life. He wanted finally to acquire a college degree and settle down with a nice girl, get married, and start a family. While doing library research for his Soviet handlers, he would occasionally take time out to examine university brochures and course catalogues to get a feel for what various college chemistry departments were offering. Acceptance at an elite institution would be a dream come true, paving the way for a fruitful scientific career.

He began to submit applications, but the results were not promising. The better schools were unimpressed with his Drexel diploma, while others would not accept his Penn and Drexel courses toward a chemistry degree; he'd have to start from scratch. Gold realized his college career had been "very unorthodox," a "jumble" of credits that did not impress four-year institutions. And with all of them, money remained an issue. Yet, all these "discouragements," as Gold referred to his admission inquiries, no doubt pleased his Soviet superior, whose "opposition" to his "going to school" remained firm.

On the marital front, however, Gold was increasingly optimistic. He was never remotely close to being a ladies' man, and his history of romantic relations was nearly a blank book. Throughout his youth, Gold was gripped by a shyness that would gradually become less obvious but would never totally disappear. Most people knew him as a reticent, "nervous individual." This was especially apparent around women. Gold would grow silent or stammer, and "his face would become flushed." Normally quiet, he "would sometimes converse a bit with . . . men, but would only talk with women when he had a job for them to do." Some women did not feel "comfortable in his presence" and would only speak to him "on matters regarding their work in the laboratory."[54] But after a number of unsuccessful ventures, he believed his luck in the field of romance was changing.

In 1933 Gold became "seriously" interested in a girl named Helen Tavelman. Short, with "long blond hair," Helen was "the first one to whom I was ever attracted," but unfortunately the feeling was not reciprocated. To Harry's great dismay, she always referred to him as "her second best boy friend."[55] He had the misfortune of watching her marry "a young man who had considerably more funds" and better social skills. Though despondent, he still managed to remain "good friends" with her.

Gold's next foray in the dating arena was with Florence Reiss. After a year, just when he believed they were on the verge of becoming "quite serious," he "discovered that she was running around with other fellows," and "not in a very nice fashion." The disconcerting news was a blow to Gold, and so he "dropped her."

Things were finally beginning to look up, however. Gold was now dating a friend of Helen Tavelman's. Her name was Shirley Oken, and their relationship was progressing smoothly enough that although he had not given her a ring, Harry considered them practically engaged.[56] The relationship was not trouble free, however. Mrs. Gold "completely disapproved" of her son's choice.

Celia Gold rarely "attempted to interfere" in Harry's romantic life, but she was not enthralled with the "various gentile girls" with whom he associated. She regularly encouraged him "to marry one of our own religion," believing that "marriage was a difficult enough problem of adjustment without having the problem of . . . religion" in the mix.[57]

Despite his mother's reservations, Harry believed he and Shirley Oken were truly in love. He could easily picture them sharing a life together. But a far more serious hurdle than his mother stood in the way: his covert work for the Soviet Union. Harry felt that he "could no longer carry on work of such a nature and be able to conceal it from my wife." As he pondered his situation, he hoped that his Soviet handler would become "sufficiently disgusted" with his lack of productivity, his repeated expressions of interest in returning to college, and his modest list of prospective recruits. Maybe Fred, on learning of his impending marriage, would just "give up on [him] as a bad job" and declare him more trouble than he was worth.[58] But it was not to be.

A "very important government official"

Fred was unrelenting in his demands. The Soviet Union had invested a lot of man-hours training Gold; he knew too much. And he had potential. Fred was determined to whip him into shape. His efforts would leave a lasting impression on his reluctant pupil.

Many years later, Gold could still rattle off examples of his Soviet superior's ruthless commands and dictatorial behavior. One such incident occurred during this period of Gold's increasing concern about his secret activities. It was August 1938, and Gold had just come home after several late nights working at the refinery. After getting drenched in a rainstorm, all he could think of was a hot bath and a good night's sleep. On arriving home he told his mother, "Should God ring me up I would not be there to answer the phone." Celia, ever protective and troubled by Harry's late hours and busy schedule, expressed her pleasure that he was "at last" showing "a little sense."[59]

No sooner had he climbed the stairs to the second floor and "start[ed] the water for the bath the phone rang . . . it was Fred." He curtly ordered Gold to "catch a train right away and come up to New York City." Because the meeting place was an unusual location in the Bronx, Gold assumed the matter must be of "tremendous import." He skipped his bath, "hurriedly put on dry clothes, called a cab, and dashed to the North Philadelphia station," where he was "almost killed getting on the train." Once at Penn Station, he took the subway to the Bronx and met Fred after 11:00 P.M. on a dark street corner.

His Soviet superior immediately launched into a vicious verbal attack. According to Gold, Fred "wanted to skin [him] alive because [he] was not producing." As Gold recounted years later, "He ripped me up the back and up and down again several times." It was a "very, very complete" and scathing indictment of his fleeting value. Fred wanted results, not excuses. Unable to get a return train to Philadelphia until 2:30 in the morning, Gold arrived back home just before sunrise and the start of a new workday.[60]

The withering broadside was not the "sole purpose" of that late-night journey. Gold was also given a directive that would propel him into the next phase of his career as a courier and military espionage agent.

After severely lambasting him for his many failures, Fred made a surprising announcement. Gold could "redeem" himself, he said, by going back to school full time and acquiring his college degree. But it couldn't be just any American college; it had to be a "school in the mid-west." It was not that the Russians had had second thoughts and realized the importance to their little Philadelphia chemist of earning a legitimate college degree. His matriculation at a specific location was designed to mask a much more significant mission: making contact with a "very important government official" who worked in the area.[61] Gold was told little more about the mission, but Fred did inform him he had a specific academic institution in mind—the University of Cincinnati. It was known at the time primarily as a technical school with an excellent engineering department, but its real selling point for the Russians was its location. Gold was further told he'd receive ample financial assistance to complete his education and was advised to "invent the excuse" for general consumption that he had a new "job in the mid-west."[62]

Gold was stunned by the offer. He wasn't thrilled about leaving his job at the refinery, his girlfriend, or his close-knit family, but he thought himself far more fortunate than his friend Tom Black, who had been ordered to Mexico to join a Trotsky death squad. Moreover, the opportunity to return to school full time, with a good portion of his expenses paid, was particularly attractive. It gnawed at Gold that Shirley Oken actually considered him a "full fledged chemist," while he "knew that without a college degree" he would forever remain "dependent on the mercy of the Pennsylvania Sugar Company for [his] rating." But the fall term was to start in just a few weeks, and he hadn't even submitted an application.

Gold promptly told his family that through a stroke of luck he had acquired a new "job in the Midwest." His employer was told the same, and he requested a leave of absence in case this new opportunity proved unsatisfactory. He then scheduled a flight to Cincinnati to see about expedited admission at the university, where the admission officials gave him a "very discouraging reception." After reviewing his records, administrators in the dean's office told him they would accept him, but only if he was willing to start as a freshman in the school's co-op program. This was a profound blow to Gold. He had already completed "almost two years at the University of Pennsylvania" and earned a "diploma in chemical engineering in the Drexel Institute Evening School." Starting "as a freshman in a co-op course," which meant one "worked six months and went to school six months," would have meant a six-year ordeal. As he reflected at the time, "I could hardly think of putting in two years at college, let alone putting in six or seven years." It was totally unacceptable.[63]

When he arrived back in Philadelphia and communicated the results of his meeting with University of Cincinnati officials, Fred was "highly upset." Once again, it seemed, his plans to jump-start his American agent had been sabotaged. While Fred mulled over the alternatives, Gold accidentally stumbled upon one himself through the intercession of Morrell Dougherty, a close friend and co-worker at the sugar refinery.

Dougherty had begun working at the Pennsylvania Sugar Company in 1929 and developed a friendship with Gold in the early 1930s. In addition to working together under Dr. Reich in the refinery's research department, both men "attended night school at Drexel," where Gold assisted Dougherty with his schoolwork and helped him get through the program.[64] Although Dougherty was a family man, the friendship grew over the years. Many co-workers viewed the two men as "inseparable friends," Dougherty, the outgoing one, was usually "doing most of the talking," while Gold, the "much more intelligent of the two," "stayed in the background and talked to very few people."[65] Their friendship became so well known around the plant that fellow workers referred to them as the "Gold Dust Twins."[66]

Despite their close relationship, Gold never spoke to Dougherty of his Soviet connections, but he did confide his frustration on learning he'd have to repeat years of schooling if he went to the University of Cincinnati. "While you were in Cincinnati," replied Dougherty, "why didn't you go to Xavier" and see what kind of deal they would offer you? A small Jesuit school with little national reputation, it had recently drawn attention with a highly improbable "upset over Indiana University in football."[67]

Gold thought Dougherty's suggestion was an excellent idea, but fall classes were about to start. Could he gain admission at such a late hour? Once again, his friend came to the rescue by suggesting he schedule a meeting with the "dean of men at St. Joseph's College," another small Jesuit school on the outskirts of Philadelphia. Maybe with his recommendation, Xavier admission officials would give the education-hungry Jewish boy the academic equivalent of papal dispensation.

Almost immediately, Gold went to St. Joseph's campus on City Line Avenue and sat himself down in the dean's office, waiting for an audience with anyone who could help him navigate the admissions bureaucracy at Xavier in Ohio. Hours went by without anyone of consequence asking him into an office, but Gold refused to take the hint. Finally, a Father McKune, a high-ranking administrator, met with him. Gold thought the man must have wondered "how in the world could he give me an introduction or a recommendation when he had never seen me until this very moment." But, in fact, he did. Impressed with the young man's sincerity and determination, Father McKune said to Gold that "any man who waited four hours for him . . . must really want to go to school."[68]

Introduction and recommendation letters in hand, Gold flew back to Cincinnati and met with Xavier admission officials. It was the first week of September and the first day of classes, but the dean, the Reverend John Benson, "stayed until almost eight o'clock that evening, making the necessary arrangements and covering the necessary details" for Gold's admission and his selection of courses. Gold was deeply moved and very appreciative of this "unusual" and "heart-warming experience." For the rest of his life he would remark "how extremely wonderful the people" at Xavier were.[69] This religious and intellectual bond would only grow stronger during the next two years, and Gold would call his time at the Catholic university the most enjoyable period of his life.

CHAPTER 5

. . . .

Semenov, Slack, and Brothman

O
n the surface, it was an unlikely match: the working-class Jewish student from South Philadelphia whose mother taught
Yiddish and Hebrew to neighborhood children, and the small
Catholic college in southern Ohio. But it turned out to be a
collegial union. Both revered knowledge and respected those willing to
put in the long, difficult hours to attain it. Slightly older than most students, but with an inquiring mind and a monastic, workhorse approach to
learning that Jesuit scholars could identify with, Gold repeatedly proved
himself a star in the classroom. His willingness to share information and
tutor others made him a hit with fellow students as well.

Gold relished his time at Xavier. Everyone associated with the school,
he later wrote, was "so friendly, so decent, and so cooperative" that he
couldn't help but take "a tremendous liking to the place." He particularly
appreciated the kindness shown him by the faculty, which contrasted
strongly with his earlier collegiate experiences.[1] Father Mahoney, who
was in charge of the English department, Father Stechschulte, who ran
the physics department, and Father Miller in the chemistry department
—all extended a helping hand to aid his adjustment and foster his intellectual development.[2] Gold never detected any sign of discrimination or
bias at Xavier. On the contrary, he encountered people "good of heart"

and "utterly sincere," characteristics he tried to emulate when dealing with others.[3]

Gold majored in chemistry but also took courses in English literature. Both subjects were of long-standing interest: one as an intellectual challenge that would contribute to his professional career, the other as "an avocation" pursued for his own enjoyment. He avoided courses in economics and political science; they "bored" him.

Though he put in many hours in the classroom and in the library studying, Gold made sure to immerse himself in the full spectrum of college experiences. He "really rooted" for all of Xavier's athletic teams. Years later he believed the school's football and basketball teams might still remember him for his devotion. He occasionally traveled with the squads to away games, and "even delayed my Christmas vacation so that I could see a team play."[4]

He was happy; he was a full-time college student once again and pursuing the scientific and intellectual paths of his choosing. He would often tell people that his time at Xavier was incredibly fulfilling. Money was no longer the constant concern it had been.[5] He was by no means financially secure—Gold would always live near the edge economically—but between his own funds and the $400 the Russians gave him, he was able to pay his tuition and afford room and board at a modest private residence. Old habits were hard to break, however, and his generosity caused occasional shortages. He tried to send his mother a monthly $35 check, in part because his family needed it and in part "to keep up the terrible fiction that I had a job" in Ohio.[6] He also sent funds to help his girlfriend, Shirley Oken, "cover some debts." Once he called his friend Morrell Dougherty and asked him "to round up a number of people who owed" him money and get them to pay up.[7]

Despite the periodic money woes, Gold was enjoying "two of the most pleasant" years of his entire life.[8] He did well in his classes, was popular with his fellow students, and was receiving "very fine letters from the girl" back home. As he fondly wrote later, "Everything seemed just wonderful."[9] There was just one blemish in this idyllic life, but it was a significant one.

"An extremely important government official"

Reality unexpectedly intruded on Gold during his first Thanksgiving holiday in Cincinnati. He had just completed "mid-semester examinations, was very tired," and had picked up "a number of books of plays from the

Xavier University Library" to read during the break. He was staying in a rented room at the home of Alys Brooks, an elderly widow who lived in the Hartwell section of Cincinnati.

The holiday was perfectly planned. He'd spend a relaxing morning reading in bed, have an early Thanksgiving dinner with Mrs. Brooks, and then travel back to school for the "football game between Xavier and the University of Toledo" later that afternoon. Gold was still in his pajamas, reading plays in bed as a light snow fell outside his window, when there was a knock at the door. It was Mrs. Brooks informing him that he had a phone call.

Gold "couldn't imagine" who it was, since most of his schoolmates were with their families, and he "knew very few people in Cincinnati." Mrs. Brooks replied, "Well, I must say that he is a very peculiar friend, your person." She said she had told the caller that "Mr. Gold was in bed and left orders that he was not to be disturbed." She was shocked to hear the caller heatedly reply that he didn't care, "Get him out of bed." Mrs. Brooks was taken aback. "He certainly is arbitrary, isn't he?" she said to her now alarmed boarder.[10]

Gold instinctively knew who it was. "This could only be Fred," he thought, "and surely enough it was." Gold had not given Fred his address —in fact, he had had no communication with his Soviet handler since he left Philadelphia for Xavier in late August—but somehow Fred had tracked him down. He was in Cincinnati and wanted to meet Gold immediately. He gave him ten minutes to get downtown. Gold objected, saying it would take nearly an hour from his location on the outskirts of the city. Fred, "very grumpy" as usual, told him, "Get down here as fast as you can."

Gold quickly dressed, skipped breakfast, and tried to mollify Mrs. Brooks, who had prepared a lovely Thanksgiving Day meal and now had no one to share it with. The snow had begun to turn to rain, making for slush on the streets and a "very disagreeable day" to travel. Yet custom was maintained, and the two men "walked around . . . downtown Cincinnati for quite a while."

Gold was surprised to find Fred "no longer angry"; his handler even "tried to be quite amiable." A "very wonderful event" or opportunity had presented itself: a "great prospect" was living in the "neighboring town of Dayton, Ohio." The man "was an extremely important government official," and Gold's assignment was "to get in touch with him . . . right away."[11]

Gold protested; he said he had "previous engagements" and tried to come up with other excuses. He said he was "carrying a very heavy load in school" and could no longer work as he had in Philadelphia. Fred would have none of it. "The devil with them," he replied. "I'm giving you orders." He then ushered his unenthusiastic American agent to the main Cincinnati train station and demanded he "leave immediately" for Dayton.

Gold was furious. He had always resented Fred's manner, but this was too much, and on Thanksgiving no less. His plans for an idyllic morning of reading in bed, a hearty meal, and much-anticipated football game had been hijacked. This was one of those rare occasions when Gold refused to be bullied. As with the directive to sever his relationship with Tom Black and the equally disturbing order to recruit new members, Gold chose to disobey his superior.

Once Fred had dropped him off at the train station, Gold "waited for a period of time" to be sure that the Soviet operative had left the area. He then walked out a different door and "went to the football game" as originally planned.[12] It was an unusual show of independence, but short-lived. Two days later he was on a train to Dayton.

"You will be finished"

Gold had little to work with apart from two names: that of his Dayton contact and the name Stan. He had absolutely no knowledge of Dayton, but a bit of sleuthing and a telephone directory revealed his contact's address. After a fifty-mile journey by train, directions from several Dayton residents, and an additional fifteen-minute bus ride, Gold arrived at the surprisingly "modest home" of this "extremely important government official."

Gold knocked on the front door and asked to see Mr. Smilg. The person who opened the door appeared to be in his mid-twenties and identified himself as Ben Smilg, but "didn't seem disposed" to talk. Gold mentioned that he was a friend of Stan's and asked if he could come in. He was shown into the living room, where a number of people were gathered. He was quickly introduced to them but paid little attention to their names. Smilg "seemed anxious for them to leave," and within a short time they did.

The two men attempted to make small talk; Gold would later describe the conversation as a "more or less desultory." He explained that he was a student at Xavier University and tried to bring Stan into the conversation as often as possible, even though he had no idea who Stan was or what his relationship to Smilg might be. For his part, Smilg remained aloof, Gold later recalled, "and treated me rather coolly and warily throughout" the brief visit.[13] "Pretty much at a loss," Gold finally said, "I guess I'll be going along now." Smilg seemed more than pleased at that and "very reluctantly" agreed to Gold's request for a lift to the train station. At their parting, Gold gave Smilg "a small, inexpensive gift from Stan" and said he'd probably "be seeing him at very infrequent intervals." Smilg seemed more troubled than pleased by the gift and the notice of future meetings. They parted, according to Gold, "with a great deal of stiffness and coldness on both sides." He was "quite convinced that a mistake had been made."[14]

Two weeks later in Middletown, Ohio, a small steel-mill town between Dayton and Cincinnati, Gold had the opportunity to express his doubts about the Smilg assignment. It would result in a confrontation with his Soviet superior that he would not soon forget.

Fred had journeyed back to Ohio to hear the results of Gold's mission to Dayton. Gold wasted little time in apprising him that a "blunder had been made." The man he had met in Dayton "did not at all appear like the sort of person who would cooperate" with them. Smilg was a waste of time; Gold was "absolutely sure" of it.

Fred immediately "tried to reassure" him: "Oh, he is just being exceedingly careful and cautious." Smilg was an "honors graduate in aeronautical engineering from Massachusetts Institute of Technology" and worked at the army's Aeronautical Experimental Station at Wright Field. He was "extremely capable . . . brilliant," and was going to go far in military aeronautical research. Fred didn't have to explain the reason for the Soviets' interest. But he did allude to Smilg's humble origins. "His father was in poor health" and had been "completely unemployed" in recent years, and his younger brother was "still going to school and too young to work." Smilg had earned a scholarship to MIT, but it paid only for "tuition and books." He earned extra income for himself and his family by tutoring MIT students, one of whom was Stan. The Soviets seemed to know Stan well.[15] He was also an aeronautical engineering student at MIT, and tutoring him brought the Smilgs "the first real income that the family had ever had."

Gold remained skeptical. He was sure they had misread this man; Smilg was in no way going to be cooperative. Gold told his superior, "This is not a matter of the man being cautious. This was the matter of a man who didn't want to see me. . . . I don't think I am mistaken." Moreover, he declared, there would be no more trips to Dayton. "I am not going back up there any more," he said in a rare display of assertiveness. "I've seen him for the first and last time."[16]

Unaccustomed to such bold proclamations from an American subordinate—especially the timid Harry Gold—Fred let him have it. He "reached up and grabbed me by the shoulders," Gold later recounted, and pinned him against a wall. "Look here, you," he said, "let's get one thing straight. How would you like the good Fathers to get a note, an anonymous note stating that you are an official or a member of the Communist Party and have been since you were seventeen or eighteen years of age?" Gold was assured he'd "not only land in jail" but also lose all prospects of continuing his academic career. Never again would he "ever get into any school" of higher learning. "You will be finished," shouted Fred, "and don't think we will hesitate to do this."[17]

Gold was stunned. It was "the first and only time [he] had ever been threatened," and Fred obviously knew which threats would have the greatest impact. As Gold would recall later, the incident "frightened me tremendously. In fact, I lost sleep for almost a week because I knew Fred's caliber and his mind, and I knew that he would not hesitate to do something like this."

Gold was faced with a most difficult conundrum. He could either carry out his handler's orders or confront the prospect that "an anonymous letter would be dropped in the mail directed to the Fathers at Xavier revealing enough facts to establish Harry Gold as a Communist agent."[18] The repercussions of the latter—expulsion from school, arrest, and public humiliation, and his parents' shock and shame—were too painful to contemplate.

"Web of lies"

In late January 1939 Gold phoned Ben Smilg at his Dayton home to set up a meeting. Smilg's father answered. Gold quickly "identified" himself and tried to make small talk, but the father remained unmoved. He said his son "wasn't home" and hung up. Gold came away convinced that he was being shunned and that he "could call twenty times and . . . Smilg would not be home to me, ever." If he wanted to see the young engineer, he'd have to travel to Dayton and take his chances that Ben would be home.

Gold did this several times over the next year or so, but with little to show for it. He saw and spent time with Smilg, but the visit was always strained and unrewarding. Convinced that Smilg wanted no part of him,

Gold never "made more than the most tentative possible advance." Smilg never refused him entry into his home, but it was clear he was uncomfortable and "made no effort to introduce" Gold to friends, neighbors, or "some girls next door." Gold was made to feel like a social pariah, and repeated visits only confirmed his view that the Soviets would get nothing from Ben Smilg.

Fred, of course, found this unsatisfactory and continually encouraged Gold to redouble his efforts. He periodically called and sometimes even showed up in Cincinnati for updates. Gold would later admit that on more than one occasion he "lied to him," saying that he "was keeping in frequent touch with Smilg" and trying to obey Fred's directive that his visits become more "frequent."

Gold recognized the importance of his mission. He was in Cincinnati for the "sole purpose" of making contact with Ben Smilg. The Russians had hoped and expected that the young scientist would provide information from what they believed to be America's "principal aeronautical research center." It was information they thought to be "intensely valuable."[19] But Gold, despite having relocated to the Midwest and having accepted their funds for his Xavier education, knew that the Soviets had made a terrible miscalculation. Smilg wanted nothing to do with them.

Though the Smilg matter periodically made him uneasy, Gold was growing more and more adept at shoving Fred's unpleasant assignments into isolated mental compartments. After completing them—or promising to do so—he'd go about his own business and put Fred and Smilg out of his mind. He was a full-time student again and took his course work seriously. Besides, he had his own concerns, and some of them were Fred's fault.

At some point the Soviets had apparently had a change of heart and decided that "the false story" of Gold's employment in Cincinnati "was too capable of being destroyed or shown up to be a fiction." Consequently, Fred informed Gold that he "would no longer have this fictitious job" and would now "have to give the impression of being [a] poor," struggling student. To lend plausibility to this role, Fred told him, "you actually will be poor . . . we are not going to give you any more money," at least "for a good long time."[20]

Gold was distressed, but what recourse did he have? He was forced to do just as Fred had advised him: "conserve and hoard" his money. His brief exposure to financial stability now over, he returned to the familiar position of living on the edge. Worse yet, key people in his life needed to be notified of his embarrassing situation. He called his parents and

Shirley Oken and told them he had committed a "blunder" at work and lost his job, but that he would remain in Cincinnati, continue with school, and send money when he could. Aware that his "web of lies" was growing and that things were getting "terribly involved," he felt that he had to continue the charade.

His dire situation forced him to turn to friends for economic assistance. Abe Sklar was a boyhood chum to whom Gold had repeatedly lent money over the years without ever asking him to repay it. But now he was "in need of funds" and sent a letter to Sklar asking for help. Could Sklar possibly send him the $200 he was owed? Sklar responded quickly, sending just a portion—about $60 or $80—but Gold was grateful all the same. Former colleagues at the Pennsylvania Sugar Company like Carter Hoodless were sent similar letters of distress.[21]

The Soviets still gave Gold money, but it never approached their original promise that he would be "amply supplied with funds." On one occasion Gold had to travel from Cincinnati to New York City to collect it. He was so hard up that he "didn't even have enough money for coach fare" and had to borrow from classmates and faculty. Fred had told him to register at the Hotel New Yorker, near Penn Station, and the money would be delivered to him in the lobby. It was not Fred who met him, however, but another man, who said he "was a friend of Fred's and who had a very distinct Russian accent." This new person inquired how things were proceeding with Smilg, and informed Gold that he would no longer be seeing Fred. He then gave Gold approximately $150 in small bills and left.[22] The sudden reassignment of his demanding handler—a man he "hated" but had to "respect" for his "zeal" in attaining information—was surprising, but such abrupt changes were typical of Soviet operations.[23] It was a turn of events that caused Gold no sadness.

In all, Gold received $895 from the Soviets during his two years at Xavier. The amount would be described years later by his attorney as "compensatory" and certainly "not sufficient to meet more than a fractional part" of his needs.[24] Gold made an already bad situation worse by continuing to lend money to those in need. In fact, he nearly missed his own graduation because he could not pay his graduation fees. He had given money "to other students so they might pay their fees." A frantic, last-minute plea to friends in Philadelphia was all that kept him from missing his long-awaited college graduation.[25]

Gold's financial problems also contributed to the end of his romantic relationship with Shirley. Just a few weeks before his graduation and return to Philadelphia, Gold got the stunning "news that the girl whom I intended to marry had married someone else." He couldn't help thinking that the fact that he had "absolutely no money and was an exceedingly poor prospect economically" was the reason the relationship fell apart.[26] Shirley had fallen in love with someone with money.

Returning to Philadelphia in June by coach, Gold had his college degree and summa cum laude recognition, but little else.[27] He arrived at the Baltimore & Ohio train station on Market Street in Center City and couldn't even call his parents to say he was back in town. He had eight cents to his name, just enough for trolley fare home. On July 1, 1940, he resumed his employment with the Pennsylvania Sugar Company, "but this time with the full rating of chemist and at an increased salary" of about $150 a month.

"Merely class notes from MIT"

A month or so later, Gold received a call at home. The caller had a slight but recognizably Russian accent and identified himself as a "friend of Fred's." He said he "was downtown in Philadelphia near the Fox Theater" and asked Gold to meet him.[28]

Gold arrived to find a man only slightly taller than himself who appeared to be in his early thirties. He had a "slight" build and "swarthy" complexion, and introduced himself as "Sam."[29] The Russian visitor, he would learn years later, was Semyon Markovich Semenov, an MIT-educated mechanical engineer and mathematician who worked for Amtorg, ostensibly "purchasing oil refinery equipment." He was also a very accomplished Soviet spy and, of all the foreign agents Harry Gold worked with, the one with whom he would develop the longest and closest relationship.

Almost immediately, Gold noticed Sam was different from his predecessors. He "wore his clothes" like an American, had many "mannerisms of an American," and to an untrained eye might have been "very easily mistaken" for an American. On that initial meeting, the two men walked to a restaurant on Walnut Street across from the Bellevue Stratford Hotel and had a lengthy discussion. Sam questioned Gold about his background, his family, and his interests. He admitted his "regret" that Gold had "returned to the Pennsylvania Sugar Company" and tried to interest him in exploring opportunities at the Philadelphia Navy Yard. He said that "other firms paid far more lucrative salaries" than the refinery.[30]

Gold was unmoved. He had never been motivated by money and was "quite satisfied" where he was. But he found this new Russian's less aggressive and less dictatorial attitude a welcome change. Their next two meetings were similar, but then Gold was asked for the names of potential recruits. Uncomfortable with the request but feeling pressured to produce, Gold offered the name of one of his brother's friends.[31] Gold had little reason to believe his brother's friend would be interested in the Soviet cause, and his "delaying action" lasted only so long. Eventually he would have to supply a name.

His next assignment, in early January 1941, was equally distasteful, if not more so—he was told to go back to Ohio and resume "relations with Ben Smilg." Gold "was very glad to completely forget Smilg, but Sam was not": the Dayton engineer could be of great value to Russian aeronautical scientists. The two debated the matter over several meetings. Gold did not hold back, insisting the Smilg gambit was hopeless. Somehow, he argued, "something had gotten badly mixed up and Smilg was not the man" they wanted. Sam ended the debate insisting Gold "go to Dayton . . . [to] resume contact" with Smilg and "get him to do the work" the Soviet Union desired.[32] Gold conceded, but only after Sam stated he'd travel out there as well and meet him afterward in Cincinnati to get his report. If it weren't for that, said Gold, "I would not have made the trip."

This time, however, Gold was armed—not with a weapon, but with something the Soviets considered equally imposing. Sam had given Gold "four receipts . . . acknowledging payment to Smilg." They were for sums "in the neighborhood of . . . $100 to $200" and were in the category of "periodical retainers." Included in the typewritten package were two sheets that appeared to be of handwritten drawings of "aircraft design"— "either engine design, wing design or propeller design." Gold thought they might have been "merely class notes from MIT," but he was assured that Smilg would have no doubts about their nature and importance.

The visit to the Smilg household occurred in late January or early February. Gold knocked on the front door and was let inside, but Smilg's manner was as chilly as the weather. His distaste for Gold and his mission intensified when he saw what his undesired visitor had brought. Gold said he "had something to show him" and handed over "the receipts and the written material." On seeing them, Smilg "turned completely white." Gold thought the young engineer "was going to faint."

"You should never have done this," Smilg stammered. "Do you realize what you have done? You have done a most terrible thing. You should have never done this."

Gold was practically speechless, while Smilg continued to panic. "You can't possibly realize . . . you have been badly misled," said Smilg. "You can't possibly realize what sort of a mess something like this could result in."[33]

"Let me tell you one thing," Smilg continued. "I haven't looked at these things except for those receipts. Those are receipts, which I gave Stan, which Stan insisted on in payment for tutoring him. Get out . . . get out right now."

Gold, flustered, told Smilg that he was "getting unduly upset" and that he had only shown him the documents "to remind him of his former relationship with Stan"—just "refreshing his memory a little bit." But his attempt to soft-pedal the Soviet blackmail scheme was fruitless. Smilg knew he was being extorted. As he followed Gold to the front door, he continued the verbal barrage. "I will tell you one more thing," he concluded, "before you go. From the time that you first came around, I intended to report you to the authorities. But I didn't because this would result in a terrible state."[34]

Gold, "extremely badly shaken" by Smilg's reaction, left immediately and followed Sam's instructions as to what he should do if a problem should occur. He went to the Dayton railroad station, entered a public bathroom, "burned the material," and "flushed it down the toilet." He then "got out of Dayton . . . as rapidly as he could" and reported back to Sam.

Unimpressed with Gold's account of Smilg's meltdown, Sam said it was a "lot of nonsense," and all for show. "Stan could have tutored Ben in differential equations instead of Ben tutoring Stan." He said the two MIT students had "spent months . . . talking about the Soviet Union," and "very little tutoring" had taken place. "Besides, the sums given were outrageous."

If not for Soviet money, Sam said, Smilg would be "sweeping the floors . . . in a department store," not working as an "aeronautical engineer" at a high-performance military base; he would be a porter in the "ladies lingerie section" if the Russians had not "provided the funds to put him through MIT." Despite the scholarship Smilg had won to MIT, said Sam, his "family was so impoverished, that it would have been impossible for Ben to have completed his education" without Soviet assistance.[35] When Sam finally calmed down, he suggested they "let Ben think it over" for a while. Gold was glad to hear he wouldn't be traveling to Ohio again soon.

"Don't you understand what is happening?"

About March or April 1941, Gold received a double dose of good news: not only had the Soviets decided to "drop the matter of Smilg entirely, they had decided to drop me entirely as well." Sam informed him that their "work was at an end." Gold "had given them all that [he] possibly could and there was no further point" in their taking up each other's time.

Gold was "only too glad" to be rid of the nasty, "fruitless and pointless" business. For some time he had doubted that what he was providing his Soviet superiors had any real value. He had never wanted "to recruit people" for Communism, and he certainly didn't enjoy being "hounded" to do it. He "was only too glad to be left alone to work at the Pennsylvania Sugar Company" and leave the politics to others.

The politics, in fact, was increasingly unfathomable: the bizarre trials 1936 and 1938 of revolutionary Bolshevik heroes like Grigori Zinoviev and Lev Kamenev, their executions, and especially the Nazi-Soviet Non-aggression Pact of August 1939 had Gold very upset. How, he had asked Fred, could Stalin and the Soviets have signed a pact with their arch-enemy? "You fool," replied Fred in his usual bellicose manner, "don't you understand what is happening? We need time. We will buy time from the devil if we have to, and the devil in this case is Adolf Hitler."[36]

Gold found this answer confusing and depressing. One of the things that had attracted him to the Soviet banner was the Russians' willingness to fight—to fight discrimination, to fight anti-Semitism, to fight Fascism. Now they were saying, "We have to wait." It made no sense. Hitler seemed to be gaining strength and territory with every passing day. The Nazis, as Gold saw it, needed to be fought immediately and vigorously. Now he approached Sam, his new Soviet contact, with the same question. The Russian "laughed uproariously," at the American's naiveté. Gold was then given a stern lecture articulating the Soviet Union's need for time, "precious time to really build up [its] military might" in preparation for the "proper hour" when Russia would "sweep over Germany and Hitler like nothing ever imagined before."[37] Gold remained skeptical of what was apparently the party line, but admitted he was not a political savant.

He wanted to believe that this chapter of his life was over; there would be no more secret agents, recruitment campaigns, or anti-Trotsky

spy missions. He felt his debt to Tom Black had been satisfied years earlier and hoped that his efforts on behalf of the struggling Russian people
had been of some help. He was tired of lying to family and friends, and
of the Damoclean sword of public exposure.

"Stealing Eastman Kodak files"

Gold's feeling of relief would be painfully brief. In September 1941, Sam
phoned Gold at home, saying it was "extremely important" that they talk.
Gold didn't even put up a struggle; he met Sam, as requested, in New
York City. Sam delivered a long, emotional pitch—Gold would later describe it as a "pep talk"—for resuming their relationship. As he listened
to Sam plead for his services, Gold recognized the exquisite irony. Just
months earlier, Sam had trumpeted the Soviet game plan, but "Hitler,
fully as realistic, and having gained for himself precisely what the Russians had bargained for, struck first."[38] The Nazis' brutal invasion of the
Soviet Union in June 1941 had changed everything. Russia was fighting
for its survival.

Gold asked Sam how one "isolated individual" with access to nothing
of great importance could be of value, particularly when America was
now supplying Russia with industrial and military material under Roosevelt's Lend-Lease Plan. Sam admitted the program was a step in the right
direction and would probably foster better relations between the two nations, but he complained that the flow of supplies "was exceedingly slow"
and that though many industrial firms were under "direct instructions to
cooperate," they "simply refused to do so or gave them antique information." Sam feared that by the time the Soviets got anything of value, "all
of Russia, including Siberia, would be completely in the hands of the Germans." They simply had to get information more quickly.[39]

Gold, not surprisingly, "agreed to once again resume" his role as a Soviet operative. The threat of Soviet capitulation and the specter of another Nazi triumph were reasons enough to go back into service.

A few weeks later he was called back up to Manhattan to meet Sam
and, with little preparation or explanation, "bundled off" on a bus to upstate New York. His destination: the company town of Rochester. His assignment: to meet Alfred Dean Slack, a chemist who had been in the employ of the Soviets, and deliver to him the same urgent message that Gold
had recently received from Sam: the Soviet Union was in a life-and-death
struggle and in need of his assistance.

Al Slack was five years older than Gold, had been born and raised in

Syracuse, and was employed by the Eastman Kodak Company. He was also a "convinced Socialist" who with his friend and former co-worker Richard Briggs was known among fellow employees for his "deep sympathy for the people of Russia."[40] In 1936 Briggs was "discharged" from Kodak but continued to see his friend and occasionally asked Slack for information from the company's files that he could forward to his new employer in New Jersey. As "a reward for his cooperation," Slack "was promised an executive position with a handsome salary" at Briggs's new firm.

Slack gradually realized that the "information which he was so freely gathering" was not going to another industrial concern but "being channeled to a foreign country." Confronted by his friend in 1938, Briggs admitted that he had lied and was actually giving the information to a Russian agent "known only . . . as George." Though surprised by the deception, Slack was not alarmed or angry and, in fact, went with Briggs to New York City the following year to meet "George." In a Manhattan restaurant, the men solidified their future working arrangement.

The Russian expressed his nation's appreciation for Slack's past help, hoped it would continue, and said he would prefer to "deal directly with Slack in the future." Briggs took exception to being cut out of the action and protested that he "would not agree to such an arrangement." The Russian diplomatically allowed Briggs to continue as a go-between.[41] Slack was content to go on periodically "stealing Eastman Kodak files," taking them home to be "photographed with a camera furnished by Briggs," and then giving the "negative[s] . . . containing secret reports . . . to Briggs." Later that year, however, Briggs suddenly died.[42] Apparently won over by the concept of an intermediary between Slack and themselves, the Soviets were forced to find another reliable courier. Harry Gold was the American agent they entrusted with the job.

"Contempt for paid agents"

Neither the long journey to Rochester nor the assignment excited Gold. The Dayton debacle still fresh in his mind; the last thing he needed was to run into another uncooperative contact like Ben Smilg. And lying to his parents about another long day away from home was always a concern. But Gold always tried to please people. This new agent seemed like a decent fellow, and the Soviet Union's survival was still important.

Slack met him in downtown Rochester. Gold began by emphasizing how important Slack's contributions were to the cause and tried (as his handlers had done with him) to get to know the man he was dealing with. By asking a series of questions about his life, his schooling, and his family, he learned that Slack was a graduate of Syracuse University and, like himself, enjoyed chemistry. He lived on a "small farm . . . on the outskirts of Rochester" with his wife and parents. Gold was surprised to learn that Slack's wife was Jewish, had grown up in Brooklyn, and "formerly worked as a salesgirl for Macy's."

A second meeting about a month later covered similar ground, although this time Gold tried to learn more about Slack's covert efforts in behalf of the Soviets. The Kodak chemist explained that his friend Dick Briggs had initiated his "work for the Soviet Union," but Briggs was "an alcoholic and had literally drunk himself to death." Slack had access to information about "film developers and methods of preparing film emulsion, particularly for Kodachrome film," which was universally considered the best in the business.[43] He also had access to information on aerial photography, which would prove particularly important in the coming years.

Gold traveled from Philadelphia to Rochester every couple of months to acquire whatever of value Slack had secreted out of the Kodak plant. By his third trip he was a welcome guest at the Slack farm, although it is quite unlikely that Slack's family knew what was happening. On at least two of these occasions Gold immediately passed the information he received from Slack along to two unidentified Russian messengers—"once in Buffalo and once in Rochester"; on other occasions he dropped off "very bulky packets" for Sam in New York City or brought them home to Philadelphia.[44]

Gold was also introduced to a new concept: payment for services rendered. Slack received an envelope filled with money each time he delivered a package to Gold. The payments "ranged on the order of about $200 [per] installment" and never climbed much over $1,000 in total, according to Gold, but he was still stunned by it all.[45] He had come into this work with the quaint notions of achieving justice, leveling the odds against his parents' homeland, and assisting the one nation taking up the struggle against Fascism. He expected no remuneration for his services. The money he did receive—for travel and expenses—was woefully short of his actual out-of-pocket costs. Gold was flattered when his Soviet superiors "would sort of low-rate the people who were accepting money," feeling that his honest efforts in behalf of Russia were being recognized.

Sam, however, warned Gold that "Al should not be looked down upon for this." Whereas Sam usually had "contempt for paid agents," Al was an exception because of the "prodigious amount of time and effort involved in obtaining and assembling the data" from Eastman Kodak. The material he was handing over on "special chemicals and . . . film processes" was unique and "not known to the industry as a whole." Slack, who occasionally "evinced . . . slight signs of reluctance in respect to continuing" his undercover work, deserved to be "compensated" for his services.[46]

In late 1941, under Gold's direction, Slack began dealing with Howard Gochenaur, an employee of the Du Pont plant in Belle, West Virginia. The plant produced nylon and nylon cord, in which the Soviets had a growing interest. The manufacture of nylon from "raw materials such as benzene and ammonia" at Du Pont's plant in Seaport, Delaware, was a sophisticated process of which Gochenaur had only incidental knowledge. He turned over to Slack "an exceedingly jumbled mass of information" for which he was paid between $500 and $1,000, leaving Slack and Gold to make sense of what they had been given. At Slack's upstate New York farm, they spent "almost an entire day going over . . . the haphazard jumble" of paperwork now in their possession.[47] Then they traveled to Manhattan and delivered the documents to a Russian who introduced himself as "Robert."[48]

Slack would make several more trips to New York City to meet Robert and pass along information, but at some point in late winter or early spring 1942, Gold and the Russians "lost contact" with him. Gold made a trip up to Slack's Rochester farm, only to discover that he had a new job and that his wife seemed uncertain about "just where he was going to be located."[49] Eventually they learned that Slack was working at the Holston Ordnance Works in Kingston, Tennessee.[50] Though the Soviets would miss Slack's access to Kodak's photographic secrets, they were delighted with the prospect of acquiring the latest developments from a major American munitions plant. With the move, Slack would leap from industrial to military espionage.

Gold's first opportunity to visit Slack in his new post came not in Tennessee but in Cincinnati, where Slack had been transferred as part of an orientation process. Little of note occurred at this meeting except for Gold's assurance that the Soviet Union looked forward to any information the chemist could obtain concerning explosive devices developed at Holston. Shortly thereafter, Slack left Ohio for Tennessee.

"Jewboy genius"

Al Slack was not the only American chemist supplying information to Gold and the Soviets during these years. Another college-trained chemical engineer contributing to the Soviet cause was Abe Brothman. A designer of mixing equipment, Brothman had been supplying information to Jacob Golos, one of the top Soviet spies operating in America. Golos had cultivated a stable of government and industrial contributors, but just before America's entry into the war he had turned over a number of his contacts to his lover, Elizabeth Bentley. It was her job to "meet with his sources, collect their documents, calm their fears, and flatter their egos."[51] Most of her contacts were based around Washington, D.C.; Brothman was one of the few who brought her north to Manhattan.

Brothman was one of Bentley's first assignments. Their relationship, strained from the beginning, only grew more problematic with time. Brothman knew Bentley as "Helen"; she dubbed him "the Penguin" because of his distinctive waddle. About a dozen times, they made their "prearranged rendezvous, [at] the corner of 32nd Street and Fifth Avenue, and walked to a restaurant." The Penguin would slip her a "thick envelope with folded blueprints, which she then delivered to Golos." The documents almost always concerned designs for "commercial vats, filters, and shafts used in the manufacture of chemicals"[52] or blueprints for "oil blowing kettles, resin kettles, and a urea resin plant layout."

Despite their shared interest in helping the Soviet Union, the two constantly complained about each other. Bentley found Brothman undependable, "irascible," and "annoying"; he in turn said she was technically unschooled and sexually provocative.[53] In an effort to end the bickering, please his girlfriend, and supply Brothman with a courier trained in the sciences, Golos decided to replace her with another American operative. Harry Gold got the assignment.[54] He too would find Brothman difficult to handle.

Not everyone considered Brothman an ogre. One particularly close admirer would describe him as someone whose "reasoning was so perceptive, his insight so special he could never stumble, who anticipated life's pitfalls and therefore could never be trapped by them, whose step was sure and whose decisions would always be unerringly wise." His "conspicuous intelligence" was accompanied by "consuming self-absorption and chronic lack of self-doubt."[55]

Brothman, who would play an important role in Gold's life as a spy and an even more critical role in his eventual capture, was only fifteen "when he entered Columbia College on a full scholarship." His progressive political instincts emerged early—Gold would come to believe he had "been a radical almost from . . . birth"—leading him to join "the Young Communist League as a teenager" and "gravitate towards radical activities" while at Columbia.[56] He graduated summa cum laude from Columbia's School of Engineering before he turned nineteen. Despite numerous academic awards and honors, he faced significant roadblocks.[57] He would have preferred a postgraduate fellowship at Columbia in either chemistry, physics, or engineering, but his "unhappy ability to alienate V.I.P.'s" relegated him instead to a "fellowship for six months in the Department of Mathematics . . . despite the fact that he had not pursued Mathematics as a primary interest."[58] Despite the Depression and his youth, "job offers came quickly."

Brothman's postcollege career involved a series of disappointing professional experiences. At twenty-one he was "chief engineer" at Blau Knox, a Pittsburgh manufacturer of chemical equipment primarily for the oil refining industry. He resigned in 1938 after what was described as "a hectic five-year career of strife involving disputes over salary, anti-Semitism, and refusal of company to provide adequate appropriations each year for chemical research."[59] Talkative, opinionated, and well left of center, Brothman was "scrappy" on the issue of anti-Semitism and increasingly uncomfortable with America's corporate culture. He was the target of "jesting epithets" and insults, of which "Jewboy genius" was only one.

Brothman gradually came to believe he'd be happiest setting up "his own operation as a consulting engineer so that he could exercise control over his professional life. He wanted the freedom to create without . . . a moribund corporate vision" constraining him. Unfortunately, despite his intellectual gifts and abundant self-confidence, Brothman's ventures, undercapitalized and poorly thought out, never attained the grand outcomes he envisioned for them. The result was a series of frustrations, convoluted business partnerships, and growing debt.

After returning to New York from Pittsburgh in 1938, Brothman founded Republic Chemical Machinery Company, which "obtained orders for equipment and sub-contracted the fabrication of the equipment which it designed." Republic was eventually incorporated into Hendrick Manufacturing with Brothman as vice president, but once again a combination of legal, business, and personal conflicts caused him to resign in 1942.

"Something completely new"

Politics, apparently, was no easier to master, at least as far as personal relationships went. Elizabeth Bentley's frustration was by no means unique. Almost immediately Gold experienced his own difficulties in dealing with the idiosyncratic "genius." Even their initial get-together presented unexpected hurdles. Having been given a description of his contact's automobile and the license number, Gold was to meet him on "Eighth or Ninth Avenue in upper Manhattan," introduce himself, and "accept any new material he had" in his possession. On the first two tries, he never spotted the car. Gold would always remember the date they finally met as the night of the heavyweight bout between Lou Nova and Joe Louis. Both sports enthusiasts, the two men "listened to the fight on Brothman's car radio" while discussing business.

Gold introduced himself as "Frank Kessler," a name he later claimed he had arbitrarily borrowed from the Kessler Manufacturing Company in Northeast Philadelphia, "visible from the train going to New York," and only later realized "was also the name of a former boyhood chum" from South Philadelphia.[60]

Gold and Brothman soon reverted to their hit-or-miss routine. Gold couldn't understand why meetings with agents in Rochester and Cincinnati proved so much easier than one just ninety miles away. He quickly learned that Brothman was averse to keeping appointments, especially before mid-afternoon. This came as a shock to Gold; appointments with Soviet handlers were "kept in exceedingly strict fashion . . . and if there was an occasion not to keep an appointment, there was usually a pretty good reason for it." Brothman "was something completely new"—he "had no concept of what an appointment meant" and seemed incapable of changing either his personal habits or his schedule.

Dealing with Brothman was a recurring headache and a series of "very sad experiences." Although Sam had told him to act as Brothman's organizational superior and give him orders when appropriate, Gold was unable to take on the personality of a demanding boss. "It took a tremendous amount of hounding, prodding, exhortation and so on to get Brothman to do any work." Waiting for one scheduled meeting at a Manhattan restaurant, for example, Gold drank "seven or eight Canadian Clubs" while "sitting at a table over a period of two hours." Brothman never arrived. Neither the absence nor the alcohol consumption was recommended spycraft, but Brothman seemed unable to show up for meetings. "In fact," Gold later recalled, "the rarity was for him to keep an appointment."[61] For a Philadelphia-based operative traveling back and forth to New York City, this was no minor matter.

Therefore, Gold would say years later, "I changed my method." There was no choice but to conform to Brothman's lifestyle. If Brothman was a nocturnal creature who liked "sleeping very late in the morning . . . coming to work some time in the afternoon, and working until way late in the night," Gold decided his best shot at reaching him was to travel to New York late in the day and call on Brothman at his workplace. That meant arriving back in Philadelphia well after midnight, but at least some business was transacted.

Another frustrating issue was Brothman's tendency to supply "fragments" of what he was supposed to deliver. Expected to show up with plans for a "reaction-mixing kettle," he would bring only "the design of a flange" for the kettle, and Gold have to plead for the rest of the plan. Such unaccountable behavior would leave Gold perturbed and Sam "furious."

Despite Brothman's inability to conform, the Soviets had no intention of discarding him. He had real value; he was "exceedingly able" and possessed a genuine creative streak. Many, including Gold, viewed him as "brilliant," a man of "ideas" who "dreamt on an extremely large and vast scale."[62] From the fall of 1941 to June 1943, Brothman gave Gold information on "Buna-S," a form of synthetic rubber; various types of mixing equipment; the manufacturing process for a new type of flare based on magnesium powder (that could also be used for tracer bullets); and aerosol sprays, or "aerosol bombs" as they were then called.[63]

Though mixing equipment may not seem particularly important, it is central to the chemical engineering process. Gold himself knew that manufacturing a chemical product depended upon "bringing together two or more solids and fluids to create the proper reaction." Many of the design plans Brothman passed along were his own, and "almost from the beginning" of their relationship Gold encouraged him to press the Soviets for "legitimate backing" so he could go into business on his own and "design processes on a vast scale for them." According to Gold, the Soviets "simply hee-hawed" at the concept and "wouldn't listen to it one bit." Their reasons were simple. First, they were already getting Brothman's work for free, and second, they were interested not in innovation but in "working processes, which were already in operation." Procuring "an exact copy of a working plant or a working process" was always their goal. As Gold would succinctly describe it years later, the Soviets "would settle for an inferior" manufacturing process that was already being used on an everyday basis, rather than "taking a gamble on something which was merely in the developmental stages."[64] Sam "despised anything" that was not "already in accepted operation." For this reason, and the fact that the items Brothman gave him tended to be "fragmentary and incomplete," Gold never passed along the information about magnesium powder and aerosol bombs. Brothman's most creative work drew no Soviet interest whatsoever. "We spit on it," Sam once remarked.[65]

The Soviet response frustrated Brothman. He desired to leave the Hendrick Manufacturing Company, start his own business, develop his own clients, and create his own products and processes. But the Soviets were equally frustrated. They encouraged Gold to convince Brothman "that he should go . . . work for U.S. Rubber or Goodyear" and "continue his work on synthetic rubber" in order to funnel additional industrial products their way. Brothman remained unmoved; he "had other ideas," one of them being "to work openly for the Soviets" and any other clients who could give him business.

Gold never paid Brothman for information, but on "several occasions" he was given "sums in the neighborhood of $40 or $50 to pay for any expenses he may have incurred," such as for stenographers and photocopying. The Russians appreciated Brothman's information, but they were also aware of his temperament and the difficulties agents had in dealing with him.

"Mathematician and mechanical engineer by profession"

Brothman's cavalier attitude toward meetings and document deadlines occasioned at least one memorable outburst from Sam. The dustup arose after Gold had traveled to "New York four times in a single week in a fruitless effort to obtain a report from Abe Brothman on the synthetic rubber Buna-S." Brothman had repeatedly assured him that "the data was ready" to be turned over, but each trip only yielded greater frustration. Gold became convinced that Brothman "had not even begun to write the report."

On Friday night, after the fourth trip, Gold was scheduled to meet with his superior and turn over the report. "Abe absolutely promised to have the report complete tomorrow," he told Sam apologetically, "let's make the arrangements to meet." On hearing of one more delay, his Soviet superior exploded. Gold called it "the worst rage" he had ever seen. "Look at you," said Sam angrily, "you not only look like a ghost, but you are one. You're positively dead on your feet and exhausted. What must your mother think? You goddamn fool, let me not hear one more word about coming to New York tomorrow or for several weeks to come. Go home and spend some time with your family. This is an order. The hell with this Buna-S, even if it means Moscow will fall."[66]

Sam agreed that the "son-of-a-bitch Brothman" probably hadn't even started writing the report and was "merely stalling for time." Brothman was called "heartless" for needlessly bringing Gold to New York, but Sam also blamed Gold for being such "good company." Brothman liked to talk of his accomplishments and plans for the future while Gold patiently listened "to his bragging." Gold's propensity for pleasing people, Sam told him, was his Achilles' heel.

Slowly, Sam calmed down and ushered Gold to the Ferris Wheel Bar in the basement of the Henry Hudson Hotel at Fifty-seventh Street and Eighth Avenue. He suggested that they "have a few double Canadian Clubs and some sandwiches" and try to forget Brothman. Later he would personally see Gold off at Penn Station. Still distressed over Gold's cavalier treatment by another agent, he offered to purchase his dedicated courier a "parlor-car seat and a few Corona cigars."[67]

This response fostered a strong bond between the two. Far more than Gold's other Soviet handlers, Sam seemed to be concerned about his welfare. He recognized that the American had little in his life apart from his work at the sugar refinery and his ever-expanding role as a Soviet operative. He occasionally apologized for "so often taking [him] away" from his family and "most especially" his mother. He became "particularly anxious" when Yus, Gold's younger brother, left for overseas service during the war. He "tried in every way," according to Gold, "to cut down on his trips" so as to give Harry more time with brother and parents.

"His greatest concern," however, was that his good-natured Philadelphia chemist had no wife and family. "I realize," said Sam, "it's because of this work, but . . . it's not natural or good. You are not an ascetic and you have normal instincts and desires. Obviously, you cannot take on the responsibility of marriage and still do this work." They had to find "some solution to this problem." Sam wanted Harry to know that his Soviet superiors appreciated his loyalty and work ethic: "Do not think that our people fail to recognize the sacrifice you are making." "As soon as it is possible," he assured Gold, his role in "this lousy business" would finally come to an end; then he could "completely forget it all" and "run around with girls every night in the week."[68]

Because of their long association—four years, more than Gold would spend with any other agent—these comrades-in-arms often let down their guard and confided their innermost concerns, fears, and aspirations. A "mathematician and mechanical engineer by profession," Sam "read widely" and "was thoroughly familiar with the works of Charles Dickens, Fenimore Cooper, Somerset Maugham, Sinclair Lewis, and Thomas Wolfe." It was not at all unusual for the two men to walk around the city or sit at a restaurant table discussing literature after their real business had been concluded. Sam was not reluctant to share his literary opinions on everything from "Browning's *My Last Duchess*" to Carl Sandburg (a "mediocrity and a bit of a faker"). Sometimes, feeling "weary" and a bit philosophical, Sam would "complain of the nasty job he was doing," how distasteful it was to pay agents for their services, and confess his longing "to be back in his native land." He talked often of his love for "skiing in Russia," and when his schedule allowed, he would try to see "ice hockey games at Madison Square Garden and then would remain for the ice-skating afterwards."

In addition to their love of science and literature, the two men shared an intimate understanding of the pulverizing drudgery of a secret agent's life. Most of their waking hours, it seemed, were spent "waiting apprehensively on street corners in New York and various other cities, waits which were often futile and sometimes extremely dangerous, eating in cheap, out-of-the-way restaurants, and cajoling, pleading with, and threatening various people." This line of work was now the centerpiece of their lives. But after so many years of it, they had both lost much of their initial enthusiasm and conviction. For the experienced Soviet operative and the no-longer-novice spy from South Philadelphia, espionage had become a lonely, boring job.[69]

One could not, Sam admitted, "continue in espionage work indefinitely." He said Gold had "already been in it too long" and expressed his hope that he would soon be free of it. Not only was it "an ordeal" from a physical and psychological standpoint, "but inevitably a slip would occur, and exposure would follow."

"Look, I am a chemical engineer and mathematician. You are a chemist. What are we doing running around begging people for information, cajoling them, and threatening them? I want to design things, you want to work in a laboratory. Inevitably," said Sam, they would "get caught. You can't stay in this thing forever. The trick is to get out before they do catch you."[70]

At the same time, Sam tried to buoy Gold's spirits by telling him that their "underhanded" activities "will not always be necessary. You'll see, after the war is won, there will come a great time of cooperation between all nations, and people will be able to travel freely back and forth through all nations." Gold would be an honored guest in Moscow and would meet all his friends, and they would have "a wonderful party" in his honor. Sam would show him around the city, and they would "have a great time" in the land for which he had sacrificed so much.

Gold, exhausted but committed to an Allied victory and the destruction of Fascism, certainly wanted to believe such a beautiful scenario was possible.

CHAPTER 6

. . . .

Dr. Klaus Fuchs

Nineteen forty-three was a busy year for Harry Gold. Like a traveling salesman promoting kitchen cabinets or encyclopedias, he was constantly on the move. Incredibly, only his Soviet handlers knew of his hectic schedule or his wide-ranging journeys to upstate New York, Ohio, and Tennessee, as he traded industrial and military secrets around the country while still putting in long hours at the sugar refinery in Philadelphia.

Gold was one of the best examples of how, as John Earl Haynes, Harvey Klehr, and Alexander Vassiliev write in *Spies,* "Soviet espionage networks in the United States would not have been able to function without the assistance of a number of dedicated support personnel whose role was as essential as that of the sources who actually took documents from the government offices in which they worked or communicated secrets to which they were privy."[1] Once the information had been obtained, someone had "to transmit it to the Soviets." Operatives like Gold and Elizabeth Bentley were indispensable: "The KGB needed a corps of such discreet, dedicated Americans willing to undertake unglamorous jobs that required regular travel and a low profile."[2]

"Very highly nitrated explosive"

Gold began going to Kingsport, Tennessee, to renew his relationship with Alfred Dean Slack, now a supervisor at the Holston Ordnance Works, a subsidiary of Eastman Kodak. On Gold's first visit, Slack informed him that Holston was producing a new, highly secret explosive. The explosive, known as RDX, was considered so "vital to the defense of the country" that Slack had to sign a document acknowledging that "divulging any information" about it "would constitute a violation of the espionage laws."[3]

This new explosive, Gold was led to believe, was a significant step forward in munitions development—not "that its destructive effect was any greater than that of the conventional nitrate explosives, but that it was so highly nitrated that much less of it was needed to achieve . . . a similar effect as the conventional explosives produced." The use of RDX could bring either a "substantial reduction" in the "size of a munitions dump" or, if quantity was maintained, "tremendously greater firing power."[4] It was a product of considerable value.

On that first trip to Kingsport, Gold detected a slight reticence on Slack's part, almost as if "Al was trying to avoid him," but after considerable coaxing and reassuring him the Soviets desired as much information as he could provide on the new explosive, Slack complied.[5] One night Slack left his laboratory carrying an unrestricted pass that allowed him to move around the Holston facility at will, and entered the section of the plant where RDX was stored. When he determined he was not being observed, Slack grabbed a "handful of the dry super-explosive and placed it in his pocket." Back in his own laboratory, he transferred the explosive powder from his pocket to a rubber container and took it home pending a meeting with his Soviet conduit, Harry Gold.

On his third trip to Kingsport, Gold was given the RDX, as well as the "technical write-up on the manufacturing process and the industrial know-how being employed at the plant."[6] Traveling back home on the Norfolk & Western train, he tried to convince himself he was in no danger. He repeatedly told himself that the "very highly nitrated explosive" was probably "not quite ready for final use" and required a "physical drying step" before it would explode. Since he was not yet scheduled to meet his Soviet handler, Gold "actually kept [the explosive] in his rowhouse Philadelphia home for three or four days" until he went to New York to turn it over to Sam.[7]

On Gold's next visit to Kingsport, he and Slack "played chess all afternoon." Slack provided little information but did mention that he expected to be transferred once again—probably to a "tremendous installation near Knoxville" whose name he didn't know. He was under the impression that "a highly secret poison gas" was being developed there and "couldn't understand why the place was so vast."[8] Gold had dinner with Slack and his wife, Julie, and they agreed to meet again just before Christmas.

Gold returned to Tennessee at the appointed time, armed with gifts, only to learn that Al had already been transferred. Eventually he would learn that Slack was working at the Oak Ridge nuclear site.[9] The next time he would see him, years later, it would be in newspaper photographs that showed him being arrested for espionage.

Gold also regularly saw Abe Brothman during this period. The frequency of his trips to New York would have been much reduced if Brothman had been less casual about preparing his information and able to keep to a set schedule. Hoping to light a fire under Brothman, Sam asked Gold to set up a meeting with the three of them. Sam was introduced to Brothman as "a high Soviet official" and proceeded to give him "a pep talk" on keeping commitments. Unfortunately, the get-together had little impact. Brothman remained as unreliable as ever, no doubt as a way of getting back at both men, and the Soviets in general, for their continuing lack of interest in his inventions.[10]

"Stock of lore"

As Gold dutifully carried out his many assignments, Sam occasionally reminded him of the dos and don'ts of Soviet tradecraft. It was the same list he had heard from Paul, Fred, and others: live as normally as possible to avoid attracting suspicion; refrain from discussing issues such as social inequality and discrimination, so as not to be perceived as a radical; never carry large amounts of money; always use an alias for espionage work, never his real name, and, Gold related, "under no circumstances . . . reveal where I lived or worked."[11] If ever "apprehended . . . I could not expect any help." Gold, Sam reiterated, would "just have to take the consequences." But he was told that if it were "feasible, large sums would be made available for legal aid."

Gold also had a "stock of lore," as he called it: tricks of the trade he had picked up over the years. To avoid surveillance, he would try to walk on the dark side of the street, and eat in restaurants with booths rather than at a table in the open. If he thought he was being followed, he would stop and tie his shoelaces or "take a subway train and sit fairly near the exit doors." After going several stops, he would "jump up and rush through them" before they closed, ensuring the "tail" could not follow. Crowded movie theaters were also a good place to ditch a tail, particularly those with side exits.

If Gold needed an excuse at home to explain his going on a mission, he could tell his family he was going to "see Tom Black in Newark over the weekend."[12] Gold was hardly a master of the black arts, but his unimpressive appearance and innocuous demeanor were ideal for delicate assignments. No one would ever suspect that the dumpy fellow with the odd gait and glum expression was a Soviet spy trading in industrial and military secrets.

"Brilliant chemical engineer"

In early 1943 Gold contacted Black about a "very urgent matter" and said they needed to meet as soon as possible. During the war years, the two saw each other infrequently; sometimes "a year or more would elapse between meetings and at other times" they'd meet "every month or every three months."[13]

When they met, Gold informed Black he needed a favor. He "had received his notice to take his preinduction physical examination." Despite having been classified as unfit for service in the past, Gold believed—or hoped—he was about to be inducted into the army. He told Black "he had been handling a contact who in the past had provided him with extremely valuable technical information" and was capable of "much more." But this contact was temperamental and had been "very badly handled before," leading to certain difficulties. He "could not be handled brusquely," Gold said, but required "extreme tact" and much flattery. This "contact was so valuable he didn't want to see just anyone handle him," and he was going "to recommend to his Soviet superior that [Black] be assigned the task." Gold never mentioned the name of this "brilliant chemical engineer" who was "an expert on the design of mixing equipment for the chemical industry."[14] Several years passed before Black finally met Abe Brothman. The overture went nowhere. Black too expected to be drafted very shortly.

In truth, Gold's concerns were highly unrealistic. When he showed up for his physical, he actually thought he might be selected. He had already cleared his desk at Pennsylvania Sugar, completed his work assignments, and said his good-byes to co-workers. The examination went smoothly except for his blood pressure, which was too high. Doctors checked his pressure a second time and found no change. Since neither the doctors nor Gold wanted to give up, he was told to lie down on a cot and have a bit of rest. Gold had risen very early that morning and quickly fell asleep. When doctors woke him after a lengthy nap and checked his pressure again, they were stunned to see that it had actually risen. The result, said Gold, was "a great big reject" on his official papers.[15]

Gold's Selective Service file contains some interesting items. The Pennsylvania Sugar Company requested a deferment for him in December 1941. Since "the company manufactured alcohol used in making explosives" and Gold was "an operations chemist who needed years of experience to reach his present efficiency," the company argued "that if the registrant was removed from his position, both the quality and quantity of production . . . would suffer."[16] Pennsylvania Sugar claimed that Gold "was the only person employed . . . with similar skill and training" and that "to replace him with a person of like abilities would take years of training."

Company executives weren't the only ones concerned. Celia Gold submitted an "Affidavit by Dependent" in December 1941 declaring she was "the mother of Harry Gold . . . was partially supported by him and had been . . . for nine years."[17] She said she was "fifty-eight years of age" and had "earned nothing in the past twelve months," while her son had "contributed $600 in cash to her support, as well as $400 in the form of room and board."[18] Neither Mrs. Gold nor his employer need have worried; Harry wasn't going to be wearing a military uniform. His "disqualifying defect" was "irremediable," and he was officially declared 4-F, "unfit for military duty."[19]

Gold still wished to be an actual combatant in the fight against Fascism. In 1943 he went to a Marine recruiting station, hoping to join up. After examining his Selective Service card, the recruiters asked why he was 4-F. Gold "blurted out blood pressure," and just as quickly the interview was over. They wouldn't even examine him.[20]

Undeterred, Gold visited a navy recruiting office several months later. This time he thought he'd be a "little cleverer" and keep the hypertension issue to himself. When asked about his 4-F designation, he replied, "Why don't you examine me?" And so they did, only to discover a problem, he recalled, as soon as "they put the inflated cuff on my arm." "I don't even think they even completed" the examination. "They took one look . . . and said get the devil out of here, you are wasting our time."

Gold's joining the military would have cost the Soviets one of their most dependable American operatives. One can only speculate how Gold would have felt. Would he have been troubled over abandoning Russia in its time of greatest need?[21] Gold may have provided a clue when he described his ability to focus on one task at a time to the exclusion of everything else. He found it "an extremely curious thing" that he was able to lead a seemingly normal life while carrying on his espionage activities and "still remain sane." He attributed his mastery of this delicate high-wire act to his ability "to simply cultivate a one track mind." He could focus exclusively on performing his assignments for the Soviets,[22] and then "once they were over I dropped them to such an extent that there were still around the house schedules, timetables, and possibly various other data" of importance. That carelessness would come back to haunt him.

Though he spent considerable time involved in secret Soviet missions, Gold was never totally convinced that his travels, the meetings with other agents, and the documents and blueprints he carried around really added up to anything. There were occasions when "the whole damned business seemed very futile." Adding to his doubts were the recurring frustration of keeping track of Slack's movements, Brothman's broken promises, and his rejection for military service. One other matter of concern was the emotional repercussions from his "increased absences from home." These were making his mother more and more distraught, especially after her younger son, Yus, shipped off with the army to fight in the South Pacific.[23] Like his older brother, Joe Gold had originally been "turned down . . . by the Army because of a hernia," but after having it repaired, he decided to enlist and ended up with the Signal Corps in the Pacific.[24]

After a disheartening late-night meeting with "the usually ebullient" Sam—who on this occasion was "very subdued because of some failures of his own"—Gold made up his mind "to be through with this work once and forever." As he sat at Penn Station reading the newspaper while waiting for his train back to Philadelphia, an incident occurred that would reenergize his flagging spirits. He later recalled that he was approached "by a swaying drunk who proceeded to vilify me as a 'kike bastard,' a 'sheeny,' a 'yellow draft-dodger' and as a 'lousy money-grabber.'" Gold wanted to smash the offensive lout in the face, but his training kicked in; he "could not afford to be involved in a scrape in New York," because it might involve his having to explain why he was there at all. Instead, he just "walked away." But as he did, so did his "resolution to quit espionage work."

The incident had neatly and powerfully framed the issue for Gold.

"It seemed all the more necessary," he would subsequently explain, "to fight any discouragement and to work with the most increased vigor possible to strengthen the Soviet Union, for there such incidents could not occur. To fight anti-Semitism here seemed so hopeless."[25]

The Soviets were not unappreciative of Gold's efforts. Their internal communications reveal that he was considered "a very valuable worker."[26] Some of his contacts, like Sam Semenov, understood how much time and money he had invested in helping them. Though he was orchestrating the operations of many other American agents, Semenov had grown particularly fond of the little chemist and fellow Jew from Philadelphia. It is likely he had something to do with Gold being awarded the Order of the Red Star, an honor that very few noncombatants, and even fewer from outside the Soviet Union, were accorded. When Sam informed him of the honor in late 1943, Gold was quite pleased. Though he was not handed the actual award, for obvious reasons, there was genuine satisfaction in knowing his efforts had not gone unnoticed.[27]

Sam also made sure to underscore the Soviets' appreciation for all Harry had sacrificed, including his considerable financial contribution. Sam said that "they had kept a very good account of the probable expenses" Harry had accumulated over the years, and what he claimed to have spent was "entirely insufficient" for his extensive travels and activities. They knew, Gold recalled, "[I] must have been supplying my own funds." Semenov called this practice "nonsense" and demanded that it stop. He wanted Gold to "give them an accurate accounting" and no longer spend his own money.[28] Gold began to receive a monthly stipend, but it still failed to cover all his assigned errands.

"A very aesthetic, intellectual appearance"

Not long afterward, Gold received an additional shot of adrenalin—not a vile insult hurled by a drunken anti-Semite or a prestigious Soviet medal, but an intriguing opportunity that would ultimately lead to infamy.

In early January 1944, Gold—already "considered a very valuable worker" by Soviet intelligence—was told by Sam to come to Manhattan for an important meeting.[29] When he arrived, he immediately discerned a difference in his friend. Before Sam had even said a word, Gold could tell he was "extremely excited," possibly "more so than I had ever seen him before."[30]

"Something has come up," he told Harry, something "so big and so tremendous" that he would have to devote his "complete efforts to carrying it through successfully."[31] The Soviet Union was assigning Gold a mission "of the utmost magnitude and importance." He was to drop everything else and devote himself "single-mindedly to this one thing." Specifically, he was to "absolutely have nothing to do" with Al Slack or Abe Brothman, "particularly Brothman."

"Before you make a single move," said Sam, "think, think twice, think three times. You cannot make any mistakes in connection with this. It must be carried through" to completion.

Sam then asked an unusual question: Did Harry "wish to accept the assignment?" In the past, Harry "had always been told what to do" and when to do it. And there was another thing: Sam said the assignment would be "extremely dangerous."[32]

Harry assented without hesitation. Maybe now, he thought, he'd really be making a contribution. Maybe this was the mission he'd been looking for.

Sam said that he would be meeting "a man recently come to this country from England." The man would be working with a "group of American scientists in the New York City area," and would have "information on the construction of a new type of weapon." Gold was told nothing about the weapon except that it was "completely new." "Devastating" was the term Sam used to describe it. It would be Gold's job to get information about this weapon from the new contact.[33]

Gold was to meet this "high government official" on Saturday, February 5, shortly before four in the afternoon, in the "neighborhood of the Henry Street Settlement on the East Side of New York City." He was to wear a pair of gloves and "to carry an extra pair in one hand." His contact would be on "the opposite side of the street . . . carrying a tennis ball and . . . a green bound book."[34] Once they approached each other, Gold was to ask, "What is the way to Chinatown?" as a secondary recognition signal. His contact was to reply, "I think Chinatown closes at 5 o'clock."[35]

On the day of the rendezvous, Gold arrived in New York early, bought an extra pair of gloves, and waited on the appointed street corner. The drill was painfully familiar at this point. As he waited, Gold could not help but think that whoever had chosen the place—whether it was Sam or some other Soviet operative—had done a good job: "It was an area where a lot of tenements were being torn down and replaced by housing projects." The Henry Street Settlement appeared closed, and there was an empty playground across the street. A large fence surrounded an excavation site where a building was being constructed, and on this Saturday afternoon, to Gold's delight, "no one was on the street." He thought it "beautifully deserted," an "ideal" place to meet. "No one would think anything of two people walking toward each other and making conversation."[36]

At the appointed time, Gold saw a tall young man slowly walking on the other side of the street. The man was "very thin, had enormous horn shell glasses," and had a "very pale, thin face. His hair was straight," and he possessed "a very aesthetic, intellectual appearance."

When the two men came close enough to give the proper recognition statements, Gold was surprised by the man's "very pronounced and very clipped British accent." But there were also "peculiar undertones" to his speech that Gold "could not account for."[37]

Gold introduced himself as "Raymond" and "expressed his pleasure at being chosen for such an important assignment."[38] Given Gold's propensity for obsequious behavior, this was not such an unusual admission. The gentleman said his name was Klaus Fuchs. The two men began walking along the waterfront. They did little talking. Fuchs said he had been in the country only a week or two. After approximately ten minutes, they took a cab up to Lexington Avenue in the forties and walked east, toward the river, then north up Third Avenue. When they reached Forty-ninth Street, Gold suggested they have dinner at Manny Wolf's steakhouse. After years of walking the streets of Manhattan with Soviet operatives, he knew the city well.

There was little conversation over dinner, but one exchange stood out in Gold's mind. Fuchs "rebuked" Gold for taking him to such a public establishment, saying that "it was not too good an idea to meet in restaurants." Gold immediately "realized that he was right," and that he wasn't dealing with a novice. If Fuchs could "pick out flaws in my own technique," it was safe to assume "that this man had been involved in espionage."[39]

After dinner the men went for another walk, "quite a long one." For more than an hour they discussed ground rules for future meetings, which "should be of the shortest possible duration" and "strictly business" —no personal or social matters should intrude into their conversations. They agreed to be extremely careful, especially Fuchs, who felt each time he left work that he might be followed. Two other things were agreed upon: they would never meet in a restaurant again and "never . . . meet in the same place twice."[40]

Fuchs suggested Fridays as the best day to meet. Fridays were generally reserved for staff meetings, and afterward he was "left pretty much alone." Other days were more problematic because co-workers, in an effort "to be friendly," often invited him to join them for dinner. He felt it was important not to create suspicions by rejecting these overtures. He cautioned Gold, however, that the time of these Friday meetings could not be nailed down too tightly. He must not "appear to be in a hurry to leave these staff meetings." Even so, "under no circumstances were we to wait any longer than four or five minutes at any of the meeting places."[41] Gold, who already had to budget large blocks of time for his risky New York excursions, no doubt appreciated this last condition. Brothman had routinely kept him waiting on street corners for hours; Fuchs was much more businesslike.

During this initial meeting and walk through Midtown Manhattan, Gold learned that Fuchs "was a member of the British Mission," a team of a dozen or more top scientists, "which was working with the U.S. Army on a project" of some importance. Fuchs provided no further information at that time, but Gold was anxious to learn more. His report to his KGB handlers read as follows:

We were both at the appointed place on time at 4:00 P.M.; he had the green book and tennis ball and I had the four gloves. I greeted him and he accepted my offer of a walk. We strolled a while and talked. He is about 5 ft. 10 in. thin, pale complexioned and at first was very reserved in manner; this last is good.

K. dresses well (tweeds) but not fancily. After a ride on the subway, we took a taxi and went to eat. As I kept talking about myself, he warmed up and began to show evidence of getting down to business. For instance, I would say that I had felt honored at having been told to meet him, and he said that he "could hardly believe it" when he had been told that we would like him to work with us (that was in England, of course). The following developed about K.: He obviously has worked with our people before and he is fully aware of what he is doing. Also, he is apparently one of us in spirit. K. has only been here since September, but he expects to be here for at least the duration; he may be transferred out of New York, but he is not very likely—in any case he will be able to let us know in plenty of time. He is a mathematical physicist and a graduate of the University of Bristol and Edinburgh; he is most likely a very brilliant man to have such a position at his age (he looks about 30). We took a long walk after dinner, and he explained the "factory setup."

The rest of Gold's report concerned technical aspects of the Manhattan Project.[42]

They met again less than a month later on the northwest corner of Fifty-ninth Street and Lexington Avenue, by a "bank and subway entrance" and in the "vicinity of Bloomingdale's Department Store." They intended "to walk across the Queensboro Bridge, but it was closed to foot traffic," so they walked along First Avenue instead, under the bridge, and then along the East River. It was a wintry night, and few others were out; Gold thought the area "exceedingly lonely at that time of the evening." It was a good time to conduct business.

The two men discussed establishing "an alibi if either were ever questioned about the manner in which they met." They decided that Gold would select a New York Philharmonic concert at Carnegie Hall and relay the program information to Fuchs; "and if either were ever questioned, both would state they attended that concert and happened to have adjacent seats where they struck up an acquaintance," based on a "common interest in chess and classical music."[43] Gold found it a "weak enough story," but "better than no story at all."

Briefer than their initial get-together, the meeting consisted of Fuchs giving a thumbnail sketch of his reason for being in America. It was the first time Gold had heard the name "The Manhattan Engineer Project." Fuchs named the members of the British Mission who had joined him and identified some of the other personnel he had met in New York. Sir James Chadwick, "the world famous physicist, was mentioned as the head of the Mission." Another prominent "physicist by the name of Peierls" was either Fuchs's "co-worker or direct superior."

Fuchs said it would be difficult to provide the names of everyone involved and what they were specifically working on, since everyone worked in "tight compartments, and . . . one group did not know what the other group was doing." Much of his own work dealt with "the separation of the fissionable isotope of uranium 235" through either gaseous diffusion or electromagnetic separation.[44] It was a small part of a very difficult and complicated project that he felt "was bound to be of very long duration" —so long, in fact, that "he doubted very much whether it would ever be utilized in the present conflict." Fuchs didn't believe their effort would ever have "any wartime utility." It was too complicated and "far too long range a job."[45]

The mention of an isotope diffusion process caught Gold's attention. As far back as 1937, Gold had become "interested in thermal diffusion . . . while working with Dr. Reich on the separation of carbon dioxide from flue gases (so as to make dry ice), and did a considerable amount on this and other applications."[46] He would remain captivated by the industrial potential of thermal diffusion and from "that time on bombarded Reich with . . . notes," questions, and discussions of its possibilities.[47]

Fuchs came away from that second meeting believing his American contact "had some scientific knowledge," and though Gold was probably not a physicist, Fuchs thought it quite possible "he might be a chemist."[48]

Gold reported back to his controller, the usual procedure when he had established contact "with a primary source of information." There would actually be two meetings; a brief one just to turn over a written report and a lengthier second meeting where he would give a detailed account of his impressions.[49] Gold's propensity for exactness ensured that these written reports were thorough and well received.[50]

These repeated excursions to New York consumed a great deal of Gold's time and energy, especially since he was working full time at Pennsylvania Sugar, occasionally taking chemistry-related courses at St. Joseph's College in Philadelphia, and often tutoring friends and co-workers.[51] After a long day at the sugar refinery, Gold found himself putting in even longer hours at his secret side job. By working long overtime shifts at Pennsylvania Sugar, he got management to grant him some workplace flexibility. If he had to take an espionage trip in the middle of the week, he would claim "exhaustion" and request a day or two off to recover.

These claims of exhaustion weren't a fantasy. During these years Gold was "perpetually tired." His mental health wasn't much better; he spent a lot of time "brooding" about his life as a secret agent. He was "thinking too greatly" about what he was involved in, as well as "the possible consequences" should his actions be uncovered. But questions were rarely asked. Management knew Harry wasn't lazy. He was widely known in the company as a workhorse—so much of one, in fact, many thought that outside their laboratory, the little chemist had no life at all.

During their second meeting, Fuchs said he would deliver a package containing "a complete written account of just who was working on the project . . . a general physical makeup of it," and "how far it had progressed." He promised to "put on paper" as much as he could "possibly obtain and find out."[52]

Fuchs's professionalism, commitment, and follow-through impressed Gold. He already had a reverence for scientists, but here was a man with a first-rate mind who was also politically aware and willing to jeopardize his career and freedom for what he believed. Despite the great difference in stature, Gold couldn't help comparing himself to the scholarly British physicist.

"Life was becoming dangerous"

"If ever a man was his father's son, it was Klaus Fuchs," wrote his biographer, Norman Moss.[53] The father, Emil, was a Lutheran pastor who believed that his church was directly descended from "the man who most effectively raised the banner of individual conscience against the claims to spiritual authority of the Roman Catholic Church." Emil and his children were accustomed to standing by their principles, challenging injustice, and steering clear of social fads and political passions. A Socialist and ardent opponent of Nazism, he followed the dictates of his conscience despite criticism and threats. He often wrote of his "spiritual struggle" with politics, economics, and his own religious beliefs. Eventually he would become a Quaker, devoted to helping the poor and the oppressed.

It was while he was a clergyman in the village of Russelsheim, near Frankfurt, that his second son and third child, Emil Julius Klaus Fuchs, was born on December 29, 1911. Klaus distinguished himself as a student and went on to study mathematics and physics at the University of Leipzig and later the University of Kiel. Studious and self-contained, Klaus claimed to have had a happy childhood, but he was not immune to travail and despair. His mother suffered from periodic bouts of depression and eventually committed suicide in a "particularly painful way."[54] Mental problems would continue to stalk the family; Klaus would also lose his older sister to suicide, and witness his younger sister institutionalized in a mental hospital.

Klaus became politically active in college. Like his father, he joined the Social Democratic Party and found himself devoting an ever-increasing portion of his time and energy to politics. He found Communists two-faced and too strictly wedded to a rigid party line, while he viewed the Nazi SA (Sturmabteilung), or Brownshirts, as a dangerous paramilitary order of embittered ruffians passing themselves off as a legitimate political party. Klaus passed out leaflets on the street and often ended up doing battle with Brownshirts. Politics in Germany at this time was more like a blood sport than a hobby.

The growing Nazi threat caused much debate in the Fuchs household and eventually pushed Klaus and his siblings—Gerhard, Elisabeth, and Kristel—into the Communist Party. Emil remained with the Social Democrats, but was sympathetic to his children's change of heart. He, too, was disappointed by the Social Democrats' timid response to the Nazi threat. Gradually, Klaus adapted to the strict party discipline, coming to believe that the nature of the enemy demanded it. During the early years of the worldwide Depression, the Soviet Union was the one country that seemed to have a plan to overcome it. Russia's grand experiment attracted the attention of progressive Germans as well as Americans, and the looming presence of Adolf Hitler and the "wild men of the Right" made it that much more important that there be a countervailing political force in Germany. For Germans like Fuchs, "Fascism was the real enemy, and communism a moral parable of hope in an age of anxiety."[55]

With Hitler's ascension to chancellor in January 1933, the Communist Party was banned from meeting, and demonstrations and violence on college campuses became more frequent. Opponents of the Brownshirts were frequently killed. Klaus was beaten by right-wing thugs and tossed into the river. Even within the Fuchs household, a political chill took hold. It was decided that they would "not talk politics among themselves. Life was becoming dangerous, and they did not want to know too much about one another's activities or contacts, because they could not know how they would respond to interrogation."[56] For Klaus, this self-imposed suppression became ingrained. Though political issues and government policy were of critical importance to him, future friends and colleagues never heard him talk about politics.

In the aftermath of the Reichstag fire, Fuchs, a known Communist activist, was encouraged by friends to go abroad for his own safety. The Nazi bullies who had once beaten him on the streets of Kiel now controlled the government. The arrest, torture, and murder of political dissidents were becoming commonplace. Distressed that there was so little opposition to Hitler transforming Germany into a dictatorship, Klaus became even more wedded to the Communist Party and its organizational principles. Strict party discipline no longer bothered him.

Klaus's father was arrested and dismissed from his post for voicing his outrage at the Lutheran Church's acceptance of the Nazi regime. Distancing himself from the church and its teachings, Emil looked for a more "direct link between Man and God" and believed he had found it in the Society of Friends.

"Enemy alien"

Klaus traveled to Berlin. As a Communist activist, he was a wanted man. He remained in hiding for six months and then attended an anti-

Fascist conference in Paris. He realized that he could not go back to Germany: only twenty-one and a political outcast, he was alone and penniless. In September 1933 he found a home with a progressive family in Bristol, England—joining what would become a flood of refugees fleeing Nazism. Ronald and Jessie Gunn, the English couple who took him in, were wealthy and well connected. Years later, Klaus would identify the Gunns as kindly Quakers who came to his rescue. Some scholars, however, note that there is "no record of their having belonged to any Quaker organization" and believe the Gunns were actually Communist sympathizers.[57]

The experience of being an exile, cut off from friends and family, adapting to a new language and culture, and trying to support himself during a turbulent time caused Fuchs to turn inward and become more reserved in manner and speech. Some thought him cold and distant. The formerly ardent political activist now kept his thoughts to himself. Many future colleagues and associates would claim to have never heard him utter a political comment.

The Gunns helped Fuchs find a position at the University of Bristol while he worked toward his Ph.D. He studied theoretical physics, concentrating on a new, mathematically intense area called quantum mechanics. In the privacy of his room, he read Karl Marx and immersed himself in the Marxist view of the historical process. Though no longer an activist, he had not given up his philosophical attachment to left-wing thought. His academic colleagues, unfamiliar with his background and interests, viewed the thin, anemic-looking young scholar as "industrious, very talented, and very serious." Years later, many would recount that he "talked very little and hardly ever smiled."

Fuchs lived with the Gunns for several years, improved his English, and earned his Ph.D. He began publishing in prestigious scientific journals and soon was recommended for a research position with Max Born, a renowned German physicist then at the University of Edinburgh.[58] Born found Fuchs a "gifted . . . mathematical physicist," and a "very nice, quiet fellow with sad eyes." Though less a loner than he had been at Bristol, he still seemed to have few friends and no romantic relationships. As one biographer has said of him, "He had established a moat between his own emotional life and those of others, and he was building his life on one side of it."[59]

In July 1939 Fuchs applied for naturalization papers as a British citizen, but the war intruded, and he found himself classified, like many other recent German refugees, as an "enemy alien." The British Home

Office was aware that "his passport had been revoked by the Nazis because of his Marxist leanings," but since there was no evidence that he had engaged in dangerous political activity in England, he was allowed to remain at Edinburgh.[60] That August, the Nazi-Soviet Nonaggression Pact was signed. Like thousands of Communists and Soviet supporters around the world, Fuchs was stunned and disappointed. He had always presumed the Soviet Union would be the one dependable bulwark of opposition to Hitler. With Communists deeply divided over this unexpected development, he struggled to understand the often-recited explanation that Russia, unprepared for war, was only seeking additional time. In June 1941, when Hitler's forces advanced across the Russian border, Fuchs's dilemma, like that of most other sympathizers, was resolved. Practically overnight, Britain and the Soviet Union were allies in a war against Germany. His geographical and philosophical homes were now in a death match with the nation in which he was born and raised, and from which he was now exiled.

Britain rounded up thousands of Germans living there—Communists and Nazis alike—and imprisoned them in internment camps. Some were shipped off to Australia, others to Canada. Fuchs was placed on a crowded, roach-infested ship and sent to an internment camp near Quebec City. Later, he was transferred to a camp near Sherbrooke, where prisoners were "kept in locomotive sheds" containing "five faucets and six latrines [to] serve 720 men."[61]

After Fuchs was imprisoned, several people spoke out on his behalf. Born described him as one of the "two or three most gifted theoretical physicists of the young generation," a man who could be doing "work of national importance."[62] Others declared him an ardent foe of the Nazis and a former member of Germany's Social Democratic Party. In December 1940, Fuchs was one of thousands released after the government recognized that its initial decisions on internment may have been both hasty and harsh. Though Churchill had once believed that German refugees and resident aliens represented a "malignancy in our midst," he conceded that "many enemy aliens had a great hatred of the Nazi regime" and it was unjust "to treat our friends as foes."

After his release, Fuchs was contacted by Rudolf Peierls to work in his laboratory in Birmingham. Peierls, like the physicists Leo Szilard and Hans Bethe, had fled to England with the rise of Hitler. He had heard good things about Fuchs and thought he might be someone who "could discuss theoretical technicalities." Fuchs was told only that he would be involved with "war work." In fact, he was put on a top-secret project, code-named Tube Alloys, to design and build the world's first atomic bomb.

Peierls knew that Fuchs had been politically active during his student days in Germany and that his progressive politics had caused him to flee the Nazis, but like most people he was unaware of the depth of Fuchs's commitment to Communism. British security officials urged Peierls to tell Fuchs as little as possible, and initially he was assigned to "work on some unclassified mathematical problems." Gradually his classification evolved until he was permitted to work on gaseous diffusion and more sensitive projects. As it turned out, gaseous diffusion would be a key step in the separation of uranium-235—a fissionable material—from uranium-238.

Throughout the 1930s a host of brilliant physicists had taken incremental steps in the exploration of the atom. Niels Bohr, James Chadwick, Harold Urey, Enrico Fermi, Otto Hahn, and Fritz Strassmann, among others, were captivated by the prospect of atomic energy. Others, like Leo Szilard, were dubious about the door that was about to be opened; Szilard predicted that "the world was headed for grief." In early 1940, Peierls and Otto Frisch sent Prime Minister Churchill's science adviser a memorandum entitled "On the Construction of a Super Bomb Based on Nuclear Chain Reaction in Uranium."[63] By late spring a secret committee had been established to explore the possibilities. Money was appropriated, high-level discussions with America commenced, and staff was hired. One extremely quiet but cerebral young physicist brought to the project was Klaus Fuchs.

In no time at all, it seemed, Fuchs moved from a squalid detention facility in Canada to board in the Peierls household in Birmingham. His Communist past was known to authorities, but since there "had been no apparent Communist associations" in England, he was cleared for naturalization. On June 18, 1942, Fuchs became a British citizen, declaring his "true allegiance to the British crown according to law."[64]

Fuchs proved to be of great value to Peierls's theoretical research. It was said that "he could understand and recall in detail the most complex and difficult documents in his field." He proved an "ideal analyst" in assessing the progress of German nuclear scientists pursuing isotope separation and the production of fissionable U-235, and his contributions were valued by British scientists and politicians frightened that Nazi Germany would build an atom bomb before the Allies could.

"Raymond"

Though his Communist convictions remained largely dormant and unknown to his academic colleagues, Fuchs was still very much a political
animal. In addition to keeping in touch with his father and siblings, he
made contact with members of the German Communist Party. Jürgen
Kuczynski was a German Communist of Polish parentage who had come
to England a few years before Fuchs and had begun organizing German
Communist refugees. Fuchs steered clear of organizing activities but
made it known that he was prepared "to furnish confidential and classified information . . . relating to atomic energy research."

Fuchs probably didn't know that Kuczynski had become an agent for
the GRU (Soviet military intelligence) in the 1920s to help spread world
revolution and foster the Soviet Union's great experiment.[65] Not long
after Germany invaded the Soviet Union, Fuchs asked what he could do
to help the embattled country. Kuczynski suggested he contact the Soviet
embassy in London. Fuchs informed the embassy he had vital information regarding an important Anglo-American war project that could lead
to a new and powerful explosive device, which he was willing to share
with the Soviet Union. He was immediately assigned a Russian control
agent.

Sometime in 1942 a new agent was assigned: Ruth Kuczynski, Jürgen's sister, who had been a Soviet operative even longer than her brother.
She and Fuchs would often meet in the town of Banbury, near Oxford,
reasonably close to his Birmingham base of operations. At two- or three-
month intervals, Fuchs would give her "classified and confidential . . .
written data concerning atomic energy research," which she would then
transmit to Moscow. After six meetings, however, he informed her in December 1943 that he was being sent to America as part of the British mission working on the construction of the atomic bomb. Before he left, he
was told he would be meeting a man in New York named "Raymond."

"Returning to Russia"

Harry Gold knew none of this. All he knew was that Klaus Fuchs had the
look and manner of a serious intellect. He was an accomplished man of
science who, like himself, had come to the aid of a people under siege.
Sam had told him only the barest facts about the British gentleman, and
Fuchs had said little more. "John," Sam Semenov's replacement as
Harry's control agent, was even more tight-lipped.

Only weeks before the first meeting with Fuchs, Sam had informed Gold he "had been in this country far too long and was now returning to Russia." In fact, Semenov was forced to leave. He had come under intense scrutiny and "was being followed closely by the FBI," whose constant surveillance was causing him "to miss a number of meetings with his many agents."[66] Gold was taken aback; he had grown quite fond of Sam, but he also understood the workings of Soviet espionage. Periodic shifts in personnel were customary. Gold was instructed to meet his new contact "in a rather public place . . . near Pennsylvania Railroad Station." He wasn't told whom to look out for, but after a few minutes on a street corner a dark-haired man approached, saying only that Sam had sent him. The man was approximately five feet ten and of average build, and identified himself as John. He had a pronounced Russian accent and swept-back black hair that kept falling across his brow; Gold thought he might be Georgian.[67] John suggested they have a drink together and led Gold to Child's Restaurant. When Gold "ordered Canadian Club and soda," John expressed surprise: "I had been told that you ordered Canadian Club and ginger ale invariably as a chaser." Gold was impressed by the Soviets' thoroughness. The new man, like his predecessors, had obviously done his homework.

John went over procedural matters with which Gold was well familiar. A couple of items were new. One dealt with timing: he wanted Gold to arrive for meetings at least an hour early, scrutinize the designated area for government surveillance, and never wait more than five minutes for his contact to arrive. The latter instruction was welcome; on one occasion Gold had waited for Sam on a street corner "for two hours . . . for the simple reason" that he was broke and had no return fare to Philadelphia. When Sam finally arrived, he apologized profusely for the delay; "unable to make the original meeting," he had gone to the designated location anyway on "the chance that [Gold] might still be there."

John also raised the issue of emergency meetings. Distrusting phone lines, the Soviets invented some innovative ways to reach out to field agents. John informed Gold that if he should ever "receive two tickets to a sporting or theatrical event in New York City through the mail and in an envelope with no other enclosures," he was to do this: at a definite date (usually three days after the date on the tickets) and a definite time (usually between eight and nine at night), Gold was to be "inside of a seafood restaurant/bar at the Astoria stop of the Broadway elevated line." He was to "observe extreme precaution before this meeting and was to scout the place . . . one hour in advance for signs of surveillance." At the appointed time—an odd minute like 8:23 or 8:43—Gold was to take a seat at a table. After a minute or two, he would be joined by his Soviet controller, who had been standing at the bar also looking for signs of surveillance.[68]

John and Gold had not been at Child's long when Sam joined them to say good-bye. No novice now, Gold well understood the nature of the business, but he was still sorry to see his friend depart. More than any of the other Russians, Sam was a friend, a mentor, and a true comrade-in-arms. He had shown Gold kindness where others had been curt and dismissive. Gold knew he wasn't Sam's only American agent, but he liked to think that they had formed a special bond. Despite the pressures of the job, the endless "waiting on street corners in New York and various other cities, waits which were often futile and sometimes dangerous, eating in cheap, out-of-the-way restaurants, and cajoling, pleading with, and threatening various people," he knew that Sam had a basically "happy and ebullient nature." During the years of their relationship the two men had "accumulated a store of memories and private jokes concerning past trials and difficulties with a variety of people—just as two good and very close friends often do."[69]

As they shook hands and wished each other well, Gold couldn't help thinking of Sam's promise that one day they'd all meet again in Moscow and celebrate their successes, laugh at their failures, and reminisce about their hectic, dangerous days as intelligence agents.[70]

"K. Fuchs, 128 West 77th Street"

Gold realized that his third meeting with Fuchs in Manhattan would be both important and brief. Fuchs had said that he would have something for him.

At that meeting, in March 1944, Gold received his first package of information from Fuchs. It was a cold, dark night, and the two men were to rendezvous at about nine o'clock somewhere along Park Avenue in the Eighties. Gold spotted Fuchs first, walking slowly ahead of him. When he caught up, the men veered onto an "extremely deserted" residential side street and continued walking toward Fifth Avenue. In a matter of seconds and with almost no conversation between them, Fuchs transferred to Gold vital information about the design, progress, and participants involved in the construction of the world's first atomic bomb. Gold immediately placed "the very bulky packet" of material in the inner pocket of his overcoat, and the two men parted.

Gold had not gone very far when he committed a significant lapse of judgment. His curiosity got the better of him, and he pulled out the package and cursorily thumbed through the very large bundle of legal-sized paper as he marched down Fifth Avenue. Inside were "possibly twenty or twenty-five closely written pages."[71] Realizing that this must be "tremendously important information"—and thinking of the penalty if he should be caught with it—he immediately placed the envelope back in his pocket and continued toward Midtown. After fifteen or twenty minutes, he met John, and the men moved off to a relatively quiet side street. In "ten or fifteen seconds," Gold "turned the information over to him." Just that quickly they separated. As had become routine by now, Gold arrived back in Philadelphia well after midnight. He got a few hours' rest and was back in the laboratory of the sugar refinery in the morning, beginning another twelve-hour day.

Four or five weeks later Gold and Fuchs met again, this time in the Bronx. They met at a movie theater near Grand Concourse and Fordham Road and began walking. Suspending the rules of engagement they had originally agreed upon, they went to Rosenheim's Restaurant, near 180th Street, where Gold had once eaten with Fred.[72] Over a light snack they "discussed topics ranging from contemporary world politics to music and chess." Though Fuchs had no illusion that "Raymond" was his contact's real name, there is no record of whether he believed Gold's claim that he was married and had two children. It may have been at this meeting that Fuchs said there was "a big uranium diffusion plant" being built "somewhere in the South, possibly Georgia or Alabama." This would turn out to be the Oak Ridge plant in Tennessee.[73]

It was at Rosenheim's that Gold saw the British scientist depart, albeit briefly, from his normal detachment. Gold had come to know Fuchs as "a very shy, reserved" individual who never disclosed emotion. That reserve, however, could quickly turn into strident partisanship "at the mention of Nazism or Fascism, particularly the German brand." Their shared hatred may have assuaged any lingering doubt either man had about the "underhanded" work they were involved in.

With each meeting, Harry became more familiar with the man who was supplying him with such valuable information. He was someone "who had played tag with the Gestapo with his life as the game—as the forfeit —and who did not need very much in the way of teaching regarding precaution." He was somebody to respect and admire.

Gold had a lifelong fascination with "any person of exceptional ability . . . Joe DiMaggio, Lefty Grove, and Babe Ruth in baseball . . . Robert

Browning or T. S. Eliot in literature . . . or Louis Pasteur" in medicine. He would one day write of his propensity for hero worship that "it goes for any field where a man is outstandingly excellent, but is at the same time relatively modest, I am absolutely fascinated by a person with ability. I regard it as . . . a sort of divine manifestation." Fuchs, accomplished in nuclear physics, willing to risk his life to fight Fascism, and modest regarding both, most definitely qualified for Gold's pantheon.[74]

Their next meeting occurred less than a month later, in July. They met for only three or four minutes in the Long Island City, or Sunnyside, section of Queens. Once again, Fuchs turned over a package of information. As he traveled to meet John, Gold's curiosity again got the better of him, and he took a quick peek at the material. The package contained about forty pages of handwritten material with an array of mathematical equations. Unsure of their meaning but quite sure of their importance, Gold resealed the envelope and within a half-hour had delivered them to John.

Fuchs had handed over formal reports he had written himself. While stationed in New York as part of the British delegation to the Manhattan Project, he wrote thirteen papers on uranium diffusion. Fuchs would "write out a draft in longhand, including mathematical calculations," show it to Peierls for approval, have a secretary type it, and then submit it to project superiors.[75] He kept his original, handwritten version to pass on to the Soviets.

The articles were highly technical and had titles such as *Fluctuations and the Efficiency of a Diffusion Plant* and *On the Effect of a Time Lag in the Control of Plant Stability*.[76] Relevant to the design and construction of an American uranium diffusion plant, they were of great interest to the Russians.

At their sixth meeting, near Borough Hall in Brooklyn, Fuchs began to open up about himself and his family. He talked of his sister who lived in Cambridge, Massachusetts, but might be coming to New York. She had two young children, but her marriage was rocky, and she was considering leaving her husband and bringing the children to New York. Given the sensitivity of his position, he wondered if the Soviets would frown on his taking them in.

Fuchs and Gold next met along Fifth Avenue near the Metropolitan Museum of Art. During an hour-long stroll through Central Park on a warm July day, Fuchs discussed his sister's continuing marital dilemma and also mentioned an older brother who was convalescing in Switzerland after being held in a Nazi concentration camp. More important, he said it appeared more than likely that he would be transferred. The Manhattan Project was being relocated "somewhere to the Southwest," possibly New Mexico.

Later that month or in early August, they were to meet again near the Brooklyn Museum of Art. Gold stood at the Belle Cinema and the Brooklyn Library for some time, but Fuchs failed to show up. Gold "didn't think too much of the event, though it was the first time that he had missed an appointment." He assumed that the British physicist "had gotten involved at work and was unable to leave without causing undue comment." The lengthy wait, however, caused Gold to arrive late for his follow-up meeting with John, who had already left by the time he arrived. The journey to New York had been a total waste of time. Gold followed through, keeping the time and place for the alternate meeting, but once again Fuchs did not show up. Gold now became concerned: this was no Abe Brothman; he could be counted on to observe tradecraft protocol. When Gold and John finally met, "they had a long discussion as to what should be done." Fuchs's absence was a troubling development. John finally warned Gold he should "be extremely cautious now" and said he'd have directives for him at their next meeting.

When next they met, on a Sunday morning "in late August or early September 1944 . . . in the vicinity of Washington Square," John said they had discovered Fuchs's address, on West Seventy-seventh Street near Broadway.[77] Gold was instructed to go there that very morning and "ask him what was wrong." Gold set out, but first he purchased a book, a new work by the famous German author Thomas Mann. *Joseph and his Brothers* was the fourth and final installment of Mann's sixteen-year effort to write a richly imagined account of Joseph according to his reading of Genesis. On the inside cover Gold wrote "K. Fuchs, 128 West 77th Street."[78] If he was questioned, he would say either that he had "found the book and was just returning it" to its rightful owner or that he was a "friend who was returning this book which he had borrowed."[79]

When Gold arrived at the address, he was met by the building janitor but did not talk to him. Looking at the bell box, he was pleasantly surprised to see the words "Dr. Klaus Fuchs." Just then "a woman he presumed to be the janitor's wife opened the door allowing him to enter." The janitor entered immediately behind him, and Gold asked whether Fuchs was there. He was told that Dr. Fuchs had recently moved out. They had no knowledge of his current whereabouts. Communication was difficult because of the janitor's poor command of English (Gold thought he might be a Swedish immigrant). In addition, Gold was becoming fearful that the apartment house was being watched.

Gold informed John of this disturbing news at their next meeting, just north of Columbia University. They considered writing a letter but decided it was "too risky." Neither knew the name or address of Fuchs's sister in Cambridge. Finally John ordered Gold to sit tight and wait for instructions. At the following meeting he informed Gold with "great glee" that they had tracked down Fuchs's sister, whose name was Kristel Heinemann. The two men "had a long discussion about the advisability of contacting" her.[80] While they usually erred on the side of caution, Fuchs was too important a source to lose. Gold was told to make the trip up to Cambridge.

CHAPTER 7

The Los Alamos Papers

O
ne Sunday in late September 1944, Gold traveled by coach
to Boston. He arrived at the Heinemann home on Lakeview
Drive in the early evening, but it looked as though no one was
home. Gold knocked on the door, and a woman who appeared
to be the housekeeper answered. She said the Heinemanns were on vacation and were "not expected back until some time in October." Gold
was disappointed, but he had at least established Kristel Heinemann's
address.

Gold reported back to John, and they agreed that another trip to
Cambridge was in order. He was told to visit early on a weekday morning to ensure that "Mr. Heinemann would not be present." John had
come to believe "Robert Heinemann would not be sympathetic to any
strangers coming around to his house and inquiring for Dr. Fuchs."

In late October, Gold returned to Cambridge and met Mrs. Heinemann. Apparently "in her thirties," she struck Gold as "an exceedingly
beautiful woman," not surprised to see him, and indeed "rather cordial."
There were three young children in the house: an infant, a young girl,
and a boy of about seven, named Steven.[1]

Gold identified himself as Raymond, gave her and the children a box
of chocolates, and said he was a friend of Klaus's from New York. He "was

traveling in the area" and wondered if she knew of his whereabouts. Mrs. Heinemann replied that she "did not know exactly where Klaus was." He had been suddenly transferred, and his letters were postmarked "somewhere in the Southwest." Gold did not press her any further; "she did not seem prone to discuss any of his work."

Gold spent twenty to thirty minutes in the Heinemann home, making small talk and inquiring about Dr. Fuchs. He mentioned that he had a wife and two children. Mrs. Heinemann said her brother was "very fond" of her own children and had written "that he wanted to bring the children presents" when he visited "some time during Christmas." Gold hid his delight at hearing that Fuchs would soon be back on the East Coast. He handed Mrs. Heinemann a sealed envelope that John had given him, containing the name and phone number of a person Fuchs should call when he arrived in Cambridge.[2]

Though he had expected to travel up to Cambridge during the coming holiday season, Christmas and New Year's passed without any notification from John that the moment had arrived. One weekday morning in January 1945, Gold received a phone call prior to leaving for work. He was told to come immediately to an "emergency meeting." John had called from a gasoline station at Oxford Circle, a short distance from Gold's new home on Kindred Street in Northeast Philadelphia.[3] As soon as Gold arrived, the two men boarded a streetcar to the Frankford Terminal, where John could take an elevated train back to center city Philadelphia. Before they parted, John told him he had just been notified that "Fuchs was in Cambridge."[4] Gold was instructed to go the Heinemann residence in Cambridge as soon as possible.[5]

On his second visit to Cambridge, Gold succeeded in meeting Fuchs. Shortly after Kristel Heinemann opened the door and announced to her brother that he had a visitor, she departed (to "buy groceries or . . . pick up her children who were at a kindergarten"). Alone, the two men expressed their pleasure in seeing each other again, but Fuchs quickly informed Gold that he wanted his sister's house to be used as a meeting place only in an emergency.[6] He took Gold upstairs to the room he was occupying, to ensure no one would walk in on them, and handed him "a considerable mass of information"—a thick, tightly sealed bundle, which would remain that way. Gold suppressed any temptation to examine the "exceedingly bulky" package he now had charge of.

Fuchs had handed him a cross-section of vital information, including papers on the bomb assembly process, the problems with "predetonation of plutonium through spontaneous fission, the advantages of the implosion method of detonation over the gun method and the critical mass of plutonium," and a report on "current ideas on how to initiate with high-explosive lenses a uniform detonation around a sphere that would compress the plutonium to critical-mass size."[7] In short, the package's contents were nothing short of exceedingly valuable.

There would be one more attempt at a transaction in the Heinemann home. The fact that it was never completed only increased Gold's respect for the British scientist. John had given Gold $1,500 in an envelope to pass on to Dr. Fuchs. According to Gold, there were "a few fives, mostly tens, and quite a few twenties." It was in appreciation of Fuchs's fine work and designed to cover "any expenses he might have" or to help if he was "running short of funds." Gold broached the issue in a "very tentative . . . delicate" manner. Fuchs rejected the offer, but his rebuff was so diplomatic and "positive in nature" that Gold couldn't help but admire the man. When Gold returned the money to John in New York, the Russian did not seem surprised. Obviously there had been past attempts to give Fuchs money.

After gracefully refusing the envelope, Fuchs showed Gold a map of Santa Fe, New Mexico, and "indicated where they could meet" in future. John had led Gold to believe that Fuchs would come east fairly often, but Fuchs quickly put that notion to rest. It was impossible, he said; "it was all that he could do to make this one trip." Leaving his base of operations was out of the question. "They were far too busy to permit anything like that."

Fuchs was now, he said, "working at a place called Los Alamos," about "forty miles from Santa Fe," which at one time "had been a very select boys' military school or boys' preparatory school."[8] Although they were all working very hard to master the intricacies of atomic energy and put it to military use, Fuchs remained pessimistic.[9] "He did not think that it would . . . be ready in time before the completion of the war against either Germany or Japan." Fuchs thought a "trial run" of this new weapon would not be possible before the summer of 1946. Moreover, he predicted, if the war ended "before a trial run could be made," he was "pretty sure that the project would be broken up and would never be carried to completion." The entire effort consumed a staggering array of human and material resources.

Before Gold left the Heinemann residence, and without his Soviet superior's authorization, he agreed to meet Fuchs in Santa Fe in early June. They set an exact place and time: a Saturday between three and four o'clock in the afternoon on the Castillo Street Bridge, over the Rio Santa Fe.[10]

Los Alamos

On November 16, 1942, after several dozen forays across a range of isolated New Mexico landscapes, J. Robert Oppenheimer and General Leslie Groves finally agreed that a quiet mesa along the Rio Grande Valley, between the snowcapped Jemez Mountains to the west and the picturesque Sangre de Cristo Mountains to the east, would be the site of one of the most controversial construction projects in history.[11] Within days the remote and beautiful countryside that was home to the Los Alamos Ranch School would begin its transformation into a bustling scientific laboratory hosting some of the greatest minds in the world.

As if the intellectual challenge of creating the first atomic bomb were not overwhelming enough, the logistics were almost as daunting. The laboratory would have to be built from scratch in a near wilderness lacking housing and electricity, not to mention phones, libraries, medical facilities, and public sanitation. Everything would have to be imported from back east—not only the creative minds but also the laboratory equipment, generators, and cyclotrons that were integral to the project's success.

Academic luminaries recruited to work at the site were both amazed and appalled by their first visits. Hans Bethe, for example, found the locale "absolutely beautiful" but was "shocked" by the accommodations. The "shoddy buildings," the constant threat of fire, and the sheer isolation of the place were disheartening.[12]

Coordinating this massive project was a frail, ascetic-looking theoretical physicist from Berkeley. Initially thought by colleagues to be ill suited to the management of such a complex undertaking, Oppenheimer was known as a "man of pure science" focused on "exploring the deep secrets of nature." No one who knew him would have listed administrative abilities among his strengths. He had never managed anything more complicated than a graduate seminar class. But after a few rough patches, Oppenheimer evolved into an accomplished administrator and much-loved leader.

Pressured by Manhattan Project colleagues to devote as much thought to human resources as he was to the awesome infrastructure challenge he faced, Oppenheimer came up with a simple but effective organizational chart. He envisioned "four broad divisions within the laboratory: experimental physics, theoretical physics, chemistry and metallurgy, and finally, ordnance."[13] The scientists within each division would report to the division chiefs, and the division chiefs would report to Oppenheimer. Dr. Klaus Fuchs was part of the theoretical division.

"Committing acts of betrayal"

Not long after Hans Bethe was designated head of the Theoretical Division at Los Alamos, he requested that the temperamental and difficult Edward Teller, the leader of the T-1 group (Hydrodynamics of Implosion and Super), be replaced with Rudolf Peierls. Initially reluctant to come aboard, Peierls accepted on the condition that he could bring along two young British scientists, Tony Skyrme and Klaus Fuchs. Fuchs left New York on August 11, 1944, and arrived in the remote and seemingly secure scientific base of Los Alamos on August 14. In one of the Soviet Union's greatest strokes of good fortune, it became his home for the next two years.

British Mission scientists, feeling locked out of certain discussions, suspected that their American colleagues held back information, but Robert Chadwell Williams believes that they "were allowed access to many different divisions of the Manhattan project, [and] often had a better overview of the research than did Americans, who for security reasons were more compartmentalized."[14] Though small in number, the British made significant contributions. Otto Frisch was part of a unit that discovered how to achieve a critical mass of uranium-235; James Tuck helped develop the implosion lenses for the plutonium bomb; and Geoffrey Taylor worked with Fuchs on the hydrodynamics of implosion. Fuchs was in charge of developing "mathematical calculations for the yield and efficiency of an atomic bomb, for which there were two possibilities: the gun-type uranium bomb ultimately used on Hiroshima and the implosion-type plutonium bomb tested at Alamorgordo and dropped on Nagasaki."[15]

As a member of the British team, Fuchs rigorously maintained his quiet, detached manner. Bethe, who had known him since the mid-1930s, thought of him as a "brilliant, unassuming" loner. "If he was a spy," Bethe reflected years later, "he played his role beautifully." Said to have "worked days and nights" as if he "had nothing better to do," the soft-spoken bachelor, according to Bethe, "contributed very greatly to the success of the Los Alamos project." But for all his brilliance, Fuchs was still among the second-tier minds. Besides Bethe and Oppenheimer, the august brainpower at Los Alamos included names like Bohr, Von Neumann, Teller, Frisch, Chadwick, Szilard, and Kistiakowsky. In all, twelve Nobel laureates and several future laureates were working at Los Alamos.

Fuchs worked on his assigned tasks around the clock. From early in the morning until very late at night one could find him in his office surrounded by books and paper, deep in thought. As one of his biographers suggests, he was "operating on two planes which were quite separate from one another, the political and the personal."[16] Even as he was trying to be more open, friendly, and collegial with his scientific compatriots and their wives, who often invited him to dinner and social outings, "on the political level he was committing acts of betrayal." Though he was less cold and detached than when he first left Germany, the political foundation that had been laid years earlier had only been reinforced with the passage of time. His homeland ruled by a band of killers propagating a deadly philosophy, a brother and father imprisoned, his brother's wife and son dying in a concentration camp, one sister a suicide—all this deepened his philosophical commitment to what he saw as the logical antidote to Fascism. No one could doubt Fuchs's hatred for the Nazis, and no one suspected him of divided loyalties. As he would write years later:

I used my Marxist philosophy to establish in my mind two separate compartments. One compartment in which I allowed myself to make friendships, to have personal relationships, to help people and to be in all personal ways the kind of man I wanted to be and the kind of man, which in personal ways, I had been before with my friends in or near the Communist Party. I could be free and easy and happy with other people without fear of disclosing myself because I knew that the other compartment would step in if I approached the danger point. I could forget the other compartment and still rely on it. It appeared to me at the time that I had become a "free man," because I had succeeded in the other compartment to establish myself completely independent of the surrounding forces in society. Looking back at it now the best way of expressing it seems to be to call it a controlled schizophrenia.[17]

This capacity to compartmentalize thoughts and actions was one all secret agents had to acquire. As one Soviet agent pointedly said, "Compartmentalization is a basic rule of all clandestine work."[18] Harry Gold, too, gradually perfected the ability to play diametrically opposite roles with consummate skill and what seemed like flip-of-the-switch adroitness. A devoted and meticulous laboratory investigator who impressed all with his single-minded ability to work incredible hours, he was on other occasions an equally committed and well-schooled political operative working in behalf of a totally different economic philosophy. Both he and Fuchs, to varying degrees, were outsiders, uncomfortable with human interaction and on the fringe of any social gathering, but blessed with the psychological wiring required to ply the trade of a secret agent to perfection. They were solitary figures: quiet, modest bachelors who

didn't need constant praise or the approval of others and could live in opposing universes simultaneously. Though they considered themselves
men of science, it was politics and world events that gradually captured
their imagination and efforts, and ultimately consumed them.

"Extremely vital"

For Harry, a cross-country journey to New Mexico on a mission of such
magnitude was no small matter. Each time he considered such an undertaking he came back to the same three impediments—money, time,
and his mother. He began borrowing money. He borrowed $500 from his
employer, the Pennsylvania Alcohol and Chemical Corporation, a subsidiary of the Pennsylvania Sugar Company. He was also hitting up the
many people to whom he had given money over the years.[19] He even, it
seems, did more than borrow. According to his lawyer, Gold's "expenses
so exceeded the funds given him . . . by the Soviets that he was put to pilfer alcohol on occasions from his employer which he sold to meet his financial demands."[20]

Finding the time for such a long trip was equally difficult. Things were
"exceedingly busy at the distillery at that time," and it was impossible for
Harry to consider taking a two-week vacation. Even five or six days off
would be "very difficult." Still more difficult would be explaining to his
mother where he was going. In all his practice sessions he was never able
to come up with a good excuse. He had no doubt that she would think he
"was probably having a romantic rendezvous with a girl at some summer
resort."[21]

One of Gold's first meetings with his Soviet superior, after he returned
from seeing Fuchs in Cambridge, occurred at Volk's, a Midtown Manhattan restaurant around Third Avenue and Forty-second Street. Ostensibly, the meeting was meant to ensure that Gold would indeed go to
meet Fuchs in New Mexico, but in addition to "the pep talk," other issues
arose that underscored the meeting's significance. Presumably as a security precaution, John insisted Gold follow "an extremely round about way"
to New Mexico. He wanted Gold to travel "all the way to California and
then double back by means of several buses" to Denver and El Paso before finally arriving in Santa Fe.

Gold immediately objected. Such a convoluted itinerary, he said, "was
completely out of the question." He could spare neither the time nor the
money. John supposedly made "some sort of tentative offer" of financial
assistance, but this game had been repeatedly played over a number of

years and with several Soviet handlers. Gold, like Fuchs, wanted his contribution to the Soviet people to be genuine, wholehearted, and uncor-
rupted by the perception of economic gain. He knew that the Soviets
looked down on those who exchanged information for money, and that
they had high regard for those who helped them out of sincere political
or philosophical commitment. Fuchs was a prime example of such devotion and a perfect role model for Gold. But even before Fuchs came on
the scene, Gold had given a good bit of his own money for his Soviet inspired journeys. Even after he started receiving monthly stipends, he
often had to dig into his own pocket to pay his expenses. Once again, with
a lengthy and expensive cross-country trip in the offing, Gold declined
John's offer of assistance and, he later recalled, "assured him that I was
making a very nice salary, and that I didn't need" the help.[22]

With that matter resolved, John insisted they "make arrangements" to
meet "as soon as possible" after Gold got back, "to turn the information
over to him." The Soviet Union wanted it without delay.

At this point Gold assumed his meeting with John was over, but he
was in for a surprise. John informed him that while he was in New Mexico he'd like him "to take a little side trip . . . to see another man." There
was "a man in Albuquerque," John told him, "who also worked at Los
Alamos and who was ready to furnish us with information."

Gold was taken aback by this breach of *konspiratsia*, or recommended tradecraft. As he said years later, "I protested very bitterly about
this additional task. I complained that it was jeopardizing the whole matter of the information I was getting from Fuchs. It represented an additional delay, and additional period or interval in which something could
happen, and I just for once got up on my hind legs and almost flatly refused to go to New Mexico."[23]

John was adamant, saying that the mission "was very important." He
called it "extremely vital" they "get this information." John proceeded to
assure him that the material supplied by Fuchs was still "paramount," but
that Gold "should endeavor to obtain this [additional] information." Gold
was given the man's name and address in Albuquerque and told that if the
man wasn't home, "his wife would have the information." John also gave
Gold $500, explaining, "This man might possibly need some money for
expenses."[24] He handed Gold a small piece of torn cardboard, part of a
Jell-O box, for recognition purposes.

These instructions, as well as the password, "I come from Julius,"
were "an unacceptable infringement of procedure," according to at least

one KGB operative who wrote of the event years later. The decision to have an agent contact two different suppliers on the same trip went "against the most elementary rule of compartmentalization."[25] The extra assignment would prove disastrous for Soviet intelligence gathering in the United States and devastating to a Lower East Side couple, unknown to Gold, but deeply involved in the conspiracy.

An "extremely bulky envelope"

Gold traveled to Chicago by train, and there secured an upper berth to Albuquerque. He could have taken a more direct route to Santa Fe by way of Lami, New Mexico, but that was basically a train station mostly used by Los Alamos workers, and Gold didn't want people to "wonder who the stranger was riding along with them." After ten years of such work, he was savvy about the rules of the game.

As soon as he arrived in Albuquerque, on this first Saturday of June 1945, he caught a bus to Santa Fe. Arriving in the small town with time to spare before his four o'clock meeting with Fuchs, he killed time in a local museum, where he examined historical displays and picked up a map of Santa Fe similar to the one Fuchs had shown him months earlier. The map would create considerable problems when Gold was questioned about it by federal agents five years later.

At the designated hour, Gold was standing on the Castillo Street Bridge over the Rio Santa Fe. As he waited for the British scientist to arrive, he amused himself by thinking about how different locales name geographic features. The so-called river he stood over would be "hardly more than a creek" back home. But here in the Southwest, it was a river, and the dirt road that passed over it was a street.

Gold repeatedly looked at his watch. It was unlike Fuchs to be late, even by a few minutes. Gold was increasingly uncomfortable; Santa Fe was a small town, and Castillo Street and nearby Alameda Street contained very few houses. It "was no place for a stranger to be standing around doing nothing."[26] When Fuchs finally arrived, driving a battered blue Buick that Gold described as a "rattletrap old car," the two men went for a short drive "across the river bridge to a deserted lane where they sat in the car" and then took a short walk.[27] Fuchs had an "extremely bulky envelope" in his possession, but as was their practice, he would not transfer it to Gold until they were about to part. From the start of their relationship, Fuchs had insisted that if ever they were "apprehended to-

gether, the information would still be on his person, and that the actual
apprehension or arrest would have to take place at the very moment when
we were parting and when the transfer of information was taking place."

Almost immediately, Fuchs brought up the subject of their next meeting. He suggested a meeting in a month or two, but Gold said it was impossible: he could not take another vacation that soon. The best he might
do was take some time in September. With that Fuchs handed Gold the
package, and the men went their separate ways. Gold took the first bus
back to Albuquerque.

The documents he now held outlined the plutonium bomb that was
to be tested at Alamogordo and dropped on Nagasaki. "The bomb," wrote
Fuchs's biographer, "would have a solid plutonium core, detonated by a
complex system of polonium initiators, a tamper, an aluminum shell, and
the high-explosive lenses. Fuchs identified the two high explosives, neither of which he understood himself. The forthcoming Trinity test was expected to produce an explosion equivalent to 10,000 tons of TNT; Fuchs
provided information on the test date and site. He told Gold that the
United States intended to use the bomb against Japan," though he remained convinced that the war would end before a viable bomb could
be developed.[28]

Gold would subsequently reflect on how inaccurate the British scientist's prediction had been. For all his brilliance, Fuchs had "terribly
underestimated . . . the tremendous industrial potential of the United
States," as well as "the tremendous individual spirit which led to the completion of [the] project."[29]

The several dozen pages of "very small, crabbed handwriting" that
Gold now had in his possession "contained everything." There was a
"tremendous amount of theoretical mathematics," but there were also
lengthy descriptions of the bomb's "practical set-up." It was, as expected,
extremely valuable material. The next rendezvous, subsequent to the
bomb's first real test, which Fuchs had told him would occur in the New
Mexico desert sometime in July, would be just as important.

Gold left the meeting with a "splitting headache," which he attributed "to the extremely high altitude of Santa Fe." He arrived back in Albuquerque in the early evening and spent the rest of the night "wandering around trying to get a hotel room." Compared with quiet Santa Fe,
Albuquerque was a bustling metropolis. With more than one military base
nearby, the town "was literally jumping. There was absolutely no room to
be had anywhere."

"I bring greetings from Julius"

While Gold wandered around the town searching for a room, he decided to carry out his other assignment. He jumped on a bus that traveled along Central Avenue, Albuquerque's main street, but soon regretted it. The address he sought turned out to be only a half-dozen blocks away, a distance he could have walked.

Gold found the house fairly quickly; it was on North High Street, a quiet, shady street near the University of New Mexico. He knocked repeatedly on the front door until an elderly man came and allowed him to enter the screened-in porch. The man told him the family he was looking for "was not home. They had gone out for the evening." Gold thanked him and said he would stop back in the morning. He was ill at ease and anxious to return home. Ordinarily, after transacting business he "would have taken the train back," but considering John's orders and the importance of the material, he decided to make another attempt the following morning. [30]

After wandering through the streets of Albuquerque until one in the morning, Gold finally found a place to sleep—"a hall of a home which had been converted for the weekend into a temporary rooming house." His "rickety cot" was partially surrounded by "a little screen containing some light gauzy material around it." Not surprisingly, he slept fitfully; besides his uncomfortable accommodations, he was constantly aware of "this huge mass of information from Fuchs" in his possession. He "was very anxious to get it over with and get out of Albuquerque." [31]

Early the next morning he left the rooming house, checked his bag at the railroad station, and went back to 209 North High Street. The same old man answered the front door, but this time he said "they were in." Gold walked up the flight of stairs and knocked on the door. A dark-haired young man answered. He was slightly taller than Gold, about five feet seven, and although he displayed "a pleasing grin," Gold "almost fell down the stairs" in shock. The man wore a pajama top with "Army pants," and behind him on a hook was an army sergeant's uniform. John had never told him his contact would be a soldier. Gold was "completely surprised"; he had "never dealt with an Army man or a military man before." [32]

Despite his surprise, Gold gave the recognition signal, saying, "I bring greetings from Julius." By the time of his arrest five years later, Gold had forgotten the exact name he had supplied, having never used it again. When recounting the exchange for his lawyers in Holmesburg Prison, he said it "was something on the order of 'Bob sent me,' or 'Benny sent me' or 'John sent me' or something like that."[33] Two months later, in August 1950, Gold's recollection of the incident wasn't much better. He told a federal prosecutor and FBI agents that he had said he brought "greetings from Ben in Brooklyn."[34] This discrepancy would provide fertile ground for Gold detractors in the years to come.

Gold introduced himself as "Raymond Frank" and pulled out the second part of the recognition signal, the Jell-O box top.[35] The soldier was handed the other part of the Jell-O box by his wife, and he gave it to Gold, who was able to match the pieces perfectly. David Greenglass then invited the stranger inside. He "did not seem too surprised," Gold recalled later. "If anything [he was] rather pleased." According to Greenglass's biographer, Sam Roberts, "pleased" is an understatement. David was "exhilarated" by his "first contact with a professional spy."[36] Though he may have originally been expecting his New York acquaintances, Ann or Mike Sidorovich, to knock at his door, he was not startled or upset by this unknown replacement. Gold was still a representative of the Soviet Union.

The apartment was very small, basically two rooms. He was introduced to Mrs. Greenglass. The Greenglasses had been married only a short time. She had come out to Albuquerque just a month or two earlier and hadn't found a job yet. Both of them commented on the many differences between Albuquerque and Manhattan, one of the chief ones being "the difficulty of getting Jewish food." The absence of "delicatessens in a place like Albuquerque" was particularly disconcerting. They said their families back in New York regularly sent them packages of salami and pumpernickel bread.[37]

Gold then asked for the information he was sent to pick up. The soldier admitted "he didn't have it quite ready in complete form" and asked if he could turn it over in the afternoon. Gold was not pleased, but since he "had gone this far," he told himself that he would just have "to carry through with it." Mrs. Greenglass offered him a glass of milk and asked if he'd like something to eat, but he declined and said he'd be back in a few hours to pick up the material. Though he always had a healthy appetite, Gold had more than food on his mind. He wanted out of New Mexico.[38]

Before his visitor left, Greenglass told him, "You know, there are several men at Los Alamos who might also be willing to furnish information. If you want me to, I can go right ahead and talk to them."[39]

"The devil you can," said Gold, and "really ripped into" Greenglass for suggesting "such a preposterous thing." Gold lectured him furiously: "You just don't approach people like that and say, 'Say, can you get me information on the atom bomb?' He told the young soldier, 'We didn't even approach people for industrial information in that fashion.' It took careful preparation and careful buildup. You had to be completely sure" of the person you were thinking of asking.

Caught off guard, Greenglass became "very much subdued," almost like a child. Though he only wanted to be helpful and make amends for not having the documents ready, he now "realized he had said the wrong thing." For his part, Gold saw he was dealing with a complete novice. Despite the soldier's good intentions, "his extreme youth" and "naïve" attitudes could cause problems. Gold wondered, "Who in the world ever got this guy into this business? Does this poor baby know what the heck he is fooling with? Does he know what he is doing even?"[40]

"Recruiting his fellow GI's to the Communist cause"

David Greenglass, the youngest of four children, grew up on New York's Lower East Side in an unheated tenement. His father repaired sewing machines for a living, and his mother was a housewife who was preoccupied with religion and economic security, and always had considerably more of the former than the latter. David's sister, Ethel, was seven years older and in love with the theater. According to her biographers, Ronald Radosh and Joyce Milton, although she was "not conspicuously talented either as an actress or singer, she nevertheless exuded determination that made others respect her."[41] Bright and hard working, she skipped several grades, graduated from high school at fifteen during the height of the Depression, and found work as a clerk in a shipping office. Four years later "she was fired for organizing 150 women co-workers in a strike that culminated in the women lying down in the middle of Thirty-sixth Street to block the way of the company's delivery trucks."[42]

Ethel's political fervor was matched by that of her boyfriend, Julius Rosenberg. A studious youth whose parents hoped he'd eventually become a rabbi, Julius lived with his parents and four brothers in circumstances slightly better than the Greenglasses'. By the time he was sixteen and graduating from high school, however, his interest in Hebrew studies had waned and been replaced by an increasing interest in politics. He entered City College of New York, chose electrical engineering as a major, and began hanging out with a group of Jewish students with a penchant for both science and left-wing politics. He started the Steinmetz Club, the campus equivalent of the Young Communist League (YCL), and looked forward to becoming an active member of the Federation of Architects, Engineers, Chemists and Technicians, an aggressive white-collar union with strong Communist tendencies.

According to Ronald Radosh, whose book *The Rosenberg File* is the classic work on the case, Julius wasn't the "intellectual star or even the natural leader" of the YCL, but he displayed a level of enthusiasm and commitment that got him noticed. Though friends such as William Mutterperl and Joel Barr may have been more intellectually gifted or naturally talented, Julius was tenacious, doctrinaire, and someone "who never missed a leafleting session, a demonstration, or a meeting."[43]

Spirited political argumentation was a staple of life at CCNY during the 1930s. With the Depression at home and the rapid rise of Hitler overseas, there was no shortage of issues for the students to discuss and debate, and each alcove of the university's main building seemed to have its own hard-core philosophical adherents. According to Miriam Moskowitz, a CCNY undergrad in the late 1930s and early 1940s, most of the students were "offspring of Jewish, working class stock who made their living as furriers, electrical workers, and garment workers." These "first generation Jewish-Americans" were "very aware of the importance of unions, the problems in Europe, and the pervasiveness of anti-Semitism." It was easy to "become very left." Moskowitz recalls it as a "time of tremendous intellectual challenge and ferment." There were always "lively arguments between the left and the ultra-left" on any number of issues. The "Communists dominated these debates," said Moskowitz, "but the Trotskyites usually gave a good showing as well."[44]

Although not a political science or history major, Julius Rosenberg could more than hold his own in these battles, but politics was beginning to affect his studies. His girlfriend, Ethel Greenglass, who was three years older, had left the sheltered world of school for a job in the real world. She "insisted he drop his friends" and curtail the time he spent on politics so he could buckle down academically and graduate. Julius began spending considerable time at the Greenglass kitchen table studying, which brought him into contact with Ethel's family, particularly her younger brother, David. It wasn't long before Ethel and her boyfriend were proselytizing the sixteen-year-old youth, extolling Communism and the benefits of the Soviet system. Initially, the youth didn't care for Julius, the amounts of time he was spending at their apartment, or his propagandizing, but the "gift of a chemistry set won David over."[45]

In addition to encouraging his interest in science, Julius made sure

David was informed about contemporary world events and periodically nudged him to join the Young Communist League. David gradually bought into socialism, began looking up to Julius as a role model, and entered Brooklyn Polytechnic Institute after graduating from high school. But he dropped out after one semester; his interests were centered more on earning money and marrying his girlfriend, Ruth Printz. In the fall of 1942, David and Ruth married and moved into a cold-water flat, but they remained active in the YCL. The following April, David was drafted. Although he hated leaving his new wife, he looked forward to fighting Fascists and "recruiting his fellow GI's to the Communist cause."[46]

Julius and Ethel had married in 1939, the same year Julius graduated from CCNY and joined the Communist Party. They moved to a three-room apartment in the Knickerbocker Village housing project on the Lower East Side. Julius was hired as a civilian employee of the U.S. Army Signal Corps, inspecting electronic parts while maintaining his political activism and becoming "chairman of Branch 16B of the Party's Industrial Division." In 1943, a watershed year for them, Julius and Ethel surprised their friends by dropping out of party activities. Though the Rosenbergs made excuses for this withdrawal, including the birth of their first child and the Signal Corps' dubious view of their political affiliations, Radosh and Milton persuasively argue that the decision to "disappear from Party functions fit the pattern followed by those who were tapped for some form of secret work."[47]

The newly married Greenglasses, for their part, seemed equally committed to the cause. Now separated by David's military obligation, they concluded many of their romantic letters to each other with reassuring political observations, such as "We are in love and have our Marxist outlook" and "Victory shall be ours and the future is socialism's."[48] As an army machinist, David was moved to different military bases around the country, and at each he kept a keen eye out for new philosophical recruits. As he wrote in a June 1944 letter to his wife from a Mississippi ordnance plant, "Darling, I have been reading a lot of books on the Soviet Union. Dear, I can see how far-sighted and intelligent those leaders are. They are really geniuses every one of them. . . . Having found out all the truth about the faith and belief in the principles of Socialism and Communism, I believe that every time the Soviet Government used force they did so with pain in their hearts and the belief that what they were doing was to produce good for the greatest number. . . . More power to the Soviet Union and a fruitful and abundant life for their peoples."[49]

"Count me in dear"

Greenglass was moved from one ordnance base to another, including stops at Aberdeen, Maryland; Santa Anita, Monterey, and Pomona, California; and Jackson, Mississippi. In July, he was transferred to Oak Ridge, Tennessee, a secret military installation that wasn't even on area maps. Julius Rosenberg, however, thought he knew what was occurring there. Having immersed himself in the Soviet cause and the recruitment of like-minded young engineers with access to sensitive information, he had heard rumors of a secret military base in Tennessee. In less than a month, though, Greenglass was transferred again, this time to a desolate stretch of New Mexico desert where something of great importance was happening. Censorship of mail and phone lines was now the order of the day. Greenglass told his wife that everyone was being watched, and their practice of signing letters "Your sweetheart, wife and comrade" and "Your husband, lover, and comrade" would have to end.

As the *New York Times* reporter Sam Roberts has written in his book *The Brother,* David Greenglass "couldn't have arrived at Los Alamos at a more propitious moment. The Manhattan Project needed machinists," and the Soviets were always on the lookout for well-placed contributors. The Soviet Union, already blessed with the assignment of its dedicated agent Klaus Fuchs to the secret New Mexico installation, now seemed to have the potential of another. (Ted Hall, then still doing graduate work in physics at Harvard, would not volunteer information on the Manhattan Project for several months yet.) The Soviets' glee at this unexpected development was described by KGB agent Alexander Feklisov. When he informed his Soviet boss that the brother-in-law of his new agent, Julius Rosenberg, had just been assigned to "Enormous," the Russian code name for the secret project in the American Southwest,[50] "my boss was unable to hide his excitement. He jumped to his feet and began walking around the room as he interrogated me in great detail. He immediately understood that David Greenglass was working at Los Alamos on the Manhattan Project."[51]

Within days the Soviet agent had discussed with Rosenberg the prospect of recruiting Greenglass and been assured that the young machinist was "devoted to our cause and one hundred percent reliable." He is "the same blood as my wife," argued Rosenberg, who went on to boast, "I'll give my right hand to be chopped off if he lets us down."[52] Feklisov says that he remained skeptical that "a 21 year old mechanic" could prove of much use, but his own superiors saw Greenglass as an "asset [who] with time and training could be developed into a valuable source." It wasn't long before Ruth Greenglass was incorporated into the plot as a possible "intermediary who could enlist David and then, without arousing suspicion, move to New Mexico to serve as his courier." Soviet cables described her as an "intelligent and clever girl" and a member of the Communist Party. On October 3, 1944, Moscow approved the recruitment of the Greenglasses and "recommended Harry Gold as their contact."[53] Writing to his wife a month later, David cryptically concluded: "My darling, I most certainly will be glad to be part of the community project that Julius and his friends have in mind. Count me in dear or should I say it has my vote. If it has yours, count us in."[54]

According to the account David later gave to federal prosecutor Myles Lane, the couple went for a walk on Route 66, just outside Albuquerque. When Ruth informed him he "was working on the Atom Bomb Project," David was "surprised." He asked how she knew, and she replied that Julius and Ethel had told her, and that they wanted him to provide "information for the Russians." As Julius had argued, "Russia was an ally and as an ally was entitled to the information." Ultimately, said David, that argument was "the main factor" in his decision to provide information. Ruth, he recalled, had been reluctant and "didn't want to tell me about it," but "Ethel Rosenberg then told her, well, at least let him know about it."[55]

David claimed to be "very much taken aback," "frightened," and "worried," but he "thought it over and the next day told his wife he would give her the information." He followed through on that promise by providing her with a description of "what the installation looked like, how many people were there," and "some of the big names" he knew "were working on it."

Julius also wanted to know the layout of the facility, how well it was guarded, and what progress had been made on the project. David replied that he'd have some answers in a few weeks, when he was back in New York on furlough. That discussion was held during the first week of January 1945, when the brothers-in-law discussed what David had garnered of the bomb's construction and the general configuration and operating pattern of Los Alamos. David made a few notes and some rough sketches of a lens mold, a key component of the bomb's trigger mechanism.

That week, over dinner at the Rosenbergs' apartment, Ruth and David met Ann Sidorovich. Her husband, Mike, had been Julius's high school classmate, and the two had briefly worked together for an aeronautical firm. Prior to that, Mike had joined the Spanish Civil War as a member of the famed Abraham Lincoln Brigade, fighting on behalf of the Spanish Loyalists. After Ann left the apartment, Julius informed the Greenglasses that she might be the person who should periodically visit them in Albuquerque to collect whatever atomic secrets David had extracted from Los Alamos. Julius wanted her to "get to know who [they] were." But, asked Ruth, what if Ann couldn't make it? How would she and David recognize a substitute messenger?

David said Julius took his wife and Ruth into the kitchen while he perused a book and listened to some music in the living room. When they returned, "Julius took the side of a Jell-O box and cut it in an odd fashion." He then gave one half to Ruth—"the one with the recipe"—saying the other half "will be brought to you by another party and he will bear the greetings from me." Ruth then put the scrap of cardboard into her wallet and put the wallet into her purse.[56]

After dinner Julius explained to David "how the Atom Bomb works." David later said that Julius "described what the Russians already knew" and stressed that it was up to David to tell them "what has gone on in the making of the bomb," and the "materials, methods of use, and experiments" needed to perfect it. Both Ruth and Ethel were present, David recalled, but he assumed that "most of it went over their heads." He believed "it didn't mean anything to them" beyond "the fact that it had something to do with an Atom Bomb."[57]

During that first week of 1945, Julius asked David to meet him one evening outside a saloon on Forty-second Street. David borrowed his father-in-law's car and drove to the bar, where Julius introduced him to a man who, David thought, might have been Russian. The stranger and David then drove around the neighborhood for about twenty minutes, during which the stranger asked a series of "questions about the bomb," and David told him "stuff about it." The nature and design of the lens mold seemed to be of particular interest.[58]

David returned to Los Alamos, and Ruth went on working for the American Jewish Congress. The next few months would be stressful for her as she learned she was pregnant, left her job, and moved to Albuquerque, found a small apartment, and then became quite ill and suffered a miscarriage. By May, she seemed to have recovered enough to camp out by an Albuquerque Safeway store, armed with her Jell-O box top and waiting for a courier. After an hour she departed. She repeated the maneuver the following Saturday, and again no one showed up—either because she had misunderstood her instructions or because she had brought David to the second meeting; she was not sure. Just a week later, a knock at their door brought them face to face with "a stocky, moonfaced man wearing a suit and an expression of barely concealed surprise."[59]

"He would soon be returning to England"

When Harry Gold returned to the Greenglasses' Albuquerque apartment that afternoon, they had an envelope prepared for him. David was already in uniform, and Ruth was getting dressed. Glancing at the envelope, Gold guessed that it held several sheets of paper, most of them typewritten but some handwritten, and "one very small, rough sketch." This was considerably less than what he had received from Fuchs, and unlikely, Gold thought, to have the same scientific value.[60] He had the impression that Greenglass was a "physicist's helper" or, more likely, an "electrician, semi-skilled machinist or possibly a draftsman." Regardless of Greenglass's specific position, Gold had pegged him as an intellectual lightweight, "his activities concerned to a very limited field."[61]

Gold's assessment was correct. Greenglass had neither Fuchs's theoretical and scientific background nor his overall understanding of the complicated project. He confused plutonium with uranium and had a shallow understanding of lens mold technology and its importance. But his information confirmed what the Soviet Union had learned from Fuchs: "the United States was moving from the gun-type uranium bomb to the implosion plutonium model in its race to build a weapon for use against Japan."

After turning over the envelope, the soldier "hinted very strongly that they were rapidly running out of money and that he had very little left with which to keep his wife in Albuquerque." He mentioned her miscarriage, the doctor bills, and the cost of medicines. That prompted Gold to hand Greenglass the envelope containing $500, a considerable amount at the time. Unlike Fuchs, Greenglass quickly accepted the money. As he would tell Sam Roberts a half century later, the envelope "had a nice feel to it."

Once Ruth had joined them, they left the apartment together, walked a few blocks, and then parted as they approached a USO (United Service Organizations) facility. When the Greenglasses were sure Gold had gone, they returned to their apartment and counted the money.[62]

Gold made the same convoluted train trip back home. He would have preferred to fly, but as usual he was short of funds. He left Albuquerque around six o'clock on a train to Chicago. "Running desperately short" of time and fearful that he might have to wait overnight for a train to take him back east, he decided to board a plane to Washington and then another train to New York, where he was scheduled to meet John. Arguably the least noticeable person on any of these vehicles, he was also the only individual in the world outside Los Alamos with possession of plans and drawings for the first atomic bomb. That unique honor was one he would have been quite happy to be relieved of at the time.

After arriving at Penn Station, Gold took public transit to Brooklyn, where he and John met "somewhere near the point where Metropolitan Avenue runs into Queens." It was a "very deserted area . . . near a cemetery." The exchange was completed and the men parted ways in a "matter of seconds." They both understood that in a week or two they'd meet again for a lengthy discussion of what had happened in New Mexico.

Gold turned over two different folders. The thicker package was labeled "Doctor," while the much thinner folder that Greenglass had produced was labeled "Other."[63] Immediately after the drop-off, Gold retraced his steps to Penn Station and boarded yet another train to return, after several exhausting and pressure-filled days, to his unsuspecting family on Kindred Street and his co-workers at the sugar company. They would ask him if he enjoyed his vacation.

Soon afterward John informed Gold that the information he had collected on his New Mexico adventure was well worth the trip and that the Greenglass material "was extremely excellent and very valuable." Gold soon had indications that the Greenglass data were less stellar than they had seemed at first.[64] In early fall 1945, Gold asked John if he should meet the soldier again. Greenglass expected another furlough sometime in September and had suggested they meet in New York. John instructed Gold "to mind his own business" and not involve himself with Greenglass, who "was being adequately taken care of by other people."[65] Some time later, Gold made a similar suggestion and "was rebuked even more sharply." He suspected that the information from Greenglass "had not been of very much consequence at all and that [the Soviets] believed that the risk attendant upon seeing him did not make any such effort worthwhile."[66]

Gold's second trip to New Mexico came after the Trinity test blast in July, and after a uranium bomb had been dropped on Hiroshima and a plutonium bomb on Nagasaki in early August. The mysterious and terribly destructive new weapons were all over the news. But if the bombs themselves were no longer secret, their ingredients and construction still were. Gold's trip, like his first venture, was "fraught with difficulties" centering on time and money. Taking the second part of his split vacation in mid-September, and carrying what he thought were sufficient funds, he departed Philadelphia for Santa Fe. But by the time he arrived in Chicago, on September 16—the "Jewish day of atonement," according to Gold's recollection—he was already desperate. From the Palmer House, where he spent the night, he called his old friend Tom Black in New Jersey and asked him to wire $50 to Chicago.[67]

Gold finally arrived in Albuquerque on September 19, registered at the Hilton, and took a bus to Santa Fe. He was scheduled to meet Fuchs on the outskirts of the city, on "Bishop's Lodge Road between Hillside and Kearney Avenues."[68] He was told to look for "a large church" or "mission" near a "boys' preparatory school." Fuchs was "quite late . . . somewhere around twenty minutes late," which unnerved Gold, who was always ill at ease when he felt exposed. When Fuchs finally arrived in his "rickety car" around sunset, he explained "he had to drive slowly . . . because they had quite a few bottles of liquor" in the vehicle, bought for a party.[69] He had also dropped off several people in town. The small complement of British scientists, like everyone else at Los Alamos, were ecstatic the conflict was over, their scientific quest a success, and their return to England one large step closer. Parties were being organized; wives planned festive meals; amateur thespians arranged entertainment with performances by renowned physicists like Otto Frisch. Fuchs declined to perform in public, but he did have a car and therefore volunteered to shuttle people and alcohol to their destinations. Everyone was in a celebratory mood; the bombs had ended the war.[70]

Fuchs, casually dressed in "pants, sneakers, and a sports shirt," took Gold for a ride along Bishop's Lodge Road into the desert, and then up the side of a mountain, where they could "barely see the lights of Santa Fe blinking below" as darkness fell. Driving through mesas and scrublands, Fuchs talked. He had been present at the Trinity test in July and described the explosion and an immense flash of light that was visible in Los Alamos, nearly two hundred miles distant. He admitted he had "grievously underestimated" America's industrial potential and expressed concern about the weapon it had produced.[71] The enormous death tolls at Hiroshima and Nagasaki had stunned him. Gold took notice that one of the scientists who had created the weapon seemed "somewhat shaken and in awe of what had been created." Few had predicted such destructive power.

Fuchs admitted to being both "happy" and "disgusted" by the reaction of Santa Fe townspeople. Initially, he and others had felt area residents were cool to the Manhattan Project scientists. They were seen as intruders whose feverish work in the desert disturbed the quiet harmony of the land and its longtime residents. But now that they saw the results of those efforts, they viewed the scientists as heroes. Fuchs was "disgusted that it had taken the achievement of such a weapon of destruction to bring them into favor with the townspeople."[72]

Fuchs also described a noticeable cooling of relations between the British and the Americans at Los Alamos. "Since the explosion of the bomb over Hiroshima and the surrender of the Japanese," he said, "the period of cooperation" between the two countries "was rapidly coming to a close." "Departments at Los Alamos which formerly had been open to him were now closed." He had "received . . . hints from the people in the British Mission that he would soon be returning to England."[73]

By "December of 1945 or January 1946," Fuchs thought, he "would again be in Cambridge" (Massachusetts), and shortly thereafter in England. In case this prediction was wrong, however, and "he should be suddenly transferred," he suggested that they arrange a London rendezvous. They agreed on a time and place: a "Saturday evening at eight or eight-thirty" at an "underground subway station."[74]

Though Gold considered it unlikely that he would be sent to meet Fuchs in London, he couldn't rule it out. His presence in the New Mexico foothills was proof that such a scenario was possible. More likely, he would "relay this information to John so that someone could later meet [Fuchs] in London."[75] Fuchs had come up with a plan whereby his contact would camp out by the assigned tube station "the first Saturday of the month beginning with January and February." As a recognition device, the person would be carrying five books tied with string under one arm, and "the other arm was to be carrying Bennett Cerf's collection of funny stories."

"A very bulky package of information"

As they watched the lights of Santa Fe flicker in the distance and noted the probable end of their relationship, Fuchs expressed his desire for a time when people and nations could work cooperatively and hostilities would cease. Someday, he said, he and Gold might be able "to meet in England or in the United States or possibly anywhere in the world, and be able to meet openly as friends and speak of music, and other matters, but not speak of war." Gold said he too looked forward to such a time and admitted he had long desired "to see the famous literary landmarks in Great Britain where Walter Scott, Robbie Burns, Wordsworth, Housman, and Shakespeare had worked." Fuchs replied that he looked forward to such a visit.[76]

Then the normally controlled Fuchs shared a side of his personality that Gold had never witnessed. For the British scientist who had fought so long against the Nazis and sacrificed so much, what did it mean, asked Harry, to know that Hitler was dead and Fascism had finally been crushed? As he listened to Fuchs's response, he took note of a rare change in his demeanor; he would subsequently describe it as "the closest to sentiment that I have ever known Klaus to come."

It was at this point that Fuchs asked Gold for a favor. As the Allied armies moved across Germany, he said, there was a chance that they would get to his hometown and the University of Kiel before the Russians and thus come into "possession of the Gestapo records of the very early thirties," which included a "very complete dossier" of his political activities. As a well-known Communist activist from a well-known family, he "had escaped from Germany with his life only by the very, very narrowest of margins." He repeated the story of how his brother, Gerhard, "had been imprisoned and tortured in a concentration camp." His father had escaped this brutal treatment because of his standing in the community, but he was completely penniless and living with a small grandchild whose parents had been put to death in a concentration camp.

Fuchs feared that his father—whom he considered "quite garrulous and completely unworldly"—would "give him away to British intelligence if they should come to Kiel" before the Russians. Fuchs assumed (fairly accurately) that British intelligence "had no idea whatever of [his] Communist background," and he wanted it to remain that way. But he had already "been approached by British intelligence with offers to try and remove his father to England." In an effort to "reward me and compensate me," he said, "they are going to bring my father to England so that I can be with the old man in his remaining years. But if they do, he is bound to prattle about my activities in the Student Communist Party. And then people will begin to wonder about my background, and once they begin to pry you know what will happen."[77]

If his background were known, said Fuchs, it "would permanently end . . . or impair his working on atomic energy."[78] On the other hand, if he opposed "this presumed kindness" by the British government, he would arouse suspicion. Gold immediately understood the physicist's quandary. Fuchs asked him to pass along the request that if Soviet troops got to Kiel first, they should search out and destroy any Gestapo police records that had his name on them. He would have to hope for the best regarding his father. Gold tried to assuage his concern, arguing that he gave his father too little credit, and that if British intelligence had shown no interest in his political affiliations to this point, they were unlikely to change now. The well-intentioned optimist's counsel would prove correct.

Before they drove out of the mountains, Fuchs made it clear that if they should lose contact, Gold should "keep in touch with his sister" by paying her a visit in the "very late fall or in the early winter."[79] He "would try and be in Cambridge around Christmastime," but the deteriorating relations between America and Great Britain made it impossible to predict where he would be.

Fuchs drove Gold back to the outskirts of Santa Fe, dropping him off in "one of the Mexican sections," and handed him "a very bulky packet of information." The two men shook hands and wished each other well. It was the last time Fuchs ever saw the little courier who called himself Raymond.[80]

After a short walk, Gold found his way back to the bus station, where he had to kill almost two hours before the bus arrived for the return trip to Albuquerque. He had brought a copy of *Great Expectations* with him, but his nerves were unsettled. He would read a few pages, walk to the front door in hope of seeing a bus, sit down, read a few more pages, and then begin "observing people around [him] for any hint of any investigating agent."[81] The entire process would then be repeated.

Gold knew he was carrying something far more explosive than dynamite. After three atomic blasts—one in the New Mexico desert and two in Japan—there was no doubt the package Fuchs had given him was incredibly important. It was at times like this, when he was in a place where he "had absolutely no business" being, that his adrenaline would start pumping, his heart would race, and he'd have to do all he could to control himself.[82] He couldn't just drop everything and run back home as he had done as a child hawking newspapers on an unfriendly Philadelphia street corner. He had to stick it out. The bus eventually came, but not before he had endured what he would call "the longest hour and a half that I have ever spent." He felt as if he didn't take a normal breath until he reached Albuquerque nearly two hours later.

At about two-thirty in the morning, a ringing phone startled Gold in his hotel room. It was an American Airlines agent informing him that the airline had a seat for him on its next flight for Kansas City. He hurriedly dressed, got to the airport, and flew to Missouri. Unable to book another flight, he took a train to Chicago. At the station he helped an elderly, heavyset woman and her grandson board the train while others "simply stood callously around" watching their clumsy struggle. The old woman, the boy, and their several suitcases were nearly overrun by "the mob that was milling around" trying to board the overcrowded train. After helping both of them get seats and store their bags, he was left without a seat himself and had to sit on his valise for the entire journey to Chicago.[83] It was typical of him to help strangers while transporting his nation's most precious secrets to a foreign competitor.

The train arrived near midnight. Gold "dashed for the LaSalle Station," where he boarded a New York Central train, and arrived in Manhattan with little money to spare. He had borrowed money, skipped meals, and skimped on the ones he did have, but the mission had been a success, except for one very important thing.[84] He had arrived in New York too late to meet John. He would have to take the secrets of the atomic bomb back to his Kindred Street row house in Northeast Philadelphia and return the following day. Gold did just that, but John did not show up. This was very much unlike the Soviet handler. John was normally very punctual, particularly when important documents were to be transferred, and Gold could think of few documents more important than those he was carrying. Something significant must have happened.

All Gold could do was wait for their scheduled backup meeting about two weeks later, in early October.

CHAPTER 8

. . . .

The Postwar Years

I n early October Gold returned to New York. He could not understand why his handler had made no effort to reach him. Direct contact, especially by phone, was frowned upon, but this was an exceptionally delicate situation. Gold was holding documents that were so valuable that he hadn't let them out of his sight for days. He carried them to work and when he shopped for groceries on Castor Avenue; wherever he went, the documents went with him.

Gold anxiously looked forward to the next scheduled meeting, which was set to take place between Jackson Heights and Flushing in Queens. To his great relief, John showed up and took custody of the Fuchs package. Gold could almost feel a drop in his blood pressure. As expected, the documents contributed much new material about the Trinity plutonium implosion design, including the increase in the production rate of both U-235 and plutonium and the critical mass of each. This would enable the Russians to estimate how many bombs Los Alamos was capable of producing. There was more information on plutonium itself, a metal whose peculiar characteristics baffled metallurgists and scientists alike.

"Plutonium is so unusual as to approach the unbelievable," said its discoverer, Glenn Seaborg. "Under some conditions, plutonium can be nearly as hard and brittle as glass, under others, as soft and plastic as lead. It will burn and crumble quickly to powder when heated in air, or slowly disintegrate when kept at room temperature. It undergoes no less than five phase transitions between room temperature and its melting point. Strangely enough, in two of its phases, plutonium actually contracts as it is being heated." Soviet scientists were no doubt ecstatic to receive anything at all from Los Alamos, particularly information about a metal that Seaborg described as "unique among all of the chemical elements."[1]

In his definitive account of the making of the hydrogen bomb, Richard Rhodes concludes that "Fuchs' revelations made it possible for Soviet scientists to approach the difficult business of plutonium fabrication well-informed."[2] The Fuchs material also covered subjects like "initiators," bomb assembly, lens design, and uranium filtration. By the time he handed his package of information to Harry Gold, Fuchs was one of the better-situated and better-informed members of the Manhattan Project team. The bits and pieces that David Greenglass added "would usefully corroborate Fuchs's scientifically accurate account."

Although the Soviets had other sources of Manhattan Project information, including Ted Hall and George Koval—and one or two yet to be determined—Fuchs was "by far the most important informant," and the information he provided almost single-handedly advanced the development of a Russian atomic bomb by several years.[3] Alexander Feklisov, a key Russian operative in America during these years, unequivocally called Fuchs "the greatest atomic spy of all."[4]

Gold, Fuchs's only courier during his time on the Manhattan Project, would have a subsequent meeting with John that fall "somewhere near the Hotel St. George in Brooklyn." From the start, the Russian seemed on edge; Gold would later describe him as "very touchy and very apprehensive." John emphasized that they both "had to be extremely careful" but offered no elaboration. Gold had the impression that his Soviet handler "had the wind up."

Two additional meetings were scheduled that fall—one in the Jamaica section of Queens and one "near the Earle Theatre in the Bronx"—but John kept neither appointment.[5] After a decade of clandestine work, Gold was used to fruitless waiting at rendezvous points, but John was normally reliable and prompt. The handler's growing concern about safety, combined with his increasing inability to make scheduled meetings, was disturbing.

"Cheap little men pulled by strings from Moscow"

There was a good reason for John's behavior. Just a few weeks after the end of the war, Igor Gouzenko, a low-level cipher clerk for military attaché Colonel Nikolai Zabotin at the Russian embassy in Ottawa, had upset the Soviet espionage apple cart. When he defected on September 5, he brought with him more than one hundred documents illuminating the wholesale theft of Canadian and American industrial and military secrets, including the latest in atomic and radar development.

Citizens of the United States and Canada, including of course Harry Gold, remained in the dark about Gouzenko's defection and the Soviet espionage triumph while both governments scrambled to figure out how to handle the fiasco. The normally smooth GRU and NKGB (Soviet intelligence and secret police) operations were about to receive a second blow as well. Just as the Soviets and Americans were debating their responses to the Gouzenko revelations, another key operative was launching her own broadside against Soviet intelligence.

Elizabeth Bentley, a Vassar graduate and Communist sympathizer, was the girlfriend of Jacob Golos, a high-ranking Soviet agent who coordinated several particularly effective spy rings in the United States. Golos, ostensibly the director of a Soviet-sponsored tour business, trained Bentley as an assistant and courier who collected information up and down the East Coast from his suppliers. One of these suppliers was Abe Brothman, who was later turned over to Harry Gold.

When Golos died suddenly of a heart attack in 1943, Bentley dutifully continued to direct the spy network. She grew disenchanted, however, when her Soviet bosses insisted that she turn over to them the operation that she had labored so loyally to maintain. She resisted and began to drink heavily, and her relations with them grew increasingly testy. In an effort to mollify her, Moscow awarded her the Order of the Red Star, the same prestigious honor Harry Gold had received a year earlier. It was hoped that the award package of money, air conditioners, and fur coats that came with it would soften her resistance and ease the transfer of Golos's network to Soviet authorities.[6]

Though Bentley grudgingly complied and ended her career as a courier by January 1945, her Soviet superiors began to worry about her stability and the likelihood that she could fall into the hands of American counterintelligence authorities who were already suspicious of her relationship with Golos. They suggested that she leave the country for her own safety, as well as that of their spy network. Once again she resisted.

As months passed and relations worsened, both parties began to consider extreme measures. Bentley contemplated going to the FBI; the Soviets contemplated killing her.

Bentley probably did not know of Gouzenko's defection that fall, but she was certainly aware of Louis Budenz's getting religion and walking out as editor of the *Daily Worker* on October 11, 1945. This change of heart by an old and reliable source of information drew front-page headlines and gave her notice that she might find herself under increased FBI scrutiny. She no doubt read the many articles detailing his rediscovery of "the faith of my fathers" and plans for a "nationwide lecture tour to expose the Communist menace."[7] It did not take a sharp mind to figure out that Bentley's name would come up in any discussions between Budenz and the FBI.

As Bentley would subsequently write, "the effect of Mr. Golos wearing off, the effect of the Russians brutally showing their hand to me . . . and suddenly coming in contact with high functionaries of the Communist Party . . . and discovering that they were just cheap little men pulled by strings from Moscow" precipitated her decision to go "back to being a good American."[8] She went to the FBI. Like Gouzenko, she discovered it wasn't an easy process. She would have to overcome a good deal of institutional mistrust before Hoover's Bureau came to believe her. Her lengthy interrogation resulted in a 107-page confession that named more than sixty individuals. As Bentley's biographer Kathryn S. Olmsted has written, "Gouzenko was the first person to alert U.S. officials that the Soviets had constructed a vast web of espionage in North America. He blew a hole in this web. Elizabeth, in turn, would tear it apart."[9]

"He was married and had two children"

The stunning twin defections led the NKGB to suspend intelligence gathering in the United States for nearly two years.[10] The formidable and elusive Soviet spy machine was shaken to its core. Many operatives were withdrawn from active duty and sent back to Russia; others were instructed to go into hibernation. Some sources, however, were just too important to walk away from, even temporarily. Possibly the most important of them was Dr. Klaus Fuchs.

Despite their much-reduced communications during the latter part of 1945, John made it known that Gold had to maintain knowledge of Fuchs's whereabouts, if not make actual contact with him. The Soviets could not afford to lose their prime supplier of atomic bomb information. An earlier severing of ties had caused much recrimination in Russian intelligence circles; no one wanted to see it repeated. Now that the existence of the bombs was public knowledge, the war was over, and speculation was rife that the British Mission would be going home, the question of immediate importance was, where exactly was Fuchs: in America or Great Britain?

The answer was neither. Beginning in late September, with their work complete, many Los Alamos scientists and workers returned to their homes, universities, and places of employment. Most of the British left, but Fuchs was asked to stay on for a few months, and he agreed. Before getting back to work, however, he was invited to join the Peierls and the Tellers on a two-week holiday in Mexico. Even though their car broke down on the journey to Mexico City and they had to wait for parts to arrive, Fuchs and his friends thoroughly enjoyed themselves, taking in the floating gardens of Xochimilco, the Basilica of Guadelupe, and other attractions. Fuchs opted out of going to the bullfight, maintaining that it was "cruel to the bull and the horses."[11]

When the group returned to Los Alamos, Fuchs departed for Montreal, where the British were recruiting members for their own atomic energy program. Because of his Manhattan Project experience and the recommendations of top British scientists, he was offered a senior position. Once again, he seemed about to insinuate himself into a high-level atomic energy program from which he could feed information to his Communist colleagues. The British—and the Soviets—were getting an accomplished physicist who had contributed to critical theoretical and design debates regarding atomic energy. Many of those discussions concerned "the super," the hydrogen bomb.

Back at Los Alamos, Fuchs had to watch others preparing for America's first postwar atomic bomb test, scheduled for late 1946 at Bikini Atoll. As a British citizen, he was not a participating member of the research team. He was, however, given a role in investigating the tragic death of Louis Slotin, a physicist who was overcome by a burst of radiation in a laboratory accident. Fuchs's involvement in probing this rare and deadly accident, and the growing threat of radiation poisoning, foreshadowed similar concerns regarding radiation exposure once he returned to England.

All of this was unknown to Soviet intelligence, which knew nothing of his activities and whereabouts after Gold had received the package from Fuchs in mid-September. For all they knew, Fuchs had already left for England. It was imperative that they reestablish communications with him. His longtime contact was instructed to go to Cambridge, Massachusetts, and learn what he could from his sister, Kristel Heinemann.

Gold traveled up to Boston in late January or early February 1946. There was still snow on the ground, but he did not have any difficulty making his way to Cambridge and the Heinemann home. Though he had made sure it was a daytime visit, Gold was "surprised," when Kristel Heinemann ushered him inside, to come face to face with Mr. Heinemann. Tall, with dark hair, glasses, and what Gold described as a "gentle, scholarly appearance," Robert Heinemann had an "abstracted air" about him.

Gold was "very much ill at ease." He remembered what his handler had told him about Kristel's husband and his attitude about visitors, but he "tried to appear as nonchalant as possible." Heinemann may have been putting up a good front as well, for he was "quite friendly and seemed to accept me as a friend of Klaus." He explained that he wasn't usually home at that time of day, but because a turbine breakdown had left the utility plant where he was employed without power or heat, everyone had been sent home. With him in the kitchen was a man introduced as Konstantin Lafazanos, who seemed to be "a long-standing friend of the family." Years later Gold would recollect that he was "a teacher of philosophy or a teacher of languages," probably of "Greek ancestry," and may have been unemployed at the time.[12]

Gold was encouraged to take a seat and have something to eat, and the four chatted briefly. He told them he was a chemist living near Pittsburgh and that he was married and had two children—a ruse he commonly employed in his spy work "to create an obstacle toward his discovery or identification."[13]

Kristel's brother, he learned, was still in Los Alamos. Klaus had planned on visiting the Heinemanns over Christmas, but for the second year in a row he was unable to make it. He was described as being "very disappointed at not being able to come to Cambridge" and bring presents to the children. His sister seemed unsure when she would see him again. The entire visit was no longer than half an hour; although he didn't reestablish contact with Fuchs, Gold at least learned where he was.

Gold immediately returned to New York and went directly to the Earle Theatre in the Bronx, near the Grand Concourse and Yankee Stadium. He was supposed to meet John in the men's room, but John didn't keep the appointment. Traveling for hours and then waiting by a row of urinals for someone who didn't show up was becoming a common experience for Gold. He had no idea what the problem was. Eventually he returned to Penn Station, and from there to Philadelphia. Return trips to New York for "emergency meetings" proved equally fruitless. While he waited for further orders, Gold was left pondering what could have disrupted his handler's usual dependability.[14]

"Get up, sleepyhead"

Within weeks, Gold had a more important problem on his hands. He and a number of other long-standing Pennsylvania Sugar Company employees were "released" in late February. This was a significant blow. The refinery had been his only employer since 1928. Like many companies after the war, Pennsylvania Sugar was confronting difficult financial times. Competition from abroad, an aging plant, and growing labor unrest would only exacerbate the problem and led to a series of ownership and managerial changes in the late 1940s and early 1950s.

Exhausted by a full schedule of legal and illegal work and now stunned by the loss of his job, Gold went into a slight depression. For the first week he seemed to sleep around the clock. Even after that, he appeared to be in no hurry to find another job. Instead, he tried to find employment for his friends and former co-workers, Morrell Dougherty and Regina Lookabaugh. Though he told his mother he was looking for work, he didn't really start to pursue another job until April, when he attended a meeting of the American Chemical Society in Atlantic City.[15] There he received a tentative job offer from J. H. Bowen, who worked in the personnel department at the Philadelphia Navy Yard. With the war over, the naval base was looking for assistance in corrosion proofing of armaments and ships.

The offer of work at the Navy Yard was ironic, considering how some of his former Soviet handlers had pushed him to get such an assignment, but Gold had no great interest in rust-proofing battleships; he wanted to be in a lab. An opportunity appeared: Abe Brothman, the brilliant but unreliable chemical engineer from New York, was looking for a head chemist for his laboratory. A dreamer and accomplished talker, Brothman sold his former Philadelphia courier on his company's potential. He already had business contracts with major players in at least two countries —China and Palestine—and expected to do even better in the future.[16] All he needed was an accomplished chemist like Gold to run the lab while he guided the organization's front office.

Gold was captivated by Brothman's promises. He knew that a relationship with one of his former suppliers was at best problematic, and most likely would be forbidden by his Russian bosses, but perhaps his career as a secret agent was behind him. He hadn't heard from anyone in the Soviet espionage orbit for months. He wasn't disappointed that his days of running dangerous errands around the country were over, and he needed a job.

Gold visited Brothman's operation a few times in late spring to check it out and listen to Brothman's attractive sales pitch. A small business office was located on Thirty-second Street in Midtown Manhattan, and the laboratory was in Elmhurst, Long Island. He started work in June 1946 for $100 a week. Since their initial contact in 1941, Gold had used the name Frank Kessler with Brothman. Now in his employ, Gold revealed his real name and some of the work he had done for the Soviets[17]—but not his work with Klaus Fuchs or the atomic bomb. Harry's new co-workers knew him as Kessler, a devoted family man from Philadelphia.[18]

He had to find somewhere to live. After some early leads proved futile, Miriam Moskowitz, Brothman's secretary, business partner, and lover, generously offered the company's new chief chemist a place to stay for the summer.[19] Moskowitz had just celebrated her thirtieth birthday when Gold joined the company. A City College of New York graduate, she had worked at the Immigration and Naturalization Service and the War Manpower Commission before taking a secretarial position at the Brothman firm.[20] Within a short time, she became a partner, a somewhat common scenario at the undercapitalized firm. To maintain staff, Brothman offered partnerships in lieu of salary when he could not make the payroll.[21] Moskowitz opted for one of these partnerships.

When she first met "Frank Kessler," Moskowitz claims, he struck her as "the most woebegone person I had ever known." His accounts of an initially blissful but then failed marriage, and the lovely twin children whom he could only see from "a distance in a playground on Saturday afternoons," were emotionally "wrenching." His story grew more somber when he described how his aged parents grieved for his brother, a paratrooper killed in New Guinea during the war.[22]

Happy to assist an important new member of the organization, Moskowitz offered Gold "temporary hospitality" while her apartment mate was visiting her parents for the summer. He offered to pay, but she refused, saying her apartment mate had already paid her share in advance. Though she expected him to return to Philadelphia on weekends, "he seemed to prefer to stay in Manhattan" and adapt his routine to her schedule and activities. It was not unusual that summer for him to join in when she went to a movie, had friends over for dinner, or visited her parents.

In close proximity with a woman other than his mother for the first and maybe only time, Gold found that his efforts at friendship could be easily misinterpreted. Though he only wanted to help, his offers of assistance sometimes became a nuisance. "He made me uncomfortable in the office," said Moskowitz. "He was always trying to do things for me that I didn't need done." He "went overboard" trying to ingratiate himself with people, and "lent money" and "did favors for people he didn't even know."[23]

One incident at her apartment was particularly unsettling. One morning, according to Moskowitz, Gold entered her room, sat down on her bed, and shook her awake, while calling out, "Get up, sleepyhead, get up." Moskowitz claimed she was so shaken by the incident that she told Brothman, who insisted that Harry find new living accommodations. Gold was so embarrassed, according to Brothman, that he "broke down and cried."[24]

Despite that incident, Gold and Brothman established a "genuine friendship," working together in the lab, playing handball, and swimming at a Midtown gym. They would periodically steal away to catch an afternoon ballgame at Ebbets Field or the Polo Grounds. Moskowitz recalled them as a team: Brothman, a manic talker, would state his opinion on an issue, and Gold would break his silence only to repeat the last few words of his boss's comment. "He would always repeat the tail end of what you said," wrote Moskowitz. "It was some kind of compulsive behavior, but he was so nice."

"You have wrecked everything"

One afternoon between Christmas and New Year's, Gold received a telephone call at Brothman's Elmhurst laboratory. He immediately recognized the voice: it was John. Almost a year had passed since their last communication, and Gold had begun to think he was through with the nasty business of spying. "Have you been well?" asked the Russian. The question was part of a code system the Soviets used "to make things seem normal and everyday"; it was designed to determine whether the receiver of the call had been under surveillance. Gold replied he had been fine, thereby letting his Russian handler know that he was not being observed, and that the phone lines were not being tapped.[25] John asked if Gold could meet him that night at the same place as before at about eight. Gold knew exactly where he meant.

On his way to the Earle Theatre that evening, Gold was not surprised

Harry Gold, born Heinrich Golodnitsky in 1910 in Bumplitz, Switzerland, sits on his mother's lap with a toy in one hand and a piece of chocolate in the other. His father stands behind them. (Joseph Gold Papers, Special Collections, Temple University Libraries, Philadelphia)

Celia Ominsky, Harry Gold's mother, traveled from the Ukraine to Paris to become a dental technician. Bad luck and a shortage of funds forced her to earn a living in cigar factories in Paris and Bern, Switzerland. (Joseph Gold Papers, Special Collections, Temple University Libraries, Philadephia)

Samson Golodnitsky, Harry Gold's father, had sufficient education for a career in business, but as a disciple of the Russian writer Leo Tolstoy, he chose instead to work with his hands as a carpenter and cabinetmaker. (Joseph Gold Papers, Special Collections, Temple University Libraries, Philadephia)

Harry Gold, c. 1914. As a child, Gold had a pronounced sweet tooth, loved chocolate, and enjoyed his mother's humorous old world yarns and fables. His father considered him his "golden boy." (Joseph Gold Papers, Special Collections, Temple University Libraries, Philadelphia)

Harry Gold as a teenager. Shy and smaller than most boys his age, Gold faced frustration on the athletic field that was offset by his love of books and his success in the classroom. (Joseph Gold Papers, Special Collections, Temple University Libraries, Philadelphia)

Harry Gold, c. 1928–1929. During his high school years, Gold feared he would never be able to earn a living despite his academic prowess and growing interest in chemistry. (Joseph Gold Papers, Special Collections, Temple University Libraries, Philadelphia)

Brothers Joe (left) and Harry Gold enjoying a day trip to the beach in Atlantic City in the mid-1930s. It would be another decade and a half before Joe learned that his older brother was secretly gathering intelligence for the Soviet Union. (Joseph Gold Papers, Special Collections, Temple University Libraries, Philadelphia)

Gold's Pennsylvania Sugar Company identification card. Though he started as a janitor doing lowly chores like cleaning spittoons, his remarkable work ethic and interest in science soon had him working in the sugar refinery's chemistry department. (Joseph Gold Papers, Special Collections, Temple University Libraries, Philadelphia)

Based at the intersection of Delaware Avenue and Shackamaxon Street along the Delaware River waterfront, the Pennsylvania Sugar Refinery was one of the world's largest sugar refineries. Gold worked there from 1929 to 1946. (Temple University Libraries, Urban Archives, Philadelphia)

Semyon Semenov, the M.I.T.-educated Soviet spy who directed Gold's activities during the early years of the war, was instrumental in Gold's receiving the Order of the Red Star. (SVR RF)

Anatoly Yakovlev (Anatoly Yatskov) succeeded Semenov as Gold's Soviet handler and would prove to be his last. Yakovlev directed Gold in his dealings with Klaus Fuchs and also made the unorthodox decision to order Gold to pick up information from David Greenglass, who was a machinist at Los Alamos. (U.S. National Archives, FBI landmark cases folder, College Park, Maryland)

Klaus Fuchs, 1960s, after he was released from prison. Though he initially disdained the strict party discipline and Communist philosophy in general, he had become a believer by 1933, as the Communists seemed to be the only ones willing to oppose the rise of Hitler and Nazism in Germany. (NSA Cryptological Museum, Fort Mead, Maryland)

Abe Brothman (left), Harry Gold (center), and an unidentified individual. Brothman was a bright Columbia graduate with grand aspirations, but his business acumen never matched his love and knowledge of chemical engineering. (Special Collections, Diamond Law Library, Columbia University)

Abe Brothman and Miriam Moskowitz became friends and colleagues of Gold after he was laid off at the sugar refinery and began working at Brothman's chemical design firm in New York City. Gold told authorities that the three of them conspired to deceive a 1947 Federal Grand Jury. Brothman and Moskowitz each served two years in prison. (Special Collections, Diamond Law Library, Columbia University)

FBI surveillance photo of Harry Gold, mid-May 1950. Many such photos were shown to Klaus Fuchs in Wormwood Scrubs Prison in the hope that he would identify the man he gave Manhattan Project documents. (U.S. National Archives, FBI landmark cases folder, College Park, Maryland).

Even before his arrest, Gold cooperated with the FBI by letting them take photos of him. This was taken in May 1950. (Temple University Libraries, Urban Archives, Philadelphia)

Harry Gold always felt most comfortable around test tubes, petri dishes, and various calibration gadgets. This undated photo from the Urban Archives at Temple University shows one of Gold's workplaces. (Temple University Libraries, Urban Archives, Philadelphia)

FBI Special Agents Thomas Scott Miller (left), 1949, and Richard Brennan, 1946. Agents Miller and Brennan were sent from the FBI's New York office to Philadelphia to investigate the strong possibility that Gold was Fuch's contact in America. They would eventually spend hundreds of hours with him as he divulged everything he knew about Soviet espionage. (FBI)

Handcuffed and escorted by deputy marshals, Gold is led into Federal Court for appearance before Judge McGranery, May 1950. (Temple University Libraries, Urban Archives, Philadelphia)

Gold and an unidentified deputy marshal arriving for an appearance before Judge McGranery in Federal Court, May, 1950. (Temple University Libraries, Urban Archives, Philadelphia)

Thousands of Philadelphians gathered at the intersection of Ninth and Market Streets to get a glimpse of the atomic spy entering Federal Court in May 1950. (Temple University Libraries, Urban Archives, Philadelphia)

Newspapers across the country devoted banner headlines to Gold's arrest. The May 24, 1950, edition of the *Philadelphia Inquirer* signified the event's importance. (Author's private collection)

John Hamilton (seated) and Gus Ballard prepare documents for Gold's defense, June 1950. A seasoned litigator and corporate rainmaker, Hamilton took on the unpopular Gold case despite considerable criticism. Ballard, just a couple of years out of law school and a member of a famous legal family, was selected by Hamilton to assist him. (Temple University Libraries, Urban Archives, Philadelphia)

Federal Judge James McGranery (pictured here at an unrelated event) gave Gold a thirty-year sentence, five years more than the prosecution requested. (Temple University Libraries, Urban Archives, Philadelphia)

FBI Special Agent Robert Lamphere, 1950. FBI Director J. Edgar Hoover assigned Lamphere the difficult task of tracking down the man who had passed the secrets of the atomic bomb from Klaus Fuchs to Soviet agents. (NSA Cryptological Museum, Fort Mead, Maryland)

Ethel and Julius Rosenberg during their espionage trial in New York in March 1951. (AP/Wide World Photos, Temple University Libraries, Urban Archives, Philadelphia)

David Greenglass, Ethel Rosenberg's brother, in July 1950. When Gold arrived at Greenglass's Albuquerque address to pick up Manhattan Project secrets, he was surprised to see that his contact was an American soldier. (National Archives, landmark cases folder, College Park, Maryland)

One of Gold's obsessive-compulsive behaviors was his habit of writing detailed lists of things to do or, in this case, what he wanted emphasized in court. Lists were often rewritten many times. (Author's private collection)

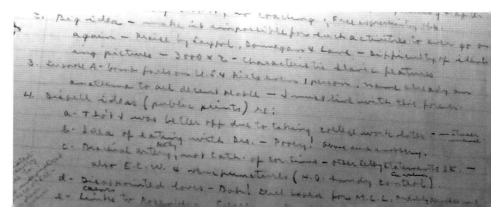

HARRY GOLD 19312-NE

19312 NE

By the time of his admission into Lewisburg Penitentiary in 1951, Harry Gold had lost considerable weight. Small, shy, and judged a traitor to his country, he was expected to have a difficult adjustment, according to his orientation papers. (Author's private collection)

Just after Harry's arrest in late May 1950, Joe Gold tries to comfort his distraught father. (Temple University Libraries, Urban Archives, Philadelphia)

While incarcerated at Lewisburg Federal Penitentiary, Gold periodically had his photo taken to send back home to his father and brother. This photo, taken in the late 1950s or early 1960s, underscores the passage of time behind bars. (National Archives and Records Administration, College Park, Maryland)

Joe trying to lift his father's spirits while Harry is in prison, early to mid-1960s. (Joseph Gold Papers, Special Collections, Temple University Libraries, Philadelphia)

Harry Gold (center) on his release from Lewisburg Federal Penitentiary in May 1966, accompanied by his attorney, Gus Ballard (left), and his brother, Joe (right). Though pelted by rain, Harry Gold said, "The sun is shining for me." (Temple University Libraries, Urban Archives, Philadelphia)

Harry Gold returning to his Northeast Philadelphia home in May 1966. He would be met by a phalanx of newspaper reporters and photographers hoping to capture the former spy's emotional reunion with his aged father after a sixteen-year separation. (Temple University Libraries, Urban Archives, Philadelphia)

Harry Gold during an interview with a reporter after his release from prison in 1966. (Temple University Libraries, Urban Archives, Philadelphia)

Harry Gold (far right) at a graduation celebration for new medical technicians at John F. Kennedy Hospital, c. 1970. (Joseph Gold Papers, Special Collections, Temple University Libraries, Philadelphia)

Gold and an unidentified student at the John F. Kennedy Hospital graduation, 1970. Though initially shunned by hospital staff, Gold quickly became a much loved and respected teacher, friend, and colleague. (Joseph Gold Papers, Special Collections, Temple University Libraries, Philadelphia)

by the Soviet's effort to reach out to him. A few weeks earlier, he "had received a couple of tickets in the mail, tickets to a prizefight in New York," the signal for an emergency meeting. The date on the tickets and the actual event were insignificant; the mere arrival of the tickets meant the recipient was to go to "a prearranged place at a prearranged time." In this case, however, Gold never showed up. Instead of being addressed to Gold's residence at 6823 Kindred Street in Philadelphia, it was sent to 6828 Kindred Street. By the time the letter reached Gold, he said, it was too late to make the rendezvous.

Entering the lounge at the Earle that night, Gold looked for John but was quickly approached by another man. He was a "large, rather tough looking character," who, said Gold, "moved very lightly . . . on the balls of his feet," giving a sort of "tigerish impression." He gruffly identified himself as "Paul" or "Pavel" and "handed Gold the torn piece of the sheet of paper containing the heading 'Arthur H. Thomas Company,'" which Gold and John had prepared as a recognition device.[26] Once they had established their bona fides, the Russian said: "Give me what you have from the doctor."[27]

Gold was taken aback by the demand. He hadn't seen or heard from Klaus Fuchs since he was in Santa Fe fifteen months earlier, but somehow the Soviets presumed that he had. When he said he had nothing, the man became "enraged"; Gold feared that the Russian would become violent. Fortunately, he regained his composure, leaned toward Gold, and whispered, "The Third Avenue Bar in an hour or as quick as you can get there."[28]

The bar at Third Avenue and Forty-second Street was another familiar meeting place; Harry and John had been there many times. Gold had been standing on the corner for only a few minutes when John showed up and suggested that they move to a restaurant in the twenties near Second Avenue. They sat at a booth, and John immediately apologized for the long break in communication. He did not mention that Soviet espionage operations in the United States had been curtailed because of the Gouzenko and Bentley disasters, saying only that "something serious had come up." Gold chose not to question him.

John asked if Gold had any news about Fuchs or any information of value. No, Harry replied, he hadn't seen Dr. Fuchs since his trip to Santa Fe more than a year earlier. John "seemed very disappointed," even annoyed, but said only, "Well, never mind."

At that point Gold brought up a piece of news he believed was relevant: Fuchs "had been questioned in Great Britain relating to giving information to the Soviet Union," according to an article in the *Herald Tribune* that, Harry said, he had not actually seen but had been told about (by Abe Brothman).[29] John reacted coldly, aware that Gold had been fed inaccurate information. To the best of his knowledge, no one knew of Fuchs's covert activities, and he wanted it to remain that way. (Brothman wasn't totally off the mark: Alan Nunn May, a British scientist of some standing, had been convicted of funneling information to the Soviets.)[30]

The Russian had no desire to prolong this discussion. The Soviet spy network had been fractured by the Gouzenko and Bentley defections, many GRU and NKVD colleagues had been sent back to Russia, and he too was being reassigned. Worse, there was a threat of more damage to come. John told Gold not to concern himself with such stories; the Soviet Union would "obtain aid for Klaus" if he should need it.[31]

John asked where Gold was now working. Presuming that he already knew, Gold replied, "Of course I am working for Abe as his chief chemist." The Russian agent was aghast, then apoplectic. Gold believed that the news "shocked him far more than the story about Klaus Fuchs, and he jumped up from the table as quickly as possible." In two years of dealing with him, Harry had never seen him so angry.

John asked, "Don't you know that this man is under extreme suspicion?"

"No," replied Gold, "I don't remember anything about it."

"I'm sure we must have told you," said John angrily. "You have wrecked everything. You have absolutely ruined years of work." He got up, and threw some bills on the table. While Gold fumbled for an explanation, John dashed out of the saloon, so excited that he didn't even realize he had left far more than the cost of their two drinks. Gold didn't bother with the money either; he chased after his Soviet boss as fast as he could. On the street, John was only slightly less angry. Gold couldn't get a word in as John repeated that he "had wrecked eleven years of preparation by his foolish move." Scheduled to depart the next day for France, where he was to assume new duties at the Soviet embassy in Paris, John was no doubt delighted to be extricating himself from this "disaster."[32]

Gold felt terrible. He hated to disappoint people, and "this seemed to have affected [John] far more than anything" else he could remember. So much so, in fact, that it kept him from giving Gold a new assignment, which he had assumed was the real reason for the meeting. Harry could only surmise that by going to work for Brothman, he had somehow exposed himself. In fact, he had done exactly that. Unaware of developments in the Gouzenko and Bentley cases, he was never properly coached by Soviet agents as to how he should proceed now that the FBI had intensified its efforts to uncover Soviet spies and their American contacts. The Russians had cut off all communications with him many months earlier, possibly believing that, as one of their more experienced operatives, he was savvy enough to recognize that Bentley's explosive relationship with Brothman presented a hazard. Yet whether through naiveté, his need for a job, or his desire to be the chief chemist of a laboratory, Gold had publicly reunited with Brothman. It was a decision for which he would pay dearly. At the time, however, he just tried to block the unfortunate episode from his mind. As he would tell his lawyers years later, "I actually thought no further of the incident at all."[33] He continued to work at A. Brothman & Associates.

But Brothman was indeed a person of interest to the FBI.

A "master mind of Soviet espionage"

During the winter and spring of 1947, Gold's primary concern—shared with all the employees at Brothman's firm—was whether they would get paid. The business never lived up to its founder's grandiose vision. During the last week of May, however, Brothman's financial concerns would take a back seat to a far more serious event, a visit by two federal agents investigating his relationship with the self-proclaimed spy Elizabeth Bentley.

Gold had been in the lab all day when he had to get some data from the public library in Manhattan. Afterward, he decided to stop by the office and see Brothman. He ran into a co-worker on the street who told him "some government men were there questioning Abe." Gold wasn't alarmed; he figured it was the Internal Revenue Service investigating another of Brothman's occasionally dubious tax returns. When he entered the office, however, he could see that the situation was far more serious. "Brothman was in a state of almost feverish excitement."

He grabbed Gold and said, "Look Harry, the whole thing is up. The FBI was just here. They know all about us. They know that you are a courier. They even had pictures of you and I. Look, we have got to tell the same story."[34] He and Gold were in serious trouble. "It must have been Helen who ratted."

The agents were at that moment headed over to the Elmhurst lab to interview Gold; Brothman had had to promise them that he would not talk to Harry of their conversation. It was imperative he get his story right. Harry had to tell the FBI that he knew Jacob Golos, Bentley's deceased lover, and that he and Brothman were just two innocent chemists who were contracted to assess chemical processes and had hoped to solicit additional business. Brothman then gave him a "pretty accurate description of a photograph which the FBI had shown him" of Jacob Golos.

On the subway back to the lab a million things ran through Gold's head, but he was pretty sure he could outwit the agents. The twenty-five-minute ride back to the lab allowed him time to cook up a plausible story to tell the investigators. Two FBI agents, Don Shannon and Frank O'Brien, arrived at the lab shortly after Gold. Apparently they didn't even know what Gold looked like: when they entered the lab, they scanned everyone there and then asked, "Is Mr. Gold here, Mr. Harry Gold?"[35]

Gold identified himself. The agents said they'd like to talk to him, preferably after everyone, including Miriam Moskowitz, had left for the day. The interrogation session began at about five-thirty and lasted until almost nine o'clock. Gold told the FBI that at an American Chemical Society meeting in Philadelphia in either 1940 or 1941, Carter Hoodless, the son of one of the owners of the Pennsylvania Sugar Company, had introduced him to a man named John Golos. Later that day, the two men met at a restaurant and talked for several hours about chemistry and potential business prospects. Golos said he was a mechanical engineer always on the lookout for good opportunities; he knew of a chemical engineer, Abe Brothman, and was anxious "to check the validity of some processes which Brothman had devised." Gold told the agents that Golos asked him to investigate Brothman's authenticity and evaluate his work product.

Gold believed that this story was both plausible and safe, especially since neither Hoodless nor Golos would deny his claims, as both were dead. Though shaken by the lengthy interrogation, he thought his story had passed muster. After the agents had left, Brothman and Moskowitz came back to the laboratory to ask Gold how it had gone. Moskowitz "assured Brothman that Gold had been extremely nonchalant when the agents arrived." The trio then went to Sunny's, a Chinese restaurant on Queens Boulevard, to assess their respective performances. Somewhat guiltily, Brothman asked, "Harry, you don't blame me for having brought your name into this, do you?"[36] Brothman explained that he figured "they would eventually uncover you and it would be better" if he brought it up "in the very beginning." He knew that Gold had worked as a Soviet courier, but he did not know the extent of his activities. Gold's decision to take the Brothman position over the Navy Yard offer was coming back to haunt him.

Either that night or the next, while Brothman and Moskowitz were driving Gold to Penn Station, "a heated argument concerning Tom Black" broke out between the two men. Voices were raised, accusations were hurled, and "a fist fight almost resulted," prevented only by Moskowitz's intercession. Brothman blamed Gold for bringing Black into his orbit. Black had first heard of Brothman a few years earlier, when Gold thought he might be accepted by the military and broached the notion of Black's taking on a new supplier. Once he went to work for Brothman, Gold informed Black that his boss "was an expert on mixing machinery and continuous processes" and, more important, "was designing a penicillin production plant for Russia."[37] This caught Black's attention, for in 1942 he was traveling the country obtaining information on biologicals for the Soviet Union.[38]

Gold brought Black to Brothman's laboratory on a couple of occasions during the spring of 1947, and Brothman was won over; he offered Black a job as a consultant. He needed an experienced chemist who was willing to travel to Russia to get the penicillin plant up and running. Black listened but declined the offer. Though disappointed, "Brothman did not press the issue any further." Now that he was the focus of a federal grand jury investigation, Brothman feared that Black might have been behind his legal problems. He considered Black a serious player, maybe even a "master mind of Soviet espionage," and at the very least an informer.[39]

"They were phony"

Gold tried to disabuse Brothman of this notion, but he had his own problems. He had to return to Philadelphia, as he had obligingly given the FBI permission to search his home on Kindred Street. Once there, he quickly tried to throw out as much incriminating material as possible. For an inveterate collector who rarely even discarded old train ticket stubs, it was impossible task. Two agents from the FBI's Philadelphia office arrived at his home on Memorial Day, 1947, and conducted what he would later call "the most cursory search." They were looking only for drawings from Brothman's former employer the Hendrick Company.[40] This superficial search would turn out to be a major blunder by the Bureau, for Gold's house was littered with remnants of his excursions around the country in behalf of the Soviets. A dutiful undercover operative on the road, he nevertheless neglected to destroy many artifacts of his dealings with Brothman, Slack, Fuchs, and others. A more thorough investigation would have turned up Kodak documents, appointment schedules, blueprints of mixing equipment, some of Slack's work, cross-country train tickets, and street maps of cities in New Mexico. But the agents, working on a holiday and in the home of a diminutive, moon-faced bachelor with heavy-lidded eyes and an obsequious manner, no doubt thought they were dealing with a most unlikely security threat.

Brothman, however, was becoming increasingly irritated. Summoned to appear before the federal jury, he had second thoughts as the date approached. He felt the entire thing was "ridiculous, that a farce was being perpetrated," and he wasn't about to "lie and squirm" on the witness stand. He planned on making "a clean breast of the whole matter" and own up to his relationship with Golos.[41] Several days later, at Topsy's Restaurant on Queens Boulevard, Moskowitz informed Gold that she and Gibby Needleman, Brothman's attorney, had finally succeeded in convincing Brothman of the foolhardiness of testifying that he had given information to the Soviet Union.[42]

On July 22, 1947, Brothman appeared before the grand jury. He was forced to admit he had been a member of the Young Communist League and had done some business with Jacob Golos, as well as his secretary, a woman named Helen. He had given her blueprints of mixing devices, but explained that everything he supplied was equipment he had developed himself and already part of the published literature in the field. Brothman appeared to be on shakier ground when he was unable to explain why he didn't know Golos's business address, or for that matter Helen's. And even though he had met her at Manhattan restaurants a dozen times, he did not know her last name. He said Harry Gold was someone he had hired after meeting him through Golos. It was Gold, in fact, who had warned him against Golos and Helen, saying that he was "very suspicious of them" and that "they were phony." Gold had told him that they "couldn't deliver on these big promises" and that he and Brothman "were wasting our time" dealing with them. Over time, said Brothman, he started paying Gold to do research that he couldn't do himself but that Gold could do at the more sophisticated Pennsylvania Sugar laboratory. When the sugar company let Gold go, Brothman decided to hire him as his firm's chief chemist.[43]

Ill at ease and on the defensive early, Brothman became more confident as the questioning progressed. He adopted a strategy of obfuscation that Gold would employ as well. When asked a question about Gold's relationship to Golos and Helen, he launched into a convoluted disquisition that incorporated everything from "the tremendous cost in money and labor" of developing a patent and the difficulty of acquiring license agreements in England to the Belgian Army and the complexity of foreign royalty rights. Obviously exasperated, the prosecutor finally cut him off, saying, "I do not think that is necessary. I think we have enough."[44] Broth-man was impressed with his own performance and boasted to confeder-ates that he had "neither cringed, flinched, or begged."[45]

If the weak-kneed Brothman was able to tap dance around the pros-ecutor's questions, Harry Gold was Fred Astaire. He held firm to his story of meeting Golos at an American Chemical Society function and follow-ing up on the Russian's request that he determine whether this Broth-man fellow was pushing "paper chemistry" or was on to "something that was really sound." When asked if he was a member of the Communist Party or "any Communist-front organizations," Gold could sincerely reply, "I would never belong to anything like that." He hit a low point when he asserted that despite doing work for Golos, he never had his address or phone number, but amply rebounded. Appearing harmless and well in-tentioned, he was willing to go into great depth about arcane aspects of chemistry. He gave long answers about Dr. Reich's work habits at Penn-sylvania Sugar and the many uses of "urea formaldehyde cold setting glue" and other obscure chemicals—answers that surely bored the mem-bers of the grand jury.[46] Once a timid youth who feared neighborhood games around the train tracks, Gold deftly parried the prosecutor's ques-tions in a setting that would have terrified most people.

To the government's chagrin, the coordinated performances of Broth-man and Gold were a complete success. Without corroboration of Bent-ley's allegation, the grand jury returned no bill of indictment. Gold had hoped to appear as an innocent chemist, at worst a "blunderer" ensnared by people and events he didn't quite comprehend. "Far from blunder-ing," as Richard Rhodes notes, Gold's "skillful evasions had thrown off the grand jury," allowing him and Brothman to walk.[47]

As Gold would admit several years later, "I tried, and I think very suc-cessfully, to give the impression of a small, scared individual who had been involved just on the fringe, possibly, who had been approached about Soviet espionage, but who had gotten frightened and possibly never even committed an overt act and had never done anything."[48] Neverthe-less, his grand jury appearance put him on the FBI's radar screen. He appeared to be no more than a fringe player, but it was enough to cause at least one agent at the Bureau to remember him.

"A big money man"

With the end of summer in 1947, Gold began to feel that all government heat—from both Americans and Russians—was off. He and Brothman

had evaded the FBI's web, and months had passed since he last heard
from any Soviet agents. Maybe he could get back to what he enjoyed the
most: working in the lab. He was putting in so many hours that his mother
said he was beginning to "look like a walking ghost." Because of Brothman's nocturnal lifestyle, Gold would end up with Brothman in the lab at
two, three, and four in the morning, working and talking. Alarmed at this
"atrocious schedule of hours," his mother became worried that his health
"would break completely under the strain." Compounding the problem
was the growing frequency of missed pay periods. Gold found himself, he
later recalled, "digging into my own savings and into my family's savings
to continue working in New York."[49]

On September 27, 1947, he was called at work with the painful news
that his mother had died of a severe brain hemorrhage while hanging
clothes in the backyard of her beloved Kindred Street home. Celia Gold
was only sixty-one, but she had a long history of hypertension and heart
problems. With the stabilizing rock and galvanizing force of the Gold
household now gone, her husband and her two bachelor sons would have
to make do on their own. It would not be an easy transition.

Celia's well-attended funeral, at Har Nebo Cemetery, brought sur-
prises for some of those who had gathered to pay their last respects. In
addition to neighbors and Harry's former co-workers from the Pennsylvania Sugar Company, there were representatives from the Brothman
firm in New York, and Tom Black from North Jersey. For Moskowitz, the
most interesting aspect was not who showed up but who did not: she
thought it odd that Harry's wife and children were not there—or at the
shiva house later that week. Even an estranged wife, she thought, should
come at a time like this. And who was this young man named Joe? Could
he really be Harry's younger brother, the paratrooper who was supposedly
shot down in the South Pacific during the war? She asked Brothman what
was going on, but he shrugged off her questions.[50]

Gold would have to deal with the unraveling of his lies at some point,
but just then his greatest regret was the vast amount of time he had spent
away from his mother and the many lies he had told her to explain his absences. The more he thought about how much of his life he had wasted
on his far-flung errands as a Soviet courier, the more he realized, as he
would subsequently write, "the damage I had done." He began to see
"the full implications involved in this spying, and to come grimly to the
horrible and sickening realization that it had all been such a tragic and irremediable mistake."[51]

That winter Gold tried to support and console his brother and elderly father from his base of operations in Manhattan and Long Island. He spent most weekends in Philadelphia. His brother was working at the Northeast Philadelphia Naval Air Supply Depot near their home, only a block from their mother's grave. Yus was also dealing with recurring bouts of malaria, contracted in the South Pacific. There were no more federal agents snooping around or meetings with Soviet operatives, allowing Gold to concentrate on the Brothman firm's business projects, but the company's revenue stream was anemic. By spring 1948 a number of employees were going unpaid. Brothman, for all his brilliance as a chemical engineer, was no entrepreneur, and his businesses seemed to survive on a shoestring.[52] Now there was the threat that his latest firm would not survive.

Things came to a head in late May when Brothman and Moskowitz took a weeklong trip to Switzerland. The excursion was ostensibly designed to foster some contracts for the firm, but others in the office were dubious. Gold was especially hurt; as the chief chemist, he thought he should be the one to accompany Brothman. He couldn't figure how a secretary merited such a role. She was also a part owner, but so were many of her co-workers. When others at the firm found documents that appeared to show Brothman entertaining the notion of selling the business, heated arguments broke out. Employees felt their economic futures in jeopardy.

Gold had always admired Brothman's creativity and intellect. He had enjoyed spending time with Abe and his wife, Naomi, at their house in the city and their summer home in the mountains; he liked working with Abe in the lab and enjoyed going to ball games with him; but he hadn't been paid in almost a year. He claimed Brothman "owed him approximately $4,000 in back pay." Now that he had "more or less abandoned all hope of ever getting it," Gold figured it was time to go back home, rejoin his aged father and brother, and get a paying job. On June 2, 1948, he quit and returned to Philadelphia.[53] Brothman reacted to his departure with a number of parting shots. One of them was a recommendation that Gold remember the story he had told the grand jury about Golos.[54]

"I had never been happier"

Gold was not only leaving New York; he was also leaving industrial chemistry. He was about to enter the world of biochemistry and two of the most rewarding years of his life.

His new job came by way of Beatrice Schied, a former Pennsylvania

Sugar employee who was friends with Jean Lookabaugh and Morrell Dougherty. Gold and Schied had met on various occasions over the years, and he was sufficiently taken with her to ask her out on dates, but his overtures were always turned down. When she learned that he was returning to Philadelphia, she suggested to her friends that he check out Philadelphia General Hospital. Her own position had just been terminated there, but she knew they wanted a biochemist for a new heart project that had just received funding. She had heard good things about his competence and professionalism from Lookabaugh and Dougherty and had no difficulty in recommending him for the job.[55]

Gold began work on September 20, 1948, as a senior research biochemist at PGH's Heart Station. This quickly proved to be a most agreeable career move. After Brothman's small operation, the old city hospital was a beehive of activity. He found the projects interesting and important, and the staff friendly and dedicated. Drs. Thomas McMillan and Samuel Bellet were accomplished physicians and serious researchers dedicated to fighting heart disease. The many other doctors and researchers Gold interacted with were equally committed and talented. Co-workers found him a good fit for the unit. They described him as "pleasant," an "excellent worker," and "the type of individual who would do anyone in the Heart Station a favor at any time."[56] He quickly became known for his generosity and his long hours. Decades later, former PGH personnel still remembered him. "He was a bit of a withdrawn figure," recalled Dr. Robert Stone, a medical intern at the time. "Gold was a quiet, chubby, unassuming character who always wore drab clothing. I often saw him fiddling with an electrocardiogram machine in the Heart Station."[57] Dr. Richard Monheit, then just starting out as a cardiologist, spent considerable time in the Heart Station. He remembers Gold as "very quiet, and reserved. You'd never hear any spontaneous chatter from him. He spent a lot of time doing electrolyte studies and the impact of potassium on electrolytes with Dr. Bellet." Monheit recalled that Gold "didn't mingle much, never talked politics, and seemed to be very self contained. He was very devoted; he'd always be working on something."[58] One doctor remembered him for donating "a small scale such as druggists use to measure milligram weights" when the Heart Station wasn't able to procure one of its own.[59]

Gold gave more than scientific instruments. The unit's tests of new medical theories and experimental techniques required steady supplies of blood. Since he did "not like the idea of going into the wards and taking [blood from] people indiscriminately" and regarded himself as "readily available," he began to take his own blood and encourage the doctors and nurses to do the same. He had at least one painful "arterial stick" and volunteered for several others, which the nurses "refused to do."[60]

Gold would say of those two years, "I had never been happier . . . in my life."[61]

PGH supplied Gold not only with a paycheck and scientific mission but also with a love interest. Her name was Mary Catherine Lanning, and she was a biological chemist who came from "an extremely fine family."[62] Although she wasn't Jewish—she was Presbyterian—Gold was immediately taken with her and would always remember the day and time he first laid eyes on her: it was late on a Friday afternoon in September 1948. "It really happened . . . just like that," he would write of the event several years later. "I knew that here was the girl I had been searching for all my life." Gold introduced himself, and the two colleagues started dating. The more he got to know her, the more intense his feelings became. "The wish to make her my wife," he admitted later, "became an overpowering drive in life."[63]

Gold was smitten; he cherished "her unassuming manner, forthright honesty, and complete lack of artificiality." And her "snub nose completely captivated me." He "could have gone on for hours" listing her attributes, but there was a shadow over the glorious visions he had for the two of them. "Even at the very beginning a warning bell sounded. Suppose that the Federal Grand Jury investigation in the summer of 1947 is really not the end of all inquiry into my life? And who knew better than I on what a precarious tottering house of cards my whole life rested." Gold said he realized from the beginning there was something holding him back, and Lanning often remarked that he "never seemed to be totally relaxed and at ease in her presence. But she never suspected the true cause."[64]

"Later, when we became much more intimate," he would write,

and after I had proposed marriage for the first time in August of 1949, Lanning remarked that only once, during a walk along the upper Wissahickon (section of Fairmount Park), did I seem completely natural; at this time she came very close to accepting me. However, at our next meeting several days later during a trip to the Poconos, I froze altogether—yes, I froze as badly as a tyro on a high scaffold; and Lanning complained that I did not really love her, and cited my lack of ardor, it was fear of exposure; and fear not for myself, but a horror at the thought that the disastrous revelation might come after we had been married for, say, 3 or 4 years, with children and a home of our own. It might then be asked why I, perceiving all this, continued to see Lanning. To this I can only feebly reply that I was hopelessly and genuinely in love.

Further, I knew this: What Lanning fancied was lack of ardor was really also an awareness of the fact that I could never marry her without telling of the whole miserable story of my past. This I knew I had to do; I loved her far too much to be so cruelly unfair as to conceal it. But strangely enough, I did not fear that she would turn away from me because of what I had done. No, mistaken as these deeds had been, I honestly thought that Lanning, if truly in love with me, would find it in her to forgive me, particularly since these acts had been so well intentioned.[65]

Tormented by his love for Lanning and the terrifying fear of exposure, Gold "cast around for a source of advice." To whom does one turn in such an exceptional situation? Ironically, he gravitated toward the Catholic Church. As he would write of this distressing time years later, "The only ones I could think of were the Jesuit priests at Xavier University, and in particular, Father Mahoney, who had done so much to open up the beautiful world of English literature to me." Father Mahoney was somebody he felt he "could talk to in confidence," even though he was not a Catholic. Still, he kept postponing the trip to Xavier.[66]

Another option was the parish priest at St. Ambrose, a church along Roosevelt Boulevard near Gold's old Feltonville home. Harry was in the habit of talking with the priest every morning in front of the church while waiting for the bus to take him to work. They had also met one day on the campus of the University of Pennsylvania near PGH, and the priest asked him to drop by the church when he had time. Gold promised he would, but never did. Much as he wanted to, he never confided in either priest; he "just kept putting it off. Besides," he would admit later, "I had the awful certainty that their counsel would only amount to one thing: Go and make a clean breast of it to the authorities."[67]

If Gold did make such a dramatic revelation, if he divulged everything, what would happen then? He thought he'd "disappear—vanish completely" in the hands of the FBI. And how would the news affect his father and brother? If it didn't kill them outright, he thought they might "go crazy" from shock and embarrassment. He knew he "was not being very logical," but how could one be rational in such a "state of confusion and mental agitation"?

And how would the news affect his PGH colleagues, whom he had become so fond of? Dr. McMillan, the "infinitely gentle . . . white-haired chief of the Heart Station would recoil in horror if the news should come out. And Dr. Bellet, so absorbed in pursuing cardiac research" when he could have had twice the income in private practice. The cardiologists had trusted Gold, allowed him to build up the lab, and provided him with a workplace that could be a "lasting source of happiness." And Drs. Bill Steiger, Harold Rowland, Isidore Cohen, and John Urbach—how would they react? Urbach had come to the United States as a boy, a "refugee from Hitler's Austria"; he was "so anti-Communist, what would he think?"

Gold already knew the answer. "I confess," he would write, "I just could not bring my courage up to the point where a voluntary admission of my crime would ensue. It was cowardly, true, but until forced to by circumstances, there could be no disclosure to the authorities; such was my mental environment."[68] His work, as usual, became his solace and escape: long hours, dedication to detail, unfailing friendliness, and offering of himself as a periodic test subject for clinical trials. In return, he was awarded with a promotion, a salary increase, and greater job security. But the sword of Damocles was about to fall.

. . . .

CHAPTER 9

The Hunt for Raymond

The ringing startled Gold awake. He had fallen fast asleep on the living room couch; he tried to regain his senses. The ringing sounded again, and he realized it wasn't the phone, it was the doorbell. He gathered himself and wondered who could be visiting this late on a Saturday night.

Gold hadn't arrived home until after seven, exhausted from a long workweek at the Philadelphia General Hospital lab. After washing up, he donned his pajamas and had a sandwich and some coffee. He looked forward to lounging in his pajamas, watching television, or listening to music with his father. His brother Yus, though still feeling the effects of malaria, had decided to go out with some friends. For Gold, these quiet evenings after a long day of work were much appreciated.

Realizing his father must have gone up to bed, Harry moved toward the door and opened it, expecting to see the boy who delivered butter and cheese on Saturday evenings. A stranger stood there. "He mumbled something that I couldn't understand and thought at first that it was some solicitor." There were many new homes in the area, and salesmen had become a constant nuisance.[1] As Gold began to close the door, the man said, "Remember John and the Doctor in New York."[2] Despite the stranger's heavy accent, Gold understood the message. The man showed Gold a piece of paper with directions for contacting him. It was "torn in a jagged fashion," and Gold "recognized it as an identifying piece of paper" he had given Sam Semenov years before. Somewhere in his own vast, disordered collection of papers was the other half.

Gold let the man in. He was an inch or two taller than Harry, about 175 pounds, well built, with "classic Slavic" features. He took a seat and asked if Gold had any information for him. Even without further prompting, Gold knew that he meant information from Klaus Fuchs.[3] Gold was surprised; he hadn't dealt with or heard from Fuchs for years, and told the Russian that. The man appeared disappointed but asked Gold how he had been. Gold replied that he had been well, enjoyed being back in Philadelphia with his father and brother, and was especially pleased with his new job.

When the Russian asked what kind of work he was now doing, Gold said he was a research biochemist at PGH. The Soviet agent made a dismissive-sounding comment in Russian and asked, "Can't you get a job in industry where you may be of some use?"[4] Gold stuttered, searching for an appropriate response, but seething inside. He had no intention of leaving his job at PGH and would have liked nothing better than to forget his past work for the Soviets.

The Russian then asked, "Why didn't you keep the meeting?" Did he not receive a letter notifying him of a forthcoming meeting? Gold "fumbled around" and finally said that he had forgotten just where the meeting was to be held. He had, in fact, received a letter earlier that summer with the address of the Prince George or St. George Hotel in Brooklyn Heights. The letter had been signed "John" and said only that the writer was back in New York and looking forward to seeing him. Gold had done his best to forget it. He had no interest in attending any more meetings or doing any more secret work for the Soviet Union. He wanted an end to that business, but the Russian now in his living room persisted. He proceeded, Gold recalled, to "bawl me out": "Don't you know that three days after the date on the letter that you are to be in the vicinity of Borough Hall in Brooklyn?"[5]

Gold was no neophyte; he knew the drill. No doubt the Russians had something in mind for him, and it soon came out. His visitor asked him about the grand jury appearance in 1947. What had Gold and Brothman told the grand jury? Gold was taken aback. As he told his lawyers two years later, "While none of this had appeared in the paper and as far as I know none of it is a matter of public record, still this man appeared to have a pretty complete idea of the testimony that I had given and that Brothman had given before the grand jury."[6]

The Russian soon left, but not before telling Gold they would have to meet again, this time in New York. Gold was no doubt sickened by the thought of starting up with the Soviets again, but he must have believed in the Soviets' capacity and willingness to expose him as a secret agent. Perhaps if he had stood his ground and threatened to expose his own work with the Russians, particularly his role in passing along the secrets of the atomic bomb, they would have backed off. The Gouzenko and Bentley defections had done great damage; they didn't need another such blow. But in Gold's tormented and fearful mind, there was little chance of such an escape. The agent's willingness to come direct to his home was proof of that. From his perspective, they were both ruthless and relentless. And though he was never physically threatened, the assassination of Trotsky, the suspicious death of Soviet spy Walter Krivitsky, and other chilling reports he must have heard over the years were enough to spark concern for his own and his family's safety. He felt he had no choice but to comply.

The next meeting would take place on Main Street in Flushing, at the end of the Flushing elevated train line. He was to be on a specific corner at 10:00 A.M. on the first Sunday of the month, and then every other month thereafter. Arrangements were also set up for how Gold should make contact in an emergency.

Worse, the Russians had grown extremely cautious. Gold was to "arrive in New York the day before, not register at any hotel, but spend the day and night wandering around from one cafeteria to another and to make sure he was not being trailed." Only then, and after several evasive measures near the meeting place, should he show up for the ten o'clock meeting.[7] As he listened to the bizarre plan, he made up his mind that he would never utilize it. All he wanted was to "completely wipe out the past" and marry Mary Lanning. As he would tell his lawyers, "There was enough that I would have to tell her before I married her, without getting further involved. In addition, I had, to a great extent, lost a good deal of faith in the good intentions of the Soviet Union."

Nonetheless, Gold followed the Russian's directives and traveled to New York for two meetings. The first was on October 6, 1949, in Forest Hills, Queens. Though it was raining heavily and Gold was without an overcoat, the two men walked the streets for hours. At first, Gold was pumped for more information about his 1947 grand jury appearance. He tried to reassure the KGB agent that the jurors had viewed him as "a well-meaning dupe" with only the slightest connection to anything nefarious.[8] The Russian cautioned him about the supposed naiveté of American jurors and then remarked that it might be best if he left the country. Gold was stunned. The Russian agent explained why the trip was necessary and how it would be orchestrated: Gold would go first to Mexico and then eventually to a country in Eastern Europe before finally, perhaps, ending up in Russia. He would be given money to live on, and his needs would be taken care of "should an emergency arise." At the end of the long walk, Gold was not only drenched but "horrified" and "speechless."[9]

The next meeting occurred a little over two weeks later, on October 23, near the Bronx Zoo. Gold was told to use extreme caution and be sure to follow the established meeting schedule. Even if no one showed up to meet him, someone would be there to "observe that he was still at large and had not been arrested." It was a tense time.

"Unusual and brilliant"

When President Harry Truman announced to the world on September 23, 1949, on the heels of the stunning Communist victory in China, that the Soviet Union had exploded an atomic device, it was shocking news. America's nuclear monopoly had lasted only four years. Joseph Stalin, no longer our ally but an increasingly fearsome adversary, now had the power to destroy cities at will. Few had predicted the Russians would master the intricacies of manufacturing an atom bomb so soon. As America's nascent counterintelligence community debated whether the Soviets had breached the Manhattan Project, a secret Russian cable, deciphered by a team of cryptanalysts, seemed to prove exactly that: information about the construction of the bomb had been smuggled out of Los Alamos.

Of the two scientific breakthroughs—America's code breaking and Soviet nuclear advances—Russia's possession of the bomb was clearly more newsworthy. Only a handful of people knew that the United States had cracked the code the Soviets used to transmit their diplomatic cables. As John Earl Haynes and Harvey Klehr write in their definitive account of Soviet codes and the American effort to break them, what came to be known as the Venona Project originated during the war, out of the fear that "a separate peace between Moscow and Berlin would allow Nazi Germany to concentrate its formidable war machine against the United States and Great Britain."[10] An elite group of army code breakers was organized to examine all diplomatic cablegrams between the United States and Moscow and try to determine if Stalin was planning such an agreement with Hitler.

Breaking the Soviet code proved an onerous task. As Haynes and Klehr explain, the Soviets used "a complex two-part ciphering system involving a 'one-time pad' code that in theory was unbreakable." Even with intense analysis and the "painstaking examination of thousands of coded telegraphic cables," the challenge appeared too imposing until a Soviet procedural error allowed a point of interpretive entry. Ironically, by the time the first messages had been translated into readable text, the war was over, and the original purpose of the effort was forgotten. But the deciphered messages proved alarming in a different way: the Soviets had mounted a major espionage campaign against the United States. More shocking yet, early messages seemed to confirm that they had placed agents inside the Manhattan Project.

Almost overnight, the Venona Project became a top priority, known only to very few people. The effort was housed in Arlington Hall, a former girls' school across the Potomac from the District of Columbia. Scores of people were involved, led by an "unusual and brilliant" college professor, Meredith Gardner, who spoke seven languages, including Sanskrit, and had spent the war breaking Japanese codes. To facilitate this, he had shocked his colleagues by learning Japanese in just three months.

The Soviet codes would prove equally imposing. Under Gardner's direction, the Army Security Agency (ASA) team chipped away at seemingly inscrutable messages, slowly deciphering words and occasionally phrases. Meanings remained elusive because of the fragmentary nature of the messages—complicated by the Soviets' extensive use of code names for everything from individuals to institutions and places. Teasing meaningful sentences from the mazelike codes was a singularly complicated mission.

One item that proved invaluable in this exercise was a partially burned Russian codebook discovered by the Finns on a battlefield in 1944. William Donovan, then head of the Office of Strategic Services, purchased hundreds of pages of it and turned them over to the ASA. By the end of the war the Soviets had changed their codes, but the codebook proved a priceless point of reference for Gardner.

One of the few people outside the ASA who were aware of the Venona Project was Robert J. Lamphere, a young FBI supervisor who had been assigned to act as a liaison between the Bureau and the ASA. Initially, relations between Lamphere and the "shy, introverted" Gardner were rather cool, but as progress was made, a friendship developed. Each week, beginning with that decisive moment in 1948 when Gardner made his breakthrough, Lamphere would receive "additional deciphered messages and new fragments of messages" that had been partially deciphered earlier. As messages were read, ongoing investigations could be developed and new ones set in motion.

As Lamphere would write years later, "I stood in the vestibule of the enemy's house, having entered by stealth. I held in my hand a set of keys. Each would fit one of the doors of the place and lead us, I hoped, to matters of importance to our country. I had no idea where the corridors in the KGB's edifice would take us, or what we would find when we reached the end of a search—but the keys were ours, and we were determined to use them."[11]

"A man interested only in his work"

Early in September 1949, before the president's announcement of the Soviet atomic explosion, a newly deciphered cable from 1944 suggested that the Russians had been collecting "data and theories" from directly inside the Manhattan Project. This one-two punch—the KGB message and the news of a Russian atomic bomb—confirmed for Lamphere that the "Russians had indeed stolen crucial research" from the United States.[12]

With the help of Ernie Van Loon, another FBI agent, Lamphere aggressively tracked down the few leads the message provided toward the identity of the mole inside the Manhattan Project. These clues suggested the KGB had placed "an agent within the British Mission" in 1944 and that he had probably been part of the bomb development effort in both New York and Los Alamos. Three scientists quickly came under suspicion; two of them were Rudolf Peierls and Klaus Fuchs. Additional information—a captured Gestapo document identifying Fuchs as a German Communist who should be arrested on sight, and Fuchs's name in an address book belonging to a Canadian Communist who had been discovered through the Gouzenko papers—seemed to confirm that Fuchs was the Soviet spy.[13]

Lamphere prepared a secret letter to British intelligence saying that a deciphered message and two additional pieces of information pointed to Fuchs as the prime suspect.

Fuchs was among a handful of British scientists who had worked at Los Alamos and had now set up shop at Harwell, Great Britain's Atomic Energy Research Establishment. Harwell was an old Royal Air Force airfield on the windswept Berkshire Downs, fifty-five miles from London and eighteen miles from Oxford. Fuchs had arrived there in early August 1946 with a comfortable salary, especially for a bachelor, and a newfound sense of security and stability. He was more sure of himself, "no longer alienated from his surroundings," and at ease with his growing number of friends and professional colleagues. As one of his biographers wrote, he now "had a homeland and not just a country of asylum, a career and not just a job."[14] One holdover from his old habits, however, was his continuing effort to funnel secret atomic information to the Soviets.

Fuchs became a well-known personage at Harwell: tall, pale, with a receding hairline and a seemingly imperturbable manner as he strode the grounds from one building to another. He was viewed as ascetic, serious, scholarly, and unmarried, "a man interested only in his work." He was known for his remarkable memory. Those unable to attend formal presentations often asked him to recount what was said. Invariably and without any difficulty, he "went over the whole lecture, bringing in all the points in the correct order." It seemed he didn't forget anything.

During Britain's harsh winter of 1946–47, Fuchs was able to have a brief reunion with his brother, Gerhard. English cities were still cratered and strewn with rubble from bombings, food and fuel shortages were common, and the weather was ghastly. Peierls and his wife decided to escape the gloomy scene by taking a skiing holiday in Switzerland, and they asked Fuchs to join them. He did and was able to meet his brother for the first time in more than a decade. Gerhard was sick with the tuberculosis that would take his life a few years later. Still a Communist, he told Klaus he planned to move to the Soviet-controlled section of Germany. On his return to England, whether motivated by this conversation or simply doing what he had always planned, Fuchs started to provide the Russians with information.

One of the first pieces of news he passed along was something unknown to most cabinet ministers: Britain had embarked on its own atomic bomb project. It is likely that "few people at Harwell—perhaps no one —knew as much about Atomic Bombs as Fuchs, so he was assigned to do the theoretical work." Once again the Soviets had extraordinary luck. Their man at Harwell was near the top of the British scientific food chain. He periodically informed them about plutonium production rates, details of a new plutonium reactor being built, and the problems associated with spontaneous fission in plutonium. He kept them abreast of data he was collecting on the Hiroshima and Nagasaki bombs, and the progress on Britain's first fast breeder reactor. All of this proved tremendously valuable to the Soviets at a time when Stalin had made the development of an atomic bomb a top priority.

When British scientists heard the news that the Soviet Union had successfully tested an atomic device, they were as shocked as their American counterparts. Most were "dumbfounded; some suggested foul play" and a leak at Los Alamos. Fuchs told his colleagues the Russians might have discovered a theoretical "short-cut," saving them many unnecessary steps, but he was as surprised as everyone else that the Soviets had achieved atomic success so quickly. His miscalculation was similar to the one he had made with the Americans: "he had underestimated not their scientists, but their industrial capacity."

In September Fuchs learned his father had accepted a professorship in the theology department at the University of Leipzig. The school was in the Soviet-occupied zone—what would soon be known as the German Democratic Republic. His father's new post presented Fuchs with a sobering set of concerns. Could he confidently and securely lead the British quest for the atomic bomb while his father held an academic position in a Communist country? What was the potential for blackmail or other forms of pressure? He began a series of discussions with a Harwell security officer, Henry Arnold. Arnold liked Fuchs and enjoyed his company but always sensed something strange about him. He felt their relationship contained an element of "game-playing." As he would say years later, "I can't call him a friend exactly, but I had affection for him. . . . Well, was it affection? More than friendship, I felt sorry for him, because I knew for a long time how it would end."[15]

"Controlled schizophrenia"

His father's new post turned out to be the least of Fuchs's concerns. MI5's counterespionage branch had quickly agreed with the FBI's assessment that Fuchs was a likely Soviet spy. They kept him under surveillance, tapped his phone, and informed Arnold of their suspicions. Arnold was still having friendly chats with Fuchs; on occasion he was sure that the scientist was going to relinquish his prestigious position at Harwell. He knew there was something on Fuchs's mind but didn't think he was the right man to question the physicist. MI5 decided to send William Skardon to Harwell and see if he could coax an admission of guilt out of Fuchs.

Skardon, known as a skillful interrogator, had handled some prominent criminal cases when he was a detective pursuing murder investiga-

tions for the London police. He had joined MI5 during the war but maintained close ties with Scotland Yard. When he was introduced to Fuchs
by Arnold, Skardon said he wanted to talk about his father's new position
in East Germany. The dialogue began on December 21 and continued off
and on for a month. None other than Kim Philby would describe Skardon's method as "scrupulously courteous, his manner verging on the exquisite, nothing could have been more flattering than the cozy warmth of
his interest" in your life. But letting one's guard down could bring "disastrous results."[16]

Fuchs was encouraged to talk about his family, his father's ministry, his
brother's sad history of imprisonment and illness, and his sister's life in
America. In short order, Skardon had him talking about his days as a
Communist student activist in Germany, his need to flee the country, and
his years in England. Presenting a disarming image, the investigator took
no notes as he sucked on his pipe and tried to draw Fuchs out of his
tightly closed shell. It was while they were discussing Fuchs's time in New
York that Skardon asked him, "Were you not in touch with a Soviet official or a Soviet representative while you were in New York? And did you
not pass on information to that person about your work?" Fuchs's reply
—"I don't think so"—was remarkably mild, considering the implications
of the questions.

The two men played cat and mouse for days, with Skardon occasionally bringing up names and events that had much less to do with Emil
Fuchs and more to do with Klaus's dubious choices and associations over
the years. Curiously, now that Skardon was practically accusing him of
giving information to the Russians, Fuchs could only muster an "offer to
resign from Harwell." He seemed in a mental fog about the repercussions of the acts they were discussing, not to mention the penalty for
them. Skardon believed "there was a good chance" that Fuchs would confess with just a bit more gentle prodding. Fuchs was discussing things he
had never broached with anyone.[17] He was clearly troubled by some of
his past actions; he had growing doubts about the Soviet Union, and his
once-firm convictions were considerably less firm. He often seemed on
the verge of telling all.

The delicate dance continued for weeks, during which Skardon often
felt that a confession was just out of his reach. One day when Fuchs and
Arnold were having lunch, the physicist remarked that he would like to
see Skardon again. At that point Arnold came right out and asked if he
had passed information to the Russians. Fuchs said that he had.

In late January 1950, after a day of emotional discussions between

Skardon and Fuchs, the time had come. Exhausted and guilt-ridden, the scientist asked his inquisitor, "What do you want to know?"

Skardon proceeded to ask about Fuchs's associations and activities over the years. He had been under the impression only one or two things had happened, and was stunned when Fuchs said, "I started in 1942 and had my last meeting last year," meaning 1949. When the detective asked him what was the most important information he passed on, Fuchs promptly stated, "Perhaps the most important thing was the full design of the atom bomb."[18] Skardon wasn't prepared for this and didn't think the British government would be either; he had no idea he was dealing with an investigation of such magnitude. Over the next hour Fuchs talked about what had happened in America, the risks he had taken, and his increasing disillusionment with the Soviet Union.

During the last week of January, in what observers called a trancelike state, Fuchs wrote a four-thousand-word confession and illuminated "how he divided his mind into two compartments, so he could be a good and honest friend in one while his other activities as a spy for the Soviet Union were locked away in the other." He referred to his divided life as "controlled schizophrenia."[19]

One Fuchs biographer, Robert Chadwell Williams, has argued that his "vagueness and confusion" leading up to his confession may have kept him from fleeing or taking "more drastic action, such as suicide." In public, Fuchs was an accomplished scientist, occasionally personable, but privately he was shy, withdrawn, and egocentric. His years in the small communities of Los Alamos and Harwell were a form of self-imposed imprisonment in which he had admirers but few friends. The private Fuchs was a "political true believer in Communism"—a belief system that was antithetical to Fascism and reinforced by a Quaker upbringing that emphasized "ethical righteousness and moral idealism." Germany's political turmoil, combined with the "devastating suicides of his mother and sister" contributed to the adolescent Fuchs's "retreat into the world of Communism and espionage," a place where he could feel morally good and politically fulfilled.[20] As time went on, however, the mental and physical effort of maintaining opposing belief systems became untenable. The controlled schizophrenia gradually crumbled under its own weight.

The case of Klaus Fuchs was whisked through the British courts. He was tried on March 1 at the Old Bailey in front of dozens of news reporters, members of the general public, and even representatives of royalty. The length and depth of his infamy, combined with a perception of the incompetence of British security operations, demanded a quick and clean process. Already orchestrating damage control, the British authorities claimed to have broken the Fuchs case without FBI assistance. J. Edgar Hoover is said to have "fumed" over this.[21] It would not be the last British decision to infuriate him. Because of the lack of independent evidence and because the Soviet Union was not an enemy of Great Britain at the time of the crime, Fuchs escaped the charge of espionage and was charged with violating the Official Secrets Act. The decision may have saved his life. He received a fourteen-year prison sentence, the maximum term allowed.

Though the British dearly hoped Fuchs's imprisonment would end the embarrassing saga, events across the Atlantic were just beginning to pick up steam. In what Hoover would describe as "one of the most difficult and most important quests ever undertaken by the FBI," and what the lead agent of the assignment would call "a raging monster of a quest," the Bureau turned its massive machinery toward finding Fuchs's American contact.[22]

"Flee the country or commit suicide"

The object of that hunt was beside himself with fear.[23] "I was stunned," said Gold, "when I first saw the news in the newspapers and frankly did not know what to do and what to expect next. The news broke on a Friday and on Saturday when I went to work, I was extremely apprehensive, and every time that the door opened or the phone rang, I literally jumped out of my shoes."[24]

In a panic, Gold reached out to Tom Black, the one friend whom he could talk to about this terrible turn of events. Black remembers getting "an excited phone call from Harry. He insisted in a frantic voice that we meet that very evening." It was obvious something serious had happened, and "Gold was in a distraught condition." They met on Monday evening in Center City Philadelphia and went for a long walk through the darkened streets. Even though Black was a dear friend—as well as the person who got him involved in this business—it was difficult for Gold to summon the courage to say what the crisis was. As Black remembered it, Gold asked, "You've read about the arrest of Fuchs and that the FBI is searching for his American contact?" He then paused for a few moments and finally said, "Tom, I am that contact."[25]

Black was "horror stricken."[26] According to Gold, "Black was possibly more shocked than I was." Black knew that his friend had traveled to the Southwest during the war and suspected he was doing something for the

Russians out there, "but he had no idea how deeply Gold was involved." For years they had kept their respective political assignments from each other, but Fuchs's arrest had serious implications for both of them. According to Black, Gold was so upset he could see only two alternatives: "flee the country or commit suicide."[27]

Black says he "tried to dissuade him" from such thoughts. Though Gold never admitted to considering either option, he gave Black credit for "reassuring" him that "it would be a long trail" for anyone trying to find him. Gold countered that even though Fuchs didn't know his real name—Harry had identified himself only as "Raymond"—the physicist might still be able to identify him. The same was true of Fuchs's sister in Massachusetts.[28]

The two men talked "at great length," Gold periodically stressing his concern for his father and brother. He knew the impact the story would have on them.

Finally, exhausted, Black and Gold agreed that "there was no point in speculating" any further. Each promised to be alert for any signs they were being followed or under investigation, and to keep each other informed of developments. They agreed to meet "only on Thursday evenings . . . in the library of the Franklin Institute."[29]

"The city of Philadelphia was mentioned"

In Washington, Hoover vacillated between anger and indignation. He was "furious" at the British for not allowing a Bureau official to interview Fuchs, and "outraged" that Fuchs's contact in America had not been found.[30] From Hoover's perspective, the British never would have nailed Fuchs if it had not been for the FBI, and by blocking access to him, they were preventing the capture of his American contact.

The director's mood had become so foul that high-ranking FBI officials had been demoted or transferred; others—like Robert Lamphere— were thinking "seriously about quitting the Bureau." Hoover, "wildly impatient" and "on a rampage" over slights real and imagined, made unrealistic demands for the "prompt solution to the identity and whereabouts of the American KGB agent." Whether or not he actually believed it, Hoover was treating the case as "the crime of the century."[31] The order and his irate demeanor placed extraordinary stress on individual agents and the organization as a whole. "The pressures," said Lamphere, "were unmerciful." It was becoming clear that until the American contact was caught, "there would be no peace for any of the 52 FBI field offices working triple shifts in the long, frustrating search. Failure would not be tolerated."[32]

The only redeeming feature of this frenzy was that no expense would be spared and no reasonable effort blocked; the campaign was deemed so important that the search for "Raymond" would "command all the Bureau's resources." This, however, presented its own dilemma: "there could be no excuse for not finding him."[33]

While the FBI haggled with British authorities to gain access to Fuchs's cell at Wormwood Scrubs Prison, the effort to track down anyone who had encountered Fuchs in America was in full swing. Two of the more promising sources of information turned out to be the spy's own family members, Kristel and Robert Heinemann.

The postwar years were difficult for Klaus Fuchs's sister. Perhaps because of her unhappy marital situation, perhaps because of a familial predisposition toward psychological problems, Kristel was in a mental institution by the time the FBI started looking for her. She had been placed in McLean Hospital on March 20, 1949, on the petition of her husband, and was transferred to Westboro State Hospital approximately two weeks later. Though diagnosed as "schizophrenic-melancholic," for which she would undergo shock treatments, she proved to be lucid and helpful when interviewed by FBI agents.[34]

Kristel told agents she recalled a man visiting her a few weeks before her brother came to visit in February 1945. She said she had first noticed him "walking down the street" and was "surprised when the man came to her door and rang the bell," since she "did not recognize him as a friend or neighbor." When she opened the door, he asked if she was "Mrs. Heinemann, the sister of Klaus Fuchs." After she replied that she was, the man "identified himself by name," but she could no longer recall what it was. She did remember his saying he was a chemist who had worked with her brother. He stayed a short time, joined Kristel and one of her children for lunch, and then left, presumably taking public transit to Harvard Square. She thought he might have come by train from Chicago because he at one point stated that "he was tired because of a long train ride."[35]

The FBI then acquired from either Kristel or her husband the letter Fuchs had sent from Los Alamos offering his apology for missing the upcoming Christmas holiday.[36] She remembered telling the stranger that her brother hoped to visit them shortly after the holiday.

Kristel recounted what she recalled of the chemist's next two visits. The first came the day after Klaus arrived on his holiday. The man arrived "in the late afternoon," she said, and "presented me with a then popular work of light fiction, entitled *Mrs. Palmer's Honey.*" A day earlier, when she had told her brother that a chemist had come a few weeks earlier to see him, Fuchs "seemed surprised and somewhat annoyed," but eventually seemed less troubled and said, "Oh, it's all right." Now that the man had come again, she could see her brother "definitely knew the chemist by name and it was not necessary for her to introduce the two men." The chemist and her brother "talked for 15 or 20 minutes in the Heinemann living room," but she did not know what they discussed and was unaware of anything having passed between them.

On his third visit, Kristel recalled, the chemist brought gifts for her and the children. When he learned that her brother was not there and "not expected in the immediate future," he asked about Fuchs's next visit, but she had no information. She vaguely recalled her husband and a friend, Konstantin Lafazanos, being present at the time, as well as the chemist's mentioning that "he had a wife" and was the "father of two children."

Mrs. Heinemann was far less cooperative in a subsequent interview. On February 17, 1950, special agents showed her hundreds of photographs (including one of Harry Gold, who by this time was the subject of their investigation), but she "refused to point out any similarities between any of the some 200 photographs and the chemist" who came to her home. In fact, the agents reported, she gave "a negative answer . . . to every photograph before she had had an opportunity to actually examine the photograph." One can imagine any number of reasons for Mrs. Heinemann's uncooperative behavior, such as her mental issues or the sudden realization that she might be placing one of her brother's colleagues in serious jeopardy. Fortunately for the Bureau, she had earlier described the unknown visitor as about forty years old, five feet, eight inches tall and 180 pounds, with a stocky build.[37]

Robert Heinemann, who readily admitted to having a long association with the Communist Party, confirmed much of what his wife said and added a few bits of information.[38] In his one brief meeting with the chemist, he recalled the man's alluding to "the extremely heavy snowfall in Buffalo, New York," leaving the impression that the caller might have resided in the Buffalo area and have "arrived in Boston by train." Unlike his wife, Heinemann recalled no reference to Chicago but did remember that "the city of Philadelphia was mentioned." Asked to examine scores of photographs, he selected three that most resembled his brother-in-law's friend. One of them showed Harry Gold. In the end, however, he put those three aside "in favor of a suspect who had already been otherwise eliminated."[39]

FBI agents also interviewed Konstantin Lafazanos, who had been at the house that day. He recalled the heavyset guest as "under five foot eight, possibly five foot six, and weighing about 200 pounds." Lafazanos contributed a few new pieces to the puzzle. He said the man "talked [about] the value of vitamins" and argued "that the exact value of vitamins had not been determined because all experiments had been on mice." He was left with the impression that "the visitor was a bacteriologist" or some other kind of scientist who might be connected to a wholesale manufacturing company.[40]

"We've got our man"

The description of a short, overweight, white male in his forties could have fitted several million American citizens. It did, however, match the one provided by Fuchs himself, and one other item in Fuchs's confession helped narrow the search. In his official statement to Dr. Michael W. Perrin, a physicist attached to the British Ministry, Fuchs said that "the Russian agent with whom he was in contact during his whole period in the United States (while at New York and Los Alamos) was rather more capable of understanding the information which he was given than had been the case with his contact in the United Kingdom. Fuchs described him as being perhaps an engineer or chemical engineer. He clearly had no detailed knowledge of nuclear physics or of the sort of mathematics with which Fuchs was competent to deal."[41]

Lamphere and Van Loon agreed that the most promising clue to the identity of the unknown subject—"Unsub" in official Bureau documents —could be his scientific expertise. The Bureau came up with "nearly a thousand men" who had such a professional background and similar physical characteristics. Photographs of the most likely Unsub candidates were flown to London and shown to Fuchs in his prison cell. While Hoover fumed over the British authorities' refusal to let his agents interview Fuchs until his legal appeals were exhausted, the convicted physicist examined dozens of photographs of potential accomplices with no indication of recognition. Finally, on March 13, 1950, he thought he recognized the man he knew as Raymond. The photo was taken to the Heinemanns for confirmation, but they denied that he was the man that had come to their home. Additional investigative work disclosed that the man Fuchs selected "could not have been in New York or Cambridge or Santa Fe at the times when Fuchs had met Raymond."

In his book about the hunt for Raymond, Lamphere describes the frustration of starting again at square one. Continuing to pursue the scientific lead and possible East Coast connection, the Bureau began to collect data on chemical laboratories. It seemed a good idea until the numbers started to come in. They were shocked to learn there were some "75,000 license permits issued to chemical manufacturing firms in New York City in the year 1945 alone."[42] Lamphere and Van Loon were looking for a needle in a haystack.

Van Loon turned back to the Bentley-Brothman connection. Abraham Brothman wasn't too far from the working profile of Unsub, and his business had a handful of politically like-minded chemists on board, such as Harry Gold, Oscar Vago, and Jules Korchein. Because of their appearance before the grand jury in 1947, Brothman and Gold were among the first people Lamphere had considered as likely suspects. The two chemists had convincingly claimed that their associations with Golos and Bentley were harmless, but Lamphere and others at the Bureau thought "both men were lying through their teeth." Unfortunately, they couldn't prove it, and Fuchs had dismissed their photos.

Van Loon wasn't persuaded, and Lamphere wasn't far behind. According to Richard Rhodes, with their suspicions raised and their desperation increasing, Hoover "evidently authorized a bag job on Abe Brothman's offices." FBI agents broke into Brothman's files "sometime in February or early March" and came up with several documents of "extreme significance." Though one document dealing with thermal diffusion had no name attached, it was thought that the author "was very likely Fuchs's cut-out."[43]

The more they went over their leads and physical descriptions, the more certain Lamphere became. "I know I'm right," he told his anxious superiors. "We've got our man."[44] He meant Harry Gold.

The FBI's office in Philadelphia was ordered "to open a very active investigation" of Gold. The agents' interest mounted as reports came in. Gold seemed to be the man, but how would they deal with Fuchs's inability to identify his photo? Could Fuchs be purposely deceiving them? Was he trying to protect his American partner? Or was it the photo itself? "Often," Lamphere and Van Loon agreed, "a witness will be unable to identify a file photo of a man, but will later readily identify a better photo, or one that had been taken closer to that time in the past when the witness had known the suspect." They ordered agents in Philadelphia to "surreptitiously obtain some still and motion pictures" of Gold.[45]

In early May, when the appeal process had concluded, Hoover finally received authorization from British officials to interview Klaus Fuchs.

Still angry about the long delay, he was further outraged when informed of a new condition: a British security agent had to be present for the interview. For Hoover, all the heightened security precautions after the horse had been stolen were merely another example of British incompetence. More important, they were impeding the search for Fuchs's American contact, who might still be actively engaged in espionage.

"Mr. Brothman and other matters"

Lamphere was surprised and delighted to be chosen to interview Fuchs in London. It was a critically important assignment, and though he was arguably the most knowledgeable agent involved in the hunt for Raymond, he was still a relatively junior member of the organization. He would eventually call "the chance to interrogate Klaus Fuchs one of the great opportunities of my life."[46] At the time, however, his excitement was tempered by the appointment of Hugh Clegg, the FBI's pudgy chief inspector whom some called "Troutmouth," as his traveling companion. Hoover apparently wanted a more senior official to accompany Lamphere, if only to stroke the delicate sensibilities of British officials. Clegg, far from an expert on espionage, was generally viewed as an "ill-tempered trainer of recruits and evaluator of field office performance" who relentlessly pursued "violations of the clauses and sub-paragraphs in the FBI field manual."[47] When a high-ranking Bureau official asked him what he thought of Clegg joining him on such an important mission, Lamphere replied: "Not worth a damn."[48]

Agents in Philadelphia were ordered to take additional film footage. Lamphere wanted as many still and moving pictures of Gold as possible. In addition, agents in several cities fanned out to interview anyone who knew Gold, including Abe Brothman, Miriam Moskowitz, and their business partners. FBI agents arrived at Brothman's Manhattan office at 1:00 P.M. on May 15. Brothman and Moskowitz immediately refused to be interviewed until they had spoken with an attorney.[49] After they were told that they should cooperate, the interview began. Brothman was asked about the origin of his company, his clients, and the services and products he provided. He mentioned his business dealings with the Chinese government and also talked of his troubled relations with Henry Golwynne, a former partner who, he claimed, cheated him out of partial ownership of a firm they were part of. The interview continued the following day with questions centering on Brothman's association with Jacob Golos, Elizabeth Bentley, and Harry Gold.

Moskowitz was interviewed on both days as well. Initial questions dealt with matters related to the Brothman firm. When questions turned to Gold, she claimed "she did not know Harry Gold prior to the time he came to work for the firm in May or June 1946, but he had been around the office and lab once or twice prior to that." She said that she did "not know how he came in contact with Brothman"[50] and that she and the others at the firm "first became aware of his name" when the various partners concluded that they were in "need of a chemist to work in the laboratory." Gold was mentioned as "a good man."

When agents asked "what reason Brothman had given to her for his being questioned by FBI agents and his subpoena by the Federal Grand Jury in 1947," she was less forthcoming. She replied that she didn't know why he was questioned and never thought to ask. When agents pointed out how unbelievable that was given their close relationship, she allowed that, on second thought, "he may have stated it was spy scare stuff." Moskowitz went on to explain that "the newspapers at the time were full of stories about Elizabeth Bentley and her allegations, and Moskowitz assumed . . . that Brothman's questioning was in connection with that matter."[51] Though initially terse and sure of herself, she became more talkative as her anxiety grew, especially when criticizing her former co-worker, Gold. She effusively shared with the agents the many untruths he had told at the office. When FBI agents informed him what Moskowitz had been telling them, he was only too willing to return the favor. As she wrote in her memoir many years later, "It was a classic trap and I tumbled in, head first." At the time, Gold had not divulged anything to the FBI that was injurious to her or Brothman, but she assumed "Harry Gold was talking to them because of the information they seemed to have."[52]

Having informed the agents that "she did not think Harry Gold had ever been a member of the Communist Party" and had left with "the firm still owing [him] approximately $2,500 representing about a half-year's salary," she rather quickly turned into an adversary. As she states in her memoir, "I judged that it would be wise to try to head [the FBI] off from reaching some unfavorable conclusions about us so I warned them that not everything Harry said was true."[53] She repeated his stories of a wife who was "a former model at Gimbels Store," the twin children, and his brother, a paratrooper who had been killed in the Pacific. She described for the FBI how Gold became "hysterical" when she suggested he list his wife and children as dependents on his tax return.[54] Fearing that Gold would tell all to the FBI—or already had—Moskowitz was determined to damage his credibility.

Others at the troubled Brothman enterprise, like Jules Korchein, Oscar Vago, Gerhard Wollan, and Emil Barish, were also interviewed on May 15. After the interviews had been completed and analyzed, Hoover received a report that argued, "While it cannot be conclusively stated, it would appear from the interviews" and previous known information "that Gold may be identical with Unknown Subject."[55]

Some ninety miles south of New York, FBI agents prepared to initiate another interview.

· ·

CHAPTER 10

The Fatal Words

A t 3:00 P.M. on Monday, May 15, 1950, Harry Gold still saw many hours of work ahead of him. He rarely left the Philadelphia General Hospital Heart Station laboratory at five with the other employees. His days were long and taxing, but he enjoyed them.

This day would be different. Shortly after three o'clock, two serious-looking men wearing business suits appeared at the Heart Station. They didn't look like doctors or hospital administrators, and they asked for Harry Gold. It was a scenario he had dreaded since the announcement of Fuchs's arrest. "Before they showed me their identification," he would write later, "I knew who they were."[1] When they were finally directed to Gold, they said they wanted to speak with him "about Mr. Brothman and some other matters."[2] Gold needed no monitor to know that his unstable blood pressure was climbing rapidly.

It was the seemingly innocuous "and some other matters" that he found most alarming.[3] Like any prey, he had become hypersensitive and immediately discerned the threat in the FBI agent's request. As he would subsequently write, "That last phrase sent a disturbing tremor through me."[4]

Others who confronted similar threats had taken measures of varying desperation. Joel Barr and Alfred Sarant would flee the country; Morton Sobell would try to flee, only to be returned by Mexican authorities; Abe Brothman and Miriam Moskowitz sought legal counsel. Gold opted for affability and the appearance of helpfulness as his first and only defense.[5] He agreed to meet with the agents at their headquarters, on the fourth and fifth floors of the Widener Building, as soon as his workday was over. He would be interrogated there well into the night, enduring an on-slaught of questions in the hope that he could deflect and outwit his interrogators. His "talkative mood," as Kim Philby would later sarcastically describe it, was equivalent to collaborating in his own downfall.[6]

"One last night"

The two agents picked Gold up at the hospital shortly after five, drove the twenty blocks to their office, and began asking questions at 6:30. As Gold would tell his lawyers three weeks later, "Most of the conversation concerned my relationship with Brothman, the story about Carter Hoodless, and the false story of how I came to meet Brothman with Jacob Golos."[7] As the hours passed and the questions kept coming, Gold worked to establish an image of innocence. "So that night in the Bureau's offices," he would write later, "I stubbornly repeated the story Abe and I had concocted in 1947 about how we had met; how I had got to know Jacob Golos (a man I actually never met, and of whose existence I had been unaware until told by Brothman); and, as I had three years previous, I tried desperately to create the illusion that I was genuinely doing all in my power to cooperate."[8]

This strategy, "at first, seemed to be going well." Then he was asked about his vacations. How many had he taken in the last five or six years? Questions regarding "trips to New York (with Morrell Dougherty on legitimate Penn Sugar business) and to Peoria (to confer at the Hiram Walker Distillery) were ominous," potentially leading to explosive subjects he hoped to avoid. To be asked, "Were you ever west of the Mississippi?" was, "to put it mildly, very upsetting." Gold answered that he hadn't, but disarmingly said "he had taken his mother to New York on one occasion."[9] Throughout the evening he did his best to hide any sign of discomfort and "appear affable and helpful."[10]

Near eleven o'clock, the agents decided to call it a day, but only after Gold agreed to meet with them again. Gold was offered a ride home, but respectfully declined, since he had more work to do back at the Heart Station laboratory. The agents were getting their first glimpse of their suspect's dedication. Special Agent Robert Jensen said that would be no problem, as he had to drop off Special Agents T. Scott Miller Jr. and Richard Brennan at the Thirtieth Street Station, only a few blocks from the hospital. Jensen, like Gold, lived in Northeast Philadelphia and would drive him home.[11] Though Harry had had enough of FBI agents over the past five hours, he thought it best not to argue.

Jensen waited in his car outside the hospital while Gold worked on the Heart Station's ultrafiltration apparatus. Then he drove Gold back to his Oxford Circle home. It was as they were approaching his neighborhood via Roosevelt Boulevard that Gold realized that Agent Jensen wasn't just doing him a kindly favor; the FBI was "trying to make sure that I would not get in touch with anyone else."

On Tuesday, Gold worked until seven in the evening and then went to the monthly meeting of the Philadelphia Physiological Society, on the campus of the University of Pennsylvania medical school. He felt comfortable; he knew everyone there. But just as the program was about to get under way, "two young men who diffidently entered just as the session started, and who left after five minutes could only have been FBI men."

On Wednesday, Agent Jensen appeared again in the heart lab. "I just happened to be in the neighborhood," he said, "and so I thought I'd stop in and see what your place was like."[12] The agent's appearance confirmed Gold's worst suspicions. He "realized that these people were not now so much interested in Brothman as they were in me and were checking up on whether I was there." As he subsequently wrote, "For an hour I showed him around, trying to be as cordial as possible, with all the cold reality gripping me that I was under surveillance. Why? What did they know?"[13]

For the rest of the day and evening, Gold tried to carry out his assignments as if nothing extraordinary was happening, but as he sat through Dr. Bellet's 8:00 P.M. lecture, he couldn't help thinking they were closing in for the kill. He arrived home late that night and was at the hospital early Thursday morning, but he had already decided to leave work at a reasonable hour. Fearing the worst, he hoped to "spend at least . . . one last night peacefully with Pop and Yus."

On Friday after work, Gold did as he had promised: he showed up at six at the Center City office of the FBI. Without legal counsel, without even his good friend Tom Black, he continued to play out his hand in what had become a risky game. There were other options. He could have gone into hiding, as others would soon do. He could have retained a sharp

antigovernment attorney to advise him. He could have just stopped cooperating, as Ted Hall did, and waited to see if the government could
make a prosecutable case against him. But he did none of those things.
He walked into the belly of the beast and said catch me if you can. Was
he emotionally shell-shocked and physically drained from years of leading a double life, or perhaps overconfident because he had fooled the
FBI and government prosecutors three years earlier? But the stakes were
much higher this time, and his opponents seemed vastly more determined.

"They just ran out of steam"

Agents Miller and Brennan were back in Philadelphia, and it didn't take
them long to "really open up." They started with more questions about
Brothman and Moskowitz and then presented a series of photographs for
identification. Included in the batch were photos of Kristel and Robert
Heinemann taken many years earlier. The one of Robert, in fact, appeared from his abundance of hair to be a college picture. Gold did his
best to show no hint of recognition. He was relieved to see that "they
were not police or FBI photographs."

Then came "the shocker." The agent said, "Do you know who he is?"
and placed another photograph in front of him. It was "the white, staring
and, somehow dully expressionless face, with those huge glasses—Klaus
Fuchs."[14] Gold would say later that it looked "almost like a caricature."
The "huge horn-shelled glasses and the extremely white face, all looking
almost like a death mask."[15] Gold's air of detachment became considerably more difficult to maintain. "Well?" said the agent. "I do not know
him," said Gold. "It's a very unusual picture. I recognize the picture from
Newsweek Magazine as that of Dr. Klaus Fuchs, the Briton who got in
trouble over there, but I don't know him. I've never been in England."

"Oh yes, you know him," said the agent. "You met him in Cambridge,
Massachusetts."

"Never been there in my life," Gold replied as convincingly as he
could.[16]

There is no FBI record of Gold's physical reaction to seeing the Fuchs
photo, but his own accounts suggest that despite his best efforts, there
was a change in his expression. The agents hammered away, insisting the
two men had met in New York, in Boston, in New Mexico. One agent
said to Gold that "two people 4,000 miles apart had picked [his] photograph from among several thousand photographs as the person whom

they knew had passed information from Klaus Fuchs to the Soviet Union."

Gold denied everything the agents threw his way, but he realized that "time was growing short." As he would write later, "All that I wanted to do, frankly, was to fight for a little extra time, before my family would become aware of this terrible thing that I had done."[17]

Hour after hour passed, with Gold fielding a steady barrage of uncomfortable questions. After so many hours he couldn't help noticing how the "FBI men . . . placed themselves strategically" around the table. "One man would be directly facing" him across the table at all times while others sat at an angle to ensure that "they could watch my every reaction" to each question. Legally, he would have been well within his rights to say, "That's it, this session is over" and walk out, but he didn't. Like Fuchs a few months earlier, he continued to participate in the painful dialogue, listen to one accusation after another, and face the questioners' expressions of disbelief at his denials. By midnight, Gold was exhausted. No doubt the agents were as well, but they couldn't relent. Hoover was driving them mercilessly, Gold was their prime suspect, and they needed to break him.

"It was a big deal," recalls Special Agent Paul Hagen, who periodically passed by the interview room where Harry was being verbally worked over; "Gold was very important." Getting him to admit his part in the conspiracy was a "very big deal in the office."[18] Even agents not on the case took notice. The innocuous-looking man attracting so much attention may have seemed inconsequential compared to most of the criminals they dealt with, but every agent working out of the Widener Building knew he was significant.[19]

Gold refused to budge on the Fuchs photo. Just when he thought Miller and Brennan were finished for the night, they opened a new line of attack. They asked for eight to ten pages of handwriting samples, both printing and cursive. And would he permit them to take photographs and motion pictures of him? "Certainly, I would be glad to," he incredibly replied. Short of admitting he was the man they were searching for, Gold could not have been more accommodating. Maybe it was the compliant, obliging aspect of his character that kept the agents working well after midnight. Even Gold sensed that nothing short of an admission of guilt was going to stop them.[20]

Around two in the morning, "Miller and Brennan appeared to give up," Gold wrote later; "they just ran out of steam . . . before I did." He agreed to meet the agents again the next afternoon, even though the contest was becoming more and more one-sided. Scotty Miller and Richard Brennan had a formidable law enforcement and intelligence agency behind them; Gold had nothing, yet he kept giving them second and third and fourth chances to get him.

Agent Jensen drove him home. With little or no sleep, Gold was back at PGH early the next morning. And so was the tail; Harry saw the "thirtyish young fellow in the powder-blue suit and the snap-brim straw hat follow me to the back gate of the hospital" and knew the man wasn't "merely out for the pleasant spring air."[21]

That Saturday turned out to be particularly busy. Gold's work for Drs. Lewis and Cohen kept him at the medical school through the mid-afternoon, but he had not forgotten his appointment. He called the Bureau and said he'd be a bit late and then, still unable to leave PGH, called a second time to apologize. An emergency had arisen, but he assured them he'd eventually get there.[22] The agents must have marveled at this mild-mannered, considerate individual who had thrown their director into a panic and inspired one of the largest manhunts in FBI history.

But just in case, to reassure themselves that their prime suspect hadn't gone on a desperate and belated run for the Mexican border and was not making calls from Missouri or Texas to gain time, agents Miller and Jensen drove over to PGH. They arrived in time to see Gold helping "Dr. John Urbach working on a patient who was exceedingly ill." Gold's job was to perform the chemical analysis and lab work. Neither Gold nor the agents considered letting the questioning interfere with his hospital duties.

The trio finally arrived at FBI headquarters much later than they had anticipated. Gold was hit with many of the same questions as before. There was one new item: they wanted his permission to search his home. Sticking to the established pattern, Gold said he "would be glad to [have them] do so," but there was "one stipulation." They must do it when his father and brother were not at home, as he "did not wish to alarm them." The agents agreed, and they "set the date for the search as Monday at eight or eight-thirty o'clock in the morning."[23] Both Sam and Yus would have left for work by then.

The scheduled search provided Gold with more than twenty-four hours to rummage through his possessions and destroy any provocative or questionable material. In the end, however, he didn't make even a superficial effort. If he was hoping for a cursory search like the one the FBI performed in 1947, he was sorely mistaken.

After an abbreviated Saturday night session—they were all exhausted from the marathon effort the night before—Jensen once again drove him home. Gold was grateful for the lift but again well "aware that the motive was not entirely humanitarian."

Rather than do the vitally important housecleaning on Sunday morning, Gold went back to the hospital. It was a common practice of his, and one that had never translated into larger paychecks. As he would subsequently write,

I worked Sunday morning . . . at the hospital and . . . over at the medical school to see Dr. Diz Cohen and our experimental dog, on whom a gastrectomy (tying off of the intestine) had been performed. Diz had been sleeping in the lab with the animal for the past two days and would stay with it till the expiration. When would this be? Possibly about 8 tonight, or even much later. I would return at 8. So I collected my specimens and set up containers for the new ones. Back at PGH I helped "Smitty," the surgeon, locate some data in our lab records. Then out again to the fifth floor of the Widener Building where from 3 till 7 PM, I cautiously and desperately parried each of the probing questions. One more hazard: I could not afford to let the name Tom Black come into the picture; he was too vulnerable. Nor a mention of the many loans from friends and from the Corn Exchange Bank. I was literally walking on eggs. But somehow, as it seemed that Miller and Brennan began to droop with defeat. I strangely enough began to feel sorry for them; they had given it such a good try. Yes, I was almost in the clear. However, instead of going directly home and frenziedly cleaning out all of those terribly damaging bits of evidence which I knew were there (though even I had no conception as to the prodigious extent of the bonanza), I went to see Diz Cohen and the dog at the med school. But Dr. Isadore Cohen had left and I had a terrible time getting in; finally a Dr. Coe and I succeeded in seeking out a guard. The lab was locked but I could see that the dog was still alive and after some further difficulty, I contrived to get a message to Dr. Cohen at the Graduate Hospital. I got home about 9:30 and Diz called at 10:30. "Relax," he said, "you won't have to come back now; the animal will last till tomorrow," and I knew that Dan Lewis . . . could take care of matters on Monday morning.[24]

During the four hours he spent with Miller and Brennan between his two hospital visits, Gold was shown additional photographs. Pictures of Earl Browder, Steve Nelson, Louis Budenz, Elizabeth Bentley, and Jacob Golos were among them. As he had told the agents earlier, the only ones he recognized were Golos and Bentley. Photos of Golos had been paraded before him by "agents Shannon and O'Brien" in 1947, and Bentley had "appeared in the newspapers in 1949." In addition to the photo lineup, he was pressed for his "whereabouts on various days . . . in 1943,

1944, and 1945." The agents were after information about vacations, traveling companions, and business trips for Pennsylvania Sugar during those years.

"I cannot reject them"

While members of the FBI's New York and Philadelphia offices were busily attempting to break Gold's will, Bob Lamphere and Hugh Clegg were trying to wear through the Germanic resolve of the now infamous Klaus Fuchs and get him to name Harry Gold as his partner in crime. Lamphere and Clegg had traveled from Washington to New York and then to London, but not before stopping in Philadelphia to pick up a very important package. The still photos and motion pictures they now possessed were critical to getting Fuchs to identify Gold as his American contact. John Cimperman, the Bureau's liaison with British intelligence, met Lamphere and Clegg at Heathrow Airport and drove them to their hotel. The short journey sadly showed that London had not yet recovered from the war. Bomb damage was still visible, debris was surprisingly widespread, and they would learn that staples like meat and butter were still being rationed.

The three Americans plotted how they would approach Fuchs. They decided to avoid any news organizations and say as little as possible of their efforts to MI5—though Lamphere noted the British government's insistence that an MI5 representative be present for all interrogation sessions.

On the morning of Saturday, May 20, 1950, Lamphere and Clegg were taken to the bleak and imposing Wormwood Scrubs Prison. William Skardon, who had expertly elicited Fuchs's original confession, joined them. The three men were taken through several locked gates to a room normally reserved for inmates to meet and talk with their attorneys. They sat around a table and waited for Fuchs to be brought to them. Lamphere believed he had done his homework and was prepared to do battle with one of the great spies of the twentieth century. He had studied the physicist's life history, had learned a good bit about the damage he had done, and had even been coached by scientists on the nuances of atomic bomb development. He was also well aware of the mission's importance to the Bureau and its demanding director.

Lamphere would subsequently write about seeing Fuchs for the first time: "The man whom I had waited so long to confront looked much as

I had expected him to: thin-faced, intelligent, and colorless. He was thirty-nine years old, of average height but a bit stoop-shouldered. His complexion was sallow, his eyes were brown and he wore glasses; his hair was receding and his scalp balding. When he pondered something, his forehead wrinkled, and there was a very noticeable vein that ran from the level of his eye across the temple and up into the hairline. His teeth were darkened from cigarette smoking, and he had a prominent Adam's apple; he swallowed hard, frequently and audibly, when under pressure. His hands were long, with wrists that were fairly wide in proportion. He blinked his eyes more than most people, and spoke English fluently, with a soft voice and a German accent."[25]

Skardon made the introductions and then sat back to observe. Fuchs appeared unmoved and uninterested; he was under no obligation to assist the FBI. He had already been sentenced to fourteen years behind bars, and nothing he said or did would alter that. He made it known fairly early that he didn't intend to say anything that might put his American friends in jeopardy. It was not a promising start, but Lamphere perceived that Fuchs was particularly concerned about his sister's welfare. He knew that Kristel Heinemann had suffered some form of mental breakdown, and he thought her safety might be the key element in getting Fuchs to talk.

Lamphere therefore assured Fuchs that his sister had been "most cooperative" in their few meetings and that agents had talked to her only "after consultation with her doctors." He said he knew Kristel had not been involved in espionage, but she had had contact with "Raymond." Lamphere was playing his hand delicately. Fuchs might consider the FBI as ruthless as "the Gestapo or the Soviet secret police," likely to take strong action "against an innocent person such as Kristel Heinemann" in order to get what it wanted. Lamphere admitted that he "was not above letting Fuchs conclude that if we were the bastards he posited us to be, Kristel would continue to be in jeopardy."[26]

Fuchs remained outwardly indifferent, but he had to be thinking of his sister's fragile mental health and the FBI's capacity to aggravate her situation. Lamphere then told the prisoner they had come a long way to see him, and he should at least look at some photographs. Fuchs knew they were hunting for Raymond. Reluctantly, he agreed to look. He was shown a dozen photos, at least half of which were of Harry Gold. Some were old; others had been taken recently. Fuchs quickly dismissed those that were not of Gold and then the older ones of him. Lamphere and

Clegg tried to hide their anticipation as Fuchs focused on the three remaining photos.

"I cannot reject them," Fuchs finally said. Lamphere's "heart leapt" at this, but it wasn't the sort of confirmation that would please either his boss or an American court of law. Pressed further, Fuchs complained that "the photos weren't clear enough for him to state unequivocally that they were of Raymond."[27]

It was probably not the quality of the photos, their age, or anything else that hindered Fuchs's identification of his American accomplice. Fuchs did not want to put an ideological ally in a prison cell. The "Red Foxes of Kiel," as the family had become known, believed in the importance of following one's conscience and not being stampeded by unthinking mobs or ruthless governments. Klaus, moreover, had been in dangerous political battles going back to the early 1930s; he knew the importance of honoring fellow soldiers in the struggle, and how much informers were reviled.[28] Even if he had known Harry's real name, it is unlikely he would have offered it up. His relationship with Gold was not a once-only, passing acquaintance on a dark street. The two had met at least nine times, in different parts of the country, and in bright daylight as well as at night. They had walked the streets for hours together, shared meals, and discussed everything from Fuchs's life and family history to science and the arts. Unprepossessing as Harry Gold was, once you knew him you were unlikely to forget him, particularly if you had spent as much time with him as Fuchs had. In addition, of all Fuchs's intellectual strengths, the one most often commented on by associates and students was his extraordinary memory.

After the interview, Lamphere and Clegg went back with Cimperman to his office, communicated their progress to Washington, and strategized. How to get Fuchs to give them unwavering confirmation that Gold was their man?

"Fatalistic and apathetic"

Back in Philadelphia, Harry Gold had been continuing to aid the FBI investigation. Now his help lay less in his undergoing endless hours of questioning than in his decision to refrain from clearing his home of incriminating evidence. When he returned home late Sunday night, he should have begun throwing out anything that suggested dubious travels—all the artifacts, documents, and mementos accumulated during years of secret work. Instead, "extremely tired" after busy stints at two different hospitals and a grilling at FBI headquarters, he went to bed.

There were other reasons for this behavior besides exhaustion. Gold would later admit that "to a certain extent" he had become "fatalistic and apathetic." He could feel that "the noose was being drawn tighter all the time"; he had little chance of escaping the inevitable.[29] He was alone; he was receiving no advice, and his poorly conceived strategy of cooperating with authorities to underscore his innocence was proving unsuccessful. Moreover, he did not wish to alarm his father and brother by rushing through the house throwing things out. He felt that his arrest as a spy and Soviet courier would prove much more disturbing to his father and brother than the housecleaning would, but he was no longer thinking rationally. He saw his life rapidly coming to an end.

As he would shortly tell his attorneys, "I realized that I could have taken several days off and made a thorough search of the house before the [FBI] visits and clean everything out, possibly one way or the other, but I didn't, and this, however, I realize there was a mass of circumstantial evidence against me. This would have meant that I would in any case sooner or later be arrested. People such as Dr. McMillan, the chief of the heart division, Dr. Bellet, the various residents, Dr. Lewis, Dr. Urbach, my father and brother, my close friends, Mr. Dougherty and so on, would all, I knew flock around me, that is, rally around me, and how terrible would be their dismay and disappointment where eventually it were proven definitely that I was the person who had received information from Klaus Fuchs because I knew by then that Klaus would inevitably identify me or at least Mrs. Heinemann would."[30]

And yet Gold awoke at 5:00 A.M. on Monday and tried to cast off the despair that had come to dominate his thinking. With a modicum of renewed hope, he began to search the house for "the accusatory items of evidence," only to be horrified by what he discovered. "Good Lord," he would write later, "here was a letter from Slack dated February 1945; a stub of a plane ticket from Albuquerque to Kansas City; a rough draft of a report on a visit to Cambridge; a street map of Dayton, Ohio; a card containing instructions from Sam relating to a procedure for approaching Ben Smilg; all this was here and more—I tore it up and flushed it down the toilet and some was shoved down near the bottom of our rubbish can in the cellar."

As his father and brother left for work, he told them he "had a report to complete before going into the hospital" but would be leaving shortly. He thought he "had taken care of everything."

"I am the man"

When the doorbell rang, Gold was still in his pajamas. He allowed Miller and Brennan to enter, and it was agreed that they would start in his bedroom. He sensed that "they could hardly wait to get upstairs" but was still feeling somewhat confident. "At first," he wrote, "all went well, very smoothly indeed. There was a lot of stuff, but it was all school notes and lab notes and chemical literature references, and my books were all volumes on mathematics and physics and chemistry—plus some two or three hundred pocket book reprints, some poetry and other anthologies, but mostly mystery stories. Then it began. First, a copy of Paul de Kruif's *Microbe Hunters* in a pocket book edition turned up and in the lower right-hand corner of the inside cover was a tiny tag: Sibley, Kerr, and Lindsay."[31]

"What's this?" asked Brennan.

Gold recognized it right away as a book he had picked up on one of his trips to Rochester when dealing with Slack. Sibley, Kerr, and Lindsay was the name of the Rochester department store where he purchased the book. He tried to hide his alarm and said, "Oh, I don't know, must have picked it up on a used book counter somewhere."

Just then Miller asked, "What's this, Harry?" He was holding a Pennsylvania Railroad train schedule that had printed on the top, "Washington-Philadelphia-New York-Boston-Montreal."

"Goodness knows," replied Gold. "I probably picked it up when I went to New York with Dougherty."[32] He had used it when traveling to Cambridge to visit Kristel Heinemann.

He was shaken, but so far these slip-ups were "not too bad. Not conclusive." There was still a chance he could get through this ordeal. The two agents kept pulling papers, pamphlets, and books off his shelves, thumbing through them, inspecting certain items more carefully, looking for anything that signaled a secret life.

"Then came the stunning blow," Gold would later write. "From in back of my bulky, worn copy of Walker, Lewis, and McAdam's *Principles of Chemical Engineering*, Dick [Brennan] pulled a sickeningly familiar tan-colored street map of Santa Fe." The pamphlet was entitled "New Mexico, Land of Enchantment," and "marked on it was the Alameda Street Bridge over the Rio Santa Fe" where Gold had met Fuchs.[33] "Oh God," he thought, "this I had overlooked. I knew that it existed, but in my hasty scrutiny that morning, could not find it, and so assumed that at some previous time it must have been destroyed."[34]

"So you were never west of the Mississippi," said Brennan, holding up the map. "How about this, Harry?" Miller, who had been rummaging through Gold's desk, recognized the importance of the find and stood up, waiting for his answer.

"Give me a minute," said Gold. He took a seat in the chair the agent just vacated, accepted a cigarette, and sat quietly for a few moments. A "torrent of thoughts poured through my mind," but he tried to focus. He thought of saying that because of his interest in U.S. history and the "Southwestern stories of J. Frank Dobey," he had sent for this map, but he could barely complete the thought, much less get it to come out of his mouth with any conviction.[35] Inconclusive as the map was, and sure as he was that he could mount a reasonable defense and a coterie of supporters, he could not fathom becoming some sort of cause célèbre, declaring his innocence, and mounting a public campaign while knowing all along that he was guilty of the crime. He couldn't imagine dragging family and friends into such a quagmire. "They would all rally around me," he would one day explain, "and how horrible would be their disappointment and let down when finally it was shown who I really was."[36]

It was over; he had no more fight left. He had "lied desperately for a week" while trying "to give the appearance of cooperating," but he could no longer keep up the charade.[37] Shy, generous, and well intentioned, the chemist who began stealing insignificant industrial documents fifteen years earlier was about to be collared for the biggest scientific and military heist of the twentieth century. Pressure, fear, the exhaustion had worn him down. He was ready to say the "fatal words."

"Yes," he finally said, "I am the man to whom Klaus Fuchs gave the information on atomic energy." Miller and Brennan were ecstatic. Gold, looking very much like the beaten man he was, went on: "There is a great deal more to this story. It goes way back to 1936, and I would like to tell it all."[38] He would be given every opportunity to elaborate. For days on end he would be probed and prodded and nudged until every last drop of information was squeezed out of him.

"That is my American contact"

That same day in London, Lamphere, Clegg, and Cimperman were having another go-around with Fuchs at Wormwood Scrubs. This time, they brought movie footage of Harry Gold that they hoped would jog the physicist's memory. After guards placed curtains in front of the windows and door of the solicitors' room, they started the projector. Fuchs watched impassively as the figure on the screen walked along a city street.[39] When the film was over, Fuchs is reported to have said, "I cannot be absolutely positive, but I think it is very likely him. There are certain mannerisms I seem to recognize, such as the too-obvious way he has of looking around and looking back."[40]

Their excitement building, the agents encouraged Fuchs watch the film a second and then a third time. They drew the projector further from the screen to enlarge the image. They wanted definite confirmation. Again, with no sign of emotion, Fuchs said, "very likely" at the conclusion of the two screenings. Two days later, on May 24, Fuchs was shown "new motion and still pictures of Harry Gold" that had just arrived from Philadelphia. He was not informed of Raymond's real name or Gold's confession. After viewing the still photos, Fuchs unemotionally said, "Yes, that is my American contact."[41]

Lamphere and Clegg returned to Wormwood Scrubs two days later to get Fuchs to write on the back of two photographs of Harry Gold, "I identify this photograph as the likeness of the man whom I knew under the name of Raymond—Klaus Fuchs—26th May, 1950." Lamphere would later write that "an unbelievably great weight seemed to lift from my shoulders."[42] The mission to London was a success.

For decades, Cold War partisans would debate which of the two men informed on the other first. Even Alexander Feklisov, the KGB agent who retrieved secrets from Western powers on both sides of the Atlantic, was "convinced that Harry Gold had betrayed Klaus Fuchs" and that "the famous map of Santa Fe" had actually been handed "to the FBI . . . during the summer of 1949."[43] Only under these circumstances, said Feklisov—who seems to have been desperate to salvage Fuchs's reputation—would the scientist have admitted his guilt in moving the secrets of the atomic bomb to Moscow. Though he and others would remain skeptical about the timing of Gold's and Fuchs's respective statements, nothing supports such skepticism. The FBI's performance in the hunt for Soviet spies was underwhelming at best during the 1930s and early 1940s, but the Bureau-wide effort to track down Fuchs's American contact was one of the high points of its history. Solid detective work, informed hunches, and resolute persistence eventually brought Gold's arrest almost simultaneously with his identification by Fuchs as the elusive "Raymond."

"My son, what have you done?"

As agents Miller and Brennan drove him back to the Widener Building, Gold unhappily reflected on what he had done, how it had all gone so wrong, and the likely impact on his family, friends, and co-workers. The arrest of Fuchs several months earlier had started the countdown. As soon as Miller and Brennan showed up at the PGH Heart Station on May 15, Gold knew the game was over. With a strategy predicated on an encore performance of his 1947 grand jury presentation, it was only a matter of time. As he would write of his inexplicable actions,

Why . . . had I fought as I did, fully aware that inescapably—in a month, or six months, or a year; once these men were on my trail—I would be run to earth? Why did I not spare myself this ordeal? The reasons were two, very good and very simple ones, both based on the fact that I was fighting for time: First, I was trying to salvage a few more precious hours with my pop and Yus, hours in which they would still remain in ignorance of what I had done. And, on the first preceding nights of Sunday and Saturday and Thursday, I had savored these few moments to the full. I can still recall Saturday and the good supper that Yus had ready when I came wearily in; and then his going out later to get the *Sunday Bulletin,* as was our custom. Then Sunday after 10 PM with pop sitting in his usual place near the TV set and I stretched exhausted on the sofa and Yus hovering over the set. The battle was not in vain here for in this I gained a victory. Second, I wanted time to complete as much of the work as possible at the Heart Station. This accounted for my working every possible minute on Tuesday and Wednesday and Saturday, plus the extra hours put in on Sunday. Even while Miller and Brennan were searching, I excused myself and called . . . the lab; and later that morning, just before we left for downtown, I again called and said I would definitely not be in today.

Riding downtown, Gold considered his next steps. He decided he "would confess fully to having been a Soviet agent for eleven years, but would only disclose the activities where they involved Klaus Fuchs and myself—the others I would cover up." He couldn't imagine himself as a "rat or squealer." During his childhood on South Philip Street, everybody had known that "one never told anything to the police." Their willingness to accept bribes from bootleggers, their sadistic assaults on prisoners, and their general corruption meant that neighborhood squabbles were best handled by neighbors. "The squealer who went to them," he would write, "was looked upon with the bitterest possible venom and hatred. And so this idea fastened itself upon me . . . Harry Gold was guilty and he was willing to accept his punishment—but he would not rat."[44]

For nearly five hours, Gold kept to his script. What had he done over the past fifteen years? Whom did he do it with? How was each act orchestrated? He talked, but he made sure to say nothing about Black, Brothman, or Smilg, or the David Greenglass incident, which in any case he had "completely forgotten about."

The FBI brass in Washington were elated with Gold's confession but determined that "it was imperative that this matter be kept quiet and that there be no leaks concerning it." Arthur Cornelius, the agent in charge of the Philadelphia office, was instructed as to "the importance of this case and the necessity for him to closely follow this matter personally."[45] Since Gold had not yet been technically arrested, Cornelius was told to "obtain a waiver from Gold . . . indicating his willingness to be interviewed and remain with the Bureau agents" while they completed their interrogation. Cornelius then asked his superiors if Gold could have a brief visit with his brother. He said Gold desperately wanted to tell his father and brother what had happened "prior to the time there is some publicity made in this case."[46] Though it was initially thought best to "hold off bringing" Joe Gold to the office "until it is absolutely necessary," Harry's insistent concern finally persuaded the FBI to have "an agent go out after work today and bring the brother to the office . . . thus ensuring [Gold's] continued cooperation and setting his mind at ease."[47]

At approximately 5:00 P.M., after hours of interrogation and the signing of confession statements, Gold was allowed to call his brother. "Yus," he said, "I'm down at the FBI headquarters, and I'm in serious trouble. Don't tell pop, but a car will pick you up at 7 PM and bring you here. We'll talk then."

When his brother arrived and was ushered up to the fifth floor of the Widener Building, Harry didn't waste any time. "Yus," he said, "it was I who worked with Klaus Fuchs, the English spy when he was in America." Joe Gold, who had won medals for the New Guinea, South Philippine, and Luzon campaigns, was stunned.[48] His normally dark complexion turned "blank white." Agents Brennan and Jensen quickly moved toward him, thinking "he was going to collapse."[49]

Regaining his composure, Joe finally said, "How could you have been such a jerk?" Harry remained silent. "Look, Harry," said Joe earnestly, "maybe it's all a mistake and you're taking the blame for someone else. You couldn't possibly have done this, not you, you're my brother."

Harry reassured his street-smart brother that it was so, "beyond a shadow of doubt." He would subsequently write of that painful confrontation, "As I looked at that awfully stunned, and still not fully comprehending face of my brother, a good half of that mountainous mental barrier that I had erected against squealing, went crashing down." Later that night, presented with another photo lineup of his Soviet handlers, he identified Semyon Markovich Semenov as his friend "Sam" and Anatoli Antonovich Yakovlev (Yatskov) as "John."[50] Both were significant KGB operatives who directed large intelligence operations in the United States.

Gold would have another visitor that evening; Robert Heinemann was brought in from Boston. With Kristel Heinemann still incapacitated, the FBI had Klaus Fuchs's brother-in-law come down to Philadelphia to see if he could identify Harry as the man who had visited their home in 1945. Gold recognized Heinemann immediately, "but Heineman [*sic*] did not or would not identify" Gold. The agents were told to "have Heineman [*sic*] return to Boston."[51]

Harry would not return home that night, or for many years thereafter. The first two nights he would be placed in a room under guard at the Ben Franklin Hotel, a few blocks from the FBI offices. He had not yet been arrested or charged. On May 23 he endured another long day of questioning and examined "several thousand photographs." He still did not divulge everything. At one point an agent informed him that they were going to take a short break and that he should take an important phone call from his brother. Yus said that their father "sensed that something was wrong." Why hadn't Harry come home the previous night? Sam Gold refused to listen to any further excuses. Agents told Harry that, if he wanted, he could see his father.

The brothers also briefly discussed finding a lawyer, possibly with the help of Sam Haftel, a very old friend of Harry's from South Philadelphia, or Morrell Dougherty. Harry had told the FBI that he planned to tell them everything but that he needed legal counsel to "advise him what is going to happen to him, what the legal proceedings will be, and how this is going to effect [*sic*] his father and brother, especially as to their jobs."[52]

The issue of legal representation was a thorny one for the Bureau. As the agents saw it, the more time they had to interview him, "the better our position will be from the standpoint of information and evidence obtained." But they were also concerned about making a case for prosecutors, especially about "McNabb and related decisions under which the courts may hold that regardless of the technicality of voluntary action on the part of the subject, he was actually under arrest and should have been arraigned immediately and, therefore, the confession is not admissible."[53]

Prior to the 1943 McNabb decision, law enforcement authorities could effectively delay a suspect's appearance before a judicial officer in order to obtain a confession. But since that ruling, arresting officers had had to keep an eye on the clock. Gold's willingness to be detained and continue talking was tempting, but a forceful defense attorney might cause a judge, not to mention the public, to look askance at such tactics.[54] After embarrassing foul-ups in a previous case, Hoover wanted to avoid any more courtroom setbacks.[55] FBI officials, knowing they were playing a game of constitutional brinkmanship, encouraged agents to get as much information as they could as quickly as they could, before Gold hired an attorney or a ruling by the attorney general or a judge terminated their access to him.

That evening, Yus brought Sam Gold to the Widener Building. The seventy-year-old stood no more than five feet tall and still spoke just a smattering of English. This was the scene Harry had always dreaded more than anything else: telling his simple, hardworking father of the crimes he had committed. As they sat in the interrogation room listening to his father and brother coming down the corridor, Dick Brennan gave Gold "a small encouraging slap on the back." Gold would write later that he needed it; he wasn't sure he could hold up.

Gold "haltingly" told his father why he was being held. Sam began to cry and said, "My son, what have you done?" Gold could only stammer and try to comfort his father. Then the old man asked, "This won't affect your job at the Heart Station, will it?" In that heartrending moment, Gold would write later, "Down went another section of the mountain."[56]

"Conviction would be very difficult"

A few hours earlier, in Washington, a high-level conference was held in the office of Deputy Attorney General James McInerney. Joining him were his deputies Peyton Ford and William Foley and FBI representatives D. M. Ladd, Louis Nichols, and A. H. Belmont. It was quickly decided that they would "proceed against Gold under Section 34 of Title 50, United States Code, charging a conspiracy to violate Subsection (a) of Section 32 of Title 50" of the espionage statute. Criminal prosecution would originate in the Eastern District of New York, although they could as easily have chosen Santa Fe or Boston. It appears the decision was fairly arbitrary. One top FBI administrator suggested: "From the standpoint of public relations it might be desirable to handle this in the Eastern District of New York as we have not given them a big case for a long time."

There was much concern about the strength of the government's case. As many of the officials recognized, and as Belmont stated in his departmental memo, "the case stands chiefly on the confession of Gold." While they appreciated his willingness to confess, there was "no assurance he will continue to feel this way." In addition, they were not certain they "could obtain Fuchs as a witness against Gold or whether Fuchs's statement . . . could be used in the absence of Fuchs." Given these legal impediments, they agreed to aggressively push forward and acquire as much corroborative evidence as possible. But it was clear that if Gold's confession proved inadmissible, "conviction would be very difficult."[57]

A courtroom defeat was a sobering concern. If the British refused to release Klaus Fuchs from his prison cell to testify in an American court of law, and Gold's attorney persuaded his client to adopt a new attitude and plead not guilty, what Hoover was calling "the FBI's toughest case" would become its most embarrassing case.[58]

It was also determined that either Ford or McInerney would call "Judge McGranery in Philadelphia for the purpose of having Judge McGranery handle the arraignment of Gold in Philadelphia."[59] It was Arthur Cornelius, the head of the FBI's Philadelphia office, who ended up making the call.

During their conversation later that evening, Judge McGranery "inquired as to what bail was recommended." When this question was placed before the attorney general, McInerney "advised that the department recommended $100,000 bail." Cornelius forwarded this recommendation to the judge.

As they waited for a complaint to be signed and a warrant issued, "agents had called from the home of Judge McGranery at 10 PM" saying they and the judge expected to be in the judge's chambers within a few minutes. By 10:35 the attorney general's office, the FBI, and Judge McGranery had agreed on the date for the preliminary hearing. Cornelius would call from the judge's chambers "as soon as the arraignment had been held." It was held right away. With only a few reporters and photographers watching, Judge McGranery had Gold read the complaint, set bail at $100,000 and—after a week of voluntary interviews—heard the prisoner ask for an attorney.[60] By 11:15 it was over.

Reporters hoping to get a feel for the controversial man who had supposedly done such great damage to his country were disappointed to hear him speak only twice. He admitted he was Harry Gold and requested permission to telephone his brother to get him a lawyer. The FBI offered a couple of quotations, presumably from Gold. "I thought that I would be helping a nation whose final aims I approved along the road to industrial strength. Particularly was I taken with the idea that whatever I did would go to help make living conditions far more advanced along the road as we know them here in the United States." And he "felt that as an ally I was only helping the Soviet Union obtain certain information that I thought it was entitled to."[61]

This late-night court session was a hurried improvisation. Gold had been prepared to divulge more names and activities and had agreed to remain in the hands of the FBI even though he was not under arrest. On May 23 the order came from Washington that he was to be arrested immediately and taken before a judge that very night. The abrupt shift in plans was caused by a leak about the impending arrest. Hoover was furious. Up to that point the investigation had been orchestrated to perfection. An incredible departmental effort that had started with approximately a thousand suspects had "finally [been] narrowed down to about five people and then finally narrowed down to two and on Sunday . . . down to one."[62] Hoover had not even told the president—"the whole thing was very secret" in order to allow his agents, Lamphere and Clegg, time to work on Fuchs in London while others talked with Gold in Philadelphia. Gold had given the Bureau a "wealth of material," and Hoover was "anxious to run down these leads." But now both the politicians and the media had been tipped off. "With a leak of this kind," the livid director wrote to his deputies, "the only safe move we can make is an arrest but the case is practically lost from the point of view of developing a large espionage ring."[63]

Hoover pointedly informed high-ranking officials at the attorney general's office, late on the afternoon of May 23, that "it was vitally important that we know who disclosed this information." If the source was "on the other side of the Atlantic we ought to know that too." He "had hoped . . . to hold this arrest until next week," thereby giving his men in London and Philadelphia time to complete their investigative work. Apparently Gold and his father and brother were willing to be part of this plan. But "if it is known to the newspapers we could not afford to wait any longer."[64]

The unexpected rush to arrest Gold and go public ahead of the news stories caused some harsh feelings among some of Hoover's most favored reporters, who had grown used to prior notification of major events. A reporter from the *New York Daily News* called the Bureau and "remonstrated . . . that she had been made to look like a fool in her office because she had no indication that a story of this nature was going to break."

The reporter, who "had done numerous favors for the Bureau in the past and secured favorable editorial comment for the Bureau" felt she had been cut out from her normal position as a Hoover favorite.[65]

"An attorney of more ability and stature"

Joe and Sam Gold were faced with the task of getting Harry a lawyer. Joe called local FBI chief Arthur Cornelius shortly after the arraignment at 3:00 A.M. and expressed a few concerns. He suggested that Harry might have been "too cooperative" with the FBI and put Aaron Miller, a local attorney, on the phone to ask exactly what Harry was being charged with. Miller followed that conversation with an early morning visit to the FBI offices. He wanted more information regarding the charges and said he was "considering whether he should represent" the Gold family.[66] Cornelius had the delicate task of dissuading the attorney from taking the case, but not so ardently as to alienate him if he chose to do so. It was imperative the Bureau still have access to Gold.

Cornelius needn't have worried. Miller called him back a little after noon and said he "was not taking the case and was going to so inform Joseph Gold." After weighing all aspects of such a high-profile case, Miller had come to "the opinion that Harry Gold would need an attorney of more ability and stature than he." Moreover, he "did not want to get mixed up in a case of this type."[67]

What had dampened the attorney's initial enthusiasm was the blizzard of front-page newspaper headlines, photos, and articles on the morning of May 24. Gold's arrest was the biggest story in the country.

Part 2
The Prisoner

CHAPTER 11

· ·

Conversion

Wednesday, May 24, 1950, was far from a slow news day. The Selective Service Act had just been extended another two years; Field Marshal Viscount Wavell, the one-eyed British general who crushed the Italian army in Africa, had died at 67; and General Motors and the United Auto Workers had signed a new wage agreement. Those stories, however, were all pushed aside by the arrest of the spy who had passed the secrets of the atomic bomb to the Russians. A three-inch banner headline atop the *Philadelphia Inquirer* announced, "Chemist Arrested Here as Atom Spy, Gave Fuchs Stolen Secrets to Reds."[1] The *Evening Bulletin* led with "Scientist Seized Here as Atom Spy; Passed Secrets to Russia, FBI Says."[2] In the *Philadelphia Daily News,* "Phila. Man is Held on 100Gs Bail as Fuchs' Atom Spy Aide in Red Thefts" covered the entire front page.[3]

The story was much the same across the country. The *New York Times* announced "Philadelphian Seized as Spy On Basis of Data From Fuchs."[4] National news magazines were mesmerized by "a mild, shy man with a dilettante's interest in symphonic music and the ballet," who had never been arrested or involved in left-wing activity, committing such a horrendous crime.[5] Under the headline "Good Boy Gone Wrong," *Newsweek*

219

asked: "What was the lure which made brilliant young people the spies and dupes of the Soviet police state?"[6]

Even the FBI was taken aback by the publicity. In the spy's home town the news coverage easily matched that of VE Day and VJ Day or anything else in living memory. Articles and photographs told of the spy's ignominious acts, what his neighbors thought of him, where he went to school, and where he worked. There were columns devoted to his favorite music, books, and hobbies. He was the subject of everything from an eleven-part newspaper series to crossword puzzle entries.[7]

Newspapers and reporters tried to outdo each other in pursuing new leads and little-known personal tidbits that their competitors hadn't mentioned. The many photos showed a small, moonfaced man with downcast eyes and double chin, wearing a drab suit and his tie tucked into his trousers. Handcuffed and wearing a perpetually glum expression, he was shown being shuffled in and out of vehicles and buildings by heavyset U.S. marshals. Though he looked harmless, the FBI assured the public Harry Gold was the real deal—an accomplished spy who had aided Klaus Fuchs in giving the atomic bomb to the Russians.

"This little, quiet, mousy guy"

The public was transfixed, but those who knew Gold were "flabbergasted." The *Philadelphia Inquirer* described the "shocked amazement" of neighbors on Kindred Street. "I just can't believe it," said one resident. "He seemed like such a nice fellow. He was so quiet."[8] Another neighbor, Marie Frignito, said she "couldn't believe Harry was involved with a spy ring unless he was tricked. He doesn't seem the type. He's very generous-hearted and intelligent."[9]

Former teachers remembered him as being "exceptionally bright" and studious, and certainly not disposed to this type of activity. "He was very mild and quite a little introverted, but he had top marks," recalled Matthias Richards, principal of South Philadelphia High School for Boys.[10]

At Philadelphia General Hospital, doctors and nurses "seemed amazed at the news of the arrest." There was widespread agreement that of the hundreds of staff members at PGH, Gold was the least likely to involve himself in such a serious adventure. "You wouldn't really take a second look at him," commented Dr. Pascal F. Lucchesi, the hospital's medical director, who said he was "terribly shocked" by the news. "He's only about five feet four inches tall, has stooped shoulders and always seems to mind his own business."[11] Dr. Daniel W. Lewis, a research fellow in cardiology at PGH, said, "Gold was extremely conscientious and hard-working" and "frequently put in more time on his job than he was called to do." Dr. Lucchesi remarked, "We all used to comment among ourselves when he worked long after regular hours, sometimes until 11 o'clock at night."

Dr. Richard Monheit had always viewed Gold as a "self-contained, little guy" who was "very dedicated, hard working," and "never talked about politics." Astonished by Gold's arrest and the subsequent press coverage, Monheit said he and the other hospital personnel "couldn't understand this little, quiet, mousy guy could have caused all this furor."[12] Dorothy Bell, the Heart Station technician who had taken Gold's calls on Monday and Tuesday saying he wouldn't be coming to work, said, "He was the most considerate man I had known. He was very competent and he was all business."[13]

Speculation that Gold had been planted at PGH as a spy by the Russians became so intense that physicians had to reassure the public that there was nothing to spy on. "There is no secrecy concerning the work at the hospital," said Dr. Herbert Baganz. "There is no secret projects [sic] here, and nothing that has to do with atomic energy, radium or anything in that line."[14]

Reporters flocked to the Gold home on Kindred Street, where Sam and Joe were barraged with painful questions. When asked about his brother's political beliefs, Joe angrily replied, "All I know is my brother is not a Communist. He never has been a Communist. My father, Samuel, is not a Communist, and neither am I."[15] "Harry was a good boy," Sam told reporters, and weakly suggested that "maybe they gave him some drug." He spoke "between sobs as he paced the living room nervously" and enumerated his son's many good deeds over the years. "During the Depression, when I was working only one or two days a week, Harry gave us $1,000 so that the family could eat."[16]

"This makes all the difference in the world"

After his early morning arraignment hearing, Gold was taken to Moyamensing Prison at Tenth and Reed streets in South Philadelphia. This was his first time in a prison, and he was fortunate to be given a cell of his own and kept "under constant watch throughout the night." Newspaper readers were told he had a "sleepless" night. Later that day he was transferred to Holmesburg Prison, another city jail in Northeast Philadelphia, near the confluence of Pennypack Creek and the Delaware River. Holmesburg was a nineteenth-century fortresslike structure usually reserved for the city's worst offenders. Ten dreary cellblocks radiated from a central hub or rotunda in the classic spoke-and-wheel pattern that Philadelphia prison architects and Quaker reformers had developed and offered to the world for emulation. The compound was enclosed by a thirty-five-foot fieldstone wall.

The prison superintendent, Dr. Frederick Baldi, claimed that Gold was transferred because "Moyamensing is pretty well overcrowded," but the real reason was that Holmesburg was the more secure facility and held the city's more dangerous criminals and those with the highest bails.[17] Though Gold didn't look particularly menacing, the public was assured that he qualified on both counts. Inside Holmesburg, however, where muscle and intimidation trumped press releases, prison officials quickly recognized that the diminutive connoisseur of stage plays and Italian opera was out of his element. Gold was given a cell of his own and placed in administrative segregation under close watch. Warden Robert Beveridge said "the isolation was to protect Gold from possible violence from other prisoners."[18] Traitors have never been popular on the nation's cellblocks.

While many around him were concerned for his physical welfare, Gold, characteristically, was preoccupied with other matters. Sensitive and important medical experiments required his attention at the Heart Station.[19] Gold "realized he was not in a position to be asking any favors" at Holmesburg, but "wondered if one thing could be arranged"—a phone call to someone in the lab so that he "could explain the status of each of the experiments" and what needed to be done. He repeatedly brought this concern to the attention of prison officials and visiting FBI agents. No doubt they told him he had more important things to worry about. He would remain both embarrassed and "resentful" that this request was refused.[20]

On May 26, prison officials contacted the FBI to inform them that Gold might soon have an attorney. William A. Gray, "a prominent criminal attorney" in the city, had notified them that Joseph Gold had requested his services. Gray said that if he took the case, it would be "for the money" and that his involvement "would help and not hinder the FBI." Cornelius, the local FBI chief, had Gray checked out. He was "one of the top three criminal attorneys in the state of Pennsylvania" and was viewed as "friendly" to the FBI and "not a left-winger," with "no indication that he is crooked."[21]

Gray followed up with a call to Cornelius. He reported that he had an appointment to see Gold at the prison but would take the case only "if he pleaded guilty." Gray also told Cornelius that it would be better if he represented Gold "rather than . . . some other attorney with a different viewpoint." Gray's comment is indicative of the anger and revulsion many people felt. The attorney seemed to suggest that he would be performing a public service if he kept Gold from mounting a reasonable or aggressive defense.[22]

Cornelius had another important conversation that day. He and Judge McGranery discussed the interrogation sessions the FBI was continuing to hold with the defendant. McGranery suggested "the Bureau might want to clear it with the [Justice] Department before attempting to talk with Gold in order that the Department could not later say that the matter should have been cleared with them." Cornelius informed the judge that it was Gold who "requested the agents come to the prison to talk to him and had requested that the interviews be continued." Moreover, said Cornelius, "Gold as yet did not have an attorney." Apparently satisfied, McGranery replied, "This makes all the difference in the world." The agent understood this to mean that "the interviews were entirely satisfactory under these circumstances."[23] As far as Cornelius and his Washington superiors were concerned, the interviews would continue, but once Gold had retained a lawyer, the interviews would not be resumed without "express permission of the attorney."

The FBI paid close attention to the Gold family's efforts to secure legal counsel. They took note of newspaper articles that revealed the family's "appealing for assistance to get an attorney," which indicated a "shortage of funds."[24] The money issue, as well as the notoriety of the case and public hostility toward the Soviet Union, no doubt played a role in Gray's eventual decision not to represent Gold.[25] Few would criticize Gray; no one wanted to risk his reputation on a defendant who had sold his country down the river.

On their first trip to Holmesburg, Sam and Joe Gold had to wait almost and hour and a half before being allowed to see Harry. They may have been family, but the FBI agents had first crack at him and were in the midst of another lengthy interview. When Sam and Joe were allowed in the visitor's room it was only for fifteen minutes, long enough for them to become "shaken" and "teary-eyed."[26] Harry tried to encourage them, told them not to worry, and said he was even getting some outdoor exercise now. He did not mention that he could go outdoors only after the exercise yard was cleared of other inmates. The warden kept him isolated to ensure that his high-profile prisoner was not assaulted. Gold walked the yard alone, contemplating his reviled acts and gloomy future, and listening to periodic catcalls from other prisoners. Before they left, Sam and Joe again impressed upon Harry how important it was that he have an attorney.

Back at the Gold residence in Oxford Circle, Sam was on a regimen of doctor-ordered sedatives. Despite his anguish, the cabinetmaker defended Harry to anyone who might listen. "My son is not a Communist. If he did anything, he was only trying to help Russia to become strong like America." "He was my golden boy," he said in broken English. "He wouldn't hurt this country. He may have wanted to help the Russians but he would not hurt this country, his own father and brother." Sam talked about the family's struggles in South Philadelphia, how they shared what little they had with those who were less fortunate, and how Harry was "brought up to help the poor. He always brought stray cats and dogs into the house to be fed." Looking forlorn and frightened, the old man asked, "They won't hang him, will they? It all happened so fast and I want to see him and help him. He is of my flesh and blood."[27]

On May 29 Gold asked Prison Superintendent Frederick S. Baldi if he could talk to Judge McGranery. With little money to hire an attorney of his own, and unwilling to deplete his father and brother's modest savings, he was hoping the judge would appoint an attorney to help with the myriad legal issues he faced. He was only requesting an attorney because of Sam and Joe's urging—Harry was sure the statements he had already made had "cooked" him and that he "couldn't implicate himself any worse."[28] He made it clear that if Gray or another lawyer advised him to stop talking, he would disregard that advice, unless, of course, someone "convinced him that further talking would involve him and his family in worse fashion than he was already involved."[29] The next day Gold was taken down to the Federal Building for a ten-minute meeting with the judge.[30] He said he was prepared to plead guilty to acting as a "courier for a Russian atomic bomb spy ring" but would not admit to trying deliberately to harm the United States. "I had no intention of hurting my country," McGranery quoted Gold as saying. Harry also stipulated that he wanted court-appointed counsel "whose patriotism is unimpeachable, with the entire respect of the court, public and bar." He didn't want anybody who had any suggestion of radical or "red leanings."[31] Lastly, he desired "to continue cooperating with the FBI."[32] The judge assured him that he would consider his request and give due deliberation to which member of the Philadelphia legal community should take such an unrewarding legal case.

McGranery, some might argue, had a grand sense of humor. A law school graduate and Philadelphia ward politician who worked his way up the political ladder, he had waged losing campaigns for Congress and the district attorney's office before finally winning a seat in the House of Representatives in 1937. He served until 1943, when he was appointed an assistant attorney general of the United States. In addition to the Immigration and Naturalization Service and the Bureau of Prisons, he also had oversight of the Federal Bureau of Investigation. In 1946 he was appointed to the federal bench for the Eastern District of Pennsylvania.

With the Gold case, which was critically important to the FBI and Director Hoover, McGranery was performing on a national stage. Gold had made himself available to FBI investigators for well over a week; the Bureau had even kept watch over him in a hotel room for two nights. They were pushing the constitutional envelope, but Philadelphia's legal community was in no great hurry to get involved. Members of the bar who could usually be counted on to take high-publicity cases were nowhere to be found. McGranery allegedly made a few phone calls but had little to show for them. "There wasn't a long line of takers," recalled one observer. "Nobody was . . . in a big hurry to try this case."[33]

McGranery came up with a novel and creative choice for Gold's defense counsel: John D. M. Hamilton. To most observers, Hamilton and Gold must have seemed as odd a couple as one could imagine sharing a defense table in a criminal courtroom.

"I'm going everywhere"

A child of comfort and privilege, John Daniel Miller Hamilton was born in 1892 in Fort Madison, Iowa. His father was an attorney for the Atchison, Topeka & Santa Fe Railroad.[34] Sent east for his education, he attended "the famous and fashionable Phillips Andover Academy" in Massachusetts and then in 1913 went on to Northwestern University, where he earned a law degree.[35] Despite being married and well connected, and therefore protected from the draft, Hamilton joined the army and served in a machine gun company during the First World War. After the war he rejoined his family in Topeka, Kansas, and found that he had a flair for politics.

Hamilton quickly rose from assistant state attorney to the bench, but in a somewhat surprising move gave up the position for electoral politics.[36] He served three terms in the state legislature and became Speaker of the House. A gifted orator and natural politician, Hamilton rapidly assumed the leadership of both the American Legion and the Kansas Republican Party. In the process he developed a friendship with Governor Alf Landon, another Kansas politician with a growing national reputation. As their careers and reputations thrived, and despite being "on different sides of the Republican fence—Landon was a liberal Republican and Hamilton a conservative Republican in the intra-party scrapping of those days"—both men saw 1936 as their year.[37]

When Landon won his party's nomination for president, he asked Hamilton to take over the National Republican Committee. Then an energetic, red-haired, forty-four-year-old lawyer, Hamilton set about developing a winning campaign.[38] The past year had brought some hope that the Depression might be ending, and Franklin Roosevelt had rejuvenated the Democratic Party, yet Hamilton envisioned a Republican victory. He believed he could win Florida and Texas, and victory was almost assured in states like Oklahoma, Nebraska, and Missouri. "I'm going everywhere," he said. "An airplane will take me and I'm going to do it awful fast. My headquarters will be in Chicago, but I'll jump around a lot. Two states [a day] isn't so hard when you've got a fast plane and there's work to be done."[39]

Election day proved to be a resounding disaster: Landon won just two states. Still, Hamilton stayed on as party chairman for the next four years and helped Republicans win handsomely in the 1938 congressional elections. When Wendell Willkie received the party's nomination in 1940, he appointed his own man party chair, and Hamilton left politics. Instead of returning to Kansas, however, he was persuaded by the powerful and influential Pew family to relocate to Philadelphia.

The Pews saw Hamilton as an able and active leader who had visited thousands of GOP county chairmen around the nation and rebuilt much of the party. In the right law firm, a man with such connections could be a serious rainmaker. They placed him in one of the most respected firms in the city, Pepper, Bodine, and Stokes, alongside one of the most respected names in American jurisprudence, George Wharton Pepper. Widely considered the dean of the Philadelphia bar, Pepper was born just two years after the Civil War and had graduated from the University of Pennsylvania Law School. Appointed to the U.S. Senate in 1922 to finish the unexpired term of Boies Penrose, Pepper served with such Senate giants as Henry Cabot Lodge, William Borah, and Robert LaFollette, but he was rejected by the party in 1926 in favor of the Philadelphia political boss William S. Vare. Undeterred, Pepper went on to distinguish himself as a lawyer, constitutional scholar, and law professor at Penn, where he taught for more than two decades. Some of his cases became judicial landmarks, such as the Agricultural Adjustment Act case (*United States v. Butler*), in which he persuaded the U.S. Supreme Court that a significant section of Roosevelt's New Deal economic recovery program was unconstitutional.

At Pepper, Bodine, and Stokes, John Hamilton became known as a sage political adviser and strategist and a much-appreciated raconteur. With well-heeled conservative clients like the Pew family, neither he nor the firm was predisposed to representing left-wing radicals or Communist activists, much less atom bomb spies. This was the firm to which Judge McGranery presented the unenviable task of representing Harry Gold.

"Will serve without pay"

The fifty-nine-year-old Hamilton was on the West Coast on business when the FBI arrested Gold. Although the event inspired front-page headlines in California, he paid little attention. It was not until mid-afternoon on June 1, when he was back in Philadelphia, that he took an interest in the case. On that day McGranery called him to explain that Gold "had no means of his own" to acquire legal counsel and "had made a request that the court appoint counsel for him." The judge stated that he "had consulted with several of his colleagues on the District bench and that they thought that [Hamilton] fitted into the picture."

No one would have been surprised if Hamilton had chuckled at the suggestion and respectfully declined, but he didn't. Instead he went to the judge's chambers to discuss the case, and as he listened he gradually grew intrigued. In the end he accepted the assignment, with two conditions. As he would subsequently write, "I had no compunction about acting in th' matter, but I did think that in fairness to myself I should be protect a statement of the court indicating quite clearly that I had not the matter or freely entered into the status of Mr. Gold's att agreed that that should be done as a matter of protecti

Hamilton's second condition was that he wante' the Pepper firm to be appointed as co-counsel. M the custom at elite law firms of young lawyers assi ners, had no problem with that. While they waite be brought from Holmesburg to meet his new coun. in a stenographer to take down a statement for Hamilton contacted his secretary and asked that Aι new member of the firm, come over to the courthouse. Hamilton, Ballard, and Gold "then had a long conversation . . . in the judge's chamber." After Gold gave his assent to the appointment of Hamilton and Ballard as his legal representatives, McGranery called a press conference and issued the following statement:

I have given great consideration to the appointment of counsel in the Harry Gold matter, and as I stated to you yesterday, it was the defendant's own request that the counsel I should appoint to use his precise words "that he did not want a lawyer who would make a show, that he have no radical connections whatever, no leftist or pinkish background whatever." Because of the gravity of the charge and its possible far reaching international implications, it behooves the court to appoint a lawyer whose patriotism would be above reproach, who has public confidence and the respect of the Court, and a deep understanding of the Anglo-Saxon principles as stated in our Constitution of every defendant having the right to be represented by counsel of his choice. With all these factors in mind, the Court could think of no one at the Philadelphia bar who more fittingly fits into that description than Mr. John D. M. Hamilton, who is a law partner of former Senator George Wharton Pepper, the dean of the Philadelphia bar. Mr. Hamilton has consulted with the defendant, Harry Gold, at my invitation and has agreed to accept this appointment of him as official counsel for Gold in the public interest, for which the court is grateful to Mr. Hamilton. Mr. Hamilton has suggested that I name, together with him, Mr. Augustus S. Ballard as associate counsel. Mr. Ballard is a young man at the bar in whom the Court has explicit confidence and I am delighted to name him as associate counsel as Mr. Hamilton has requested.[41]

The appointments drew headlines around the country. "John D. M. Hamilton Will Defend Gold on Soviet Atom Spy Charge" was the headline in the June 1 edition of the *New York Times*. Out of the national news arena for almost a decade, Hamilton may not have been all that pleased that his reappearance came in association with an alleged Russian spy. Perhaps it was just as well that the *Times* did not mention the Pepper firm, though the story did note that "the former chairman of the Republican National Committee . . . will serve without pay."[42]

"He was bored and restless"

at the firm of Pepper, Bodine, and Stokes were shocked by the announcement. "Some of the partners were very upset," recalled Gus Ballard, who had joined the firm just two years earlier and now found himself at the center of one of the biggest legal cases in America. "Many of the partners in the law firm were from old established Philadelphia families and Hamilton didn't quite fit in. A lot of people considered Pepper and Hamilton odd bedfellows in the first place. Hamilton had come roaring out of the West and though he was a good trial lawyer, there was always a noticeable difference between him and the rest of the firm."[43]

Hamilton would admit that his initial reaction to McGranery's request was "a firm No." He had a "violent distaste for everything the Communists represented." Such an appointment "would bring him no money, only criticism." But as he told his senior partner, former Senator George Wharton Pepper, "Somebody has to do it. Every man deserves a defense. I can't very well ask somebody else to do what I wouldn't do." Pepper said simply, "You have to live with yourself, John."[44] Not all of his partners were as understanding.

The disenchantment at the firm paled in comparison to the disillusionment expressed by one of its major corporate clients—the Pew family. "The Pew brothers at Sun Oil were upset with Hamilton," said Ballard. "The Pews were some of the most right-wing people going."[45] Their consternation must have been particularly galling, since they were the ones who had brought Hamilton to Philadelphia. They couldn't fathom why the former GOP chairman would take such a potentially career-killing case.

Ballard, who spent significant time with Hamilton, thought he knew why Hamilton would risk damaging his career, irritating his partners, and upsetting the firm's more influential clients. "He took the case because he was bored and restless. Sure, he thought it was a disgrace that the Philadelphia bar wasn't going to defend this guy, and Harry certainly didn't have a lot of friends in high places, but it was more than that. Hamilton was looking for a little excitement. He was looking for something to sink his teeth into."[46]

Hamilton's decision was all the more surprising because it was exactly counter to what his doctors were telling him. John D. M. Hamilton was not a well man. He had suffered a heart attack shortly before his appointment—something known only to a few family members and close friends. "His doctors," said Ballard, "told him to take it easy. They told him a big case could kill him, and advised he give up trial work altogether." As a big name with significant national connections, he could have done very well as a rainmaker for the firm, attracting clients with deep pockets and letting others do the spadework. But he took Gold's case. "And when he stuck out his jaw and gritted his teeth, you couldn't argue with him after that. He wanted to do it, so he did it."[47] Had Mc-Granery known of Hamilton's fragile health, he probably would not have appointed him, but he didn't and thereby drafted the nationally known Republican to handle one of the most watched cases in America.

"He told me it was a big case"

For Ballard, things were happening at such a rapid clip that it was hard to keep up. Only two years out of law school—just a "kid lawyer," according to his brother[48]—he was assisting someone "rumored to be to the right of Attila the Hun" in the defense a self-confessed Communist spy. It was not a case that would bring a lot of money or new friends. Hamilton recognized the risks of such a controversial undertaking and wanted to know if his young assistant was up for the challenge.

"Hamilton asked me if I wanted to bail out," said Ballard more than half a century later, recalling the enormous pressure they were under. It wasn't a popular case; his own family members questioned its merits. Some considered it a "remarkable opportunity," while others thought it could be a severe blow to a career that had barely started. "I had some apprehension," admitted Ballard. "No competent attorney in the city would take it. The judge had polled the leading criminal lawyers and no one wanted it. There was no money in it and the damn thing could destroy your reputation."[49]

Augustus Stoughton Ballard was one of a long line of Philadelphia Ballards who had made a name for themselves in the legal arena. His grandfather had founded one of Philadelphia's most prominent law firms; his father, Frederick C. Ballard, served as chief counsel for the Philadelphia Transport Company, the city's large mass transit system; and an uncle had founded a law firm in Chicago. Each of Gus Ballard's three brothers would play prominent roles at influential Philadelphia law firms.

Gus grew up in the city's Andorra section and went to Chestnut Hill Academy and the St. George School in Newport, Rhode Island, where he developed an interest in sailing. His education at the University of Pennsylvania was interrupted by service in the South Pacific during World War II. After four years in the army, he returned to Penn Law School and earned his law degree in 1948. He could easily have joined the family's firm, Ballard and Spahr, but he had an independent streak and was set on making his own way. He chose George Wharton Pepper's firm and was learning the nuances of corporate law when a senior member of the outfit plucked him out of nowhere to participate in the hottest criminal case in the country.

Ballard was "delighted" by the selection, "but Hamilton told me to be prepared. He said every kook in the world is going to call you names and say why don't you go back to Russia. He told me it was a big case, but I didn't know how big. Hamilton didn't pull any punches; he told it like it was. He let me know we were going to have a rough time of it."[50]

Hamilton knew whereof he spoke; there was no shortage of disdain for anyone siding with the spy. The newspaper columnist Earl Selby, for example, wrote a piece entitled "Harry Gold: An Intimate Picture of a Spy," which angered a good many who read it. Selby described Gold as "reconciled . . . to a long prison term" and trying to do the right thing. "He is not talking as a stool pigeon who's trying to explain away his own guilt. He consistently has shied away from legal outs & dodges. He does not appear to be talking in hopes of a lighter sentence." Selby went on to describe the "stoop-shouldered man with a moon face . . . and half-shuffle walk" as a man with an "excellent memory—an asset to the Russians when he was a courier-spy is now working against them as he goes back into the last 15 years to name & document detail after detail in his work & contacts with other Soviet agents."[51]

Readers were incensed: how dare Selby say anything positive about a "self-confessed spy"? Gold "deserves no pity," wrote one outraged reader. "Gold is a criminal of the worst kind," and there were "more interesting topics for Selby than the defense of a traitor."[52] Another reader wrote that Selby's article "smells bad." Gold was "a confessed spy and naturally a liar. Anything he says is so much bunk . . . let's keep such trash out of our newspapers."[53] Hamilton, who anticipated such reactions, had clearly given up any notion of re-entering politics.

In his first meeting with his new attorneys, Gold had stated his intent to plead guilty to the charges, but with one reservation. He vehemently denied that "he did the acts charged with an intent to injure the United States." He had acted in the "belief that he should help Russia and an ally of the United States and as an opponent of Fascism."[54] Hamilton wanted to pursue that distinction, given its importance to Gold and the fact that the charge was central to the government's case and not likely to be swept away. He also wanted to determine how the FBI was treating Gold, as well as the conditions he was being kept under at Holmesburg Prison. After meeting him and seeing his modest build and mild manner, Hamilton realized that he might be in some danger among other prisoners. Gold had stated that he wanted to continue cooperating with the Bureau and had developed a comfortable relationship with agents Brennan and Miller. He also claimed he was "being treated perfectly at the prison and had no complaints." If Gold had a concern, it centered on his elderly father and brother. He was "particularly anxious that his brother not pay the penalty" for what he had done. He wanted to make sure his brother didn't lose his job at the Naval Air Supply Depot and that both Joe and Sam be informed he finally had legal representation.[55] And yes, there was one other thing: could Mr. Hamilton facilitate a phone call between him and a co-worker at the PGH Heart Station? He was worried that with his absence no one would be able to complete an experiment he had been working on.

The next day, June 2, Sam and Joe Gold visited John Hamilton's office to discuss Harry's case. In the minutes of the meeting, Hamilton described Sam as "a very small man, not much over five feet, thin, gray and has only one tooth in an otherwise toothless upper jaw. I would say he was about 75 years old." He recorded the old man's early life in Kiev, his work as a cabinetmaker at RCA, and his difficulties providing for his family in America. "He speaks English very badly; in fact it is hard to understand him at all," but it was clear that he was "thoroughly broken by this affair."[56]

Joe Gold was described as "about the same general appearance as Harry" and as having "served with merit in the United States Army." Both father and son described "Harry's need to work throughout his school years" and the generally "bitter struggle" required for him to complete his education. Joe, in particular, talked about his brother's "unselfish" behavior, his willingness to help others, and his regular donations of blood. Looking back, said Joe, the root of the problem was Harry's gullibility: "He could always be tricked into things." As a boy, Harry had been a "goat" whom "his companions in school used . . . for all sorts of trickery."

Hamilton came away believing "that neither of these men knew anything about the affairs with which Harry is now charged"; it was "perfectly apparent that they had lived a clean, wholesome, and a rather happy life."[57]

"At some point he said the hell with it"

As they immersed themselves in the facts of the case and repeatedly traveled up to Northeast Philadelphia to interview their client in Holmesburg, the two lawyers began to see that without Gold's confession and ongoing cooperation, the government's case against him was very weak. Hamilton and Ballard were thus presented with a dilemma: should they launch a vigorous, full-scale defense of their client? Claim his innocence and emphasize to the jury that he had been interrogated by the FBI for days on end and in effect imprisoned in a room at a Center City hotel, all without the benefit of an attorney? Such a strategy might work, but it would also raise the stakes of the entire exercise as well as ruin their names and that of their firm. Hamilton and Ballard had no desire to become renowned left-wing attorneys, specializing in defending Communists and radical bomb throwers.

Their client pulled them back from that precipice. He had already resolved to plead guilty. "We considered a more aggressive defense," said Ballard, "but Gold was so full of mea culpa. He wanted to come clean. There was no changing his mind. He was such a decent guy. He was ashamed of having betrayed his country."[58]

Ballard and Hamilton explained to Gold that "the government had no evidence," just a lot of "cloak and dagger stuff." But Gold never expressed second thoughts about the confession or his cooperation. "He wasn't a steely-nerved criminal" looking to get away with something, Ballard recalled.

With the appointment of legal counsel, Gold would write, "down went more of what remained of my mental mountain." He started telling the FBI and his attorneys things that he had held back in earlier statements. He became more forthcoming about people like Smilg and Slack. He began to remember small details, and also some larger matters—among which was the David Greenglass incident. Though Harry "had forgotten his name completely," he now recalled his "shock at discovering that he was a GI . . . the location of his apartment . . . and that he had a small salami and a pumpernickel loaf sent to him from New York every week."[59]

Even before his first meeting with Hamilton and Ballard at Holmesburg, Gold had already "exposed the rest: Ben Smilg, Abe Brothman, Miriam Moskowitz, Vera Kane, Fred Heller, Joe Brodsky, and the Soviet agent coming to his home."[60] The South Philly boy imbued with the neighborhood ethos of shunning informers was now a permanently open spigot. He helped the FBI as enthusiastically as he once helped the Soviets. As he would come to say of these two intense weeks of interrogation and revelation, "I shall openly brag . . . for I am proud to have contributed to an outstanding bit of police work."[61]

Rather than fight the charges, Gold dedicated himself to making amends. "He just decided to fold his cards. At some point he said the hell with it," Ballard recalled.[62] "Harry was convinced he wanted to go that route and there was no turning him back."[63] In early June, Gold wrote his father and brother from Holmesburg Prison that he was "co-operating to the most complete extent with the investigating agents," and intended to continue doing so.[64]

Hamilton and Ballard visited Gold regularly. Soundscriber disc recordings—a relatively new dictation mechanism that recorded sounds on vinyl discs—were made of most of their interviews. To respond to the government's complaint, the lawyers needed to know everything: how long had he worked as a spy, whom had he worked with, what acts were committed, what if any money he was paid. Gold remained insistent that "he had no intention of hurting his country."

Sitting for hours in the attorney-client visiting area, peppering Gold with questions, asking for explanations, trying to better understand his lengthy career as a spy and courier, Ballard had a front-row seat to one of the strangest alliances ever to come before a federal court in Philadelphia. The young lawyer referred to them as "the atom spy and the old political warhorse. Boy, it was almost worth the price of admission."[65] Early on, Hamilton commented to his assistant on how exceptional a character Gold was. He brought the prisoner reading material to take his mind off things.[66] Ballard saw Gold as a "very meek and mild sort of fellow," but Hamilton would say, "This guy's got more brains than you would give him credit for."[67] "I thought Hamilton must have insight I don't have," said Ballard. "Hamilton and I didn't agree on much, particularly politics. He looked at everything in a different way than I did. He was from Kansas. But for all his reputation as a hard-nosed guy, he was intrigued by Harry. Harry appealed to him in some way. Hamilton said, 'If we don't defend him, he's a goner.' He was talking about the death sentence. We were scared to death of it."

The more time they spent with him, the more Ballard understood why Hamilton was so captivated. "When he was first arrested he was bewildered. As time went on he got with it. He was a funny little fellow. We were both inclined to believe him. He was easily misled, a sucker for those people who wanted to use him. He was very naïve and all too ready to believe people, but for all the terrible things he was charged with he was really a very decent, caring individual." Pretty soon, Ballard admitted, "I was carrying the torch myself."[68]

"Never discussed politics"

As Hamilton and Ballard were beginning to do their homework, the FBI was well into mining everything it could about Gold. His modest bank statements and loan record were gathered, neighbors and co-workers were interviewed; the Bureau even researched what books he had bor-rowed from the library.

Rarely did interviewees diverge in their assessments of Gold. Dr. Samuel Bellet, his superior at PGH, described him as "a very hard worker, pleasant, a type of individual who would do anyone in the Heart Station a favor at any time."[69] Dorothy Bell, a lab technician, called the prisoner "very pleasant," a "hard worker," and someone who would always be "will-ing to do anyone in the Heart Station a favor. . . . Nothing has ever oc-curred which would cause her to question his loyalty in any way."[70]

To Dr. William A. Steiger he was a "very likeable person, easy going," and an "extremely hard worker" who never gave anyone reason to ques-tion his loyalty. "Never," according to Steiger, did they "discuss political matters or world affairs."[71] Margaret A. Tierney, a stenographer-clerk, said much the same but added that during "the past two months, she had noticed a gradual change in Gold's mannerisms, in that he became in-creasingly nervous." Others who recognized this change, being unaware of the significance of the Fuchs arrest, attributed it to Gold's long work hours. The interviews became so repetitive that agents finally decided to list the names of doctors, nurses, and lab technicians beneath this head-ing: "The following individuals . . . could furnish no information in addi-tion to what had previously been set forth."

Gold's former Pennsylvania Sugar Company co-workers said much the same. Dr. Gustave T. Reich, the mentor who had nurtured the pris-oner's interest in chemistry and from whom his pupil later stole trade se-crets, called his protégé "industrious, hard-working, and an intelligent chemist."[72] Another co-worker, Clarence Hunt, told the FBI "he just could not believe that Gold would knowingly do anything that was wrong."[73] Morrell Dougherty, Harry's best friend, couldn't believe "he was so close to Gold yet . . . knew nothing about him or his activities." Gold "never discussed politics" or read the *Daily Worker*. The nearest thing to a political statement Dougherty ever heard from him was a ref-erence to Father Coughlin as a "rabble rouser." Gold "regularly took the Jewish holidays off" and once, in the mid-1930s, stayed out of work "28 days during which time a strike was in progress." Asked about trips out-side the Philadelphia region, Dougherty said all his excursions with Gold —such as a visit to Chicago, Pekin, and Peoria, Illinois, in June 1945— were work related and "for the purpose of obtaining . . . methods of dis-tilling grain alcohol."[74]

The FBI even tracked down Mary Catherine Lanning, Gold's former girlfriend, who was now working in a laboratory at Children's Hospital of

Philadelphia. She admitted that "Gold had at one time proposed marriage to her" but that she had "declined his offer." She also said that Gold
had mentioned "a visit to New Mexico" and "having been in the city of
Santa Fe." She thought she remembered Gold telling her that "Pennsylvania Sugar had some interest in a Coca Cola bottling plant in that
area."[75]

Back at Holmesburg, Gold was doing double duty as the centerpiece
of intense and lengthy interrogation sessions with both the FBI and his
attorneys. No one inside Holmesburg's ominous walls could recall anyone
spending so many hours telling of his exploits and associations. As Ballard
remarked, "Harry was tireless in his cooperation with the government.
He was a compulsive worker."[76] Gold spent his mornings with FBI investigators, who would then have to leave in the afternoon when the attorneys arrived. The agents would often reappear in the evening for an
additional session. For the agents and lawyers it was like shift work, with
time for recuperation between interviews; for Gold it was nonstop. Never
did he plead exhaustion or send his visitors away, even though the hours
were staggering and would be used by his lawyers to show the judge—
and later the parole boards—the extent and sincerity of his cooperation.
Through it all, the embattled defendant maintained an equanimity that
impressed the federal agents, his lawyers, and correctional staff. Gold
even found occasional humor in the proceedings. He once compared
himself to the popular radio character Fibber McGee. "Old Fibber and
I have something in common," he said to the agents: "Neither one of us
ever got to clean out that closet."[77]

As Robert Lamphere, the lead FBI agent assigned to track down
Fuchs's American contact, would one day write, "The quantity of information that was coming from . . . Harry Gold was enormous; as important, its factual content tended to verify our earlier notions about KGB
networks inside the United States." For Lamphere, the unthreatening
Gold was a "really important espionage figure" whose long active career
documented his importance to Soviet operations in America.[78] "Cases
developed from the confession of Harry Gold were breaking everywhere . . . more than they could handle"; he and Ernie Van Loon found
the "crush so great" that they "didn't have time to stick to normal Bureau
procedures." "Harry had an excellent memory," said Lamphere, and that
contributed to a heavy workload. "I ended up working 22 hours a
day . . . we had a raging monster underway."[79] Every time they sat down
with him, new information and names seemed to come forth. Special
Agent Scott Miller, who along with his partner Dick Brennan had devel-

oped a rapport with Gold, compared interviewing him to "squeezing a lemon; there was always a drop or two left."[80]

During an afternoon interview in early June, John Hamilton suggested that Gold might want to jot down his own account of how he got himself into this mess. It was a casual, spontaneous suggestion—Hamilton did not yet know his client well enough to anticipate Gold's workhorse approach. Ballard remembered Hamilton saying on the way back from the prison that day, "He's a compulsive writer; maybe we'll get something out of it." Hamilton and Ballard were astounded when Gold presented them with a 123-page handwritten treatise on his career as a secret agent. "The Circumstances Surrounding My Work as a Soviet Agent" covered everything from the Golodnitsky family's arrival in America and their struggles to survive in South Philadelphia during the Depression to his decision to help the Russians by stealing documents from Pennsylvania Sugar and his relationship with the infamous Klaus Fuchs. Even more impressive is that Gold must have rewritten it in pencil at least half a dozen times before he felt that it adequately conveyed what he hoped to communicate. The document would prove invaluable, both to his attorneys and to the FBI, as well as to congressional investigative committees and Cold War scholars in later years.

The first of the many legal issues that the lawyers had to deal with was the official complaint. Hamilton read it aloud to Gold, underscoring two sections: "Whoever with intent or reason to believe that it is to be used to the injury of the United States" and subsection A, "in time of war, shall be punished by death or by imprisonment for not more than thirty years."[81]

When Gold was asked if he was aware of the specifics of the statute, he admitted that he was not. But when Hamilton followed up with the key question, "Do you have any change of heart [regarding your plea]?" Gold replied, "No, I do not."

Hamilton then moved on to related issues: whether to waive the government's need to show "preliminary proof"; accepting or opposing Brooklyn as the origin of the indictment; and Gold's strong opposition to the government's claim that he had acted with "harmful intent to the United States." Since Gold had already received "enough harmful publicity," Hamilton didn't see why he should suffer through another wave of headlines; therefore they would waive the government's need to show proof. On the matter of a trial site, Hamilton argued that "whatever weight [Hamilton] might have in this case would be best" utilized if the trial took place in Philadelphia. Gold agreed, not wanting to burden his father and brother with trips to New York. As for "harmful intent," Hamilton said it would be a difficult clause to excise, but they would try and would also ask the judge to consider "any other ameliorating circumstances" that might affect the sentence.[82]

Hamilton and Ballard then had a series of conversations with Gerald A. Gleeson, an assistant attorney general for the Eastern District of Pennsylvania. They wanted the "intent" item taken out of the complaint, Gold's trial to be conducted in Philadelphia, and some kind of assurance the death penalty would not be a government priority. Gleeson was noncommittal on all three, a stance that irritated Hamilton. He was not asking for a pass—he knew the seriousness of the charges against his client —but he was hoping for some sign of compromise. Did the government have to be intransigent on every point?

Ballard and Hamilton knew they "didn't have a leg to stand on, but we wanted a favor and if they weren't going to extend themselves we would have to play it tough as well."[83] Hamilton told Gleeson, "Look Buster, if we pull Harry out of the case you don't have anything," Ballard recalled. "We threatened to withdraw the guilty plea" and have Gold "renounce his confession." That caught Gleeson's attention.

Hamilton's client had been interviewed for hours on end for more than a week and been confined for two nights in a hotel room under guard without the benefit of a lawyer—all before he was even arrested. With the Venona decrypts unavailable for courtroom presentation and little else to document Gold's involvement, without his evidence the prosecution's case would hinge almost entirely on the presence and participation of Klaus Fuchs. And that was looking increasingly problematic. British officials were progressively more resistant to allowing Fuchs to testify in an American courtroom. A written deposition from Fuchs might be the most the prosecutors would have to work with.[84] It wasn't an encouraging prospect, and aggressive lawyering by Gold's legal team would only muddy the waters. Gleeson said he would get back to them.

"Hi Kike"

After Hamilton's acceptance of the Harry Gold case put him in the public eye for the first time in years, Leon J. Obermayer, a prominent Philadelphia attorney, wrote Hamilton a letter: "Today, more than ever, I am delighted that you are a 'Philadelphia lawyer.' In representing Gold you are observing and preserving the best traditions of the law and showing a fine example of unselfish American citizenship."[85] Hamilton appreciated the note from a fellow member of the local bar, because he was having a rough time of it. Not everyone was as enthusiastic about his taking the case. "I am having some calls from the bigoted and intolerant," he replied to Obermayer, "but I put that down to ignorance of the higher duty and tradition which you mentioned."[86]

Hamilton also received a welcome letter from the nation's capital. "I do want to take this occasion to express to you my appreciation of the excellent cooperation which you have extended to the FBI, and particularly to our Philadelphia office in the Gold case. If you get to Washington again, please drop by my office so that I may have the opportunity to say hello to you."[87] The author of this note, J. Edgar Hoover, had every reason to be well disposed toward him. Hamilton and Gold were now marching in lockstep with the FBI. Hamilton thanked Hoover for the note, calling it "particularly welcome as a matter of personal satisfaction. I at no time entertained any doubt as to my obligation as an attorney to accept Judge McGranery's appointment and while there has been a most complimentary press, some seem to think I have acted unwisely. A full and active life has led me to the conclusion that at times the intolerant and the bigoted threaten our national security as well as those engaged in subversive activities."[88]

The Golds were also getting mail and phone calls, but theirs, unlike Hamilton's, were relentlessly negative. "Hi Kike," read one note to Sam Gold. "Your son Harry should be hung, and all Jews who call themselves 'Russians' and who love Russia more than the USA. What we need here is a Hitler to decimate Jews, Yids & Kikes." The note was signed "A1-Citzen."[89] Sam and Joe received so many crank and hate-filled calls that within twenty-four hours of the first headline they were forced to get an unlisted phone number.[90]

"Our lives have been ruined," Joe Gold soberly admitted. "I suppose I could call Harry a snake and a viper, the way some columnists have done, but then I'd feel like a viper myself. Harry has been a good brother to me." Despite having served with distinction in the military, Joe received several death threats and was constantly on the lookout for assailants now that his photo had appeared in the newspapers. "Fortunately," he said, "I'm not particularly handsome or ugly, and nobody seems to recognize me. I never did a bad thing in my life, nothing exceptional at all. I suppose now I'll never get a car or get married. The lives of Pop and myself are ruined, I guess, but what can we do? We can't criticize Harry, though we have no sympathy for his views. Harry is Harry. He is in a public fishbowl now, and what he thought he was doing will all come out at the public hearing."[91]

"The crowd booed"

Gold made a brief appearance in front of Judge McGranery on June 12, for a hearing on the government's request to transfer him from Philadelphia to Brooklyn. Hamilton argued for and received "more time to study the indictment." On the issue of where to try Gold, Gleeson was no longer obstructionist but did observe, "If Gold wants to enter a plea of guilty here he must first obtain [the] consent . . . of U.S. Attorney J. Vincent Keogh of Brooklyn."[92] What was occurring on the streets outside the courthouse was more newsworthy. Thousands of Philadelphians had gathered for a glimpse of the spy. Traffic came to a standstill as people packed four and five deep at the intersection of Ninth and Market streets pushed and shoved for a view of Gold. To prevent an ugly incident, deputy U.S. marshals hurried the prisoner out a side door and into a waiting car. "The crowd booed" and hurled epithets as Gold, heavily shackled, was hustled into the car.

Within days, both Alfred D. Slack and David Greenglass were arrested in what the newspapers would call "one of the most sweeping crackdowns on suspected spies and subversives in the history of the country."[93] Harry Gold, who had performed so dutifully for so many years for the Soviets, was now the source of a reign of terror from which the KGB would never recover.

· ·

CHAPTER 12

To Make Amends

The year 1950 would see many important events, notable personal achievements, and significant firsts. Ezzard Charles successfully defended his heavyweight boxing title three times, and Man o' War was named the greatest horse of the first half of the century. William Faulkner won the Nobel Prize for literature, *All the King's Men* got the Academy Award for best motion picture, the federal minimum wage was raised to seventy-five cents an hour, and the longest vehicular tunnel in the United States, the Brooklyn-Battery Tunnel, opened in New York City. But for a particular segment of the population, 1950 would be remembered as an unsettling period of angst and recrimination that would usher in years of political discord. Whether America had become a sieve for foreign agents or a victim of political hysteria, the ideological battle was engaged, the debate was bitter, and the psychological scars were deep enough to sustain a half century of internal conflict.

Beginning with Alger Hiss's second trial for perjury in January and continuing through Harry Gold's sentencing later that December, the year was full of high-profile arrests, arraignments, and sensational trials of Americans accused as Soviet spies and Communist operatives. The formal allegations involved only a handful of people, but the accusations were so startling and the media coverage so bold that it must have seemed to many Americans not a week went by without someone's being charged with treason. One man, a mild-mannered biochemist from Philadelphia with a passion for opera and baseball, fingered many of them and put many behind bars. Pressing forward through public scorn and endless debate, Harry Gold seemed dedicated to undoing everything he had done since the Depression. Was he oblivious to the pain he was causing, or just reaffirming his love of America? The recipient of the Order of the Red Star turned out to be a windfall for the FBI: as FBI supervisor Robert Lamphere wrote, "The quantity of information that was coming . . . from Harry Gold was enormous. Gold would name all his contacts, and we would find them and get them to confess and to lead us to still more Soviet agents."[1] By the time they were through "mining Gold's information," Lamphere continued, "we had opened forty-nine separate cases." Many targets were convicted and jailed; others fled and were "never seen again in the United States."

The Mountain Had Been Leveled

On Thursday, June 15—just a month after special agents Scotty Miller and Dick Brennan walked into Philadelphia General Hospital's Heart Station looking for Harry Gold—FBI agents arrested Alfred Dean Slack in Syracuse. One day later, David Greenglass was picked up in New York City for having passed secret atomic data while working at Los Alamos in 1945, when he was a sergeant in the army. Greenglass then named his sister and brother-in-law as part of the effort. Harry Gold's wagon train of misery and regret was on the move.[2]

Month after month, suspected Soviet operatives were arrested, charged, and jailed. Gold was the centerpiece of what the FBI would call "a wide manhunt for persons connected to him." The exercise took on darker meaning in late June with the start of the Korean War. Many believed the North Koreans would not have invaded the South if the Soviets had not had the bomb.

Slack and Greenglass confessed even faster than Gold had. At his Syracuse arraignment, Slack admitted giving the Soviets a sample of and the data behind RDX, the powerful new explosive being manufactured at the Holston Ordnance Works in Kingsport, Tennessee, in 1943 and 1944. But he denied having ever been a Communist. "I am not now and never was a member of the Communist Party," he said, "and never would be." When asked by a reporter whether he knew Harry Gold, he replied, "I don't recall ever knowing anybody by that name."[3] Two days later, handcuffed and shackled, Slack was placed in a car under heavy guard and taken to Tennessee, where he would ultimately be tried.

On New York's Lower East Side, Julius Rosenberg repeatedly warned his brother-in-law David Greenglass to gather his family and leave the country immediately. Greenglass dithered and fell into the arms of the FBI. Gold quickly identified photos of his Albuquerque contact and then took it as a badge of accomplishment when one of the arresting agents came back and informed him, "Even though Dave had gained 65 pounds and was five years older and far more mature in appearance, as we entered the apartment, four lines of the verbal description furnished by you leaped to my mind—and I know that we had the right man."[4]

Later that summer, when drafting a history of his life as a secret agent, Gold would explain how he and FBI agents finally came up with the names of the married couple who had given him information in Albuquerque. "For the life of me," he wrote, "I could not recall David Greenglass's name. So this was done. A list of some twenty last names was selected; first we eliminated the least likely ten; then we cut the list further; finally a group of the three most likely was chosen, and lo, Greenglass's was at the top." A similar strategy was used to acquire his wife's name, "and again Ruth headed the list."[5]

Gold had mixed feelings about these latest disclosures; he recognized that they ensured that his own "punishment would be most severe." He was forced to ask himself, "Why, therefore, had I acted so?" Ratting people out and destroying their lives "was a terribly shameful and depraved thing" to do, especially when he had "tried to behave with a measure of dignity." He was ashamed of providing names, but "there were reasons and cogent ones."[6]

At the top of the list, said Gold, was that "everything I had done for the past fifteen years . . . was based on falsehood and deception." "Every time I went on a mission," he would write, "or even a simple trip to New York, I must have lied to at least five or six people—so possibly to expect an instantaneous change to complete truthfulness literally overnight was too much." He would have to "rigidly condition and train" himself to tell the truth—"a total reversal of all that went before."[7]

To make amends and address his "horrible sense of shame and disgust," Gold would have to divulge everything. His imprisonment at Holmesburg gave him the isolation and "sufficient time" to realize that "every last particle of truth" needed to be turned over to authorities so that he "not appear so completely the despicable character." Prison, he found, was "a great place in which to order one's thoughts and to think clearly and logically." It was "most peculiar" that somebody who had always been, as he put it, "so scrupulously accurate and correct in my scientific work" had lied "so devilishly and so capably throughout an entire 15 years." Alone, reviled, and locked away, he decided he must finally do the right thing.[8]

"Red spy network"

Eventually, after weeks of regurgitating every bit of his life as an industrial spy and Soviet courier, and having identified every item from his "Fibber McGee's closet" filled from floor to ceiling with chemistry books, novels, paperback mysteries, documents, and blueprints from years of secret missions, Gold was done. Confined in one of the worst city jails in America and facing severe punishment, he felt "at peace for the first time in more than a decade and a half." He noted that his "blood pressure, which had steadily stayed at an average of 190/110, sometimes going as high as 205/125, is now an amazingly normal 140/80." It wasn't just his rapid weight loss, suddenly reduced work schedule, or reprieve from cross-country travel that effected this change. He attributed "the startling decrease from hypertension to normalcy" to his decision to come clean.[9] If that affected the lives of former accomplices, so be it.

One of those accomplices was Tom Black, a loyal and devoted comrade, a scientific mentor, and someone who knew his parents and had shared meals in his home. Black had saved the Gold family from losing their home in South Philadelphia during the early years of the Depression, but he was also the one who had pulled Gold into spying for Russia. Before meeting him, Gold had never had much interest in politics; Communism and the grand experiment taking place in the Soviet Union had no appeal for him. It was Black's repeated pleas, the social gatherings at Vera Kane's Greenwich Village apartment, and his own sense of obligation that ultimately wore him down. He stole documents from Pennsylvania Sugar as much to repay Black as to help the struggling Russian people.

Black himself suspected his days of freedom were numbered after Gold gave him the stunning news that he was Fuchs's unknown American courier. At the time, he tried to assure Harry that a great deal of extraordinary detective work would be needed to connect him to Fuchs, but he must have known that he too was at risk. From May 15, when FBI agents walked into PGH, Gold was careful not to contact Black, for fear of implicating him. When Gold's arrest became front-page news on May 24, Black knew the end was near. "Since I had recruited him," Black would subsequently write, "I realized my secret would soon be known to the authorities."[10]

Within days, Black received a phone call from a "Miss Watkins," a code notifying him of an emergency meeting with Soviet agents. He was supposed to "rendezvous under the marquee of the Translux Theatre on Broadway between 7:15 and 7:18 PM next Tuesday." Black would later claim that he had "no intention of obeying" the prearranged directive, but his resolution turned out to be irrelevant: agents turned up that very day.[11] He must have known that his friend would not withstand grilling by the FBI.

Inside Holmesburg in early June, Gold told the FBI how he acquired the job at Holbrook Manufacturing in February 1933, and about Black's subsequent attempt "to get me to join the Communist Party" and supply "information from the Pennsylvania Sugar Company relative to processes" that would aid the long-suffering Russian people and advance "the Soviet Union along the road to industrialization."[12] Gold went on to describe the difficulties of photocopying the stolen documents, transporting them to New York, and eventually meeting with the Soviet agent "Paul Smith" in late 1935. In subsequent confession statements, he would inform the FBI of Black's pursuit of "information on penicillin" in 1942 and the related effort to obtain "information on biologicals for the Soviet Union" with trips to Pittsburgh, New Castle, and Chicago. He identified Black as a source of travel money when he was low on cash and as an understanding confidant with whom he could discuss troubling situations like his connection to Klaus Fuchs.[13]

Confronted by the FBI, Black said he knew little of Gold's activities. The agents didn't press the issue, but he knew they would be back. He would later write, "I knew that I must find the courage to come clean without reservations." He thought he "was clear" of any "treasonable acts" and would claim he had "more to fear from Stalin's executioners than my own government." Black soon phoned the FBI and made an appointment, hoping to "disentangle" himself from the "Red spy network" and afford himself "reasonable assurance of dying a natural death."[14]

When it was Black's turn to answer questions, he too revealed everything. He identified the people who had sparked his interest in Communism: friends like Fred Heller, Ernie Segressemann, and Vera Kane. He recounted his exploits as a Soviet operative and mentioned that his Soviet bosses had even offered to "send him to the California Institute of Technology for a graduate degree." The Russians, he said, had a great respect for the scientific work under way at MIT and Caltech and were willing to provide "liberal expense accounts" for individuals with the academic qualifications to enter such elite institutions.

Black was lucky. To Robert Lamphere's chagrin, "the Justice Department decided that the information about industrial processes that he'd passed had not affected the national defense," and therefore did not indict him for espionage. This decision is curious when one considers how many less-involved people were prosecuted or had their lives disrupted during these years. In Lamphere's eyes, and probably Gold's as well, Black was a spy. But he escaped legal consequences.

"No recollection of ever meeting him"

Other figures from Gold's past were less willing to come forward. Vera Kane, the Communist cheerleader who threw frequent parties in her Lower Manhattan apartment for a wide assortment of leftists and Bohemians, and who had encouraged Gold to become a party member, played dumb when FBI agents arranged for them to meet in their New York office. When the agents ushered Gold into the office, he said, "Hello Vera" and offered his hand. Kane "acknowledged the handshake and asked Gold if he knew her."[15] When Gold said yes, he knew her well, she made the mistake of asking where they had met. While agents watched, "Gold proceeded to tell her that they had met in her apartment in Greenwich Village in 1933" and went on to name "Tom Black, Fred Heller, and Ernest Segressemann as other individuals present at the time." He then described her apartment, Tom Black's apartment in Newark, and her later apartment at the Hotel Carteret in New York City, all in great detail. He also mentioned the time they and Black saw the Clifford Odets play *Waiting for Lefty*. Gold even recalled that Kane became so emotionally involved in the play that at one point "she jumped up and cried out, 'Strike.' "[16]

Kane should have known better than to test Gold's memory. Though she is said to have "overcome her original nervousness" toward him, she must have found it uncomfortable to hear Gold relate these events and descriptions, as well as more sensitive matters such as their effort to photocopy the documents he was stealing and her suggestion that he "take the material to the Hudson Blueprinting Co. in New York City." Yet she continued to insist "she had no recollection of ever meeting him," and "denied that she was aware of any espionage activities on the part of Gold or Black."

Feeling guilty for drawing Kane into such a mess, Gold told her "he had not mentioned her name until six or seven weeks after his arrest" and had always had "a very favorable impression" of her. He "held no malice towards her and regretted that they had to meet again under such circumstances."[17] A day after the staged meeting, he theorized that "Kane's reluctance to acknowledge him . . . may possibly be due to her not wanting her son to know about her past." Her son, about eight years old at the time they met, would now be a young man probably not very accepting of her earlier political views. The country had a very different attitude now toward Communism and the Soviet Union.

"Completely fictitious"

Gold did not spare Abraham Brothman and Miriam Moskowitz. On the afternoon of July 29, FBI agents swarmed into the office of the Ulster Chemical Company in Cliffwood, New Jersey, and arrested Brothman and Moskowitz for lying to a federal grand jury in 1947. They were arraigned one day before the three-year statute of limitations would have run out.[18] The charge of giving "false, fictitious, and manufactured information to the 1947 grand jury" carried a maximum sentence of two years in prison and a $10,000 fine.

Though lying to a grand jury paled in comparison to some of the other transgressions Gold had owned up to, even this allegation received front-page coverage. The defendants' attorney was heard to say, "It is most regrettable that the spying activities of persons other than the two defendants have distorted this case to the public out of all proportion."[19] But Gold wasn't some minor operative; he was now universally known as the "atomic spy." Even J. Edgar Hoover thought of him as a "master Soviet spy," so anything he said was newsworthy, particularly when he was naming fellow spies.[20] Newspapers struggled to explain the convoluted nexus of Gold, Brothman, Elizabeth Bentley, and Jacob Golos, noting that "the original scent had grown almost cold" before Gold made his revelations.[21] Whereas Bentley's initial disclosures were "received with . . . skepticism," Gold was now confirming the accuracy of her allegations against Brothman. Harry explained how he and Brothman had fooled the grand jury in 1947 by "painstakingly going over the story time and again while walking the streets in the neighborhood of Brothman's Sunnyside, Long Island home."[22]

"Absolutely false, completely fictitious," Gold now said of his 1947 performance. It was a "product of my imagination."

At a new grand jury hearing in 1950, Bentley preceded Gold on the witness stand and told the jury that Brothman, a contact of hers in 1940 and 1941, had given her "many blueprints" to pass on to Golos, the head of the espionage ring. She said she "also collected his party dues, brought him party directives and instructed him in the latest Communist doctrines." Although they never got along, Brothman "objected strenuously" and "seemed frightened" when Bentley told him he would be getting a new contact. Golos had to impress on him his obligation as a party member to accept orders.[23]

Gold was equally damaging. He told the jury how he and Brothman had conspired to ensure that their stories would "hang together." He enumerated the items Brothman had passed to the Russians: two hundred or three hundred pages on Buna-S, the synthetic rubber; three hundred pages on mixing equipment; "the aerosol insecticide bomb"; and the "magnesium powder used in flares and tracers." He said that Miriam Moskowitz was present at many of the discussions designed to throw off prosecutors and the earlier grand jury, had actively dissuaded Brothman from telling the truth, and was "greatly overjoyed" when Gold declared that he had convinced the earlier grand jury of his innocence.[24]

At their trial in November, Gold was equally impressive. Slouching in the witness chair, and speaking in "a precise, even voice," he was seen by those in the courtroom as "unhesitatingly" candid. When defense counsel tried to show that the witness had not always been honest, Gold frankly admitted that he had told many lies to perpetuate his double life: "It became easier to continue the fiction than to straighten out the whole hideous mess, but it's a wonder that steam didn't come out of my ears at times."[25] On his position in the Brothman firm, the confessed spy explained with a wry smile, "When there was no money, I was a partner and when there was money, I was an employee."[26]

"One a vindictive liar and the other a fantasist"

In contrast to Gold's disarming frankness, Abe Brothman and Miriam Moskowitz punctuated their grand jury appearances with frequent repetitions of "I decline to answer on the ground that it might tend to incriminate me." Moskowitz's use of the Fifth Amendment irritated the prosecutor and must have frustrated members of the jury, who could not understand why she would evade such seemingly innocuous questions as whether she had ever worked for the Social Security Board or the War Manpower Commission. Her decision to plead the Fifth on whether it was her handwriting on a U.S. Civil Service Commission document was another matter. She had checked "no" when asked if she was a member of a "Communist or German Bund organization."[27]

Brothman and Moskowitz's subsequent trial, in which they seemed to damage their case further by not taking the witness stand to defend themselves, would eventually be viewed by historians as a dry run for a more important one the following year. "We were a dress rehearsal" for the Rosenberg trial, said Moskowitz. "It was the same judge, the same prosecutors, the same witnesses. They tried out their skills and their witnesses. I didn't initially recognize it, but Abe saw immediately what the system was doing."[28] Not taking the stand exposed them to questions and innuendos, but as Moskowitz explained a half century later, testifying might have been worse. "We knew the prosecution would have focused on our relationship and I, particularly, would have been the object of savage interrogation," she wrote in 2003. "Roy Cohn, no less, had hoped to uncover evidence of 'moral turpitude' on our part and had inspired FBI Director J. Edgar Hoover to send the American Legal Attaché in London to Switzerland to search the hotel records and determine if we had 'cohabitated' when we were there on business. For all that effort they learned that Abe and I had registered in separate rooms. Nevertheless, Saypol and Cohn would have strayed far from the legal charge against us; they would have turned the trial into a frenzied expose of sex and scandal and would have spun the heads of the jurors and the media with prurient entertainment."[29]

Their illicit relationship was not the pair's only concern; their politics was equally troubling—they were both ardent Communists. As Moskowitz would eventually admit, "There was also the question of our old political ties. I had been a member of the Communist Party. Abe had joined the Young Communist League as a teenager. The trial would have become a syllogistic phantasmagoria: we were Communists; all Communists are spies; ergo, we were spies."[30]

And the FBI knew it. Moskowitz had been an active member of the "Hetti Lapatine Club of the Communist Party" in the Chelsea area and had participated in heated discussions of party leadership and policies.[31] Co-workers at the Brothman firm recalled that Brothman and Moskowitz "favored the expulsion of [Earl] Browder (then head of the Communist Party) and the election of William Z. Foster to head the Party." One FBI informant recalled hearing Moskowitz say she "had lost her wallet containing her Communist Party card."[32] It was asserted that the "general atmosphere at Brothman's firm was pro-Communist and pro-Soviet Russia."

Many decades later, Moskowitz was comfortable expounding on the "dedicated work of Communist Party workers for a whole series of good works including rent control, opposition to anti-Semitism, civil rights, unemployment insurance, and social progress in general."[33] In 1950, however, it is unlikely that the judge would have entertained discussion on the merits of such social issues. "With the wisdom of hindsight," wrote Moskowitz, "it is doubtful that we would have won acquittal even had we testified. The temper of the times . . . and the willingness of a poorly informed public and a naïve jury to believe what the prosecution and the media told them would have drowned us in preconceived guilt. Worse yet, we were trapped in a deadly game in which we were merely pawns; we had to fall. The judge and the prosecution team in our trial would be the same who would try and prosecute Ethel and Julius Rosenberg and Morton Sobell four months after our trial. To assure a conviction in that case it was imperative for the prosecution to establish the credibility of Elizabeth Bentley and Harry Gold since they would testify in the later event also. With our conviction they became unimpeachable witnesses."[34]

On November 22, 1950, after deliberating for just over five hours, the jury found Brothman and Moskowitz guilty of obstructing justice during an espionage investigation. They got the maximum terms allowable. Brothman received a two-year sentence on one count and a five-year sentence on another plus a $10,000 fine, Moskowitz a two-year sentence for one count of obstruction and a $10,000 fine.[35] Judge Irving R. Kaufman made it clear that he regretted he "could not impose stiffer penalties," angrily noting that he had "no sympathy or mercy for these defendants; none whatsoever." They had engaged in behavior designed destroy "the judicial process. It is beyond my comprehension," said Kaufman, "that anyone would commit a crime such as this. What is strange is that the very country that they sought to undermine gave them a fair and impartial trial, something they could not have obtained from the very country they sought to aid."[36]

"There are so few safe havens remaining on earth today," Kaufman continued, "and it seems to me that these defendants sought to undermine the staunchest supporter of freedom in the world today. I cannot understand. I said that when the verdict came. I repeat again I just cannot comprehend why these defendants and others seek to destroy that which protects them from tyranny."[37] Six months later he would preside over a case that had far more significance.

Miriam Moskowitz spent almost fifteen months behind bars at the

Federal Reformatory for Women in Alderson, West Virginia, and remained firmly convinced that Gold had given "false testimony" against her. She would always insist she was not present when Abe and Harry plotted to present a fictitious story to the grand jury. Gold "had no cause for the gratuitous damage he had inflicted on me," Moskowitz bitterly wrote in her memoir. "He had made himself at home in my apartment; he had shared my friends and the routine of my life."[38] As for her lover, Abraham Brothman, "his life had begun full of promise but it was brought to an unproductive, even premature end by an unstable woman and a very frightened little man." That would be Elizabeth Bentley and Harry Gold. "Both of them, one a vindictive liar and the other a fantasist and, in his lucid moments, a fake and a fraud, were used (willingly) by a powerful coven of amoral, ambitious toads seeking to advance their careers by any means possible."[39]

Moskowitz was not always filled with vitriol at the thought of her former co-worker and housemate. "He was so alone," she recalled in a 2007 interview. "He had no one to talk to. He didn't confide in anyone, not even to a lawyer. He thought through [the dilemma] the best he could and the best was the worst."[40] Reflecting on her trial, she said, "Harry knew he was doing something abominable when he testified against us. He wanted to save his life. He was burdened, he couldn't take the pressure anymore."[41]

"Opposing ideologies"

When he testified against Brothman and Moskowitz, Harry Gold had not yet appeared at his own sentencing. Throughout the summer and fall of 1950 he was regularly transported from Holmesburg to the Federal Courthouse and back. At one hearing in October, prepared to plead guilty and receive his sentence, Gold heard U.S. Assistant Attorney General Gleeson and Judge McGranery debate whether it should be an open hearing or a closed one, how much sensitive security information the government wanted to expose, and the government's request for another continuance. Gleeson said new "investigative phases" of the case had developed, which "we would like an opportunity to explore." He argued that such an important case deserved some latitude and that the government's ability to pursue a thorough investigation is "greatly lessened after the defendant is sentenced." He requested a new sentencing date be set "after the first of the year."[42] Law enforcement agencies were only too familiar with informants terminating their cooperation once they had been sentenced, and the government expected Gold—the first American tried for atomic spying—to do the same.

John Hamilton said he and his client were amenable to another continuance, but underscored that Gold "will have been in confinement for nearly seven months" by January. He wanted assurance that McGranery would "give due credit for the confinement which he has suffered."

Judge McGranery expressed some irritation with the prosecution. He had originally expected to issue a sentence in early September, and now, a month later, the government was requesting another delay. Such delays interfered with the "efficient administration of justice"; moreover, there was "no reason" for the government to seek another delay. The new year, he believed, should start with "clean books"; "I certainly will not grant any continuance until that time."

In an effort to be helpful, Hamilton said Gold could live with another continuance so long as it was understood by all parties that it would be the last. McGranery replied that he knew of "no case on record where sentence has been deferred for so long a time." He said he had made his own "independent investigation" of the Gold case: "I have discussed it with Mr. Hoover [and] there is nothing that would warrant continuing this until after January. I am going to fix a date."[43]

The trial judge had just admitted in open court to having highly improper *ex parte* communications with a key arm of the prosecution team. Documents from the FBI suggest that McGranery, already unduly friendly with the Bureau, had held conversations with agents both before and after Gold's arrest, counseling them on what they could and could not do with Gold while he was confined but without an attorney. Even though McGranery's *ex parte* transgressions pale in comparison to Judge Kaufman's indiscretions in the Rosenberg trial, his actions are still troubling.[44]

Although one could argue that judicial etiquette was different in 1950, McGranery's announcement of private conversations and "independent" fact finding should have drawn skeptical questions, if not an objection, from the defense counsel. It was even quoted in the next day's newspaper accounts of the trial.[45] Hamilton and Ballard's silence on the revelation is curious. It could have been due to their inexperience in high-profile criminal cases, their fear that raising the issue would damage their client's chance of a reasonable penalty, or their client's apparent commitment to a guilty plea. Accusations of judicial misconduct would only have muddied the waters.

Prosecutor Gleeson made one last pitch for a continuance. Although he claimed he could not "reveal the investigative phases of the case" that justified the delay, he argued that "we have very good reason for asking for this continuance until after January 1."

"No," replied McGranery firmly. "I will not do it, and will fix December 7 for final disposition and sentence."[46]

Gold's distraught father came to many of these hearings, hoping for a miracle. Seeing his son chained, handcuffed, and guarded by burly officers was emotionally draining. In one brief meeting in the building's third-floor cell room, Sam kissed his son's hands through the bars. He was heard to say as he left for the courtroom, "He was a misguided boy. He's lost a lot of weight."[47]

Meanwhile, some of those Gold had named had already been sentenced and begun serving their time. Alfred Dean Slack was brought into federal court in Greenville, Tennessee, on September 18, 1950, and pleaded guilty to violating the espionage laws. He owned up to everything, from his early industrial espionage at Eastman Kodak to supplying the "super-explosive" RDX to the Soviets when he worked at the Holston munitions plant during the war. He tried to make Gold the heavy, claiming that he had been "reluctant to furnish military information to a foreign government," but Gold had threatened to expose him as a Communist operative. Even the U.S. attorney assigned to prosecute the case, James M. Meek, came to believe that Slack might not have committed these acts if not for "the threats of the man who dominated his every move."[48] It is unlikely that Meek ever came face to face with Harry Gold, the timid operative who could not even persuade his contacts to show up on time for meetings. Apparently, U.S. District Judge Robert L. Taylor didn't buy the argument, rejecting the prosecutor's recommendation of a ten-year sentence for a crime the judge found so "shocking" that it could only "be contemplated . . . with detestation." Against a backdrop of "opposing ideologies" and "the threat of a devastating war" between the United States and Soviet Russia, Taylor sentenced Slack to fifteen years' imprisonment.[49] He was not the only judge during this period to reject a prosecutor's recommendation in favor of a tougher alternative.

"Reticent and introverted"

Back in Philadelphia, Hamilton and Ballard prepared for Gold's December sentencing. Arguing his innocence was no longer an option, but they could present their client's best side, try to explain what led him to commit his crimes, and emphasize that many people spoke extremely well of him. Because of Gold's tremendous value to the government in identifying other Soviet operatives, they were pretty sure he would avoid the death penalty, but a sympathetic presentation might avoid the maximum prison sentence as well. Could he get the kind of sentence that Fuchs and Slack received?

As soon as they took the case the two lawyers reached out to anyone who had known their client, from his early years in South Philadelphia, his places of employment, and the various institutions of higher learning he had attended. Throughout the summer and fall they received phone calls and letters of support that were some of the most positive and moving they had ever read about anybody. They didn't know what impact the letters would have on McGranery, but they certainly confirmed what the defense team had already discovered: their client was well liked and respected. For all his gullibility, excessive generosity, and odd mannerisms, it was easy to like him.

Sam Haftel, who claimed he was "Harry's closest friend during all of elementary school and most of high school," described Gold as a "regular fellow" growing up in one of the city's "toughest neighborhoods . . . where fighting, cheating and stealing were the rule rather than the exception, but Harry stood above all this and maintained a high moral code." Although "he was not an athlete, he was always interested in sports" and developed "an affinity for physics and chemistry." He said science was "Harry's one undying love and coupled with a brain that I always regarded as superb, he could have become one of the fine scientists of the times were he not sidetracked, evidently, by false conceptions of idealism."[50]

"In all the years I knew him," added Haftel, "Harry never once displayed . . . any predilection for Communism nor any special sympathy for Russia." He said Gold had an "almost monastic absorption in his work and academic pursuits . . . and must have been ensnared by some professional Communists through their usual and subtle insidious methods." Money was not an answer to this riddle, since Gold was "an almost completely unmercenary person." Nor was "personal glory," because of his "reticent and introverted" personality. However, Haftel thought it quite likely that the "the source of his seduction" was Harry's tendency to be "naïve and trusting in his social relationships." Haftel had not seen his old friend in many years and had no doubt his "traitorous" acts were "undeniable and uncondonable," but still he felt compelled to point out the Harry Gold he knew "would not lie to save his skin." He had seen Harry "take many a beating when we were kids rather than lie or squeal on a friend. If he is squealing now, I would attribute it to a realization of the horrible wrong he participated in."[51]

A fellow student from Drexel Evening School wrote that everyone in the class "recognized his superior intelligence . . . and his willingness to help other students." Gold was obviously devoted to his family, shouldered much of the economic burden, and was "very close to his mother." The classmate said he and others had lost touch with Gold during the war and now presumed he was "avoiding all of his old friends because he did not wish to involve us in any way in his criminal activities."[52]

Another old friend who wrote to Hamilton and Ballard was one whose name Gold had appropriated on certain occasions to conceal his true identity. Frank Kessler, who had met Harry in 1922 when they were both twelve years old, knew the Gold home well and said "it was the poorest, but the cleanest I had ever seen." Kessler had always been impressed by his friend's generous spirit and ability to handle adversity. "Harry left Penn and went to work" when the family fell on hard times during the Depression, he wrote, "but he never uttered a word of regret or resentment concerning his bad fortune." Yet "away from his Bunsen burner and test tubes, he seemed lacking in a worldly sense. Harry never seemed to know when someone was taking advantage of him. It was the easiest thing in the world to sell him a bill of goods." Speaking for his old South Philly crowd, Kessler summed up by stating: "Harry was the nicest, most generous, sympathetic, and dependable person we had known. When I saw his picture in the newspaper and read the story I was a very sick person. Knowing Harry the way I did, it is still hard for me to believe that it is the same person."[53]

"He never measured time by hours"

Kessler's account pales in contrast to the communication from Gold's former Heart Station colleagues. Entitled "Statement As To The Work, Conduct and Character of Harry Gold While Employed At The Heart Station, Division of Cardiology, Philadelphia General Hospital," the five-page single-spaced document underscored Gold's many contributions during his two years as their biochemist. Not long after he was hired, Harry's supervisors noticed his interest and enlarged the scope of his work "beyond that which might be expected from one holding his particular position." He was introduced to doctors with whom a lab biochemist wouldn't normally associate and was taken to medical conferences that biochemists didn't normally attend. He not only mastered a new piece of complicated equipment, called a flame photometer, that measured the concentration of chemicals in the body, but was asked by the manufacturer "to write an article as to both the operation and procedures" to help other hospitals instruct lab workers in its use. Gold was commended for his work ethic: "He never measured time by hours, but by the tasks to be done." The time he put in exceeded anything that "might be expected of a conscientious research worker. He was ready and willing to do anything asked of him irrespective of the inconvenience or the length of time required." If an experiment "started at three o'clock in the morning, he was there and remained there until it was completed." During a 1949 transit strike, he volunteered to "sleep in the clinic in order that he might be available, and this he did."

Gold also frequently volunteered his blood for necessary tests in amounts far in "excess of what might normally be taken from any single individual. This he did although he suffered from hypertension," which made donation far more risky. He even volunteered for experiments where he would be injected with substances that were known to be "quite toxic to humans."[54]

"Outside of his professional and related activities," wrote his colleagues, "Gold's life seemed normal in all respects." He followed sports, "particularly baseball," and displayed no great interest in politics except for his supporting "the ideologies of the Roosevelt and Truman administrations." In fact, the authors wrote, when "the Wallace Convention" was in town and "immediately opposite the hospital, he took no apparent interest in its proceedings and did not attend any of its sessions. He did, however, attend one or two sessions of the Democratic Convention of the same year." Never was there any indication of "leftist or radical sympathies."

Co-workers also detected no latent or patent psychopathic tendencies, though "he was undoubtedly driven by an obsessive compulsion," which presented itself most obviously in "the necessity for getting his experiments done and done accurately." Toward hospital personnel, he was "unselfish" and "solicitous to the point of fault," "the easiest touch in the world," "the most generous person we have ever known," and "a gentle person who would give you the shirt off his back." In conclusion, his former colleagues "unqualifiededly" stated that "his reputation for truthfulness, veracity and as a law abiding citizen was of the best." This testimonial, more suited to a retiring hospital president than an imprisoned spy, was signed by Drs. Thomas M. McMillan, Samuel Bellet, John R. Urbach, and William A. Steiger, and Dorothy E. Bell, a lab technician.[55]

Hamilton and Ballard weren't sure how much credence Judge Mc-Granery would give to such a glowing letter signed by such esteemed members of the Philadelphia medical community, or how much weight all the letters would be given, but they themselves were impressed. Even priests at Xavier University had written to them, describing Harry as "brilliant," "an earnest scholar" with a "serious" approach to learning.[56] Though he had committed a truly serious crime, they did not want to see him destroyed by it.

While Ballard collected the many letters of support for their client, Hamilton was developing his own correspondents. In an effort to bring himself up to speed on all aspects of the Gold case, he immersed himself in everything from the Great Depression to the rapidly worsening relations between the United States and the Soviet Union. Exploring the new term "Cold War," for instance, he consulted the respected political columnist Walter Lippmann, who apprised him of the term's French origin and current political connotation.[57]

Gold was writing as well, mostly to-do lists and notes to himself regarding subjects his attorneys asked him to elaborate on, as well as his big project: his admission in open court that he was a spy. He saw his sentencing hearing as his opportunity to tell his family, his friends, his professors and co-workers—in fact the entire world—how sorry he was for the crimes he had committed and to say that he hoped one day to make amends. Alone in his Holmesburg cell, Gold catalogued what needed to be done, ways he could help his lawyers, and items that might aid the FBI agents who regularly stopped by to talk. No matter how much abuse he received from other prisoners for assisting the government, he never turned them away.

A prolific writer of notes to himself, Gold would start with sheets of loose-leaf paper and scribble an item per line on a vast array of subjects. His list for one day in August, for instance, began:

1) Lack of faith in democratic processes
2) That I was better off due to taking college work later
3) Thrill of seeing people discharged from the hospital
4) Disappointments—Loves
5) Anybody has idea that this work was thrilling is doomed to disappointment—Drudgery—way of life idea
6) Name anathema to decent people
7) Realize that I have forfeited right to ask re. Work at the Heart Station
8) The way an admission comes—fighting in/out in cell.[58]

A second list fleshed out the thirty-odd points in the first list. "Suppose A-bomb falls on U.S.A. [and] kills even one person. [My] name is anathema to all decent people—I must live with this forever." On the subject of "Disappointed loves," he wrote: "Bah! Still hoped for M.C.L. [Mary Catherine Lanning] Probably despises me now." And under "Dispel other ideas," Gold underscored a series of points including "Against emotionalism—F[ather] visits; not seeking sympathy re. Pop, but he is old man. How could I have ever done this to family?" "Everyone has been more decent to me than I deserve. Dispel idea of any complaints re. FBI —G[rea]t treatment at Holmesburg; Max. security block—want no more no less than other inmates."[59]

Gold may have made an additional list or two, further embellishing his central points, before he started to draft his formal statement for the court. With his crime the centerpiece of his existence at the moment, he worked on his trial statement with single-minded ardor. Guilt ridden, cursed with an obsessive-compulsive disorder, and desirous of explaining himself, he uncompromisingly grabbed hold of his chance to tell his fellow Americans who he really was and why he had acted so shamefully.

"Your Honor," his statement began, "I feel that an explanation is due to the people of the United States, to this court, which represents these people, to my family, to my friends and to the people with whom I have worked—all of whom I have besmirched by my crime." His "horrible and heinous" actions had created a "far more terrible weapon than any atomic bomb . . . namely, Harry Gold, Soviet courier, a name which is now an anathema to all decent people. Listen to the evolution of this weapon. I promise you that I shall be more merciless than any prosecutor."[60]

"This is my country and I love it."

Gold's twenty-five-page statement, written in pencil, began with the debt he owed Tom Black and went on to recount his meetings with Semenov and Yakovlev, his Xavier experience, the activities with fellow spies like Slack, Brothman, and Greenglass, and his more notorious espionage activities with Fuchs—everything was laid out. With no thought of masking his sins, he said his "long experience" in the secrecy business and "dealing with people of diversified backgrounds" helped produce the "perfect courier" and secret operative. Having learned the tradecraft, he traveled "inconspicuously around the country obtaining our most cherished secrets from persons foolish enough to give them to me."[61]

And though not wanting to sound boastful, he said anyone desiring to do the things he did, for as long as he did, must have "a hard inner core of resolve and determination." His success required a "one-track mind" able to focus on the "mission . . . to the exclusion of all other thoughts." He believed that the same traits that enabled him to become a competent chemist—a capacity for "hard work"—contributed to his lengthy career as a spy. Rather than being a "great original thinker," he was able to rise in his nefarious profession "by the sheer weight of extra effort." Few could compete with him in that department. Gold could work a twelve-hour day at his regular job, travel to New York, wait on a cold street corner for two hours to receive a package, promptly pass it on to a third party, and then travel back to Philadelphia and the next day's work routine without even an hour's sleep. Though he was physically unimposing, few others had his mental toughness and physical endurance.

"Peculiar as it sounds," he proclaimed himself happy that it had all come to an end. "Traveling on these missions," he wrote, "resulted in a perpetual state of tiredness and exhaustion, which in turn kept me from doing any extensive thinking about these deeds and effectively dulled my moral sense." It was always necessary to make an "effort to forget" what he was involved in. He admitted to "doubts, grave ones" about the country for which he was risking his life: the Soviet invasion of "small countries such as Finland" and the "horribly farcical trials and confessions in Russia" in the late 1930s continually troubled him. But those doubts were countered by his "lack of faith in the democratic processes" of his own country, especially during the Depression, and America's timid response to the rise of Nazism.

He found pleasure in working with people who sacrificed themselves for a higher cause. Semenov and Fuchs, for example, were "extremely cultured individuals" who also had the courage to fight for what they believed. "Even the drudgery had become a part of my life . . . passing time in cheap movies, long dreary rides in buses and day coaches, and coming home late at night. And I knew all the time that I was giving up a normal life: a wife, a family of my own, and leisure time, and I was very envious of my friends who had these blessings. I can definitely aver that anyone who has any romantic ideas about espionage work is due to be disillusioned. Still I continued with these activities. For there was the previously mentioned inner core of resolve."[62]

"Violently anti-Fascist" and terrified of Hitler's increasing strength in Europe, Gold had seen a beacon of hope in the Soviet Union, "the foremost and most constant fighter against Fascism." He had come to believe that anti-Semitism, with which he was very familiar, had been declared a crime against the state in Russia. "How mistaken I was."

Finally, Gold wanted it known that he had "never intended any harm to the United States. For I have always steadfastly considered that first and finally I am an American citizen. This is my country and I love it." He brought up his love of movies like *The Best Years of Our Lives, A Letter to Three Wives*, and *The Red Shoes*; his "fondness for the Philadelphia Orchestra"; his reverence for "sports heroes such as Lefty Grove, Babe Ruth, and Joe DiMaggio"; and what the Soviets would call his "petty-bourgeois" affection for comic strip characters like Steve Canyon, Pogo, and Li'l Abner. He even had a "liking for Arthur Godfrey," the radio entertainer. "My life is here and so is all that I cherish and love," he wrote, "why should I turn against it? Life elsewhere would be unthinkable."[63]

His appreciation of the "wonderful free spirit here which is unknown elsewhere in the world" extended to his own attorneys. "Possibly the greatest single illustration of this spirit is the fact that I, a lifelong voting Democrat am represented in this court by a former chairman of the Republican National Committee, Mr. Hamilton, and he and Mr. Ballard have toiled long hours, without a cent of pay, and at a great personal sacrifice, all in an effort to see that I got the proper legal representation."[64]

As for his "accomplishments" as a chemist, his role as part of the PGH team fighting heart disease, and the "wonderful girl" he found himself in love with—all of that had fallen victim to his other life: "I had constructed a gigantic house of cards, built on a foundation of deception and lies, and it took the removal of only one card to bring the whole structure tumbling down."

In an effort "to make the greatest possible amends," he promised to recall "every single mission" that he had ever undertaken and to name everyone he had ever worked with. "I have sought for no legal outs," he concluded, "and I have attempted to make no deal. And as a man I shall take my punishment."[65]

"Every Man Deserves a Defense"

Hamilton informed Gold that it was a very fine statement indeed, but the judge was highly unlikely to let him read the entire twenty-five-page mea culpa in court. He suggested Gold pare it down to three or four points, which he would deliver in court, while the full document would be formally entered for McGranery's consideration. As usual, Gold complied.

Gus Ballard recalls that his boss was having similar difficulty with his own sentencing presentation. Hamilton, says Ballard, didn't know when to quit; he had a "tendency to make the sentencing statement too long." Both men spent considerable time on it, and its length became their "biggest point of contention." There were other issues as well: Ballard believed it should be "case specific" and stick to "the law of the matter," while Hamilton thought an impassioned explanation of Gold's motivations was in order. Their man was guilty; that wasn't going to change. Hamilton believed they had to explain what had motivated this mild, law-abiding citizen to act in such a manner. This strategy, however, was leading toward a lengthy dissertation. Ballard may have also been concerned that Hamilton was not up to the mental and physical challenge of a long courtroom presentation, and that the old Kansas pol would run out of steam and look foolish in the most heavily watched performance of his career. He did not say as much to Hamilton but focused on the court's attention span: "These people will go to sleep before you ever finish."

"Don't worry about that," replied Hamilton. "Believe me, they'll stay awake."[66] Ballard was unconvinced, but as a junior member of the firm, he was in no position to argue. Despite their disagreement over the presentation, Ballard said Hamilton "was a fun guy to work with. We had wonderful talks on our trips up to Holmesburg to interview Harry. Younger guys at the firm got a kick out of him. At the drop of a hat Hamilton would launch into some story about people he had met over the years. It was fascinating stuff."[67] Folksy as his stories were, Ballard was still unsure how the old GOP warhorse would do defending a Communist spy in front of two hundred people.

As the December sentencing date drew near, the lawyers spent almost all their time in preparation. They debated a number of critical issues, including whether to bring in character witnesses. Eventually they decided to dispense with a parade of Gold partisans. Some had already received hate mail and negative comments; others were nervous at the prospect of saying complimentary things about a spy in what would surely be a media-saturated event. Gold himself, from the very beginning, had strongly opposed putting his friends, family, and co-workers on the spot. It was one of the central reasons he did not fight the charge; he did not want to draw anyone else into the quagmire he had made of his life. He felt similarly toward his lawyers. "Harry didn't want to get us in any more trouble," said Ballard. "He knew there was pressure on us and the firm." Some partners were hoping Hamilton would keep a low profile at his client's sentencing. Others respected Hamilton and Ballard for sticking their necks out in such a hopeless cause. That summer Hamilton had been the subject of a *Philadelphia Inquirer* magazine article entitled "Every Man Deserves a Defense."[68] Years later, his defense of Gold would be used as a model for young lawyers asked to "represent clients against whom there is likely to be strong public sentiment."[69]

"I have discussed it with Mr. Hoover"

Ushered into court at 9:59 A.M. on December 7, handcuffed, shackled, and surrounded by deputy marshals, Gold was "haggard" and much thinner than at the time of his arrest just six months earlier. He was almost invisible until the marshals departed and he took his seat next to his attorneys.[70] When Judge McGranery entered the courtroom and the clerk called out "the United States of America versus Harry Gold," the defendant showed little emotion. The room was packed; many who had hoped to view the drama were left standing on the sidewalk.

Assistant Attorney General Gleeson began by stating: "Harry Gold became interested in the Communist Party in 1933."[71] In fact, Gold never joined the party. Gleeson went on to describe Gold's career as a spy, his assignments, and his associations, including the Russians who gave him orders, and the disloyal Americans who supplied valuable information on everything from industrial processes to atomic energy. Gleeson concluded by informing the judge that seated beside him was "the agent of the FBI who was in charge from the beginning."

"Because of the public interest" in the case, said McGranery, he wanted to hear from the agent. T. Scott Miller Jr., was sworn in. Answering a question put to him by Gleeson, he said, that "Harry Gold was one of numerous individuals that we thought might be identical with the American espionage contact of Dr. Klaus Fuchs."[72] Special Agent Miller was asked a few more questions about Gold's attempt to recruit another man at Wright Field in Ohio and the last time he had contact with the Russian, Yakovlev. Hamilton then surprised McGranery and Gleeson by requesting an opportunity to cross-examine Miller. He wanted to underscore the fact that Gold had directly contributed to the arrests of Slack, Brothman, Moskowitz, Greenglass, and others while never once asking for a deal or "promise of a reward." Miller agreeably said, "That is very correct, sir."

Judge McGranery then asked Miller if he knew of "any reason why sentence should not be pronounced." Miller answered that he hadn't given it much thought or talked to his superiors about it. McGranery assured the agent that he had already looked into the matter. "I have discussed it with Mr. Hoover," said McGranery, "and he personally told me that he saw no reason why sentence should not be pronounced.[73] There is no case outstanding at this time in which Mr. Gold is a defendant."

"Yes, there is one," said Gleeson. He was referring to the Rosenberg trial, due to begin in New York in just a few months.

McGranery and Hamilton expressed surprise. They were under the impression the defendant had been "named as a conspirator" but no more. In any case, all parties agreed that sentencing could continue. Gleeson asked Hamilton to deliver his prepared remarks before the government made its recommendation.

"As the twig is bent"

Hamilton told the court he did not intend to dispute the "sordid picture" that had emerged of his client's secret life as a Soviet spy. Yet he wanted to bring out in "the full light of day . . . how easily a man may become mired down in the intrigues of those who are willing to put to infamous use the ideals of another as an instrumentality for the attainment of unworthy objectives." Just as "no man is altogether noble nor altogether trustworthy, no man is altogether bad. I believe that when I have finished your honor will conclude so it is with Harry Gold . . . where malice, vindictiveness, revenge, greed or other base characteristics of man are found it is often simple to divine the intent which motivated the crime. But when none of these are present we must search deeper if an explanation is to be found." He quoted Alexander Pope: "'Tis education forms the common mind: just as the twig is bent so the tree is inclined."[74]

Hamilton described the circumstances of Gold's parents in "Czaristic Russia," the constant threat of "Cossack Knouts," and their struggle to acquire an education. The bright, inquisitive Celia wound up in a cigar factory; Samuel, devoted to Tolstoy's vision of "the dignity of human labor," became a cabinetmaker. The lawyer went into detail discussing the young couple's marriage, the birth of a son in 1910, and their fateful decision to come to America. He talked of their eventual settlement in South Philadelphia, their constant "struggle to live," and Celia's frequent refrain, "If we have less money we eat less." Harry, a weak, sickly child, was eligible for the school district's summer program for "undernourished children."

In "the years during which the twig is bent," Gold grew up in a poor but loving household that cherished "the fundamental rights of men," sympathized with the "great masses of people" who struggled each day to survive, and regularly reminded him that "he who does not help his fellow men may not look to God."[75] Harry, too, became a supporter of the downtrodden. Often shunned by other children because of his "reticence and shyness," the boy "withdrew more and more to himself." He became a "prodigious reader" and found great satisfaction in helping others in their schoolwork. "This desire to help others became . . . the dominating characteristic of Harry Gold's later life," said Hamilton.[76] He described his client as an "extraordinarily selfless person, in fact, the most selfless person I have ever met in my life."[77]

At this point in Hamilton's remarks, not a cough or whisper could be heard in the crowded courtroom. As Ballard slowly scanned the room, he realized that he need not have worried about Hamilton's boring listeners with the minutiae of their client's troubled life. The old Kansas lawyer could tell a story. "Hamilton was in good form that day," Ballard would recall five decades later. "He was a pretty fair litigator and was good in front of an audience. I was nervous about the speech, I thought it was much too long, but . . . there was intense interest by everyone there that day."[78]

The listeners stayed interested as Hamilton moved on to Sam Gold's experience of prejudice and low pay at RCA Victor, Celia's effort to earn extra money teaching Hebrew to local youngsters, and Harry's high school graduation, employment at the sugar refinery, and thwarted desire to go on to college and become a chemist. After nearly two hours, Hamilton had reached his client's introduction into industrial espionage. Judge Mc-Granery decided that everyone needed a break and recessed the court for an hour. Many refused to leave for fear they would lose their seats and not be allowed back in to what had become the hottest ticket in town.

After lunch, Hamilton launched into Fred's reappearance in Gold's life on Thanksgiving Day, 1938, his client's deepening involvement with Soviet agents and American suppliers, and his increasing role as a "messenger boy" for a Russian spy ring. Underlining Gold's lowly position and the insignificance of most of the information he was passing, Hamilton argued: "I have never heard of an instance where the responsibility of the servant was greater than that of the master; where the accomplice or the fence were guiltier than the principal or the thief."

The court was also reminded of the Nazis' "treatment of racial and religious minorities" and that "many Americans looked to Russia as the one active force which stood in opposition to Nazism." There was never "any intent to injure the United States and . . . at the time he transmitted the information Soviet Russia was an ally of the United States." He quoted Churchill at the time Hitler invaded Russia: "The Russian danger is, therefore, our danger, and the danger of the United States, just as the cause of any Russian fighting for his hearth and home is the cause of free men and free peoples in every quarter of the globe." Hamilton would quote Churchill yet again and remind his audience that "high government officials, educators, clergymen, scientists and leaders in every phase of our national life were glorifying Russia." Surely, he argued, "it is abhorrent to the Anglo-Saxon conception of justice that a man should be held to criminal responsibility for an act which was not a crime at the time of its commission." The same was true of "ex post facto sentences which would give a crime a degree of seriousness measured by public reaction at the time of imposition rather than that at the time of commission. I submit that reason and justice require the gravity of Harry Gold's offence and motive in which they were carried out shall not be weighed in the temper of these times but as they would have been weighed had he come before your honor for sentence at the times they were committed."[79]

Hamilton concluded his nearly one-hundred-page speech by quoting from the Bible and underscoring the interdependence of justice, truth, and mercy. Before he had even had the opportunity to sit down, Judge McGranery called the presentation "one of the most brilliant" he had ever heard, especially given the "very difficult matter" Hamilton had been handed. Many in the courtroom would never again hear such an oratorical tour de force. Newspapers said Hamilton "held the room spellbound"; one lawyer called it "the most brilliant performance that I have ever witnessed in any court room."[80]

But Hamilton's client had already pleaded guilty.

When McGranery finally asked Gleeson for his sentence recommendation, the assistant U.S. attorney began by reacquainting everyone with the defendant's crimes, in far more colorful and severe language than had been heard that morning. He reminded the court that the defendant was not some fallen hero. Gold had "betrayed his employer" and repeatedly stolen company documents, shown "contempt for legally constituted authority," and forsaken the good men and mission of Xavier University, the school he claimed to love, for the "shadowy, tawdry, melodramatic figures" behind Communist espionage in America. Despite his appearance as a witness before a grand jury and at a trial, Gold deserved to "suffer imprisonment for a period of twenty-five years."[81]

There was a hush in the courtroom. Many looked for Gold's reaction, but there was none. Ballard, however, was angry. He thought Gleeson had gone too far, especially with his "egregious remarks about the church and Xavier." After court that day, Ballard walked over to Gleeson and said, "Jesus, Gerry, you're reaching pretty far into the well on that one."[82]

Judge McGranery thanked both attorneys, as well as Special Agent Miller. He told the agent that "all Americans should have a proper pride in the Federal Bureau of Investigation" and that the Gold case "adds new luster to the record of the FBI, long recognized for fidelity, bravery, integrity and for its advanced techniques of inquiry." McGranery also commented that "there has been some view that has gone about that this case probably was first exposed by Fuchs. That is not true. This matter was uncovered by the Federal Bureau," and Fuchs had not cooperated "in any way, shape or form until after the arrest of Harry Gold." When McGranery asked Miller if that assessment was correct, the agent said, "The identification of Harry Gold's picture was not made until after Gold signed a confession."

McGranery asked Miller to "convey to Director Hoover the commendation of the Court for a tremendous task well done." He added that he had done his own "privately conducted investigation" that included a psychiatric examination of the defendant, and assured Hamilton, "You need have no fear as to his mental situation."[83] Stating that he would like to reflect on the recommendations made to the court, the judge set Saturday at 11:00 A.M. as the time he would pass sentence. Gold thanked Hamilton, held out his wrists to be handcuffed, and returned to Holmesburg Prison.

"I was pissed off"

On December 9 Gold was brought back to court. Neither his father nor brother was there; it was said that Joe Gold had taken Sam for a hospital follow-up visit after a recent operation. Outwardly calm, but somber, the defendant chatted briefly with his attorneys, "clasping and unclasping his hands." Occasionally he would move "to the edge of his chair, lean forward, and bow his head as if in meditation."[84]

Judge McGranery took the bench at 10:14 A.M. and asked Gold if he cared to make a statement. Gold, now dozens of pounds lighter and with dark circles under his eyes, nodded and stepped to the bar. "If your honor please," he began in the manner of an attorney beginning a plea. There were just four points he wanted to make.

First, nothing has served to bring me to a realization of the terrible mistake that I have made as this one fact, the appointment by this court of Mr. Hamilton and Mr. Ballard as my counsel. These men have worked incredibly hard and faithfully in my behalf, and in the face of severe personal criticism and even invective, and they have done this, not for the reason that they condoned my crime, but because they believe that as a basic part of our law I was entitled to the best legal representation available.[85]

Secondly, I am fully aware that I have received the most scrupulously fair trial and treatment that could be desired [and] most certainly this could never have happened in the Soviet Union or in any of the countries dominated by it.

Third, the most tormenting of all thoughts concerns the fact that those who meant so much to me have been the worst besmirched by my deeds. I refer here to this country, to my family and friends, to my former classmates at Xavier University, and to the Jesuits there, and to the people at the Heart Station of the Philadelphia General Hospital. There is puny inadequacy about any words telling how deep and horrible is my remorse.

Fourth, and very last, I have tried to make the greatest possible amends by disclosing every phase of my espionage activities, by identifying all of the persons involved, and by revealing every last scrap, shred, and particle of evidence.[86]

Gold thanked the court and went back to his seat. Many in attendance that day, impressed by his smooth delivery, thought he must have memorized and rehearsed his words. His much-revised handwritten statement actually had a few additional points he had chosen not to make. One expressed his disdain for deal making with authorities and his sense that negotiating a reduction in his sentence in return for testimony would be dishonorable.[87]

Judge McGranery informed the defendant that he had listened carefully to the "cogent and analytical statement" presented by his "distinguished counsel, Mr. Hamilton," as well as the prosecution's recommendation. After weighing "the protection of society" and "the discipline of the wrongdoer," along with Gold's "attempt to atone" for his crimes "by actively cooperating with the government," he had decided "not to follow the recommendation of the Attorney General." The need "to deter others in the future from the commission of similar offenses" mandated "that you, Harry Gold, shall be confined in a federal penitentiary for a term of thirty years."[88]

A collective gasp filled the courtroom, and everyone strained to get an unobstructed view of the defendant. Gold showed no sign of emotion, but his attorneys were stunned. "I was pissed off," Ballard admitted. In the few moments they had before Gold was taken away, Hamilton and

Ballard apologized. "God damn it, Harry, I'm bitterly disappointed," said Ballard. "Don't worry about it, Gus," replied Gold. "I just wanted to plead guilty and get my side of the story out."

"We felt ridiculous about the sentence," said Ballard later, "but Harry never bitched or moaned about it. . . . I thought he'd really be angry, but he wasn't. He was ashamed of what he had done and knew he deserved to be punished." Hamilton and Ballard would later discuss how they felt blindsided. Though some people praised their effort as having saved their client from the electric chair, they were hoping for a sentence more like that Fuchs or Slack had received. The thirty-year maximum was totally unexpected. Hamilton thought the judge was afraid to be "perceived as soft on Communism." Decades later, Ballard said of McGranery and Hamilton that "when you were in their company, . . . you were in the company of two seasoned politicians. I had no doubt Hamilton knew what had motivated McGranery's harsh sentence"[89]

As he was escorted out of the courthouse for the trip back to Holmesburg, Gold watched smiling Christmas shoppers walking in and out of department stores on Market Street with their packages. He knew he might never again share in such a festive experience. His fortieth birthday was just three days away.

"Traitorous Americans"

Gold was still too important to be sent off to a federal prison to begin serving his time. The government was going to use him for as long as he was willing to testify. Less than a week after receiving his sentence, he was transferred from Holmesburg to the Tombs in New York City, to play his part in connecting the Greenglasses and Rosenbergs to the theft of information from Los Alamos.[90]

The process that had started so spectacularly, with the FBI's capture of Fuchs's American contact, had hit a stone wall. Gold had given up names, places, and details of tradecraft, and the Bureau aggressively mined everything he knew. But after they had identified and successfully prosecuted a host of Soviet agents and American operatives such as Semenov, Yakovlev, Black, Slack, Brothman, Moskowitz, and the Greenglasses, the trail had stopped with Ethel and Julius Rosenberg, and Morton Sobell. The Rosenbergs and Sobell, unlike many others, would not roll over; they denied everything. Harry Gold was vital to convincing the jury of their guilt.

Ironically, while waiting for the trial to commence, Gold received what would normally have been good news. The U.S. Patent Office had granted him a patent, to be shared with Abe Brothman and Philip Levine, for a process that "could be used in making plastics and possibly . . . for synthetic rubber." The process's commercial potential, however, was hindered by the fact that two of the three patent holders were in prison.[91]

Although Gold and especially his attorneys may have been distressed by his harsh sentence, the government's decision to demand the death penalty for the three defendants on trial in New York showed that things could have been worse.[92] Hamilton and Ballard would have no role in any of Gold's activities outside Philadelphia. He was on his own. And as a sentenced prisoner, he could not leverage his testimony for a reduced sentence, even had he wanted to.

The prosecutor in the Rosenberg case, U.S. Attorney Irving Saypol, was the same one who had handled the Brothman-Moskowitz case several months earlier. Calling the three defendants "traitorous Americans . . . worshiping and owing allegiance to Soviet Russia and to world communism," Saypol said in his opening statement that the three "had conspired to steal and deliver to the Soviet Union the one weapon that might well hold the key to the survival of the world—the atomic bomb."[93] "The evidence will reveal to you," Saypol told the jury, "how the Rosenbergs persuaded David Greenglass, Mrs. Rosenberg's own brother, to play the treacherous role of a modern Benedict Arnold while wearing the uniform of the United States Army." Gold was "their co-conspirator," according to Saypol, and the one to whom Greenglass "turned over at a secret rendezvous sketches and descriptions of secrets concerning atomic energy and sketches of the very atomic bomb itself."[94]

"Dave from Pittsburgh"

When Gold took the stand on March 15, 1951, as the government's eighth witness, the jury was already familiar with his name. Apart from the extensive news coverage of his arrest and trial, the previous two witnesses, David and Ruth Greenglass, had underscored his role in the affair. Both had recounted their dealings with Gold after his unexpected visit to their Albuquerque apartment in June 1945. The *New York Times* described Gold as "the Government's star witness" and the first to directly link the defendants to Soviet espionage.[95]

Assistant U.S. Attorney Myles J. Lane began with a series of questions dealing with Gold's occupation, education, and family background. He highlighted Gold's bona fides as a spy by having him admit he was "named a co-conspirator in the [current] indictment" and was currently serving a thirty-year sentence for espionage.[96] Lane then had Gold tell in detail his history with Yakovlev and Fuchs, describing meeting places, conversations, and modus operandi for his spy missions.

The defense counsel strenuously objected to such testimony. Emanuel H. Bloch, Julius Rosenberg's attorney, opposed any mention of "the Soviet, Gold's Soviet superior, the Soviet Union, Soviet espionage, or Soviet activities." Judge Irving R. Kaufman cautioned Block that Gold probably had information "even more damaging" to their cause. After a brief courtroom huddle, the four defense attorneys apparently "decided that the 41-year old jurist might be right."[97]

Still hoping to limit the damage, Edward Kuntz, one of Morton Sobell's lawyers, irritated Judge Kaufman by arguing that "judges usually sustained valid objections to testimony."

"Don't you give me any course of instruction in running a courtroom," Kaufman shot back. "I'm running this courtroom and I think I understand how a courtroom should be run. I don't want to hear any more from you."

"But the government must prove that a foreign power is involved," added Bloch. "It must prove that fact."

Annoyed, Kaufman turned to Gold and said, "And the fact is that you pleaded guilty to an indictment charging espionage for the Soviet Union?"

"Yes I did," replied Gold.

Kaufman then turned back to Block, and with a "wry smile" said, "All right, proceed."[98]

Equally problematic for the defense was Gold's demeanor on the stand. His "forthright delivery," keen memory, and expansive explanations contrasted sharply with the "murmuring tones of earlier witnesses," who clearly would have preferred to be somewhere else. Though small, round-shouldered, and sallow after months in prison, Gold delivered his comments in a "robust" and authoritative manner. When asked, for example, where he had first met Yakovlev, he replied, "I met Anatoli Yakovlev in March 1944, in New York City. It was on the north side of Thirty-fourth Street between Seventh and Eighth Avenues, and somewhat closer to Eighth Avenue. The exact spot was in front of the bar entrance of a Childs restaurant." Many of his answers went on for several minutes, as if he were a college professor in a lecture hall.

The jury found Gold's description of Soviet espionage operations and his dealings with Fuchs interesting, but the truly critical features of his testimony concerned his June 1945 trip to the Greenglasses in Albuquerque. He told how he "protested" when Yakovlev first assigned him "an additional mission besides the one to see Dr. Fuchs." He recalled that "a woman was supposed to go in place of me, but she was unable to make the trip." Gold told the court how he had argued that it was poor tradecraft and "highly inadvisable to endanger the very important trip to see Dr. Fuchs with this additional task." The Russian, however, said the extra assignment "was extremely important," and Gold had to go to Albuquerque. "That is an order."[99]

Yakovlev then gave him a sheet of onionskin paper that included the name Greenglass and an address on "High Street" in "Albuquerque, New Mexico." The last item on the paper, said Gold, was a "recognition signal. I come from Julius." This, the most explosive and controversial comment from his several hours on the stand, would be roundly attacked for decades afterward by Rosenberg partisans.

From the time of his arrest in May 1950 until the Rosenberg trial the following March, Gold was unsure of both the recognition signal and the pseudonym he had chosen for himself. When recounting the Albuquerque episode with his lawyers in early June at Holmesburg Prison, Gold thought he might have told David Greenglass, "Bob sent me or Benny sent me or John sent me or something like that." He was equally mystified as to his own alias. He told Hamilton and Ballard, "I know that I did not use my own name, that I possibly used the name of Mr. Frank, possibly Raymond Frank, possibly Frank Martin. But I know that I did not use my name."[100] Interrogation by FBI agents on this point was no more fruitful. Despite his recalling numerous other aspects about Ruth and David Greenglass, their apartment, and items from their conversation, including their receiving delicatessen items from back East, the alias and recognition signal continued to elude him.

At the Rosenberg trial, however, Gold displayed no uncertainty. He said he had identified himself as "Dave from Pittsburgh" and used the code "I come from Julius."[101] These identifiers would provide much grist for the Rosenberg propaganda mill.

A few years later, playwright and screenwriter John Wexley would combine an active imagination, amateur psychoanalysis, and his zeal to exonerate the Rosenbergs into a bizarre portrait of Gold. Wexley saw the congenial but guilt-ridden Philadelphia chemist as the archetypal "insane witness" who delights in outwitting judges and juries and enjoys "hoaxing the entire world" and "seeing his name in headlines."[102] Prison for this lonely, disturbed soul, said Wexley, was "a sanctuary, a retreat," and the special treatment he was accorded in the Tombs only fed his need for attention.[103] Gold's cell was in the "Singers Heaven or the Singing Quarters," where informants and other prized miscreants could "loll about" and enjoy "good food, and special privileges." "What possible reason was there," Wexler wrote, "for Gold and Greenglass to be lodged in the same prison unless it was for the express purpose of their collaboration? The Tombs is not a Federal prison."[104] Why wasn't Gold moved to a prison in Pennsylvania after he pleaded guilty on July 20? Wexley's answer: it was the government's "express purpose" to synchronize their testimony.

In fact, Greenglass and Gold were in the Tombs for separate and legitimate reasons: Greenglass because he had not yet been sentenced, and Gold because, notwithstanding the fact that he had not yet been assigned to a federal prison, the Tombs was the closest jail to where the Rosenberg trial was being held. For Wexley, however, their presence in the same facility was more sinister. "It is more than suspicious," he argues, "that the two were lodged in the same prison together for the entire period before the trial." Wexley pictures Gold "coaching his bunk-mate, Greenglass, on the mysteries of the atom bomb secrets about which the latter was to testify."[105]

Ronald Radosh and Joyce Milton persuasively argue in their definitive study of the Rosenberg case that "Gold and Greenglass were less cozy than the scenario would have it . . . nor was there any need for the kind of wholesale manufacture of testimony Wexley envisions. The version of their June 1945 meeting that Gold and Greenglass had given the FBI independently agreed in their important essentials."[106] Both David and Ruth Greenglass distinctly remembered that Gold introduced himself as "David from Pittsburgh." Though Gold resisted this name for some time, a meeting between the two confessed spies in late December seemed to jog Gold's memory, especially after Greenglass said he mentioned when they met that they both had the same name. Gold now thought that was a "distinct possibility."[107]

The name Julius was even more difficult for Gold to reconcile. The Greenglasses did not recall "greetings" from anybody, though Gold said he always "brought greetings" from someone in accordance with standard procedure. David Greenglass argued that the expressions "Julius sent me" and "I come from Julius" were the only signals that would have made sense to him. Gold left their December 28 meeting still unsure. It was not until "the day before the Rosenberg-Sobell trial began that Gold expressed some degree of certainty that 'I come from Julius' was the expression used on first meeting David Greenglass in Albuequerque." The

Rosenberg jurors would never know of Gold's difficulty in arriving at the two key phrases, but the later release of FBI documents would illuminate the Bureau's efforts to coordinate the statements of its two key witnesses. If one was content to disregard the many facts Gold and Greenglass agreed on, these documents would conclusively demonstrate a government conspiracy.

"Smoke coming out of my ears"

Only slightly less contentious for Rosenberg defenders was Manny Bloch's decision not to cross-examine Harry Gold. Gold's testimony had been exceedingly damaging, and leaving it unchallenged did much to confirm the Rosenbergs' guilt, strengthen the belief that Bloch was not up to such a high-profile case, and add to the controversy surrounding the trial.

The Rosenbergs needed a high-powered defense attorney skilled in the management of capital cases. Though certainly committed to his clients, Bloch was not that attorney. "Manny Bloch was the most incompetent lawyer in America," said Gus Ballard, who followed the court proceedings. "He was a family friend and not a competent criminal lawyer. Here was the principal witness for the United States and Bloch passed on him. He didn't ask Harry a single question. It was incredible."[108]

Many observers, especially those who knew of the witness's statements in the Brothman-Moskowitz trial, had anticipated a lively confrontation. Gold's admission of "smoke coming out of my ears" from all the lies he was forced to tell in order to conceal his spy missions should have provided fertile ground for vigorous cross-examination. A thorough skewering of Gold's veracity by a clever litigator might have instilled a doubt or two in the minds of jurors. Bloch's decision to allow Gold's account to stand—particularly the phrase "I come from Julius"—was deeply perplexing. Even a moderately skilled trial attorney could probably have got Gold to admit that his recollection of the recognition statements was weak and had been encouraged by prosecutors.

In their assessment of this pivotal decision, Radosh and Milton convincingly argue that Bloch may have thought that he and his clients had got off easy: "Gold's testimony might have been even more damaging than it actually was."[109] They quote Louis Nizer's suggestion that fear played a compelling role in Bloch's decision not to cross-examine Gold: "Fear that Gold, if pressed, might blurt out something which, whether true or false, might sink the Rosenbergs."

Gold had no need to speculate. He believed he had told the truth and begun to make amends for his colossal errors in judgment. Over the next few weeks, he would learn that the Rosenbergs and Sobell had been found guilty. Julius and Ethel received the death penalty; Sobell thirty years. For his cooperation, David Greenglass was given a relatively light fifteen-year sentence and his wife her freedom.

For Gold, the months of question-and-answer sessions, of grand jury and courtroom testimony, were finally over. It was time to begin serving his sentence.

CHAPTER 13

· ·

Prisoner 19312-NE

On June 26, 1951, Harry Gold entered Lewisburg Federal Penitentiary in north-central Pennsylvania.[1] The enormous walled facility, sitting ominously amid gentle rolling hills and languid pasturelands, would be Gold's home for the next three decades.

There are no personal letters, documents, or witnesses to tell us what Gold thought about while handcuffed and shackled along with three dozen other prisoners on the uncomfortable eight-hour bus ride from Manhattan's West Street Detention Center to Lewisburg. But he surely grasped, as easily as one sees the difference between New York City's skyscrapers and rural Pennsylvania's endless countryside, that a part of his life was over and a new, equally daunting one was beginning.[2] Though imprisonment was no longer a complete novelty to Gold—he had already spent more than a year behind bars—he was now entering the "Big House," a formidable federal institution for men convicted of major crimes and sentenced to significant time. In the lexicon of the criminal underworld, his thirty-year sentence meant he was "buried."

Few would seem as ill-equipped for such a brutal environment as the bookish and unimposing chemist. Gold's arrest, prolonged interrogation, and high-profile courtroom appearances had taken a toll on him both physically and psychologically. Most obvious was his weight loss—he had shed a good sixty to seventy pounds since his arrest the previous May and now looked more like a somewhat haggard tax accountant than a pudgy adolescent. But he was in no shape to contend with the hardened criminals on Lewisburg's raucous and occasionally violent cellblocks.[3] For a mild-mannered Jew who had lived with his mother his entire life, enjoyed the Philadelphia Orchestra, loved Italian operettas, and read Charles Dickens, Somerset Maugham, and Thomas Wolfe, Lewisburg was most definitely a world apart.

"An experiment in penology"

In the late 1920s, America's nascent and troubled federal prison system consisted of three penitentiaries—in Leavenworth, Kansas; Atlanta; and McNeil Island, Washington. There was also a youth facility and an institution for female offenders. The whole system was overcrowded, unable to classify inmates scientifically or provide meaningful work assignments, and incapable of offering needed training to its officers and staff. To rectify these problems and provide some authority and direction, the U.S. attorney general's office in 1929 selected Sanford Bates, commissioner of the Massachusetts Correctional System, to reorganize the Bureau of Prisons and become its first superintendent.

Bates envisioned a total overhaul of the federal prison system that would incorporate both legislative and programmatic changes. One item on his agenda was the construction of a new prison for the northeastern United States, to be situated somewhere east of Pittsburgh and north of Delaware's southern border. In an effort to take politics out of the decision, Bates came up with a sixteen-point ranking system that included such factors as accessibility, the importance of neighboring towns, topography, and the fertility of the land. An additional factor was that the tract should not cost more than $100,000.[4]

A hundred applications were submitted, and Bates and his team visited seventy sites. The location with the highest score was a large tract near the little college town of Lewisburg, Pennsylvania, home of Bucknell University. Known to local residents as the Buffalo Valley, the rugged landscape sat between the Appalachian Mountains and the west branch of the Susquehanna River. Level terrain would facilitate construction, fertile soil could provide food for the inmates, and the Reading Railroad was willing to run a spur line to the institution. A purchase price of $95,000 sealed the deal.[5]

Alfred Hopkins, one of the preeminent prison architects of the day, was hired to plan the new facility. Dispensing with the custom of building prisons to resemble grim medieval fortresses, Hopkins instead designed it "in an exquisite Italian Renaissance style, using cast stone, concrete blocks, and rough kiln bricks, that gave it the appearance of a monastery or university."[6] The institution's unusual but attractive red tile roof could be seen for miles around.

The prison's interior was equally unconventional. Hopkins departed from the traditional spoke-and-wheel configuration in favor of a seven-hundred-foot main corridor intersected by a series of three-story cell-blocks and administrative units containing gymnasiums, chow halls, and clinics that ran at right angles from the central corridor. Just coming into its own in both Europe and America, this "telephone pole" penal design, along with the other institutional innovations, signaled the Bureau's intent to approach punishment in a more modern, scientific way. As one local newspaper declared, the $3.5 million project would be "the most advanced penal institution in the world. . . . Modeled after the most modern prisons in the United States and Europe, it will express the last word in up-to-date theory concerning the treatment of criminals."[7] Sanford Bates was interested in more than architecture; his primary goal was inmate rehabilitation.[8]

Northeastern Penitentiary opened in November 1932 and soon became a testing ground for dozens of experimental ventures in housing, training, education, classification, and community development. Whatever worked was maintained and encouraged throughout the federal penal system; whatever failed was jettisoned. Bates described Northeastern as "an experiment in penology," a world-class penal institution that allowed the Bureau to "carry out some of the newer ideas for which we are all striving."[9]

At first, the twelve hundred prisoners incarcerated at Lewisburg were those deemed most capable of reform: the younger, less violent offenders, with less threatening criminal portfolios than the inmates sent to Atlanta, Leavenworth, or the recently opened Alcatraz. But rehabilitation slowly gave way to more mundane concerns like systemwide overcrowding, and Northeastern began to resemble its older, more menacing cousins. "The best of America's prisons," no longer the last word in scientific penology, gradually received its share of mobsters, bank robbers, kidnappers, and murderers.[10] By the onset of the Korean War, Northeastern was demographically almost indistinguishable from any other maximum-security federal institution. In any case, for a first-time offender like Harry Gold, fine distinctions among inmate populations could hardly have mattered.

Inmate 19312-NE

Entering a maximum-security federal prison at the start of a long sentence, even seasoned felons take a deep breath and brace themselves. Harry no doubt did the same.

A World War II–era conscientious objector named Alfred Hassler wrote of his first sight of Northeastern's awesome walls and reinforced entrance, "Except for the impression of a mass of brick buildings with red-tile roofs, I didn't really get much of a look at my new home from the outside. I was too busy concentrating on that high gray wall and the barred gate: the highest, meanest . . . looking wall and gate I had ever seen in my life. . . . I think we all felt as though we should hunch up our shoulders and get ready for something pretty unpleasant."[11]

Gold had even more reason to be pessimistic. He wasn't a conscientious objector accepting a two- or three-year prison term because of a principled religious stand; he was a longtime Soviet agent convicted of giving the Communists the secrets of the Bomb. He was a high-profile traitor, a convicted spy about to serve a lengthy sentence in a time of war —a war that some argued he had helped create.

Even worse, Gold had spent enough time in Holmesburg and the Tombs to know how the inmate population felt about "rats" and "snitches." Informants shared the lowest spot on the prison food chain with child molesters. In the past year, Gold had been a fountain of information for the FBI, had helped put numerous former associates in prison, and had been instrumental in sending a husband and wife to the electric chair. There may have not been a better known or more loathed stool pigeon in the federal prison system.

After entering the gates and watching the several-inch-thick steel and wooden doors close behind them, Gold and the others were escorted off the prison bus and taken down a flight of stairs to an area designated "Receiving & Discharge." Here they were stripped, ordered to shower, given quick medical exams, and handed their new prison garments. They were then taken to another area to be fingerprinted and photographed. This was followed by a trip to a large room above the prison hospital where a more thorough medical exam looked for communicable diseases, such as syphilis and tuberculosis.[12]

The new inmates were then placed in one- or two-man cells while undergoing the Admission and Orientation process. A&O could last from three to four weeks and was designed to determine what kind of individual the prison was receiving and which institutional programs best fitted him. Apart from the many interviews, the only time the men left their cells was to go to the chow hall and, occasionally, the exercise yard. In both areas, new arrivals were kept separate from the facility's regular inhabitants.

The classification process consisted of a series of interviews, written examinations, medical assessments, criminal histories, and an array of pre- and post-sentence reports that would eventually determine an inmate's living quarters (cellblock or dormitory), his job assignment (working in the kitchen, working in prison industries, mopping the floors, and so on), and whether he presented a risk to himself or anyone else.

Bob Smith, a former Lewisburg correctional officer, described the exhaustive process. "When you're putting a guy out in general population, you have to know all about him, if he needs psychological counseling, if he presents a threat of violence to anyone or if he's liable to hurt himself." And, Smith added, "You also better know if anybody in the institution could be a threat to him." In a maximum-security penitentiary, the threat of violence is ever present. For some inmates, the classification process was critical to their survival. Smith said of Gold, "Anyone could have picked up Harry and thrown him for some distance."[13]

Gold's inmate file, already thicker than most, soon grew even bigger. The voluminous paperwork he arrived with was supplemented by a report from the U.S. attorney general's office underscoring his "most cooperative" assistance in the FBI's investigation of others and his "testifying as a government witness in other trials";[14] Judge McGranery's verdict and sentence; the FBI's lengthy parole report; and Lewisburg's own extensive and detailed analysis of its notorious new resident.[15] Little escaped the classification committee's observation: Gold's "hammer toes" and "slightly lopsided facial appearance," his "superior" intelligence, his mother's "domineering influence" on the family, and his claim of graduating from high school at fifteen. The intake form noted his recent weight loss, high blood pressure, and "terrifying nightmares"; a "repaired congenital hernia"; and the fact that Harry required orthopedic shoes. The committee recommended "moderate duty" prison work assignments.[16]

Gold's psychiatric assessment noted his "cooperative, courteous" demeanor, his "slight anxiety" during interviews, and some "compulsive personality traits" that led to "difficulty in relating to other people." The assessment team characterized him as a "rather deep individual, who at times appeared somewhat obsequious" during the interview process. Gold displayed "considerable remorse" but also seemed to "rationalize it quite well," raising questions of his "sincerity." The psychiatric section concluded by noting the subject's denial of "homosexual activities," his "deeply repressed hostility," and "some emotional insecurity." The final diagnosis was "mixed psychoneurosis."[17]

A battery of intelligence and psychological tests showed above-average intelligence and an IQ of 119 nonverbal and 121 verbal. Not surprisingly, his occupational interest inventory yielded a high score for science and lower ones for mechanical and artistic aptitude. Business-related subjects barely registered. The educational assessment also mentioned Gold's "moderate ambivalence in assuming an aggressive or passive role in life, marked suspiciousness, and a tendency to project difficulties."[18]

On the lighter side, Gold told interviewers of his interest in sports, particularly basketball, football, and handball, and somehow gave the impression that he'd be "active in these sports" while at Lewisburg. He also said that while he and his family were members of a synagogue, his father attended irregularly, his mother had not been observant at all, and he himself "hadn't attended any synagogues for 25 years." But he admitted that "if I had gone, I probably wouldn't have done the terrible thing I did."

Despite his request to work in the prison hospital or in some teaching capacity, Gold was assigned a job in the cannery. He was also to be quartered in a cell, as opposed to the more relaxed environment of a dormitory. "Close custody" was recommended due to the "length of his sentence and the nature of the offense."

Though the Lewisburg inmate classification report was less negative than the Holmesburg neuropsychiatric report of September 1950, which cited his "resentful ideas," "psychosexual" development, and "fanatic" qualities, it forecast an ominous future for Gold.[19] His prospects for adjustment were described as somewhere between daunting and impossible. In one especially poignant passage, the evaluator commented: "This man gives the impression of being rabbit-like in appearance and manner. One wonders how he ever got enough nerve to do any kind of espionage work. He has been quartered in a cell and it is suggested that he be kept in this type quarters. When he tried to play basketball with the other men at the stockade, they left the court. The only men that will have anything to do with him are the other men of the Communist Party. He has made no requests of the officers in A/O and apparently feels safer in his cell as he has never made sick line. Keeps his cell clean enough and is pitifully eager to please in every way. Prognosis for his future adjustment is very doubtful."[20]

Not many Lewisburg staffers—or inmates—would have bet on this timid newcomer's surviving long in such an unforgiving environment. "Rabbit-like in appearance," "pitifully eager to please," and shunned by the inmate population, federal prisoner no. 19312-NE seemed destined for a very bad end.

"Well-adjusted and well-satisfied"

Gold, it turned out, was made of sturdier stuff than people gave him credit for. Tremendously resilient, capable of incredible determination, and able to endure considerable discomfort, he in many ways personified such long-standing prison adages as "Do your own time" and "Don't serve time, let time serve you."[21] He had the ability to compartmentalize difficult chores, focus on the task at hand, and grapple with challenges regardless of distractions, impediments, or overwhelming odds of failure. Understandably seen as unlikely to survive what Alger Hiss—another high-profile Lewisburg inmate—called a "citadel of lonely men" and a "fortress of frustration," Gold tolerated extreme hardship far better than most.[22] And he could do it without succumbing to what Hassler called the "great temptation to indulge in orgies of feeling sorry" for oneself.[23]

Gold was put in a six-by-ten-foot cell furnished with a metal bed, desk, chair, and toilet, on a block reserved for hardened criminals.[24] No doubt others on the block found this strange little man with the odd gait and submissive demeanor a curiosity. Those who knew of his treasonous crimes surely loathed him and were probably not shy about expressing their feelings. Gold, by all accounts, was indifferent to his reception. He had been called names and physically threatened before. His lengthy imprisonment was just another assignment to be carried out.

In fact Harry was pleased to be at Lewisburg. He had wanted a transfer from his Manhattan detention facility to a federal prison for some time. A year of nonstop meetings with FBI agents, federal prosecutors, and his own attorneys, plus emotionally charged courtroom appearances, had made him long for the point when he could begin doing his own time. He was ready to do penance. As he wrote to his attorney, John D. M. Hamilton, in June 1951 from the White Street holding facility in Manhattan, "I have today been notified by federal authorities that my transfer to the penitentiary at Lewisburg will take place sometime during the week of June 25th. . . . Naturally, I am very pleased by all this, as it represents an opportunity to settle down to regular schedule of both work and study."[25]

But this was not a faculty appointment at Bucknell. Lewisburg Federal Penitentiary had all the noise, odor, and danger of any maximum-security penal institution. Unimpressed, Gold went about his business.

In his first letter to Hamilton from Lewisburg, Gold wrote, "I have been out in the general population since the end of July and I'm getting along very well. My work assignment is a twofold one: In the mornings I am stationed in the cannery, and in the afternoons I work in the hospital laboratory; the cannery is a seasonal job, lasting till about February, and it is possible that after that I may be assigned full-time to the hospital laboratory—at least, I hope this does transpire."

Far from succumbing to self-pity or fear for his physical safety, Gold sounds calm, even upbeat.[26] The only hint of dejection relates not to himself but to his beloved Philadelphia Phillies. "One final note: Boy, was I off on that prediction about the Phils!—Good pitch, good field, no hit. Oh well, wait till next year."[27] Closing baseball commentaries had become routine in Gold's and Hamilton's letters to one another and would remain so throughout their relationship.

Having a wife or children no doubt makes imprisonment harder for some inmates. Gold's equanimity may be attributed partly to the absence of such attachments. His fellow Lewisburg inmate David Greenglass had a difficult time adjusting to prison life and separation from his family. Gold had his father and brother, and being already guilt-ridden about the hurt he had caused them, he was determined not to trouble them any more than necessary.[28] He remained positive in his correspondence in order to lighten their worry about his safety.

Prisons constrain choices, narrow opportunity, and squeeze the life out of an individual's sense of independence. Harry Gold was better than most at dealing with such limitations, especially if he had a laboratory to pass the time in. He was good at submitting to authority, following orders, and completing tasks. Such attributes greatly facilitated his assimilation into the repetitive rigidity of prison life. As one former inmate said of his own days at Lewisburg, "Time in here drags with an indescribable slowness. I used to get up in the morning with a sense of anticipation for what the new day would bring; here one begins with the knowledge that the overall pattern of the day will be precisely what the overall pattern was yesterday, and the day before that. And what it will be tomorrow, of course! . . . Time in prison simply cannot be measured by the standards used outside. The unvarying routine, the constant tension, the sense of humiliation—all these make every day a week and every week a year."[29]

The boredom and routine of imprisonment could be interrupted by sudden bursts of extreme violence. Those with reputations as Communists or informants had to be particularly wary. Prisoners like Hiss, Gold, and Greenglass, whose cases had drawn national attention, needed to be vigilant, each in his own way. Greenglass, who had outdone Gold in infamy by testifying against his own family, was particularly unnerved and repeatedly reached out for reassurance and protection from authorities.

In response to a Bureau query regarding Greenglass's safety, Lewisburg's warden G. W. Humphrey wrote, "Of course, there are those in our population who label anyone who testifies against another as a 'rat.' . . . Some of these may have been taunting him because they realize they can disturb him and put him 'on the run.' He has withdrawn himself from most of the normal activities of the institution, which does not improve this situation. Generally speaking, he is fairly well shunned by the general population."[30]

The warden went on to explain that Greenglass was "in as protective status as we can place him without making it too obvious. . . . The only other action we could take to further protect him would be to place him in Administrative Segregation. . . . If you feel we should go that far we will do so, but once done it would be next to impossible to work him back into the population."[31] "As for any open violence against him," Humphrey added, "I doubt that there is any danger."

The flurry of letters and departmental memos regarding the safety of Greenglass and other high-profile Communists reflected the tension, anger, and roiling political emotions on Lewisburg's cellblocks. Eventually, Greenglass would acclimate himself to his surroundings, but not before numerous alarm signals and requests "to send me to Danbury [Connecticut] or some like institution."[32]

Harry Gold appears to have had a far less traumatic adjustment. In 1952 a "Special Progress Report" for inmate no. 19312 stated that "Gold is well-adjusted and well-satisfied on his current program and no recommendation for change is made at this time." He was described as a "quiet, reserved individual, with very few close, intimate associates," who nonetheless appeared "to get along well with the inmate body in general" and displayed a "favorable attitude at all times." The report added that Gold "maintains his person and quarters in a neat, orderly condition at all times. Most of his spare time is used on the Hepatitis program, but when free from this project he does a great deal of reading in quarters and listening to the radio. He attends very few recreation activities of the institution."[33]

Gold received "excellent work reports" from his supervisor on the canning detail and was "considered outstanding along the lines of technical improvement of food processing." When the canning season ended, he was assigned to the hospital, where he was made a laboratory technician and spent a good deal of time on a hepatitis study being conducted by the U.S. Public Health Service. Harry's supervising officer reported that he "performed a large number of laboratory tests, particularly urinalysis," which involved "the use of delicate instruments and other expensive equipment." He was of "great aid in the processing of blood samples taken from the volunteers" and was noted for taking "great care of the equipment" and carrying out the various procedures "with dexterity and a great sense of responsibility and accomplishment."[34]

The former biochemist no doubt relished his time in the prison hospital laboratory. The world of flasks, beakers, and precise scientific instruments had always been an oasis and an intellectual challenge for him. Though rudimentary by the standards of Philadelphia General Hospital's Heart Station, the Lewisburg laboratory was better than no lab at all. It meant his years of imprisonment wouldn't be wasted, and his training and education would be used for something worthwhile. The presence of the Public Health Service's research team confirmed that important science was underway.

Though Gold's first "inmate progress report" mentioned the Public Health Service's hepatitis project, it failed to cite an earlier study in which Gold volunteered as a test subject. Apparently, during the spring of 1952, the U.S. Army began a research study at the prison designed "to develop a serum which will prevent yellow jaundice."

According to an FBI memo addressed to "Mr. Hoover," Gold had become both researcher and test subject at the federal facility. "The Korean campaign," the memo stated, "has demonstrated that wounded soldiers supplied blood plasma have developed severe cases of yellow jaundice. In an effort to assist the Army in developing this serum, . . . Gold subjected himself to an injection of contaminated blood and developed yellow jaundice." He went from being a hospital technician "running blood tests for the U.S. Army" to requiring hospitalization himself.[35]

Gold's decision to become a human guinea pig is not that surprising considering his background, mindset, and circumstances. Cut to the core by the allegation that he had done deliberate harm to America, Gold looked for ways to show his patriotism. Serving as a experimental subject in a research project at a laboratory where he worked, in support of American soldiers overseas, was an opportunity to do this. Gold wasn't the first prison inmate or hospital aide to subject himself to fever, discomfort, and bouts of diarrhea, but he may have been the only one of interest to the FBI to do so during the early years of the Cold War.[36]

Gold's selfless act apparently never received public mention—and may never have been reported to some prison officials, since inmate participation in medical research often wasn't—but the clinical trial may have had lasting effects on his health. Many years later, suffering from chronic chest discomfort, shortness of breath, and fatigue, Gold told a friend that a prison medical experiment had worsened his general health and aggravated his heart problems.[37] Joe Gold knew of his brother's decision to become a test subject but believed that he had "contracted a severe case of hepatitis while working on his prison research."[38]

Another not altogether surprising item found in Gold's progress report was his decision to begin regular attendance at Jewish religious services. Though Gold had had a bar mitzvah and as a child had enjoyed his mother's Yiddish fables, as an adult he was indifferent to religion and never went to synagogue, even on the High Holidays. Imprisonment changed all that. Like many newly imprisoned people, he sought spiritual comfort and the collegiality of like-minded individuals.

Chick Goodroe, another Jewish inmate who served time at Lewisburg and who eventually ran the kosher kitchen at the institution, said it wasn't unusual for nonobservant Jews to rediscover their heritage in jail. "People would get active because it introduced you to your peers," said Goodroe. "There's always a desire to hook up with people you have an affinity with. As a Jew you were part of a very small minority in prison, maybe a dozen in the whole joint. I was a criminal so I knew people, but for somebody like Gold it must have been terribly difficult. Camaraderie is very important in prison. You're always looking for a more welcoming environment." It helped, said Goodroe, that a "rabbi would come in to hold services and counsel you, you could celebrate the High Holidays with others like yourself, and services would usually end with bagels, cream cheese, grape juice, and gefilte fish."[39]

It wasn't the Waldorf Astoria or even South Philip Street, but Harry Gold was getting along far better than the case managers for the Bureau of Prisons had predicted. Even his brother Joe seemed pleased: he mentioned Harry's "excellent spirits" in a letter to FBI Special Agent Scotty Miller. "My brother," he wrote, "has an interesting job at Lewisburg and he gets along well with everyone."[40] Guards like Al From came to like and trust Harry. "He was no problem at all," recalls From, a correctional officer who began his career at Lewisburg in the early 1950s. "Harry kept to himself, spent time in the prison library, and was a good asset to the hospital. He never bothered anybody, people seemed to like him."[41]

During these early years of confinement, Gold's only complaints concerned the many inaccuracies in press accounts of his actions and motives as a Soviet agent, and his inability to get books—scientific and otherwise. Hamilton and Ballard received a number of letters from Gold expressing concern over his portrayal in newspaper and magazine articles. He never denied his guilt, but he was exasperated by accounts that embellished his role or completely distorted the truth. He wrote long, detailed missives to his lawyers separating fact from fiction in the hope that Hamilton or Ballard would set the record straight.[42] After trying at first to correct egregious falsehoods, his attorneys gradually tried to get him to recognize that such efforts were hopeless; he'd always be political fodder for columnists. Moreover, there was no sense stirring the pot: the less said about him in the media, even to correct inaccuracies, the better.[43] Gold continued to craft long explanatory rebuttals, but fewer and fewer were forwarded to the offending parties.

Of at least equal concern were Gold's tortured attempts to stay in contact with Mary Lanning, the woman to whom he had once proposed marriage. He had written to her from his Manhattan holding cell in the spring of 1951 and thanked her for having the "courage" and "Christian charity" to stop by and visit with his father and brother after his arrest. He understood how "horrified" she must be by his crime. His father and brother, he said, "try to excuse me but—and here is the rub—I cannot excuse myself. Ever."

Gold admitted how frightened he had been "that they too, would turn against me . . . but they have stuck by me. Nothing I can ever do will make for restitution." He meekly asked if he could write to her "occasionally, say every couple months or so . . . that would be grand?"

In another letter to Lanning from his Manhattan cell, Gold plaintively tried to assure her that nothing was expected of her in return. "Please let me make it clear, I shall be writing to an old friend—no more than that, and if you should care to answer my letters that would make me very happy, not to speak of helping me keep in touch with the outside world."

"Regarding our past friendship," he wrote, "it was just that and no more. We enjoyed the same things and . . ."; he struggled to find the right words. Three times he began. "I just don't . . . I don't know whether . . . I don't know whether any. . . ." Apparently, neither the thought nor the sentence could be completed. This went beyond Gold's usual struggles with obsessive-compulsive disorder; too much had transpired, and too much had been lost.[44]

Gold's letters to Lanning from Lewisburg, including the drafts he never mailed, were no less difficult and would eventually stop. His many practice letters in pencil would begin "Dear Mary . . . Dearest Mary," further illuminating his quandary. Beset by conflicting emotions and never quite able to strike the right tone, he filled pages with heartfelt words, phrases, and occasionally paragraphs that he would then cross out. In the letters that made it into the mail, Gold tried to keep the tone light and refrained from any comment on their former relationship. He'd mention his job, the hepatitis study on which he was "only too happy" to work, and his graying hair, but he dared not bring up what she had once meant to him.[45]

Gold began one letter by informing Lanning that he'd come "to realize one often curious (and insidiously dangerous) feature of existence in prisons . . . [the belief] that time stops outside and everything and everyone on our return will be exactly as we left the free world. But, of course, time doesn't stop and changes do occur."[46] Despised by much of "the free world," severed from his few remaining friends and family members, and buried alive in a brick and steel crypt, Gold resided in a reviled netherworld—not dead, but not quite alive either.

Roy Cohn

As the days passed ever so slowly for the twelve hundred men inside Lewisburg, Harry went about his assignments in his normal businesslike fashion. He seemed impervious to both his daunting sentence and his surroundings. Unlike most prisoners, especially those with a scarlet *C* attached to them, he never communicated any concern for his safety. Letters home were either upbeat or resigned. He wrote to Hamilton in early fall 1953, "I am well: my weight is still at a normal 140 lbs. And I don't ever intend to become 'sloppy fat' again; however, my hair is visibly gray at the temples, very much so, in fact. Oh well."[47]

Work, as usual, was the centerpiece of his life. "A great source of satisfaction has been my work assignment here," he wrote; "the project in question should come to a successful completion probably about July of next year. A friend once said with much truth, 'just put Harry in a laboratory and he's happy.' For a while I worked rather long hours, which left no leisure time, but lately the pace has slackened off, and I've been reviewing my mathematics—as I've intended for many years."

To someone unfamiliar with Gold's situation, his letters might sound like those of a family breadwinner at a distant work assignment or a college student writing happily from an out-of-state campus. His frequent references to recent sporting events would have encouraged this impression: "I heard some of the World Series games on the radio here; and we get football broadcasts over the weekend: lately 'my cup runneth over,' since Penn beat Penn State Saturday for the first time in 17 years."[48]

Some letters were more ebullient than others. In early November 1953, Gold announced to his lawyers, "I have what I trust will be good news." During a recent interview with Senator Joseph McCarthy's committee, Roy M. Cohn, the committee's chief counsel, had pulled Gold aside and informed him that "there now existed a tremendous sentiment (including that within Government circles) acknowledging the fact that I had received too great a penalty." Gold said Cohn had spoken to "Judge McGranery in Washington and the Judge had stated that it was now his belief he had imposed a too severe sentence upon me."[49] Surprised and excited by this comment, Gold reminded Hamilton that "Cohn was one of the U.S. Attorneys in both the Brothman and the Rosenberg trials and . . . I was a witness in these two cases." Gold was anxious to pursue this unexpected development and asked his attorney to "write Judge McGranery and Mr. Cohn" for confirmation.

Hamilton wasted little time in writing to Cohn but counseled his client that "the matter . . . is much too delicate to bring up with Judge McGranery other than as a matter of personal discussion." Written communication over such a sensitive issue was out of the question; Gold would have to wait until Hamilton had the opportunity to talk with the judge personally.[50]

Hamilton's tactful letter to Roy Cohn can be read as the work of an aging and experienced lawyer whose instinct has told him that he and his client should be wary. They had been burned once. Hamilton was still troubled by the severity of Gold's sentence, and he was in no mood to be manipulated by McCarthy's slick young aide-de-camp, who was riding the anti-Communism horse for all it was worth.

Hamilton made it clear to Cohn that he was "not assured that the time is now propitious to take any steps looking to a commutation of Mr. Gold's sentence," but "when that step is taken" he wanted to know where everyone stood. He asked Cohn to put on paper "the conversation between Judge McGranery and yourself," as well as Gold's lengthy record of "cooperation since the date of sentencing." Hamilton didn't want his client's many contributions to the government to be forgotten: he wanted them acknowledged now, in writing.[51]

Gold wrote to Hamilton saying he understood "that the matter of approaching Judge McGranery about the severity of my sentence is a most delicate business." Gold had been irritated when the issue found its way into a newspaper gossip column.[52] A sentence reduction would not be "accomplished easily—if, indeed, it is at all possible," and he agreed with Hamilton that "the time to try this is not now. Definitely."

Gold also underscored his belief that if anyone knew the "extent of my continued cooperation with the Government" it was "Mr. J. Edgar Hoover." "Ever since my sentencing on December 9, 1950," he reminded Hamilton, "I have been in frequent and constant touch with his agents and have given, and shall continue to give, whatever definite and accurate information I have on a variety of, as yet, 'unfinished business.'" He told his lawyer, "Some of this has appeared in the papers, but a good deal has not—and possibly may never do so."[53]

In short, Gold was delighted to hear from a government official that the federal judge who had sentenced him was having second thoughts, but he wasn't going to get his hopes up based on the words of a Senate staffer, even one as well connected and familiar with his case as Roy Cohn. Even if his sentence was reduced, he would be in prison for a very long time.

Joe Gold

In the summer of 1954, Gold received his second "special progress report." It is hard to imagine a federal prisoner in a maximum-security facility receiving a more positive assessment. Gold's laboratory supervisor was practically gushing, praising him for "doing an outstanding job" as a "laboratory technician and special nurse in the hospital." He had "shown a great deal of interest in his work," he was "careful with fragile and expensive equipment," and it was not unusual to see him "working evenings and weekends." Never once had Gold "refused any request to perform special services." His contributions were significant; now sensitive laboratory work could be performed at Lewisburg "instead of being sent to other laboratories."[54]

Gold's cellblock record reported no conduct infractions; he was described as "courteous, cooperative," and was said to spend most of his time on the block "reading, writing, and listening to the radio." He attended Jewish services regularly, participated in group activities, and was receiving "numerous visits from his father and brother." The report also mentioned a letter from Gold's attorney "relative to a communication with a Mr. Roy Cohn . . . relative to possible adjustment on his sentence which the attorney proposes to take up with the sentencing Judge sometime in the future on a personal basis."[55]

That Gold had apparently adapted to his new home did not mean that things couldn't be improved. Though he was highly unlikely to complain to officials about perceived inequities or lobby for additional benefits, his brother was not so reticent. Joe Gold was six years younger than Harry and as a child had looked up to his older brother for guidance and protection, but as an adult Joe was considerably more streetwise. He had served in the Pacific during the war, and knew how his brother could be manipulated. Harry's incarceration must have kept him constantly on edge. Joe saw Harry as a lamb on the banks of a canal filled with alligators.

Joe Gold constantly championed his brother's cause—whether Harry liked it or not. Both Harry's lawyers and his keepers received the treatment. Everything from institutional limitations on reading material to cavalier treatment by federal prosecutors was grist for the Joe Gold complaint mill. Although he was occasionally undiplomatic and often a pain to deal with, no one could question his loyalty or dedication.

Joe drove officials and agencies to distraction in his efforts to get his brother the reading material he desired. Harry was a voracious reader and may well have gone through every book in the penitentiary library. He regularly sent his brother penciled lists of books he wanted to read or reread. One list included Charles Dickens's *Great Expectations* and *David Copperfield,* Irving Stone's *Lust for Life,* Thomas Mann's *Magic Mountain,* Tolstoy's *War and Peace,* and Somerset Maugham—"anything he ever wrote."[56]

But classics and popular novels weren't the only items on Harry's reading agenda; he also hoped to stay current with the latest scientific developments and routinely requested access to chemistry journals and books. If the prison library wouldn't pay for a subscription, Joe and his father offered to cover the cost. It was the least they could do for a loving, dedicated son and brother who had never—until recently—caused them a bit of trouble and was due to spend the next thirty years behind bars.

When such modest requests were rejected, Joe was beside himself with frustration and would initiate a letter-writing campaign. John Hamilton and Gus Ballard, the Lewisburg warden, and numerous Bureau of Prison officials would all hear about the latest outrage. Ballard, who by 1954 had been working on Harry Gold's case for four years without a penny of remuneration and would do so for many years to come, found Joe to be "a complete pain in the ass." "Harry appealed to me," said Ballard. "There was something about him. He was just a very appealing guy. His brother, however, was a bloody bore. Joe Gold was always complaining." Ballard said the "difference between the brothers was absolutely astonishing." On top of that, "Joe didn't seem to understand the concept of paying your lawyers."[57]

Even the FBI found itself on the receiving end of Joe's outrage and appeals for assistance. In September 1954 an FBI memo to Hoover recounted a lengthy list of Joe's grievances, including the "publications" issue. It informed the director that even though the Gold family was sending "the necessary money to purchase . . . publications" at Lewisburg, they were repeatedly rebuffed "due to prison regulations." "Joseph Gold," the memo went on, "stated it is a known fact that prisoners receive books from the outside concerning auto repair, refrigerator repair, and in general books which will assist prisoners in learning a trade. It is difficult to understand, according to Joseph Gold, why Harry Gold cannot receive books which will assist in human repair."

The memo also mentioned a letter in which John Hamilton cautioned Joe that complaining to the Justice Department might "harm Harry" and cause "prison officials to become antagonistic" toward him. Joe, unimpressed, decided to do an end run around the department and contacted the FBI in the hope that Harry's "past cooperation" would translate into assistance.[58]

It was more than the availability of books and magazines that concerned Joe Gold. He presented the FBI with a list of concerns ranging from "the unfavorable publicity" his brother had received, despite his becoming a "cooperative government witness," to a remark supposedly uttered by the Lewisburg warden: "No Communist gets good time or pay for any work done at Lewisburg."

Joe found the latter issue particularly irksome. He believed his brother was being lumped in with "Alger Hiss, William Remington and others," who denied their Communist activities, whereas Harry had been "a cooperative government witness . . . identifying all individuals who were associated with him in Soviet espionage."[59] For the past three years Harry had been "averaging 18 hours a day on hepatitis research without compensation." This, Joe pointed out, was due to the warden's "purposely not paying Harry Gold for work because the warden has included Harry with Hiss and Remington."

Joe concluded by informing the FBI that he was airing these issues out of "brotherly duty" and recognition that his brother "would not mention the problems himself."[60] Harry, the model of decorum in practically all his personal transactions, would never have been so demanding. But Joe was trying to protect his brother as best he could from 150 miles away. That familial instinct would be sorely tested very soon.

"A hatred of Communists"

William Walter Remington was another of the high-profile Communists incarcerated at Lewisburg. A tall, handsome Dartmouth graduate, Remington had been the target of a series of well-publicized grand jury hearings and trials in the early 1950s prompted by allegations that he had been a Soviet spy and dues-paying member of the Communist Party. Remington's name first surfaced in the media when Elizabeth Bentley named him as someone whose CPUSA dues she had picked up years earlier, when he was a young economist with the War Production Board. In addition, she claimed he had also supplied her with "War Production Board information . . . on airplane production, high-octane gasoline, and synthetic rubber."[61]

The FBI began investigating Remington in 1947, and for the next several years he endured a string of legal battles with a cross-section of federal agencies, including the Atomic Energy Commission and the Civil Service Loyalty-Security Review Board. In addition, he was involved in a much-publicized libel suit against NBC, which had broadcast Bentley's accusations on *Meet the Press*.[62] Although the FBI and Justice Department believed Bentley's allegations of Remington's espionage, they felt they had a better chance of winning a court verdict against him if they focused on his unpersuasive claim that "he had never been a Communist or participated in Communist activities."

Remington was indicted by a grand jury in June 1950 and convicted in December after prosecutors persuaded his wife to testify against him. A three-judge panel threw out the conviction on a technicality and ordered a new trial. Fearing that the case against Remington could be lost on an array of thorny issues, including a troubling secret business relationship between Bentley and the grand jury foreman, assistant prosecutor Roy Cohn "suggested a different tactic." He argued for a new grand jury. Starting from scratch would alleviate most of their current concerns, allow the use of additional information garnered from the last trial, and place the focus "on matters where the government had witnesses and evidence refuting Remington's denials."[63]

Remington's second perjury trial began in January 1953. As she had done two years earlier, Remington's wife provided critical testimony. With the combined recollections of former Dartmouth students and other colleagues, Remington's association with the Young Communist League and the CPUSA appeared well documented. On January 28, 1953, he was found guilty on two of five counts and sentenced to three years in Lewisburg Penitentiary.

Though described as "brilliant of mind, handsome in appearance, and engaging in manner," William Remington was headed to a place where these weren't the most enviable personal traits. Being a court-certified Communist didn't help. Men like Hiss, Gold, Greenglass, and Remington, said Federal Bureau of Prisons Director James V. Bennett, were more than "merely newspaper headlines or academic figures, they were present in the flesh"—provocative bait for the prison system's more dangerous and unstable inmates.[64]

Remington did his best to blend in, and after a year and a half was promoted to the facility's honor quarters, with its unlocked doors and greater freedom. But a bureaucratic bungle placed Lewis Cagle Jr. and George McCoy in a room directly opposite his. Neither Cagle nor McCoy warranted such a choice housing assignment. The thirty-four-year-old McCoy claimed to belong to the infamous McCoy family that had feuded for generations with the Hatfields after the Civil War. A misfit and troublemaker of long standing, his right arm bore the tattoo of a naked woman. On the left was his social security number. With an IQ of 61, he had "found it necessary to burn it permanently into his flesh in order to remember it."[65]

Cagle, only seventeen, was much younger than the other men in Lewisburg but had already proven himself a predator at several juvenile institutions, where his menacing behavior had won him a transfer to the more secure federal pen. No longer top dog, he carried a half-pound brick stuffed into a white sock for protection. He was especially frightened of McCoy. The one thing that united them was their distaste for Remington. In addition to his good looks and Ivy League degrees, Remington, according to McCoy, acted "high hat." More important, McCoy hated Communists. "I would like to line up a bunch of Communists," he once said, "and shoot them down with a machine gun just like cutting wheat."[66]

During October and November 1954, Remington and his roommate were victimized by pranks ranging from theft to arson. "The whole floor is irritated at the fire incident," Remington wrote home. "It puts on the heat . . . the officers will be more apt to discover and crack down on the various illicit activities normally in process. . . . Some fellows have a good idea of who's doing the stealing and who tossed the match, but naturally they won't say. However, they are emphatic that no one is in any physical danger."[67] They were wrong.

Early on the morning of November 22, Cagle and McCoy quietly entered Remington's room. He was alone, asleep. Cagle, with no warning, began swinging his brick weighted sock at Remington's head. Stunned and bleeding profusely, Remington was unable to ward off the blows. McCoy then finished him off. "A spy," "a traitor," "a damn Communist [who] tried to sell us out," McCoy is reported to have called Remington.[68] He died the next day of massive head injuries.

The murder of a high-profile inmate sent a shiver through the Bureau of Prisons. It did more than that to the other Communist prisoners in the system, particularly those at Lewisburg. Even the FBI took notice. In addition to investigating the murder, they had to determine how best to protect the remaining Communists. Some were still being interviewed as part of ongoing investigations; the FBI couldn't afford to lose them to violence. "The feasibility of future interviews with Gold and Greenglass" became a paramount concern.[69]

Warden Fred T. Wilkinson was candid with the FBI; "there was no doubt in his mind that other inmates at Lewisburg Penitentiary had as deep a hatred of Communists" as Cagle and McCoy did, and "if given the opportunity would probably take the same actions against other convicted Communists presently incarcerated at Lewisburg."[70] Wilkinson advised the FBI "that Harry Gold and David Greenglass . . . have been labeled as Communists by other inmates" and furthermore were "regarded as 'rats' and 'informers' . . . which, of course, adds nothing towards popularity or amicable feelings."

In the aftermath of Remington's murder, two "convicted Smith Act subjects" who had been found guilty of belonging to revolutionary groups were transferred out of Lewisburg for their own safety. Wilkinson cautioned the FBI against conducting any further interviews with Gold and Greenglass at the prison. Considering "the deep seated feelings of some of the inmates," he warned, further meetings between the FBI and the espionage prisoners would make things worse. The warden knew that

George McCoy's sentiment about Communists, that "somebody ought to knock their heads in," was shared by many in the institution.[71]

Wilkinson initiated "precautionary measures" to protect Gold and Greenglass and told the FBI that Greenglass, who was practically apoplectic about the situation, "would probably be transferred."[72] Gold, meanwhile, acted as if nothing had happened. No letters of alarm were rushed to his attorneys or family members in Philadelphia; there were no pleas to Bureau of Prison officials for reassignment to a less violent institution, no distress calls went out to the many FBI agents with whom he was now on a first-name basis. Though quite possibly the smallest and most timid prisoner in the institution, Gold was surprisingly fearless.[73]

"Harry had considerable courage," says Gus Ballard. "If you were interested in harming him you sure wouldn't have to go very far. But you wouldn't be able to intimidate him. Sure, he was a quiet little man and quite shy in person, but he had an indomitable will." Ballard said his client was "like any other new federal prisoner, intimidated by the prospect of doing a lot of time behind bars and Harry was doing thirty years. But he never expressed his fears."[74] His many letters from prison over the years show that he was more concerned with how his father and brother were getting along in his absence.

Gold's ability to push himself was again called into service. Possibly he viewed the threat of bodily harm from other prisoners as just another burden he'd have to shoulder for his terrible crime, or as simply a brutal fact of life in prison; but he was determined not to be paralyzed by his menacing environment. Gold believed he had important work to do and wanted to redeem himself, or at least add an asterisk to the judicial and historical record that had so decisively stamped him as a traitor to his country.

. . . .

CHAPTER 14

State of Mind

Gold spent as much time as he could in the Lewisburg Penitentiary hospital laboratory. In a roiling sea of discontent, this island of pipettes, precise measuring devices, and good intentions allowed him to immerse himself in something more positive than the stark confines of his cell or the contemplation of his gloomy future.

As a combination of hospital aide, head nurse, and chief lab chemist, Harry was not only a one-man first-aid station but also a person of rising prominence and respect within the institution. Medicine-related assignments are some of the choicest positions behind bars. Getting someone with previous medical experience is a bonus; a workaholic like Gold was an exceptional find. His willingness to subject himself to tainted substances and experimental drugs only heightened his value and image in the prison.

Many human experiments done in prisons entail possibly fatal danger. Imprisoned test subjects who died while participating in malaria, dysentery, mononucleosis, and hepatitis studies were commended by the Bureau of Prisons, the Public Health Service, and the Department of Defense for their "courage and patriotism" and thanked for their "outstanding service in aid of the defense effort" during wartime.[1] When John F. Gavin, a twenty-five-year old burglar, died in 1952 of complications from his participation in an infectious hepatitis experiment at Lewisburg, it is quite likely that Harry Gold was either his nurse or a patient in the next bed—possibly both.[2]

In addition to serving as a test subject in at least one medical experiment (and probably two or three more), Gold became a regular contributor to Red Cross blood drives. Though most inmate blood donors were primarily interested in the modest remuneration it offered, a few gave blood for more principled reasons—patriotism, altruism, scientific advancement. Harry, a member of the "Gallon Plus Club," was proud of his growing record of contributions and awards.[3] Records show that he gave blood every few months and occasionally every month, something that doctors aware of his hypertension issues probably would not have recommended.[4]

Though obviously hampered by the prison laboratory's lack of sophisticated equipment, Gold pursued a number of scientific projects he had begun thinking about or working on years earlier. While at Philadelphia General Hospital, he had begun research on "a quantitative chronometric method" to "test for the presence of glucose" and other chemicals in the human body. His experience in Lewisburg made him even more aware of the difficulties of practicing medicine in remote and technologically limited parts of the country, and he launched a search for blood-testing methodologies that could be used in "places without extensive medical facilities."[5]

In 1953 and 1954 he invented a blood sugar test using manganese heptoxide combined with potassium and concentrated sulfuric acid.[6] Over the next few years, he would perfect the test using an array of different chemical agents, explore its medical utility with lab directors at university hospitals, and begin seeking out purveyors of medical equipment to help him patent and market his inventions.

"A screwball pink"

In the mid-1950s, Gold's role as a key government witness was renewed. In June 1955, he made a rare excursion outside the penitentiary walls to testify for the prosecution against Benjamin Smilg, the Wright-Patterson Air Force Base aeronautical engineer he had attempted to recruit for the Soviets in the late 1930s.

Smilg, who had risen to chief of the dynamics branch of the base's aircraft laboratory, was suspended from his position when Gold named him as a potential contact after his arrest in 1950.[7] On November 22,

1952, Smilg was indicted on three counts for lying to the loyalty-security hearing board at the base. According to the *New York Times,* "He denied that during the time he knew Gold he also knew that Gold was engaged in espionage work."[8] He faced a maximum penalty of $6,000 in fines and fifteen years in prison.

The trial began in Dayton in June 1955. Gold, looking small, meek, and ghostly, with a pronounced prison pallor, testified that "he had visited Mr. Smilg on several occasions" but "could not get the information" he desired.[9]

Smilg claimed he considered Gold a crackpot, "a screwball pink, and not a spy." Gold, however, testified that Smilg knew more than he was letting on and had once scolded him, shouting, "You don't know what you have done. I ought to call military intelligence right away. I was going to report you the first time you came to me, but after all, you are Jewish and I am Jewish, and it would be a terrible reflection on the Jewish people."[10] It was on that occasion, in March 1940, said Gold, that he came "right out and asked Ben for specific information on technical data concerning production and performance of aircraft engines."[11]

The verdict was handed down on June 18. The jury needed seven ballots before acquitting the forty-two-year-old defendant of lying to an Air Force Loyalty Board. Smilg was "tearful and grateful." His outright rejection of cooperation and Gold's confirmation of his refusal were no doubt central to the successful defense.

Defenders of the Rosenbergs used the Dayton verdict to attack Gold and champion a jury that had rejected this strange little man's unsubstantiated accusations. The *Daily Worker* sneered that "one of the key informer-witnesses . . . in the FBIs frame-up of Ethel and Julius Rosenberg, self-styled 'atom spy' Harry Gold of Jell-O box top fame, has now been judged unworthy of belief."[12] The article repeatedly slammed Gold as "a discredited informer/witness" who was "incapable of belief."

The *Daily Worker*'s Gold bashing would continue unabated. Subsequent articles repeated the "discredited informer-witness" tag, relishing the outcome of the trial: "Smilg walked out of court a free man," while "Gold was headed back to Lewisburg Penitentiary." "The rotten fabric of the government's carefully built frame-up" was finally being "exposed."[13]

Also quick to pounce on the decision was the Committee to Secure Justice for Morton Sobell. A spokesman for the group said Sobell, who was also serving a thirty-year term, "should be freed on the ground that the testimony of Gold . . . had now been discredited because of the jury's action in Dayton."[14]

A year would pass before Gold's next trip out of the institution, but this journey, to the Capitol for an appearance before a Senate subcommittee, would provide a less constrained atmosphere than a criminal courtroom and considerably more opportunity to clear the air regarding his long career as a secret agent. It would also allow him to respond to critics and try to stem the continuing flood of half-truths and outright lies that had washed over his life.

"And that is how I began it"

Escorted along with David Greenglass to Washington, D.C., by "four husky deputy U.S. Marshalls" to testify before the Senate Judiciary Committee's Internal Security Subcommittee on April 26, 1956, Gold proved contrite, informative, and occasionally captivating.[15] Senator Herman Welker of Idaho chaired the hearing, and committee staffers Robert Morris and Benjamin Mandel would also play a prominent role. The hearing's purpose was to "determine the nature and the scope of Soviet activity in the United States." Senator Welker announced to those in attendance that Gold would shed light on the activities of "Amtorg Trading Corp., the vice consul of the Soviet Union in New York, the Soviet delegation at the United Nations and other official agencies of the Soviet Union in this country."[16]

Chief counsel Morris began the session by asking the witness about his country of birth, his family's arrival in America, and his formal education, but Senator Welker, obviously restless, interrupted to ask, "Mr. Gold, when did you first become a member of the Communist Party?"

"I have never been a member of the Communist Party," replied Gold matter-of-factly.

"You were never what we call an open member of the Communist Party?"

"I was never a member of the Communist Party," Gold said again, "and never had any desire to be one."

"You never had any desire to be either an open or a secret member of the Communist Party?" asked Welker, incredulously.

"That is correct," said Gold.[17]

Morris then asked the witness to describe the "concrete circumstances surrounding your introduction into espionage for the Soviet Union" and "your state of mind" at the time.

Gold, "now 45 and dressed in a light brown suit and blue shirt," began by describing how he "ran out of funds" and was forced, early in 1932, to leave the University of Pennsylvania and return to his previous job at the Pennsylvania Sugar Company.[18] This was during the worst years of the Depression, said Gold, and he was soon laid off. Another chemist at the plant, Ferdinand Heller, knew of a possible opening at the Holbrook Manufacturing Company in Jersey City, New Jersey, and suggested that Gold contact a friend of his named Thomas L. Black. Black had found a better-paying position, opening up his Holbrook job.

Gold told the committee how, desperate for work, he had traveled up to Jersey City late one night, met Black, and was immediately informed, "You are a socialist. Fred Heller has told me that. I am a Communist, and I am going to make a Communist out of you."[19] Black spent "from January to September of 1933" pressuring Gold to join the Communist Party. Gold agreed to attend several Communist Party meetings in Jersey City and New York and was constantly "propagandized" by Black, but he refused to join.

When asked by Morris what kind of people came to these meetings, the witness didn't flinch: "I was actually repelled by the people that I saw who belonged to the Communist Party." They were a "rather dreary" bunch; some were missing teeth, others pontificated on boring subjects, a few were immersed in obscure discussions of "Marxian dialectics." They were a "frowsy lot of characters," said Gold. "I felt ashamed of being with people like that."[20]

When the federal National Recovery Act program allowed Gold to return to his old job at the Pennsylvania Sugar Company in September 1933, Black, now a good friend, kept pushing him to join the Philadelphia branch of the Communist Party. Finally Black relented but said, "There is something [else] you can do," something that "would be very helpful to the Soviet Union." He asked Gold to supply him with "processes on industrial solvents," presumably simple things like shellacs and lacquers. The people of the Soviet Union were desperate, said Black, and needed these processes. He assured Gold that whatever he supplied would be "turned over to the Soviet Union" for the betterment of the Russian people.

Without a noticeable pause or stammer, Gold matter-of-factly stated, "And that is how I began it."[21]

"They did a superb psychological job on me"

Counsel for the committee asked the witness to describe "his first acts of espionage," how information was relayed to his Russian handlers, and the role Amtorg, the Russian trading corporation, played in the transfer of information. Gold began a lengthy discourse on his career as a spy, how he moved from industrial espionage into military espionage, and his brief foray into "espionage in connection with Leon Trotsky, or the followers of Leon Trotsky."

In the beginning, said Gold, he gave information about various solvents to Tom Black, but soon an array of blueprints and other items belonging to Pennsylvania Sugar followed, so much that Amtorg agreed to photocopy all of the material Gold was bringing in. The impressive haul won Gold his first meeting with a Russian, "Paul Smith," who became his first Soviet handler. Obviously cultured and a linguist, Smith ordered Gold at their first meeting to filch certain items, "never to see Black again," and to write a detailed family history for his perusal. Smith also told him how they would meet in the future and supplied a sophisticated contingency plan in case one of them did not show up for a meeting.

At this point, Senator Welker asked, "Harry, did you ever ask yourself this question: 'Why am I doing this against my country?'" For Gold, this was a psychological tripwire. It was a question he had asked himself a thousand times and a story he had long wanted to tell.

"At that particular phase," said Gold in an earnest, firm voice, "the question of doing it against the United States had not arisen. It was more a question of strengthening the Soviet Union. You see this is also part of a pattern. I realized much later that these people operated with me in the very manner that a virtuoso would play a violin. They did a superb job on me, now that I come to think of it. They knew what would appeal to me and what I would be repelled by. For instance, as we went along, I was not a paid agent, but I paid other people for their efforts, and they would continually commend me in very indirect fashion, of course, and would sort of low-rate the people who were accepting money from us. You see, they knew that I would feel good." Not motivated by money like the rest, Gold saw himself as a true champion of the Russian people.

Welker, looking for the key to Gold's character, asked if he might have "had an inferiority complex" at the time of his initial involvement with the Russians. "Could that be true?"

Gold was tired of being psychoanalyzed by opinionated amateurs with pedestrian notions of the human psyche. Such people couldn't begin to comprehend his motives for doing what he did. He was fed up after years of armchair character assassination. He seized the chance to respond to all the magazine articles and newspaper columns.

"I don't think I have ever had what is called an inferiority complex," said Gold, warming up to the challenge. "I have, I think, a lot of drive. I like to get things done. And I have a sort of one-track mind, that once I get started on something, I go right ahead to the finish of it. It takes quite something to stop me."

Did the Russians think "these compliments . . . would make you very happy?" asked Welker.

"Yes," said Gold. "I said they did a superb psychological job on me, I didn't realize it at the time."

"You had never had much happiness, I take it, in your life?" asked Welker, again probing the witness's psychological history.

"No," replied Gold immediately. "I have been very happy."

"You have?" said Welker.

"That is something I would like to hammer and nail down right now," replied Gold, obviously agitated by the line of questioning. "There has been such an incredible mountain, or a whole mountain range of trash that has appeared anywhere from saying that I got into this because I was disappointed in love—well, I haven't been uniformly successful, but anyhow, I didn't get into it for that reason—through reasons that I felt inferior, and I wanted the adulation of people. It would take literally months to refute all of it, and it is sheer balderdash."[22]

"I was cocksure," he said. "That was my only trouble. I was always sure I was doing the right thing. I did have qualms. I knew this much, I was committing a crime. I knew that. And where we lived in South Philadelphia, it was, as I said, a poor neighborhood, but criminal deeds were looked down on."

"I couldn't kid myself, I was stealing. And to add to that, I was stealing from Dr. Gustave T. Reich, who was research director for the Pennsylvania Sugar Company. And Doc Reich, well, so to speak, he sort of raised me from a pup. I started to work in the lab, cleaning spittoons, and when I finally left the Pennsylvania Sugar Company, I think I was a capable chemist.

"Reich taught me a lot and made a lot available to me. He raised me from the very beginning. I was violating the man's confidence. I was going into his files. I was stealing from a man who trusted me. And believe me, I had qualms. I wasn't happy about it. But it seemed to me that the greater overall good of the objective merited the means or justified the means that I was using."[23]

"It was a dreary, monotonous drudgery"

Gold told the committee about his Soviet handlers, their relationship to Amtorg, and their suggestion, once he had picked Pennsylvania Sugar clean of secrets, that he find another position at the Philadelphia Navy Yard or the Baldwin Locomotive Works. He described his brief role in tracking down Trotskyites and how it coincided with a similar assignment Tom Black had been given. Although he'd been directed to stay clear of Black, Gold "continued to see him, in direct defiance of the orders. . . . I didn't always follow them out slavishly." Black informed Gold that "he had canceled all of his industrial espionage activities and that he was devoting himself to one thing, and that was trying to worm his way into the confidence of followers of Leon Trotsky and report back to the Soviet Union."

Gold spoke of the men he was supposed to track as part of a wider plan, he subsequently learned, "to kill Trotsky." Asked by Senator Welker what effect this had on him, Gold frankly stated that he "wasn't happy with it. I don't think any executioner is ever happy no matter how small his part."

Welker asked how anyone could "carry out a little leg work . . . that might result in the death of a fellow human being?"

Gold compared his dubious activities to a progressive illness. It "started off in a very innocuous fashion. What, after all, are chemical solvents? We started off in a very innocuous fashion, a very innocent fashion. But then, step-by-step, they advanced the tempo; they advanced the level on which we worked. . . . And you got used to it. It got to be a way of life with me.

"It was a dreary, monotonous drudgery. If anyone has any idea that there is anything glamorous or exciting about this, let them be disabused of it right now. It is nothing but dreary drudgery. You work for years trying to get information. Sometimes you are unsuccessful. You spend long hours waiting on street corners. The success, the amount of success actually in the work is very small in proportion to the effort you put in. And what became even more important, I was gradually losing my identity and my desire to be an individual. I was becoming someone who could be told what to do and who would do it."

"In other words," said Welker, "you were in so deep you could not back out; is that correct?"

"It was not a matter of backing out," replied Gold. "It was a matter that I had become conditioned so . . ."

"You did not want to back out?" interjected Welker.

". . . that I didn't want to back out," continued Gold. "I was set in this way. It was a way of life with me."[24]

As the hearing continued, the witness told the committee of the Soviets' desire for proven technologies rather than cutting-edge formulas and processes that hadn't yet been put into operation. He recalled his difficulty trying to get Ben Smilg to divulge information, his dealings with Abe Brothman and Al Slack, and his initial meeting and critical relationship with Klaus Fuchs. Gold was peppered with questions about all of them, but Fuchs and the heist of atom bomb secrets drew the most interest.

Gold related how he was first informed that he was about to undertake something "so big . . . so tremendous," but also "very dangerous"; the many clandestine meetings with Fuchs in New York, Boston, and Santa Fe, and the tremendous workload entailed in combining a demanding occupation with the many intense hours required by his espionage activities. It was all-consuming, and much of the time he was exhausted, both physically and psychologically. "I took my whole life and I didn't realize at the time I was taking my whole personality, my entire soul, and I was turning it over to these people. I didn't realize how far it was getting."

The committee, obviously fascinated by the Los Alamos plot, asked about Gold's dealings with Fuchs, the information and monetary transaction with David Greenglass, recognition signals, and the passage of the critical Los Alamos information back to his Soviet handler. At one point during the lengthy session and probably to the amusement of his listeners, Gold surprised everyone by launching into a detailed account of a professional football game. Asked if he had ever met with Julius Rosenberg, Gold, always in search of ways to support his recollection of particular events—especially controversial ones—brought up a game between two teams of the old All-American Football Conference to underscore that he had the right date in mind.[25] Before the panel knew what was happening he was describing New York's "two huge tackles, one of whom was Arnie Weinmeister . . . breaking through San Francisco's line" to impede the progress of "Joe Perry, the San Francisco halfback and Frankie Albert, the quarterback" who was known for "his fancy hipper-dipper stuff."[26]

It was likely the only time a congressional hearing on the theft of nuclear secrets digressed into a play-by-play account of a long-forgotten football game. But sports were an established part of Harry Gold's life, and it was only natural for him to use athletic events as signposts to confirm his recollection of other events.

Though a committee staff member was quick to document the accuracy of Gold's memory, Senator Welker and chief counsel Morris quickly put an end to the sports discussion.[27]

"They played me very shrewdly."

Returning to the matter at hand, Gold was asked about his dealings with Abe Brothman, Shura Swan, and Al Slack. The last name led to Gold's surprising comment that "the most damaging" thing he had done on behalf of the Soviet Union was the theft of Eastman Kodak's processes for color photography. Gold believed the material Slack gave him "could not be duplicated anywhere else in the world" and was therefore extremely valuable from a scientific and commercial point of view. Slack had told him that Kodak production secrets were heavily guarded; work was compartmentalized, and patents were never taken out, in order "to keep them as industrial secrets." "There was no way . . . that the Soviet Union could duplicate this material except . . . by either stealing it from Eastman Kodak or . . . start[ing] an organization fully as large, if not larger . . . with a number of superbly trained organic chemists—and those you don't come by overnight." Such a project, if it were even possible, would be "an immense undertaking."

Some were surprised by Gold's emphasis on the Kodak color emulsion process and his assertion that it was equal or superior in importance to the theft of atomic information. Gold proceeded to argue that "once it was known that the atom could be split, anyone could do it with sufficient technical and industrial potential. Given the time and the potential and the equipment and the industrial background for it, it could be done eventually. . . . There is no question about it, because the theory was known." With the film process, however, "there was no theory. It was just a matter of know-how on minutiae, very, very, little things, but things which might take 2 or 3 years to find out." According to Slack, said Gold, "some of these photographic emulsions had 6 or 7 layers of color emulsions. So it is a tremendous job speaking purely as a chemist."[28]

At this point in the hearing, Gold steered the conversation away from purloined technical processes and toward the Soviets' mastery of psychological co-optation. "These people did a superb job of psychological evaluation on me," he said, "and they worked on three principal themes. The first was the matter of anti-Semitism." In 1933, Tom Black and Vera Kane repeatedly argued that "the only country in the world where anti-Semitism is a crime against the state is the Soviet Union." And the Soviets he met did the same, always "hammering away at it."

Even when he had reservations about what he was doing, Gold informed the committee, the Soviets knew how to play him. He recalled the time, shortly after the Soviet-German Pact was signed, when he asked Fred, his Russian handler, "What in the world goes on?"

"You fool," Fred shot back dismissively, "Don't you understand what is happening? We need time. We will buy time from the Devil if we have to, and the Devil in this case is Adolph Hitler. We need time to get prepared. In the meantime, you get busy and get us things with that time . . . get us information that we need, military information . . . and when we are ready we will strike, and we will wipe Nazism from the earth. It will disappear forever."

This was one of the ways, said Gold, in which "they hammered at this subject of anti-Semitism. As I said, they played me very shrewdly, and I worked on this thing on the basis that we were doing a dirty, disgusting, miserable job, one which we had no pride in and no liking for, but that we had to do it. It was one of the many unpleasant things which you have to do in this life." Whenever such concerns were about to engulf him, Gold fell back on "the idea of helping the people of the Soviet Union, helping these people live a little better than they had before."

As time went on, especially in the mid- to late 1940s, Gold admitted that his reservations about the Soviet Union grew. "I had doubts . . . all along. There were first these doubts about violating the confidence of the man for whom I worked. There were doubts when I was asked to recruit people, which I never did. There were doubts that arose all along," he said, but "after 11 years of very steady work for these people so that it became a way of life." Not until after the war and "this hiatus . . . of two years or so" did he have a "chance to think." "I looked at what was happening in the countries that the Soviet Union was taking over. I thought I was helping destroy one monstrosity, and I had created a worse one, or helped strengthen another one. That is what I had done.

"And even more than that, I came to realize—the thing that hit me the deepest was that I had completely lost my free will; I had actually turned over my complete personality, my complete soul, and everything. I wasn't living the life of a normal person." Gold informed the committee that he had been "instructed not to marry . . . and they even told me to try and break my family ties. They felt that I was too closely knit with my family and I wasn't likely to take chances."

Someone like Tom Black, Gold continued, "an orphan, with only old maid aunts," someone "completely loose and free in the world, who would take any number of chances, who would deliberately live the life of an eccentric . . . was what they wanted. Black represented to them the ideal espionage agent. They wanted someone that they could take over completely."

"I had built up this huge, flimsy house of cards"

Gold was now letting his innermost thoughts tumble out. He had puzzled over his own behavior for some time; his actions—and failures to act—perplexed even him. How had he let himself get involved in such a mess?

"You are just not human if you come to realize that you have to be ensnared to that extent, willingly," he told the committee, "and ensnared to that extent, and not rebel against that. I think; I know I have done damage, a tremendous amount of damage. We just spoke about Eastman Kodak and the matter with Klaus Fuchs and with Abe Brothman and so on, all of that.

"It is true. But actually, I wonder if the biggest damage, the greatest damage, wasn't the damage that I did in completely turning over myself to these people. We are free. We should be free. A person should be free. It is his right."[29]

Fascinated by his story, the committee members allowed Gold to go on. He related how his double life affected his personal relationships, how it cast a dark shadow over his romantic life, and how his fear of capture grew. "I will tell you frankly I was afraid," he said. "We are not all noble. I was scared. I was scared of what would happen, and I was particularly frightened, of what people who trusted me, the people with whom I worked at the Heart Station in the Philadelphia General Hospital, the people who knew me, my intimate close friends, my own family, especially; what would they think about it if something like this ever came to light?"

Gold recounted how, with no friends or family members he could turn to for guidance, he contemplated seeing Father Mahoney, a priest at Xavier University, with whom he had developed a close friendship, and whom he could trust to keep his secret. But he knew "what his answer would be." Instead, he resorted to "what fallible, human people do. I kept putting it off in hope that it would never come to light."

But it did come to light. Robert Morris, the committee's chief counsel, asked Gold to comment on his arrest. Gold talked of the 1947 grand jury hearing with Brothman, the event that first put him on the FBI's radar screen, the FBI agents' appearance at the PGH Heart Station one day in May 1950, and their search of his home. Reflecting on his career as a secret agent, Gold admitted that he knew "exposure was inevitable."

I had built up this huge, flimsy house of cards. It was a horribly tangled skein. All you had to do was take one thread and pull it, and the whole thing had to come apart.

Every time I went to New York on a trip, I would lie to a half a dozen people, my family and the people I worked with. The whole thing had to come
apart. I knew that. I couldn't cover up. But I lied for a week, and I lied very
desperately.

I lied for only two reasons. First of all, I had to figure out how I was going
to tell my family. I couldn't figure out how I was going to tell my family. I
couldn't figure out how I was going to break the news.

The second thing was that I wanted to complete as much of my work at
the Heart Station in the Philadelphia General Hospital as possible. There
were a number of projects which had been carried almost to a finish and
needed just a little more work, and I wanted to leave things in as good shape
as possible.

"As if it were something unclean"

Gold described his psychological turmoil the night before the FBI agents
were scheduled to search his house. He knew he should have been home
"tearing the place from top to bottom, looking for anything that might in
any way be incriminating," but instead he was at the Heart Station and the
University of Pennsylvania's medical school completing an important
project. The same obsessive-compulsive trait that served the rigors and
duties of a secret agent kept him from forsaking his hospital obligations
for his own self-preservation. Gold admitted that when he went on a mission, "a job to obtain information, I set myself to go in one direct fashion,
just like turning a switch. I went right for that objective. I obtained information. Nothing was going to stop me. And I turned it over to the Russians.

"Then I came back to Philadelphia and I turned that switch again and
I became Harry Gold, the hard-working chemist—'Isn't it a shame to
work overtime all the time? He works overtime all the time.'"

But the switch began to malfunction under the pressure of a nation-
wide manhunt. When Gold needed his faculties and his decision making
to be at their sharpest, they failed him. Through physical and mental exhaustion, accumulated guilt, or just his foolish belief in his own powers
of persuasion, he made one bad decision after another. A day or two of
thorough housecleaning, the destruction of incriminating evidence, guidance from a Soviet superior or consultation with sharp defense lawyer
could have put off the "inevitable"—possibly forever.

Instead, Gold chose a strategy of slow, agonizing dissembling. He collaborated in his own demise by trying to give the appearance of cooper-

ating, sitting down for hours on end, day after day, with federal agents and without an attorney. Ultimately he allowed the FBI to search his evidence-saturated home. As Agents Miller and Brennan went through his room and discovered one incriminating souvenir after another from places he claimed he had never been, the owner of all the suspicious material saw his long-held secret unraveling before his eyes.

"I was aghast," he told the Senate panel. "There were railroad schedules, train schedules. There was all sorts of stuff there that if anyone dug deeply enough, it was bound to tie me in." The discovery of a well-worn "New Mexico—Land of Enchantment" brochure was the last straw.[30]

Senator Welker, obviously intrigued by the lengthy career and eventual fall of the unassuming little man before him, inquired, "Did you ever think of using the Fifth Amendment?" Gold answered that he never considered that strategy; he was "a scientific man," someone who deals with "facts in a laboratory," and he "knew that as a scientist, as a technical man, that I could not go on forever lying and covering up."

Moreover, Gold continued, he felt the "extreme repugnance," the "horror," of becoming an informer. He invoked the character played by Victor McLaglen in the 1935 John Ford film, *The Informer*.[31] There was a poignant scene, he said, where that character "was waiting in the British Army Headquarters, when the British soldiers have gone to pick up Frankie Phillips, his buddy, on whom he had informed. The news comes over the phone. The British officer picks it up, and he says, 'Yes, he has been shot. He has been shot. Very well. That is all.' And he hangs up the phone.

"Then he takes his swagger stick, and on that table is some money, and he pushes the money with his swagger stick, as if it were something unclean, over to the other end of the table where McLaglen is sitting. That burned very deep into me."

Gold said the scene made him think of Fuchs, Semenov, and the others, men for whom he had developed a deep respect. They were friends made under the most difficult of circumstances, friends he "could not see myself turning in" and sending to prison. Yet in his heart he knew "that I was going to turn them in."

"At first," Gold admitted, he tried "to cover up." He'd provide an accurate physical description of one of his contacts, but then place him "in an entirely different locale" to throw the authorities off. He'd say someone worked in Syracuse, for example, rather than Rochester. Eventually, said Gold, he knew he was "going to tell the truth. . . . It took a while. It took . . . about 2 months before I got it all down as it had occurred." Over time, he began "remembering little details on various occurrences."

Had he now disclosed "everything you know to the Federal Bureau of Investigation?"

"Completely," Gold responded.

The committee's chief counsel then pointed out for Senator Welker's benefit, "The testimony here this morning, in strong contrast to the testimony of most witnesses we have had, is most revealing."

"If I could only take it back"

After three hours in the witness chair, Harry Gold had provided the Senate panel, the media, and the general public with much to chew on. The "small, nervous man with a prison crew cut" had led quite a life as a foreign agent.[32] Who would have believed it?

Chief counsel Morris brought up Gold's detractors, "the forces at work in the United States that are trying to present the story told by Harry Gold as an incomplete story." Gold responded by mentioning again the "whole mountain of trash" that one could "spend months, months and months to try and refute." "Some scurrilous things were noted in these books," he said, obviously disturbed, "and they are just plain out-and-out lies."

Although Lewisburg Penitentiary had "a very good library," Gold continued, the prison did not allow books or other materials "connected to any individuals in the penitentiary," and therefore he wasn't able to read everything published about him. But he had heard many of the allegations, things that were "totally out of context" or "outright lies." Unless you knew the real "facts" of the case, he said, you were "just dealing in fairy tales."

Though not specifically asked about his lawyers, Gold also took a moment to publicly thank John Hamilton, for his "very hard, extremely hard" work in his behalf. "One of the things that hastened my completely revealing what I had done was the appointment of Hamilton as my court-appointed attorney. He saw me day after day . . . through the heat of the summer in Holmesburg Prison . . . and we accumulated a whole mountain of material." Hamilton "is a fine man," said Gold, "and I have a tremendous amount of respect for him."

It was now time for Senator Welker's summation of the day's testimony, and he did not hold back. He told the witness that "time alone will show what damage you have done to your country. Time alone will show what damage you have done to yourself." Gold, "perspiring freely" and obviously "nervous," listened as Welker lectured him: "You have lied; you have cheated; you have stolen; you have been a spy, an espionage agent; you have been a man who could be convicted of a conspiracy to murder. Maybe some of the things that you have done will bring about mass murder."

In a more forgiving tone, Welker thanked Gold for coming before the subcommittee to "tell us under oath your shocking, vicious story . . . of lying, of espionage, of sabotage, of everything that is distasteful to a red-blooded American." He asked the witness whether he thought "it was worth it all."

"It was a horrible mistake from the very beginning," said Gold contritely. "I almost can't conceive how, knowingly and willfully, I went through all these years doing these things. If I could only take it back, but I can't."

Senator Welker adjourned the hearing after telling Gold, "You have sinned wrongfully against your country, your fellow man," but "maybe after you have passed away, there will be a shaft of light thrown upon the life of Harry Gold."[33]

"Lonely creature in full manhood"

No one can say what satisfaction Gold received from his brief opportunity to illuminate the origin of his career as a Soviet spy, but he couldn't have been pleased with the media's characterization of his Senate appearance. Most news accounts focused on his emotionally charged final comments, when he called his life as a spy a "horrible mistake," and his statement about giving his "soul" to the Soviets. Little ink was devoted to his family's struggles during the Depression, his bouts with anti-Semitism, and the rise of Hitler and Fascism.

Some accounts were merely superficial, unkind, and personal. *Newsweek* described him as a "pudgy, nervous, little man" and quoted him on the subject of Jacob Golos, even though Golos was never mentioned during the hearing and Gold had, in fact, lost dozens of pounds and was probably underweight.[34]

Though Gold was accustomed to inaccuracies and personal slights, it didn't make their digestion any easier. He deeply resented being depicted as a psychological freak and a "withdrawn mousy individual" with an abnormal "compulsion to live deviously."[35] He wrote notes to himself and his attorneys cataloguing the inaccuracies and voicing his frustration that the truth, even when known, seemed so elusive. Gold and the atom bomb conspiracy had become a journalistic cottage industry that showed no signs of losing its appeal for either writers or readers. Even the few articles that contained facts he wanted highlighted also brought out details that were untrue, highly embellished, or deeply embarrassing. For example, in an article by J. Edgar Hoover, Gold was no doubt pleased to see that the FBI director had written, "To Gold's credit, he repented his treason, offered us the fullest co-operation, searching his memory for names, dates, and incidents." Unfortunately, the article, entitled "What Was the FBI's Toughest Case?" underscored the Bureau's exhaustive search for Klaus Fuchs's American courier. It didn't help that Hoover called Gold a "master Soviet spy."[36] More embarrassing yet was the mention of the Soviet Union's bestowing on Gold the Order of the Red Star. Imagining his brother and father reading of the Soviet honor gave Harry a chill.

By 1957, at least ten books had been published on the atom bomb case—what "Communists called 'the American Dreyfus Case.'" All those who claimed that the Rosenbergs had been "railroaded to their deaths" saw Harry Gold as a conductor on the train.[37] Arguably the most important of these books was John Wexley's 664-page volume entitled *The Judgment of Julius and Ethel Rosenberg*.[38] This "anatomy of a frame-up" was said to provide near-proof of a government conspiracy.[39] One observer wrote, "Communists quote the Wexley book the way Moslems quote the Koran."[40]

In his defense of the Rosenbergs, Wexley gave Gold a good workout, calling him at various times an "imposter," a "pseudologist," a "pathological liar," and a "paid agent-provocateur." At other times Gold was a "lonely creature in full manhood" and an "accomplished deceiver" with "a disordered mind."[41] Besides his creative name-calling, Wexley's chief contribution to the Gold story is probably his attention to a "small white card" from the Hilton Hotel in Albuquerque.[42] Though he was the first to question the legitimacy of the hotel registration card, a decade later other authors would give it the most intense scrutiny.

Prison rules excluded much of this material, thereby sparing Gold additional bouts of dyspepsia and allowing him to focus on the two things of most interest to him—his laboratory research and getting out of prison. Though detractors delighted in psychoanalyzing this "strange creature Harry Gold," their claim that he enjoyed prison was as specious as the rest of their commentary. Wexley, for instance, charged that prison for Gold represented "a sanctuary, a retreat."[43] Not true. Although he didn't beg to be set free or clamor for a transfer to a safer facility like David Greenglass, he was hardly enamored of prison life.

"Eradicate Soviet espionage in this country"

Gold pursued his freedom from the very beginning. On December 14, 1950, just five days after receiving his startling sentence of thirty years, he had his attorneys petition Judge McGranery for credit for time served—the "142 days in custody since his plea of guilty on July 20, 1950." McGranery duly "issued an order amending Gold's sentence to 29 years and 223 days."[44]

Gold certainly did not expect a dramatic intervention from high places, but he did believe his many hours of cooperation with FBI investigators and federal prosecutors should translate into something tangible. Gus Ballard's periodic visits to Lewisburg Penitentiary were short on pleasantries and long on legal strategy. In a memorandum to John Hamilton regarding a 1957 visit, Ballard wrote that their client had grown a "bit grayer," "weighs less," and was doing as well "as could be expected under the circumstances." Gold had informed Ballard of his long days in the hospital laboratory that sometimes included evenings and weekends, and explained that the "four days a month additional good time for his work in the laboratory" would translate into "a total of 621 days to be subtracted from his sentence."[45] Harry was keeping track of each day—not the behavior of a man who had found a "sanctuary."

The previous year, Hamilton had asked Ballard to research their client's release options. Ballard came back with a memo enumerating "three devices by which a federal prisoner can be released before the expiration of his sentence." The first, "parole," required a prisoner to have served at least a third of his sentence, something Gold would not achieve until October 1960.[46] The next option, "good behavior time deduction," looked even less promising: the sliding scale of days off per month wouldn't get Harry out until 1972 at the earliest.

The last option was executive clemency, a special pardon power accorded the president by the Constitution. This would be extremely difficult to obtain. It required that "every prisoner applying before his parole eligibility date must show why" the parole process should be circumvented.[47] Despite Ballard's understandable doubts that they had "valid grounds for applying," Gold encouraged them to file the papers.

Hamilton and Ballard remained dubious. They understood their client's desire to get out of prison, but precedent and Gold's infamous reputation were working against them. Ballard, in fact, thought the whole thing "pointless," but they decided to ask the Justice Department about their chances.[48] In late August 1957 they had their answer. The Office of the Pardon Attorney of the Department of Justice was "not persuaded" that the Gold case warranted a "special privilege . . . exception" to "established policy and practice."[49] It "cannot be deemed to be harsh," the letter went on, "to require Gold to serve one-third of his sentence" before filing for parole consideration. If at that point "Gold is denied parole," the attorneys were advised, they could then "petition for Executive clemency."

Unmoved, Gold still asked his lawyers to file the papers. Ballard cautioned him that an effort now "might have an adverse effect on his chance of obtaining a parole at a later date," but Gold was "pessimistic about his chances before a parole board."[50] During his years of captivity, he had seen how the system worked. He told Ballard that a parole board "would automatically turn him down" because of the notoriety of his case. "Parole officials," he said, were "accustomed to dealing with youthful car thieves, they do not take kindly to persons convicted of espionage."

Lawyer and client discussed a "realistic" commutation request. Gold suggested that they "should ask for five or ten years off" his enormous sentence. Ballard set a "tentative figure of fifteen years off," but reminded him that their chances of success were "very slight."[51] Brainstorming with Ballard about who "would be most likely to come to his assistance," Gold suggested an array of federal prosecutors and FBI agents. The names of Roy Cohn, James Kilshimer, Tom Donegan, Scott Miller, and Richard Brennan headed the list.

Cohn had already voiced his support and followed it up with a letter to John Hamilton in which he declared, "I know of no one who I found to be more sincerely repentant and more effectively cooperative with the United States Government than Harry Gold."[52] As part of the Rosenberg prosecution team and through various grand juries and trials to "eradicate Soviet espionage in this country," Cohn wrote, he had come "to know Gold rather well." Gold's sentence "was far too severe in view of this obvious repentance and cooperation" and his "great service in the smashing of the Communist conspiracy in this country." Cohn went on to predict that Gold would be a "model prisoner" and parole would be "granted at the earliest opportunity."[53]

Cohn invited Gold to submit his letter "to the appropriate authorities so that they would know that one of the prosecutors of the cases of which Gold was a part, firmly believes that parole should be granted." Yet the lawyers were far from sold on Cohn's benevolence and were skeptical of his offers of help. "Cohn was a terrible man," said Ballard. "He wouldn't help anyone unless it was in some way to his benefit. He was

very vengeful and hated Communists."[54] Ballard and Hamilton appreciated Cohn's involvement, but at least one of them was not persuaded of
his altruistic motives. Ballard said Cohn "wrote a good letter," but "Roy
was a menace to society."

Others on Gold's list of potential supporters included Irving Saypol,
Myles Lane, Benjamin Mandel from the Senate subcommittee, two air
force investigators involved with the Smilg inquiry, and several other FBI
agents.[55] Clearly, Gold now saw his onetime pursuers and prosecutors as
allies. As Ballard informed Hamilton, Gold believed that "his cooperation with the government has prevented further harm to the country, put
other espionage agents out of business and revealed to the FBI the methods of operation of the Soviet spy system." That, argued Gold, should be
worth something.

In addition, Gold still felt that he was "capable of doing useful work
in the field of medical research." He believed he had the "training and experience" in "chemistry and biochemistry" to do any and all "chemical
and hematological work normally done in hospital laboratories."[56]

"Excellent reaction to supervision"

The campaign for Gold's release was built more on a flimsy foundation of
longing and hope than on anything resembling legal precedent or political reality. Gold, in prison parlance, had been "banged out" with a sobering thirty-year term. That was twice what Greenglass had received, and
the man who had helped put his own sister in the electric chair was still
in prison. Moreover, the 1950s were not the most liberal of decades. Even
though McCarthyism may have hit its high-water mark and was on the
decline, court-confirmed traitors were not held in high esteem. Gold
shouldn't even have contemplated parole until he had completed at least
one-third of his sentence. But like most prisoners, he wanted out. Lewisburg was certainly not the idyllic "retreat" his critics had labeled it.[57]

In fact, Gold may have collaborated in his own predicament. By
pleading guilty, requesting patriotic lawyers of utmost integrity and devoid of leftist leanings, and renouncing any possibilities of deal making,
he had boxed himself in. Even Roy Cohn acknowledged this when he
commented to Gus Ballard, "You know, it's an interesting thing that everybody is getting favors done for them except the man who's done the
most."[58]

Pursuing this long shot, Hamilton and Ballard began marshaling their
contacts, refining their arguments, and gathering supporting data. They

catalogued the hundreds of hours Gold had spent with FBI investigators (it had taken him a week just to examine thirty-five hundred photographs of suspected Russian agents) and his many court and government appearances, along with his prison "progress reports" and medical "detection" devices. They even noted the 1955 request by the director of U.S. prisons, James V. Bennett, to sit down and meet the infamous Harry Gold.[59]

As he mulled over his chances and strategized with his attorneys, Gold went about his business, dutifully tackling his assignments in the prison hospital and laboratory. As the years slowly clicked by, Harry was becoming one of the old heads in the institution, a "seasoned con" who had long since established himself as a model prisoner. Institutional progress reports said that Gold conducted his affairs in an "exemplary fashion," accepted "responsibility for his offense," and was "most cooperative with various governmental agencies" still in the pursuit of Communist agents. In addition, there was "no evidence of psychotic" behavior or need for "psychiatric therapy."[60] Gold spent much of his free time in the prison library borrowing an assortment of "fiction and non-fiction" books and "magazines." And he was now not only a regular attendee at "Jewish services" but had become "a leader of the group." On the cellblock he maintained good relations, had an "excellent reputation," was known to be "quiet, neat and clean," and was said to have an "excellent reaction to supervision."[61]

It was in the hospital and laboratory, however, that Gold made his most significant contributions. His "performance" there was considered "outstanding"—"excellent" being the operative term most often used to describe his attitude and capabilities. He could handle "specialized tests," and he was said to be "cheerful and prompt" when "called to the hospital for emergency duties."[62] By the end of the decade he had no doubt spent more time in the prison hospital than most of the doctors hired to work at Lewisburg Penitentiary. Though quiet and timid in demeanor and small in stature, Gold had become a recognized and respected figure in the institution—someone who followed the rules, didn't cause trouble, and could be counted on in a pinch.

Not only had Gold fostered an effective and efficient hospital operation through his many hours in the laboratory, he had also single-handedly thrust Lewisburg into the select company of laboratories producing patentable medical and technological breakthrough. For years he tinkered with equipment and processes, refining or simplifying them so they could be utilized in remote areas of the country lacking state-of-the-art medical care. By 1959 he believed he had invented something quite "novel," a "practical and rapid blood sugar test" that was ready to be patented.[63] John Hamilton supplied him with the name of a Washington patent attorney, James M. Graves, to explore filing "an application for a U.S. patent." Gold, in turn, sent both lawyers a package of information detailing current medical practice, the "novel features" of his creation, its potential "utility," and a "narrative note" concerning "how [he] came to invent it."[64]

Graves "conducted a patentability search" to determine "whether or not it amounts to invention to employ indigo disulfonate in a procedure which determines quantitatively the mount of sugar in the blood." After conferring with various experts and the "patent examiner," Graves informed Gold: "I think we have a fair chance of persuading him that there is patentability in such a process."[65]

Gold's long hours of study, speculation, and experimentation looked promising. The year 1959 was ending on an upbeat note, and he and Graves would continue corresponding and researching the relevant issues to ensure the patent for his invention would come to fruition. When he received notice from Graves in October of the following year that the "patent will issue December 6, 1960 and will be numbered 2,963,360," Gold was overjoyed.[66] He had accomplished something that few other chemists had, and he had done it under less than ideal circumstances. The arrival of "the original grant of Letters Patent" at Lewisburg on December 11, 1960, must have seemed quite a Chanukah present.[67]

The blood sugar test and the patent application process drew on all of Gold's strengths. Slow, methodical, and imperturbable, he approached his institutional assignments and self-directed tasks with the same care and dedication. When he combined these qualities with his love of chemistry, above-average intelligence, and tremendous work ethic, no challenge seemed too imposing. As for those challenges over which he had little control—such as winning parole—he would confront them as he had faced so many other long-desired and long-awaited goals in his life: he'd work toward them the best way he knew how. As with the college degree that so long eluded him and the purchase of a new home for his aging parents and brother, Harry was willing to work hard without complaint or histrionics. Delayed gratification may never have had a better representative.

With the advent of a new decade—the beginning of his second behind bars—Harry Gold dreamed that the stars would finally align themselves in his favor, and that he was nearing the time when he would walk out of prison a free man. There was reason for optimism. It was 1960, the year in which he would become eligible for parole. Klaus Fuchs had been released from prison in the summer of 1959, and David Greenglass would be released a year later, but Gold did not begrudge them their freedom.[68] Even though his sentence was twice as long as theirs and he felt that he had done as much if not more to expose and destroy Soviet espionage in America, their release only caused him to redouble his effort. He believed he was more than worthy of consideration; it would only take patience and hard work, qualities he had in abundance.

CHAPTER 15

· ·

The Campaign for Parole

After almost a decade in prison, Harry had a well-established early morning routine: out of his bunk before 6:00 A.M. and the first one seated in the chow hall for breakfast. Institutional early birds could get a glimpse of the stoop-shouldered inmate shuffling down the seven-hundred-foot corridor from his single room on J Block—the prison honor block—to the prison hospital, where he could be found at his bench well before most of the others arrived, at 8:00.[1] He was also generally the last to leave. By all accounts, Gold had embraced the treadmill inescapability of prison life. Many had come to believe, as correctional officer Al From said, that "you could set your watch by his movements in the prison."[2]

"Everybody liked Harry," said From. "I don't recall anybody who disliked him. No one picked on him that I can remember. He just seemed to be well-liked by everybody."

Nonthreatening, solitary, and always willing to help those in need, Gold had established himself as not just a "very good inmate" but an "asset" to the institution. It wasn't commonplace for prison guards to feel empathy for criminals serving long bits, particularly those serving time for treason, but From occasionally felt sorry for Gold. Even his chronic orthopedic problems inspired sympathy.[3]

"He really was a pathetic little guy," recalls Bob Smith, another Lewis-burg correctional officer. "Harry always seemed to be walking with his head down like he was depressed. He was always looking at the ground. He had this duck-like walk, and he'd just move about in a slow, method-ical fashion from one end of the corridor to the other, from the prison hospital to his block and back." And always alone: "He was friendly enough if you talked to him, but he would rarely initiate a conversation."[4]

"Word got around pretty good that Harry could help you if you were sick or had a medical problem," Smith remembered. Once he showed Gold a boil on his neck. "He told me to come down to the hospital. Harry took a culture of it and told everybody in the hospital what to do. He cer-tainly knew what he was doing."[5]

Institutional records confirm Gold's medical and laboratory expertise. Some of his supervisors believed he enabled the prison hospital to be-come "more advanced than . . . outside hospitals" in the vicinity. "In a number of instances his work has directly contributed to preserving the lives of patients," they reported. Once, when Lewisburg's medical oper-ations were stretched thin and confronted with a serious medical prob-lem, Gold was said to have "worked five consecutive days with practically no sleep."[6] Such feats of endurance and steadfastness in behalf of the in-mate community did not go unnoticed. Guards, prisoners, and officials grew very familiar with the name Harry Gold.

He was now teaching other inmates the rudiments of medical labo-ratory work and spending a good deal of his time helping novice med-ical technicians prepare for their certification examinations. Annual in-stitutional reports described the long-serving inmate as "completely trustworthy," noting that he took advantage of many of the institution's programs—with the exception of organized athletic activities—and vol-unteered for such inmate programs as the radio committee and the clas-sical music appreciation class. He was said to display "an excellent atti-tude."[7] Rarely was he known to complain.

"A serious blow to Nixon's chances"

Still, Harry wanted out, and periodically pressed his lawyers to move for-ward with his application for parole. As they approached the long-awaited date of October 1960, when he would have served a third of his sentence and become eligible for parole, Hamilton and Ballard stepped up their strategy sessions.

It was Gus Ballard's belief that a number of newspaper and magazine articles could be used to their advantage. Roy Cohn's letter of support would be helpful as well. Though "Cohn's reputation had suffered with the decline and fall of Joe McCarthy," Ballard believed that "an endorsement from such a right wing source is [still] useful."[8] It was clear they'd need extra political juice from the law enforcement community, and they prepared request letters to former Judge McGranery, Robert Morris, Gerald Gleeson, and William L. White.

An astute observer of the political scene, Ballard recognized "that probably no less fortunate date than October 22d could be selected as a time when Harry Gold should become eligible for parole." The question "would be referred to rather high circles in the administration and . . . somewhere along the line it will be determined that favorable action upon the application would deal a serious blow to Nixon's chances."

Ballard therefore suggested to Hamilton that they ask the Board of Parole to postpone action for a few weeks. This, Ballard admitted, was "tantamount to labeling the Board as being subject to political pressure," but it was "foolish to suppose that a favorable ruling on the application would be handed down a few days before the election."[9] Harry was already a hot potato; Ballard didn't want him to become a focus of attention in Nixon and Kennedy's presidential race.

"The most extraordinary selfless person"

Hamilton and Ballard consulted with their client. Considering the glacial pace of the parole bureaucracy and the improbability that such a controversial application would be granted on its first request, the three men decided to move forward despite Ballard's misgivings. Hamilton, the former Republican National Committee chairman, sent an imposing ten-page letter to the U.S. Board of Parole on behalf of the notorious spy.

Hamilton began by elaborating on his long association with the applicant. He carefully explained that when he and Ballard "accepted appointment" to represent Gold, they saw it as their "constitutional duty" to do their best for him and as their "further duty to represent Mr. Gold in any subsequent proceedings." Their decade-long service, Hamilton pointed out, was an "obligation without compensation from any source."[10]

Hamilton then tackled a series of issues, beginning with the crime for which Gold was convicted. The parole panel had to understand that Harry Gold had not intended any injury to his country. At the time of his arrest Gold had "stated unequivocally that he would not plead guilty" to any indictment that read "an intent to injure the United States." Instead, he had pleaded guilty to the transfer of "information concerning the national security with the intent to benefit the Soviet Union." The indictment, Hamilton emphasized, "was devoid of any allegation of intent to injure the United States. This was not a case of treason."[11]

Second, Hamilton declared, "after nearly fifty years in the practice of my profession, I have never known an instance where a man's associates and friends spoke more highly of him than those who knew Gold." Testimonials came from laboratory workers at Pennsylvania Sugar Company, doctors at Philadelphia General Hospital, and professors at Xavier University. Hamilton reiterated what he had told Judge McGranery ten years earlier: "Harry Gold is the most extraordinary selfless person I have ever met in my life."[12] Nothing in the interim had caused him to change his mind.

His client's prison record was by all accounts exemplary. Hamilton illuminated Gold's many contributions to the prison hospital and the health of the inmate population, and further noted that a "patent application is presently pending" on the new blood sugar test Gold had invented.

Then there was Gold's cooperation with government authorities. Hamilton pointed out that his client "could have well stood mute" like a "hardened criminal" and "bargained for a lesser sentence." But he had instead chosen to "give freely all that he knew as a partial expiation and atonement for his crime." Hamilton enumerated Gold's many grand jury appearances, the trials, his hundreds of hours of meetings with FBI agents and testimony before congressional committees. He even quoted a former chief counsel of the Senate Internal Security Subcommittee who declared that Gold's "reliability and loyalty . . . has been demonstrated time and time again."[13]

Gold's sentence, Hamilton continued, was harsher than requested by the prosecution: "This nation was at a critical stage in its history when Gold was sentenced," and Judge McGranery saw a "severe sentence" as a "warning to all."[14] Granting "parole at this time . . . is in no sense stating that ten years imprisonment suffices as a deterrent." In fact, "it is saying much more," as "justice requires not only imprisonment, but complete cooperation by the prisoner in assisting the government to purge the field of crime in which he was engaged." Gold, he argued, had provided this service many times over.

Hamilton concluded with a personal appeal for leniency and understanding. This case was the only criminal case in which he had ever taken part. He expected no monetary reward or boost to his reputation. But "Harry Gold, in serving ten years in prison and having given every possible aid to the government, has atoned for his crime to the fullest extent humanly possible, and a parole should be granted by this Board."[15]

Realistically, his client's chances were slim.

"A heck of a good chemist"

Gold began to contemplate life after prison. In keeping with his compulsive personality, he prepared a series of to-do lists. One critical concern was employment. He needed to earn an income, help pay back his brother and father for their financial support over the past decade, and contribute to the upkeep of the household. Though well aware of the difficulties ex-convicts have finding work—let alone notorious offenders like himself—he believed his long experience in industrial and biomedical laboratories made him marketable. Earning a scientific patent reinforced that belief.

With the help of his brother and his attorneys, he started contacting public and private laboratories about job opportunities. They made no effort to hide or avoid his controversial history or current residence. Gold insisted that his brother tell all—including that Harry's "last act of espionage was committed in September, 1945," and that he had tried to make "all possible amends for [his] crime"—and assure prospective employers that they were not hiring a "problem."[16] He had every intention of being a loyal, hard-working employee.

Gold coordinated the job search effort like a battlefield general, giving precise directives, supplying valuable personal data, offering potential leads—and always telling his foot soldiers to "be of good cheer" despite the many obstacles ahead.[17] Harry told his brother he "preferred work as a clinical chemist" but would settle for a laboratory technician position, as long as he didn't have to work in histology and serology. He also apprised Joe of certain jobs listed in the newspapers, and further advised that "jobs listed under . . . 'Female Help Wanted' should be pursued as well, as most hospitals are only too pleased to get a male technician—women get married, etc."[18]

The confluence of Gold's exemplary prison record, his parole application, the patent award, and the job search gave rise to wishful thinking that sometimes overwhelmed reality. At one point Harry informed Joe the trouble with one job prospect "is that it will be till (at the earliest) November before I am available."[19]

In fact, many Novembers would pass before Gold was available for a job in the free world. The rejection of his parole application became an annual event. These setbacks did not send him into a psychological tail-spin, as they do to many prisoners in similar circumstances. Gold pushed ahead, completed his daily assignments, and marshaled his resources. Confident of his abilities, he believed he had mounted a strong argument for parole, was "a heck of a good chemist and laboratory technician," and would sooner or later find work on the street.[20]

"A big event in his monotonous life"

By 1962, Harry had accumulated an impressive folder of endorsements. Dr. Richard Mechanic, of Strong Memorial Hospital in Rochester, New York, had written to Joe that Harry's "diligent assistance and hard work . . . contributed in no small part" to a 1960 study conducted by the National Institutes of Health.[21] A Philadelphia pharmaceutical company had expressed interest in Gold's patent, calling the concept "excellent" and complimenting Harry "on a fine piece of work."[22] More rewarding yet was the letter from Joseph H. Boutwell Jr., director of the Clinical Chemistry Laboratory at Temple University Hospital, who had become familiar with Gold and said he was actively working to find him a position. The hospital was currently searching for a new director of its en-docrinology laboratory, wrote Boutwell, and "if he were free now, I would be glad to recommend him for the position."[23] Hamilton and Ballard made sure such letters were added to Gold's parole application file.

They began gearing up for their client's October 22 parole hearing each spring. In 1962, Hamilton had his speech prepared and arguments organized by early May. As in earlier briefs, he tried to explain how a "hard-working . . . law-abiding citizen" had fallen into "the coils of Soviet espionage." He described "the lash of anti-Semitism" the Gold family had suffered before coming to America, and Harry's "sympathies" for the "hundreds of thousands of Russians giving their lives on behalf of the al-lied cause."[24]

Hamilton wanted the parole board to understand that his client's crime was "giving aid and comfort not to an enemy . . . but to an ally of the United States."[25] It was important that Gold be "removed . . . from the label of 'Communist Traitor'" and be seen as what he really was, "a susceptible person of generous impulses lured down the trail of espionage in the hope of benefiting the country of his forebears and members of his faith."[26] The petition hit the usual notes: no intent to harm the United States, unparalleled cooperation after arrest. Gold was a key force in "unraveling the web of Soviet espionage" in America. "No man could have done more than Gold to break up the Soviet espionage system."[27] With his exemplary prison record, his contributions to the efficient and effective management of the prison hospital, a new invention that was drawing interest from the medical industry, and excellent job prospects, argued Hamilton, Gold was "eminently suited for release on parole."[28]

Once again, however, the panel turned down the application without explanation. Both the denial and the lack of any explanatory comment irritated Gold and his advocates. What was missing? What more could they do? After all these years of exemplary conduct, what did Gold have to do to earn his freedom?

After three years of denials without explanation, they decided to send a letter to the Parole Commission expressing their "disappointment" and requesting answers. The reply was unsatisfactory; the parole executive stated that he was "unable to give . . . any reason or reasons why the Board denied Gold a parole." It had been a "majority opinion," and it was "not possible for anyone to specify what factors entered the judgment of each of the Board members."[29] Hamilton and Ballard could only speculate that their client was just too hot to handle. Even after all these years, no politician of consequence, and certainly no one on the Parole Commission, wanted to be known as having let a central figure in "the crime of the century" walk out of prison.[30]

Curiously, Gold was less despondent than his attorneys. He believed they had made some progress and "attained a measure of good will" with the parole board. At least one "board member listened attentively and was personally impressed by my case." After a visit with Gold at Lewisburg, Ballard noted in a memo to Hamilton that their client's surprising take on the situation was "at variance" with Gold's earlier opinion that "he could never expect any relief from the Board, and that his only chance was a commutation of sentence by the president."[31]

Gold and Ballard talked about going over the parole board's heads and having Hamilton contact some of his influential friends in Washington, but Ballard ultimately counseled that the effort would be futile and would "probably have the effect of destroying whatever good will we now have with the Board." Ballard brought his senior law partner up to date on their client's situation at Lewisburg, describing his work for the U.S. Public Health Service in an investigation of "Arthritic and Metabolic Diseases" (for "the magnificent sum of $50") and tutoring prisoners in "hospital technicians' work."[32] Gold looked "well physically, although his hair is white at the temples and he has aged," but he "seemed nervous and on edge," probably because "he is visited by no one except his brother" and a visit from "somebody else is a big event in his monotonous life."[33]

Unbeknownst to the team, the Harry Gold case was drawing increasing interest. A member of the U.S. Senate was making inquiries.[34]

The Office of the Attorney General of the United States also renewed its interest in the notorious chemist from Philadelphia, who by this time had been residing in a maximum-security prison for more than a dozen years. A two-page letter from Hamilton to Attorney General Robert F. Kennedy in March 1963, seeking executive clemency for Gold, may have sparked their interest. The Gold team, Hamilton told Kennedy, was requesting "a commutation of sentence to a term of 18 years in order to make the prisoner eligible for immediate release." After briefly enumerating some aspects of the case and Gold's stellar record as a prisoner, Hamilton made a personal appeal to Kennedy. "In a relatively short time I shall have practiced before the Courts of this Country for half a century," he wrote. "I have never been more convinced of the correctness of my position than I am in urging upon the President that after twelve years imprisonment Harry Gold is entitled to Executive Clemency."[35]

As required, three character affidavits accompanied the clemency petition; one was from Gus Ballard. No longer the young and inexperienced aide-de-camp of his celebrated senior partner, Ballard had moved up the Pepper, Hamilton and Sheetz masthead over the years and grown into an accomplished member of one of Philadelphia's best-known legal families. In his affidavit, Ballard stressed his exhaustive research: "I believe I know more about [Gold] and his life than anyone outside of his family and the prison authorities with whom he is in daily contact, with the possible exception of special agents of the Federal Bureau of Investigation. While the files of the FBI on Gold may be more complete than my own, it is probable that no one representative of the FBI has had as long or as close a contact with the prisoner."[36]

While reiterating many of Hamilton's familiar points, Ballard also cited an aspect of Gold's character that Hamilton usually chose to play down. "Gold's unselfishness," he wrote, "makes him a gullible person and an easy mark," characteristics that were easily "played upon by agents of the Soviet Union." Once caught in "the coils of Soviet espionage" he could find no way out. Seemingly paralyzed by "mortal fear of disgracing his family, his employers and his friends," he couldn't fathom "coming forward before he was actually apprehended."[37]

Soon after the clemency petition was filed, internal memos began circulating at the Justice Department's highest levels. J. Walter Yeagley, assistant attorney general in the Internal Security Division, informed his boss that there were certainly pros and cons, but he "would recommend commutation of Gold's sentence," citing the prisoner's "grasp of the seriousness of his offense, his contriteness, and his cooperation with the government."[38] "Communists and left-wing groups . . . have over the years agitated for the release of Morton Sobell," but "never sought clemency for Harry Gold." Yeagley thought that fact "quite significant." He concluded by recommending that "the president exercise clemency in the case of Harry Gold."[39]

Something of a "Symbol" at Lewisburg

The Justice Department was not the only agency mulling over Gold's situation. His landlord was thinking about him as well.

Warden O. G. Blackwell's October 1963 memo to the assistant director of the Bureau of Prisons, H. G. Moeller, was only two sentences long, but it would have chilled the hearts of Gold and his family had they seen it. "The Classification Committee has recommended the transfer of [Gold] to the institution at Marion, Illinois."[40]

The transfer itself, let alone the destination, would be a serious assault on Gold's routine and comfort. After almost thirteen years, he had grown accustomed to life at Lewisburg. Acclimation to a new prison is not easy. Every prison has its own culture, management style, and set of personalities to negotiate. The new federal prison in Marion, Illinois, was designed to replace Alcatraz—its residents would be the most dangerous and unmanageable in the federal system. And the long distance from Philadelphia would have created hardships for Gold's brother and elderly father.

What could have precipitated such an abrupt and dramatic change? What had Gold—a model prisoner by everyone's accounting—done to deserve a transfer to what would soon become one of the most dreaded pens in the federal system? Was this another dose of punishment for his spying, or perhaps payback for his aggressive campaign for parole?

Recognizing the poor fit between the timid and easily manipulated Gold and the violent career criminals being sent to Marion, top administrators at the Justice Department's Bureau of Prisons suggested that the U.S. Medical Center for Federal Prisoners in Springfield, Missouri, might be a more appropriate place.[41] Warden Blackwell replied that "it is quite possible that Gold could and would contribute his talents to their pro-

gram." But he restated his original point: "My only thinking in suggesting Marion was that it is a new institution and developing a new program,
and his talents might very well be utilized there."[42] Blackwell's real intent
may have been more ominous. No one interested in Gold's welfare would
have suggested sending him to the latest incarnation of Devil's Island.

Although Gold was generally well liked and respected in the Lewisburg community, those feelings were obviously not universal. An internal
memo told Bureau of Prisons Director James Bennett that "some staff
members at Lewisburg over the years" believed that Gold had acquired
considerable "status and for this reason is perhaps vulnerable to manip-
ulation or is otherwise likely to take advantage of his position."[43]

When Harry informed his family of the proposed move, Joe and Sam
Gold were understandably distressed. It wasn't the first time they had
had to contend with such rumors, but each one sent a shiver of concern
through the small family. An earlier scare had inspired Joe to dash off a
series of distress calls and letters to high-profile government officials. In
one letter to a federal prosecutor, Joe wrote: "The news of this possible
transfer to Leavenworth of my brother has us all upset and worried very
much. Harry is doing wonderful work in medical research at the Lewisburg hospital and . . . my father and I keep our morale up by the visits
we occasionally can make to Lewisburg.[44] I have never asked for any favors in the past, but in consideration of the tremendous help and co-operation my brother has given the government, I would like definite assurance that this matter of the possible transfer of my brother to
Leavenworth be dropped and that he be permitted to remain at Lewisburg until he is ready for his release."[45] What assurance, if any, Joe received is unknown, but one can safely speculate that the lack of a transfer made him believe that his letter writing campaign had helped keep his
brother in Pennsylvania.

Nor did Gold's imminent transfer sit well with the prison's medical
staff. Three of the doctors wrote Blackwell to "express . . . distress at the
prospect" of losing Gold to another institution. They pointed out that he
was "providing services to the NE medical department that are at least
comparable with those of a civilian lab technician" and in addition "minds
his own business; causes no problems." They said it looked as if he were
being "penalized for the good work he does at Lewisburg."[46]

The Bureau of Prisons assistant director, H. G. Moeller, was forced to
admit to his boss, Director Bennett, that he had "some difficulty understanding the urgency of moving Gold at this point." Granted, he had become something of a "symbol" at Lewisburg, but Moeller could find no

evidence of Gold causing a problem; according to Bureau records, he had "not presented overt difficulties" at any time.[47] Incredibly, Harry Gold, now fifty-three years old and in failing health, had stature in the eyes of the prison community. Though it was never his desire or goal, he was perceived as a big shot. It was a stunning turnaround for someone whose "adjustment" behind bars was once declared "very doubtful."[48]

Several months later Blackwell sent Moeller another memo, to clarify his earlier recommendation. Although it was "through no fault or encouragement of Gold," Blackwell wrote, "he has gradually grown, over the years, into a position whereby he is considered by some employees on a level or above an employee and is strongly resented by other employees. This, as you can well imagine, does not result in an ideal situation."[49]

Blackwell admitted that "the majority of the medical staff have a very high regard for Gold's work performance." He had no doubt that Gold was "obviously an outstanding chemist and a good laboratory technician" and that his transfer to another institution would "upset" Lewisburg's medical department. "On the other hand," Gold "could very well be a definite asset to Marion. He has been at Lewisburg in one routine for some twelve years now and whether he recognizes this or not, probably a change would be good for him."[50] It is painfully easy to read between the lines here. The move had nothing to do with what was good for Harry. The reason for the proposal was that he had adapted to prison life more successfully than many on the Lewisburg staff (possibly including Blackwell himself) felt a prisoner should.

"60 years of work ahead of me"

Though the talk of a transfer must have been upsetting to Gold, one wouldn't have known it by his comments or actions. He had always been adept at compartmentalizing personal problems and difficult assignments. Obstacles had always been a part of his life; he would deal with them. The impact of such a move on his brother and ailing father was his greatest concern.

There was already much on his plate: his campaign for parole, his effort to secure a job once released, following up on his recently patented blood test with a medical instrument supplier, and his latest research project, a new glucose tolerance test. The new project grew out of Gold's work on a Public Health Service diabetes study between April 1962 and June 1963. He was enthusiastic about the effort, part of a "world-wide program . . . to establish criteria for the detection of various chronic diseases, so that these ailments may either be completely checked or at least be prevented from wreaking all of the damage they would otherwise do." If this program were properly implemented, argued Gold, "the people of the world would thus be spared an unmeasureable amount of physical agony and distress and the span of life would be correspondingly length- ened, but lengthened so that even the last years would be enjoyable."[51]

Besides taking and analyzing the blood of "480 inmate volun- teers . . . every two months" for the diabetes study, Gold also tinkered with the existing "blood urea nitrogen (BUN) test used to evaluate kid- ney function and damage." The procedure he was developing would be fast ("only two minutes"), "ridiculously inexpensive," and useful in "small hospitals with limited facilities and personnel."[52]

In addition, Gold was working on "a much simplified protein-bound iodine (PBI) test . . . for detecting thyroid disease." In a letter to Gus Bal- lard updating him on his myriad lab projects, Gold admitted he had his hands full. "My big problem," he wrote, "is that I now have 60 years of work ahead of me. And if I work for a few years more, I'll probably have enough to keep me busy for the next 140 years."[53]

Locked into the daily routine that had started when he walked into Lewisburg many years earlier, Gold kept busy as the passing weeks and months brought professional satisfaction and personal frustration. Prob- ably due to its illogicality and petty inspiration, the threatened transfer never materialized, but neither did his long-awaited and much-desired parole or executive clemency. Gold plodded along, seemingly blessed with endless patience. Klaus Fuchs and David Greenglass had been out of prison for several years now, and Gold believed his time would even- tually come.

"One of the best inmates in Honor Quarters"

The March 1964 issue of *Lab World* carried an article entitled "Blood Sugar Test Patented." The highlighted description of the process, by "au- thor-inventor, Harry Gold, Lewisburg, Pa.," and its importance must have been exceedingly uplifting.[54] This was the sort of media attention that Gold could live with.[55] The seven-paragraph article in a scientific maga- zine substantiated his accomplishment.

Further confirmation came in the form of letters from both the pub- lic and the private sectors requesting additional information on Gold's blood sugar test.[56] Established names like Ames, Pfizer, and Smith, Kline contacted his representatives, as did large public entities like Chicago's Board of Health and Philadelphia's Albert Einstein Medical Center.[57] Not only did Gold's newfound notoriety lack any hint of illegality or embarrassment, it also was fully consistent with his goal of advancing science and contributing to the public health.

The Gold brothers and Harry's lawyers wasted little time. Gus Ballard sent a letter to the federal parole board informing it that the *Lab World* article had "stirred considerable interest among hospitals, physicians and manufacturers of laboratory equipment"; he hoped this noteworthy feat would "have pertinence" for Gold's parole application.[58] The article didn't trigger the bureaucratic reaction they had desired, but they also knew it couldn't hurt.[59]

In fact, it generated much correspondence for Gold. Inquiries continued to come in, from as far away as Canada and New Zealand as well as from nearby. Just down the road from Lewisburg, in Williamsport, Pennsylvania, was Divine Providence Hospital. Sister M. Isabelle, who helped coordinate the hospital's laboratory operations, was one of the first to inquire about Gold's invention and soon followed with a visit. Gold bonded with the Catholic nun, as he had many years earlier with the nuns and priests at Xavier, and they became devoted pen pals. Gold would occasionally offer "procedural" suggestions to help resolve problems in the hospital's laboratory, and Sister Isabelle would respond with additional questions regarding improved techniques to enhance their productivity.[60]

As rewarding as the opportunity to provide useful information was the satisfaction Gold received from Sister Isabelle's vivid descriptions of life outside the walls of Lewisburg Penitentiary. For someone who rarely left the gray confines of the prison's interior even for the exercise yard, Sister Isabelle's colorful accounts of "flowering shrubs like a huge bouquet," the "violet of the grape hyacinths" on the Williamsport hospital grounds, and a rare albino robin sighted among the "lacey green, pink and white bushes" must have been exhilarating.[61]

About to turn fifty-five years old, Harry Gold hoped 1965 was the year he would finally attain his freedom. While Gold was incarcerated, Dwight Eisenhower had served two terms as president, his successor had been assassinated, the American Federation of Labor and the Congress of Industrial Organizations had merged, polio had been conquered, and the New York Yankees had been in thirteen World Series. Five years had passed since he became eligible for parole, but he remained confined. His many hours attending to the ill in the prison hospital, his contributions in the laboratory, and his newfound recognition as an inventor seemingly made no difference to the parole board. He would soon be confronted with one of the most disturbing and frustrating dilemmas in his life.

As always, his annual Parole Progress Report glowed with praise: "outstanding," "excellent" skills, "one of the best inmates in Honor Quarters." The "prime mover" behind the prison's classical music program and a key participant in other educational endeavors, Gold was well liked and respected for his "good attitude" and willingness to work "quite a bit of overtime."[62] Most prison administrators, not to mention most inmates, had never seen anything like him. He was unique, but apparently not exceptional enough to win parole.

Gold's spirits were lifted momentarily when he was scheduled for a special interview with the parole board in May 1965. Moreover, because of the "complicated nature" of his case, "a Board member and not a parole examiner would be holding the hearing."[63] It seemed to be a good sign. In his presentation, Gold stressed to the board that "everyone in his case is on the outside," that he had helped the government round up other spies, and that he could be useful to society from "a medical standpoint."[64] Months passed without any change.

"The more sympathetically we can portray him"

Though his health had deteriorated in recent years and he'd soon need surgery to have gallstones removed, Gold maintained his normal schedule of activities.[65] That summer, however, he received a shock as powerful as a punch to the solar plexus. It was made all the worse by Gold's realization that he had collaborated in this stunning blow. John Hamilton and Gus Ballard were no less appalled: furious at those who had deceived them, as well as at themselves for falling for a con job.

The story began with an innocent-sounding request several years earlier, when Hamilton received a letter from Walter Schneir stating that he and his wife were "currently working on a book which deals, in great part, with a former client of yours—Harry Gold."[66] Schneir was effusive in his praise of Hamilton, saying he was "extremely impressed" with Hamilton's courtroom efforts and the "staggering amount of research" that was required for such a formidable presentation. He requested an interview with Hamilton. He wanted to hear his "recollections and anecdotes about the case" and to listen to the Holmesburg Prison audiotapes of Gold. He also requested a copy of Gold's "confession," a lengthy handwritten manifesto entitled "The Circumstances Surrounding My Work as a Soviet

Agent." There was sure to be "much fascinating biographical data" in this document.[67]

Hamilton wrote back that he had "no authority to turn over" his client's papers. He would first have to seek Gold's permission.[68]

Schneir persisted and quickly set up a meeting with Hamilton and Ballard. The meeting was cordial, and the attorneys showed Schneir their letter to the parole board among other items. Schneir said he was impressed by the "very strong case" they had presented; he intended, he wrote Hamilton, to follow up with a letter to Gold requesting permission to "hear the tapes" and "see the handwritten interview notes and reports."[69] "For a writer," Schneir told Ballard, "this sort of material is often a gold mine."[70]

Schneir's letter to their client, meanwhile, promised "a full and fair portrait of Harry Gold" if Schneir and his wife were given access to certain "material so as to hear your story in your own words." Perhaps hoping to disarm Gold by using his attorney's own words, Schneir wrote, "I came here to explain a crime and not to excuse one."[71]

Gold never got to see the letter. Since the Schneirs were not on his "authorized correspondence list," it was never delivered.[72] Walter Schneir asked Gus Ballard to pass the message along. He repeated that if he and his wife couldn't "spend a week or so" with Gold, "listening to the tapes" would be the next best way for them to gain the "essential feel for our subject that makes a book come alive." "Hopefully, more public awareness of Gold's case may make his release more likely and, certainly, the more biographic information we have about Gold the more sympathetically we can portray him."[73]

As everyone would eventually discover, a sympathetic portrayal of Harry Gold was the last thing the Schneirs would deliver.

Ballard could not have known this at the time. Though Gold's treatment by the press over the years had made the attorney suspicious of journalists, the Schneirs had won him over. He wrote to Gold of the request, admitting that he and Hamilton had "always been somewhat skeptical about publications involving your experience in espionage," but noted that Schneir had done considerable research and could probably "proceed with a book whether or not we accede to his request." More important, Ballard added, cooperation might "lead to more sympathetic treatment than a refusal of cooperation at this point." Saying that he and Hamilton were "favorably impressed with both Mr. and Mrs. Schneir," Ballard said he was "hopeful that their approach will be fair" and encouraged Gold to think over the request.[74]

For the rest of his life, Gus Ballard would deeply regret this advice. He also maintained a lifelong distaste for the Schneirs. Gold, trusting his attorneys, authorized Ballard "to permit Mr. and Mrs. Walter Schneir to use whatever tapes and other materials are in your files relating to my case."[75]

The Schneirs were "pleased to hear" of Gold's decision and informed Ballard that they would come to Philadelphia in the first week of June 1961, find a hotel room, and thoroughly investigate the "great number of tapes and hundreds of pages of notes" related to the case. Though they saw it as "a rather arduous undertaking," they believed it would be "well worthwhile" and the only way to "really know the man we are writing about."[76]

"An effort to destroy my life"

Four years later, late in the summer of 1965, *Invitation to an Inquest* by Walter and Miriam Schneir arrived in bookstores. Its theories of governmental conspiracy, FBI mendacity, and psychopathic personalities—with Harry Gold as the centerpiece of a monstrous hoax—were so unexpected, so shocking, that Gus Ballard, though on vacation, fired off a letter to his client. He informed him that the Doubleday publication went into "some detail" regarding "the espionage activities of you and others." He would get Gold a copy of the book as quickly as possible. More important, he advised his client "not to discuss the case with anyone except officials of the prison and the Department of Justice." Ballard also said he would arrange to meet with Gold at Lewisburg to "discuss the book" as soon as he returned to his office.[77] Thus put on notice, Gold must have been overcome with apprehension.[78]

When he got his hands on the book, Gold was thunderstruck. Once again he faced a battery of unflattering physical descriptions ("a pudgy, sad-faced little man") and psychobabble ("his considerable imaginative talents," "eagerness to please," and "prodigious ability to lie convincingly"). More important, he was pegged as a delusional pawn of a right-wing government on the edge of fascism intent on prosecuting innocent dissenters who posed absolutely no threat to the nation's security. Gold had gone out of his way to help the Schneirs and afforded them a unique opportunity to examine his life and legal papers, and all he asked in return was a fair and honest accounting. Instead, he was carved up as a "deviously complex man" and "pathological liar" with a critical role in a government frame-up and the execution of two innocent people.[79]

The book makes "very serious charges against me," wrote Gold to his attorney. [80] If read "cold," without any other knowledge of the case, "the book is frighteningly convincing. To a large extent, it amounts to an effort to destroy my life."[81]

Gold's lengthy letter to his attorneys addressed the book's main points: that he had "concocted the entire story of a non-existent event"; that the "registration card at the Albuquerque Hilton Hotel was a fake"; that "either deliberately or because of my extreme suggestibility I changed my story . . . thus influencing Judge Kaufman to give the death penalty"; and a number of other controversial points, from the "cut-out box top" to numerous attacks on Gold as a "weirdly twisted creature" who "easily confused self-created fantasy with reality."[82]

In addition to laying out the Schneirs' most damaging charges and suggesting ways to refute them, Gold also illuminated for his attorneys the potentially fatal flaw in such a plan. Though *Invitation to an Inquest* had injured him more than any of the many other books and magazine articles written about the case over the previous decade and a half—especially since he had allowed the authors access to his files, and at a time when he was hoping for some good news from the parole board—he was no longer a legal and media novice. First, wouldn't "engaging in controversy only provide more publicity for the Schneirs' book?" Second, wouldn't aggressively "show[ing] the charges to be false" make him appear to be "seeking notoriety, one of the reasons the Schneirs have advanced to account for my actions"? Third, "the huge factor working against us is the undeniable public revulsion at the execution of the Rosenbergs. So here we support an unsympathetic cause." No matter how many people wanted to believe otherwise, "there was a spy ring and the Rosenbergs' death did permanently close off that line of investigation. Martyrs? Yes, to the Soviet Union, their one allegiance."[83]

The Schneirs' "charges cannot be let stand unanswered; the affair is too far-reaching," Gold felt. But who was to answer them, and how? Gold suggested the American Bar Association or possibly "the newspapers," but neither seemed a particularly good alternative.

Gold saw a "very evident pattern" in the book's methodology that even a partial reading could discern. The authors, he said, had used "a very clever series of omissions from my various statements and from my recordings and writings for Mr. Hamilton" to construct their narrative.[84] Their cut-and-paste job portrayed Gold "in a slanted manner," thereby giving credibility to the most ridiculous of charges. His supposed "contentment" behind bars exemplified their misrepresentations. "Aw heck!" wrote Gold. "Then why have I tried so hard to get out?"[85]

In conclusion, Gold called the book "a particularly nasty hatchet job" and told his attorneys that the "best way to answer it is to offer as many factually based denials as possible" and to do it "simply and unemotion-ally."[86]

For Hamilton and Ballard, the sixteen-page letter was typical Gold —lean, well thought out, and helpful. It was typical in another way too: not once did he remind his lawyers that they had landed him in this mess. It only reaffirmed why Hamilton and Ballard liked Harry so much.

"Very evident bias"

As he had promised, Gus Ballard drove up to Lewisburg to discuss the book. He brought more bad news with him. There were now indications that Morton Sobell's attorneys would be using the Schneir book to re-open his case. Could it get any worse? Attorney and client decided that they would not assist in this venture and that Gold would not consent to an interview with William Kunstler, Sobell's attorney.[87]

Ballard later informed Gold that Sobell's lawyers intended to have him "brought to New York to be questioned" in their effort to reopen the case. Ballard and Gold decided on a firm stand of noncooperation. Since his "apprehension by the FBI Gold had told the truth"; there was noth-ing more to be said.[88]

Though he shared his client's indignation over the "assertions and characterization made by the Schneirs," Ballard advised against "any af-firmative action . . . at this time." There was "a better than even chance" that the effort to reopen the Sobell case would be denied, making *Invi-tation to an Inquest* "no more than an addition to the already voluminous literature on the Rosenberg-Sobell case." Trying to refute it would only focus more attention on the controversy and improve Kunstler's chances.

Ballard was fairly sure that any judge reviewing the Rosenberg-Sobell trial would look with "extreme skepticism" on reopening a matter so long closed. Still, he thought it worthwhile for Gold to continue his "analysis of the Schneir book and to commit to paper your conclusions." If Ballard was wrong in his assessment and Gold was ordered to testify, the analy-sis would come in handy.[89]

Every time Gold read a newspaper or magazine review of what the *New York Times* called a "major event in the history of the celebrated case," his already high blood pressure would get a further workout. See-ing himself repeatedly called "abnormal," "unsavory," a "strange human specimen," and a man with "a need to do great deeds and to suffer for them," he alternately cringed and raged.[90] Letters from friends, acquaintances, and even former government officials strengthened Gold's impulse to counterattack. Ben Mandel, the former Senate staff aide, wondered how Gold could have granted the Schneirs permission to use his lawyers' tapes and other material, considering the authors' "very evident bias."[91] Hamilton and Ballard also had to field questions. A prominent Philadelphia attorney and highly respected former city councilman wanted to know if the Schneir "theory" was correct and "the hapless Mr. Gold" was "either nuts or . . . made up his testimony against the Rosenbergs and Sobell."[92] Burdened with addressing all these challenges, Hamilton and Ballard were also reminded that they had fostered their client's predicament. They never bothered concealing their anger at the Schneirs.[93]

"One adjusts, and without sniveling"

Gold followed his attorney's suggestion to analyze the Schneir book and "commit his conclusions to paper."[94] Though he called his September 24, 1965, mailing to Ballard a "statement," the eighty-nine-page handwritten document more closely resembled a dissertation, footnotes and all. Considering the depth of the injury he had sustained and his compulsive nature, this was not surprising. To Ballard, the lengthy document was typical of Harry. Gold had meticulously scrutinized, dissected, and rebutted every aspect of the Schneir "polemic."[95] From supposedly "concoct[ing] the entire story" and helping the FBI "manufacture" and "forge" the Albuquerque Hilton Hotel registration card to his "extreme suggestibility" and "weirdly twisted" psyche, Gold painstakingly answered every allegation like a college professor proving a convoluted theorem.[96]

In trying to "exculpate" not only the Rosenbergs but the Soviets as well, wrote Gold, "the Schneirs round up everyone and everything from Mary Surratt to Alfred Dreyfuss to the Sacco-Vanzetti Case to put across the idea that the Rosenberg-Sobell Case is a legitimate matter for controversy." All this was "balderdash."[97] The key "accusation that I was fed information, coached, intimidated, and brainwashed" was "complete inanity—perversion, in fact."[98]

Concerning the much-debated events of June 3, 1945, and the question of the authenticity of the hotel registration card—first raised years earlier by John Wexley, and now used by the Schneirs to argue that Harry had never been to Albuquerque—Gold offered several explanations. It was conceivable that the hotel "stamp was accidentally advanced by a day" and that the hotel clerk's normal script could have been altered due to "an awkward or cramped [writing] position" or the turmoil of a busy hotel lobby, but it was certainly not an FBI forgery.[99] He proposed an analysis of the ink on the card and a close examination of the registration cards' serial numbers, as well as the machine stamp on the cards "immediately preceding and following" his own that day.[100]

Far from being "a nobody seeking notoriety," said Gold, he had specifically asked of Judge McGranery that there be "no circus" at the trial. Consistent with the Schneirs' tactic of excising whatever didn't fit their "preordained thesis," those words were nowhere to be found in their book.[101]

As for his "apparent desire for life in prison" and "happiness there"—contrasted with Greenglass's "stunned appearance" at the time of his release as if he had "gone through an ordeal"—that was "twaddle." To "create this perversion," the Schneirs quoted "fragments from a letter I wrote Mr. Hamilton in 1953. But if life in a penitentiary was what I wanted, then why have I tried so many times (and even before my earliest parole date) to be set free?" The rest of the time, wrote Gold, "Yes, I got along in the penitentiary; one adjusts, and without sniveling."[102]

In page after page, each of the Schneirs' charges is addressed. Toward the end of this intellectual exercise, Gold seems ready to explode in frustration. "The Schneirs say there is no solid evidential proof that Klaus Fuchs and David Greenglass were spies, that these two men ever gave me data on atomic weapons, and that there is nothing available to establish that I ever passed on the information to Yakovlev. Do the authors really expect that a notary public, stenographer and cameraman should have been taken along to record these events for posterity?"[103] Though locked away for fifteen years and now the victim of a public character assassination, Harry Gold had not lost his sense of humor.

Gus Ballard found Gold's treatise "very thorough and convincing," though it took him a weekend to digest it. "Since the initial flurry of excitement created by the publication of the book" things had quieted down considerably, which was "all to the good." In addition, there had been no further communication from Sobell's attorney. Ballard advised his client that "while I appreciate your understandable indignation at the characterization of you indulged in by the Schneirs, I suggest that we take no affirmative steps at the present time." But if proceedings emerged requiring "refutation of the Schneirs' book, you have already prepared yourself fully and in detail."[104]

Though the noise surrounding the book gradually declined, Gold was still frustrated that the Schneirs' scurrilous accusations and ludicrous scenarios remained largely uncontested. In late November he would receive more bad news. Once again the parole board had denied his application for parole. In a letter to the board, Ballard voiced his "disappointment" and expressed his hope "that some day in the not too distant future the Board will act favorably on Mr. Gold's application so that others similarly situated will be encouraged to follow his unparalleled example of repentance and atonement."[105]

That same day he reassured his client of his and John Hamilton's "continued conviction that you should be released and our readiness to plead your cause to the fullest extent which your circumstances permit."[106]

It had not been a good year for Harry Gold. He was already despised as a traitor to his country, a secret agent for America's most feared adversary. Now ideological partisans had declared him a weird, psychopathic personality who had colluded with a repressive government to engineer the execution of two innocent people. More important, he had hoped to be free by now and doing important research in a medical laboratory at a hospital. How many more years would he have to serve? And what additional public abuse was in store?

CHAPTER 16

. . . .

Return

By 1966 Gold had been a prisoner for more years than he had been a spy. Like everyone else in Lewisburg Penitentiary, he was focused on getting out. Regrettably for Gold, few of the other two thousand prisoners had as infamous a reputation. Even Warden Blackwell, in a news interview after another Gold parole rejection, soberly commented, "He's been here a long while."[1] Despite the repeated setbacks, Gold never gave up hope that the board would eventually see the merit of his application for parole. More than three years earlier, he had said in a letter to his brother, "I'm glad to hear that Gus and John [Ballard and Hamilton] are going right ahead with efforts to obtain my release. I just have the feeling that it will not be too long before I'm home again."[2]

"Best of intentions"

After these annual rejections, Gold usually tried to lift the flagging spirits of his family and supporters. "Accentuate the positive," he would periodically write to his brother. "It could even be that in the next couple of weeks we will get that big decision and . . . be home again to you and pop. Pleasant prospect indeed."[3] His own spirits were buoyed by any tidbit of news regarding his life after prison, especially his employment prospects. On learning that a hospital laboratory was still interested in him despite another unfavorable parole decision, Harry wrote to Joe, "Gee whiz, the way it's shaping up, maybe things are breaking our way at last. Well, after all this time we can certainly do with a good dollop of Happy Days are here again, huh?"[4]

Single-minded as usual, Gold had his brother order him the latest medical and laboratory textbooks. He wanted to be up to speed on developments in medicine and lab technology. He knew he wouldn't have a level playing field greeting him in the job market and did not want his many years in cold storage to be more of an obstacle than they need be. As he wrote to Joe, "I keep right on with my studies and work: really want to be ready for the job in that medical facility—when I come home, that is. So with that in mind, I've pretty well cut back on the leisure-type activities, mystery stories, TV and any other items that would use up time, pleasurable as these might be."[5]

Gold also tried to cut back on unhealthy food consumption. After admitting that he had visited the prison commissary and "slurped up an extra pint of ice cream," he felt the need to reassure Joe that his "weight was down to 130 lbs., so the ice cream was really therapy. Almost convincing, wasn't I? Okay, so I'm a bit of a fraud, but I mean well: that's my trouble, in fact, I always did have the best of intentions."[6]

"Joe asked if I would do him a favor"

Gold also cut back on his hours in the prison hospital. At fifty-five he was battling increasing infirmities. His gall bladder had been removed, his hypertension problems seemed to recur more frequently, and his participation in medical experiments may have taken its toll. The fourteen- to sixteen-hour days in the prison hospital had dropped to nine- or ten-hour days. After leaving the hospital at 5:30, he'd take a shower and lie on his bunk until 11:30 or so, reading the *Technical Bulletin of the Registry of Medical Technologists* or *Analytical Chemistry*.[7] Lighter fare included news shows like the *Huntley-Brinkley Report* and a new British mystery series entitled *Secret Agent,* which Harry seemed especially well qualified to judge.

Sixteen years in a closed community offered few highlights, but Harry looked forward to his brother's regular visits. In the early 1950s Joe would make the long drive from Philadelphia to Lewisburg with his father. When the trip became too much for the old man, Joe would drive alone.

Over the years he developed his own health problems. Diabetes would eventually lead to the amputation of a leg. The journeys became less frequent, and Joe requested the assistance of a Kindred Street neighbor, Milton Bolno.

"When I learned that my next door neighbor was a spy," said Bolno, "I didn't feel too good about it. I saw an article in *Life* magazine about Harry Gold and couldn't believe I lived next to the guy." One day in 1955 "Joe asked if I would do him a favor. He asked me to drive him to Lewisburg. I really felt pity for the guy. You could see he was very dedicated and really loved his brother. And the father was very emotional about Harry's situation. He used to cry right away if Harry's name came up. I said okay, I'd drive them up. I thought it would be a one-time thing, but it turned out to be every other month for ten years."[8] When he was feeling up to it, Sam Gold would sit in the back seat and prepare himself emotionally for the always unnerving reunion and painful goodbye. They would leave at 4:30 on Sunday morning, stop for breakfast on the highway, and arrive at the prison around nine.

Bolno never went into the inmate visiting area; he would sit in his car or in the prison lobby. He would normally have to wait for hours, until visiting hours ended, to begin the long trip back. Initially Bolno was reluctant to say which inmate he had brought his neighbors to see: "I thought the guards would look down on me." Once he did, however, he was surprised to hear that the guards "loved" Harry. Gold, they said, "was a model prisoner." One guard told Bolno, "Everybody likes him."[9]

"I sat down and cried"

Gold kept busy, working in the prison hospital and trying to stay current with national and world developments, such as the resumption of bombing raids on North Vietnam and General Motors' apology to Ralph Nader for spying into his private life. Literature and sports always piqued his interest, and he made note of Bobby Hull's becoming the first hockey player to score fifty goals in a season and Truman Capote's book *In Cold Blood*. The prison often showed movies, and he and Joe compared their evaluations of such films as *Ship of Fools, The Ipcress File,* and *King Rat.*

Gold spent hours trying to perfect his laboratory creations and improving his experimental "thermal diffusion technique," watched his favorite television shows, read magazines like the *New Yorker,* and assiduously followed all manner of sports. He anxiously awaited the start of each baseball season and expressed his hope that "our Phils make a run for the pennant this year."[10] He led the prison's Passover Seder services.

He exchanged weekly letters with his brother. Harry's letters tended to be short: two pages on his health, the ongoing work of his lawyers, his aspirations for the future. Gaining parole and starting life again as a member of a hospital team were recurring themes. Reading these letters puts to shame the long-standing canard propagated by Rosenberg defenders that Gold wanted to be punished and enjoyed prison life.

John Wexley was typical of those who, in their zeal to discredit the little man who brought down the Rosenbergs, painted Gold as divorced from normal human relationships. It was "all the same to him," wrote Wexley, "wherever he happened to live, whether in prison or outside." Prison, in Wexley's view, represented a friendly oasis to Gold, a "sanctuary" where reality never intruded and his abundant fantasies could take flight. "Gold found much more serenity within his safe, monastic surroundings that in the hazardous tension-ridden world without."[11] Because he didn't break down or plead for mercy as David Greenglass and other convicted spies had done, Gold's detractors assumed—or wanted people to believe—that he found prison life agreeable. Repeated often enough by writers like Wexley and Walter Schneir, the image of Harry Gold as a conscienceless psychopath immersed in a delusional world of intrigue that he was happy to spin out in a courtroom became the standard view. It seemed to explain the testimony of an unassuming little man who no one could believe had really been a secret agent. As his neighbor Milton Bolno said of him after they eventually met, "You'd never in a million years believe this guy was a spy. He didn't look like a spy. He was a little nothing."[12]

Harry Gold knew himself, though, and knew he wanted to be back on the street. Not a day went by that he didn't think about, dream about, and work toward his freedom.

Finally on April 1, 1966, Gold was notified the parole board had acted favorably on his application. "I have been paroled," Gold proudly led off the letter that day to his brother. He didn't know his exact release date yet, "but the big thing is that I am coming home in about seven weeks. I got the news tonight, just about a half-hour before it was announced on the Huntley-Brinkley news program."[13] After all those years, Harry Gold was still national news.

He asked Joe to immediately phone Gus Ballard. "How wonderful it is that all of his and John Hamilton's efforts through all these years are finally bringing me home to you and pop," he wrote. "Right now I'm a mixture of stunned confusion and happiness. Golly, and it will be great to be able to work in a medical facility back home. Am sure I can be of use. So more even than before (and you know how I've been working away at my studies) I'll be digging into those textbooks. And I'll try to get done what I can in the way of verifying those improvements on the blood lead and the CO_2 content methods." Gold also cautioned his brother "there'll be something in the newspapers, but we'll take that as it comes."[14]

The next day he wrote with news of his release date: May 18. There was a chance it could be altered, "but, by golly, the big thing is that I am coming again next month to you and pop." He noted again "how much Gus and John had to do with my release. I'm sure their efforts on my behalf must have impressed many people in the Justice Department."[15]

During the following days, Gold was, he said, "literally walking on air." The time until his release was "going by at a most satisfactory rapid rate." He told his brother he thought the "newspaper accounts" of the parole board's decision "were all correct and unbiased." He was described as providing the "most dramatic moments" of the Rosenberg trial, and his own sentence was said to have "stunned most observers" by its severity. Gold's prison record was reported as exemplary, and the press noted that he had "developed new techniques in blood chemistry analysis" while working in the prison's medical laboratory.[16]

Though Gold was discomforted to find himself still front-page news, he was "pleased that none of the local papers gave our home address." He didn't want his brother and ninety-year-old father burdened with another round of vicious hate mail. A related concern was the formal release process, the planning for the trip home, and the possible presence of news media at the prison's front gate and his Kindred Street home. He knew running that gauntlet might be too much for his temperamental brother. As he had done so often in the past, Gus Ballard came to the rescue. Harry wrote to Joe on hearing the news, "I was delighted to hear that Gus is coming with you to Lewisburg on the day of my release. Very gratifying and reassuring this is indeed. It is most kind of him and it does settle so much."[17]

John Hamilton had retired to Florida in the late 1950s but still kept in touch with Ballard concerning Gold's status and other important business at his old firm, now called Pepper, Hamilton and Scheetz. Ballard was by now one of the most experienced and respected lawyers at the firm, with a roster of impressive clients. But he still made time to handle the affairs of a longtime federal prisoner from whom he had never received a dime.

"Hamilton and Gus maintained their loyalty to Gold," said Francis Ballard of his brother's extraordinary commitment. "They had established a relationship with their client. The fellow needed help and Gus could help him. It took a lot of chutzpah on his part and he never made a cent on it." Ballard recalled that his brother had influential clients over the years, clients like "the Pews and the Sun Oil empire," and had been involved in the massive and complicated Pennsylvania Railroad bankruptcy, which led to the formation of Conrail; yet he probably considered representing Gold "the apex of his career. He considered it his most significant legal matter."[18]

Joe Gold may have occasionally taken Hamilton and Ballard's contributions for granted, but Harry was ever mindful and forever grateful. "Am still overwhelmed by his kindness in coming up here with you on my release date," said Harry of Ballard's offer to drive him back home. The expressions of appreciation were a recurring theme of his letters home. Harry didn't make a move, whether it was an innovative concept to market one of his lab creations, a job prospect at a local hospital, or an appeal to the parole board, without first consulting Ballard. Ballard always replied quickly with judicious advice. Now he was taking the time to escort Gold home through a swarm of reporters. Gold had an extensive history of putting himself out for people, but he was not used to being the recipient of such benevolence. He knew how lucky he had been to have Hamilton and Ballard on his side.

Once, their long and consistent support brought Harry to tears. He was in his cell reading his mail and had just received congratulatory letters from both men. Their joy at his success and their earnest expressions of best wishes for the future overwhelmed him. He had been treated by many as a pariah and frequently been shunned, but his lawyers had never wavered. When other attorneys refused to take his case, Hamilton and Ballard had done the honorable thing, and then had stood by him all those years. "All this at one time was just too much and so I sat down and cried," Harry told his brother. "In particular, the one [letter] Mr. Hamilton wrote affected me by reason of its complete kindness and concern."[19]

As the release date drew near, the brothers discussed Joe's plans to spruce up Harry's old room and "moldy" wardrobe. Sixteen years older and sixty-five pounds lighter, Harry was concerned about the expense of new clothing. "But I should be working very soon," he wrote, "and will be turning over my paycheck to you—you've got much more sense in such matters."[20] Although Joe was concerned about his brother's clothes, Harry was preoccupied with something else. "One of the very first things I want to do is visit mom's grave. We had the most wonderful woman for a mother—doubt if many others have been so fortunate."[21]

"They were cheering for Harry"

On May 18, 1966, Joe Gold and Gus Ballard arrived at Lewisburg Federal Penitentiary and saw reporters and camera crews camped in front of the institution. Ballard hoped that someone else of prominence might be leaving prison that day, but he knew that Harry's luck had never been that good. The reporters and media trucks were there for him. Even a heavy rain could not keep them away.

Ballard and Hamilton had discussed just such a possibility, and both men agreed they "ought to avoid any further publicity if . . . feasible." Hamilton had come up to Philadelphia from Clearwater, Florida, to discuss Gold's impending release. They wanted the transition to go smoothly, both to minimize the emotional strain on Gold and to avoid "jeopardizing Harry's chances of getting a good job" if any of them made "some statement for which we could be criticized." Ballard had been receiving media requests for interviews with Gold since his parole was announced. The two lawyers even considered scheduling a press conference to deal with the media onslaught all at once and then hope for some period of peace.[22]

Ballard corresponded with Jacob Parker, the current warden of the penitentiary, in hope of preventing a circus; he even explored the possibility of a late-night release. Once again it was decided they would just have to endure Gold's notoriety. Ballard informed Warden Parker that he'd be at the prison's front gate at 8:15 A.M. "Harry's best interest lies in as little publicity as possible, but it seems unlikely that his being freed after sixteen years is going to escape the attention of reporters, photographers and camera men, therefore, we must content ourselves with making the ordeal as brief and painless as possible."[23] Ballard asked the warden if "your guards might see to it that Harry and I and Joe Gold were not followed too closely . . . by the exodus of the press, radio and television people in their cars."

Parker admitted to Ballard that he was going to miss his prisoner. "Whoever hires Harry," said the warden, "is making a tremendous find. He doesn't know when the closing bell rings. Gold's a tremendous worker. He'll work till he drops. Whoever gives Harry a job is going to have trouble getting him to go home."[24]

That morning, Ballard entered the institution while Joe waited in the car. Standing in the large lobby, he experienced one of the strangest events of his life. Still pondering the best way to deal with the press and evade a media frenzy occurring in the parking lot or, worse yet, having reporters follow them for hours on the highway, he heard yells and shouts coming from within the prison. They grew into a blizzard of screaming and banging of metal cups and plates. Ballard, along with other visitors in the lobby, became increasingly concerned. That was all he needed—a riot on the day his client was getting out of prison. As a corporate lawyer, he had little contact with the criminal justice system. Visits to Harry at Holmesburg were the extent of his familiarity with penal institutions.

Increasingly unnerved, Ballard noticed that the lobby guard continued to do paperwork, indifferent to the racket that now seemed to fill the entire prison. He went over and asked if there was a problem. The guard looked up at Ballard with an amused smile and said, "There's nothing wrong, counselor. That's for your client. They're saying goodbye to Harry."[25]

"I was absolutely flabbergasted," Ballard recalled. "But the guard was right. It wasn't any kind of riot or cellblock brawl. It was for Harry. The whole damn place was screaming for Harry." As they passed from the administration building through an open courtyard surrounded by cellblocks, all the windows opened and inmates waved newspapers, magazines, bedsheets, anything at their disposal through the barred widows.

"As soon as we hit the clearing," said Ballard, "the place exploded in cheers. It was like fans in a stadium cheering a football hero. . . . Here was this world famous, notorious spy and they're cheering for him. It was incredible. . . . They were cheering for Harry."

Harry seemed embarrassed by the noisy demonstration and never looked up. He walked across the clearing in that unusual waddle of his while prisoners rained shouts of "Good luck, Harry," "Hang in there, Harry," "Give 'em hell, Harry" and generally wished him well.[26] Many thanked him for some bit of tutoring or medical assistance he had provided them over the years.

Despite his diffidence at this outpouring of affection, Harry must have found it gratifying, especially as the predictions for his survival in such a dangerous and unforgiving environment had once been so pessimistic. Shunned as a rat and a traitor in the early days and no doubt occasionally threatened, Gold never complained, never asked authorities to put him in protective custody or transfer him to a less threatening institution. Remington had been murdered inside Lewisburg, Greenglass had pleaded to be transferred out, but Gold did his time, kept busy, and found a way to make a contribution—all while actively planning a best-case scenario for his eventual release. In handling a difficult situation like a man, he earned the respect of a population that prized toughness, revered grit, and disdained complainers and squealers. By the end, Harry had become a big man in one of the most savage milieus in contemporary America.

"The hideous mistake"

Once Gold and Ballard were outside the prison, Joe Gold met them at the front gate, and they walked to the parking lot where the media were waiting. Ballard tried to keep the umbrella over Gold's head, but they were all getting soaked. Gold had lost considerable weight since his arrest—he had gone from 190 pounds to 125—and looked uncomfortable in his prison-issued dark navy suit, light blue shirt, and blue and gray striped tie. In recent years he had seldom needed to wear a suit and tie.

Just as Gold and Ballard couldn't avoid being pelted by the rain, they wouldn't escape the reporters who had trekked to rural Pennsylvania to collect a few words from the infamous World War II spy. Ballard had planned just to push his way through the crowd, but Gold, knowing he would have to face the press sooner or later, thought he might as well get it out of the way. The last thing he wanted was a crowd of reporters knocking on his family's door or, worse, the doors of neighbors.

"I'm looking forward to working in a medical facility," Gold replied when asked what he would do now that he was a free man. "I have a few feelers, but no definite job yet. I think I'd like to wait awhile—long enough to get used to being at home."[27]

Of his crime, he said, "One of the reasons I got into trouble was my inability to say 'no' to anyone. But I was not misled in the sense of a poor innocent lamb. I made a hideous mistake. It just seemed to me at the time, starting back in 1934 with industrial secrets, that it wasn't so bad."[28] He added, "It had started on such a small scale. And then it grew and grew and grew and snowballed, and I couldn't have got out of it without a full disclosure. And when I was threatened with exposure, I kept quiet and kept doing it."

To make amends, said Gold, he had disclosed everything, "everything I know, every shred, about everyone who gave secrets to the Soviet Union. I know nothing more, nothing." He said he had not been questioned by the FBI for many years.

Asked if he expected a difficult readjustment to the free world, a world in which those convicted of espionage are not particularly welcome, he soberly replied, "You get bumped in this life. But I'm prepared to face up and take it. I think I am a capable laboratory worker, and I think I can contribute to life."

As Ballard opened the car door for Gold, someone said it was a shame a happy occasion was being ruined by such bad weather. "The sun is shining for me," Gold replied.

The 170-mile drive back to Philadelphia was interrupted just outside Harrisburg when the three men stopped for lunch at a diner. Harry had a real fountain-made ice cream sundae, something he had not tasted in a long time. It was nearly 4:00 P.M. when they arrived at Gold's row house on Kindred Street in Northeast Philadelphia. Once again, reporters were there to greet them, and once again Gold entertained their questions as if it were a required stipulation of his parole. While adults peeked from behind curtains and blinds, pretending to have little interest, and children gathered on the normally quiet street to see what all the excitement was about, Gold assured his obviously irritated brother, "I think it will be all right," and looked for confirmation from his attorney. Harry appeared to be the least tense of the trio and seemed in no way reluctant to answer questions or discuss life in prison. He repeated that he hoped "to go to work in a medical facility, either as a biochemical technician or as a biochemist in medical research. I haven't had any job offers, but I understand that my brother and Mr. Ballard have had some." He hoped that such offers would be based "on what I can do in a laboratory and not on any notoriety concerned with this case."[29]

When asked about life behind bars, Gold did not take it as an opportunity to trash his former fellow inmates. "There are some fine men inside penitentiaries," he said, standing on the front lawn where his mother had planted two trees, a cedar and spruce, many years earlier. After his long absence, he must have noted how tall they had grown. One was ramrod straight; the other had a slight but noticeable tilt. Surrounded by reporters under now sunny skies, Gold continued to tell of the men he had met behind Lewisburg's walls and mentioned their contributions to the Red Cross. "In 15 years not one inmate has failed to give blood," he said with some pride. "You get to be selective and you find some good people in prison."[30]

As he had done earlier in the day, Gold spoke of his great remorse, "the hideous mistake" he had made, and how things had "snowballed" and become "a way of life. I couldn't have gotten out of it without a full disclosure. When I was threatened with exposure, I kept quiet and kept doing it. I have tried to make the greatest possible amends by disclosing every phase of my espionage activities and by identifying all the persons involved and by revealing every last scrap, shred and particle of evidence."

Of his tremendous weight loss, Gold said: "It was intentional. I did it with malice aforethought. I was eating myself to death." It was only when the questioning moved to the Schneirs' book, *Invitation to an Inquest*, that Gold displayed any irritation, but Gus Ballard intervened at that point, and Gold was ushered up the front steps of his home. He would hug his father, now ninety and bedridden, for the first time in sixteen years and say how sorry he was. He would learn that during his imprisonment his father had lost his sight and was now blind.

"I adored him"

Harry Gold was front-page news again, and television, no longer in its infancy, also gave prominent coverage to the former secret agent's return home. A new generation would learn of Klaus Fuchs, Julius and Ethel Rosenberg, and the Soviet Union's theft of atomic secrets.

Marylou McKeough read the articles with interest. She was too young to remember the actual arrest and trial, but something else about the stories on Gold had caught her attention. She was in charge of the blood bank at John F. Kennedy Hospital in Northeast Philadelphia and was intrigued to read that a hospital chemist had got himself into such serious trouble. She went to work the next day and said to her colleagues in the hospital's lab, "If I know Iossifides, he'll hire this guy."[31]

McKeough was prescient. Within a short time Kennedy Hospital, a small community hospital at Langdon Street and Cheltenham Avenue, had a new clinical chemist. Dr. Ioulios Iossifides was the hospital's chief pathologist, and according to McKeough, he had a strong predisposition toward "giving people a second chance." And Gold certainly qualified. McKeough remembers that "Dr. Iossifides introduced Harry at a meeting one morning" during the summer of 1966. He "didn't care about a person's past," as long as he or she was competent. Though none of the hospital's lab staff had the power to countermand Iossifides's decision, she recalled, "word got around who Gold was and what he had done. No one liked him." But the hospital's medical personnel would quickly discover that it was hard to dislike Harry Gold.

Almost immediately, Harry proved himself not only competent but also considerate, generous, "nice to everyone," and a workhorse. Donna Bralow, a recent Washington High School graduate who was training to become a medical technician, arrived at the hospital each morning before 6:30 expecting to be the first one there, only to find Gold already at work. "Harry never slept," she said. "You could go in there at two and five in the morning and he'd be there working."[32]

Bralow began her training at Kennedy in 1968. Part of Gold's job was to teach chemistry to the aspiring medical technicians. According to most of them, they could not have been assigned a better teacher. "He was very quiet and reserved," said Bralow, "but dedicated and very intelligent. We thought he was a wonderful person. He gave us a wealth of knowledge. He was certainly instrumental in my career."

For the longest time, said Bralow, she "had no idea who he was." When she heard about him from older staff members, she was stunned. "I adored him so much," said Bralow, "I didn't want to hear anything bad about him." He was just a kindly, gentle little man who would do anything you'd ask of him. His generosity became legendary. "I once asked him if I could borrow a dollar to buy a soda in a vending machine," said Bralow, "and he'd quickly pull out a bill and gave it to me. But it wasn't a dollar; it was a ten-dollar bill. When I told him it was too much and tried to give it back, he'd just say take it. Don't worry about it."

Diane Reibel, a heart researcher at Thomas Jefferson University in Philadelphia, remembers Gold's "unbelievable patience" when she was a high school intern during the summers in the early 1970s. "He'd sit there and teach me all this complicated material. He explained everything and even if you didn't get it he'd sit there and explain it to you until you understood it. He was a very kind, brilliant guy. Everybody loved him."[33] When she was applying to colleges, Reibel thought of asking Gold for a reference, but her mother cautioned her, "I wouldn't do that," and then explained who Harry Gold was. "I asked him for a reference," said Reibel, with obvious pride.

Fred Himmelstein had a similar experience. A sophomore at Northeast High School with aspirations of becoming a physician, Himmelstein threw himself into his tenth grade science project, which required access to and information from Kennedy Hospital. He spent most of his time in the hospital's laboratory, and remembers it as a complex of basement rooms where the hematology, microbiology, and electrophoresis work was performed, with the morgue nearby. Everyone he came into contact with was working on something, but one staff member seemed particularly busy. "I just walked up to him and asked what he was doing," said Himmelstein. It was the beginning of one of the most important relationships of his formative years. "I guess I gravitated towards Harry because he spent more time helping me than anyone else there," recalled Dr. Himmelstein, now an emergency medicine specialist.[34] "He took the time to explain things to me. He could have said, 'I'm too busy, kid. Come back some other time,' but he never did. He spent a lot of time helping me with that science project. I adored him. He really took me under his wing." Gold was very professional, but Himmelstein got a kick out of his unusual mannerisms. "He had a strange little waddle of a walk, and he was so short his white lab came down below his knees making him look a little bit cartoonish." Harry also loved to eat. His trim 125-pound prison physique didn't last long on the outside. "He loved to nosh," said Himmelstein, "and he would occasionally talk to himself while puttering around the laboratory. He could be quite eccentric and was always losing things. I remember one day there was a big panic in the lab when he couldn't find his keys. After a long, frenetic hunt we found them in his lunch bag."

Like most others who arrived at Kennedy Hospital after Gold's first summer there, Himmelstein had no idea that Harry had once been notorious. Two decades after he left Kennedy, "I was reading a magazine article one day about the Rosenbergs, and there was a photograph of him. I couldn't believe it. I said, 'My God, that's my Harry.'"

Gold's co-workers rarely mentioned his past and didn't go out of their way to notify new employees. If the subject arose, Gold never flinched, lied, or provided phony excuses. "He always said he was guilty," recalls McKeough. "He would talk about it openly and freely if you brought it up. He never denied it. He said he had made a horrible mistake."[35] That is not to say, however, that he enjoyed talking about his past. Unexpected reminders of those days could prove terribly unsettling. Bralow witnessed one such incident while Gold was a patient in the hospital.[36] "We were all around him one afternoon while he was lying in his hospital bed," said Bralow. "We were all joking and making conversation when all of a sudden he started yelling, 'Shut it off,' 'Shut it off,' 'Shut the television off.' He startled all of us. I looked up at the TV to see what had disturbed him so and it was the Mike Douglas Show. They had a photo of David Greenglass on the screen. They were talking about the Rosenberg case and Harry got very emotional. It took us some time to settle him down."[37]

"He lived and breathed science"

Although a few of his co-workers would not believe it, Gold had a life outside the hospital laboratory. He enjoyed lounging around the house in his pajamas watching baseball games on television, listening to classical music, and reading a wide assortment of books and magazines. Gold relished these quiet times with his father and brother. That life, and a good hospital job, were all he had dreamed of while buried behind bars.

Milton Bolno, the neighbor who drove Joe Gold up to Lewisburg, remembered Harry "sitting in a living room chair listening to classical music. He was an intellectual and read a lot of books and newspapers. He would always come home late at night. Joe would usually pick him up and bring him home. He really worked a lot of late hours." When Joe introduced him to Harry shortly after he came home from prison, Bolno wasn't particularly impressed. For someone who had caused so much mayhem, Gold was very ordinary. "He was very quiet. He rarely sat outside and talked to his neighbors. He was into his music and books. He talked a little about sports and what was going on in the world, but not much more than that.

"To the end," said Bolno, "I never really felt Harry knew what he was doing with those Russians. He didn't realize what he was getting in to. They really finagled him." Years later, Bolno and his wife had a shock when they toured the FBI building in Washington and came upon a "giant photo of Harry" in a display on espionage. "We had no intention of looking for anything on Harry," he said. "It really gave us a chill."[38]

Gold did a bit of traveling once he regained his freedom, but it almost always involved a scientific conference of some sort. At a meeting of the Clinical Chemists Association in Denver in 1969, he met Howard Harner. Also a Philadelphia area chemist, Harner had given a talk at the conference and recalled "this little guy coming up to me asking some follow-up questions about the separation of molecules." During their brief discussion, Harner gradually became more intrigued and suggested a collaboration, but his new acquaintance replied, "You may not want to work with me. My name is Harry Gold." When Harner showed no immediate sign of recognition, Gold said, "I was the courier who passed the secrets of the atomic bomb to the Russians." Harner was taken aback; he was not exactly a left-wing activist. "I was really hesitant," admitted Harner. "I picketed the pickets who protested the Rosenberg executions."[39] Gold related that his application to the national chemists' association had not been without controversy. "The right-wingers," said Harner, "opposed his membership and it became quite a fight." Only through the intervention of the national chairman did Gold attain his membership. He was delighted to become an active member of the organization and went on to deliver a paper on liquid thermal diffusion at the annual conference in Seattle. In April 1972, at the convention of the Association of Clinical Scientists in Elkhart, Indiana, he gave another presentation, entitled "The Application of Thermal Diffusion to Separation of Bio-chemical Entities."[40]

From the very first, Harner was taken with Gold's honesty, politeness, and sincerity. His "ideas were interesting" as well. Two weeks after their conversation in Denver, Harner visited Gold's lab at Kennedy Hospital, and the two quickly became friends. "He was really sorry for what he had done and wanted to be known for something good," said Harner, who was impressed that Gold didn't make excuses for his criminal activity. He observed how rigorous and how meticulous Gold was in his research. They discussed Gold's long-standing interest in thermal diffusion and how it might be used in medical diagnosis. It was clear, said Harner, that Harry "lived and breathed science." Harner also heard stories of how Gold extended himself for people. Hospital staffers told him how Gold had "helped a six year-old child who had suffered anaphylactic shock. Harry stayed up with the kid for two full days and kept that kid alive."

The two chemists occasionally socialized together. "Harry never drank to excess," said Harner. "He'd have one or two beers at the most" and discuss everything from Gilbert and Sullivan and his beloved Phillies to his distaste for the Schneirs and Roy Cohn, to the possibilities of thermal diffusion. Gold was also very concerned about other people's health, though he wasn't nearly as conscientious about his own. "He gave me a pipe," said Harner, "in an effort to get me to quit smoking cigarettes. He was worried about me." But Gold was having his own problems. "He was very chubby and overweight," said Harner, who had never seen the slimmed-down version of Gold on his release from prison. And his stamina was a growing problem. Harner said, "I think that hepatitis experiment at Lewisburg and the other experiments he participated in as a guinea pig weakened his heart."

"The most gentle man I ever knew"

Gold was slowing down, but you wouldn't know it from his work hours. He put in so much time in that Bralow came to believe "his best friend was the laboratory."[41] Lab workers, however, became fond and protective of him and brought him to all their social occasions. "We had him over for dinner," said McKeough, "and brought him to the house at Christmas time. We took him to parties, weddings, everything."[42] "We all loved him," added Bralow. "He was like an adorable little pet we all wanted to take care of."

The downside was that "some of the girls bossed him around," said McKeough, "and he took it. Students abused him. He was easy."

By the early 1970s, Gold was overweight and slowing down, but still pushing himself through extremely long, intense days. Some of his consultations with physicians now concerned his own health. Doctors determined that he suffered from "aortic regurgitation due to a faulty heart valve."[43] This congenital defect would only grow worse with time until the heart valve eventually failed. A replacement valve was cutting-edge surgery at the time, and many doctors thought it too risky. Dr. Iossifides, the head of Kennedy Hospital's pathology unit, was one of them. He said the procedure had not been perfected yet. Gold, however, went ahead and scheduled the surgery when his boss was away.

"Harry wanted the operation and the valve replaced," said Harner. "He was having chest pains and slowing down. His excessive weight only complicated the situation. He knew there was a possibility of death. He was a very smart man, but he decided to go ahead with it anyway." Harner visited Gold before he went into the hospital for the surgery, and the two men exchanged a "bear hug rather than a handshake" when Harry said, "I'm going in, goodbye." Harner said he was "pretty sure Harry knew this could be the end."[44] Over the two years of their acquaintance, he had learned what a struggle life had been for Gold. He was worn out.

Gold had the operation on August 28, 1972, at Albert Einstein Hospital in Philadelphia. It was a high-risk procedure in those early days of delicate open-heart surgery. He died on the operating table. The official cause of death was listed as "prosthetic replacement of aortic valve." He was sixty-one years old.

When word of Gold's death got back to Kennedy Hospital, his co-workers were devastated. "When I got the call and heard that Harry had died during surgery, I was hysterical," said Donna Bralow. Doctors and students were heartbroken. They began telling each other stories about Harry, his dedication, friendship, and extraordinary patience, what they remembered best about him. "He was always patient," said one colleague. "And if he did yell at somebody, he'd give everybody a rose the next morning. He was a very gentle man."[45] Dr. Iossifides added that Harry was the "most gentle man I ever knew. We were all his friends. He was preoccupied with his work, and he was excellent at it."[46]

Another of Harry's students remembered that after he died, "we were all here the next day, upset, crying. I was crying. We were all here and the place was empty."[47]

"I do not propose to whimper"

August 30, 1972, was a warm, sunny day. Dozens of Harry Gold's friends came to Har Nebo Cemetery to say goodbye. The man from South Philadelphia who had led such an unusual and tragic life would now be buried near the most important person in his life. His public persona was that of a traitor: a reviled spy who gave his country's most precious scientific secrets to the enemy. But to those who knew him and worked with him, he was a friend and treasured colleague. A number of mourners that day may have been completely unaware of Harry's infamous past; to them he was just a loving, generous soul who had brightened their lives.

There was no public announcement in local newspapers; no obituary carried notice of his death. Joe Gold, who idolized his brother, wanted it that way. He and his father had had enough of the ugly headlines, the hate mail, the endless articles analyzing his brother's infamy. But people heard of Harry's death and came to the gravesite. Many were from Kennedy Hospital. "Everybody was fighting as to who was going to the funeral," recalled Marylou McKeough. "No one wanted to work the lab that day. They all wanted to go. Supervisors wanted to go, trainees wanted to go. I guess we all just wanted to say goodbye. Everybody liked Harry."

As the mourners gathered around the burial plot, Diane Reibel noticed how many people had come to pay their last respects: "I was astounded by how many people showed up. I never saw so many people at a funeral. He was loved by everyone."[48]

Howard Harner, Harry's friend and now a pallbearer, noted the level of grief Harry's passing had stirred. For those who just knew him by his newspaper clippings, such an outpouring of affection was incomprehensible. But those who knew the real Harry Gold, from lawyers and doctors to foreign agents, were captivated by him. Even prison inmates, notoriously hard to impress, came under his spell. At least one inmate was moved to dedicate a poem to him.[49]

In his letter to Judge McGranery at the time of his arraignment on July 20, 1950, Gold wrote that he had "tried to behave with dignity, as a man should" in such difficult times. He said that he "sought no legal outs . . . no deals" and would "take my punishment" like a man. He quoted "The Hollow Men" by T. S. Eliot: "This is the way the world ends, not with a bang, but a whimper," and added: "I do not propose to whimper. I have done my best to make amends, but I know that somehow, sometime, somewhere, I shall, with God's help, make an even greater restitution."[50]

Epilogue

The public did not learn of Harry Gold's death for another year and a half. Alvin H. Goldstein, a writer-producer for the National Public Affairs Center, discovered it while preparing a television documentary on the Rosenbergs. Unable to locate Gold and failing to find his name through a routine obituary search, he placed an advertisement in the *New York Times* asking anyone who knew the whereabouts of Harry Gold to contact him. Within a week he received a call notifying him that Gold had died in August 1972. Goldstein planned on releasing this news in his documentary, *The Unquiet Death of Julius and Ethel Rosenberg*, but he was scooped. The story appeared on television and in newspapers around the country in mid-February 1974.

When reporters went to Gold's former home in Philadelphia to confirm his death and ask why it had not been reported, Joe Gold was less than cordial. The media had never been a friend of his brother's, said Joe; why should he go out of his way to inform them of Harry's passing? Gus Ballard was only slightly friendlier. "The poor bastard was hounded all his life, and his brother was sick of it," he said. Ballard says there was "no deliberate attempt" to keep the death secret. A death certificate had been filed and a will probated, "but nobody picked them up."[1]

When pressed further, Joe stated, "My brother died in August, 1972. We made no announcement of services. We didn't want no publicity. We didn't need it."[2] Joe had always been offended by news accounts of his brother's crimes, particularly by journalists' willingness to print the bizarre characterizations periodically trotted out by the Wexleys and the Schneirs of the world. He no doubt added Alvin Goldstein to the list when his documentary aired on television shortly after the announcement of Harry's death. It was not a flattering portrait.

Gus Ballard was incensed. Once again he had given help to an independent researcher—this time a filmmaker—in the hope that his client would get a fair shake, only to find another declaration of the Rosenbergs' innocence. "For the record," wrote Ballard to Goldstein, "I would like to lodge with you a complaint concerning the characterization given my client. . . . While Harry can no longer be personally hurt, his brother and friends, including his counsel and Dr. Iossifides, are distressed at your posthumous attack on his credibility." Ballard wrote that he had "provided . . . information and leads sufficient to enable you to present a balanced review of the Rosenberg case as it involved Harry Gold. You chose instead to enlist Walter and Miriam Schneir as your writers. I think you should have identified them as such in the credits at the end of the film."[3]

Long after Gold's death, Ballard remained infuriated by the ongoing slander campaign. As he wrote to one New York lawyer at the time of the documentary, "My only concern is the credibility of my deceased client, Harry Gold, which continues to be attacked by apologists for the Rosenbergs." The Goldstein documentary "continued the characterization of Harry as a pathological liar. This annoyed Harry during his lifetime and continues to upset his surviving brother and the loyal friends he made following his release on parole in 1966."[4] In his note, Ballard included a *Philadelphia Daily News* article announcing the death of Gold that contained the warm comments of his Kennedy Hospital colleagues.[5] He said the article presented "the best view of Harry and the kind of man he was. It gives you an idea why I never gave up on him over a period of 22 years."[6] Though he was unaware of the correspondence, Milton Bolno, the Golds' Kindred Street neighbor, would not have been surprised by it. "That lawyer fought like hell for Harry," he said.[7]

Friends of Harry Gold were not the only ones who were upset with *The Unquiet Death of Julius and Ethel Rosenberg*. Some in law enforcement were perturbed, particularly Robert Lamphere, the FBI supervisor who led the hunt for Klaus Fuchs's American contact. "In agreeing to be interviewed and later to a filming," wrote Lamphere to Goldstein, "I had one specification—that your documentary would not be slanted. To this both you and . . . your producer, agreed. You did not keep this agreement."[8] Lamphere could understand wanting to "create interest" in a product by building "some controversy," as well as arguing that "the punishment of death" was unjustified, but "in the last two-thirds of your film, neither your commentary nor your allotting of time was balanced. It was clearly slanted in the direction of suggesting that these people were not guilty of the crime with which they were charged." Lamphere was bothered that "the Schneirs said that in their view the entire case was a frame-up and that only the FBI could have engineered it."

Lamphere's letter enumerated inaccuracies and gross distortions of fact, and expressed surprise that "Public Television would slant a so-called documentary to the extent that you did." Was this supposed to be an example of "unbiased reporting"? Likening the film to "the efforts to portray various conspiracies out of the assassination of President Kennedy," he concluded: "I consider you personally responsible for the unmistakable bias and for breaking the agreement made with me and I am sure with others."[9]

How must Harry Gold have felt over the years as the punching bag of choice for many Rosenberg defenders, who subjected him to a level of scrutiny that Julius and Ethel never could have withstood? Yes, Gold admitted to lying. He created a fictional family with a wife, two children, and a brother who had fought and died in the war. But during his years as an agent, he could hardly tell everyone he met that he was a spy for the Russians who lived with his parents in Philadelphia. As for his many trips to New York, Ohio, Tennessee, and New Mexico, he could hardly tell his parents that he was traveling for espionage on behalf of the KGB. Of course he lied, that is what spies do. As John Earl Haynes, Harvey Klehr, and Alexander Vassiliev state in *Spies,* "Espionage is a secret business. It is rare that agents engaged in it . . . speak honestly and openly about what they have done because the incentives to lie, dissemble, and continue to deceive are so strong for all concerned."[10]

But when Gold was caught and decided to tell all, he told the truth. He devoted hundreds of hours to recounting and explaining to the FBI and federal prosecutors everything he had ever done as a secret agent for the Russians. Some Americans found this endeavor not only redemptive but also refreshing. One observer wrote that such openness "distinguishes you from the rest of our traitors insofar as they usually circumvent, lie and even perjure themselves trying to deny their guilt, whereas you have had the grace, honesty and humility to admit yours."[11]

Such candor, however, was anathema to many on the left. They much preferred and steadfastly supported those who were accused of espionage but fervently denied it. Hiss, Sobell, and the Rosenbergs inspired street marches and had organizations established in their honor. Chambers,

Bentley, and Gold came under constant attack. Gus Ballard was outraged at how supposedly liberal, intelligent people treated Gold. "The poor guy tries to make amends for committing a terrible crime," argued Ballard, "and is viciously attacked for it. Not for the original crime, but for owning up to it. They wanted to punish him for telling the truth."[12]

In addition to all the fictionalized accounts of Gold's life and psychology by supposed nonfiction authors, Ballard also had to endure a novelist's attempt to portray his former client.[13] Though the novel was actually more fact-based than the propaganda from the Rosenberg camp, Ballard still had his problems with it, particularly the sex scene portraying Gold as the victim of coitus interruptus.

As the years passed, those moved by evidence and scholarship, as opposed to "articles of faith," began to recognize that Gold and others had told the truth. *The Rosenberg File*, by Ron Radosh and Joyce Milton, was a landmark piece of investigative scholarship that conclusively demonstrated, through the use of the Freedom of Information Act and scores of interviews, that Julius Rosenberg was a central actor in Soviet espionage. Though Ethel had a limited role, she knew of and supported what her husband was doing. Radosh, a son of progressive activists and *Yiddishkayt* culture, came under withering attack for daring to dislodge two bedrock principles of the American Left: that "communists were just another group of dissenters who posed no threat . . . to American national interests" and that the Rosenbergs "were the victims of a government frame-up."[14]

The last decade of the twentieth century was especially difficult for Rosenberg defenders. The release of Soviet archival material and long-secret National Security Agency decrypts underscored the breadth and depth of Soviet espionage in America. Gold's significant role was once again confirmed. Code-named "Goose" and later "Arno," he was mentioned numerous times in secret Soviet cables between Moscow Center and the Soviet embassy in New York City.[15] His meetings with "Rest" (Fuchs), "Calibre" (David Greenglass), "Wasp" (Ruth Greenglass), and "Chrome Yellow" (Abe Brothman) were all there.[16] His trips to Cambridge, Massachusetts, to see Fuchs's sister, Kristel Heinemann ("Ant"), and his monthly stipends from the Soviets were also mentioned. The decrypts even captured lengthy comments by top KGB authorities on the value of supplying "Arno" with the cover of his own laboratory as a way to free him up for more secret missions.[17]

Most recently, Haynes and Klehr joined with former KGB officer Vassiliev to produce *Spies*, a compilation and analysis of secret Stalin-era

KGB documents that offers the most complete account yet of Soviet intelligence operations against the United States. One can now say with complete certainty that Harry Gold was a long-serving spy and courier for the Soviet Union. His account has been fully confirmed. From his initial recruitment and theft of minor industrial documents in the mid-1930s through his progress as an undercover agent and assignments to work with contacts like Ben Smilg, Alfred Dean Slack, Abe Brothman, and David Greenglass, to his most important assignment as a courier for Klaus Fuchs and the theft of Manhattan Project secrets, Gold was a key figure in Soviet intelligence gathering in the United States.

Vassiliev's notebooks not only confirm but also provide context for the brief Venona decrypts. Regarding the Soviet insistence that Gold complete his college education in Ohio, the Vassiliev documents disclose that "Goose" (Gold) "was brought to Cincinnati specifically for a connection with Lever" (Ben Smilg) and even mention that he was a "good student" at the university, received "excellent grades," and was "happy to have been given the opportunity to get an education."[18] The documents also make clear that "Lever" wanted no part of "Goose" and "that he had wanted to denounce Goose in November of '38, but decided not to, b/c Goose was a Jew, and that would have been detrimental to the entire race."[19]

Vassiliev's notebooks show that as the years passed, Gold's value and professionalism as a spy and courier were repeatedly commented on. He was said to have "matured," become a "good worker," and "very valuable" as a "group handler."[20] Maybe the "best assessment of Arno's [Gold] work is the prestigious state award," the Order of the Red Star, that was presented to him in 1944 and thought to be a stimulant "for even better work" in the future.[21] Unsurprisingly, many notebook entries concerning Gold deal with his very important relations with "Charles," or "Rest" (Fuchs), but other entries illuminate his relations with contacts like "Chrome Yellow" (Brothman),[22] his injuries on the job,[23] and the unbelievable prospect of taking his mother with him on his journeys to meet Fuchs in New Mexico.[24]

There may someday be additional revelations from an American or Russian archive or possibly a memoir from a former clandestine operative, but they will only embellish what we now know well: Harry Gold—however unlikely it seems—was a critical component of Soviet espionage in America.

And what of the fates of others mentioned in this story? Sam Gold died on February 7, 1973, six months after he had buried his firstborn son, his "golden boy." A small, unpretentious man who enjoyed working with his hands, Sam was by all accounts a master woodworker and an accomplished but poorly paid cabinetmaker. Though his son's conviction and lengthy imprisonment nearly killed him, father and son shared six years together after Harry's release from Lewisburg. Sam died at ninety-six and is buried next to his wife, Celia, at Har Nebo Cemetery.

John D. M. Hamilton, Gold's attorney and the head of the Philadelphia firm of Pepper, Hamilton and Scheetz, died at eighty-one on September 25, 1973. His death was attributed to a combination of emphysema and heart disease.[25] The onetime GOP chairman who had coordinated Governor Alf Landon's campaign for the presidency in 1936 and helped direct Senator Robert Taft's unsuccessful campaign for the Republican nomination in 1952 spent the last years of his life in Clearwater, Florida.[26] Despite criticism from some members of his firm and personal attacks from others for agreeing to represent a confessed Soviet spy, his dedicated representation of Gold and principled stand that everyone deserves legal counsel earned much respect for both him and the firm. His role in the Gold case is now prominently showcased on the Pepper, Hamilton Web site.

Klaus Fuchs died in East Germany on January 28, 1988, at the age of seventy-six. Upon his release after nine years in a British prison, he immediately traveled to the part of his homeland that was under Communist control. He married a woman he had known years earlier at the University of Kiel, reestablished his scientific credentials, and became a revered member of the East German scientific community. He was given various Communist Party and government honors, including the Karl Marx Medal—the country's highest civilian decoration—and the title "distinguished scientist of the people." At his death he belonged to both the East German Communist Party and the East German Academy of Sciences. Said to have been "a man driven by conscience," he was described at his trial as a Jekyll and Hyde figure who used "his magnificent brain in the cause of science" but was also guilty of "betraying his oath of allegiance, his vows of security and the friendship of his friends." The official announcement of his death noted his significant scientific accomplishments but made no mention of his espionage.[27]

Former FBI agent Robert J. Lamphere passed away at eighty-three in a Tucson hospital on January 7, 2002, from a combination of prostate cancer and Parkinson's disease. A successful member of the FBI's criminal unit when he was transferred to the Soviet espionage squad, he was said to have worried that counterespionage "would not be as satisfying as the criminal cases he had been working on. It turned out to be anything but monotonous." Lamphere had his hands full with Fuchs, Gold, the Rosenbergs, and the Venona and Manhattan projects.[28] Of the Soviet spying apparatus, Lamphere said, "The enemy just went on and on. When you got rid of one spy, another would take his place." Although he protected the secrecy of the Venona Project for four decades, in hindsight Lamphere wondered if it might not have been better to reveal Venona's existence "to dramatize for doubters that Soviet espionage was, indeed, widespread." After leaving the FBI in 1955, Lamphere held high positions with the Veterans Administration and later became an executive with the John Hancock Mutual Insurance Company. His memoir of combating Soviet intelligence operations in America, entitled *The FBI-KGB War*, was published in 1986.

Joe Gold died on October 22, 1989, of either a stroke or heart attack while taking a bath. He was seventy-two years old. Lacking his older brother's warmth, generosity, and intellect, Joe was far more street savvy and won several commendations during World War II. After retiring from the Naval Air Supply Depot, he took care of his father and brother for the rest of their lives. Neighbors remembered Joe dutifully driving Harry to and from work at Kennedy Hospital. In the late 1980s, Joe asked Gus Ballard for advice in making out a will; he wanted to know what he should do with his savings and house. "Well, you might consider paying your attorneys," suggested Ballard.[29] Like his brother, Joe Gold never married. He is buried a few yards away from Harry at Har Nebo Cemetery.

The Gold case was Gus Ballard's only foray into criminal defense work. Like his brothers and father, he established himself as a creative and highly competent corporate lawyer who represented some of the nation's largest firms. He was chairman of Pepper, Hamilton from 1972 to 1984 and co-chair for the next two years. He retired as an active partner in 1989 and served in an "of counsel" role through 1995.[30] Along with being an active member of the Philadelphia, Pennsylvania, and American bar associations, he was also a president of the Mental Health Association of Southeastern Pennsylvania. He played bridge and sailed, was an avid reader, and had memorized long stretches of poetry. "I think he really wanted to be a writer, a poet, but his father pushed him pretty hard," recalled his son, Wainwright Ballard. "If you're a Ballard you're supposed to be a lawyer."[31]

For all his prominent clients, legal achievements, and substantial retainers over the years, the case Gus Ballard worked on for more than two decades without earning a cent was, as his brother Francis said, the "apex of his career."[32] Gus Ballard's children agree. "My dad was always talking about the Harry Gold case," said Frances Ballard. "It was the high point of his legal career."[33] At the start, and at several later points, he had his doubts. "Here was a guy pleading guilty to a very serious crime concerning national security during the McCarthy era, and here I am trying to defend him," Ballard recalled. "I always wondered what the hell am I doing with this case?" But, like his mentor, John Hamilton, Ballard knew exactly what he was doing, especially when things became difficult, epithets like "Commie lover" were being thrown around, and partners and clients were unsupportive. "I knew there were partners in the law firm who would have been happier if I hadn't shouldered the burden for Harry after Hamilton moved to Florida in 1957," recalled Ballard in a 2007 interview, "but I was hooked. There was something very appealing about Harry. It affected Hamilton first, and then me. He was just such a decent guy."[34] Ballard died of pulmonary fibrosis on February 9, 2008, at the age of eighty-six.

In the conclusion of *Spies,* Haynes, Klehr, and Vassiliev point out the "tendency to romanticize sometimes dangerous but usually tedious" aspects of high-stakes espionage, and the public's "insatiable appetite for fictional accounts of spying. Such literature, even when skillfully executed, often cannot match the oddities of the real world." Harry Gold was one of those oddities. His life was a long and troubled endurance contest. He had a few good years—the two years he spent at Philadelphia General Hospital, the two years at Xavier, his year at Penn, his final years at John F. Kennedy Hospital—but the rest was a never-ending struggle. The legend of Harry Gold will forever be associated with an infamous crime and infamous people, but for those who knew him, the riddle will always remain. How did such a gentle, apolitical person get caught up in the "crime of the century"?

Gold knew the stigma of his crime would never wash off. For his friends, the mystery, the sheer incomprehensibility of it all, would remain long after he was gone. But he did want the judge at his trial and everyone beyond to know one very important thing. As he wrote from his cell at Holmesburg Prison, "I have never intended any harm to the United States. For I have always steadfastly considered that first and finally I am an American citizen. This is my country and I love it."[35]

Notes

Preface

1. J. Edgar Hoover, "What Was the FBI's Toughest Case?" *This Week Magazine,* February 20, 1955, p. 10.

2. Author's interview with Milton Bolno, August 20, 2006.

3. J. Edgar Hoover, "The Crime of the Century," *Reader's Digest,* vol. 58, May 1951, p. 150.

4. John Wexley, *The Judgment of Julius and Ethel Rosenberg* (New York: Cameron and Kahn, 1955), p. 39.

5. Author's interview with Donna Bralow, August 2, 2007.

6. Author's interview with Miriam Moskowitz, July 22, 2008. Interestingly, for all of Moskowitz's anger toward Gold for naming her as a participant in a scheme to deceive a federal grand jury, she was also capable of showing great compassion toward her accuser. In my first interview with her at New York University she was brought to tears when describing the isolated and "lonely" life Harry Gold led as a spy. She said, "He was so alone. He had no one to talk to. He didn't confide in anyone. He was a tragic figure." When I directly asked her, "He put you in prison, but you still feel sympathy for him?" "Yes," was her reply. Author's interview with Miriam Moskowitz, April 5, 2007.

7. Robert J. Lamphere and Tom Shactman, *The FBI-KGB War* (New York: Random House, 1986), p. 160.

8. Wexley, *Judgment,* p. 39.

9. "Scope of Soviet Activity in the United States," hearing before the Subcommittee to Investigate the Administration of the Internal Security Act and other Internal Security Laws of the Committee on the Judiciary United States Senate, Eighty-fourth Congress, second session, April, 26, 1956, p. 1055.

Chapter 1. South Philadelphia

1. Transcripts from Soundscriber discs of interviews with Harry Gold by John D. M. Hamilton and Augustus S. Ballard at Holmesburg Prison, June 6, 1950, reel 5, pp. 12–14. (Hereafter cited as Soundscriber interviews.)

2. A. N. Wilson, *Tolstoy* (New York: Norton, 1988), p. 326.

3. Harry Gold, "The Early Life of Harry Gold—A Report," October 23, 1950, p. 4. Legal Papers of Augustus S. Ballard, Special Collections, Paley Library, Temple University. (Hereafter cited as "Early Life.")

4. Soundscriber interviews, June 6, 1950, reel 5, pp. 4–8.

5. According to Gold, his mother was talked into "transporting bombs" from "one place to another" in a "market basket" by a young revolutionary to whom she had been attracted. Though she was subsequently interrogated "by several secret servicemen," she was never incarcerated. She would subsequently inform her son "to beware of the people who led these various revolutionary movements" as they are not always as "idealistic as they might have you believe." Ibid., pp. 8–11.

6. Ibid., p. 11.

7. Ibid., p. 14.

8. Ibid., p. 15.

9. "Early Life," p. 4.

10. The S.S. *Lapland* was a two-funnel, four-mast, 17,540-gross-ton ship, built in 1908. Capable of carrying twenty-five hundred passengers, the *Lapland* could do seventeen knots and made numerous ocean crossings under various flags before it was decommissioned and scrapped by the Japanese in 1934.

11. Curiously, the ship's manifest of passengers lists the profession of Samson Golodnitski as "Baker," though there is no other confirmation that Sam Gold had this skill. Samson, Zipa, and Heinrich are all designated as "Hebrew" and "Russian." Their last permanent residence is "Switzerland, Bumplitz," and their country of origin is "Smilla, Kieff" (Kiev). From "List or Manifest of Alien Passengers for the United States" of the S.S. *Lapland.*

12. "Early Life," p. 5.

13. There exists the possibility that the Gold family traveled to Little Rock, Arkansas, where they may have had relatives, but Harry Gold, who was four years old at the time, was "not sure" of this. His earliest recollection is of being in Chicago. Soundscriber interviews, reel 1, p. 20.

14. The Second Street residence was remembered by Gold as the "only sore spot" throughout his parents' "entire married life." Dubious about an attractive offer to buy, Sam Gold rejected the deal, to Celia Gold's great chagrin. His mother, wrote Gold, "often bemoaned this lost opportunity." Ibid., pp. 7–9.

15. Rakhmiel Peltz, *From Immigrant to Ethnic Culture* (Stanford, Calif.: Stanford University Press, 1998), p. 15.

16. Though the origin of "the Neck" is unclear, the area south of Oregon Avenue along Stonehouse Lane was a unique piece of real estate populated by folks found nowhere else in the city. As former South Philadelphia resident and author, Murray Dubin, states: "Neckers looked different, they talked different, they dressed differ-

ent—they were a rural, primitive people who lived a different type of life. Their children were laughed at in the public schools, but you wouldn't want to fight them." Interview by author with Murray Dubin, September 24, 2007.

17. Peltz, *From Immigrant,* p. 25.

18. Sandy Wizov, *A Corner Affair* (Philadelphia: Self-published, 1999), p. 7.

19. "Early Life," p. 13

20. Ibid., p. 8.

21. Ibid., p. 20.

22. Author's interview with Dr. Arthur Coltman, November 22, 2006.

23. The old Jewish quarter of South Philadelphia was a "densely populated area." Wizov, *Corner Affair,* p. 7.

24. Author's interview with Yetta Silverstein, March 8, 2007.

25. Harry Gold, "The Circumstances Surrounding My Work as a Soviet Agent —A Report," October 11, 1950, p. 1059. This report, which was made at the request of Gold's attorneys, can be found in various repositories, including the FBI Archives, Temple University's Paley Library Special Collections, and the Diamond Law Library at Columbia University. One of the handiest copies is part of the U.S. Senate hearing before the Subcommittee to Investigate the Administration of the Internal Security Act and other Internal Security Laws of the Committee on the Judiciary United States Senate, Eighty-fourth Congress, second session, April 26, 1956.

26. Ibid., p. 1060.

27. Ibid. and "Early Life," p. 9.

28. Ibid., p. 55.

29. John D. M. Hamilton's Defense Presentation at the Sentencing of Harry Gold, Philadelphia, December 7, 1950, p. 8. Legal Papers of Augustus S. Ballard, Special Collections, Paley Library, Temple University. (Hereafter cited as Hamilton, Sentencing Presentation.)

30. Soundscriber interviews, June 1, 1950, reel 1, p. 23.

31. "Early Life," p. 10.

32. Author's interview with Yetta Silverstein, March 8, 2007.

33. "Early Life," p. 10.

34. Ibid., p. 20.

35. Celia Gold detested hypocrisy and routinely pointed out examples to her son. The local grocer, for instance, made a show of his devotion to God and his Jewish faith by "beating his breast" on the "holiest of days" as the shofar was blown, but would then go back to "his store and once again place a thumb on the scales while weighing out the corned beef." Ibid., p. 19.

36. Ibid., p. 72.

37. Hamilton, Sentencing Presentation, p. 9.

38. A Social Democrat who loathed "dilettantes" and "political drones," Celia Gold was constantly telling her children that "the only kind of worthwhile work was that which contributed to the welfare of society," and "no matter how menial the task, as long as it provides a necessary service, then the man doing it can hold his head high." "Early Life," pp. 71–72.

39. Ibid., p. 72.

40. Gold greatly enjoyed his two summers at the camp. He gained seven or eight pounds to his "very puny" frame in each of the summers of 1923 and 1924, developed a "tremendous appetite" for the first time in his life, and met and became inspired by the Penn athletes who were camp counselors. "Early Life," pp. 62–63, and Hamilton, Sentencing Presentation, p. 43.

41. "Early Life," pp. 18–19.

42. Ibid., pp. 38–39.

43. Author's interview with Yetta Silverstein, March 8, 2007.

44. Author's interview with Sylvia Weiss, May 20, 2006.

45. Author's interview with Ted Krakow, February 27, 2009.

46. Author's interview with Mary Frank, March 7, 2006.

47. Hamilton, Sentencing Presentation, p. 10.

48. In a paper he wrote for one of his classes at Xavier, Gold said he read his first book "about Bre'r Rabbit and his family" at the age of eight. Within a year he was "avidly following the adventures of Tom Swift" in submarines and airplanes. The Frank Merriwell series by Burt L. Standish soon became a favorite. Gold's literary tastes were maturing, and he started tackling more difficult subject matter, such as Dickens and Shakespeare, but his love of the "printed word" was not respected in "the mean and rough world of South Philadelphia." Regrettably, such pursuits were "invariably taken as a sign of weakness," and resulted in Gold enduring much suffering. "The Printed Word and I," college paper, September 29, 1939.

49. "Early Life," p. 22.

50. Hamilton, Sentencing Presentation, p. 34.

51. Gold's stint as a candy seller at the Broad Street Theatre was short-lived because, as he recalled, he "was too frightened to call out my wares between the acts" and "only sold one box." "Early Life," p. 26.

52. Ibid., p. 39.

53. Soundscriber interviews, June 6, 1950, reel 1, p. 40. Hamilton, Sentencing Presentation, p. 40. Gold admits to being "extremely puny at this time," but still greatly desirous of making his high school basketball or football team. Though this wish just resulted in him being "laughed at," he was once allowed to scrimmage with the fourth team and "on the very first play . . . received what amounted to a dislocated hip which put me in bed for almost two weeks. It was exceedingly painful." "Early Life," p. 27.

54. Ibid., pp. 27, 28, 34.

55. Ibid., p. 41.

56. Author's interview with Sam Dinerman, August 28, 2006.

57. Author's interview with Ted Krakow, February 27, 2009.

58. "The Circumstances Surrounding My Work as a Soviet Agent," pp. 1059–60.

59. "Early Life," p. 44.

60. Gold would look back on his fear of neighborhood bullies with some wonderment. He did "not understand" how as an adult he was able to "face very real physical danger without flinching, situations where others with far greater bone and muscle equipment than I possessed, trembled with fear." Ibid., p. 41.

61. "The Circumstances Surrounding My Work as a Soviet Agent," p. 1060.

62. "Early Life," p. 70.

63. Ibid., p. 44.

64. Ibid., p. 49.

65. "Scope of Soviet Activity in the United States," hearing before the Sub-committee to Investigate the Administration of the Internal Security Act and other Internal Security Laws of the Committee on the Judiciary United States Senate, Eighty-fourth Congress, second session, April, 26, 1956, p. 1065. Reprint of "The Circumstances Surrounding My Work as a Soviet Agent—A Report."

66. "Early Life," p. 74.

67. Hamilton, Sentencing Presentation, p. 10.

68. "Early Life," p. 63.

69. Ibid. p. 65. Even in his late teens, Gold seemed to have been excessively sheltered from street language and sexually explicit locker room talk. When trying out for the Penn cross-country team, Gold overheard a well-publicized running prodigy make some crude remarks about a coed he had spent time with the previous night. The combination of a star athlete using "filthy and crude" language about a young woman "almost made [Gold] ill." Ibid.

70. Ibid., p. 66.

71. Ibid., p. 50.

72. Jeffrey M. Schwartz, *Brain Lock* (New York: Regan Books, 1996), pp. xii–xviii. In fact, mental health professionals today would probably categorize Gold as suffering from a lesser form of the impairment. Obsessive-compulsive personality disorder (OCPD) is "far less disabling" and takes the form of "personality quirks or idiosyncrasies" rather than the more troubling characteristics of OCD. Ibid., p. xxiii.

73. "Early Life," pp. 50–51.

74. Ibid., p. 26.

75. Ibid., p. 52.

76. Ibid., p. 75.

77. Ibid., p. 31.

78. Gold must have been impressed with Frank Kessler, for he would appro-priate the name many years later and introduce himself as Kessler—as he did to Abe Brothman and Miriam Moskowitz—when working as a secret agent.

79. "Early Life," pp. 32–33.

80. There were other reasons for the growing separation, of which Gold listed his "espionage activity for the Soviet Union" and, "with the advent of Klaus Fuchs," his decision "to avoid . . . old chums . . . that they may not suffer the inevitable endless investigation, plus the disgrace of being known as my friends." Ibid., pp. 36–37.

81. Ibid., pp. 74–75.

82. Ibid., p. 31.

Chapter 2. A Debt Repaid

1. Transcripts from Soundscriber discs of interviews with Harry Gold by John D. M. Hamilton and Augustus S. Ballard at Holmesburg Prison, June 1, 1950, reel

1, p. 52. Legal Papers of Augustus S. Ballard, Special Collections, Paley Library, Temple University. (Hereafter cited as Soundscriber interviews.)

2. John D. M. Hamilton's Defense Presentation at the Sentencing of Harry Gold, December 7, 1950, p. 11. Legal Papers of Augustus Ballard, Special Collections, Paley Library, Temple University. (Hereafter cited as Hamilton, Sentencing Presentation.) The FBI interviewed the Philadelphia School District regarding Gold's academic record and was told by George J. Mentz that Gold "was a very good student," was a "member of the Latin Club and the Science Club," and "graduated in the upper ¼ of his class." FBI memo from SA Joseph E. Spivey to SAC re. Harry Gold, May 25, 1950, p. 1.

3. Soundscriber interviews, June 1, 1950, reel 1, p. 53.

4. "Now Employs 1100; Reorganized 1912 by Geo. Earle, Jr." *Philadelphia Inquirer,* February 16, 1936.

5. Hamilton, Sentencing Presentation, p. 14

6. Ibid., p. 54.

7. Soundscriber interviews, reel 1, p. 56.

8. Ibid.

9. FBI memo from SA Joseph E. Spivey to SAC, May 25, 1950. FBI files procured from the Diamond Law Library of Columbia University Law School disclose that Gold received "Good" to "Distinguished" grades for drafting, German, and English, but had difficulty in chemistry and math, requiring "second examinations," and received a "Passing" grade for both during his first term at Penn. He did considerably better his second term, earning "Distinguished" grades for his two English courses, German, and drafting, while getting passing grades in physical education and two math courses. He was forced to take a chemistry course examination a second time in order to earn a "Passing" grade. During his abbreviated second year at Penn he actually "failed" a physics course.

10. Harry Gold, "The Early Life of Harry Gold—A Report," October 23, 1950, p. 40. Legal Papers of Augustus S. Ballard, Special Collections, Paley Library, Temple University. (Hereafter cited as "Early Life.") Soundscriber interviews, June 1, 1950, reel 1, p. 61.

11. "Early Life," p. 22.

12. Soundscriber interviews, June 1, 1950, reel 2, p. 11. Also "Early Life," p. 28.

13. "Early Life," p. 27.

14. Soundscriber interviews, June 8, 1950, reel 2, p. 14.

15. Hamilton, Sentencing Presentation, p. 16.

16. Ibid.

17. Ibid., p. 17.

18. Ibid., p. 19.

19. "Early Life." p. 74.

20. Hamilton, Sentencing Presentation, p. 19.

21. "Early Life," p. 75.

22. "Scope of Soviet Activity in the United States," hearing before the Subcommittee to Investigate the Administration of the Internal Security Act and other Internal Security Laws of the Committee on the Judiciary United States Senate,

Eighty-fourth Congress, second session, April 26, 1956, p. 1060. Reprint of "The Circumstances Surrounding My Work as a Soviet Agent—A Report." This report was made at the request of Gold's attorneys while he was incarcerated in Holmesburg Prison.

23. Ibid.

24. Margaret B. Tinkcom, "Depression and War, 1929–1946," in *Philadelphia: A 300-Year History,* edited by Russell F. Weigley (New York: Norton, 1982), pp. 601–26.

25. Frederick M. Miller, Morris J. Vogel, and Allen F. Davis, *Philadelphia Stories* (Philadelphia: Temple University Press, 1988), p. 44.

26. "Scope of Soviet Activity in the United States," p. 1061, and "Early Life," p. 14.

27. Author's interview with Joseph Rovner, May 15, 2008. The Rovner family resided on Daly Street in the Jewish quarter of South Philadelphia. Joseph's father, a mechanic, was laid off shortly after purchasing a new 1931 Ford. Within a few months, he was unable to make the car payments and had to return the vehicle.

28. Miller, Vogel, and Davis, *Philadephia Stories,* p. 46.

29. Author's interview with Ted Krakow, February 27, 2009.

30. "Scope of Soviet Activity in the United States," p. 1061.

31. Robert Weinberg, *Stalin's Forgotten Zion* (Berkeley: University of California Press, 1998), p. 15.

32. Arno Lustiger, *Stalin and the Jews* (New York: Enigma Books, 2003), p. 60.

33. By the mid-1920s the Organization for Jewish Colonization in Russia had been organized. It initiated an "intense campaign around Birobidjan" and encouraged "American Jews to fulfill their duty toward realizing the future Jewish state." Melech Epstein, *The Jew and Communism: The Story of Early Communist Victories and Ultimate Defeats in the Jewish Community* (New York: Trade Union Sponsoring Committee, 1959), p. 169.

34. Author's interview with Aaron Libson, September, 25, 2006.

35. Author's interview with Doris Kaplan, January 30, 2006.

36. Ibid.

37. Epstein, *Jew and Communism,* p. 177.

38. Ibid., p. 179.

39. A Philadelphian by birth, Ferdinand Phillip Heller had graduated from Northeast High School in 1926 and from Penn State in 1930. After graduate work at the University of Virginia, he began working at the Pennsylvania Sugar Company in 1931. Heller described himself to the FBI as "pink politically," a reader of *New Masses,* the *New Republic,* and the *Daily Worker.* He said he considered the "Soviet Union a progressive country" and thought "there were many good things about the Soviet system," but "was never sympathetic enough to join" the Communist Party. Memorandum from SA Cornelius to Director and SACS June 17, 1950, pp. 1, 2.

40. Soundscriber interviews, June 23, 1950, reel 6, p. 38.

41. "Scope of Soviet Activity in the United States," p. 1061.

42. Rep. Francis E. Walter, "Harry Gold's Atom Spying Called 'Crime of the Century,'" *Philadelphia Inquirer,* March 3, 1958, and Bob Considine, "Meeting of

Fuchs, Gold Changed World History," *Philadelphia Inquirer,* fourth part in eleven-part series, December 1951.

43. "Scope of Soviet Activity in the United States," p. 1061.

44. Ibid., p. 1062.

45. According to Gold's testimony before a Senate Subcommittee in the mid-1950s, the first words out of Black's mouth on their initial meeting were, "You are a Socialist. Fred Heller has told me that. I am a Communist, and I am going to make a Communist out of you." Ibid., p. 1011.

46. Ibid., p. 1062.

47. Hamilton, Sentencing Presentation, p. 22.

48. "Scope of Soviet Activity in the United States," p. 1062.

49. Hamilton, Sentencing Presentation, p. 22.

50. Ibid.

51. When interviewed by FBI agents, Ernest Segressemann discussed the political debates his roommate, Tom Black, had with Harry Gold. It was clear to Segressemann that Gold was not taken with Black's pro-Soviet arguments; in fact, "Gold appeared to be anti-Communist." Memorandum from SA Reginald C. Vincent to SAC S. K. McKee, June 20, 1950, p. 3.

52. Ibid.

53. "Scope of Soviet Activity in the United States," p. 1012.

54. Ibid., p. 1062.

55. Those who attended these meetings reminded Gold of "Plodersacken," which he said was the Swiss term for "endless, boring talkers." Ibid.

56. Ibid., p. 1012.

57. Thomas L. Black and Eugene Lyons, "I Was a Red Spy," *New York Sunday Mirror,* June 10, 1956, p. 6.

58. Ibid., p. 5. Following his father's death, Black would legally file to change his first name in the Union County (Pa.) Common Pleas Court from Tasso Lessing Black to Thomas Lessing Black. Memorandum from SA Reginald C. Vincent to SAC S. K. McKee, June 20, 1950, p. 9.

59. Memorandum from SA Reginald C. Vincent to SAC S. K. McKee, June 12, 1956, p. 20.

60. Ibid., p. 23.

61. "Scope of Soviet Activity in the United States," p. 1062.

62. Ibid.

63. Gold initially thought Kane was a lawyer at the Wall Street firm of Fraser, Speir, Meyer and Kidder, but would subsequently learn that she was not. She was probably a paralegal or a member of the secretarial staff. Ibid., p. 1012

64. Hamilton, Sentencing Presentation, p. 23, and Soundscriber interviews, June 23, 1950, reel 6, p. 44.

65. Soundscriber interviews, June 23, 1950, reel 6, p. 44.

66. "Scope of Soviet Activity in the United States," p. 1063.

67. Ibid., p. 1063.

68. Ibid., p. 1077.

69. Gold's first-term course load included physical chemistry and two organic

chemistry courses. Though he generally received either As or Bs, he did earn two Cs during his first year at Drexel. Memorandum from Joseph E. Spivey to Special Agent Chief, May 25, 1950.

70. Soundscriber interviews, June 8, 1950, reel 2, p. 5.

71. "Scope of Soviet Activity in the United States," p. 1013. In his other accounts of this critical event, Gold has given the date as "November or December of '34 or possibly January or February of '35" or "very early in 1935." Similarly, Gold's prison treatise entitled "The Circumstances Surrounding My Work as a Soviet Agent" presents this meeting as occurring at Vera Kane's apartment in New York City, and Kane and Black informing Gold they had met an Amtorg official who was "desirous of obtaining" an array of "chemical processes," including "filter materials," "vitamin D concentrates from fish oils," "sulfonated oils," and other such products. The confusion may be due to Gold's recollection regarding a precise date for this discussion or more likely the progression of events from when Gold first started to comply with Black's request, when material started to be photocopied by the Amtorg office in New York City, and when he met his first Soviet handler, Paul Smith.

72. Soundscriber interviews, June 23, 1950, reel 6, p. 45.

73. Hamilton, Sentencing Presentation, p. 24.

74. Ibid.

75. Ibid., p. 25.

76. "Scope of Soviet Activity in the United States," p. 1065.

77. Ibid. Gold felt that combating anti-Semitism in America was "a pretty hopeless business." He believed that "once a person became an anti-Semite, he stayed that way." Educational venues preaching tolerance, plays, and the reading of books were already subscribed to by the tolerant, but had no attraction whatever for the intolerant. "The only possible approach," argued Gold, "to combat racial hatred in America, and which appeared at all reasonable, was a long-range program starting with the children, but unfortunately it was these same children's very parents who would incubate the virus of hatred." Ironically, Gold would point out, he who was so very troubled by anti-Semitism and wished to stamp it out had now by his own act of treason "done so much more to aid in its spread." Ibid.

78. Ibid., p. 1066.

79. Ibid., p. 1067.

80. Simon Sebag Montefiore, *Stalin: Court of the Red Tsar* (New York: Vintage, 2003).

81. "Scope of Soviet Activity in the United States," p. 1067.

82. Ibid., p. 1068.

83. Ibid.

84. All the chemicals came from either Pennsylvania Sugar or its subsidiaries, the alcohol distillery and the Franco-American Chemical Works at Carlstadt, near Rutherford, N.J. Ibid., p. 1064.

85. Soundscriber interviews, June 23, 1950, reel 6, p. 57. Also "Scope of Soviet Activity in the United States," p. 1068.

86. Soundscriber interviews, June 8, 1950, reel 2, p. 19. Also "Scope of Activity in the United States," p. 1015.

87. "Scope of Soviet Activity in the United States," p. 1015.

88. Ibid., p. 1068.

89. Ibid. There are numerous FBI documents describing Black "being pressured by his Soviet superiors to develop new contacts," such as "Thomas L. Black's Version of Gold's Introduction to Espionage," in file PH 65-4307, June 2, 1950, p. 4.

Chapter 3. The Novice Spy

1. "Scope of Soviet Activity in the United States," hearing before the Subcommittee to Investigate the Administration of the Internal Security Act and other Internal Security Laws of the Committee on the Judiciary, United States Senate, Eighty-fourth Congress, second session, April 26, 1956, p. 1016.

2. Ibid.

3. Transcripts from Soundscriber discs of interviews with Harry Gold by John D. M. Hamilton and Augustus S. Ballard at Holmesburg Prison, June 8, 1950, reel 2, p. 21. (Hereafter cited as Soundscriber interviews.)

4. Ibid., p. 1017.

5. Christopher Andrew and Vasili Mitrokhin, *The Sword and the Shield* (New York: Basic Books, 2001), p. 69.

6. Kim Philby, *My Silent War: The Autobiography of a Spy* (New York: Modern Library, 2002), p. xxviii. Philby, one of the most accomplished Soviet espionage agents, defines an agent as "a simple courier carrying messages between two points; it can mean the writer of such messages; it can imply advisory or even executive functions."

7. Gold, like many other progressive Jews around the world, was inspired by the Soviet Union's call for radical change. There are numerous accounts, such as Walter Krivitsky's *In Stalin's Secret Service*, that illuminate the idealistic vision the Soviet Union presented at the time. One of the "great illegals," Krivitsky was born Samuel Ginsberg and was "passionate" in his desire to oppose the "oppressiveness of the world." For him, the Bolshevik Revolution represented "an absolute solution to all the problems of poverty, inequality and injustice." Walter Krivitsky, *In Stalin's Secret Service* (New York: Enigma Books, 2000), pp. 243, 244.

8. Sidney Hook, *Out of Step* (New York: Harper and Row, 1987), p. 33.

9. Author's interview with Aaron Libson, September 25, 2006.

10. Author's interview with Francis Gabow, August 28, 2006.

11. Author's interview with Murray Friedman, May 15, 2006.

12. Ibid.

13. Hook, *Out of Step*, p. 135.

14. Steven T. Usdin, *Engineering Communism* (New Haven: Yale University Press, 2005), pp. 6–8.

15. Tim Tzouliadis, *The Forsaken* (New York: Penguin, 2008), p. 1.

16. Ibid., p. 5.

17. Usdin, *Engineering Communism*, p. 8.

18. The OGPU operated between 1923 and 1934 and was one of a series of So-

viet state security operations, running from the Cheka in 1917 to the KGB, which was formed in 1954.

19. Katherine A. S. Sibley, *Red Spies in America* (Lawrence: University Press of Kansas, 2004), pp. 31–32.

20. In order to thwart Western counterespionage measures and enhance deniability, the main responsibility for intelligence collection was shifted from "legal" to "illegal" residencies, which operated independently of Soviet diplomatic and trade missions. In many cases, it took years of "painstaking construction of legends to give the illegals false identities" to further their intelligence gathering efforts. Ibid., pp. 35, 42.

21. The English novelist Graham Greene was so taken with the talents and skills of spies like Kim Philby that he suggested Philby's autobiography, *My Silent War*, should be subtitled *The Spy as Craftsman*. Philby, *My Silent War*, p. xix.

22. Krivitsky, *In Stalin's*, p. 263.

23. Philby, *My Silent War*, p. 161.

24. Ibid., p. 148.

25. Sibley, *Red Spies*, p. 2. "In the first two months of 1941," according to Sibley, "roughly 8,500 espionage cases were initiated," and by the end of the year there would be "nearly 100,000" of them. FBI manpower would also swell. Between 1940 and 1945 the number of "agents mushroomed from nine hundred to almost five thousand."

26. Ibid., p. 35.

27. Thomas L. Black and Eugene Lyons, "I Was a Red Spy," *New York Mirror*, June 13, 1956, p. 1.

28. Ibid., p. 17.

29. Ibid., p. 18.

30. Ibid., p. 18.

31. "Scope of Soviet Activity in the United States," p. 1017.

32. Ibid., p. 1018.

33. Andrew Meier, *The Lost Spy* (New York: Norton, 2008), p. 123.

34. Soundscriber interviews, June 8, 1950, reel 2, p. 21.

35. Ibid., p. 22

36. David J. Dallin, *Soviet Espionage* (New Haven: Yale University Press, 1955), p. 21.

37. Soundscriber interviews, June 8, 1950, reel 2, p. 22.

38. Ibid., p. 23.

39. Ibid.

40. Krivitsky, *In Stalin's*, p. 246.

41. Dallin, *Soviet Espionage*, p. 10. In addition, agents were instructed to never "visit one another in their homes or make telephone calls from home," letters "should never be sent to members of a group" unless "cover addresses of sympathizers" were used, "written messages must be destroyed," and all "accumulating documents . . . constitute criminal acts."

42. Pennsylvania Station in Midtown Manhattan was the terminus of the Pennsylvania Railroad. The Reading Railroad terminated at Jersey City, where passen-

gers boarded a ferry to Lower Manhattan. Author's interview with John Tucker, November 13, 2007.

43. Soundscriber interviews, June 23, 1950, reel 6, p. 56.

44. John D. M. Hamilton's Defense Presentation at the Sentencing of Harry Gold, Philadelphia, December 7, 1950, p. 27. Legal Papers of Augustus S. Ballard, Special Collections, Paley Library, Temple University. (Hereafter cited as Hamilton, Sentencing Presentation.)

45. Soundscriber interviews, June 6, 1950, reel 2, p. 25.

46. Ibid., June 23, 1950, reel 6, p. 68.

47. Ibid., p. 66.

48. FBI Memo from SA Joseph Spivey to Special Agent Chief, May 25, 1950, pp. 6–7.

49. Ibid., p. 5.

50. Soundscriber interviews, June 1, 1950, reel 1, pp. 38–39.

51. Ibid., June 6, 1950, reel 2, pp. 20–21.

52. Ibid., p. 19. Zolinas, a "laboratory assistant" with "little formal education," fathered a very large family consisting of "somewhere around eleven or twelve children," and was always "in dire need of money." Gold would "pretty regularly" loan him money—"anywhere from $1 or $2 to $15 or $20." At Christmas, he'd bring "presents for the children . . . and cash for Charley." Celia Gold appreciated her son's desire to help the needy, but when the full scope of his generosity was examined it no doubt proved of considerable concern.

53. Ibid., August 9, 1950, reel 7, p. 41.

54. Rosenberg grand jury records, August 2, 1950, p. 9118.

55. Soundscriber interviews, June 23, 1950, reel 6, pp. 39–40.

56. Ibid., August 9, 1950, reel 7, p. 41.

Chapter 4. The Evolution of a Secret Agent

1. Transcripts from Soundscriber discs of interviews with Harry Gold by John D. M. Hamilton and Augustus S. Ballard at Holmesburg Prison, June 6, 1950, reel 3, p. 2. (Hereafter cited as Soundscriber interviews.)

2. Ibid., p. 3.

3. "Scope of Soviet Activity in the United States," hearing before the Subcommittee to Investigate the Administration of the Internal Security Act and other Internal Security Laws of the Committee on the Judiciary, United States Senate, Eighty-fourth Congress, second session, April 26, 1956, p. 1077.

4. Internal FBI Memo, Thomas L. Black's Version of Gold's Introduction to Espionage (PH 65-4307), p. 14.

5. Ibid., p. 17.

6. "Scope of Soviet Activity in the United States," p. 1019.

7. Internal FBI Memo, Thomas L. Black's Version of Gold's Introduction to Espionage (PH 65-4307), p. 18.

8. Soundscriber interviews, June 23, 1950, reel 6, pp. 67–68.

9. Ibid., June 8, 1950, reel 3, p. 1.

10. "Scope of Soviet Activity in the United States," p. 1074.

11. Soundscriber interviews, June 23, 1950, reel 6, p. 58.

12. Ibid., p. 59.

13. Ibid., p. 60.

14. Confession Statement by Harry Gold to Special Agents T. Scott Miller Jr. and Richard Brennan, May 22, 1950, p. 8.

15. Gold's own self-doubt about the importance of the work he was doing would be borrowed by his critics on the left and Rosenberg defenders to minimize his actual role and contributions. Miriam Moskowitz, for example, would years later refer to Gold as "just a courier, a messenger transporting lacquers and solvents. Nothing important." Author's interview with Miriam Moskowitz, July 22, 2008.

16. Confession Statement by Harry Gold, p. 8.

17. Soundscriber interviews, August 9, 1950, reel 7, p. 42

18. Confession Statement by Harry Gold, p. 8.

19. "Scope of Soviet Activity in the United States," p. 1074.

20. John Earl Haynes and Harvey Klehr, *Venona* (New Haven: Yale University Press, 1999), p. 287.

21. "Scope of Soviet Activity in the United States," p. 1074.

22. "Bricks Hurled in Sugar Strike," *Philadelphia Evening Bulletin,* March 4, 1937, p. 1.

23. "Workers Reverse Sit-Down Order," *Philadelphia Evening Bulletin,* March 5, 1937, p. 1.

24. "Refinery Picket Badly Beaten," *Philadelphia Evening Bulletin,* March 6, 1937, p. 1.

25. Harry Gold, "The Early Life of Harry Gold—A Report," October 23, 1950, p. 72. The Legal Papers of Augustus S. Ballard, Special Collections, Paley Library, Temple University. (Hereafter cited as "Early Life.")

26. FBI Memo from SA John A. Hebenstreit regarding Harry Gold, file 65-4307-83, May 26, 1950, p. 2.

27. "Early Life," p. 73.

28. Ibid., p. 1. There is no record of what Steve Schwartz, his Soviet handler, thought of Gold's actions, but one can speculate that he would have advised Gold to refrain from doing anything that would have drawn attention to himself. It is quite likely that Gold never told Schwartz of the refinery strike or his controversial decision to leave the plant and support the strikers.

29. FBI Memorandum from SA Joseph E. Spivey to SAC concerning Harry Gold. May 25, 1950 (65-4307-78), p. 5.

30. John D. M. Hamilton's Defense Presentation at the Sentencing of Harry Gold, Philadelphia, December 7, 1950, p. 29. Legal Papers of Augustus S. Ballard, Special Collections, Paley Library, Temple University. (Hereafter cited as Hamilton, Sentencing Presentation.)

31. "Scope of Soviet Activity in the United States," p. 1022.

32. Ibid., pp. 1022, 1023.

33. Soundscriber interviews, June 8, 1950, reel 3, p. 7.

34. FBI Memorandum from SA Richard Brennan and T. Scott Miller regarding Harry Gold's Confession, June 2, 1950 (65-4307), p. 18.

35. Simon Sebag Montefiore, *Stalin: The Court of the Red Tsar* (New York: Vintage, 2003), p. 44.

36. "Scope of Soviet Activity in the United States," p. 1020.

37. Soundscriber interviews, June 8, 1950, reel 3, p. 10.

38. Ibid.

39. Ibid. In addition, FBI documents such as "Harry Gold's Suggested Espionage Recruits," file PH 65-4307, June 4, 1950, pp. 12 and 13, disclose the names Joseph Schultz, Herbert Epstein, Daniel Kline, and Malcolm Schwartz as potential Soviet recruits. Gold discloses that Schultz and Schwartz "were names picked out of the telephone book." Epstein was "an absolutely fictitious individual" he made up, and Kline was someone who "graduated with his brother from high school," and who was only suggested "as a delaying action."

40. Soundscriber interviews, June 8, 1950, reel 3, p. 11.

41. Ibid., p. 12.

42. "Scope of Soviet Activity in the United States," p. 1020.

43. Soundscriber interviews, June 23, 1950, reel 6, p. 39.

44. "Scope of Soviet Activity in the United States," p. 1020.

45. Ibid.

46. Ibid.

47. Thomas L. Black and Eugene Lyons, "I Was a Red Spy," *New York Mirror,* June 11, 1956, p. 5.

48. Ibid.

49. Ibid.

50. Black would learn after his arrest that "Dr. Schwartz," aka "Robert," was actually Dr. Gregor Rabinovich, a physician. Ostensibly a Red Cross officer in New York, Rabinovich had actually "been sent to the United States at the height of the purge with the assignment of investigating Trotskyites and organizing the assassination of Leon Trotsky." David J. Dallin, *Soviet Espionage* (New Haven: Yale University Press, 1955), p. 407.

51. Black and Lyons, "I Was a Red Spy," June 11, 1956, p. 5.

52. Ibid.

53. Andrew Meier, *The Lost Spy* (New York: Norton, 2008), p. 236.

54. Special Report for the FBI on Harry Gold by Special Agents Robert G. Jensen and William B. Welte Jr., May 31, 1950, p. 27. (Hereafter Jensen and Welte, Special Report.)

55. Soundscriber interviews, June 6, 1950, reel 2, p. 14.

56. Ibid., p. 13.

57. Ibid., p. 22.

58. Ibid., June, 8, 1950, reel 3, p. 15.

59. Ibid.

60. Ibid., p. 16.

61. Ibid., June 23, 1950, reel 6, p. 71.

62. Ibid.
63. Ibid., August 9, 1950, reel 7, p. 3, and June 6, 1950, reel 2, p. 8.
64. Jensen and Welte, Special Report, p. 34.
65. Ibid., p. 24.
66. Ibid., p. 32.
67. Soundscriber interviews, August 9, 1950, reel 7, p. 2.
68. Ibid., p. 4.
69. Ibid., p. 5.

Chapter 5. Semenov, Slack, and Brothman

1. Gold's attorney, John Hamilton, described in his sentencing presentation how Jesuit faculty members took to Gold and how one instructor even "arranged for a regular period of calculus at six o'clock in the morning" so that Gold could overcome a "deficiency" in that area of study. John D. M. Hamilton's Defense Presentation at the Sentencing of Harry Gold, Philadelphia, December 7, 1950, p. 30. Legal Papers of Augustus S. Ballard, Special Collections, Paley Library, Temple University. (Hereafter cited as Hamilton, Sentencing Presentation.)

2. Transcripts from Soundscriber discs of interviews with Harry Gold by John D. M. Hamilton and Augustus S. Ballard at Holmesburg Prison, June 6, 1950, reel 2, pp. 9, 10. (Hereafter cited as Soundscriber interviews.)

3. "Scope of Soviet Activity in the United States," hearing before the Subcommittee to Investigate the Administration of the Internal Security Act and other Internal Security Laws of the Committee of the Judiciary United States Senate, Eighty-fourth Congress, second session, April 26, 1656, p. 1070.

4. Soundscriber interviews, June 8, 1950, reel 2, p. 12.

5. Gold was always on thin ice financially, especially so during the Depression. In just the two years prior to departing for Xavier, he took out "about ten loans from the Corn Exchange Bank in Philadelphia." He even applied for some of these bank loans using the 1037 North Delaware Ave. address of the Pennsylvania Sugar Company, so as "to keep knowledge of these loans from my family." Ibid., June 8, 1950, reel 2, p. 15.

6. Ibid., reel 7, p. 7.

7. Ibid., p. 16.

8. According to John Hamilton, "the Fathers and instructors" at Xavier took an immediate liking to Gold. They were "sympathetic with a man who had struggled as Gold had for an education." "At Xavier," according to Hamilton, "Gold could work to his heart's content with men rooted in the sciences who like himself knew no hours and who gave him encouragement at every step of the way." Hamilton, Sentencing Presentation, p. 30.

9. Soundscriber interviews, June 8, 1950, reel 3, p. 18.

10. Ibid., pp. 19–20.

11. Ibid., p. 21.

12. Ibid., pp. 21–22.

13. "Harry Gold's Version of His American Contacts," from Harry Gold, Con-

fession Statement to FBI Agents T. Scott Miller Jr. and Richard Brennan, June 2, 1950 (PH 65-4307), p. 5.

14. Soundscriber interviews, June 8, 1950, reel 3, pp. 24–26.

15. Ibid., p. 23.

16. Ibid., pp. 26–27.

17. Ibid.

18. Hamilton, Sentencing Presentation, p. 33.

19. Soundscriber interviews, August 9, 1950, reel 7, p. 45.

20. Many years later Gold and Tom Black would make a "great joke of this" bitter change of Soviet plans, "but at the time that it happened it did not seem so funny." Ibid., p. 9.

21. Ibid., pp. 16–17.

22. Ibid., p. 12.

23. "Scope of Soviet Activity in the United States," p. 1074.

24. Hamilton, Sentencing Presentation, p. 34.

25. Ibid., p. 36.

26. Soundscriber interviews, June 8, 1950, reel 3, pp. 31–32.

27. Gold was pleased not only with his academic success at Xavier but also with his recognition as a summa cum laude graduate. He knew his "scholastic average merited it," but his Drexel experience left him with expectations of "discrimination." Individuals he had tutored at Drexel received "honors," while he, equally deserving, did not. "Scope of Soviet Activity in the United States," p. 1070.

28. Soundscriber interviews, June 8, 1950, reel 3, pp. 32–33.

29. Internal FBI Memo from SAC, New York to Director, FBI, regarding UNSUB—SAM, May 31, 1950, p. 1.

30. Soundscriber interviews, June 8, 1950, reel 3, p. 35.

31. "Edward Klein" was a "high school friend" of Joe Gold and was actually "employed at the Navy Yard." Ibid., p. 36.

32. Ibid.

33. Ibid., p. 64.

34. Ibid., pp. 64–65.

35. Ibid., p. 65.

36. "Scope of Soviet Activity in the United States," p. 1046.

37. Ibid., p. 1072.

38. Ibid.

39. Soundscriber interviews, June 8, 1950, reel 3, p. 69.

40. Transcript of Proceedings, *United States of America v. Alfred Dean Slack,* United States District Court, Greenville, Tennessee, Criminal No. 5593, p. 2. (Hereafter cited as Transcript of Slack Proceedings.)

41. Ibid., p. 3.

42. In a show of sympathy and appreciation for his past service, the Soviets gave Slack "$300 to help defray the funeral expenses of Briggs." Ibid.

43. Soundscriber interviews, June 8, 1950, reel 3, p. 72.

44. FBI Memo from SAC, Philadelphia to Director, FBI, concerning Harry Gold's Confession Statement of May 22, 1950, p. 2.

45. Soundscriber interviews, June 8, 1950, reel 3, pp. 73–74.

46. "Scope of Soviet Activity in the United States," p. 1076.

47. Soundscriber interviews, June 8, 1950, reel 3, pp. 78–79.

48. Transcript of Slack Proceedings, p. 4. Most likely Sam adopted the name "Robert" when dealing with Slack.

49. Soundscriber interviews, June 8, 1950, reel 3, p. 80.

50. After his arrest, Slack had apparently communicated to authorities that he had developed reservations about his work for the Soviets and hoped his transfer would end his dealings with Gold and the Soviets. At his trial, prosecutors described "the mysterious telephone call" Slack received at his "Cincinnati apartment." The call, from Gold, was described as "the tentacles of the Russian espionage system . . . again reaching out for him." Transcript of Slack Proceedings, p. 7.

51. Kathryn S. Olmstead, *Red Spy Queen* (Chapel Hill: University of North Carolina Press, 2002), p. 36.

52. Lauren Kessler, *Clever Girl* (New York: HarperCollins, 2003), p. 80.

53. Author's interviews with Miriam Moskowitz, February 5, 2007, and June 25, 2008. Moskowitz said Brothman was frustrated by Bentley's lack of scientific sophistication and her inability to "understand blueprints." He said it was "an agonizing thing for her." She just "couldn't comprehend" what he was talking about and supplying her with. In addition, Brothman said, "Bentley wanted to go to a hotel with him." There were occasional "sexual overtures."

54. Elizabeth Bentley informed the FBI that she had told Abe Brothman at "Paddy's Clam House on West 34th Street" that he would be receiving a new courier for his material. In her discussions with the FBI, Bentley speculated that "the Brothman material was sufficiently important" to "Red Army Intelligence" and that his new contact would probably "be connected with Red Army Intelligence." FBI Report on Harry Gold by SA Joseph C. Walsh Jr., New York, May 29, 1950, p. 22.

55. Miriam Moskowitz, unpublished manuscript entitled "Phantoms of Spies Run Amok and an Odyssey of Survival in the Cold War" (May 2003). A copy of the manuscript is in the Special Collections of the Diamond Law Library at Columbia University Law School.

56. Moskowitz, "Phantoms," p. 243, and Soundscriber interviews, June 8, 1950, reel 3, p. 50.

57. In the late 1920s and early 1930s Brothman won a range of honors, including the Harkness Scholarship Award, Phi Beta Kappa, Tau Beta Pi, the Whitehead Award for General Excellence, the Elseberg Award for Proficiency in Physics, the Dupont Award for Highest Ranking Scholar in the School of Engineering, and the Mathematics Colloquium Award. FBI Report on Abraham Brothman by SA John R. Murphy Jr., June 30, 1950.

58. FBI Memo, SA John R. Murphy Jr., Brothman Investigation, June 23, 1950, p. 1. Legal Papers of Augustus S. Ballard, Special Collections, Paley Library, Temple University

59. Ibid.

60. Soundscriber interviews, June 8, 1950, reel 3, p. 41.

61. Ibid., p. 39.

62. Ibid., p. 52.

63. "Scope of Soviet Activity in the United States," pp. 1056–57.

64. Soundscriber interviews, June 8, 1950, reel 3, pp. 50–51.

65. Harry Gold's handwritten court statement, July 20, 1950, p. 8. Legal Papers of Augustus S. Ballard, Special Collections, Paley Library, Temple University.

66. "Scope of Soviet Activity in the United States," pp. 1074–75.

67. Ibid.

68. Ibid.

69. Ibid., p. 1074.

70. Ibid., p. 1046.

Chapter 6. Dr. Klaus Fuchs

1. John Earl Haynes, Harvey Klehr, and Alexander Vassiliev, *Spies* (New Haven: Yale University Press, 2009), p. 393.

2. Ibid., p. 394.

3. Transcript of Proceedings, *United States of America v. Alfred Dean Slack,* United States District Court, Greenville, Tennessee, Criminal No. 5593, September 18, 1950, p. 7. (Hereafter cited as Transcript of Slack Proceedings.)

4. Soundscriber interviews, June 14, 1950, reel 4, p. 2.

5. Ibid.

6. Transcript of Slack Proceedings, p. 8.

7. Soundscriber interviews, June 14, 1950, reel 4, p. 3.

8. Ibid., p. 4.

9. Gold would receive a "very warm and friendly letter" from Slack sometime later. At the time of Slack's arrest in 1950, Gold would learn that Julie—who had "just about given up hope" she would ever bear children, due to "an obstruction in her cervix"—had "given birth to two children." Gold said he was "very much saddened" to think "these two youngsters will forever be tainted with an ineradicable stigma." "Scope of Soviet Activity in the United States," hearing before the Subcommittee to Investigate the Administration of the Internal Security Act and other Internal Security Laws of the Committee on the Judiciary United States Senate, Eighty-fourth Congress, second session, April 26, 1956, p. 1076.

10. Soundscriber interviews, June 14, 1950, reel 4, p. 5.

11. "Information Relative to Soviet Espionage Operations as Known to Harry Gold," forty-five-page document on Gold's recollection of the tradecraft maintained in the Legal Papers of Augustus S. Ballard, Special Collections, Paley Library, Temple University. (Hereafter cited as "Soviet Espionage Operations.")

12. Ibid.

13. FBI Report by Francis Zangle on Thomas L. Black, January 17, 1951, New York, file 65-5338, p. 4.

14. Ibid.

15. Soundscriber interviews, June 6, 1950, reel 2, p. 1.

16. FBI Report by Robert G. Jensen on Harry Gold, Philadelphia, May 31, 1950, p. 50.

17. If FBI documents are accurate, it would seem Pennsylvania Sugar Company and Celia Gold filed applications for a military deferment for Gold within days of each other and just a few short days before the Japanese attack on Pearl Harbor. Though the fact that all three events occurred in the first week of December 1941 is most curious, there is nothing more to show than it was anything other than coincidence.

18. FBI Report by Robert G. Jensen on Harry Gold, Philadelphia, May 31, 1950, p. 50.

19. Ibid., p. 51.

20. Ibid., p. 2.

21. It is also possible that Gold's scientific training would have caught the eye of military officials and he could have been assigned to an installation like Edgewood Arsenal, where the U.S. Army's Chemical Corps was based.

22. One individual who knew Gold during the 1940s said he was "always looking at his watch . . . constantly moving according to some schedule he was following." Author's interview with Miriam Moskowitz, June 18, 2008.

23. "Scope of Soviet Activity in the United States," p. 1072.

24. FBI Memorandum from A. H. Belmont to Mr. Ladd, May 24, 1950.

25. "Scope of Soviet Activity in the United States," p. 1072.

26. Vassiliev Papers, Black Notebook, KGB file 40159, pp. 111, 255. The Vassiliev documents can be researched at the Manuscript Division of the Library of Congress and on the Web.

27. "Scope of Soviet Activity in the United States," p. 1075. In retrospect, Gold thought there might have been an additional reason for the award. He gradually came to believe that the "staged presentation of the Order of the Red Star" was "to prepare me for the coming Fuchs affair."

28. Soundscriber interviews, August 9, 1950, reel 7, p. 21.

29. Allen Weinstein and Alexander Vassiliev, *The Haunted Wood* (New York: Random House, 1999), pp. 176–77.

30. Soundscriber interviews, June 14, 1950, reel 4, p. 7.

31. "Scope of Soviet Activity in the United States," p. 1024.

32. Ibid., p. 1025.

33. Ibid.

34. Soundscriber interviews, June 14, 1950, reel 4, p. 9.

35. Haynes, Klehr, and Vassiliev, *Spies,* p. 95. The exact wording of the verbal recognition signal is in some dispute. Norman Moss, one of Klaus Fuchs's biographers, believes Gold inquired, "Can you tell me the way to Grand Central Station?"

36. "Scope of Soviet Activity in the United States," pp. 1025–26.

37. Soundscriber interviews, June 14, 1950, reel 4, p. 10.

38. Admission Statement of Emil Julius Klaus Fuchs to FBI Agents Hugh H. Clegg and Robert J. Lamphere at Wormwood Scrubs Prison, May 26, 1950, p. 44. (Hereafter cited as Fuchs, Statement.)

39. "Scope of Soviet Activity in the United States," p. 1026.

40. Harry Gold, Confession Statement to FBI Agents T. Scott Miller Jr. and Richard Brennan, May 22, 1950, p. 3. (Hereafter cited as Gold, Confession Statement.)

41. Soundscriber interviews, June 14, 1950, reel 4, pp. 11–13.

42. Harry Gold, Report on his initial meeting with Fuchs, February 5, 1944. Vassiliev Papers, Yellow #1, pp. 68–69.

43. Gold, Confession Statement, p. 18.

44. Ibid., p. 17.

45. Ibid.

46. "Scope of Soviet Activity in the United States," p. 1081.

47. Though they sound somewhat similar, gaseous diffusion is a process different from thermal diffusion. Gaseous diffusion was used at Oak Ridge, Tenn., while thermal diffusion would be used at the Hanford Plant at Washington State. Though the FBI would eventually find papers of Gold's on thermal diffusion, they were his own work. Neither Fuchs nor Greenglass had worked on the process. Soundscriber interviews, June 23, 1950, reel 6, p. 28.

48. Norman Moss, *Klaus Fuchs: The Man Who Stole the Atom Bomb* (London: Grafton Books, 1987), p. 53.

49. "Scope of Soviet Activity in the United States," pp. 1027–28.

50. After his initial meeting with Fuchs on February 5, 1944, Gold filed this report: "The following developed about K. [Klaus]: He obviously has worked with our people before and he is fully aware of what he is doing. . . . He is a mathematical physicist . . . most likely a very brilliant man to have such a position at his age (he looks about 30). We took a long walk after dinner and he explained the 'factory' [code name for Enormoz used between Gold and Fuchs] setup. He is a member of the British mission to the U.S. working under the direct control of the U.S. Army. . . . The work involves mainly separating the isotopes of 'factory' and is being done thusly: The electronic method has been developed at Berkley, California, and is being carried out at a place known only as 'Camp Y'—K. believes it is in New Mexico. . . . Simultaneously, the diffusion method is being tried here in the East. . . . Should the diffusion method prove successful, it will be used as a preliminary step in the separation, with the final work being done by the electronic method. They hope to have the electronic method ready early in 1945 and the diffusion method in July 1945, but K. says the latter estimate is optimistic. All production will be done in the U.S.; only preparatory work is being carried on in England. K. says that the work is being done in 'watertight' compartments, but that he will furnish us with everything in his and [Rudolf] Peierls's divisions and as much of the other as possible; Peierls is K.s superior, but they have divided the work between them. The two countries had worked together before 1940, and then there was a lapse until 1942. Even Niels Bohr, who is now in the country incognito as Nicholas Baker, has not been told everything. We made careful arrangements for meeting in two weeks, when K. will have information for us." Weinstein and Vassiliev, *Haunted Wood*, p. 187.

51. In 1943 Gold was transferred to Pennsylvania Alcohol and Chemical laboratory, a subsidiary of the Pennsylvania Sugar Company. In conjunction with that

move, he began taking courses in "fermentation, distillation, and glass blowing" at St. Joseph's. The choice of a Jesuit college is not surprising, considering Gold's fond memories of Xavier. FBI Report on Harry Gold by SA Robert G. Jensen, file 65-4307, June 7, 1950, pp. 5, 10. (Hereafter cited as Jensen, Report.)

52. "Scope of Soviet Activity in the United States," p. 1028.

53. Moss, *Klaus Fuchs*, p. 2.

54. After many bouts of depression, she one day in October 1931 took her own life by swallowing hydrochloric acid. Ibid., p. 6.

55. Robert Chadwell Williams, *Klaus Fuchs: Atom Spy* (Cambridge, Mass.: Harvard University Press, 1987), p. 21.

56. Moss, *Klaus Fuchs*, p. 10.

57. It is believed that in order to deflect any investigations of the Gunns for their political beliefs and Communist sympathies, Fuchs identified them as practicing Quakers. This tendency to protect fellow Communist activists would become most prominent at his arrest for espionage and his reluctance to name Harry Gold as "Raymond." Ibid., p. 12.

58. After receiving his doctorate from Bristol, Fuchs would have been expected to acquire a college teaching post, but his mentor at the time thought him "too uncommunicative to be a good teacher" and recommended him to Born. Ibid., p. 19.

59. Ibid., p. 21.

60. Williams, *Klaus Fuchs*, p. 30.

61. Ibid., p. 33.

62. Ibid., p. 35.

63. Ibid., p. 38.

64. Ibid., p. 42.

65. The GRU was the overseas intelligence branch of the Soviet Army.

66. Weinstein and Vassiliev, *Haunted Wood*, p. 189.

67. FBI Report on Harry Gold, by SA Robert G. Jensen, May 31, 1950, p. 83.

68. "Soviet Espionage Operations," p. 31.

69. "Scope of Soviet Activity in the United States," p. 1074.

70. In actuality, Semyon Semenov did not leave for Russia immediately. Unbeknownst to Gold, he remained in the country. He had planned to surprise Gold with another meeting prior to his actual departure, but Gold never made the meeting. He had been scheduled to meet John in New York sometime in July 1944, but his mother was "terribly disturbed" that she had not heard from her other son, who was stationed on various islands in the South Pacific. When Gold notified her that he would not be home until "late that evening she seemed so depressed that [he] decided not to go to New York at all." When Gold and John next met, Gold was informed, "it was pity" he couldn't make the last meeting, as Semenov had surprisingly stopped by the Ferris Wheel Bar "to say goodbye to [him] in person." John informed Gold that Sam "had waited for three hours" for Gold to show. In 1945, however, John brought "greetings" from Sam on two occasions, the "messages worded so that they were indubitably from [his] friend." Soundscriber interviews, June 14, 1950, reel 4, p. 21.

71. Ibid., pp. 18–19, and "Scope of Soviet Activity in the United States," pp. 1026–27.

72. Jensen, Report, p. 16.

73. Moss, *Klaus Fuchs*, p. 54.

74. Ibid., pp. 32–34.

75. Ibid., p. 55.

76. Ibid.

77. Fuchs, along with others of the British Mission, had arrived on American shores at Newport News, Virginia, and immediately traveled to New York City. He and others initially stayed at the Taft Hotel near Times Square, but then moved to a more upscale residence at the Barbizon Plaza overlooking Central Park. Two months later, "he rented a furnished apartment at 128 West 77th Street, in a four-story converted brownstone house." Ibid., p. 50.

78. "Unfortunately," according to Gold, he never disposed of the book. Although he "completely scratched out the address," the FBI gained control of the book when it eventually searched his house in Philadelphia. Soundscriber interviews, June 14, 1950, reel 4, p. 30.

79. Jensen, Report, p. 17, and Soundscriber interviews, June 14, 1950, reel 4, p. 30.

80. Ibid.

Chapter 7. The Los Alamos Papers

1. Transcripts from Soundscriber discs of interviews with Harry Gold by John D. M. Hamilton and Augustus S. Ballard at Holmesburg Prison, June 14, 1950, reel 4, p. 37. (Hereafter cited as Soundscriber interviews.)

2. Gold didn't know the individual whose name he thought was "Jerome Kaplun" and was never sure he "ever called the number." FBI Report on Harry Gold by SA Robert G. Jensen, file 65-4307, June 7, 1950, p. 18. (Hereafter cited as Jensen, Report.)

3. The Gold family had left South Philadelphia in 1938 when it moved to another rented house at 5032 Boudinot Street in the Feltonville section of the city just off of Roosevelt Boulevard. In 1944, the Gold family bought its first home at 6823 Kindred Street in the Oxford Circle section of Northeast Philadelphia. Although vast stretches of this section of the city were farmland, the postwar period would witness a tremendous construction and population shift to this relatively unused portion of Philadelphia. The Oxford Circle neighborhood that encompassed portions of the fifty-third and fifty-fourth wards would develop a very strong Jewish, middle-class flavor, particularly so the streets between Bustleton Avenue and Castor Avenue, where the Golds resided.

4. Richard Rhodes, *Dark Sun: The Making of the Hydrogen Bomb* (New York: Simon and Shuster, 1995), p. 120.

5. Soundscriber interviews, June 14, 1950, reel 4, p. 39.

6. Jensen, Report, p. 19.

7. Robert Chadwell Williams, *Klaus Fuchs: Atom Spy* (Cambridge, Mass.: Harvard University Press), 1987, p. 78.

8. Soundscriber interviews, June 14, 1950, reel 4, p. 41.

9. Fuchs was not alone in his pessimism. The winter of 1944–45 saw morale

plummet at Los Alamos. Scientists had not achieved a viable bomb design for plutonium and no deliveries of either plutonium or uranium-235 had yet arrived from Hanford or Oak Ridge. The lack of progress did not contribute to an upbeat or optimistic mood at the New Mexico site.

10. Soundscriber Interviews, June 14, 1950, Reel 4, p. 42.

11. Kai Bird and Martin J. Sherwin, *American Prometheus* (New York: Vintage, 2005), p. 206.

12. Ibid., p. 215.

13. Ibid., p. 208.

14. Williams, *Klaus Fuchs,* p. 76.

15. Ibid.

16. Norman Moss, *Klaus Fuchs: The Man Who Stole the Atom Bomb* (London: Grafton Books, 1987, p. 58.

17. Ibid, pp. 58–59.

18. Alexander Feklisov and Sergei Kostin, *The Man Behind the Rosenbergs* (New York: Enigma Books, 2001), p. 152.

19. Soundscriber interviews, June 14, 1950, reel 4, p. 44.

20. Defense Statement by John D. M. Hamilton at the Sentencing of Harry Gold, U.S. Federal Court, Philadelphia, December 7, 1950, p. 35. Legal Papers of Augustus S. Ballard, Special Collections, Paley Library, Temple University. (Hereafter cited as Hamilton, Sentencing Presentation.)

21. Soundscriber interviews, June 14, 1950, reel 4, p. 44.

22. Ibid., p. 47.

23. "Scope of Soviet Activity in the United States," hearing before the Subcommittee to Investigate the Administration of the Internal Security Act and other Internal Security Laws of the Committee on the Judiciary United States Senate, Eighty-fourth Congress, second session, April 26, 1956, p. 1032.

24. Soundscriber interviews, June 14, 1950, reel 5, pp. 34–36.

25. Feklisov and Kostin, *Man Behind,* p. 317.

26. Soundscriber interviews, June 14, 1950, reel 4, pp. 48–49.

27. Letter from Robert J. Lamphere to Pat Lynch of ACR "Close-Up," December 9, 1981. Special Collections, Georgetown University Library. (Hereafter cited as Lamphere, Letter.)

28. Williams, *Klaus Fuchs,* p. 79.

29. Soundscriber interviews, June 14, 1950, reel 4, pp. 55–56.

30. Ibid., pp. 52–53.

31. "Scope of Soviet Activity in the United States," p. 1034.

32. Ibid.

33. Soundscriber interviews, June 14, 1950, reel 5, p. 40.

34. In addition to the recognition statement, Gold had difficulty recollecting the name he used to identify himself. He told the federal prosecutor he may have given the name Dave. Statement of Harry Gold to United States Attorney, Southern District of New York, August 1, 1950, p. 11. Statement made to Myles J. Lane, chief assistant U.S. attorney, and Special Agents William F. Norton and John A. Harrington.

35. Gold did not use his real name. When meeting with his lawyers in Holmesburg Prison, he said he could have "possibly used Raymond Frank or possibly Frank Martin." Soundscriber interviews, June 14, 1950, reel 5, p. 40. The Jell-O boxtop is described in "Scope of Soviet Activity in the United States," p. 1035.

36. Sam Roberts, *The Brother: The Untold Story of Atomic Spy David Greenglass and How He Sent His Sister, Ethel Rosenberg, to the Electric Chair* (New York: Random House, 2001), p. 130.

37. Soundscriber interviews, June 14, 1950, reel, 5, pp. 39–40.

38. Before leaving that morning, Gold would be given a piece of paper that had the name and phone number of a Greenglass relative in New York City that he could use if he needed to be in contact with Greenglass during his coming "furlough about Christmas of 1945." When questioned by his attorneys in June 1950, Gold could no longer remember the name or phone number he had been given. Ibid., pp. 40–41.

39. Julius Rosenberg had told David he should provide him with a "list of all the people on the project who seemed susceptible to giving information to the Russians." Though Harry would admonish David for this perceived amateurish indiscretion, it was really Julius who had encouraged it. Statement of David Greenglass to United States Attorney, Southern District of New York, August 1, 1950, p. 70.

40. "Scope of Soviet Activity in the United States," p. 1035.

41. Ronald Radosh and Joyce Milton, *The Rosenberg File* (New York: Holt, Rinehart and Winston), 1983, pp. 49–50.

42. Ibid.

43. Ibid., p. 51.

44. Author's interview with Miriam Moskowitz, June 25, 2008.

45. Rhodes, *Dark Sun*, p. 134.

46. Radosh and Milton, *Rosenberg File*, pp. 52–53.

47. Ibid., p. 56. It should also be pointed out that more current revelations in the Vassiliev Papers suggest that Julius Rosenberg may have been a Soviet operative several years earlier, beginning in late 1941 and certainly by 1942. John Earl Haynes, Harvey Klehr, and Alexander Vassiliev, *Spies* (New Haven: Yale University Press, 2009), pp. 334–35.

48. Haynes, Klehr, and Vassiliev, *Spies*, p. 59.

49. Rhodes, *Dark Sun*, p. 137.

50. Feklisov and Kostin, *Man Behind*, p. 152.

51. Ibid.

52. Ibid., p. 153.

53. Roberts, *The Brother*, p. 83.

54. Ibid., p. 84.

55. Statement of David Greenglass to United States Attorney, Southern District of New York, August 1, 1950, p. 65. A close reading of the Vassiliev Papers, however, paints a slightly different picture of the Greenglasses' decision to assist Soviet espionage efforts. David and Ruth were said to be quite excited to mine information at Los Alamos for the Soviet Union. This information, of course, was passed along to the Soviets by their brother-in-law Julius Rosenberg, whose devotion to the Soviet Union is a matter of record.

56. Ibid., p. 68.

57. Ibid., p. 67.

58. Ibid., p. 71.

59. Roberts, *The Brother,* p. 123.

60. Greenglass would subsequently admit that he wrote "about lens molds in much detail, about the growth of the project," as well as providing "a pretty substantial list of names of both possible recruits and of scientists who worked there," including "Kistakowsky and Bohr." Statement of David Greenglass to United States Attorney, Southern District of New York, August 1, 1950, p. 73.

61. Soundscriber interviews, June 14, 1950, reel 5, p. 41.

62. Gold's subsequent report to his KGB superiors would include the following item concerning the Greenglasses: "By the time it was 8 o'clock and they had left for the whole evening—he came home for the weekend. Therefore, so as not to seem too anxious, and b/c it was already too late to leave 'S.' [Sernovodsk/Albuquerque]. I came back the next morning. I identified myself, and they gave me a very warm welcome. 'D' [David Greenglass] asked me to come back in the half of the day, b/c he had very important material for me. He said that they had not been expecting me for another two weeks, but that he would get the material ready in a few hours, as was understood. I left them a considerable sum of money, which they were both happy to receive. . . . I met with 'D' in the afternoon, received the materials from him." Arno's (Gold's) Report on visits to Wasp (Ruth) and Calibre (David Greenglass) on June 2 and 3, 1945. Haynes, Klehr, and Vassiliev, *Spies,* p. 108.

63. "Scope of Soviet Activity in the United States," p. 1036.

64. Rhodes, *Dark Sun,* p. 132.

65. "Scope of Soviet Activity in the United States," p. 1037.

66. Soundscriber interviews, June 14, 1950, reel 5, p. 43.

67. When interviewed on June 27, 1950, by the FBI, Black said that Gold had called him from Albuquerque, New Mexico, not Chicago. And the request for funds had come prior to, not after, the dropping of the bombs on Hiroshima and Nagasaki. FBI Report on Thomas Lessing Black, July 7, 1950, file 65-59181, p. 7.

68. Lamphere, Letter.

69. Soundscriber interviews, June 14, 1950, reel 4, p. 58.

70. Richard Rhodes believes the party was a "formal British Mission" event that could have only been known to someone who was there at the time, like Gold. Such a recollection, he argues, "is significant confirmation of [Gold's] veracity." Rhodes, *Dark Sun,* p. 190.

71. Ibid., p. 190.

72. Soundscriber interviews, June 14, 1950, reel 4, p. 65.

73. Ibid., p. 60.

74. To the best of Gold's recollection, the suggested station had the words "Paddington" and "Crescent" in it. Paddington Station is one of London's busier transit stops and can be reached on the Highsmith and City Line, the Bakerloo Line, and the Circle Line. Mornington Crescent, the more likely candidate for this rendezvous, is a less trafficked station on the Northern Line. Ibid., p. 64.

75. Ibid., p. 63.

76. "Scope of Soviet Activity in the United States," p. 1077.

77. Ibid., p. 1038.

78. Soundscriber interviews, June 14, 1950, reel 4, p. 71.

79. Gold was never clear on Kristel Heinemann's knowledge of her brother's activities or her allegiance to the Soviet Union. Although he knew Klaus and Kristel to be "very, very close," and her unusual willingness to "welcome into her home a total stranger . . . at rather odd hours, leaving him notes," there was no firm proof she was a conspirator. Gold had little doubt she was "sympathetic to Communist ideas," but most of this was due to Klaus and Kristel's exceedingly close relationship.

80. Gold's written account of his meeting with Charles [Fuchs] included the following: "For the first time since I have known him Charles [Fuchs] was late—by fifteen minutes. But he did come along in a car and picked me up. We drove out into the mountains beyond S.F. [Santa Fe] and he explained the reason for his tardiness by telling that he had great difficulty in breaking away from his friends at Zapovednik [Los Alamos]. He said, further, that we had made an error by choosing to meet in the evening in SF [Santa Fe] and that it would have been better to have come together in the afternoon when everyone was busy shopping. In fact, Charles said, it was very bad for me to come to SF in any case but that we would not have foreseen this since the last meeting. He was very nervous (the first time I have seen him so), and I was inwardly not too calm myself. His first remark had been, 'Well, were you impressed?' I answered that I was even more than impressed, and in fact was even somehow horrified. Charles said that the test shot had far exceeded expectations but that these had been purposely toned down because the results of the calculations showed them to be so incredible. Charles was present at the test shot, some 20 miles away.

"As regards the future, Charles says that a research institute will be established in 'Ostrov' [Britain], but he will most likely be here till at least the beginning of the year. He agreed, however, that it was a good idea for making an arrangement for meeting in Ostrov. The city is London; the place Mornton Crescent, along the Crescent; the date is the first Saturday of the month after which Charles returns, and so on the first Saturday of the month thereafter; the time 8 o'clock in the evening; Charles is to carry a copy of *Life* Magazine, our man is to carry three books tied together with a stout twine and held by a finger; Charles's remark is: 'Can you tell me the way to Harvard Square?' (Charles is to speak first), our man's remark is 'Yes, but excuse me a minute—I have an awful cold (and our man is to blow his nose into a handkerchief). Charles gave me the material, which is excellent and fully covers everything. He dropped me off in the outskirts of SF. The next meeting will be in the city of Charles's sister, probably in November or December. I am happy to keep in touch with her so as to be advised when. After a few bad moments of waiting for the bus, I left SF with no mishap." Haynes, Klehr, and Vassiliev, *Spies*, p. 103.

81. Soundscriber interviews, June 14, 1950, reel 4, p. 72.

82. Gold admitted his attitude toward these missions with Fuchs was "somewhat fatalistic." Though he knew he could "carry on a deception to a certain extent" and a pattern of "continuous lying" for some time, he seemed to understand that it

was "impossible" that it could go on forever. One day his luck would run out, and he would be "apprehended." At that point, he "would try to destroy what information" he had in his possession and "would not try to implicate anyone," but merely own up to what he had done. Ibid., p. 73.

83. Ibid., pp. 73–74.

84. Though Gold was known as an "easy touch" and loaned money to those in need on a regular basis (in most cases never to have it returned), there were also occasions when he was forced to ask for a loan. Friends and co-workers would be hit up for anywhere between a few bucks to fifty dollars, while there were occasions— such as before one of his Los Alamos trips—where he would borrow $500 from a bank or his employer, the sugar refinery. Ibid., pp. 77–78, and June 14, 1950, reel 5, pp. 1–2.

Chapter 8. The Postwar Years

1. Richard Rhodes, *Dark Sun: The Making of the Hydrogen Bomb* (New York: Simon and Schuster, 1995), p. 192.

2. Ibid.

3. Katherine A. S. Sibley, *Red Spies in America* (Lawrence: University Press of Kansas, 2004), p. 168.

4. Alexander Feklisov and Sergei Kostin, *The Man Behind the Rosenbergs* (New York: Enigma Books, 2001), p. 317.

5. FBI Report on Harry Gold by SA Robert G. Jensen, file 65–4307, June 7, 1950, p. 22. (Hereafter cited as Jensen, Report.)

6. Sibley, *Red Spies*, pp. 117–18.

7. Kathryn S. Olmsted, *Red Spy Queen* (Chapel Hill: University of North Carolina Press, 2002), p. 95.

8. Sibley, *Red Spies*, p. 119.

9. Olmsted, *Red Spy*, p. 93.

10. Sam Roberts, *The Brother: The Untold Story of Atomic Spy David Greenglass and How He Sent His Sister, Ethel Rosenberg, to the Electric Chair* (New York: Random House, 2001), p. 168, and John Earl Haynes, Harvey Klehr, and Alexander Vasilliev, *Spies* (New Haven: Yale University Press, 2009), p. 104.

11. Norman Moss, *Klaus Fuchs* (London: Grafton Books, 1987), p. 87.

12. Soundscriber interviews, June 14, 1950, reel 5, pp. 24–25.

13. Jensen, Report, p. 23.

14. Ibid.

15. Soundscriber interviews, June 14, 1950, reel 5, p. 26.

16. Miriam Moskowitz, unpublished manuscript entitled "Phantoms of Spies Run Amok and an Odyssey of Survival in the Cold War" (May 2003). A copy of the manuscript is in the Special Collections of the Diamond Law Library at Columbia University Law School.

17. "Scope of Soviet Activity in the United States," hearing before the Subcommittee to Investigate the Administration of the Internal Security Act and other

Internal Security Laws of the Committee on the Judiciary United States Senate, Eighty-fourth Congress, second session, April 26, 1956, p. 1040.

18. Some of Brothman's partners and employees already knew Gold as Frank Kessler. He was introduced as a friend and chemist with whom Brothman had occasional business dealings. Years later, Gold would explain the pseudonym as a safeguard against "having his employer, the Pennsylvania Sugar Company . . . hear about his other efforts at remunerative work," or that he was using their facilities to do research work for other entities. FBI Memo, SA John R. Murphy Jr., Brothman Investigation, June 23, 1950, p. 4.

19. Ibid.

20. FBI File on Miriam Moskowitz, file 70887, February 3, 1954, p. 4.

21. Moskowitz, "Phantoms," p. 240.

22. Ibid., pp. 337–38.

23. Author's interview with Miriam Moskowitz, June 25, 2008.

24. Moskowitz, "Phantoms," pp. 338–39.

25. "Scope of Soviet Activity in the United States," pp. 1038–39.

26. Robert J. Lamphere Papers, Section on Harry Gold, Special Collections, Georgetown University Library, p. 35.

27. "Scope of Soviet Activity in the United States," pp. 1038–39.

28. Soundscriber interviews, June 14, 1950, reel 5, p. 47.

29. Gold was informed by Abe Brothman that he had seen such a news article on Fuchs's apprehension. In fact, the story was about another atomic spy, Alan Nunn May.

30. Alan Nunn May was a British scientist who had joined the British atomic bomb project in 1942 and started working a year later at Chalk River, the site of the Canadian natural uranium reactor. Approached by GRU agents to funnel them information, he complied and passed along a series of documents, some of them concerning what he had learned at the Manhattan Project's atomic reactor in Chicago. He also passed along uranium isotope samples to the Soviets. As John Earl Haynes and Harvey Klehr describe in *Early Cold War Spies: The Espionage Trials That Shaped American Politics* (New York: Cambridge University Press, 2006), p. 52, legal standards differed wildly between America, Great Britain, and Canada, and even though May had been identified in the Gouzenko files, it was still problematic if he could be convicted without more substantial evidence. After Drew Pearson reported news of the Gouzenko defection in February 1946, the pace of events rapidly increased. Thirteen individuals were arrested on February 15. May initially proclaimed his innocence, but "when confronted with incriminating evidence," confessed his guilt, though he refused to provide names of Soviet contacts. He was convicted in March and sentenced to ten years in prison.

31. Soundscriber interviews, June 14, 1950, reel 5, pp. 49–50.

32. Richard Rhodes, *Dark Sun: The Making of the Hydrogen Bomb* (New York: Simon and Schuster, 1995), p. 291.

33. Soundscriber interviews, June 14, 1950, reel 5, p. 51.

34. Ibid., 77.

35. Ibid., June 23, 1950, reel 6, p. 2

36. FBI Report on Miriam Moskowitz by SA Agent Thomas Zoeller, July 27, 1950, file 100-96341, p. 5.

37. FBI Report on Thomas Lessing Black for Director, FBI, file 65-59181, July 7, 1950, p. 6.

38. Ibid., p. 1.

39. Ibid., p. 7.

40. Soundscriber interviews, June 23, 1950, reel 6, p. 11.

41. FBI Report on Miriam Moskowitz by SA Agent Thomas Zoeller, July 27, 1950, file 100-96341, p. 6.

42. Gibby Needleman was also the attorney for Amtorg, the Russian trading corporation, and was thought by the FBI to be "in frequent contact with Communist Party members and Communist Party functionaries." Ibid., pp. 5–6.

43. Testimony of Abraham Brothman, Transcript of Federal Grand Jury, July 22, 1947, pp. 849–89.

44. Ibid.

45. Rhodes, *Dark Sun,* p. 293.

46. Testimony of Harry Gold, Transcript of Federal Grand Jury, July 31, 1947, pp. 971–1001.

47. Ibid.

48. "Scope of Soviet Activity in the United States," p. 1048.

49. Soundscriber interviews, June 6, 1950, reel 2, pp. 22–24.

50. Moskowitz, "Phantoms," p. 115.

51. "Scope of Soviet Activity in the United States," p. 1070.

52. FBI Report on Harry Gold by SA Agent Robert G. Jensen, May 31, 1950, p. 77.

53. Ibid., pp. 73–76.

54. Soundscriber interviews, June 23, 1950, reel 6, p. 12.

55. FBI Report on Harry Gold by SA Agent Robert G. Jensen, May 31, 1950, pp. 31–32.

56. Ibid. p. 41.

57. Author's interview with Dr. Robert Stone, December 4, 2006.

58. Author's interview with Dr. Richard Monheit, December 1, 2006.

59. FBI Report on Harry Gold by SA Agent Robert G. Jensen, May 31, 1950, pp. 31–32.

60. Soundscriber interviews, June 6, 1950, reel 2, p. 8.

61. Ibid., reel 6, p. 12.

62. Ibid., reel 2, p. 17.

63. "Scope of Soviet Activity in the United States," p. 1078.

64. Ibid.

65. Ibid.

66. Ibid., p. 1048.

67. Ibid., p. 1079.

68. Ibid.

Chapter 9. The Hunt for Raymond

1. Transcripts from Soundscriber discs of interviews with Harry Gold by John D. M. Hamilton and Augustus S. Ballard at Holmesburg Prison, June 14, 1950, reel 5, p. 55. (Hereafter cited as Soundscriber interviews.)

2. Richard Rhodes, *Dark Sun: The Making of the Hydrogen Bomb* (New York: Simon and Schuster, 1995), p. 375.

3. Soundscriber interviews, June 5, 1950, reel 5, p. 56.

4. Ibid., p. 65.

5. Ibid., pp. 56–59.

6. Ibid., p. 60.

7. Ibid., p. 62.

8. Rhodes, *Dark Sun*, p. 376.

9. Ibid.

10. John Earl Haynes and Harvey Klehr, *Venona* (New Haven: Yale University Press, 1999), p. 8.

11. Robert J. Lamphere and Tom Shactman, *The FBI-KGB War* (New York: Random House, 1986), p. 84.

12. Ibid., p. 134.

13. Ibid.

14. Norman Moss, *Klaus Fuchs* (London: Grafton Books, 1987), p. 93.

15. Ibid., p. 127.

16. Kim Philby, *My Silent War: The Autobiography of a Spy* (New York: Modern Library, 2002), p. 187.

17. Moss, *Klaus Fuchs*, p. 138.

18. Ibid., p. 141.

19. Ibid., p. 142.

20. Robert Chadwell Williams, *Klaus Fuchs: Atom Spy* (Cambridge, Mass.: Harvard University Press, 1987), p. 124.

21. Ibid., p. 129.

22. Lamphere and Shactman, *FBI-KGB War*, pp. 137, 141.

23. "Scope of Soviet Activity in the United States," "Scope of Soviet Activity in the United States," Hearing before the Subcommittee to Investigate the Administration of the Internal Security Act and other Internal Security Laws of the Committee on the Judiciary United States Senate, Eighty-fourth Congress, second session, April 26, 1956, p. 1077.

24. Soundscriber interviews, June 23, 1950, reel 6, p. 13.

25. Thomas L. Black and Eugene Lyons, "I Was a Red Spy," *New York Mirror,* June 15, 1956, p. 5.

26. "Scope of Soviet Activity in the United States," p. 1077.

27. Ibid.

28. Soundscriber interviews, June 23, 1950, reel 6, p. 14.

29. Ibid., p. 15.

30. Lamphere and Shactman, *FBI-KGB War,* p. 139.

31. J. Edgar Hoover, "The Crime of the Century," *Reader's Digest,* vol. 58, May 1951, p. 149.

32. Robert Lamphere, "At All Costs," unpublished manuscript, Special Collections, Georgetown University Library.

33. Lamphere and Shactman, *FBI-KGB War,* p. 141.

34. FBI Report on Harry Gold prepared by SA Agent Joseph D. Walsh, June 8, 1950, file 65-15324, p. 31.

35. Ibid., p. 32.

36. The letter from "K. Fuchs" in "Santa Fe, New Mexico," dated December 15, 1944, was as follows: "Dear Kristel, many thanks for your letter. I am afraid I have been very busy during the last few weeks and I expect that will go on for a little time longer. But I do hope that I shall be able to take a holiday some time at the end of January. I have not even been able to do any Christmas shopping, but I will do that on Saturday. I expect Marcia and Steve will be cross if my Christmas parcel does not arrive on time. But I trust you will be able to pacify them. We have lots of snow around here and I am itching to get on skis. But before I do so I shall have to pacify my conscience and an uncle and get the parcel for your kids off. With best wishes, KLAUS." Ibid., p. 33.

37. Ibid., pp. 34–36.

38. Heinemann admitted to being active in the "Communist Party branch of Swathmore College students," and he maintained his association with the party until February 2, 1950, while attending Harvard University. He further admitted that "his Communist party name in Boston was Robert Hill." Ibid., p. 36.

39. Ibid., p. 38.

40. The FBI investigation of Lafazanos discovered that he had been rejected for military service twice and been "classified 4-F." On both occasions, he was determined to be "psychoneurotic." Ibid., p. 40.

41. Klaus Fuchs, Confession to Michael Perrin, January 30, 1950, in Williams, *Klaus Fuchs,* p. 191.

42. Lamphere and Shactman, *FBI-KGB War,* p. 142.

43. Rhodes, *Dark Sun,* p. 425.

44. Lamphere, "At All Costs," p. 2.

45. Lamphere and Shactman, *FBI-KGB War,* p. 143.

46. Ibid., p. 146.

47. Lamphere, "At All Costs," p. 1.

48. Lamphere and Shactman, *FBI-KGB War,* p. 145.

49. The attorney they consulted was Fowler Hamilton. Hamilton was the attorney Judge Ryan assigned to prepare a brief for the court regarding "the claim of Valentine A. Gubitchev that he had diplomatic immunity in connection with the Coplan-Gubitchev prosecution." FBI Office Memorandum from D. M. Ladd to the Director, May 18, 1950, p. 1.

50. FBI File on Miriam Moskowitz, February 3, 1954, file 70887, p. 10.

51. Ibid., p. 11.

52. Miriam Moskowitz, unpublished manuscript entitled "Phantoms of Spies

Run Amok and an Odyssey of Survival in the Cold War" (May 2003). A copy of the manuscript is in the Special Collections of the Diamond Law Library at Columbia University Law School, p. 345.

53. Ibid.

54. FBI Office Memorandum from D. M. Ladd to the Director, May 18, 1950, p, 8.

55. Ibid., p. 12.

Chapter 10. The Fatal Words

1. "Scope of Soviet Activity in the United States," hearing before the Subcommittee to Investigate the Administration of the Internal Security Act and other Internal Security Laws of the Committee on the Judiciary United States Senate, Eighty-fourth Congress, second session, April 26, 1956, p. 1079.

2. Transcripts from Soundscriber discs of interviews with Harry Gold by John D. M. Hamilton and Augustus S. Ballard at Holmesburg Prison, June 23, 1950, reel 6, p. 15. (Hereafter cited as Soundscriber interviews.)

3. Ibid.

4. "Scope of Soviet Activity in the United States," p. 1080.

5. Steve Usdin's book *Engineering Communism* is the best account of the Barr and Sarant experience. Morton Sobell's book *Doing Time* presents his attempt to escape authorities, and more unbiased accounts would be Ronald Radosh and Joyce Milton's *The Rosenberg File* and Allen Weinstein's *The Haunted Wood*.

6. Kim Philby, *My Silent War: The Autobiography of a Spy* (New York: Modern Library, 2004), p. 164.

7. Soundscriber interviews, June 23, 1950, reel 6, p. 16.

8. "Scope of Soviet Activity in the United States," p. 1080.

9. FBI Memorandum from D. M. Ladd to the Director, May 18, 1950, p. 11.

10. Ibid.

11. Special Agents Miller and Brennan were attached to the New York City FBI office. Special Agent Robert Jensen belonged to the Philadelphia office.

12. "Scope of Soviet Activity in the United States," p. 1080.

13. Ibid.

14. Ibid.

15. Soundscriber interviews, June 23, 1950, reel 6, p. 18.

16. Gold's reactions to the Fuchs photo are taken from ibid. and "Scope of Soviet Activity in the United States," p. 1080.

17. Soundscriber interviews, June 23, 1950, reel 6, p. 19.

18. Author's interview with Special Agent Paul Hagen, February 29, 2007.

19. Author's interview with Special Agent Albert Runbaken, March 3, 2007.

20. Soundscriber interviews, June 23, 1950, reel 6, p. 20.

21. "Scope of Soviet Activity in the United States," p. 1081.

22. Soundscriber interviews, reel 6, p. 22.

23. Ibid., p. 23.

24. "Scope of Soviet Activity in the United States," pp. 1081–82.

25. Robert J. Lamphere and Tom Shactman, *The FBI-KGB War* (New York: Random House, 1986), p. 148.

26. Ibid., pp. 148–49.

27. Ibid., p. 149.

28. The nickname originated with a German newspaper that wanted to describe the color of both the Fuchses' family hair and "the complexion of their politics." Robert Chadwell Williams, *Klaus Fuchs: Atom Spy* (Cambridge, Mass.: Harvard University Press, 1987), p. 9.

29. Soundscriber interviews, June 23, 1950, reel 6, p. 32.

30. Ibid., pp. 32–33.

31. "Scope of Soviet Activity in the United States," p. 1082.

32. Ibid.

33. Ibid., p. 1049.

34. Ibid., p. 1082.

35. Soundscriber interviews, June 23, 1950, reel 6, p. 34.

36. "Scope of Soviet Activity in the United States," p. 1050.

37. Ibid., p. 1049.

38. Soundscriber interviews, June 23, 1950, reel 6, p. 34.

39. In *The FBI-KGB War* (p. 150) Robert Lamphere makes much of the fact that the FBI had collected "films of Gold which had been taken without Gold's knowledge," but Gold informed his attorneys that, on the contrary, he had given permission to the FBI on at least two occasions to shoot still and moving footage of him. Soundscriber interviews, June 23, 1950, reel 6, p. 19.

40. Lamphere and Shactman, *FBI-KGB War*, p. 150.

41. Ibid., p. 151.

42. Ibid.

43. Alexander Feklisov, *The Man Behind the Rosenbergs* (New York: Enigma Books, 2001), p. 240.

44. "Scope of Soviet Activity in the United States," p. 1083.

45. FBI Memorandum from D. M. Ladd to Mr. Belmont concerning Emil Klaus Fuchs, May 22, 1950.

46. Ibid.

47. FBI Memorandum from A. H. Belmont to Mr. Ladd concerning Harry Gold, May 22, 1950.

48. Soundscriber interviews, June 1, 1950, reel 1, p. 9.

49. "Scope of Soviet Activity in the United States," p. 1084.

50. FBI Report on Harry Gold by SA Agent Joseph Walsh Jr., June 6, 1950, pp. 49, 51.

51. FBI Memorandum from A. H. Belmont to D. M. Ladd concerning Harry Gold, May 23, 1950.

52. FBI Memorandum from A. H. Belmont to Mr. Ladd, May 23, 1950.

53. Ibid., p. 2.

54. *McNabb v. United States*, 318 U.S. 332 63S. CT 608, 87 L. EU. (1943).

55. One source of information on the Judith Coplon case is *The Spy Who Seduced America* by Marcia and Thomas Mitchell (Montpelier, Vt.: Invisible Cities Press, 2002).

56. "Scope of Soviet Activity in the United States," p. 1084.

57. FBI Memorandum from A. H. Belmont to Mr. Ladd, May 23, 1950, p. 3.

58. "The FBI's Toughest Case," *This Week Magazine,* February 20, 1955, p. 9.

59. FBI Memorandum from A. H. Belmont to Mr. Ladd, May 23, 1950, p. 1.

60. FBI Memorandum from A. H. Belmont to Mr. Ladd, May 22, 1950, pp. 1–4.

61. "Philadelphian Seized as Spy on Basis of Data from Fuchs," *New York Times,* May 24, 1950, p. 21.

62. FBI Memorandum from John Edgar Hoover to Tolson, Ladd, and Nichols, 5:32 P.M., May 23, 1950.

63. Ibid.

64. Ibid., 5:03 P.M., May 23, 1950.

65. FBI Memorandum from A. H. Belmont to Mr. Ladd, May 24, 1950.

66. Ibid.

67. Ibid.

Chapter 11. Conversion

1. *Philadelphia Inquirer,* May 24, 1950, p. 1.

2. *Evening Bulletin,* May 24, 1950, p. 1.

3. *Philadelphia Daily News,* May 24, 1950, p. 1.

4. "Philadelphian Seized as Spy on Basis of Data from Fuchs," *New York Times,* May 24, 1950, p. 1.

5. "The Man with the Oval Face," *Time,* June 5, 1950, p. 20.

6. "Good Boy Gone Wrong," *Newsweek,* June 5, 1950, p. 20.

7. Syndicated columnist Bob Considine wrote a lengthy series of articles entitled "The Great A-Bomb Robbery" that appeared in the *Philadelphia Inquirer* in December 1951. Gold was also to become a question in a *Philadelphia Evening Bulletin* crossword puzzle on March 3, 1951.

8. "Neighbors in Northeast Call Gold Quiet, Sociable," *Philadelphia Inquirer,* May 24, 1950, p. 3.

9. "Gold Led Quiet Life, Liked Opera, Baseball," *Philadelphia Evening Bulletin,* May 24, 1950, p. 3.

10. "Very Bright but Introverted; Gold's Teachers Say of Him," *Philadelphia Evening Bulletin,* May 24, 1950, p. 3.

11. "Hospital Associates Say Gold Worked Hard, Kept to Himself," *Philadelphia Evening Bulletin,* May 24, 1950, p. 1.

12. Author's interview with Dr. Richard Monheit, December 1, 2006.

13. "Hospital Associates Say Gold Worked Hard, Kept to Himself," *Philadelphia Evening Bulletin,* May 24, 1950, p. 3.

14. "Gold's Heart Research at Hospital Is Praised," *Philadelphia Inquirer,* May 24, 1950, p. 1.

15. "Scientist Seized Here as Atom Spy; Passed Secrets to Russia, FBI says," *Philadelphia Evening Bulletin,* May 24, 1950, p. 1.

16. Ibid., p. 3

17. Ibid., p. 3.

18. "Gold Is Visited by Kin," *New York Times,* May 27, 1950, p. 7.

19. FBI Memorandum from SA Agents T. Scott Miller Jr. and Richard E. Brennan to SAC concerning Abraham Brothman, May 25, 1950, p. 1.

20. This is how Gold described the episode from his prison cell: "I am resentful about one matter; I have tried to obtain consent from all of the authorities involved for a single session, three-quarters of an hour or an hour would have sufficed, with one of the personnel at the Heart Station (say, Dr. Steiger or Dr. Urbach) so as to be able to clear up as much of the unfinished work as possible; and I would have insisted that the FBI and a competent biochemist be present, to insure that the conversation would be restricted to the details of our research. Further, I would guarantee that no publicity would ever be sought; the only desire was to help the work on heart disease continue. Permission has never been granted. I have stated the above, being fully aware that as a Federal prisoner, I no longer possess the rights I once had. However, the people at Holmesburg did permit me to write a letter to Mr. Hamilton, relating as much as could be put on paper; and Mr. Hamilton has forwarded this to PGH. For this I am grateful." "Scope of Soviet Activity in the United States," hearing before the Subcommittee to Investigate the Administration of the Internal Security Act and other Internal Security Laws of the Committee on the Judiciary United States Senate, Eighty-fourth Congress, second session, April 26, 1956, p. 1083.

21. FBI Memorandum from A. H. Belmont to Mr. Ladd concerning Harry Gold, May 26, 1950, p. 1.

22. FBI Memorandum from Arthur Cornelius to William C. Hince Jr. concerning Harry Gold, May 26, 1950.

23. FBI Memorandum from A. H. Belmont to Mr. Ladd concerning Harry Gold, May 26, 1950, p. 1.

24. Ibid.

25. FBI Memorandum from G. E. Hennrich to A. H. Belmont concerning Harry Gold, May 26, 1050, p. 1.

26. "Father, Brother See Spy Suspect," *Philadelphia Evening Bulletin,* May 26, 1950, p. 1.

27. "Father, 70, Insists Gold Wouldn't Hurt U.S.," *Philadelphia Evening Bulletin,* May 25, 1950, p. 1.

28. FBI Memorandum from SAC A. Cornelius to File regarding Harry Gold, May 29, 1950.

29. Ibid.

30. So sensitive was the Gold case, discussions were held between Judge McGranery, the FBI, and the U.S. marshals as to who should bring him from Holmesburg to the judge's chambers. Even though the FBI was interviewing Gold every day, but behind prison walls, it was concerned about "publicity attending the case" and the prospect of "misinterpretation" if its agents were seen escorting Gold down-

town. Judge McGranery agreed and asked the marshals and prison system to facilitate Gold's transportation. FBI Memorandum from SAC Arthur Cornelius to File concerning Harry Gold, May 31, 1950, p. 1.

31. Ibid.

32. "Gold Is Seen Ready to Plead Guilty to Being a Courier for Spy Ring," *New York Times,* May 31, 1050, p. 2.

33. Author's interview with Augustus S. Ballard, May 15, 2007.

34. Cal Tinney, "Man of the Week: John Hamilton," *Philadelphia Record,* July 26, 1936, p. 5.

35. "Landon's Manager," *Philadelphia Evening Bulletin,* June 11, 1936, p. 1.

36. Ibid.

37. "Hamilton to Give Farley a Run if Landon Is GOP Nominee," *Philadelphia Inquirer,* June 9, 1936, p. 3.

38. Ibid.

39. Ward Morehouse, "Hamilton Plans Flying Campaign," *Philadelphia Evening Bulletin,* June 24, 1936, p. 3.

40. Soundscriber interviews, June 1, 1950, reel 1, p. 4.

41. Ibid., p. 5.

42. "John D. M. Hamilton Will Defend Gold on Soviet Atom Spy Charge," *New York Times,* June 1, 1950.

43. Author's interview with Augustus S. Ballard, May 15, 2007.

44. "Every Man Deserves a Defense," "Your Neighbors" magazine, *Philadelphia Inquirer,* July 16, 1950.

45. Author's interview with Augustus S. Ballard, March 13, 2007.

46. Ibid.

47. Author's interview with Augustus S. Ballard, May 24, 2007.

48. Author's interview with Francis Ballard, May 12, 2008.

49. Author's interview with Augustus S. Ballard, March 13, 2007.

50. Gayle Ronan Sims, "Augustus S. Ballard, 86, High-Profile Lawyer," *Philadelphia Inquirer,* February 14, 2008.

51. Earl Selby, "In Our Town," *Philadelphia Evening Bulletin,* p. F4.

52. Alice W. Dugan, "Column on Harry Gold Rouses Readers Ire," *Philadelphia Evening Bulletin,* July 21, 1950, p. F43.

53. Thomas P. Russell, "Column on Harry Gold Rouses Readers Ire," *Philadelphia Evening Bulletin,* July 21, 1950, p. F43.

54. Soundscriber interviews, June 1, 1950, reel 1, p. 6.

55. Ibid., p. 7.

56. Ibid., p. 9.

57. Ibid., pp. 10-11.

58. Author's interview with Augustus S. Ballard, June 7, 2007.

59. "Scope of Soviet Activity in the United States," p. 1085.

60. Ibid.

61. Ibid.

62. Author's interview with Augustus S. Ballard, May 15, 2007.

63. Author's interview with Augustus S. Ballard, May 31, 2007.

64. In addition to expressing his desire to make "amends," Gold informed his father and brother that he was "very fortunate in having such men [Hamilton and Ballard] to represent me" and appreciated their exceptional kindness as exemplified by Hamilton bringing him "a book of operas and two of his own books" for his perusal. Gold signed off by telling his brother, "Keep up your courage—I am doing my best to keep up mine. And I am doing my best to make amends. No matter how it may appear to the rest of the world." Letter from Harry Gold to Joseph Gold, June 9, 1950. Papers of Joseph Gold, Special Collections, Paley Library, Temple University.

65. Author's interview with Augustus S. Ballard, May 24, 2007.

66. Hamilton sent books to Gold, such as *Stories of Famous Operas* and Thomas Wolfe's *Of Time and the River*, so that he would have something other than his depressing situation to think about. Letter from John D. M. Hamilton to Dr. F. S. Baldi, July 20, 1950. Legal Papers of Augustus S. Ballard, Special Collections, Paley Library, Temple University.

67. Author's interview with Augustus S. Ballard, May 15, 2007.

68. Author's interview with Augustus S. Ballard, May 24, 2007.

69. FBI Report on Harry Gold by SA Robert G. Jensen, May 31, 1050, p. 41.

70. Ibid.

71. Ibid., pp. 41–42.

72. FBI Memorandum from SA Robert G. Jensen on Harry Gold, June 7, 1950, pp. 9–10.

73. Ibid., p. 8.

74. Ibid., pp. 35–36.

75. Ibid., p. 12.

76. Author's interview with Augustus S. Ballard, November 15, 2006.

77. FBI Report on Harry Gold by SA Robert G. Jensen, May 31, 1950, p. 91.

78. Robert J. Lamphere and Tom Shactman, *The FBI-KGB War* (New York: Random House, 1986), pp. 160–63.

79. *Red Files*, PBS documentary series, episode entitled *Secret Victories of the KGB*.

80. FBI Memorandum from A. H. Belmont to Mr. Ladd concerning Harry Gold, June 6, 1950, p. 1.

81. On June 6, 1950, Hamilton read from Section 32 of the United States Code, under Title 50, "Whoever with intent or reason to believe that it is to be used to the injury of the United States or to the advantage of a foreign nation, communicates, delivers or transmits or attempts to, or aids or induces another to communicate, deliver or transmit to any foreign government, or to any faction or party or military or naval force within a foreign government, or to any representative, agent, employee, subject or citizen thereof, either directly or indirectly, any document, writing, code books, signal book, sketch, photograph, photographic negative, blue print, plan, model, note, instrument, appliance or information relating to the national defense, shall be punished by imprisonment for not more than twenty years, provided, however that whoever shall violate the provisions of subsection A, in time of war, shall be punished by death or by imprisonment for not more than thirty years." Soundscriber interviews, June 1, 1950, reel 1, pp. 12–13.

82. Ibid., pp. 14–15.

83. Author's interview with Augustus S. Ballard, May 31, 2007.

84. Discussions between Geoffrey Patterson and Sir Percy Sillitoe made it clear that although the British were "highly elated" with the news that Fuchs's American contact had been captured, it was highly unlikely that Fuchs would ever make an appearance in an American courtroom. FBI Memorandum from A. H. Belmont to Mr. Ladd, May 25, 1950, p. 1.

85. Letter from Leon J. Obermayer to Dear John, Legal Papers of Augustus S. Ballard, Special Collections, Paley Library, Temple University.

86. Letter from Hamilton to Leon J. Obermayer, Legal Papers of Augustus S. Ballard, Special Collections, Paley Library, Temple University.

87. Letter from J. Edgar Hoover to John D. M. Hamilton, Legal Papers of Augustus S. Ballard, Special Collections, Paley Library, Temple University.

88. Letter from John D. M. Hamilton to J. Edgar Hoover, Legal Papers of Augustus S. Ballard, Special Collections, Paley Library, Temple University.

89. Letter from A1-Citizen to Sam Gold, Papers of Joseph Gold, Special Collections, Paley Library, Temple University.

90. "Gold's Family Seeks Lawyer," *Philadelphia Evening Bulletin*, May 25, 1950, p. 20.

91. Oliver Pilat, "Joseph's Dreams Blasted by Gold's Spy Confession," *New York Post*, June 9, 1950, p. 4.

92. "Court Remands Spy Courier to Holmesburg Jail," *Philadelphia Evening Bulletin*, June 12, 1950, p. 3.

93. "More Espionage Arrests Likely," *Philadelphia Evening Bulletin*, June 17, 1950, p. 1.

Chapter 12. To Make Amends

1. Robert Lamphere and Tom Shactman, *The FBI-KGB War* (New York: Random House, 1986), pp. 160–61.

2. Lamphere divided the many Soviet operatives that Gold had worked with into three different groups. The first group consisted of Fuchs and Greenglass, who were involved with atomic espionage; the second of Brothman and Moskowitz; and the third of Black and his initial recruitment into industrial espionage. Ibid., p. 163.

3. "The Nation," *New York Times*, June 18, E1.

4. "Scope of Soviet Activity in the United States," hearing before the Subcommittee to Investigate the Administration of the Internal Security Act and other Internal Security Laws of the Committee on the Judiciary United States Senate, Eighty-fourth Congress, second session, April 26, 1956, p. 1085.

5. Ibid.

6. Ibid.

7. Ibid., p. 1086.

8. Gold admitted that it was "most peculiar" that somebody like himself who had always been "so scrupulously accurate and correct in [his] scientific work" could

have been able to lie "so devilishly and so capably throughout an entire 15 years." Ibid.

9. Ibid.

10. Thomas L. Black and Eugene Lyons, "I Was a Red Spy," *New York Mirror,* June 15, 1956, p. 5.

11. Ibid.

12. Confession of Harry Gold witnessed by Richard E. Brennan and T. Scott Miller Jr., June 2, 1950, file 65-59181-84, p. 1.

13. Confessions of Harry Gold witnessed by Richard E. Brennan and T. Scott Miller Jr., June 4 and 5, 1950.

14. Black and Lyons, "Red Spy," p. 3.

15. FBI "Urgent" Memo concerning Vera Kane, Washington from New York, April 27, 1951 (SAC Scheidt to Director), p. 1.

16. FBI Memorandum concerning Harry Gold by Joseph C. Walsh, July 5, 1951, p. 2.

17. Ibid.

18. "2 Named by Gold in Spy Network Arrested by FBI," *Sunday Bulletin,* July 30, 1950, p. 1.

19. "2 Plead Not Guilty in Spy Conspiracy," *New York Times,* August 3, 1950, p. 10.

20. "The FBI's Toughest Case," *This Week Magazine,* February 20, 1955, p. 10.

21. "2 Named by Gold In Spy Network Arrested by FBI," p. 7.

22. Ibid.

23. Thomas P. Ronan, "Brothman a Spy Says Miss Bentley," *New York Times,* November 15, 1950, p. 17.

24. Federal Grand Jury Testimony relating to Abraham Brothman and Miriam Moskowitz, July 29, 1950, pp. 9030–85.

25. Thomas P. Ronan, "Gold Says Soviet Let Brothman Go," *New York Times,* November 21, 1950, p. 14.

26. Ibid.

27. Federal Grand Jury Testimony relating to Abraham Brothman and Miriam Moskowitz, July 29, 1950, pp. 9030–85.

28. Author's interview with Miriam Moskowitz, June 25, 2008.

29. Miriam Moskowitz, unpublished manuscript entitled "Phantoms of Spies Run Amok and an Odyssey of Survival in the Cold War" (May 2003), p. 243. A copy of the manuscript is in the Special Collections of the Diamond Law Library at Columbia University Law School.

30. Ibid.

31. FBI Memorandum on Miriam Moskowitz, Newark Office, file 70887, February 3, 1954, pp. 1, 6.

32. FBI Memorandum on Miriam Moskowitz, New York Office, file 100-963341 MFH, December 28, 1950, p. 4.

33. Author's interview with Miriam Moskowitz, June 25, 2008.

34. Moskowitz, "Phantoms," pp. 243–44.

35. Brothman would successfully challenge the legality of his five-year sentence and have it overturned. He, like his co-defendant, would stand guilty of one count of conspiracy to obstruct justice and a two-year sentence.

36. Edward Ranzal, "2 in Spy Case get Maximum Penalty," *New York Times*, November 29, 1950, p. 8.

37. FBI Memorandum on Miriam Moskowitz, New York Office, file 100-963341 MFH, December 28, 1950, p. 5.

38. Moskowitz, "Phantoms," p. 362.

39. Ibid., p. 255.

40. Author's interview with Miriam Moskowitz, April 5, 2007.

41. Author's interview with Miriam Moskowitz, June 25, 2008.

42. Transcript of *United States v. Harry Gold*, Criminal No. 15769, Eastern District of Pennsylvania, Philadelphia, Pennsylvania, October 19, 1950, pp. 2–3.

43. Ibid., pp. 4–5.

44. The best account of Judge Kaufman's *ex parte* indiscretions in the Rosenberg case can be found in the definitive account of the Rosenberg case In Ronald Radosh and Joyce Milton, *The Rosenberg File* (New York: Holt, Rinehart and Winston, 1983), pp. 277–79.

45. "Gold Sentence Delayed to December 7," *Evening Bulletin*, October 19, 1950, p. 1.

46. *United States v. Harry Gold*, p. 5.

47. "Hearing on Gold Expected in Fall," *Evening Bulletin*, July 21, 1950, p. F1.

48. Transcript of *United States v. Alfred Dean Slack*, Criminal No. 5593, Eastern District of Tennessee, Greenville, Tennessee, September 18, 1950, p. 10.

49. Ibid., p. 14.

50. Ibid.

51. Ibid.

52. Letter from Harry Kraiker Jr. to Augustus S. Ballard, August 29, 1950, p. 1. Legal Papers of Augustus S. Ballard, Special Collections, Paley Library, Temple University.

53. Letter from Frank Kessler to Augustus S. Ballard, August 27, 1950. Legal Papers of Augustus S. Ballard, Special Collections, Paley Library, Temple University.

54. Letter from Division of Cardiology to Augustus S. Ballard, August 9, 1950. Legal Papers of Augustus S. Ballard, Special Collections, Paley Library, Temple University.

55. Ibid., p. 5.

56. Letter from V. C. Stechschulte, S.J., to Augustus S. Ballard, July 3, 1950, p. 1, and Letter from Charles F. Wheeler to Augustus S. Ballard, July 6, 1950, p. 1. Legal Papers of Augustus S. Ballard, Special Collections, Paley Library, Temple University.

57. According to Lippmann, "the phrase 'cold war' was in its French form 'guerre froide' in circulation in France during the 1930s and was applied to Hitler's war of nerves." Lippmann went on to say that although a series of articles he wrote in September 1947 for the *New York Herald Tribune* probably spurred wide use of the term, it was probably first used by "Mr. Baruch . . . before the summer of 1947."

As for dating the origin of the Cold War, Lippmann suggested a series of possible events, including the Yalta and Potsdam conferences, Secretary Byrne's visit to Moscow, and the Soviet blockade of Berlin, but he personally leaned toward "President Truman's message about Greece and Turkey announcing the so-called Truman Doctrine." Letter from Walter Lippmann to John D. M. Hamilton, June 21, 1950. Legal Papers of Augustus S. Ballard, Special Collections, Paley Library, Temple University.

58. Harry Gold To-Do List #1, Holmesburg Prison, August 8, 1950.

59. Harry Gold To-Do List #1a, Holmesburg Prison, August 8, 1950.

60. Harry Gold, Sentencing Statement, July 20, 1950. Legal Papers of Augustus S. Ballard, Special Collections, Paley Library, Temple University.

61. Ibid., pp. 11–12.

62. Ibid., pp. 17–18.

63. Ibid., pp. 19–20.

64. Ibid.

65. Ibid., p. 25.

66. Author's interview with Augustus S. Ballard, May 15, 2007.

67. Ibid.

68. "Every Man Deserves a Defense," "Your Neighbors" magazine, *Philadelphia Inquirer,* July 16, 1950.

69. Letter from Murray Milkman and Berel Caesar to John D. M. Hamilton, March 17, 1954. Legal Papers of Augustus S. Ballard, Special Collections, Paley Library, Temple University.

70. "U.S. Wants Gold Jailed for 25 Years; Sentence Put Off," *Evening Bulletin,* December 7, 1950, p. 1.

71. *United States v. Harry Gold,* p. 2.

72. Ibid., p. 15.

73. This was the second time Judge McGranery mentioned having *ex parte* discussions with Director Hoover of the FBI, and once again neither the defense nor the prosecution voiced a concern, though an argument can be made both had reason to question the propriety of such an act. It is also curious that Gleeson and the attorney general's office were quite invested in gaining a continuance, though Hoover according to McGranery saw no reason for one.

74. John D. M. Hamilton's Defense Presentation at the Sentencing of Harry Gold, Philadelphia, December 7, 1950, p. 4. Legal Papers of Augustus S. Ballard, Special Collections, Paley Library, Temple University. (Hereafter cited as Hamilton, Sentencing Presentation.)

75. Ibid., p. 9.

76. Ibid., p. 10.

77. "U.S. Wants Gold Jailed for 25 Years," p. 1.

78. Author's interview with Augustus S. Ballard, November 15, 2006.

79. Hamilton, Sentencing Presentation, pp. 69–70.

80. Letter from Joseph Moss to John D. M. Hamilton, January 5, 1950. Legal Papers of Augustus S. Ballard, Special Collections, Paley Library, Temple University. Moss felt obligated to write to Hamilton that he had practiced law "for over 40 years"

and had heard "many court lawyers here and elsewhere, but never in my entire career did I hear such an able, carefully prepared, and logical presentation of a most difficult case." Moss would go on to write that he had dropped in to the courtroom intending to stay for only a few minutes but stayed for five hours and returned on Saturday to hear the sentence. He called Hamilton's presentation "simply magnificent" and thought Gold would receive "about ten years." He admitted to being surprised by the actual length of the sentence, but said, "It is not for me to criticize my good friend, Judge McGranery."

81. *United States v. Harry Gold,* p. 131.

82. Author's interview with Augustus S. Ballard, May 31, 2007.

83. Ibid., pp. 132–33.

84. "Harry Gold Gets Maximum Term As Spy: 30 Years," *Sunday Bulletin,* December 10, 1950, p. 1.

85. *United States v. Harry Gold,* p. 138.

86. Ibid., p. 139.

87. Harry Gold, Pre-Sentence Statement, December 9, 1950, p. 2. Legal Papers of Augustus S. Ballard, Special Collections, Paley Library, Temple University.

88. *United States v. Harry Gold,* pp. 141–43.

89. Author's interviews with Augustus S. Ballard, November 15, 2006, and May 15, 2007.

90. "Harry Gold Brought Here," *New York Times,* December 16, 1950, p. 6.

91. "Gold Spy, Gets Patent; Brothman a Co-Inventor," *New York Times,* January 6, 1951, p. 10.

92. "U.S. Will Ask Death Penalty for 3 in Spy Trial," *New York Times,* March 6, 1951, p. 8.

93. Meyer Berger, "Theft of Atom Bomb Secrets in War Stressed at Spy Trial," *New York Times,* March 8, 1951, p. 1.

94. Ibid.

95. William R. Conklin, "Admitted Spy, Gold Is Star Witness," *New York Times,* March 16, 1951, p. 1.

96. "Extracts from Testimony Given by Harry Gold at Spy Trial," *New York Times,* March 16, 1951, p. 8.

97. Conklin, "Admitted Spy," p. 8.

98. Ibid.

99. "Extracts from Testimony,"p. 8.

100. Soundscriber interviews, June 14, 1950, reel 5, p. 40.

101. "Extracts from Testimony,"p. 8.

102. John Wexley, *The Judgment of Ethel and Julius Rosenberg* (New York: Cameron and Kahn, 1955), pp. 70–71.

103. Wexley was no doubt more familiar with Hollywood than with the Tombs, which he made sound like the Waldorf Astoria South. As someone who has worked in prisons, studied them, and observed their operations, I would call Wexley's assessment of the so-called Singing Quarters exaggerated if not imaginary.

104. Wexley, *Judgment,* p. 205.

105. Ibid., 70.

106. Ronald Radosh and Joyce Milton, *The Rosenberg File* (New York: Holt, Rinehart and Winston, 1983), p. 159.

107. Ibid.

108. Author's interview with Augustus S. Ballard, May 15, 2007.

109. Radosh and Milton, *Rosenberg File*, p. 216.

Chapter 13. Prisoner 19312-NE

1. United States Penitentiary, Lewisburg, Pa. Notorious Offender File, Admission Summary, for Harry Gold.

2. Interviews with several former federal prisoners and Lewisburg inmates, including Louis "Junior" Kripplebauer and Charles "Chick" Goodroe, whose careers are covered in part in Allen M. Hornblum, *Confession of a Second Story Man* (Fort Lee, N.J.: Barricade Books, 2006). In addition, the journey from New York City to Lewisburg in the early 1950s before the advent of interstate highways is described in Tony Hiss, *The View from Alger's Window* (New York: Knopf, 1998), which describes his father's forty-four months at Lewisburg.

3. United States Department of Justice, Lewisburg Penitentiary, Prison Photo of Harry Gold, June 26, 1951. Gold's dramatic weight loss was widely mentioned in news accounts. Though most accounts, as in *Newsweek,* for example, commented on Gold having "slimmed down from 195 pounds to 125" upon his release from prison, the bulk of that weight had in fact been lost prior to his admission to Lewisburg.

4. John W. Roberts, "The Origins of USP Lewisburg," in *The History of the Federal Penitentiary at Lewisburg,* by John W. Roberts (Lewisburg, Pa.: Union County Historical Society, 2005), p. 6.

5. Ibid., p. 8.

6. Ibid., p. 10.

7. Diana Medina Lasansky, "The Federal Prison at Lewisburg," in *The History of the Federal Penitentiary at Lewisburg,* by John W. Roberts (Lewisburg, Pa.: Union County Historical Society, 2005), p. 42.

8. Ibid., p. 22

9. Roberts, "Origins," p. 13.

10. Alfred Hassler, *Diary of a Self-Made Convict* (Chicago: Regnery, 1954), p. 4. Newspaper articles at the time made note of Lewisburg's transformation from a "country club" to an institution holding more dangerous "life termers." "Harry Gold to Go to Lewisburg," *Philadelphia Evening Bulletin,* January 21, 1951.

11. Hassler, *Diary,* p. 41.

12. Author's interview with Robert Smith, June 6, 2007. Smith, a former Lewisburg correctional officer and caseworker, worked in a number of federal prisons and came into contact with Harry Gold on a daily basis.

13. Ibid.

14. Gerald Gleeson, *Report on Convicted Prisoner by United States Attorney,* August 28, 1951.

15. Lewisburg Penitentiary's workup of Harry Gold was quite professional.

There were thorough and detailed commentaries on the prisoner's crime, his subsequent assistance to law enforcement, social history, early life, education, and employment history.

16. United States Penitentiary, Lewisburg, Pa. Notorious Offender File, Admission Summary for Harry Gold, Medical Report.

17. Ibid., Psychiatric Assessment.

18. Ibid., Psychological and Educational Assessment.

19. Ibid., Case Analysis and Planning for Harry Gold. Though the complete "neuropsychiatric" report on Gold from Holmesburg Prison is no longer available, a portion of it was incorporated into the Lewisburg Penitentiary Admission and Orientation report.

20. Ibid., Admission and Orientation report.

21. Maxims and slogans directed at new inmates entering prison systems are of long standing. Most are designed to ensure that new inmates avoid trouble, do their own time, stay away from bad influences, and get out of prison as quickly as possible. Hassler, *Diary,* p. 44, and Yusef Anthony in Allen M. Hornblum, *Sentenced to Science* (University Park: Penn State University Press, 2007), p. 42.

22. Hiss, *View,* p. 222.

23. Hassler, *Diary,* p. 48.

24. Ibid., p. 44. Also interviews with other Lewisburg prisoners, including Louis Kripplebauer, Charles Goodroe, and Doug Ealy.

25. Letter from Harry Gold to John D. M. Hamilton, June 16, 1951. A letter from Gold to Hamilton six months earlier underscored Gold's intentions. "For the present," he informed his attorney, "my plan is to do thusly: to observe meticulously the rules wherever I am committed, to work diligently at whatever work is assigned, and to make the best use of my time—by a regular program of study and by engaging in whatever additional useful activities as are permitted." Letter from Harry Gold to John D. M. Hamilton, January 5, 1951.

26. Hassler, *Diary,* p. 48.

27. Letter from Harry Gold to John D. M. Hamilton, September 6, 1951.

28. In a 1953 letter of apology to Bureau of Prisons Director James Bennett, Greenglass explains his "petulant attitude" in an earlier letter being due to "considerable mental strain" and the "anger and frustration" of his situation. He goes on to state, "All I want from this life is to be reunited with my wife and children and to be allowed to earn a living for them." In another frantic letter to his lawyer, Greenglass wrote in July 1953, "I am sorry that I get into such a state that I have to unburden to someone. Up until last Saturday I had no mail from Ruth for eleven days." Letter from David Greenglass to Bureau of Prisons Director Bennett, July 28, 1953. Bureau of Prisons, Notorious Offender File, National Archives, College Park, Md. Gold did not have such family pressures and was normally the model of decorum in his correspondence with government officials.

29. Hassler, *Diary,* p. 18.

30. Intra-Bureau Correspondence from Warden G. W. Humphrey to Bureau of Prisons Director, December 29, 1952.

31. Ibid.

32. Danbury was another federal penitentiary, in Connecticut, but held younger, less serious offenders. Letter from David Greenglass to Bureau of Prisons Director James Bennett, July 28, 1953.

33. United States Penitentiary at Lewisburg, Pa. Special Progress Report for Harry Gold, September 25, 1952.

34. Ibid.

35. FBI Memo from SA Edward Scheidt to Mr. Hoover, July 11, 1952. Also, Lewisburg and several other federal prisons were involved in medical research during the postwar years. "New hepatitis research programs were initiated at McNeil Island, Lewisburg, and Ashland" in 1951. The programs were "carried out under the auspices of the Laboratory of Biologics Control, National Microbiological Institute." The U.S. Public Health Service coordinated similar and additional research programs. The research confirmed that "blood derivative plasma can carry the virus of infectious hepatitis but blood derivatives albumin and gamma globulin apparently did not." From United States Department of Justice Annual Report of Federal Prisons, for 1951, 1952, 1953.

36. A vast array of vulnerable, institutionalized subjects such as the mentally retarded and orphans were used as raw material for medical research in postwar America, but prison inmates were probably the guinea pigs of choice for researchers. Generally uneducated, locked behind prison walls, and hoping their participation would translate into an early release or a few extra dollars for the commissary, inmates were a cheap and readily available pool of test subjects for doctors and pharmaceutical companies. A few, like Nathan Leopold at Stateville Penitentiary in Illinois, were both hospital aides and test subjects. Leopold wrote about his experience as a prison inmate and test subject in *Life Plus 99 Years* (Garden City, N.Y.: Doubleday, 1958). Another inmate's personal account of participating in prison medical experiments is narrated in Hornblum, *Sentenced to Science*. The most detailed account of the history and use of prison inmates as test subjects is Allen M. Hornblum, *Acres of Skin* (New York: Routledge, 1998).

37. Author's interview with Howard Harner, June 20, 2004.

38. Joseph Gold Papers, Special Collections, Paley Library, Temple University.

39. Author's interview with Charles "Chick" Goodroe, January 5, 2008

40. Letter from Joseph Gold to SA FBI Scott Miller, March 19, 1952. This letter was intended less to announce his brother's successful acclimation to federal prison life than to request the FBI agent's help in getting Harry's sentence reduced in view of his contribution to the government's prosecution of Soviet spies.

41. Author's interview with Al From, December 19, 2007.

42. Letter from Harry Gold to John D. M. Hamilton, May 8, 1951. Though "pleased" with the May 8, 1951, *Reader's Digest* article that noted his "cooperation with the government authorities," Gold was distressed by the "unfortunate . . . condensation" of the facts that led to distorted "impressions" that were "different from the actual purport of these events." Mention of his being awarded "the Order of the Red Star" was "very difficult" for Gold. He never wanted it mentioned or printed, "so great was [his] sense of shame." "An unremitting stabbing pain" was how he referred to "the harm" he had done. "Scope of Soviet Activity in the United States," hearing

before the Subcommittee to Investigate the Administration of the Internal Security Act and other Internal Security Laws of the Committee on the Judiciary, United States Senate, Eighty-fourth Congress, second session, April 26, 1956, p. 1075.

43. Numerous communications between Gold and his attorneys concern media inaccuracies. After reading a *Time* magazine article mentioning "Gold's last meeting with Yakovlev," Hamilton tells his client, "I desire to write a letter to the editor of 'Time' asking for a suitable correction. I am not writing the letter in the thought of having it published but simply in order that the statement as contained in the article shall not go unchallenged in the thought that some day this might be used against you in a hearing before a parole board." Letter from John D. M. Hamilton to Harry Gold, March 22, 1951.

44. Letter from Harry Gold to Mary Lanning, May 20, 1951. Papers of Joseph Gold, Special Collections, Paley Library, Temple University.

45. Letter from Harry Gold to Mary Lanning, June 25, 1951. Papers of Joseph Gold, Special Collections, Paley Library, Temple University.

46. Ibid.

47. Letter from Harry Gold to John D. M. Hamilton, October 5, 1953. Legal Papers of Augustus S. Ballard, Special Collections, Paley Library, Temple University.

48. Ibid.

49. Letter from Harry Gold to John D. M. Hamilton, November 1, 1953. Legal Papers of Augustus, S. Ballard, Special Collections, Paley Library, Temple University.

50. Letter from John D. M. Hamilton to Harry Gold, November 6, 1953. Papers of Joseph Gold, Special Collections, Paley Library, Temple University.

51. Letter from John D. M. Hamilton to Roy M. Cohn, November 6, 1953. Legal Papers of Augustus S. Ballard, Special Collections, Paley Library, Temple University.

52. Letter from Harry Gold to John D. M. Hamilton, November 17, 1953. Legal Papers of Augustus S. Ballard, Special Collections, Paley Library, Temple University. At least one newspaper column mentioned Judge McGranery's change of heart regarding the Gold case. Leonard Lyons's "Gossip of the Nation" piece in the *Philadelphia Inquirer*, November 3, 1953, noted that "Ex-Attorney General McGranery, who as a Federal Judge gave a 30-year sentence to Harry Gold, may join the list of those asking clemency for the atom bomb spy."

53. Letter from Harry Gold to John D. M. Hamilton, November 17, 1953.

54. United States Penitentiary, Lewisburg, Pa. Special Progress Report on Harry Gold, July 19, 1954.

55. Ibid. It is not clear whether prison authorities learned of Cohn's comments on Judge McGranery's reconsideration by reading Gold's mail or whether Gold informed his caseworker about them.

56. List of desired books, Papers of Joseph Gold, Special Collections, Paley Library, Temple University.

57. Author's interviews with Augustus S. Ballard, September 20, 2007, April 24, 2007, and May 15, 2007.

58. FBI Memo to Director, FBI, September 2, 1954. Special Collections, Paley Library, Temple University.

59. Ibid.

60. Ibid.

61. John Earl Haynes and Harvey Klehr, *Early Cold War Spies* (New York: Cambridge University Press, 2006), p. 74.

62. Ibid., p. 75.

63. Ibid., p. 77.

64. Gary May, *Un-American Activities* (New York: Oxford University Press, 1994), p. 4.

65. Ibid., p. 5.

66. Office Memorandum from SAC, Philadelphia, to Director, FBI, December 27, 1954. Special Collections, Paley Library, Temple University.

67. May, *Un-American Activities*, p. 7.

68. Ibid., p. 8.

69. Memorandum from SAC to Director, FBI, December 27, 1954. Special Collections, Paley Library, Temple University.

70. Ibid.

71. Ibid., p. 2.

72. Ibid.

73. From day one of his thirty-year sentence, Gold was set on doing his time near his family and Philadelphia. In fact, there is reason to believe that he was more alarmed by rumors of his being transferred to another federal penitentiary than by the threat of violence targeting convicted Communists. His father and brother were mobilized by rumors of transfer; there is little sign that the Remington murder had the same impact.

74. Author's interview with Augustus S. Ballard, December 12, 2007.

Chapter 14. State of Mind

1. "Medical Research Volunteer Dies at Lewisburg Prison," *Philadelphia Evening Bulletin*, December 16, 1952.

2. Ibid. Gavin, a resident of Washington, D.C., was serving a sentence of sixteen months to four years. Test participants were entitled to $9 a month from the army during the length of the experiment and time off their sentence for good behavior.

3. Gold accumulated several donation cards of the Northeastern Pennsylvania American Red Cross Blood Program based in Wilkes-Barre, Pennsylvania. He was also awarded a Certificate of Appreciation from the same organization for being a member of the Gallon Plus Club.

4. Gold had a long history as a blood donor. His medical colleagues at PGH submitted a lengthy statement on his work habits and character during the summer of 1950, noting his "unselfish" work habits and blood contributions "in excess of what might normally be taken from any single individual," especially one who "suffered

from hypertension." Statement as to the Work, Conduct and Character of Harry Gold while Employed at the Heart Station, Division of Cardiology, Philadelphia General Hospital, Philadelphia, Pennsylvania, by Drs. McMillan, Bellet, Steiger, Urbach, and Dorothy Bell, August 9, 1950, p. 3.

5. In an effort to win support and ultimately patents for his research discoveries, Gold crafted a document entitled "Background Material and Notes re the Indigo carmine Patented Blood Sugar Method." The five-page document lists the research initiatives, years of study, and medical importance, among other items. In addition, Gold became interested in solving some of the research dilemmas of rural physicians after talking with Dr. Harold Rowland, a PGH medical resident from Harlan County, Kentucky.

6. Ibid., p. 2.

7. "Perjury Laid to Gold Friend," *New York Times,* November 22, 1952, p. 7.

8. Ibid.

9. "Spy Case Figure Freed," *New York Times,* June 19, 1955, p. 54.

10. "Spy Harry Gold in Court Again," *Philadelphia Evening Bulletin,* June 15, 1955, p. F4.

11. Ibid. Press coverage of the Smilg case sparked Gold's lawyer, John Hamilton, to write to his client and suggest they bring his "files up to date" in order that they be ready when Harry would eventually petition the government for "clemency." Hamilton informed Gold he (Hamilton) was "getting along in life," had recently suffered a severe illness, and didn't know how much time he had left, but if he did pass away and Gold attained new counsel, he wanted to be sure all Harry's legal work was up-to-date and in order. In a June 16, 1955, letter, he asked Gold to list all his grand jury appearances, cases he was a witness in, hours he spent with FBI agents, and appearances before congressional committees. Hamilton believed Gold's worth to the government had been invaluable and wanted to make sure his client received the credit he deserved. Two weeks later Hamilton received a letter from Gold enumerating his many appearances before Congress, various grand juries, and as a prosecution witness. Interestingly, Hamilton had asked James V. Bennett, director of the Federal Bureau of Prisons, for the same information. Bennett had no problem with compiling the information, but cautioned Hamilton that in light of the Remington murder and the threat of violence faced by informers "it would be much better for Mr. Gold . . . if this information were not in any way made public." Letter from James V. Bennett to John D. M. Hamilton, July 11, 1955. Legal Papers of Augustus S. Ballard, Special Collections, Paley Library, Temple University.

12. Virginia Gardner, "Jury Disbelieves Harry Gold," *Daily Worker,* June 21, 1955, p. 3. The *Daily Worker* article also pointed out that William Hopkins, Smilg's defense attorney, brought into court a new book by John Wexley that argued the Rosenbergs had been framed "and used it in the cross-examination of the witness."

13. "Rosenberg Witness Found Lying by Jury," *Daily Worker,* June 25, 1955, p. 5.

14. "Spy Case Figure Freed," p. 54.

15. "Repentant Gold Says He Gave 'Soul' to Reds in 'Horrible Mistake,'" *Philadelphia Inquirer,* April 27, 1956, p. 1.

16. "Scope of Soviet Activity in the United States," hearing before the Subcommittee to Investigate the Administration of the Internal Security Act and other Internal Security Laws, Committee on the Judiciary, United States Senate, Eighty-fourth Congress, second session, April 26, 1956, p. 1010.

17. Ibid., p. 1011.

18. John G. McCullough, "Spy Harry Gold Tells Probe He 'Gave His Soul' to Reds," *Philadelphia Evening Bulletin,* April 27, 1956, p. 1.

19. "Scope of Soviet Activity in the United States," p. 1011.

20. Ibid., p. 1012.

21. Ibid., p. 1013.

22. It is not an exaggeration to state that a cottage industry of Gold detractors had emerged by the time of the Senate subcommittee hearing. In fact, "Mrs. Morton Sobell stood outside the hearing room and handed out a document charging that Gold had been thoroughly discredited as a liar" after the Ohio jury verdict in the Smilg case. "Repentant Gold Says He Gave 'Soul' to Reds," p. 3.

23. "Scope of Soviet Activity in the United States," p. 1018.

24. Ibid., p. 1022.

25. The All-American Football Conference was conceived by *Chicago Tribune* sports editor Arch Ward and consisted of eight teams that hoped to compete with the more established National Football League. The AAFC was in operation between 1946 and 1949 and included such teams as the Miami Seahawks, Chicago Rockets, and Los Angeles Dons. Though they had their share of big name players, the league ended when it finally merged after the 1949 season with the NFL.

26. "Scope of Soviet Activity in the United States," p. 1042.

27. Ibid. Benjamin Mandel, director of research for the committee, entered into the record an October 24, 1949, *Daily News* article illuminating New York's decisive 24 to 3 victory over San Francisco. The article went on describe "the crackling line play of Martin Ruby and Arnie Weinmeister . . . that held Frisco to only 49 yards gained on the ground."

28. "Scope of Soviet Activity in the United States," p. 1045.

29. Ibid., p. 1047.

30. Ibid., p. 1049.

31. This 1935 adaptation of Liam O'Flaherty's novel about a slow-witted Dublin brute who betrays a friend for money garnered Oscars for director (John Ford), actor (Victor McLaglen), screenwriter (Dudley Nichols), and composer (Max Steiner). The film came out the year Harry Gold began supplying industrial information to the Soviets.

32. "Repentant Gold Says He Gave 'Soul' to Reds," p. 1.

33. "Scope of Soviet Activity in the United States," p. 1055.

34. *Newsweek,* May 7, 1956.

35. Oliver Pilat, *The Atom Spies* (New York: Putnam, 1952), p. 27.

36. J. Edgar Hoover, "What Was the FBI's Toughest Case?" *This Week Magazine,* February 22, 1955, p. 10.

37. Bill Davidson, "The People Who Stole It from Us," *Look* magazine, October 29, 1957, p. 87. Gold's intimate knowledge of the events he participated in and

his compulsive nature caused him to keep track of newspaper, magazine, and book accounts that mentioned his history as a spy. His brother Joe similarly monitored newspaper accounts, and the brothers shared their articles. On one occasion Joe received a letter from the Jewish chaplin at Lewisburg Penitentiary informing him that Harry suggested he acquire two articles by George Sokolsky and Willard Edwards related to David Greenglass. The rabbi requested that Joe Gold make no mention of it when writing his brother, as "I don't want the institution to know that I wrote you." Letter from Rabbi Emanuel Kramer to Joseph Gold, July 23, 1957. Papers of Joseph Gold, Special Collections, Paley Library, Temple University.

38. John Wexley, *The Judgment of Julius and Ethel Rosenberg* (New York: Cameron and Kahn, 1955).

39. Wexley was a Hollywood screenwriter, playwright, and director, with a number of significant movies to his credit. In addition to the screenplay for *Angels with Dirty Faces* starring James Cagney, Humphrey Bogart, and Pat O'Brien, he wrote the script for several other films in the 1930s, including *The Amazing Dr. Clitterhouse* with Edward G. Robinson and Humphrey Bogart. His interest in the Rosenbergs harkened back to one of his earliest successes, a 1932 venture entitled *The Last Mile*, a film about men imprisoned on death row.

40. Davidson, "The People Who Stole It from Us," p. 87.

41. Wexley, *Judgment*, pp. 39 (pseudologist, pathological liar), 43 (lonely creature), 49 (imposter, accomplished deceiver), 53 (disordered mind), 64 (paid agent).

42. Ibid., p. 59.

43. Davidson, "The People Who Stole It from Us," p. 100.

44. FBI Parole Report for Harry Gold by SA Robert Jensen, July 29, 1951. Federal Bureau of Prisons Notorious Offender File, National Archives, College Park, Md.

45. Memorandum from Mr. Ballard to Mr. Hamilton, September 3, 1957. Legal Papers of Augustus S. Ballard, Special Collections, Paley Library, Temple University.

46. Memorandum on *U.S. v. Harry Gold,* November, 1956. Legal Papers of Augustus S. Ballard, Special Collections, Paley Library, Temple University.

47. Ibid., p. 2.

48. Author's interview with Augustus S. Ballard, December 26, 2007.

49. Letter from Kenneth V. Harvey, Acting Pardon Attorney of the United States Department of Justice, to John D. M. Hamilton, August 27, 1957. Legal Papers of Augustus S. Ballard, Special Collections, Paley Library, Temple University.

50. Memorandum from Mr. Ballard to Mr. Hamilton, September 3, 1957. Legal Papers of Augustus S. Ballard, Special Collections, Paley Library, Temple University.

51. Ibid., p. 3.

52. Letter from Roy M. Cohn to John D. M. Hamilton, October 1, 1954. Legal Papers of Augustus S. Ballard, Special Collections, Paley Library, Temple University.

53. Ibid.

54. Author's interview with Augustus S. Ballard, December 26, 2007.

55. Memorandum from Mr. Ballard to Mr. Hamilton, p. 4.

56. Ibid., pp. 3–4. Interestingly, when Ballard asked his client what hospital he thought would hire him, Harry responded with Nazareth, a Catholic hospital in Northeast Philadelphia.

57. Davidson, "The People Who Stole It from Us," p. 100.

58. Author's interview with Augustus S. Ballard, September 12, 2006.

59. Note to Augustus Ballard from ZCH, July 12, 1955. Legal Papers of Augustus S. Ballard, Special Collections, Paley Library, Temple University.

60. United States Penitentiary, Lewisburg, Pa. Special Progress Report of Harry Gold, August 1, 1957, Notorious Offender File, National Archives, College Park, Md.

61. United States Penitentiary, Lewisburg, Pa. Special Progress Report of Harry Gold, July 13, 1959, Notorious Offender File, National Archives, College Park, Md.

62. Ibid.

63. Letter from Harry Gold to John D. M. Hamilton, April 11, 1959. Legal Papers of Augustus S. Ballard, Special Collections, Paley Library, Temple University.

64. Ibid. Gold may have been working on considerably more tests than he told Graves about. According to his brother, Joe Gold, work was being done on an array of tests. In addition to the blood sugar test, there was also a "blood cholesterol test," a "blood urine test," a "blood potassium test," and a "blood sodium test" designed to measure everything from heart and kidney disease to chemical imbalances in the blood. Joe believed that advances on these fronts would "help mankind," possibly "earn some money for Harry," and, most important, "reflect favorably" on his brother's prospects for parole.

65. Letter from James M. Graves to Harry Gold, June 4, 1959. Legal Papers of Augustus S. Ballard, Special Collections, Paley Library, Temple University.

66. Letter from James M. Graves to Harry Gold, October 24, 1960. Legal Papers of Augustus S. Ballard, Special Collections, Paley Library, Temple University.

67. Letter from Eric Schellin to Harry Gold, December 9, 1960. Legal Papers of Augustus S. Ballard, Special Collections, Paley Library, Temple University. James M. Graves, Gold's patent attorney, died of a heart attack just before the patent was granted. Graves's partner, Eric Schellin, completed the application process.

68. Klaus Fuchs was released from England's Wakefield Prison on June 23, 1959. David Greenglass was released from Lewisburg Penitentiary on November 16, 1960.

Chapter 15. The Campaign for Parole

1. Gold was rewarded for his good behavior and value to the institution when he was moved off a cellblock and placed on Lewisburg's Honor Block in February 1956. The unit consisted of individual rooms slightly larger than cells. The doors were made of wood and were usually unlocked and left open. Gold was also receiving "Meritorious Pay for outstanding work" that amounted to "$10 per month with $5 to his savings and $5 to his spending accounts." United States Penitentiary, Lewisburg, Pa. Special Progress Report of Harry Gold, 1956, Notorious Offender File, National Archives, College Park, Md.

2. Author's interviews with Al From on December 19 and 20, 2007.

3. Ibid.

4. Author's interviews with Robert Smith, January 3, 2008.

5. Ibid.

6. United States Penitentiary, Lewisburg, Parole Progress Report for Harry Gold, July 23, 1960, p. 1. Notorious Offender File, National Archives, College Park, Md.

7. Ibid., p. 2.

8. Memorandum from Mr. Ballard to Mr. Hamilton, re. Harry Gold—Petition for Parole, September 6, 1960, p. 1. Legal Papers of Augustus S. Ballard, Special Collections, Paley Library, Temple University.

9. Ibid., p. 2.

10. Letter from John D. M. Hamilton to United States Parole Board, Att.: William K. McDermott, Parole Executive, September 30, 1960, p. 1. Legal Papers of Augustus S. Ballard, Special Collections, Paley Library, Temple University.

11. Ibid., p. 3.

12. Ibid.

13. Ibid. Hamilton quoted Robert Morris, former chief counsel of the Senate Internal Security Subcommittee and now president of Dallas University, that Gold "as much as anyone that I know, has revealed and exposed the machinations of the Soviets in atomic and industrial espionage. The reliability and loyalty of Gold to our side of the struggle has been demonstrated time and time again."

14. Ibid., p. 8.

15. Ibid., p. 10.

16. Letter from Harry Gold to Joe Gold, July 16, 1960. Papers of Joseph Gold, Special Collections, Paley Library, Temple University.

17. Letter from Harry Gold to Joe Gold, June 28, 1960. Papers of Joseph Gold, Special Collections, Paley Library, Temple University. Harry provided his brother with a synopsis of his educational background that could be passed along to potential employers. He told Joe he would prefer work in a "medical facility" but could always fall back "as an industrial chemist."

18. Ibid. The brothers kept each other informed of employment possibilities from newspaper want ads and shared their thoughts on how they should be pursued. Harry informed Joe of an advertisement for a "laboratory technician" at "Presbyterian Hospital" that he had seen in the *Philadelphia Sunday Bulletin.* In another letter Harry would explain to Joe that "Histological or Serological work" were things he could do, but were "more or less an unrewarding drudge. You do the work, somebody else comes in and gets the credit." Histology, he went on to explain, was "tissue sectioning" and serology was "mostly testing for syphilis." Ibid.

19. Ibid.

20. Ibid., p. 2. Gold's letters to his brother were often a mix of business (job strategies) and more light-hearted banter. The June 28, 1960, letter contained a page on job application forms, hierarchy of job preferences, and modified pep talk, as well as a page on the movies being shown that week at Lewisburg (*Never So Few* with "Gina and Frankie-boy" and *Wake Me When It's Over* with Ernie Kovacs) and a recap of the Phillies-Dodgers game Harry was listening to. He closed by telling his brother he was "thrilled" by those coming forth "trying to get a job for me."

21. Letter from Richard C. Mechanic, M.D., to Joseph Gold, April 24, 1962.

Papers of Joseph Gold, Special Collections, Paley Library, Temple University. The 1960 and 1961 studies conducted by the National Institutes of Health involved "endotoxin stimulation testing of leukocyte function" and was dependent upon the "close cooperation of the inmate staff of the prison hospital laboratory." Strong Memorial researchers were no doubt pleasantly surprised to find someone of Gold's biomedical experience working in the lab.

22. Letter from Clifford W. Price to Irwin N. Rosenzweig, August 1, 1962. Papers of Joseph Gold, Special Collections, Paley Library, Temple University. The law firm of Rosenzweig, Krimsky and Goichman was recommended by John Hamilton to handle the outreach process for Gold's rapid blood sugar test.

23. Letter from Joseph H. Boutwell Jr. to Augustus S. Ballard, October 16, 1962. Legal Papers of Augustus S. Ballard, Special Collections, Paley Library, Temple University.

24. Argument in Support of Parole Application of Harry Gold, May 5, 1962, pp. 1–6. Legal Papers of Augustus S. Ballard, Special Collections, Paley Library, Temple University.

25. Ibid., p. 8.

26. Ibid., p. 9.

27. Ibid., p. 12.

28. Ibid., p. 19.

29. Letter from Joseph N. Shore to Augustus S. Ballard, January 1, 1963. Federal Bureau of Prisons, Progress Report on Harry Gold, Notorious Offender File, National Archives, College Park, Md.

30. J. Edgar Hoover, "The Crime of the Century," *Reader's Digest,* vol. 58, May 1951, pp. 149–68.

31. Memorandum from Mr. Ballard to Mr. Hamilton, July 18, 1962, p. 1. Legal Papers of Augustus S. Ballard, Special Collections, Paley Library, Temple University.

32. Ibid., p. 2.

33. Ibid.

34. Letter from Richard Chappell to Senator John Tower, February 15, 1963. Chappell was the chairman of the U.S. Board of Parole Gold had come up for parole before several times and had been "denied." Chappell said the board had "not felt that any change was warranted in its original order denying parole," but assured the senator the board would continue to review "annually" Gold's "possibility of parole."

35. Letter from John D. M. Hamilton to the Honorable Robert F. Kennedy, March 15, 1963. Legal Papers of Augustus S. Ballard, Special Collections, Paley Library, Temple University.

36. Department of Justice Character Affidavit for Harry Gold by Augustus S. Ballard, March 5, 1963, p. 2. Legal Papers of Augustus S. Ballard, Special Collections, Paley Library, Temple University.

37. Ibid., p. 3.

38. Internal Memorandum from J. Walter Yeagley to Andrew F. Oehmann, July 23, 1963, p. 1.

39. Ibid., p. 2.

40. Memorandum from O. G. Blackwell to H. G. Moeller, October 17, 1963.

Federal Bureau of Prisons, Notorious Offender File, Progress Report on Harry Gold, National Archives, College Park, Md.

41. The United States Medical Center for federal prisoners in Springfield, Missouri, was home to the Federal Bureau of Prisons medical, mental, and dental facilities. In addition to patients and many elderly prisoners, it also had a much more relaxed level of security and oversight.

42. Memorandum from O. G. Blackwell to H. G. Moeller, November 8, 1963. Federal Bureau of Prisons Notorious Offender File for Harry Gold, National Archives, College Park, Md.

43. Memorandum from H. G. Moeller to Mr. Bennett, December 2, 1963. Federal Bureau of Prisons Notorious Offender File for Harry Gold, National Archives, College Park, Md.

44. Letter from Joe Gold to Myles Lane, undated. Initially and for many years thereafter, Gold and his attorneys were concerned about his possible transfer to Leavenworth. It was one of the oldest penitentiaries in the federal system; its location—Kansas—and its collection of hardened criminals presented serious concerns. The impact of Joe Gold's letters is unknown, but Harry was never sent to Leavenworth.

45. Ibid.

46. Ibid.

47. Ibid.

48. United States Penitentiary, Lewisburg, Pa. Notorious Offender File, Admission Summary for Harry Gold, Medical Report, National Archives, College Park, Md.

49. Memorandum from O. G. Blackwell to H. G. Moeller, c. early 1964. Federal Bureau of Prisons Notorious Offender File for Harry Gold, National Archives, College Park, Md.

50. Ibid.

51. Letter from Harry Gold to Augustus S. Ballard, August 22, 1963, p. 1. United States Penitentiary, Lewisburg, Pa. Notorious Offender File for Harry Gold, National Archives, College Park, Md.

52. Ibid., p. 2.

53. Ibid.

54. "Blood Sugar Test Patented," *Lab World,* March 1964, p. 289.

55. One other long-serving federal inmate, Robert Stroud, better known as the Birdman of Alcatraz, had also made a mark for himself in the scientific arena. His work on bird diseases would be popularly recognized in a best-selling book and subsequent Academy Award–winning movie. Gold's laboratory initiatives went relatively unnoticed.

56. Letter from M. O. Berkness to Irwin N. Rosenzweig, May 21, 1964, and letter from Jack N. Widick to Irwin N. Rosenzweig, March 30, 1964. Both Berkness's company, Physicians and Hospitals Supply Company, and Widick's, Scientific Products, were examples of the two dozen or so medical outfits seeking additional information on Gold's invention.

57. Letter from Dr. Robert G. Martinek to Irwin N. Rosenzweig, March 19,

1964, and letter from Henry Brody to Irwin N. Rosenzweig, June 21, 1963. Legal Papers of Augustus S. Ballard, Special Collections, Paley Library, Temple University.

58. Letter from Augustus S. Ballard to Joseph N. Shore, May 15, 1964. Legal Papers of Augustus S. Ballard, Special Collections, Paley Library, Temple University.

59. Letter from Joseph N. Shore to Augustus S. Ballard, May 25, 1964. Legal Papers of Augustus S. Ballard, Special Collections, Paley Library, Temple University. Shore, the "parole executive," informed Ballard that "the Board has reviewed this matter and taken into account your comments, buy we have to advise that it was not felt any action to change Mr. Gold's parole status is now indicated."

60. Letter from Sister M. Isabelle, Sisters of Christian Charity to Mr. Gold, October 1, 1964. Papers of Joseph Gold, Special Collections, Paley Library, Temple University.

61. Letter from Sister M. Isabelle, Sisters of Christian Charity to Harry Gold, May 4, 1965. Papers of Joseph Gold, Special Collections, Paley Library, Temple University.

62. United States Penitentiary, Lewisburg, Pa. Parole Progress Report for Harry Gold, April 26, 1965, p. 1, Notorious Offender File, National Archives, College Park, Md.

63. Memo on Gold, Harry, 19312-NE, May 17, 1965, Federal Bureau of Prisons Notorious Offender File for Harry Gold, National Archives, College Park, Md.

64. Ibid.

65. Memo from Mr. Heaney to Mr. Alexander, January 21, 1965. In addition to describing Gold's deteriorating condition, the interdepartmental memo addressed the possibility of "moving Morton Sobell to Lewisburg." Warden Blackwell expressed his assurance that "no problem would arise between" Gold and Sobell, but did advise that a "problem might result from one of the young hoodlums attacking Sobell for kicks."

66. Letter from Walter Schneir to John D. M. Hamilton, April 25, 1961. Legal Papers of Augustus S. Ballard, Special Collections, Paley Library, Temple University.

67. Ibid.

68. Letter from John D. M. Hamilton to Walter Schneir, April 27, 1961. Legal Papers of Augustus S. Ballard, Special Collections, Paley Library, Temple University.

69. Letter from Walter Schneir to John D. M. Hamilton, May 1, 1961. Legal Papers of Augustus S. Ballard, Special Collections, Paley Library, Temple University.

70. Letter from Walter Schneir to Augustus S. Ballard, May 1, 1961. Legal Papers of Augustus S. Ballard, Special Collections, Paley Library, Temple University.

71. Letter from Walter Schneir to Harry Gold, May 1, 1961. Legal Papers of Augustus S. Ballard, Special Collections, Paley Library, Temple University.

72. Letter from Walter Schneir to Augustus S. Ballard, May 5, 1961. Legal Papers of Augustus S. Ballard, Special Collections, Paley Library, Temple University.

73. Ibid.

74. Letter from Augustus S. Ballard to Harry Gold, May 10, 1961. Legal Papers of Augustus S. Ballard, Special Collections, Paley Library, Temple University.

75. Letter from Harry Gold to Augustus S. Ballard, May 15, 1961. Legal Papers of Augustus S. Ballard, Special Collections, Paley Library, Temple University. Iron-

ically, in the letter to his lawyer allowing the Schneirs access to his files, Gold wrote: "It has been some time since I have had the opportunity to tell you that I am fully aware of the great efforts you and Mr. Hamilton are continuing to make with regard to obtaining my freedom. Thanks."

76. Letter from Walter Schneir to Augustus S. Ballard, May 25, 1961. Legal Papers of Augustus S. Ballard, Special Collections, Paley Library, Temple University.

77. Letter from Augustus S. Ballard to Harry Gold, August 2, 1965. Legal Papers of Augustus Ballard, Special Collections, Paley Library, Temple University.

78. Despite Gus Ballard's best efforts to have a copy of the Schneir book delivered to his client, prison regulations precluded such literature from entering the institution. On at least one occasion the book was mailed to Lewisburg Penitentiary, only to be sent back to Ballard. A series of letters between Gold's lawyers and Warden Blackwell over the course of two weeks finally resolved the matter, but required Ballard to stress that "we feel it is important that [Gold] be permitted to read this book and we trust that it will be delivered to him." Letter from Augustus S. Ballard to Warden Olin G. Blackwell, August 3, 1965. Legal Papers of Augustus S. Ballard, Special Collections, Paley Library, Temple University.

79. Walter and Miriam Schneir, *Invitation to an Inquest* (New York: Doubleday, 1965), p. 410.

80. Letter from Harry Gold to Augustus S. Ballard, August 25, 1965. Legal Papers of Augustus Ballard, Special Collections, Paley Library, Temple University.

81. Letter from Harry Gold to Augustus S. Ballard, October 2, 1965, p. 1. Legal Papers of Augustus S. Ballard, Special Collections, Paley Library, Temple University.

82. Ibid., pp. 1–3.

83. Ibid., pp. 8–9.

84. Ibid., p. 10.

85. Ibid., p. 12

86. Ibid., p. 13. Gold's initial assessment of *Invitation to an Inquest* in his letter to Ballard raised some two dozen points that he would elaborate on in a more lengthy critique at a later date. Gold was particularly irked by a number of charges and allegations, such as being called a "liar" when he had had been completely open and forthcoming, even giving the Schneirs carte blanche access to his files, and their questioning the propriety of his relationship with prosecutor Cohn. As Gold said, "As for my acting as a sort of Devil's Disciple to Roy Cohn—twaddle!"

87. Letter from Augustus S. Ballard to Harry Gold, September 7, 1965, p. 1. Legal Papers of Augustus S. Ballard, Special Collections, Paley Library, Temple University.

88. Ibid.

89. Ibid., p. 2.

90. Florence Casey, "Trial by Public Opinion," *Christian Science Monitor,* September 30, 1965, and Nathan Glazer, "Dissenting Opinion," *New York Times Book Review,* September 5, 1965.

91. Letter from Ben Mandel to Harry Gold, September 21, 1965. Legal Papers of Augustus S. Ballard, Special Collections, Paley Library, Temple University. Gold would respond in most cases on his own, but with regard to Mandel, the former In-

ternal Security Subcommittee staffer, he asked Gus Ballard to reply. Gold said Mandel's "puzzlement is understandable," considering that Gold had allowed access to the Schneirs when he had turned down a *Saturday Evening Post* writer who had been introduced to him by Mandel. Letter from Harry Gold to Augustus S. Ballard, September 24, 1965. Legal Papers of Augustus S. Ballard, Special Collections, Paley Library, Temple University. Ballard informed Mandel that they hadn't an "inkling of the direction . . . the Schneirs were headed" and to the "contrary, we got the impression that the book would a refutation of such works as *The Judgment of Ethel and Julius Rosenberg* by John Wexley. In this impression we have obviously been proven mistaken in view of what you so correctly term 'the very evident bias of the authors'" Letter from Augustus S. Ballard to Benjamin Mandel, September 27, 1965. Legal Papers of Augustus S. Ballard, Special Collections, Paley Library, Temple University.

92. Letter from Henry W. Sawyer III to Augustus S. Ballard, August 31, 1965. Special Collections, Paley Library, Temple University.

93. Author's interview with Augustus Ballard, May 15, 2007.

94. Letter from Augustus S. Ballard to Harry Gold, September 7, 1965, p. 2. Legal Papers of Augustus S. Ballard, Special Collections, Paley Library, Temple University.

95. Letter from Harry Gold to Augustus S. Ballard, September 24, 1965, p. 86. Legal Papers of Augustus S. Ballard, Special Collections, Paley Library, Temple University.

96. Ibid., pp. 1–2.

97. Ibid., p. 86.

98. Ibid., p. 84.

99. Ibid., pp. 32–34

100. Ibid.

101. Ibid., pp. 66–67, 99.

102. Ibid., p. 68.

103. Ibid., pp. 84–85.

104. Letter from Augustus S. Ballard to Harry Gold, October 25, 1965. Legal Papers of Augustus S. Ballard, Special Collections, Paley Library, Temple University.

105. Letter from Augustus S. Ballard to Joseph N. Shore, November 24, 1965. Legal Papers of Augustus S. Ballard, Special Collections, Paley Library, Temple University.

106. Letter from Augustus S. Ballard to Harry Gold, November 24, 1965. Legal Papers of Augustus S. Ballard, Special Collections, Paley Library, Temple University.

Chapter 16. Return

1. Dennis M. Higgins, "Atomic Spy Broods in Prison, 15 Years of 30-Year Sentence," *Philadelphia Inquirer*, August 1, 1965, p. 3.

2. Letter from Harry Gold to Joseph Gold, January 9, 1963, p. 1. Papers of Joseph Gold, Special Collections, Paley Library, Temple University.

3. Letter from Harry Gold to Joseph Gold, March 22, 1966, p. 1. Papers of Joseph Gold, Special Collections, Paley Library, Temple University.

4. Ibid., p. 2.

5. Letter from Harry Gold to Joseph Gold, March 24, 1966, p. 1. Papers of Joseph Gold, Special Collections, Paley Library, Temple University.

6. Ibid., p. 2.

7. Letter from Harry Gold to Joseph Gold, March 26, 1966, p. 1. Papers of Joseph Gold, Special Collections, Paley Library, Temple University.

8. Author's interview with Milton Bolno, August 20, 2006.

9. Bolno agreed with Ballard as to the profound difference between Harry and Joe Gold. "Joe was not a very nice person," said Bolno. And as opposed to Harry's famed generosity, Joe was "cheap." He only gave Bolno $10 for the full day of driving to and from Lewisburg. Bolno also had difficulty remembering Joe ever thanking him for his services. Ibid.

10. Letter from Harry Gold to Joseph Gold, March 30, 1966, pp. 1–2. Papers of Joseph Gold, Special Collections, Paley Library, Temple University.

11. John Wexley, *The Judgment of Julius and Ethel Rosenberg* (New York: Cameron and Kahn, 1955), p. 70.

12. Author's interview with Bolno.

13. Letter from Harry Gold to Joseph Gold, April 1, 1966, p. 1. Papers of Joseph Gold, Special Collections, Paley Library, Temple University.

14. Ibid., p. 2.

15. Letter from Harry Gold to Joseph Gold, April 2, 1966, p. 1. Papers of Joseph Gold, Special Collections, Paley Library, Temple University.

16. Fred P. Graham, "Gold, Rosenberg Witness, Free; Irvin Scarbeck Is Also Paroled," *New York Times*, April, 2, 1966, p. 1.

17. Letter from Harry Gold to Joseph Gold, April 7, 1966, p. 1. Papers of Joseph Gold, Special Collections, Paley Library, Temple University.

18. Author's interview with Francis Ballard, May 12, 2008.

19. Letter from Harry Gold to Joseph Gold, April 14, 1966, p. 1. Papers of Joseph Gold, Special Collections, Paley Library, Temple University.

20. Letter from Harry Gold to Joseph Gold, April 18, 1966, p. 2. Papers of Joseph Gold, Special Collections, Paley Library, Temple University.

21. Letter from Harry Gold to Joseph Gold, April 22, 1966, p. 2. Papers of Joseph Gold, Special Collections, Paley Library, Temple University.

22. Letter from Augustus S. Ballard to Harry Gold, April 20, 1966. Legal Papers of Augustus S. Ballard, Special Collections, Paley Library, Temple University.

23. Letter from Augustus S. Ballard to Warden Jacob Parker, May 10, 1966. Legal Papers of Augustus S. Ballard, Special Collections, Paley Library, Temple University.

24. Author's interviews with Augustus S. Ballard, November 15, 2006, and May 31, 2007.

25. Ibid.

26. Ibid.

27. Mary G. Larkin and Judson P. Hand, "Ex-Spy Gold Free, Finds Father Blind on His Return Here," *Philadelphia Inquirer,* May 19, 1966, p. 1.

28. Douglas E. Kneeland, "Gold, Atom Spy, Released after 16 Years in Prison," *New York Times,* May 19, 1966, p. 9.

29. Ibid.

30. Larkin and Hand, "Ex-Spy Gold Free," p. 1.

31. Author's interview with Marylou McKeough, July 12, 2007.

32. Author's interview with Donna Bralow, August 2, 2007.

33. Author's interview with Diane Reibel, March 3, 2005.

34. Author's interview with Fred Himmelstein, May 2, 2009.

35. Author's interview with McKeough.

36. Recollections of those interviewed differ on just what malady caused Gold to be admitted as a patient. Some believe it had to do with Gold's progressively worsening heart condition, while others believe in broke his leg in a fall.

37. Author's interview with Bralow.

38. Author's interview with Bolno.

39. Author's interview with Howard Harner, October 20, 2006.

40. Program of the Forty-first Meeting of the Association of Clinical Scientists, April 27–30, 1972, Elkhart, Indiana. Legal Papers of Augustus S. Ballard, Special Collections, Paley Library, Temple University.

41. Author's interview with Bralow.

42. Author's interview with McKeough.

43. Author's interview with Dr. Fred Nakhjavan, December 8, 2006. When Dr. Sidney Greenstein, Gold's internist at Einstein Hospital, referred Gold to Dr. Nakhjavan, a cardiologist, for examination, Dr. Nakhjavan did not know who Harry Gold was. Greenstein then asked, "Do you know the story of Harry Gold and the Rosenbergs?"

44. Author's interview with Harner.

45. Pete Dexter, "Spy Remembered as a Gentle Man," *Philadelphia Daily News,* February 15, 1974, p. 20.

46. Ibid.

47. Ibid.

48. Author's interview with Reibel.

49. "Harry Gold: My name is Harry Gold, I am from the Quaker State. / The truth has now been told, and I have received my fate: / But this one thing I say, that truth always prevail, luck is bound to come my way and I know it cannot fail: / for he who lives above the sky looks deep in to the heart, Seeing that I has told no lie in my revealing Part: / But justice from the heart of man I don't expect to get, I look to Gods eternal hand the one who don't forgets: / he it is who will reward the goodness of this life, the just and ever-lasting God who's love will vanish strife. / Now I don't think when storm clouds gather, I am surely to be drowned: / The very darkest tempest, may so quickly pass around: / Then up above that darkness, shines ever-more the blue: / so never sink in trouble, there is always hope for you: by Floyd." Papers of Joseph Gold, Special Collections, Paley Library, Temple University.

50. Harry Gold's Arraignment Statement, July 20, 1950, p. 26. Legal Papers of Augustus S. Ballard, Special Collections, Paley Library, Temple University.

Epilogue

1. Alden Whitman, "1972 Death of Harry Gold Revealed," *New York Times*, February 14, 1974, p. 44.

2. Ibid.

3. Letter from Augustus S. Ballard to Alvin Goldstein, March 7, 1974. Legal Papers of Augustus S. Ballard, Special Collections, Paley Library, Temple University.

4. Letter from Augustus S. Ballard to Samuel S. Duryee, March 11, 1974. Legal Papers of Augustus S. Ballard, Special Collections, Paley Library, Temple University.

5. Pete Dexter, "Spy Remembered as a Gentle Man," *Philadelphia Daily News*, February 16, 1974, p. 20.

6. Letter from Ballard to Duryee.

7. Author's interview with Milton Bolno, August 15, 2007.

8. Letter from Robert J. Lamphere to Alvin H. Goldstein, March 8, 1974, p. 1. Lamphere Papers, Special Collections, Georgetown University Library.

9. Ibid., p. 2.

10. John Earl Haynes, Harvey Klehr, and Alexander Vassiliev, *Spies* (New Haven: Yale University Press, 2009), p. 541.

11. Letter from Clare R. Guidotte to Harry Gold, January 19, 1951. Legal Papers of Augustus S. Ballard, Special Collections, Paley Library, Temple University.

12. Author's interview with Augustus S. Ballard, May 31, 2007.

13. Millicent Dillon, *Harry Gold* (New York: Overlook Press, 2000).

14. Ronald Radosh, *Commies: A Journey through the Old Left, the New Left, and the Leftover Left* (San Francisco: Encounter Books, 2001), pp. 147–49.

15. "Goose," Gold's initial code name, very likely originated with his portly physique and distinctive gait. As Nigel West says, "Individual [Soviet] case officers had the discretion to choose codenames, and often picked one that helped them remember the person concerned." Nigel West, *Mortal Crimes* (New York: Enigma Books, 2004), pp. 120–21.

16. First Venona Release, July 11, 1995. National Security Agency, Fort Meade, Md.

17. The New York to Moscow message No. 1797 of December 20, 1944, on the subject of "ARNO's Cover" stated: "We have been discussing his cover with ARNO. ARNO's note about his setting up a laboratory was sent in postal dispatch No. 8 of 24 October. As the subject on which to work ARNO chose 'Problems of the Practical Application Under Production Conditions of the Process of Thermal Diffusion of Gases.' In his note ARNO envisages concluding agreements with firms. At first he said that our help was not needed: now he explains that not more than two thousand will be needed. For our part we consider that ARNO does not give sufficient consideration to all the difficulties of organizing a laboratory and has not, as yet, adequately worked out the chances of reaching agreements with interested firms—on the conclusion of agreements with which he is counting heavily. I suggested to him that he should study the possibilities in greater detail. The picture will not become clearer before the end of January. ARNO intends to open the laboratory in his own town."

18. Vassiliev Papers, Black Notebook, pp. 290–92. The Vassiliev documents can

be researched at the Manuscript Division of the Library of Congress, Washington, D.C., and on the Web.

19. Ibid., pp. 167–68.

20. Ibid., p. 255.

21. Ibid., p. 457.

22. "Arno was deactivated in the fall of '45. The last meeting—with Aleksey (Yakovlev) in Dec. '46 in NY. At this meeting Arno reported that he had been fired from his former place of employment due to cuts in the staff and had gotten a job with Chrome Yellow (Brothman), who was handled by Arno until halfway through 1945. In doing this, Arno went against our orders to break off all ties—including personal ones—with Chrome Yellow, thereby making a major oper. mistake. This mistake was aggravated by the fact that, when he went to work for Chrome Yellow on our line, he had given him his real name. Previously, when he worked with Chrome Yellow on our line, he had given false information about himself: he had gone under a made-up name, as a family man with two children, and so forth. At the meeting with Aleksey, Arno completely acknowledged his fault and promised to mend it with good work. He also promised to leave Chrome Yellow on a plausible pretext and break off any contact with him. It should be noted that before this incident, Arno had always been a disciplined athlete, and this is the first such problem that he has had." Ibid., pp. 228–29.

23. "Arno hit his head on some sort of pipe at his factory and cut open his brow. Now he has a black eye and a wound on his brow covered in dry blood. I decided it would be best if he didn't go see "Bir" (Slack) with his eye looking like that, b/c the mark is too noticeable, and even suspicious." Ibid., p. 58.

24. One of the most stunning revelations in the Vassiliev notebooks concerning Gold is that his mother, Celia, accompanied her son on his trips to meet Fuchs in New Mexico. Moscow Center was not only fine with this highly unusual venture but had actually suggested it. Gold was "suffering from constant sore throats," and the "dry climate" of the Southwest was thought to be a likely remedy. It was also agreed that Gold "would locate a sanatorium" and "take his mother along" as a "peaceful and domestic cover." Though Moscow Center no doubt believed this to be true, I remain quite skeptical. Gold's father, Sam, was close to seventy years old and in declining health. Celia's hypertension problems were worse than her son's and would contribute to her death just two years later. It is unlikely she would have embarked on a long cross-country journey and left her husband alone. Joe Gold was still serving in the Signal Corps in the South Pacific. "He served in New Guinea from January 15, 1944 to December 17, 1945." He was discharged on January 17, 1946 and returned home with three combat ribbons and "a bad case of malaria." It is therefore quite unlikely that Mrs. Gold would have put aside her home obligations for a "vacation" for herself. One additional point: Harry was always short of money for such trips. One wonders how he could have afforded transportation for both himself and his mother on two different occasions. Most likely, Gold told his KGB handlers he had taken his mother, thinking that's what they wanted to hear. It was not an unprecedented practice (occasional dealings with Smilg and Brothman were examples of such behavior). Moscow Center never would have known the difference. Haynes,

Klehr, and Vasilliev, *Spies*, p. 102, and Oliver Pilat, "Joseph's Dreams Blasted by Gold's Spy Confession," *New York Post*, June 9, 1950, p. 4.

25. Author's interview with Augustus S. Ballard, May 24, 2007.

26. "John Hamilton, GOP Strategist," *New York Times*, September 26, 1973, p. 44.

27. Eric Pace, "Klaus Fuchs, Physicist Who Gave Atom Secrets to Soviet, Dies at 76," *New York Times*, January 29, 1988, p. A1.

28. Douglas Martin, "Robert J. Lamphere, 83, Spy Chaser for the FBI Dies," *New York Times*, February 11, 2002, p. A25.

29. Author's interview with Augustus S. Ballard, May 15, 2007.

30. Gayle Ronan Sims, "Augustus S. Ballard, 86, High-Profile Lawyer," *Philadelphia Inquirer*, February 14, 2008.

31. Author's interview with Wainwright Ballard, February 14, 2008.

32. Author's interview with Francis Ballard, May 12, 2008.

33. Author's interview with Mrs. Frances Ballard, February 14, 2008.

34. Author's interview with Augustus S. Ballard, May 24, 2007.

35. Harry Gold, Sentencing Statement, July 20, 1950. Legal Papers of Augustus S. Ballard, Special Collections, Paley Library, Temple University.

Bibliography

Archives

Columbia University, Diamond Law Library—Special Collections, New York
  Miriam Moskowitz Papers
  Marshall Perlin Papers
  Sam Roberts Papers
Federal Bureau of Investigation, Washington, D.C.
  Files of Julius and Ethel Rosenberg
  Files of Harry Gold
Georgetown University Library—Special Collections, Washington, D.C.
  Robert Lamphere Papers
U.S. National Archives and Records Administration, Atlanta, Georgia
  U.S. Attorney General File of Alfred Dean Slack
U.S. National Archives and Records Administration, College Park, Maryland
  Federal Bureau of Prisons Records—Notorious Offender File
  Harry Gold Files
U.S. National Archives and Records Administration, New York
  Brothman-Moskowitz Grand Jury Records
  Rosenberg Grand Jury Records
New York University Tamiment Library, New York
  Alger Hiss Papers

Temple University Paley Library—Special Collections, Philadelphia
  Augustus S. Ballard Papers
  Joseph Gold Papers
Temple University Paley Library—Urban Archives, Philadelphia
  Philadelphia Evening Bulletin Clipping File

Court Records

United States v. Harry Gold, 1950, National Archives and Records Administration, Philadelphia
United States v. Alfred Dean Slack, 1950, National Archives and Records Administration, Atlanta
United States v. Abraham Brothman and Miriam Moskowitz, 1950, National Archives and Records Administration, New York

Secondary Sources

Albright, Joseph, and Marcia Kunstel. *Bombshell: The Secret Story of America's Unknown Atomic Spy Conspiracy.* New York: Times Books, 1997.
Alperovitz, Gar. *The Decision to Use the Bomb.* New York: Vintage, 1996.
Andrew, Christopher, and Vasili Mitrokhin. *The Sword and the Shield: The Mitrokhin Archive and the Secret History of the KGB.* New York: Basic Books, 1999.
Applebaum, Anne. *Gulag: A History.* New York: Doubleday, 2003.
Bentley, Elizabeth. *Out of Bondage.* New York: Devin-Adair, 1951.
Bird, Kai, and Martin J. Sherwin. *American Prometheus: The Triumph and Tragedy of J. Robert Oppenheimer.* New York: Vintage, 2005.
Birstein, Vadim. *The Perversion of Knowledge: The True Story of Soviet Science.* Cambridge: Westview, 2001.
Brent, Jonathan, and Vladimar P. Naumov. *Stalin's Last Crime: The Plot against the Jewish Doctors, 1948–1953.* New York: Perennial, 2003.
Budenz, Louis. *Men Without Faces: The Communist Conspiracy in the U.S.A.* (New York: Harper) 1950.
Carmichael, Joel. *Trotsky.* New York: St. Martin's Press, 1975.
Carmichael, Virginia. *Framing History: The Rosenberg Story and the Cold War.* Minneapolis: University of Minnesota Press, 1993.
Casty, Alan. *Communism in Hollywood: The Moral Paradoxes of Testimony, Silence, and Betrayal.* Lanham, Md.: Scarecrow Press, 2009.
Caute, David. *The Great Fear: The Anti-Communist Purge under Truman and Eisenhower.* New York: Simon and Schuster, 1978.
Chambers, Whittaker. *Witness.* New York: Random House, 1952.
Chase, William J. *Enemies Within the Gates.* New Haven: Yale University Press, 2002.
Conquest, Robert. *The Great Terror.* New York: Oxford University Press, 1990.
Courcel, Martine de. *Tolstoy.* New York, Scribner's, 1980.

Cook, Fred. *Maverick: Fifty Years of Investigative Reporting.* New York: Putnam, 1984.

Cowley, Malcolm. *Exile's Return.* New York: Viking, 1951.

Craig, R. Bruce. *Treasonable Doubt: The Harry Dexter White Case.* Lawrence: University Press of Kansas, 2004.

Dallin, David J. *Soviet Espionage.* New Haven: Yale University Press, 1955.

Davis, Allen, and Mark Haller, ed. *The Peoples of Philadelphia.* Philadelphia: Temple University Press, 1973.

Dillon, Millicent. *Harry Gold.* New York: Overlook, 2000.

Dubin, Murray. *South Philadelphia: Mummers, Memories, and the Melrose Diner.* Philadelphia: Temple University Press, 1996.

Epstein, Melech. *The Jews and Communism.* New York: Trade Union Sponsoring Committee, 1959.

Evanier, David. *Red Love.* New York: Charles Scribner's, 1991.

Feklisov, Alexander, and Sergei Kostin. *The Man Behind the Rosenbergs.* New York: Enigma Books, 2001.

Gentry, Curt. *J. Edgar Hoover: The Man and the Secrets.* New York: Norton, 1991.

Gold, Harry. *The Circumstances Surrounding My Work as a Soviet Agent — A Report.* (Unpublished Manuscript) 1950.

Gornick, Vivian. *The Romance of American Communism.* New York: Basic Books, 1977.

Gouzenko, Igor. *The Iron Curtin: Inside Stalin's Spy Ring.* New York: Dutton, 1948.

Halliwell, Leslie. *Halliwell's Filmgoer's Companion.* New York: Scribner, 1980.

Hassler, Alfred. *Diary of a Self-Made Convict.* Chicago: Regnery, 1954.

Haynes, John Earl. *Red Scare or Red Menace.* Chicago: Ivan R. Dee, 1996.

Haynes, John Earl, and K. M. Anderson. *The Soviet World of American Communism.* New Haven: Yale University Press, 1998.

Haynes, John Earl, and Harvey Klehr. *Early Cold War Spies: The Espionage Trials That Shaped American Politics.* New York: Cambridge University Press, 2006.

Haynes, John Earl, and Harvey Klehr. *Venona: Decoding Soviet Espionage in America.* New Haven: Yale University Press, 1999.

Haynes, John Earl, Harvey Klehr, and Alexander Vassiliev. *Spies: The Rise and Fall of the KGB in America.* New Haven: Yale University Press, 2009.

Hiss, Tony. *The View from Alger's Window: A Son's Memoir.* New York: Knopf, 1999.

Hook, Sidney. *Out of Step: An Unquiet Life in the Twentieth Century.* New York: Harper and Row, 1987.

Hoover, J. Edgar. *Masters of Deceit.* New York: Henry Holt, 1958.

Huffines, M. Lois. *The History of the Federal Penitentiary at Lewisburg.* Lewisburg, Penn.: Union County Historical Society, 2006.

Kern, Gary. *A Death in Washington: Walter G. Krivitsky and the Stalin Terror.* New York: Enigma Books, 2004.

Kessler, Lauren. *Clever Girl: Elizabeth Bentley, the Spy Who Ushered in the McCarthy Era.* New York: HarperCollins, 2003.

Knight, Amy. *How The Cold War Began: The Igor Gouzenko Affair and the Hunt for Soviet Spies.* New York: Carroll and Graf, 2005.

Koestler, Arthur. *Darkness at Noon.* New York: Time Incorporated, 1941.

Krivitsky, Walter. *In Stalin's Secret Service: Memoir of the First Soviet Master Spy to Defect.* New York: Enigma, 2000.

Labovitz, Sherman. *Being Red in Philadelphia: A Memoir of the McCarthy Era.* Philadelphia: Camino, 1998.

Lamphere, Robert J., and Tom Schachtman. *The FBI-KGB War: A Special Agent's Story.* New York: Random House, 1986.

Lens, Sidney. *Unrepentant Radical: An American Activist's Account of Five Turbulent Decades.* Boston: Beacon Press, 1980.

Lichtman, Robert M., and Ronald D. Cohen. *Deadly Farce.* Urbana: University of Illinois Press, 2004.

Liebman, Arthur. *Jews and the Left.* New York: Wiley and Sons, 1979.

Lindsey, Robert. *The Falcon and the Snowman: A True Story of Friendship and Espionage.* New York: Simon and Schuster, 1979.

Luckett, Richard. *The White Generals: An Account of the White Movement and the Russian Civil War.* New York: Viking, 1971.

Lustiger, Arno. *Stalin and the Jews.* New York: Enigma Books, 2003.

Massie, Robert. *The Romanovs: The Final Chapter.* New York: Random House, 1995.

May, Gary. *Un-American Activities: The Trials of William Remington.* New York: Oxford University Press, 1994.

Meeropol, Robert, and Michael Meeropol. *We Are Your Sons: The Legacy of Ethel and Julius Rosenberg.* Boston: Houghton Mifflin, 1975.

Meier, Andrew. *The Lost Spy: An American in Stalin's Secret Service.* New York: Norton, 2008.

Miller, Frederic, Morris Vogel, and Allen Davis. *Philadelphia Stories: A Photographic History 1920–1960.* Philadelphia: Temple University Press, 1983.

Mitchell, Marcia, and Thomas Mitchell. *The Spy Who Seduced America: The Judith Coplon Story.* Montpelier, Vt.: Invisible Cities Press, 2002.

Montefiore, Simon Sebag. *Stalin: The Court of the Red Tsar.* New York: Vintage, 2003.

Morgan, Ted. *A Covert Life: Jay Lovestone, Communist, Anti-Communist and Spymaster.* New York: Random House, 1999.

Moskowitz, Miriam. *Spies Run Amok.* Unpublished Manuscript. 2003.

Moss, Norman. *Klaus Fuchs.* London: Grafton, 1987.

Navasky, Victor S. *Naming Names.* New York: Viking Press, 1983.

Nizer, Louis. *The Implosion Conspiracy.* New York: Doubleday, 1973.

Olmsted, Kathryn S. *Red Spy Queen: A Biography of Elizabeth Bentley.* Chapel Hill: University of North Carolina Press, 2002.

O'Reilly, Kenneth. *Hoover and the Un-Americans.* Philadelphia: Temple University Press, 1983.

Oshinsky, David. *A Conspiracy So Immense: The World of Joe McCarthy.* New York: Free Press, 1983.

Peltz, Rakhmiel. *From Immigrant to Ethnic Culture.* Stanford: Stanford University Press, 1998.

Penrose, Barrie, and Simon Freeman. *Conspiracy of Silence: The Secret Life of Anthony Blunt.* New York: Vintage Books. 1986.

Perry, Roland. *Last of the Cold War Spies: The Life of Michael Straight*. New York: Da Capo, 2005.

Philby, Kim. *My Silent War: The Autobiography of a Spy*. New York: Modern Library, 2002.

Philipson, Ilene. *Ethel Rosenberg: Beyond the Myths*. New York: Franklin Watts, 1988.

Pilat, Oliver. *The Atom Spies*. New York: Putnam, 1952.

Poretsky, Elizabeth. *Our Own People: A Memoir of Ignace Reiss and His Friends*. London: Oxford University Press, 1969.

Powers, Richard Gid. *Secrecy and Power: The Life of J. Edgar Hoover*. New York: Free Press, 1987.

Radosh, Ronald. *Commies: A Journey Through the Old Left, the New Left, and the Left Over*. San Francisco: Encounter Books, 2001.

Radosh, Ronald, and Joyce Milton. *The Rosenberg File: A Search for the Truth*. New York: Vintage Books, 1984.

Rhodes, Richard. *Dark Sun: The Making of the Hydrogen Bomb*. New York: Simon and Schuster, 1995.

Roberts, Sam. *The Brother: The Untold Story of Atomic Spy David Greenglass and How He Sent His Sister, Ethel Rosenberg, to the Electric Chair*. New York: Random House, 2001.

Romerstein, Herbert, and Eric Breindel. *The Venona Secrets: Exposing Soviet Espionage and America's Traitors*. Washington, D.C.: Regnery Publications, 2000.

Roth, Philip. *I Married a Communist*. Boston: Houghton Mifflin, 1998.

Scammell, Michael. *Koestler: The Literary and Political Odyssey of a Twentieth-Century Skeptic*. New York: Random House. 2009.

Schneir, Walter, and Miriam Schneir. *Invitation to an Inquest: A New Look at the Rosenberg-Sobell Case*. Garden City, N.Y.: Doubleday, 1965.

Schrecker, Ellen. *Many Are the Crimes: McCarthyism in America*. Princeton: Princeton University Press, 1998.

Schwartz, Jeffrey M. *Brain Lock: Free Yourself from Obsessive-Compulsive Behavior*. New York: Regan Books, 1996.

Sibley, Katherine A. S. *Red Spies in America: Stolen Secrets and the Dawn of the Cold War*. Lawrence: University of Kansas, 2004.

Sobell, Morton. *On Doing Time*. New York: Scribner, 1974.

Sudoplatov, Pavel. *Special Tasks: The Memoirs of an Unwanted Witness, a Soviet Spymaster*. New York: Little, Brown, 1994.

Tanenhaus, Sam. *Whittaker Chambers: A Biography*. New York: Random House, 1997.

Theoharis, Athan. *Chasing Spies: How the FBI Failed in Counter Intelligence but Promoted the Politics of McCarthyism in the Cold War Years*. Chicago: Ivan R. Dees, 2002.

Theoharis, Athan, and John Stuart Cox. *The Boss: J. Edgar Hoover and the Great American Inquisition*. Philadelphia: Temple University Press, 1988.

Toledano, Ralph de. *The Greatest Plot in History: How the Reds Stole the A-Bomb*. New York: Duell, Sloan and Pearce, 1963.

Tzouliadis, Tim. *The Forsaken: An American Tragedy in Stalin's Russia*. New York: Penguin, 2008.

Usdin, Steven T. *Engineering Communism: How Two Americans Spied for Stalin and Founded the Soviet Silicon Valley*. New Haven: Yale University Press, 2005.

Weigley, Russell, ed. *Philadelphia — A 300 Year History*. New York: Norton, 1982.

Weinberg, Robert. *Stalin's Forgotten Zion: Birobidzhan and the Making of a Soviet Jewish Homeland*. Berkeley: University of California Press, 1998.

Weinstein, Alan. *Perjury: The Hiss-Chambers Case*. New York: Random House, 1997.

Weinstein, Allen, and Alexander Vassiliev. *The Haunted Wood: Soviet Espionage in America — The Stalin Era*. New York: Random House, 1999.

West, Nigel. *Games of Intelligence: The Classified Conflict of International Espionage*. New York: Crown, 1989.

West, Nigel. *Mortal Crimes*. New York: Enigma Books, 2004.

White, G. Edward. *Alger Hiss's Looking-Glass Wars: The Covert Life of a Soviet Spy*. New York: Oxford University Press, 2004.

Williams, Robert Chadwell. *Klaus Fuchs, Atom Spy*. Cambridge, Mass.: Harvard University Press, 1987.

Wilson, A. N. *Tolstoy*. New York: Norton, 1988.

Wizov, Sandy. *A Corner Affair*. Philadelphia: self-published, 1998.

Wright, Peter. *Spycatcher*. New York: Viking, 1987.

Zion, Sidney. *The Autobiography of Roy Cohn*. Secaucus, N.J.: Lyle Stuart, 1988.

Published Official Documents: Congressional Hearings

Hearings Regarding Communism in the United States Government — U.S. House of Representatives, 81st Congress, 2d session. Washington, D.C., 1950.

Hearings Regarding Soviet Atomic Espionage—Joint Committee on Atomic Energy, 82d Congress, 1st session, April 1951.

Hearings Regarding Interlocking Subversion in Government Departments — U.S. Senate, 83rd Congress, 1st session, April 1953.

Scope of Soviet Activity in the United States — Committee of the Judiciary United States Senate, 84th Congress, April 26, 1956.

Scope of Soviet Activity in the United States — Committee of the Judiciary United States Senate, 85th Congress, November 21, 1957.

Chronicle of Treason — Committee on Un-American Activities, 85th Congress, 2nd session, March 3–9, 1958.

First Venona Release, National Security Agency, Fort George Meade, Maryland. July 11, 1995.

Selected Articles

Benjamin, Philip. "Greenglass Freed from Prison; Served 9 1/2 Years as Atom Spy," *New York Times*, November 13, 1960, p. 20.

Black, Thomas L., and Eugene Lyons. "I Was a Red Spy," *New York Mirror*, June 10–June 15, 1956.

Brelis, Dean. "The Making of a Spy," *Life* Magazine, June 12, 1950, p. 7.

"The Case of the World's Greatest Secret," *Life* Magazine, April 16, 1951, p. 53.

Considine, Bob. "The Great A-Bomb Robbery" (Eleven-part series syndicated through International News Service—appeared in the *Philadelphia Inquirer* in-December 1951).

Craig, Bruce. "Declaration of Bruce Craig," United States District Court Southern District of New York, re. Petition of National Security Archive to Re-open the Grand Jury Records of the Rosenberg Case, 2009.

Davidson, Bill. "The People Who Stole It From Us," *Cowles Magazine*, 1957, p. 87.

Dobbs, Michael. "Julius Rosenberg Spied, Russian Says," *The Washington Post*, March 16, 1997.

Freeman, Ira Henry. "How the Russians Got the World's Biggest Secret," *New York Times*, April 1, 1951, p. 10E.

Hook, Sidney. "Why They Switch Loyalties," *New York Times*, November 26, 1950, p. SM7.

Hoover, J. Edgar. "The Crime of the Century," *The Reader's Digest*, May 1951, p. 149.

Hoover, J. Edgar. "What Was the FBI's Toughest Case?" *This Week Magazine*, February 20, 1955, p. 1.

"The Inside Story of Soviet Espionage in America," *Spies Confidential, Special Issue*, 1960.

Kenworthy, E. W. "Espionage in Real Life Can Be Duller Than Fiction," *New York Times*, October 20, 1957, p. E6.

Knebel, Fletcher. "Red Spies: The Inside Story of the People Who Betrayed Their Country," *Look* Magazine, October 29, 1957.

Mendes, Philip "The Melbourne Jewish Left, Communism and the Cold War. Responses to Stalinist Anti-Semitism and the Rosenberg Spy Trial," *The Australian Journal of Politics and History*, Vol. 49, No. 4, 2003, p. 501.

Oriccio, Michael. "The Woman Who Came In from the Cold," *The San Jose Mercury News*, September 13, 1992.

Parrish, Michael E. "Cold War Justice: The Supreme Court and the Rosenbergs," *The American Historical Review*, Vol. 82, No. 4, October 1977, p. 805.

Roberts, John W. "The Origins of USP Lewisburg"—The History of the Federal Penitentiary at Lewisburg—Union County Historical Society, pp. 6–47.

Stanley, Alessandra. "KGB Agent Plays Down Atomic Role of Rosenbergs," *New York Times*, March 16, 1997.

Tyner, Arlene. "A Promise for Tomorrow: Deconstructing the Rosenberg Case," National Committee to Reopen the Rosenberg Case, 1998.

Walter, Rep. Francis E. "Harry Gold's Atom Spying Called Crime of Century," *The Philadelphia Inquirer*, March 3, 1958, p. 1.

Interviews

Ballard, Augustus S. Interviews by author November 15, 2006, May 15, 2007, May 16, 2007, May 24, 2007, May 31, 2007, June 7, 2007, and December 26, 2007.

Ballard, Francis. Interview by author, May 12, 2008.

Bolno, Milton. Interviews by author, October 19, 2006, and November 12, 2006.

Bralow, Donna. Interview by author, August 2, 2007.

Coltman, Arthur. Interviews by author, September 12, 2006, and November 22, 2006.

Dinerman, Sam. Interview by author, June 12, 2006.

Domsky, Yetta. Interview by author, March 8, 2007

Frank, Mary. Interview by author, September 20, 2006.

Friedman, Murray. Interview by author, October 12, 2006.

From, Al. Interviews by author, December 19, 2007, and December 20,2007.

Gabow, Francis. Interview by author, August 28, 2006.

Goodroe, Charles "Chick." Interview by author, January 5, 2008.

Hagen, Paul. Interview by author, February 29, 2007.

Harner, Howard. Interviews by author. March 5, 2006, June 12, 2006, and June 28, 2006.

Himmelstein, Fred. Interview by author, May 2, 2009.

Kaplan, Doris. Interview by author, October 1, 2007.

Krakow, Ted. Interview by author, February 27, 2009.

Kripplebauer, Louis "Junior." Interviews by author, March 8, 2007, and June 5, 2007.

Labovitz, Sherman. Interviews by author, March 12, 2007, and October 8, 2008.

LaCheen, Steve. Interviews by author, April 19, 2009, and May 14, 2009.

Libson, Aaron. Interview by author, September 25, 2006.

McKeough, Marylou. Interview by author, August 12, 2007.

Monheit, Richard. Interview by author, December 1, 2006.

Moskowitz, Miriam. Interviews by author, December 5, 2007, April 5, 2007, June 18, 2008, June 25, 2008, and July 22, 2008.

Nakjavan, Fred. Interviews by author, November 30, 2006, and December 8, 2006.

Reibel, Diane. Interview by author, June 15, 2006.

Rovner, Joseph. Interview by author, September 12, 2007.

Rundbaken, Albert. Interview by author, March 3, 2007.

Smith, Robert. Interviews by author, June 7, 2007, June 18, 2007, December 18, 2007, and January 3, 2008.

Stone, Robert. Interview by author, November 4, 2006.

Tyner, Arlene. Interview by author, April 22, 2006.

Weisberg, Ilene. Interview by author, October 15, 2007.

Weiss, Sylvia. Interview by author, May 20, 2006.

Acknowledgments

My quest to unearth the real Harry Gold story was aided by many individuals. Though my repeated phone calls, visits, and endless requests to answer one more question may have often taxed their patience, they can be assured I deeply appreciate their contributions. Without their assistance this biography would have been a much less thorough and interesting work.

As a student of history who appreciates a well-told tale, I believe it is imperative to rely on more than just documents; if at all possible one must include the recollections of those individuals who knew the protagonist. Consequently, I spent considerable time tracking down Gold associates and seducing them into answering my questions. Gus Ballard, Harry Gold's long-serving attorney, was particularly critical to this venture. Though repeatedly annoyed by inaccurate and unflattering portraits of his client over the years, skeptical of any media representatives, academics, and authors promising a "fair and balanced" account, and residing in an assisted living facility, Ballard endured my many visits and endless questions for several years. Though his health would gradually decline and his mind occasionally wander, his memories of the Gold affair remained firm, and he never once declined to answer a question, especially given the chance that his client would finally receive his just due. It is with sincere regret that Gus Ballard died before publication of what I believe—and Gus no doubt hoped—would be a true accounting of the man he so faithfully represented for so many years. Miriam Moskowitz was another Gold associate who believed she had been portrayed inaccurately by the press and repeatedly declined my overtures for an interview. Eventually she relented, answered many of my questions, and even served me lunch at her home. It is my hope that she finds that I have related her comments accurately and fairly.

There are many others I would like to thank for sharing their recollections of Harry Gold, including Yetta Domsky, Mary Frank, Arthur Coltman, Sylvia Weiss, Robert Stone, Richard Monheit, Charlotte Roland, Paul Hagen, Bob Smith, Al From, Diane Reibel, Donna Bralow, Marylou McKeough, Fred Himmelstein, Fred Nakhjavan, Milton Bolno, and Howard Harner.

Others I would like to thank for sitting down with me and sharing their thoughts on Gold and the times in which he lived, as well as everything from South Philadelphia and the Great Depression to Birobidzhan and Lewisburg Penitentiary, include Sherman Labovitz, Joe Rovner, Ilene Weisberg, Arlene Tyner, Ted Krakow, Sam Dinerman, Chick Goodroe, Junior Kripplebauer, Doris Kaplan, Frances Gabow, Aaron Libson, Murray Friedman, Albert Rundbaken, Joe Rosenberg, and Steve La-Cheen.

In the always difficult and time-consuming archival paper chase a number of knowledgeable archivists and special collection librarians assisted my hunt for relevant documents. I owe a debt of gratitude to all of them, but would like especially to thank Whitney Bagnall and Sabrina Sondhi at Columbia University's Diamond Law Library; Patrick Connelly of the National Archives in New York City and Guy Hall of the National Archives in Atlanta; Michael Nash of New York University's Tamiment Library; historian and author Katie Sibley, who shared many of her own documents with me; and Thomas Whitehead of Temple University Library's Special Collections Department and Brenda Galloway-Wright and John Pettitt of Temple University's Urban Archives. I would also like to thank Russian historian Svetlana Chervonnaya for her thoughts, photographs, and friendship, not to mention her assistance in arranging my trip to Moscow and St. Petersburg. I also want to thank Franklin B. Holland of the Pepper, Hamilton law firm for his assistance in overcoming an obstacle of many years and greasing the institutional skids so that Gus Ballard's historically important Harry Gold files would be transferred to Paley Library's Special Collection Department at Temple University.

A number of former students and friends with a passion for history and a penchant for detective work aided me in my many years of sleuthing for documents and individuals. Brandon DeJulius, Santo Mazeo, and

Evan Munsing were particularly supportive in this regard. I would also like to thank George Holmes for helping locate some of Gold's South Philadelphia neighbors and Josh Camerote for his wide-ranging technical skills and help in coordinating my many Gold family photographs. I would also like to thank Greg Dober for his friendship and ardor for historical research and Bill Rosenberg for his prompt attention to my periodic computer meltdowns.

John Earl Haynes, Harvey Klehr, and Steve Usdin also deserve thanks for reviewing the manuscript and for their supportive comments. The favorable feedback from these accomplished Cold War historians assured me that both my scholarship and my judgment were sound. I also need to thank Ronald Radosh, who encouraged me in this venture and whose own experience in tackling a related espionage case underscored the fact that truth should always trump politics. I appreciate that Jonathan Brent of the Yivo Institute for Jewish Research and a Yale University Press editor-at-large was so upbeat about this project and complimentary regarding the submitted manuscript. And I cannot thank Yale University Press editor William Frucht enough for his supportive comments, critical literary eye, and the smooth shepherding of this project. Also deserving my thanks at YUP are Jaya Chatterjee, Otto Bohlmann, and Margaret Otzel, who wielded a gentle lash in their determination that my work result in a top-notch Yale product.

To my agent, Jill Marsal, I owe a dept of thanks for seeing the value in this project and illuminating the intellectual gravitas that comes with a Yale-published work. And lastly I would like to thank my copyeditor, Jane Barry, for once again undangling my modifiers, smoothing over my many grammatical errors, and clearing the decks of all extraneous verbiage.

Index